Handbook

FOR MEMBERS AND VISITORS 2009

1 February 2009 to 31 January 2010

🌺 THE NATIONAL TRUST

President: HRH The Prince of Wales

Chairman: Simon Jenkins

Director-General: Dame Fiona Reynolds DBE

The National Trust is a registered charity and is independent of government

For enquiries please write to:
The National Trust, PO Box 39,
Warrington WA5 7WD
telephone 0844 800 1895
(minicom 0844 800 4410)
or email **enquiries@nationaltrust.org.uk**
Registered Charity No. 205846

To contact the Editor email
lucy.peel@nationaltrust.org.uk

Information about the National Trust and its work, including places to visit, can be seen on the Internet at **www.nationaltrust.org.uk**

© 2009 The National Trust

Editor: Lucy Peel
Editorial assistance: Penny Clarke, Anthony Lambert,
    Penny Shapland, Wendy Smith
Production: Graham Prichard
Art direction: Craig Robson
Customer care: Alex Youel
Design: LEVEL Partnership
Database developers: Roger Shapland, Dave Buchanan
Maps: Blacker Design ©Maps in Minutes™ 2007. ©Crown
    Copyright, Ordnance Survey & Ordnance Survey Northern
    Ireland 2006 Permit No. NI 1675 & ©Government of Ireland,
    Ordnance Survey Ireland.
Origination by Zebra
Printed by St Ives, Peterborough
Printed on Charisma Silk and Cyclus Print, both made from
100 per cent post-consumer waste

NT LDS stock no: 73801/09
ISBN 978-0-7078-0407-1

Please keep this Handbook for reference, and record your membership number here:

Renewal month:

Photographic acknowledgements

National Trust Photographic Library photographers:
Matthew Antrobus, Steve Atkins, NaturePL/Niall Benvie, Andrew
Besley, Mark Bolton, Clive Boursnell, Michael Boys, Andrew
Butler, Michael Caldwell, NaturePL/John Cancalosi, Nick Carter,
Michael Allwood-Coppin, Joe Cornish, Stuart Cox, Derek
Croucher, John Darley, David Dixon, Britainonview/Rod Edwards,
Rod J. Edwards, Andreas von Einsiedel, Cath Evans, Derek
Forss, Geoffrey Frosh, Lee Frost, Dennis Gilbert, Ray Hallett, John
Hammond, Jerry Harpur, Paul Harris, Ross Hoddinott, Andrea
Jones, Chris King, Andrew Lawson, David Levenson, Nadia
Mackenzie, Leo Mason, Nick Meers, John Miller, Andrew
Montgomery, Robert Morris, David Noton, Alasdair Ogilvie,
Magnus Rew, Phil Ripley, Stephen Robson, NaturePL/Andy
Sands, David Sellman, Neil Campbell-Sharp, Ian Shaw, Steve
Stephens, Mark Sunderland, Rob Talbot, David Tarn, Geraint
Tellem, Simon Tranter, Martin Trelawny, Rupert Truman, Simon
Upton, Paul Wakefield, Michael Walters, Chris Warren, Ian West,
Andy Williams, Mike Williams, Jennie Woodcock

Additional photographs supplied by: NT/Rob Auckland, NT/Sigute
Barniskyte, NT/Bernie Brown, NT/Aerial-Cam, NT/Val Corbett,
NT/David Dixon, NT/Lucy Evershed, NT/Simon Ford, NT/Jerry
Green, NT/Jon Hicks, NT/Chris Hill, NT/Fisheye images, NT/David
Kirkham, NT/Pat McSorley, NT/John Miller, NT/Jeffrey Morgan,
NT/Peter Muhly, NT/Hugh Palmer, NT/Derek Robinson,
NT/Jonathan Sargant, NT/John Such/Scanair, NT/Lee Searle,
NT/David Sellman, NT/Edward Shorthouse, NT/Sarah-Jane
Stapleton, NT/A. Tryner, NT/David Watson, NT/Paul Watson,
NT/Tony West, NT/Derek Wilbraham

Front cover: enjoying a peaceful moment in one of the shell-headed niches on the east front of Montacute House, Somerset.
Title page, clockwise from top left: exploring Dedham Vale on the Essex-Suffolk border by boat; the Bailiff's House at Llanerchaeron, Ceredigion in Wales; the Walled Kitchen Garden at Clumber Park, Nottinghamshire; Uppark House, West Sussex; puffin on Rathlin Island, Co. Antrim.
Contents page, from top: the West Wing at Great Chalfield, Wiltshire; harvest mouse on knapweed; visitors at Sizergh Castle and Garden, Cumbria; Brimham Rocks, North Yorkshire.
Back cover: local seasonal produce from the kitchen garden at Calke Abbey, Derbyshire.

Contents

In 1895 three Victorian philanthropists, worried about the impact of uncontrolled development and industrialisation, set up the National Trust. These three forward-thinking individuals – Octavia Hill, Sir Robert Hunter and Canon Hardwicke Rawnsley – were determined to acquire threatened coastline, countryside and buildings to save them for the nation.

Now, more than a century later, the National Trust cares for 250,000 hectares (617,763 acres) of countryside in England, Wales and Northern Ireland, as well as 709 miles (1,141 kilometres) of coastline and more than 350 buildings and gardens of outstanding importance and interest.

Quench your thirst for knowledge

Many of these properties have intriguing connections to some of the most fascinating periods, and people, in history. From Anglo Saxon ruins to homes of distinguished politicians, there is something to interest everyone. So whether you are looking to brush up on your general knowledge, or simply want to experience the drama of the past by retracing the footsteps of some of Britain's most extraordinary men and women, a visit to a National Trust property will be an appetising feast for the curious.

'Treasure Forever'

Every day the National Trust cares for the nation's treasures, however this autumn we are focusing on treasures which are a bit more personal and meaningful to you and your past in our 'Treasure Forever' programme. There will be numerous fascinating events and activities, and we would like you to bring us your particular treasure and tell us the story behind it. We will give you expert tips on how to care for it, and there will even be the magnificent opportunity to put forward your favourite treasure to be displayed at a National Trust property near you!

Properties with a treasured story to tell include:

Buckland Abbey, Devon, the home of the famous sailor and adventurer Sir Francis Drake;

Chartwell, Kent, where Winston Churchill lived from 1924 until his death in 1965;

Plas Newydd, Anglesey, famous for its association with Rex Whistler, whose enormous mural was painted here;

Cragside, Northumberland, an extraordinary house which once belonged to the Victorian inventor Lord Armstrong.

The elegant Plas Newydd on Anglesey, is famous for its association with Rex Whistler

Please remember – your membership card is *always* needed for free admission

Many properties will be running lecture lunches on wonderfully diverse topics, ranging from what life was really like below stairs, to revealing portraits of past owners. These fascinating lunches give visitors the chance to pick up interesting facts and understand their favourite places in more depth than ever before.

Encouraging a more hands-on approach, several properties are revealing their conservation projects, allowing visitors to see at first hand the complex nature of restoration work. For example at Tyntesfield, one of the Trust's most well-known and recent acquisitions, even more rooms and new areas of the estate have been opened for everyone to explore.

Celebrate spring

If it's the great outdoors that excites you, then a seasonal walk is the perfect way to explore your favourite National Trust garden. As carpets of nodding bluebells cover woodland floors, a spring walk will sweep away the winter cobwebs. The sound of birds before the sun rises is a wonder of the natural world, so set your alarm a bit earlier and join one of the annual 'dawn chorus' events in April and May. For more information please visit **www.nationaltrust.org.uk/events**

Properties with beautiful bluebell walks include:

Blickling Hall, Gardens and Park, Norfolk, be sure also to explore the secret garden, woodland dell and 18th-century Orangery;

Calke Abbey, Derbyshire, also look out for deer and a 1,000-year-old oak tree in the Park attached to Calke Abbey;

Kingston Lacy, Dorset, after exploring the gardens take time to visit the elegant mansion;

Mount Stewart House, Garden and Temple of the Winds, Co. Down, Northern Ireland, this exotic and luxuriant garden, set in a unique microclimate, is a World Heritage Site.

Find the perfect space to relax and unwind

If you are looking to get out into the fresh air, unwind with friends and enjoy delicious local,

Spring sunshine and bluebells at Blickling Hall, Norfolk

seasonal food, then the National Trust has the perfect day out for you.

Relax in a pretty park, picnic at atmospheric abbeys and discover majestic ruins; the National Trust offers the perfect respite from the hustle and bustle of 21st-century life. Discover space to breathe and chill out.

For a perfect day out escape to:

Stourhead, Wiltshire, adjoining a Palladian mansion and with a magnificent lake as its centrepiece, this iconic garden is famous throughout the world;

Fountains Abbey and Studley Royal Water Garden, North Yorkshire, the fascinating ruined abbey, elegant Georgian water park and medieval deer park are also a World Heritage Site;

Stowe Landscape Gardens, Buckinghamshire, more than 40 monuments and temples are hidden within the glorious 18th-century gardens;

Lyme Park, Cheshire, as well as the fabulous mansion house there are stunning gardens, moorland and an ancient deer park to explore.

Top ten properties to visit without a car

Blaise Hamlet (page 40)
Easily reached by bus from Bristol, this delightful hamlet was designed by John Nash in 1809.

St Michael's Mount (page 93)
The iconic island of St Michael's Mount sits in one of the world's most beautiful bays. Catch a bus or walk along the shore from Penzance, then cross the causeway at low tide.

West Wycombe Park (page 163)
Good bus links pass this fine 18th-century landscape garden with its wonderfully theatrical neo-classical mansion.

Wightwick Manor and Gardens (page 263)
Although Victorian, the interiors of Wightwick Manor are pure Arts & Crafts. The garden reflects this vibrant style.

Speke Hall, Garden and Estate (page 291)
Being so close to Liverpool city centre this superb Tudor house, surrounded by fine gardens and estate, is accessible to all.

Windermere and Troutbeck (page 295)
Take a bus or walk from Windermere and lose yourself in the great outdoors. There are numerous footpaths and fantastic views.

East Riddlesden Hall (page 304)
After exploring the manor house and its formal and wild gardens, enjoy a picnic in the adjoining Aire Valley.

Aberdulais Falls (page 335)
You will be following in the footsteps of many famous artists, including Turner, when you visit these waterfalls.

Elizabethan House Museum (page 192)
Step back in time as you wander through this beautiful 16th-century house on Great Yarmouth's historic South Quay.

Treasurer's House (page 314)
This city-centre York house is close to many cycle routes and has good bus links from the surrounding areas.

Treat yourself

It's little wonder that the cream tea remains as popular today as in the 1900s – our cafés and restaurants serve a staggering three and a half million cups of tea a year. For the authentic West Country experience visit Trelissick Garden in Cornwall, where cream teas are served in the undercroft of a 19th-century barn.

Meanwhile foodies will relish discovering the Trust's many kitchen gardens, where fruit, vegetables and herbs provide mouth-watering ingredients for use in our restaurants and tea-rooms.

Visit in spring during one of our 'Food Glorious Food' events, and you will have the opportunity to celebrate local, seasonal delights. Discover sumptuous home-made recipes, experience regional specialities and pick up advice and support to help you create your own kitchen garden at home!

Tantalise your taste buds at:

Erddig, Wrexham, the October Apple Festival is not to be missed;

Wimpole Hall, Cambridgeshire, visit the Tomato Festival in August;

Gibside, Newcastle upon Tyne, there is something for everyone to enjoy at the Gibside Larder.

The best of autumn

As the nights begin to draw in and the leaves start to turn stunning shades of copper and gold, it is time to discover the best of autumn. From fiery red American maples to zesty tulip trees, the National Trust's landscape gardens are the perfect setting for an autumnal stroll. Join our 'colour walks' to discover how woodland is managed and work up a hearty appetite for a warming treat.

Top spots for an autumn stroll include:

Sheffield Park Garden, East Sussex, an internationally renowned landscape garden and parkland with many rare trees and shrubs;

Bodnant Garden, Conwy, everyone will enjoy the superb autumnal colours and stunning views across Snowdonia;

Brownsea Island, Dorset, this thriving wildlife haven is dramatically located in Poole Harbour;

Please remember – your membership card is *always* needed for free admission

Children sitting on the beach at Brownsea Island

Quarry Bank Mill and Styal Estate, Cheshire, after visiting the Apprentice House garden, take time to explore the recently opened 'Secret Garden', set in a stunningly picturesque valley.

Fun for all the family

Planning a family day out which entertains everyone can sometimes seem a tall order – but not with the National Trust. From intriguing houses, captivating castles and gardens to explore, the whole family will find all kinds of things to discover.

There are so many special places in the care of the Trust, and the wonderful thing is that you'll never know what interest you might awaken in your children, or yourself, with a visit. There is so much waiting to be discovered, from unearthing the hidden lives of gardens on a bugs and beasties trail, retracing the footsteps of the past below and above stairs to exploring turrets, battlements and basements galore, or simply making the most of the open spaces all around you … the list is endless.

Take the opportunity to get out into the fresh air. Many properties will be running quirky and exciting family events throughout the year; from Easter Egg trails and summer nature events – guaranteed to bring out the wild child within – to spooky goings on at Hallowe'en and festive grottos at Christmas, there's fun to be had whatever time of year you make a visit.
To find out more about the wide range of events on offer, please visit
www.nationaltrust.org.uk/events

If adventure and action are the buzz words for your family day out then you'll be pleased to hear that many properties offer just that. No one can resist the lure of an amazing maze or a thrilling adventure playground, and if you make sure the following properties are at the top of your visit list, then you can pit yourself against the puzzlers and get a bit of serious exercise thrown in for good measure.

For a puzzling challenge or vigorous visit don't miss:

Glendurgan Garden, Cornwall, the laurel maze will delight and baffle adults and children alike;

Belton House, Lincolnshire, once you have cracked the box maze then have fun at the Trust's largest adventure playground;

East Riddlesden Hall, West Yorkshire, the grass labyrinth and Airedale Heiffer playground will keep you and your family busy.

Benefits of Trust membership

National Trust members are entitled to:

- free entry and parking at more than 300 historic houses and gardens;

- free parking at our countryside and coastline locations;

- free members' *Handbook* – the complete guide to all of the places you can visit;

- regional newsletters with details of special events at locations near you;

- three editions of *The National Trust Magazine*;

- information about National Trust supporter groups in your area;

- free admission to properties cared for by the National Trust for Scotland;

- benefits of reciprocal agreements with certain overseas National Trusts (see page 384).

For general and membership enquiries, please telephone 0844 800 1895

The *Handbook* gives details of how you can visit National Trust properties, including opening arrangements for the period from the start of February 2009 to the end of January 2010, and available facilities. Property entries are arranged by area (see map on page 11) and are ordered alphabetically within each area. Maps for each area appear on pages 12 to 24, and these show properties with a charge for entry, together with a selection of coast and countryside places. Maps also show main population centres.

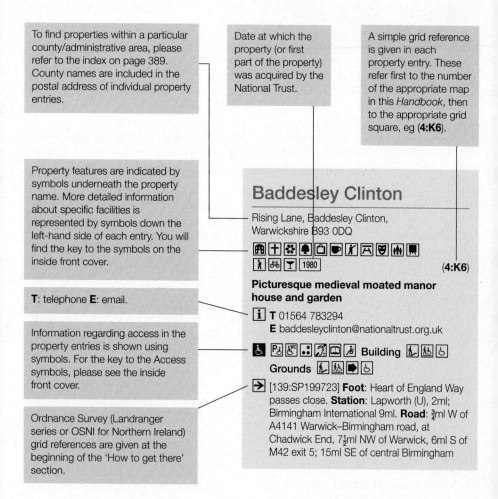

To find properties within a particular county/administrative area, please refer to the index on page 389. County names are included in the postal address of individual property entries.

Date at which the property (or first part of the property) was acquired by the National Trust.

A simple grid reference is given in each property entry. These refer first to the number of the appropriate map in this *Handbook*, then to the appropriate grid square, eg (**4:K6**).

Property features are indicated by symbols underneath the property name. More detailed information about specific facilities is represented by symbols down the left-hand side of each entry. You will find the key to the symbols on the inside front cover.

T: telephone **E**: email.

Information regarding access in the property entries is shown using symbols. For the key to the Access symbols, please see the inside front cover.

Ordnance Survey (Landranger series or OSNI for Northern Ireland) grid references are given at the beginning of the 'How to get there' section.

Baddesley Clinton

Rising Lane, Baddesley Clinton, Warwickshire B93 0DQ

1980   (**4:K6**)

Picturesque medieval moated manor house and garden

ℹ️ **T** 01564 783294
E baddesleyclinton@nationaltrust.org.uk

Building   Grounds

➡️ [139:SP199723] **Foot**: Heart of England Way passes close. **Station**: Lapworth (U), 2ml; Birmingham International 9ml. **Road**: ¾ml W of A4141 Warwick–Birmingham road, at Chadwick End, 7½ml NW of Warwick, 6ml S of M42 exit 5; 15ml SE of central Birmingham

Opening arrangements

The information is given in table format, intended to show at a glance when properties or parts of properties are open and when they are closed.

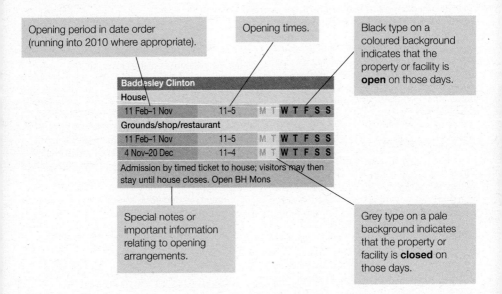

Opening period in date order (running into 2010 where appropriate).

Opening times.

Black type on a coloured background indicates that the property or facility is **open** on those days.

Baddesley Clinton									
House									
11 Feb–1 Nov	11–5	M	T	**W**	**T**	**F**	**S**	**S**
Grounds/shop/restaurant									
11 Feb–1 Nov	11–5	M	T	**W**	**T**	**F**	**S**	**S**
4 Nov–20 Dec	11–4	M	T	**W**	**T**	**F**	**S**	**S**

Admission by timed ticket to house; visitors may then stay until house closes. Open BH Mons

Special notes or important information relating to opening arrangements.

Grey type on a pale background indicates that the property or facility is **closed** on those days.

Please note the following points about this year's *Handbook*:

■ areas are shown in hectares (1ha = 2.47 acres) with the acres equivalent in brackets. Short distances are shown in yards (1 yard = 0.91m); longer distances are measured in miles (ml). Heights are shown in metres (m).

■ although opening times and arrangements vary considerably from place to place and from year to year, most houses will be open during the period 28 February to 1 November inclusive, usually on three or more days per week between about noon and 5pm.

Please note that, unless otherwise stated in the property entry, last admission is 30 minutes before the stated closing time.

■ we make every effort to ensure that property opening times and available facilities are as published, but very occasionally it is essential to change these at short notice. Always check the current *Handbook* for details and, if making a special journey, please telephone in advance for confirmation.
You can also check our website **www.nationaltrust.org.uk**

■ when telephoning a property, please remember that we can provide a better service if you call on a weekday morning, on a day when the property is open. Alternatively, call our Membership Department on 0844 800 1895, seven days a week (9–5:30 Monday to Friday, 9–4 at weekends and bank holidays).

Extra copies of *The National Trust Handbook* are available, while stocks last.

Car parking sticker

This year your car parking sticker can be found between pages 384 and 385 of this *Handbook*, lightly glued to a bookmark which can also be easily removed.

If you need a replacement or additional sticker please contact the Membership Department (see page 386).

Do please also remember that the parking sticker is not in any way a substitute for your valid membership card, which should continue to be shown to staff on request whenever you enter Trust properties and pay and display car parks.

Gift Aid on Entry

This year, most National Trust properties will again be operating the Gift Aid on Entry scheme at their admission points. Where the scheme is operating, non-members are offered a choice between paying the standard admission price or paying the Gift Aid Admission, which includes a 10% voluntary donation. Gift Aid Admissions enable the National Trust to reclaim tax on the whole amount paid* – currently an extra 25% – potentially a very significant boost to property funds.

The admission prices shown on the National Trust's website, or which are available on request from the Trust's Membership Department, are inclusive of the 10% voluntary donation where properties are operating the Gift Aid on Entry scheme, but both the standard admission price and the Gift Aid Admission will be displayed at the property and on our website.

Most National Trust members already pay their subscriptions using Gift Aid, helping the Trust to the tune of many millions of pounds every year at no extra cost to themselves. If you would like to know more about Gift Aid please contact the Membership Department on 0844 800 1895.

* Gift Aid donations must be supported by a valid Gift Aid declaration, and a Gift Aid declaration can only cover donations made by an individual for him/herself or for him/herself and members of his/her family.

The National Trust

- looks after special places for ever, for everyone.

- is a registered charity, founded in 1895, to look after places of historic interest or natural beauty permanently for the benefit of the nation across England, Wales and Northern Ireland.

- is independent of the Government and we receive no direct state grant or subsidy for our core work.

- one of Europe's leading conservation bodies, protecting through ownership, management and covenants 250,000 hectares (617,763 acres) of land of outstanding natural beauty and 709 miles (1,141 kilometres) of coastline.

- is dependent on the support of its 3.56 million members and its visitors, volunteers, partners and benefactors.

- is responsible for historic buildings dating from the Middle Ages to modern times, ancient monuments, gardens, landscape parks and farmland leased to over 1,000 tenant farmers.

- has the unique statutory power to declare land inalienable. Such land cannot be voluntarily sold, mortgaged or compulsorily purchased against the Trust's wishes without special parliamentary procedure. This special power means that protection by the Trust is for ever.

- spends all its income on the care and maintenance of the land and buildings in its protection, but cannot meet the cost of all its obligations and so is always in need of financial support.

- Our strategic aims 'to 2010 and beyond' are:

  - engaging supporters

  - improving our conservation and environmental performance

  - investing in our people

  - financing our future.

Please remember – your membership card is *always* needed for free admission

This key shows how England, Wales and Northern Ireland are divided into eleven areas for the purposes of this *Handbook*, and displayed on seven maps. The maps show those properties which have individual entries as well as many additional coast and countryside sites in the care of the National Trust.

In order to help with general orientation, the maps show main roads and population centres. However, the plotting of each site serves only as a guide to its location. (Full-scale maps can be purchased from National Trust shops.) Please note that some countryside properties, for example those in the Lake District, cover many thousands of hectares. In such cases the symbol is placed centrally as an indication of general location.

KEY:	
Map 1	**South West**
Map 2	**South and South East**
	London
Map 3	**East of England**
	East Midlands
Map 4	**Wales**
	West Midlands
Map 5	**Yorkshire**
	North West (S)
Map 6	**North West (N)**
	North East
Map 7	**Northern Ireland**

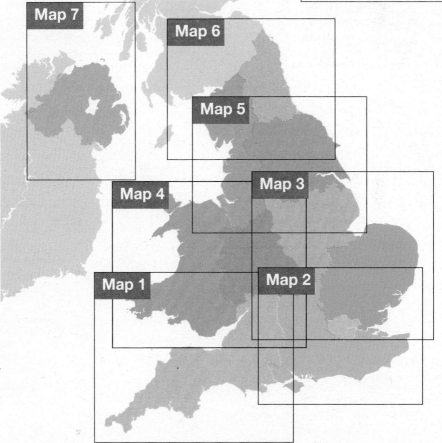

For general and membership enquiries, please telephone 0844 800 1895

Map 1

South West (p.25)

▲ Buildings & gardens

■ Coast & countryside

0 — 10 — 20 Miles
0 — 10 — 20 — 30 Km

Grid A

■ Levant Mine
■ Botallack Count House
■ Cape Cornwall
■ Mayon Cliff

Grid B

■ Pen Anglas
■ Ynys Barri
■ St David's Head
▲ St David's
■ St Bride's Bay
■ Martin's Haven
■ Marloes Deer Park
■ Marloes Sands
■ Freshwater West
■ Stackpole Estate
■ Broadhaven
■ Barafundle Bay
■ Zennor Head
■ Bosigran
■ Godrevy
■ Trengwainton Garden
■ St Ives
▲ Godolphin
■ St Michael's Mount
▲ Porthcurno
■ Kynance Cove

Grid C

■ Dina Island
Fishguard
Haverfordwest
Neyland
Pembroke
Tenby
▲ Colby Woodland Garden
■ Ragwen Point
Tudor Merchant's House
Lydstep Headland

▲ Cilgerran Castle
Newcastle Emlyn

■ Lundy

■ East Titchberry
■ South Hole
■ Boscastle
■ Barras Nose
■ Port Quin
▲ Tintagel Old Post Office
The Rumps & Pentire Point
Camelford
■ Rough Tor
Padstow
Wadebridge
■ Park Head
■ Carnewas & Bedruthan Steps
Newquay
■ Crantock & Holywell Bay
▲ Trerice
■ Chapel Porth & Wheal Coates
Truro
▲ Cornish Mines & Engines
Camborne
▲ Trelissick Garden
Falmouth
■ Nare Head
■ St Anthony Head
▲ Glendurgan Garden
Helston
■ Penrose Estate: Gunwalloe & Loe Pool
■ Lizard Point

Grid D

■ Pen Anglas
Cardigan
St Clears
Narberth

■ The Dodman
■ The Gribbin
St Austell
Fowey
Looe
■ Bodigga Cliff
Liskeard
Bodmin
▲ Lanhydrock
■ The Old Mill

Grid E

▲ Cilgerran Castle
Carmarthen
St Clears
Kidwelly
Llanelli
Burry Port
■ Aberdeunant
■ Paxton's Tower
Ammanford

■ Morte Point
■ Woolacombe
■ Baggy Point
Ilfracombe
Braunton
Barnstaple
▲ Abbotsham
Bideford
■ Buck's Mills
■ Sandy Mouth
Bude
■ Crackington Haven
Holsworthy
Okehampton
■ Finch Foundry
▲ Lydford Gorge
▲ Lawrence House
Launceston
Tavistock
▲ Cotehele
▲ Buckland Abbey
Saltash
▲ Antony
PLYMOUTH
■ Wembury Point
▲ Saltram

Grid F

■ Dolaucothi Gold Mi
■ Aberdeunant
▲ Llandeilo
Dinefwr
Henrhy

Countisbury
Watersmeet
■ West Exmoor Coast
■ Lynmouth
▲ Arlington Court
South Molton
Great Torrington
■ Castle Drogo
■ Teign Valley
▲ The Church House
Widecombe in the Moor
■ Holne Woods
■ Trowlesworthy
■ Hembury Woods
■ Plym Bridge Woods
■ Overbeck's
■ Bolt Tail
■ Soar Mill Cove
■ Bolt Head
■ Portlemouth Down
■ Rhossili
■ Gower Peninsula
Swansea
Port Talbot
■ Pennard Cliffs
Port Einon

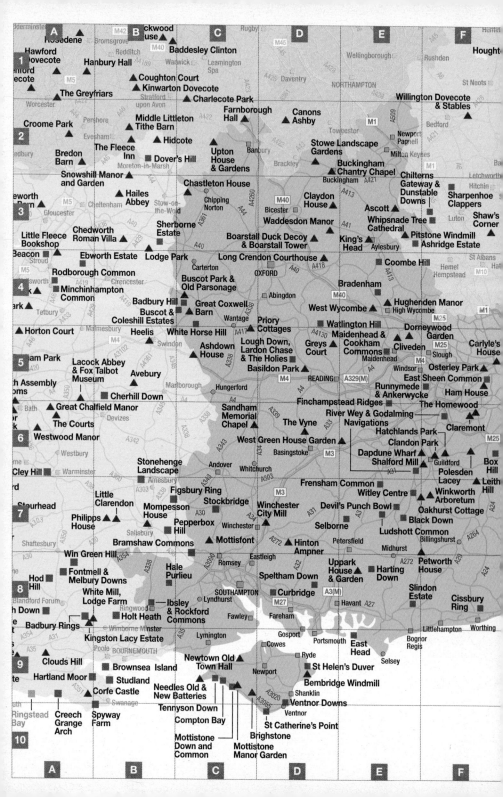

Map 3

East of England (p.181)
East Midlands (p.213)
▲ Buildings & gardens
■ Coast & countryside

0   10   20 Miles
0 10   20   30 Km

Grid references: G H I J K L across top and bottom; 1–10 down right side.

nsby
Cleethorpes
Louth   Mablethorpe
A1031
A16
A52
A158
A16   Gunby Hall
Skegness
Monksthorpe
Chapel
A52
Boston
Hunstanton   A149   Brancaster   Stiffkey Marshes   Blakeney National Nature Reserve
A16   King's Lynn   Wells-next-the-Sea   Blakeney   Sheringham Park
Holbeach   A17   A148   Morston Marshes   Cromer   West Runton & Beeston Regis Heath
A17   Fakenham   A148   Felbrigg Hall
King's Lynn   St George's Guildhall   East Dereham   North Walsham
Wisbech   A47   Blickling Hall   Aylsham
Peckover House   A10   Swaffham   A1067   Horsey Mere   Horsey Windpump
March   Downham Market   A47   Heigham Holmes   Great Yarmouth
A1122   Watton   NORWICH   A143   Elizabethan House Museum
Chatteris   A134   Oxburgh Hall   Wymondham   A146
A141   Attleborough   A140   Darrow Wood   Lowestoft
Littleport   Brandon   A11   Diss   Bungay   Beccles
Ely   A1101   Thetford   A1066   Halesworth   Southwold
St Ives   Wicken Fen   Mildenhall   A143   Eye   Dunwich Heath Coastal Centre & Beach
Waterbeach   A14   Burwell   Bury St Edmunds   Saxmundham   Leiston
Histon   Newmarket   Theatre Royal   A140   Stowmarket   Aldeburgh
A428   CAMBRIDGE   Anglesey Abbey & Lode Mill   Ickworth   A134   Woodbridge   Orford Ness
M11   A12
Wimpole Hall & Home Farm   Melford Hall   Lavenham Guildhall   Kyson Hill   Sutton Hoo
A505   A1307   Haverhill   Long Melford   IPSWICH
Royston   Saffron Walden   Sudbury   Flatford: Bridge Cottage   Pin Mill
Halstead   Thorington Hall   Felixstowe
Coggeshall: Paycocke's & Grange Barn   Dedham Vale   Harwich
Bishop's Stortford   A120   Braintree   Colchester   Bourne Mill
Ware   Hatfield Forest   A130   Witham   Copt Hall Marshes   West Mersea   Clacton-on-Sea
Hertford   Harlow   Blakes Wood   Maldon
Hoddesdon   Chelmsford   Northey Island
M25   Danbury & Lingwood Commons   Burnham-on-Crouch
M11
ton House   Brentwood   Rayleigh   Rayleigh Mount
Sutton House   Basildon   Southend-on-Sea
Road   Eastbury Manor House   Canvey Island
George Inn   Rainham Hall
man Bath
wcoat School   Red House   Sheerness   Margate
dsey Ho   St John's Jerusalem   Whitstable   Herne
en Hall   Ov   Rochester

Map 5

- North West (South) (p.265)
- Yorkshire (p.297)
- ▲ Buildings & gardens
- ■ Coast & countryside

0   10   20 Miles
0   10   20   30 Km

G
den
■ Warren House Gill

Hartlepool

Redcar

Runswick Bay & Port Mulgrave

Middlesbrough
Stockton-Tees
■ Ormesby Hall
Whitby

Stokesley
■ Roseberry Topping
Old Coastguard Station

■ Scarthwood Moor
Ravenscar & Peak Alum Works

▲ Mount Grace Priory
Farndale
■ Hayburn Wyke

Northallerton
Bridstones, Crosscliff & Blakey Topping
Scalby
Scarborough

Rievaulx ▲ Terrace & Temples
Helmsley
Pickering
Cayton Bay
■ Newbiggin Cliffs

Thirsk
▲ Nunnington Hall
Filey

Easingwold
Malton

(M)

Bridlington

▲ Beningbrough Hall & Gardens

borough
Driffield

Treasurer's House
YORK ▲ ▲ Goddards Garden
Pocklington

Wetherby

Tadcaster
Market Weighton
■ Beverley

Garforth
Selby

Castleford
Pontefract
Goole
Maister ▲ House
KINGSTON UPON HULL
Withernsea

Barton-upon-Humber

▲ Nostell Priory & Parkland

Hemsworth
Thorne
Scunthorpe
■ Immingham
Grimsby
Cleethorpes

Doncaster
Brigg

Caistor

Rotherham
Bawtry
Gainsborough
Market Rasen
Louth
Mablethorpe

Mr Straw's House
Worksop
Retford
LINCOLN

▲ Clumber Park
Washingborough
Horncastle
▲ Gunby Hall
Skegness

Stainsby Mill
Ollerton
Monksthorpe Chapel

Hardwick Hall
Mansfield

Alfreton
Kirkby in Ashfield
Southwell
Newark-on-Trent
Coningsby

Ripley
Hucknall
▲ The Workhouse
▲ Tattershall Castle

Branca

Ilkeston
NOTTINGHAM
Sleaford
Boston
Hunstanton

M1
Beeston
Belton ▲ House
Grantham

DERBY
Long Eaton
▲ Grantham House

wood

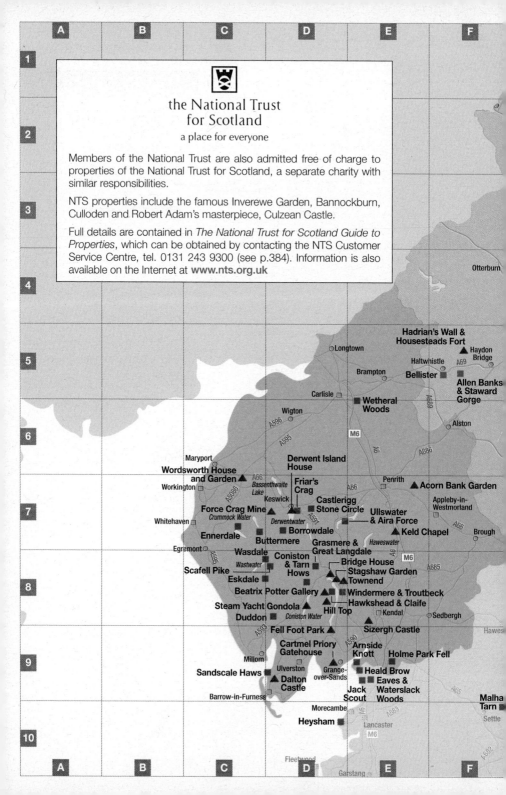

the National Trust
for Scotland
a place for everyone

Members of the National Trust are also admitted free of charge to properties of the National Trust for Scotland, a separate charity with similar responsibilities.

NTS properties include the famous Inverewe Garden, Bannockburn, Culloden and Robert Adam's masterpiece, Culzean Castle.

Full details are contained in *The National Trust for Scotland Guide to Properties*, which can be obtained by contacting the NTS Customer Service Centre, tel. 0131 243 9300 (see p.384). Information is also available on the Internet at **www.nts.org.uk**

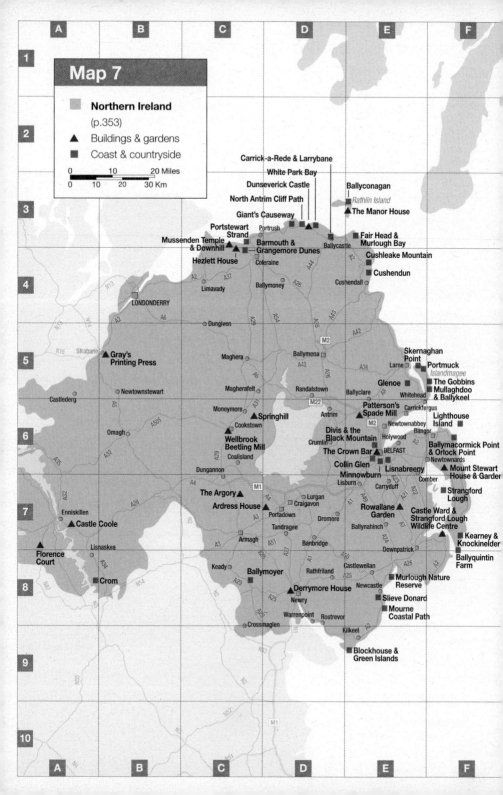

South West

The glorious South West – so varied and distinctive, so unspoilt and so beautiful – exudes a powerful magnetism. Devon and Cornwall, plus neighbouring Wessex, have mile upon mile of coastline, along with extensive areas of farmland, woodland and moorland for all to enjoy.

Two regions, six counties

Ask most people what they love best about Devon and Cornwall, and it is likely that their answer would be: the coast. The Trust protects 370 miles (36 per cent) of the coastline of Devon and Cornwall, and wherever you are in the two counties, you are never more than 25 miles from the sea: from the great sandy beaches of the north coast, where the surf comes rolling in; from the high rocky headlands like a string of fortifications; from the weedy pools, coves and tidal inlets of the south coast. And around it all runs the incomparable South West Coast Path, at 630 miles the longest national trail in the country, linking everywhere and providing unparalleled access on foot to all the lonely shores and soaring cliffs.

To the east, the region of Wessex is incredibly diverse. Spreading from Gloucestershire in the north, south through Somerset and Wiltshire, and down to Dorset, it contains spectacular stretches of coastline, chalk downland, high moorland, historic landscapes and beautiful rolling countryside. The Cotswolds, in the north, boasts many lovely villages, some of which are partly owned by the Trust – which also owns uplands, farmland and ancient woodland. Altogether the Trust cares for more than 25,000 hectares (61,700 acres) of countryside in Wessex and welcomes an estimated twelve million visitors every year.

Above: **Heddon's Mouth, North Devon**
Below: **Botallack Mine, Cornwall**

Previous page: **flower-edged garden steps at the east front at Cotehele in Cornwall**

Rock pools, fossils and fun

Among the popular spots in Devon and Cornwall are the surfing beaches of Godrevy and Chapel Porth; Kynance Cove on the Lizard, famous since Victorian times for its fantastic rocks and botanical rarities; Wembury, close to Plymouth Sound, with its rock pools and children's events; and Carnewas, overlooking the famous

Above: **children search for sea shells on the coast near Cape Cornwall**

beauty spot of Bedruthan Steps.

Families flock to such glorious beaches as Woolacombe Sands, Holywell Bay and Crantock, Sandy Mouth and Duckpool on the north coast, and South Milton Sands, Porthcurno and Gunwalloe on the south coast.

In Dorset, the Purbeck Estate boasts one of Britain's best beaches, two National Nature Reserves, as well as being home to the richest ten square miles of wild flowers in the country. The Jurassic Coast, a World Heritage Site, stretches all the way along the Dorset and East Devon coast, covering Purbeck, Burton Bradstock and Golden Cap, and Branscombe. Here lies a wonderfully varied landscape, ranging from

heathland, dunes and a mile-long stretch of sand, to shingle and sandstone cliffs – perfect for picnics, walking and fossil hunting.

Mines, forts and lookouts

In the old mining areas of Cornwall and West Devon, newly designated a World Heritage Site, you will find ruined engine houses now protected and preserved by the Trust; some of them, such as those at Botallack near St Just, clinging to the cliff edge just above the sea. In Botallack's Count House Workshop on the clifftop, you will find fascinating displays on the St Just coast's mining history.

There are many curious structures to be discovered and explored around the coasts of Devon and Cornwall. All tell stories of this peninsula's colourful past – such as the military fortifications at Froward Point near Brixham, and St Anthony Head near St Mawes, Parson Hawker's driftwood hut high on the cliffs at Morwenstow, the castellated coastguard lookout at Mayon Cliff above Sennen Cove, and the candy-striped 25.6 metre-high Gribbin daymark near Fowey.

West Dorset's historic landscape includes magnificent Iron Age hill forts, such as Hod Hill, Eggardon and Lambert's Castle. Make sure you don't miss North Somerset's Cheddar cliffs. Cheddar, Britain's largest gorge, was carved by melt-water from the last Ice Age and has been forming and changing over the past two million years. Not far away you can experience the drama of Brean Down, which extends a mile and a half into the Bristol Channel and has truly breathtaking views, as well as abundant wildlife and fascinating history – including a Roman Temple, Napoleonic era fort and Second World War gun battery.

For those who like to delve a bit more deeply into the history of wherever they are, there are detailed leaflets available covering the Trust's coast and countryside (see page 30).

A wealth of wildlife

The abundance of wildlife you will find on the Trust's coast and countryside sites in Devon and Cornwall bears

falcons (www.plym-peregrines.co.uk).

The glorious rolling heathland on the Exmoor coast of North Devon, in West Penwith and around Chapel Porth in Cornwall provides a rich habitat for birds and insects. Ashclyst Forest on the Killerton Estate and Lydford Gorge are great spots for bats and butterflies (as are the Lanhydrock and Arlington estates),

witness to many years of pioneering nature conservation work. Try walking the Rosemergy and Bosigran cliffs near Zennor in West Penwith; between Bolt Head and Bolt Tail in South Devon; or from Kynance to Mullion on the Lizard, and appreciate the swathes of wild flowers which carpet the grazed clifftops in spring and summer.

That emblematic bird, the Cornish chough, has returned to breed in Cornwall at last, on the grazed cliffs of the Lizard. If you visit Lizard Point, be sure to stop by the Chough Watchpoint next door to the café, particularly at fledging time in the summer. On an old viaduct in Plym Bridge Woods, near Plymouth, you will find the observation post for the successful Peregrine Falcon Watch, set up to protect nearby breeding

and there are numerous other sites, including areas of Dartmoor such as Hembury, where rare butterflies flourish under the Trust's protective grazing regimes.

One high-summer sight not to be missed is the astonishing display of vivid arable flowers, such as poppies and corn marigolds, along with Venus's looking-glass and weasel's snout, in the fields of West Pentire near Crantock in North Cornwall.

Some of the most important areas of chalk grassland in the country are found at Calstone Coombes, Cherhill Down and Whitesheet Hill in Wiltshire. Calstone and Cherhill Down have a wide range of wildlife, including 25 varieties of breeding butterfly, while Fontmell and Melbury Downs in North Dorset are rich in flora.

One of Dorset's largest remaining

Above: the River Lyd flowing through the woods at Lydford Gorge in Devon

Above left: a National Trust warden walking his dog on the Cornish coastline near Zennor

expanses of heathland is on the Corfe Castle Estate on the Isle of Purbeck. This is an important breeding site for heathland birds, as well as being home to sand lizards, snakes, dragonflies, grasshoppers, crickets, moths, beetles and butterflies.

At Minchinhampton and Rodborough Commons in Gloucestershire there are rare

on the River Lynher near Callington, and Branscombe and Salcombe Hill near Sidmouth in East Devon.

Further east, Burrow Mump in Somerset has stunning views across the Levels and Moors to the River Parrett and Glastonbury Tor. There are also 87 miles of footpaths, bridleways and cycle paths running across the beautiful Holnicote Estate – perfect for

Above: the tower of St Michael on the summit of Glastonbury Tor, Somerset

Above right: red squirrel on Brownsea Island, Dorset

butterflies and wild flowers, including thirteen recorded species of orchid, while Holnicote Estate in Somerset boasts thirteen species of bat, and Collard Hill in the same county is home to the rare large blue butterfly.

As well as Studland, one of the richest areas for flora and fauna in Dorset is Brownsea Island in Poole Harbour. It boasts an immensely diverse range of wildlife and habitats, and is one of the few places in the country where there are red squirrels.

A place for everyone
The Trust has provided many specially adapted or graded paths and viewpoints around the coast, and inland, such as those at Glebe Cliff by Tintagel, Loe Pool near Helston, Snapes Point and Bolberry Down near Salcombe, Cadson Bury

exploring the open moors and deep-sided valleys in the heart of Exmoor National Park. Discover Horner Wood, with its magnificent pollarded oaks and heathland grazed by red deer, or climb to Exmoor's highest point on Dunkery Beacon and enjoy the views along the coast. The Sherborne Estate, in the Cotswolds, has wonderful views, varied wildlife, water meadows and perfect picnic spots.

Or why not visit the Bath Skyline? This unique six-mile walk around the city outskirts passes through woodlands and wildflower meadows – a great retreat whether you want to picnic, fly kites or are just after some peace and quiet. Nearer Bristol discover Leigh Woods, a National Nature Reserve with numerous waymarked trails and paths. It even has an all-ability orienteering trail.

www.nationaltrust.org.uk/coastandcountryside

Coast and countryside guides

To help you make the most of your time and to discover more about the places you visit, there are nearly 40 in-depth guide leaflets available covering the coast and countryside owned by the Trust in Devon and Cornwall. For a full list, please contact either the Cornwall or the Devon office. To buy specific Cornwall leaflets, contact the shop at Lanhydrock (01208 265952); for Devon leaflets contact the shop at Arlington Court (01271 851116).

Car parks in the West Country

The Trust owns numerous coastal car parks in Dorset, Devon and Cornwall, most of which are simply inconspicuous parking spots providing access to lovely remote coves, cliffs and headlands, undisturbed homes to a host of birds, bugs and butterflies. Some of the Trust's car parks are the gateways to more popular destinations, where you will find visitor facilities such as beach cafés and WCs.

Dorset

Cogden, West Dorset	SY 503 883
Stonebarrow Hill	SY 383 933
Langdon Hill	SY 413 931
Burton Bradstock	SY 491 888
Ringstead Bay	SY 760 822
Spyway	SY 996 785
Studland	SZ 036 835

Devon

Barna Barrow, Countisbury	SS 753 497
Countisbury	SS 747 497
Combe Park, Hillsford Bridge	SS 740477
Woody Bay	SS 676 486
Hunter's Inn, Heddon Valley	SS 655 481
Trentishoe Down	SS 635 480
Trentishoe Down	SS 628 479
Torrs Walk, Ilfracombe	SS 511 475
Baggy Point, Croyde	SS 433 397
Brownsham, Hartland	SS 285 259
East Titchberry, Hartland	SS 244 270
Wembury Beach	SX 517 484
Stoke	SX 556 465
Ringmore	SX 649 457
South Milton Sands	SX 677 415
Bolberry Down	SX 689 384
East Soar	SX 713 376
Snapes Point	SX 739 404
Prawle Point	SX 775 354
Little Dartmouth	SX 874 492
Higher Brownstone	SX 905 510

Coleton Camp	SX 909 513
Scabbacombe	SX 912 523
Man Sands	SX 913 531
Salcombe Hill	SY 139 882
Branscombe	SY 197 887

Cornwall

Morwenstow	SS 205 154
Duckpool	SS 202 117
Sandy Mouth	SS 203 100
Northcott Mouth	SS 204 084
Strangles Beach	SX 134 952
Glebe Cliff, Tintagel	SX 050 884
Port Quin	SW 972 805
Lundy Bay	SW 953 796
Lead Mines, Pentireglaze	SW 942 799
Pentire Farm	SW 935 803
Park Head	SW 853 707
Carnewas (for Bedruthan Steps)	SW 850 690
Crantock	SW 789 607
Treago Mill (for Polly Joke)	SW 778 601
Holywell Bay	SW 767 586
St Agnes Beacon	SW 704 503
Wheal Coates	SW 703 500
Chapel Porth	SW 697 495
Basset's Cove	SW 638 440
Reskajeage Downs	SW 623 430
Deadman's Cove	SW 625 432
Derrick Cove	SW 620 429
Hudder Down	SW 612 428
Hell's Mouth	SW 599 427
Godrevy	SW 582 432
Carn Galver	SW 422 364

Levant	SW 368 345
Botallack	SW 366 334
Cape Cornwall	SW 353 318
Bollowall	SW 354 314
Porth Nanven (Cot Valley)	SW 358 308
Highburrow (Loe Bar west)	SW 635 249
Penrose (Loe Pool west)	SW 639 259
Degibna Chapel (Loe Pool east)	SW 653 252
Chyvarloe (Loe Bar east)	SW 653 235
Gunwalloe Church Cove	SW 660 207
Predannack	SW 669 162
Kynance Cove	SW 688 132
Lizard Point	SW 703 116
Poltesco	SW 726 156
Bosveal (for Durgan)	SW 775 276
Trelissick	SW 836 397
St Anthony Head	SW 847 313
Porth Farm (Towan Beach)	SW 867 329
Pendower Beach	SW 897 384
Carne Beach	SW 905 384
Nare Head	SW 922 380
Penare (Dodman Point)	SW 998 404
Lamledra (Vault Beach)	SW 011 411
Coombe Farm	SX 110 512
Pencarrow Head	SX 150 513
Frogmore	SX 157 517
Lansallos	SX 174 518
Hendersick	SX 236 520
Bodigga	SX 273 543
Cotehele Quay	SX 424 682

Ancient and unchanging landscapes

Opposite: **the Rumps in Cornwall**

Below: **a male common blue butterfly**

There is something dream-like about standing on one of the dramatic Wessex hill forts and surveying the surrounding countryside. Skylarks sing their melodious song high above, and the chalk downland is studded with a myriad of wild flowers. Indeed, the mix of colours is better than anything that can be created in a garden. Rare orchids, such as bee, fragrant, spotted, butterfly and pyramidal, are often seen in huge numbers, while tiny squinancywort, eyebright and salad burnet cloak anthills. Wild thyme and marjoram scent the air as they are crushed underfoot.

Great care is needed in managing these spectacular sites. Grazing by old breeds of cattle in the summer and sheep in the winter months is an ideal way of keeping down invasive vegetation. Hawthorn scrub relentlessly tries to gain a toehold, and needs cutting from the downland to prevent it overwhelming many of the special species.

Archaeology and nature conservation go hand in hand, with many of our hill forts being both Scheduled Ancient Monuments and Sites of Special Scientific Interest. There are so many examples, from Badbury Rings at Kingston Lacy, Hod Hill and Eggardon Hill in Dorset, to Whitesheet Hill at Stourhead, Cley Hill, Oldbury Castle and Avebury Henge in Wiltshire, to Dolebury Warren, Somerset, Little Solsbury Hill, Bath, and Haresfield Beacon and Crickley Hill in Gloucestershire.

In such ancient and unchanging landscapes it is easy to picture a shepherd folding his sheep among hazel hurdles, or even Thomas Hardy climbing a steep scarp slope. These are inspirational places and offer so much to visitors – whether you are interested in wildlife, history, views or simply a good healthy walk.

Simon Ford
Regional Nature Conservation Adviser, Wessex

Above: **a vivid pink pyramidal orchid at Dyrham Park, Gloucestershire**
Right: **part of the stone circle at Avebury, Wiltshire**

Hidden deep in the quaking grass, a cricket rasps, while butterflies make use of the shelter of the ramparts. Beautiful and rare, Adonis and chalkhill blue, along with marsh fritillary, nectar on the hoary plantain and rock rose. A lizard darts under some exposed flints.

A La Ronde

Summer Lane, Exmouth, Devon EX8 5BD

 1991 **(1:G7)**

Quirky 18th-century house with fascinating interior decoration and collections

This unique sixteen-sided house, described by Lucinda Lambton as having 'a magical strangeness that one might dream of only as a child', was built for two spinster cousins, Jane and Mary Parminter, on their return from a grand tour of Europe in the late 18th century. It contains many objects and mementoes of their travels. The extraordinary interior decoration includes a feather frieze and a fragile shell-encrusted gallery, said to contain nearly 25,000 shells, which can be viewed in its entirety on closed-circuit television.

What's new in 2009 Room for hands-on activities in the house – including silhouettes, shells and period costume dressing-up

★ Unsuitable for caravans/trailers due to narrow lanes and limited parking. Tel. in advance. Small and fragile rooms, so large/bulky bags need to be left in lockers at entrance and groups of 15+ must tel. in advance

ⓘ **T** 01395 265514, 01395 255918 (shop), 01395 255912 (tea-room)
E alaronde@nationaltrust.org.uk

Family activities, exhibitions

🚶 Parminter Walk

♿ Building Grounds

🛍 NT shop. Plant sales

🍴 Mary-Jane tea-room (NT-approved concession)

👪 Silhouette and shell craft activities, period costume dressing-up. Croquet. Themed quiz/craft days at Easter, summer and half-terms

🎒 Suitable for school groups

➔ [192:SY004834] **Foot**: East Devon Way borders property. South West Coast Path within ⅝ml. **Bus**: Stagecoach in Devon 57 Exeter–Exmouth to within ¼ml. **Station**: Lympstone Village (U) 1¼ml; Exmouth 2ml. **Road**: 2ml N of Exmouth on A376

🅿 Free parking. Coaches must be booked

NT properties nearby
Branscombe, Killerton

A La Ronde			M	T	W	T	F	S	S
28 Feb–8 Mar	11–5		M	T	W	T	F	**S**	**S**
14 Mar–1 Nov	11–5		**M**	**T**	W	T	F	**S**	**S**

Shop, tea-room & grounds open as house, but shop & grounds 10:30–5:30, tea-room 10:30–5. House, shop, tea-room & grounds open Good Fri. Due to the size and nature of the house, small delays may occur at busy times

Diamond-shaped window at A La Ronde, Devon: the quirky exterior contains an extraordinary interior

Antony

Torpoint, Cornwall PL11 2QA

 1961 (1:E8)

Superb early 18th-century mansion set in parkland and fine gardens

Faced in silver-grey Pentewan stone and flanked by colonnaded wings of mellow brick, this classically beautiful house is a beguiling mixture of the formal and informal, the venerable and the modern. Still very much the home of the Carew Pole family, it contains fine collections of paintings, furniture and textiles. The expansive grounds bordering the tidal Lynher estuary were landscaped by Repton and include a formal garden with topiary, a knot garden, modern sculptures and the National Collection of Daylilies. The woodland garden (owned by the Carew Pole Garden Trust) has outstanding displays of rhododendrons, azaleas, magnolias and camellias (including the National Collection of *Camellia japonica*).

What's new in 2009 New family-friendly events

★ NT members free to woodland garden (not NT) only on days when house is open

ℹ **T** 01752 812191
E antony@nationaltrust.org.uk

Building Grounds

🍽 Restaurant (NT-approved concession) in east wing. Children's menu

👶 Baby-changing facilities. Baby back-carriers admitted. Hip-carrying infant seats for loan. Children's quiz/trail. Family-friendly events

Antony								
House/garden								
1 Apr–28 May	1–5	M	**T**	**W**	**T**	F	S	S
2 Jun–31 Aug	1–5	M	**T**	**W**	**T**	F	**S**	S
1 Sep–29 Oct	1–5	M	**T**	**W**	**T**	F	S	S
Shop/restaurant								
As house	12–5							
Woodland garden								
1 Mar–31 Oct	11–5:30	M	**T**	**W**	**T**	F	**S**	**S**

Open BH Mons. Bath Pond House interior can only be seen by written application to the Property Manager, on days house is open

The dovecote at Antony, as seen from the terrace

➡ [201:SX418564] **Cycle**: NCN27, 2ml. **Ferry**: Torpoint 2ml. **Bus**: First 81 from Plymouth (passing close ≆ Plymouth), alight Great Park Estate, ¼ml. **Station**: Plymouth 6ml via vehicle ferry. **Road**: 6ml W of Plymouth via Torpoint car ferry, 2ml NW of Torpoint, N of A374, 16ml SE of Liskeard, 15ml E of Looe

🅿 Free parking, 120yds

NT properties nearby
Cotehele, Saltram

Arlington Court and the National Trust Carriage Museum

Arlington, nr Barnstaple, Devon EX31 4LP

🏛 📷 ✝ ♿ ❀ ♣ ♠ 🏠 🏠 🍵 🎧 🎭 👫

🎦 🚶 🔔 1949   (1:F5)

Intimate and intriguing Regency house, set in extensive estate, and impressive collection of horse-drawn vehicles

Arlington Court								
House/Carriage Museum		M	T	W	T	F	S	S
14 Feb–22 Feb	12–4	M	T	W	T	F	S	S
28 Feb–8 Mar	12–4						S	S
14 Mar–1 Nov	11–5	M	T	W	T	F	S	S
Shop/tea-room/garden/bat-cam								
14 Feb–22 Feb	12–4	M	T	W	T	F	S	S
28 Feb–8 Mar	12–4						S	S
14 Mar–1 Nov	10:30–5	M	T	W	T	F	S	S
7 Nov–22 Dec	12–4						S	S

Access to property by guided tour only from 14 Feb–8 March, last tour starts 3. Booking preferable. Light refreshments only 7 Nov–22 Dec. Grounds open dawn–dusk, 1 Nov–31 Jan 10

Hidden in a wooded valley on the edge of Exmoor, the Arlington Estate has numerous extraordinary collections, inside and out. The house is crowded with treasures to suit all interests, from model ships and rare 18th-century Beauvais tapestries to an amazing assortment of shells. At the stables you can discover the Trust's internationally important collection of more than 50 horse-drawn carriages, from a grand state chariot to a sombre hearse. Then meet the working horses and take a journey into the past on a horse-drawn carriage ride. Back down to earth, you will find scenic pleasure grounds, including a formal Victorian garden, to explore, picnic or play in. The restored walled kitchen garden provides cut flowers for the Victorian-style arrangements in the house. The garden's fruit and vegetable produce supplies the tea-room and is made into a range of preserves, including an award-winning chutney, available in the shop. The last owner, Miss Rosalie Chichester, encouraged wildlife on the extensive estate, including an ancient heronry. Today Arlington is recognised as being one of the top spots in Devon for wildlife, famed for its rare lichens and bats. You can spy on the colony of lesser horseshoe bats roosting in the roof of the house, live, using the interactive 'bat-cam' (best time between May and August).

What's new in 2009 Weekly 'Conservation in Action' demonstrations. Special 60th anniversary events

⭐ Carriage rides available from 14 March most days, weather permitting (please tel. 01271 851117 prior to visit to avoid disappointment). No rides on 16 May, 13 June, 4 July and 12 September. Voucher for drink in tea-room awarded to everyone arriving by bicycle. Pushchairs not admitted to house

ℹ **T** 01271 850296
    E arlingtoncourt@nationaltrust.org.uk

🎭 60th anniversary events. Harnessing demonstrations most days at 12. Open-air theatre, activity workshops for children throughout the school holidays. Experience Carriage Driving days and craft and produce fairs

🚶 Range of waymarked walks around the estate

♿ 🅿 ♿ ⠿ 📷 🦽 💻 ♿ 🚻 🔤

Building 🦽 ♿   Grounds 🦽 ➡ 🦽

🏠 NT shop. Plant sales

The Craven state coach from the carriage collection at Arlington Court, Devon

Arlington Court, on the edge of Exmoor, is an intriguing house set in an extensive estate

Old Kitchen tea-room (licensed) in the north wing of the house. Serves hot and cold meals and picnic food. Children's menu

Baby-changing facilities. Front-carrying baby slings and hip-carrying infant seats for loan. Rain covers available. Children's play area. Children's activity workshops in school holidays. Children's I-Spy sheet, quiz and Tracker Packs

Suitable for school groups. Education room/centre

On short leads in gardens, grounds and Carriage Museum. At certain times (eg during lambing season) dogs must also be on leads on the wider estate

→ [180:SS611405] **Bus**: TW Coaches 309 Barnstaple–Lynton, infrequent. **Station**: Barnstaple 8ml (1ml from bus station). **Road**: 8ml N of Barnstaple on A39. Use A399 from South Molton if travelling from the east

P Free parking, 150yds. Coaches access car park at 2nd entrance. An area will be marked off if prior warning is given

NT properties nearby
Bideford Bay and Hartland, Dunster Castle, Knightshayes Court, Watersmeet, West Exmoor Coast

Ashleworth Tithe Barn

Ashleworth, Gloucestershire GL19 4JA

[1956] (1:J2)

15th-century tithe barn

The barn, with its immense stone-tiled roof, is picturesquely situated close to the banks of the River Severn.

★ No WC

i **T** 01452 814213
E ashleworth@nationaltrust.org.uk

♿ Building

→ [162:SO818252] **Bus**: Swanbrook 351 Gloucester–Upton upon Severn (passing close ➡ Gloucester), alight Ashleworth ¼ml. **Station**: Gloucester 7ml. **Road**: 6ml N of Gloucester, 1¼ml E of Hartpury (A417), on W bank of Severn, SE of Ashleworth

P Parking (not NT) on the roadside

NT properties nearby
Bredon Barn, May Hill, Westbury Court Garden

Ashleworth Tithe Barn								
All year	9–6	**M**	**T**	**W**	**T**	**F**	**S**	**S**
Closes dusk if earlier. Other times by appointment								

Avebury

nr Marlborough, Wiltshire SN8 1RF

🚲 1943   **(1:K4)**

World-famous stone circle at the heart of a prehistoric landscape. Archaeological finds displayed in on-site museum

This internationally renowned stone circle, a World Heritage Site, partly encompasses the pretty village of Avebury. Many of the stones were re-erected in the 1930s by the archaeologist Alexander Keiller, who uncovered the true wonder of one of the most important megalithic monuments in Europe. You can picnic amongst the stones and explore this intriguing and mysterious landscape, then discover the story of the people who created it. The Barn Gallery and the Stables Gallery house the museum, exhibiting many of the fascinating finds from all the local excavations. The Barn Gallery has many exciting interactive displays to bring the area to life and children can take part in a range of activities in the crafts area. Another layer of history is provided by the buildings themselves: the dovecote is 16th-century, while the thatched threshing barn and stables are 17th-century. Nearby, the gentle rise of Windmill Hill, once the site of an important neolithic settlement, has several well-preserved Bronze Age burial mounds and boasts commanding views. West of Avebury,

the Iron Age earthwork of Oldbury Castle crowns Cherhill Down, along with the conspicuous Lansdowne Monument. With the spectacular folds of Calstone Coombes, this area of open downland provides wonderful walking.

What's new in 2009 Updated events programme, including lectures and workshops throughout the year. Seasonal events for families and children. Restoration of the Stables Turret Clock

⭐ Please note that due to on-going conservation work some sections of the stone circle may be closed. Avebury stone circle is in the guardianship of English Heritage and managed on its behalf by the NT

ℹ **T** 01672 539250
   E avebury@nationaltrust.org.uk

🗡 Short tours of the henge available in the summer

🎭 Full events programme, including family fun trails and seasonal activities, living history, archaeology week, craft workshops, talks and tours, art exhibitions and lectures

🚶 *Walking around Avebury* guide features six local walks; available from the museum (£2.50 plus 50p p&p)

♿ 🅿 ♿ ♿ ⋯ 📷 🗺 🎒 ♿ 🔊 Building ♿
Grounds ♿

🛍 In old Granary. Museum shop also sells books on archaeology

The stone circle at Avebury, Wiltshire: one of Europe's most important megalithic monuments

📷 The Circle Restaurant (licensed). The Trust's only vegetarian restaurant, specialising in vegan and gluten-free dishes, using organic and local produce

👶 Baby-changing facilities. Pushchairs and baby back-carriers admitted. Family fun trails, events and activities

🎒 Suitable for school groups. Education room/centre. Hands-on activities

🐕 On leads in stone circle and estate

🚲 Ridgeway National Trail and NCN4 & 45 pass through property and are shared with walkers

➜ [173:SU102699] **Foot**: Ridgeway National Trail. **Cycle**: NCN4 & 45. **Bus**: Stagecoach in Swindon 49 Swindon–Trowbridge; Wilts & Dorset 96 Swindon–Pewsey. Both pass close ☒ Swindon. **Station**: Pewsey 10ml; Swindon 11ml. **Road**: 6ml W of Marlborough, 1ml N of the Bath road (A4) on A4361 and B4003

🅿 Parking, 500yds (pay & display) off A4361. NT and EH members free. Parking during the Summer Solstice in late June may be limited. Tel. estate office before travelling. Overnight parking prohibited

NT properties nearby

Avebury Manor and Garden, Heelis, Lacock Abbey, Stonehenge Landscape

Avebury									
Stone circle									
All year		M	T	W	T	F	S	S	
Museum/galleries									
1 Feb–31 Mar	10–4	M	T	W	T	F	S	S	
1 Apr–31 Oct	10–6	M	T	W	T	F	S	S	
1 Nov–31 Jan 10	10–4	M	T	W	T	F	S	S	
Circle Restaurant									
1 Feb–31 Mar	10–3:30	M	T	W	T	F	S	S	
1 Apr–31 Oct	10–5:30	M	T	W	T	F	S	S	
1 Nov–31 Jan 10	11–3:30	M	T	W	T	F	S	S	
Shop									
1 Feb–28 Feb	11–4	M	T	W	T	F	S	S	
1 Mar–31 Mar	11–5	M	T	W	T	F	S	S	
1 Apr–30 Sep	10–6	M	T	W	T	F	S	S	
1 Oct–31 Oct	10–5	M	T	W	T	F	S	S	
1 Nov–31 Jan 10	11–4	M	T	W	T	F	S	S	

Closes dusk if earlier. Closed 24–26 Dec. Barn Gallery may close in very cold weather. Museums, shop & café closed 3 Dec & during weekdays 11–22 Jan 10

Avebury Manor and Garden

nr Marlborough, Wiltshire SN8 1RF

🏛 ✳ 🗂 📷 🎒 🌳 🐕 👪 1991 (1:K4)

16th-century manor house with tranquil Edwardian garden

A much-altered house of monastic origin, the present buildings date from the early 16th century, with notable Queen Anne alterations and Edwardian renovation. The charming Edwardian garden was completely redesigned in the early 20th century and provided inspiration for Vita Sackville-West, a frequent visitor in the 1920s. Visitors can relax amidst the topiary and tranquil spaces of this delightful garden, which is contained within ancient walls and clipped box hedges, creating a series of outdoor 'rooms'. Some of the features are believed to be survivals of the original priory precinct.

⭐ The manor house is occupied and furnished by private leaseholders, who open a part of it to visitors. Due to restricted space, guided tours operate and ticket numbers are very limited. Tickets are allocated on a first-come first-served basis. Tours run every 40 minutes from 2, last tour starting at 4:40. Following periods of prolonged wet weather it may be necessary to close the house and garden

ℹ **T** 01672 539250
E avebury@nationaltrust.org.uk

🐕 House only

♿ 🅿 🔲 🔲 🔲 🔲 Building 🔲 🔲 Grounds 🔲 ➡

🗂 In old Granary. Museum shop also sells books on archaeology

📷 The Circle Restaurant (licensed). The Trust's only vegetarian restaurant, specialising in vegan and gluten-free dishes, using organic and local products

👪 House not suitable for young children

➜ [173:SU100699] **Foot**: Ridgeway National Trail. **Cycle**: NCN4 & 45. **Bus**: Stagecoach in Swindon 49 Swindon–Trowbridge; Wilts & Dorset 96 Swindon–Pewsey. Both pass close ☒ Swindon. **Station**: Pewsey 10ml; Swindon 11ml. **Road**: 6ml W of Marlborough, 1ml N of the Bath road (A4) on A4361 and B4003

Charges for National Trust members apply on some special event days

P Parking in main Avebury car park, 600yds (pay & display). Located off A4361. NT and EH members free. Parking during the Summer Solstice in late June will be very limited. Tel. estate office before travelling. Parking charge may vary

NT properties nearby
Avebury, Heelis, Lacock Abbey, Stonehenge Landscape

Avebury Manor and Garden									
House									
5 Apr–27 Oct	2–4:40	**M**	**T**	W	T	F	S	**S**	
Garden									
3 Apr–31 Oct	11–5	**M**	**T**	W	T	**F**	**S**	**S**	
Admission to house by timed ticket and guided tour (max. 12 per tour)									

Barrington Court

Barrington, nr Ilminster, Somerset TA19 0NQ

1907   (1:16)

Beautiful Gertrude Jekyll-inspired gardens, kitchen gardens and Tudor manor house, let to Stuart Interiors

Influenced by Gertrude Jekyll, this enchanting formal garden is laid out in a series of walled rooms which are awash with colour. The working stone-walled kitchen garden produces a variety of wonderful fruit and vegetables, which can be enjoyed in the restaurant, while the arboretum delights visitors with vivid autumn hues. The Tudor manor house was restored in the 1920s by the Lyle family and is currently let to Stuart Interiors as showrooms. Here visitors are treated to a rather different kind of visit, with the opportunity to purchase splendid antique or reproduction furniture.

What's new in 2009 Children's history quiz in Court House. Exhibition on the restoration of the Chestnut Avenue

i **T** 01460 242614 (Infoline), 01460 241938
E barringtoncourt@nationaltrust.org.uk

Wide range of events throughout the year

Many public rights of way

Building

Grounds

NT shop. Plants and kitchen garden produce

Children enjoying the Gertrude Jekyll-inspired garden at Barrington Court, Somerset

Show your card and display sticker for free parking

📖 Strode House Restaurant (licensed). Available for functions and Christmas lunches. Booking recommended. Corporate and private lunches weekdays in Nov and Dec (groups 25–50 only). Booking essential. Beagles café

👪 Baby-changing facilities. Pushchairs and baby back-carriers admitted. Hip-carrying infant seats for loan. Children's quiz/trail. Family activity packs

🔲 Suitable for school groups

➡ [193:ST396182] **Cycle**: NCN30. **Bus**: First 632/3 Ilminster–Martock, with connections on 30A from Taunton. **Station**: Crewkerne 7ml. **Road**: in Barrington village, 5ml NE of Ilminster, on B3168. Signposted from A358 (Ilminster–Taunton) or A303 (Hayes End roundabout)

🅿 Free parking, 30yds

NT properties nearby
Fyne Court, Lytes Cary Manor, Montacute House, Tintinhull Garden, Treasurer's House

Barrington Court									
House/garden/shop									
28 Feb–1 Nov	11–5	M	T	W	T	F	S	S
7 Nov–29 Nov	11–4	M	T	W	T	F	S	S
Restaurant									
1 Mar–30 Mar	11–5	M	T	W	T	F	S	S
31 Mar–30 Sep	12–3	M	T	W	T	F	S	S
29 Mar–28 Sep	12–5	M	T	W	T	F	S	S
2 Oct–1 Nov	11–5	M	T	W	T	F	S	S
7 Nov–13 Dec	11–4	M	T	W	T	F	S	S
Café									
29 Mar–30 Sep	11–5	M	T	W	T	F	S	S
4 Oct–25 Oct	11–5	M	T	W	T	F	S	S

2 April–29 Sept: restaurant open for lunches only weekdays, for lunches and teas weekends. Café may be closed in poor weather (Oct)

Bath Assembly Rooms

Bennett Street, Bath, Somerset BA1 2QH

🏛🏠📖🎟🎧🎭👪🔲🔔☂ 1931 (1:J4)

Elegant public rooms at the heart of fashionable 18th-century Bath life

Designed by John Wood the Younger in 1769, the Assembly Rooms were at the heart of fashionable Georgian society, and were the perfect venue for entertainment and socialising. Bombed in 1942, they were subsequently restored and now visitors can fully appreciate the magnificent rooms. The Assembly Rooms are now let to Bath & North East Somerset Council, which has its Fashion Museum on the lower ground floor.

⭐ Some rooms may be closed to visitors on days when there are functions

ℹ **T** 01225 477173
E bathassemblyrooms@nationaltrust.org.uk

🎧 Seven languages

🎭 Occasional events

♿ 🚻 Building 🔧🔧 Grounds 🔧

📖 Assembly Rooms Café (not NT) in card room and formal garden. Open daily all year, available when rooms not in use for booked functions; tel. 01225 444477 for reservations

👪 Baby-changing facilities. Baby carriers available. Pushchairs admitted to ground floor. Family activities during the summer holidays

🔲 Suitable for school groups. Hands-on activities

➡ [156:ST749653] **Cycle**: NCN4, ¼ml. **Bus**: from ⬛ Bath Spa and surrounding areas. **Station**: Bath Spa ¾ml. **Road**: N of Milsom Street, E of the Circus

🅿 Parking (not NT) (pay & display), charge inc. NT members. Street parking very limited, park & ride recommended

NT properties nearby
The Courts Garden, Dyrham Park, Great Chalfield Manor and Garden, Lacock Abbey, Leigh Woods, Prior Park Landscape Garden, Tyntesfield, Westwood Manor

Bath Assembly Rooms								
1 Feb–28 Feb	10:30–5	M	T	W	T	F	S	S
1 Mar–31 Oct	10:30–5	M	T	W	T	F	S	S
1 Nov–31 Jan 10	10:30–5	M	T	W	T	F	S	S

Last admission 1hr before closing. Closed when in use for booked functions and 25/26 Dec. Access is guaranteed in Aug, but at other times visitors should tel. in advance

Captivated by Barrington Court? Then you will be amazed by the splendour at Dyrham Park

Dogs assisting visitors with disabilities are always welcome

Blaise Hamlet

Henbury, Bristol BS10 7QY

 1943   (1:I3)

Nine rustic cottages around a green

A delightful hamlet of nine very different picturesque cottages in a wonderfully tranquil location. The hamlet was designed by John Nash in 1809 to accommodate Blaise Estate pensioners.

★ Access to green only; cottages not open. Please respect tenants' privacy. No WC

ℹ **T** 01934 844518
   E blaisehamlet@nationaltrust.org.uk

👪 Pushchairs admitted

➜ [172:ST559789] 4ml N of central Bristol. **Cycle**: NCN4, ¾ml. **Bus**: First 1 from ➔ Bristol Temple Meads; also First 40 from city centre. **Station**: Sea Mills 3ml; Filton Abbey Wood 3½ml. **Road**: Entrance on Hallen Road, W of Henbury village, just N of Weston Road (B4057)

🅿 No parking on site. Not suitable for coaches. Car parking on Hallen Road

NT properties nearby
Bath Assembly Rooms, Clevedon Court, Dyrham Park, Leigh Woods, Prior Park Landscape Garden, Tyntesfield, Westbury College Gatehouse

Blaise Hamlet							
All year	M	T	W	T	F	S	S

A cottage in Blaise Hamlet, designed by John Nash

Boscastle

Cornwall

 1955   (1:D7)

Picturesque harbour and village on the north Cornish coast

Much of the land in and around Boscastle is owned by the Trust. This includes the cliffs of Penally Point and Willapark, which guard the sinuous harbour entrance, Forrabury Stitches, high above the village and divided into ancient 'stitchmeal' cultivation plots, as well as large areas of woodland and meadow in the lovely Valency Valley.

What's new in 2009 National Trust café open in former pilchard cellar

ℹ **T** 01840 250353
   E boscastle@nationaltrust.org.uk

🖈 NT *Coast of Cornwall* leaflet 3 includes map and details of circular walks and information on local history, geology and wildlife

🦽 🚻 Grounds 🧗

🏠 NT shop

🍴 New café open in the lower harbour with outdoor tables in sheltered courtyard

👪 Children's quiz/trail

➜ [190:SX097914] **Bus**: Western Greyhound 595 from Bude, 584/594 from Wadebridge (with connections on 555 at Wadebridge for ➔ Bodmin Parkway). **Road**: 5ml N of Camelford, 3ml NE of Tintagel on B3263

🅿 Parking (not NT) (pay & display), charge inc. NT members, 100yds

NT properties nearby
Tintagel Old Post Office

Boscastle							
All year		M	T	W	T	F	S	S
Shop/NT info							
13 Feb–1 Apr	11–4	M	T	W	T	F	S	S
2 Apr–1 Nov	10:30–5	M	T	W	T	F	S	S
2 Nov–29 Nov	11–4	M	T	W	T	F	S	S
5 Dec–20 Dec	11–4	M	T	W	T	F	S	S
27 Dec–3 Jan 10	11–4	M	T	W	T	F	S	S
Shop open later than 5 in high season								

The long sinuous Boscastle Harbour, on the north Cornish coast, is surrounded by Trust-owned land

Bradley

Newton Abbot, Devon TQ12 6BN

 1938   **(1:G8)**

Delightful medieval manor house, set in woodland and meadows through which the River Lemon runs

Set in an area of 'wild space' on the outskirts of the market town of Newton Abbot, Bradley Manor is a charming, unspoilt historic house still lived in by the donor family. Predominantly 15th-century, parts of the building date back to the 13th century and some original decoration survives from that time. This little-changed, relaxed family home contains a superb collection of furniture and paintings. The meadows and woodland surrounding it are a green haven for families.

★ Satellite Navigation should not be used in getting to Bradley as it will take you to the wrong side of the valley. No refreshments. No WC

ℹ️ **T** 01803 661907
E bradley@nationaltrust.org.uk

🎭 Shakespeare in the park, crafts

🚶 Woodland and meadow walks

♿ 🅿️ ⋯ Ⓐ 🔁 🖥️ 🎵 **Building** ♿♿ **Grounds** ♿♿ ➡️

👶 Hip-carrying infant seats for loan. Children's quiz/trail. Unpacked Tracker Packs

🏫 Suitable for school groups. 3D jigsaw model of house

🐕 Only in meadows and woodland surrounding manor, not in garden or house

For public transport details, see page 377

→ [202:SX848709] **Foot**: within easy walking distance of town along Totnes road.
Bus: Stagecoach in Devon X54, Country Bus 176 from Newton Abbot (passing close ▦ Newton Abbot). **Station**: Newton Abbot 1½ml. **Road**: drive gate (with small lodge) is ½ml from town centre on Totnes road (A381)

P Parking, 400yds. Free from 1:30. No coaches

NT properties nearby
Coleton Fishacre, Compton Castle, Greenway

Bradley								
31 Mar–1 Oct		2–5	M	**T**	**W**	**T**	F	S	S

5–30 Oct open weekdays by prior appointment only. Tel. at least one day in advance

The ante-chapel at Bradley, Devon

Branscombe – The Old Bakery, Manor Mill and Forge

Branscombe, Seaton, Devon EX12 3DB

🐓 ❌ 🔩 🍽 🚲 🏠 ▣ 👪 ▦ 🛠 1965 (1:H7)

Charming vernacular buildings with mill and forge restored to working order

The Old Bakery is a stone-built and partially rendered building beneath thatch, which at the time of its closure as a business in 1987 was the last traditional working bakery in Devon. The old baking equipment has been preserved in the baking room and the rest of the building now serves as a tea-room. The water-powered Manor Mill probably supplied the flour for the bakery. The forge is open daily and the blacksmith sells the ironwork he produces.

⭐ WCs at bakery and village hall

ℹ **T** 01392 881691
E branscombe@nationaltrust.org.uk

🚶 Branscombe walks leaflet available

♿ 🚻 Building 🔹🔹 Manor Mill 🔹 Grounds 🔹

🍵 Tea-room (NT-approved concession)

👪 Pushchairs and baby back-carriers admitted. Family guide

🎒 Suitable for school groups. Live interpretation

🐕 On leads and only in garden and Old Bakery information room

→ [192:SY198887] **Foot**: South West Coast Path within ⅝ml. **Cycle**: public bridleway from Great Seaside to Beer gives shared access for cyclists. **Bus**: Axe Valley 899 Sidmouth–Seaton (connections from ▦ Axminster or Honiton). **Station**: Honiton 8ml. **Road**: in Branscombe village, off A3052

P Free parking. Small NT car park adjacent to Forge, also car park adjacent to village hall; donations in well

NT properties nearby
A La Ronde, Loughwood Meeting House, Shute Barton

Branscombe								
Old Bakery								
1 Apr–1 Nov	11–5	M	T	**W**	T	**F**	**S**	**S**
Manor Mill								
29 Mar–28 Jun	2–5	M	T	W	T	F	S	**S**
1 Jul–30 Aug	2–5	M	T	**W**	T	F	S	**S**
6 Sep–1 Nov	2–5	M	T	W	T	F	S	**S**
Forge								
All year		**M**	**T**	**W**	**T**	**F**	**S**	**S**
Forge: tel. for details of opening times								

Please remember – your membership card is *always* needed for free admission

Brean Down

Brean, North Somerset

[icons] 1954   **(1:H4)**

Promontory of land with dramatic cliffs and Victorian fort

One of the most striking landmarks of the Somerset coastline, Brean Down projects dramatically for over a mile into the Bristol Channel. It offers magnificent views for miles around and is rich in wildlife and history, making it an ideal place to explore. The Palmerston Fort, built 1865, provides a unique insight into Brean's past.

★ The cliffs are extremely steep. Please stay on the main paths, keep dogs on leads and wear suitable footwear. The beach (not NT) can be dangerous. The Fort and Down are reached by a steep climb from the car park. On most Sat and Sun afternoons from Easter to end Sept, volunteers open officers' quarters and gun magazines for visitors. Also open Mon, Wed and Fri during school holidays. Groups guided on request. No WC

ℹ️ **T** 01934 844518
E breandown@nationaltrust.org.uk

🚶 Circular walks leaflet

♿ [icon] **Building** [icon]

☕ Brean Down Cove Café (not NT) by car park

🏛 Suitable for school groups. Small exhibition about Down and Fort in room opposite café entrance

🐕 On leads only

➡️ [182:ST290590] **Bus**: First 112 Highbridge–Weston-super-Mare (passing close ≅ Highbridge and close ≅ Weston-super-Mare), alight Brean, 1¾ml. **Station**: Highbridge 8½ml. **Road**: between Weston-super-Mare and Burnham-on-Sea, 8ml from exit 22 of M5

🅿️ Parking, 200yds. NT members must display cards. Situated at Brean Down Cove Café at the bottom of Brean Down. The higher Down is a steep climb from the car park and the Fort is approx. 1½ml further

NT properties nearby Cheddar Cliffs, Clevedon Court, Crook Peak, Sand Point, Tyntesfield

Magnificent view from Brean Down, Somerset

Bredon Barn

Bredon, nr Tewkesbury, Worcestershire GL20 7EG

[icon] 1951   **(1:K1)**

Large medieval threshing barn

The 14th-century barn is beautifully constructed from local Cotswold stone and noted for its dramatic aisled interior and unusual stone chimney cowling.

★ No WC

ℹ️ **T** 01451 844257
E bredonbarn@nationaltrust.org.uk

♿ **Building** [icon]

➡️ [150:SO919369] **Bus**: Astons 540/5 Evesham–Cheltenham (passing ≅ Evesham). **Station**: Pershore (U) 8¼ml. **Road**: 3ml NE of Tewkesbury, just N of B4080

🅿️ Parking very limited (land around barn not NT). Access difficult – tight corners and narrow lane to Barn. NT sign set back from road

NT properties nearby
Ashleworth Tithe Barn, Croome Park, Hailes Abbey, Snowshill Manor and Garden

Bredon Barn									
11 Mar–1 Nov		10–6	M	T	**W**	T	**F**	**S**	**S**

Closes dusk if earlier. All other times by appointment only

Brean Down								
All year			**M**	**T**	**W**	**T**	**F**	**S**	**S**

Brownsea Island

Poole, Dorset BH13 7EE

✚ 🔧 🍽 🏔 🐾 🏠 🗄 👜 🍴 🏕 🎭 🏃 🖼

🏃 | 1962 | (1:K7)

Peaceful island of woodland, wetland and heath with a wide variety of wildlife, famous for being the birthplace of Scouting and Guiding

Brownsea Island is dramatically located in Poole Harbour, offering spectacular views across to Studland, Old Harry Rocks and the Purbeck Hills. This unspoilt setting offers an escape from the noise and stress of modern life, making it a great location for walking, picnicing and exploring. Thriving natural habitats, including woodlands, heathland and lagoon, create a haven for wildlife such as the rare red squirrel and a large variety of birds and insects. Visitors to the island will be fascinated by its rich history, including daffodil farming, pottery works and acting as a decoy to protect Poole in the Second World War. Robert Baden-Powell held the first experimental Scout camp here in 1907, and the island is now known worldwide as the birthplace of Scouting and Guiding.

What's new in 2009 Range of outdoor and island activities for booked school, Scouting and Guiding groups

⭐ Brownsea Island is only accessible by boat. Ferry trips (not NT) depart from Poole Quay, Sandbanks Jetty, Bournemouth Pier and Swanage Pier. Brownsea Castle is privately leased and is not open to the public. Part of the island is leased to Dorset Wildlife Trust, please call 01202 709445. Brownsea Island is a nature reserve – assistance dogs only

ℹ️ **T** 01202 707744
E brownseaisland@nationaltrust.org.uk

🚶 Free guided walks every day – Introduction to Brownsea Island. Group tours by arrangement. Dorset Wildlife Trust reserve self-guided trail and other tours

Brownsea Island offers fantastic opportunities to explore and spot rare wildlife

To Explore the Island

Unless indicated, last admission is always 30mins before closing time

⊙ Programme of events, including family activity days. Open-air theatre (tel. 01202 251987)

🚶 Walks for all abilities: woodland, heathland, shoreline and clifftop. Self-guided trail leaflets, including red squirrel and Baden-Powell trails

♿ 🚻 ⠿ 🅿 🔼 🔼 Building 🔼 🔼 🔼
Grounds 🔼 ➡

🏠 NT shop (including red squirrel souvenirs and Scouting souvenirs)

☕ Villano Café near landing quay. Hot and cold refreshments, children's lunch boxes, ice-cream

👶 Baby-changing facilities. Pushchairs and baby back-carriers admitted. Children's guide book. Children's quiz/trail. Family outdoor activity packs. Family activity days. All-terrain baby buggies for loan (booking advisable)

🏫 Suitable for school groups. Scout and Guide groups (day or residential). Education room/centre. Hands-on activities. Baden-Powell Outdoor Centre

➔ [195:SZ032878] In Poole Harbour.
Foot: close to start/end of South West Coast Path at Shell Bay. **Ferry**: half-hourly boat service from 10 (not NT) from Poole Quay (tel. 01202 631828 or 01929 462383) and Sandbanks (tel. 01929 462383). Also service from Bournemouth and Swanage (tel. 01202 558550). Wheelchair users are advised to contact ferry operators. **Bus**: Wilts & Dorset 50 Bournemouth–Swanage, alight Sandbanks; 52 Poole–Sandbanks. Buses from surrounding areas to Poole Bridge, few min walk from Poole ferry. **Station**: Poole ½ml to Poole Quay; Branksome or Parkstone, both 3½ml to Sandbanks

NT properties nearby
Corfe Castle, Kingston Lacy, Studland Beach

Brownsea Island									
14 Mar–27 Mar*	10–4	**M**	**T**	**W**	**T**	**F**	**S**	**S**
28 Mar–17 Jul	10–5	**M**	**T**	**W**	**T**	**F**	**S**	**S**
18 Jul–31 Aug	10–6	**M**	**T**	**W**	**T**	**F**	**S**	**S**
1 Sep–27 Sep	10–5	**M**	**T**	**W**	**T**	**F**	**S**	**S**
28 Sep–1 Nov	10–4	**M**	**T**	**W**	**T**	**F**	**S**	**S**

Shop and Villano Café close 30mins before island. The island is open during winter for booked groups only.
*Limited boat service from 14 Mar–27 Mar inc. Visit website or tel. property for boat service details

Buckland Abbey

Yelverton, Devon PL20 6EY

⊺ 1948 (1:E8)

700-year-old home of Elizabethan seafarers Drake and Grenville, in beautiful Tavy Valley estate

From matins and vespers to swashbuckling tales of the sea, Buckland was home to Cistercian monks and later the seafaring adventurers Drake and Grenville. Wander through the monastic Great Barn and Elizabethan garden to reach the Abbey, with its exhibition galleries and interactive displays revealing the lives and stories behind two men who changed the shape of the house and fate of the country. Treasures include Drake's Drum which, according to legend, will sound when England is in danger to summon Sir Francis Drake from his grave to save us. Beyond the house discover meadows, orchards and four woodland walks on the bank of the River Tavy. These, along with a Letterbox Trail and Tracker Packs, provide activities for all to enjoy.

What's new in 2009 Seven-day opening in summer. Concerts in the Great Barn and extended Christmas event

⭐ The Abbey is presented in association with Plymouth City Museum

ℹ **T** 01822 853607
E bucklandabbey@nationaltrust.org.uk

⊙ Craft fairs 27/28 June (small entrance fee inc. NT members) and 14/15 Nov. Medieval re-enactment, Teddy Bears' Picnic and Christmas event

🚶 Four waymarked walks through woodland and farmland, map available from reception; Letterbox Trail

♿ 🅿 🔼 🚻 ⠿ 🅿 🔼 🔼 🔼
Building 🔼 🔼 🔼 Grounds 🔼 🔼 ➡

🏠 NT shop and plant sales. Independent craft workshops, usually open as Abbey. Woodturner (tel. 01364 631585) and countryside artist (tel. 01752 664096)

☕ Refectory restaurant/tea-room (licensed) in

the 13th-century Monks Guesthouse. Serving lunches, snacks and refreshments March–Oct. Restricted menu Nov–Feb. Open in Dec for Christmas lunches. Children's menu

🏼 Baby-changing and feeding facilities. Front-carrying baby slings and hip-carrying infant seats for loan. Children's quiz/trail. Parent and baby room. Family activities

▥ Suitable for school groups. Education room/centre. Live interpretation. Hands-on activities

→ [201:SX487667] **Cycle**: Drake's Trail, NCN27, 2ml. **Bus**: DAC 55 from Yelverton (with connections from ⊞ Plymouth) Mon–Sat; First 48 from Plymouth Suns.
Station: Plymouth 11ml. **Road**: 6ml S of Tavistock, 11ml N of Plymouth: turn off A386 ½ml S of Yelverton

P Free parking, 150yds

NT properties nearby
Antony, Castle Drogo, Cotehele, Lydford Gorge, Plym Bridge Woods, Saltram

Buckland Abbey										
14 Feb–8 Mar	11–4	M	T	W	T	F	S	S
14 Mar–30 Jun	10:30–5:30	M	T	W	T	F	S	S
1 Jul–31 Aug	10:30–5:30	M	T	W	T	F	S	S
1 Sep–1 Nov	10:30–5:30	M	T	W	T	F	S	S
6 Nov–13 Dec	11–4	M	T	W	T	F	S	S
18 Dec–23 Dec	11–4	M	T	W	T	F	S	S
Last admission 45mins before closing								

Buckland Abbey: once a monastery, the house has many seafaring connections

View of the beach (not NT) at Bedruthan Steps from Carnewas in the south looking north to Park Head promontory

Carnewas and Bedruthan Steps

nr Bedruthan, St Eval, Wadebridge, Cornwall PL27 7UW

🖼 🏠 🖤 🎭 🏠 🏼 🧍 🦅 1930   **(1:C8)**

Dramatic coastline with views over massive rock stacks

This is one of the most popular destinations on the Cornish coast because of the spectacular clifftop view of rocks stretching into the distance across the sweep of Bedruthan beach (not NT). There are magnificent walks along the coast path between Carnewas and Park Head. The Trust has rebuilt the cliff staircase down to the beach, but it is **unsafe to bathe at any time** and visitors need to be aware of the risk of being cut off by the tide.

★ WC not always available

ℹ **T** 01637 860563
E carnewas@nationaltrust.org.uk

🧍 NT *Coast of Cornwall* leaflet 6 includes maps and details of circular walks and information on local history, geology and wildlife

♿ 🅿 🚾 🧍 🎒

📷 Shop

🍽 Tea-room and garden (NT-approved concession) in Carnewas car park overlooking the coast

👪 Children's quiz/trail

➔ [200:SW849692] **Foot**: ⅔ml of South West Coast Path on property. **Bus**: Western Greyhound 556 🚌 Newquay–Padstow. **Station**: Newquay 7ml. **Road**: just off B3276 from Newquay to Padstow, 6ml SW of Padstow

P Parking. Seasonal charge

NT properties nearby
Trerice

Carnewas and Bedruthan Steps								
All year		M	T	W	T	F	S	S
Shop/info								
13 Feb–1 Mar	10:30–3:30	M	T	W	T	F	S	S
7 Mar–8 Mar	10:30–3:30	M	T	W	T	F	S	S
14 Mar–1 Nov	10:30–5	M	T	W	T	F	S	S
Tea-room								
13 Feb–22 May	11–4	M	T	W	T	F	S	S
23 May–30 Sep	10:30–5	M	T	W	T	F	S	S
1 Oct–20 Dec	11–4	M	T	W	T	F	S	S

Cliff staircase closed throughout winter from 1 Nov.
Tea-room enquiries tel. 01637 860701

Castle Drogo

Drewsteignton, nr Exeter, Devon EX6 6PB

🍵 1974 (1:F7)

The 'last castle to be built in England', set above the Teign Gorge with dramatic views over Dartmoor

What appears to be an ancient granite fortress overlooking the wilds of Dartmoor was actually the 20th-century home of self-made millionaire Julius Drewe. Employing the foremost architect of his age, Sir Edwin Lutyens, Drewe created an impressive family home – a bold statement that looks back to a romantic past, while heralding the modern era. Inside modern technology and family keepsakes – radios and gramophones, toys, dolls' houses, photographs and books – sit alongside 17th-century tapestries and inlaid tables. The servants' rooms are also fascinating and poignant. The beautiful formal garden, inspired by Gertrude Jekyll, makes a striking contrast to Dartmoor's ancient woodlands, which creep right up to the borders of the grounds. Play a family game of croquet on the huge circular lawn, while younger children enjoy the play area nearby, then explore the estate and hike down through the wooded Teign Gorge to the rushing river far below.

Castle Drogo: dramatically situated high above the wooded Teign Gorge

Charges for National Trust members apply on some special event days

What's new in 2009 Seven days a week opening in main season. Super Tuesdays, when you can discover special conservation days at Drogo

★ The property is situated at a height of nearly 300 metres within Dartmoor National Park and can experience extreme weather conditions. Approach lane is narrow with tight corners. Appropriate clothing and footwear are recommended

ℹ️ **T** 01647 433306
E castledrogo@nationaltrust.org.uk

🎭 From March–Dec inc. family trails and activities, walks, talks, art and craft workshops. Family event every day in school holidays (April–Oct)

🚶 Walks leaflet

♿ 🅿️ 🚻 ♿ ⚐ ∴ ◎ 🖥 🎒 🔔 🔲
Building ♿ ♿ ♿ **Grounds** ♿ ♿ ➡️

🏠 NT shop. Plant sales

☕ Castle tea-room in castle. Children's menu. Tea-room at visitor centre. Children's menu

👶 Baby-changing and feeding facilities. Baby back-carriers admitted. Hip-carrying infant seats for loan. Children's play area. Children's quiz/trail. Family trails and activities, walks, talks, art and craft workshops. Family events during school holidays (April–Oct)

🏛 Suitable for school groups. Live interpretation. Hands-on activities

🐕 On leads and only in car park and on estate walks

➡️ [191:SX721900] **Foot**: Two Moors Way. **Bus**: Stagecoach in Devon 173 Exeter–Moretonhampstead (passing ≣ Exeter Central) Mons–Sats. Carmel Coaches 274 from ≣ Okehampton, Suns & BHols May–Sept. **Station**: Yeoford (U) 8ml. **Road**: 5ml S of A30 Exeter–Okehampton. Take A382 Whiddon Down–Moretonhampstead road; turn off at Sandy Park

🅿️ Free parking, 400yds. Tight corners and narrow lanes

NT properties nearby
Finch Foundry, Fingle Bridge, Lydford Gorge, Parke Estate, Steps Bridge

Castle Drogo									
Castle									
14 Feb–22 Feb	11–4	**M**	**T**	**W**	**T**	**F**	**S**	**S**
28 Feb–8 Mar	11–4	M	T	W	T	F	**S**	**S**
14 Mar–1 Nov	11–5	**M**	**T**	**W**	**T**	**F**	**S**	**S**
28 Nov–13 Dec	11–4	M	T	W	T	F	**S**	**S**
19 Dec–23 Dec	11–4	M	**W**	**T**	**F**	**S**	**S**
Visitor centre/garden/shop/tea-room									
14 Feb–22 Feb	10:30–4:30	**M**	**T**	**W**	**T**	**F**	**S**	**S**
28 Feb–8 Mar	10:30–4:30	M	T	W	T	F	**S**	**S**
14 Mar–1 Nov	10:30–5:30	**M**	**T**	**W**	**T**	**F**	**S**	**S**
7 Nov–13 Dec	10:30–4:30	M	T	W	T	F	**S**	**S**
19 Dec–23 Dec	10:30–4:30	M	**W**	**T**	**F**	**S**	**S**
27 Dec–3 Jan 10	10:30–4:30	**M**	**T**	**W**	**T**	**F**	**S**	**S**
9 Jan–31 Jan 10	10:30–4:30	M	T	W	T	F	**S**	**S**

Chedworth Roman Villa

Yanworth, nr Cheltenham, Gloucestershire GL54 3LJ

🏛 🏠 💼 🍴 ♿ ⌂ 🛋 🎭 👶 🏛 1924 **(1:K2)**

Remains of one of Britain's largest Romano-British villas, set in the heart of the Cotswolds

The remains of one of the largest Roman villas in Britain provide a fascinating insight into the period. The site was discovered in 1864 by a local gamekeeper and subsequently excavated. Over a mile of walls survive along with beautiful mosaics, two bathhouses, hypocausts, a water shrine and latrine. Visitors to the museum will discover artefacts from the villa, and an audio-visual presentation brings history to life.

What's new in 2009 New family Tracker Packs

ℹ️ **T** 01242 890256
E chedworth@nationaltrust.org.uk

🎧 Adult and child version available from reception. Full interpretive guide to the villa's many exciting features (children free)

🎭 Living history events. Family trails

♿ 🅿️ 🚻 ♿ ∴ ⚐ 🎒 🔲 **Building** ♿ ♿
Grounds ♿

🏠 Wide range of Roman and archaeological books, plus Roman-themed gifts and plants

☕ Light snacks and drinks for sale in shop. Tea tent serving hot drinks and sandwiches open at weekends and during school holidays

(†) Baby-changing facilities. Pushchairs and baby back-carriers admitted. Children's guide. Children's quiz/trail. Family activity packs. Family trails. Activities for children in school holidays

(†) Suitable for school groups. Education room/centre. Live interpretation. Hands-on activities. Archaeological and living history activities for schools

→ [163:SP053135] **Station**: Cheltenham Spa 9ml. **Road**: 3ml NW of Fossebridge on Cirencester–Northleach road (A429); approach from A429 via Yanworth or from A436 via Withington (coaches must approach from Fossebridge)

Chedworth Roman Villa										
3 Mar–3 Apr	10–4	M	T	W	T	F	S	S
4 Apr–23 Oct	10–5	M	T	W	T	F	S	S
24 Oct–15 Nov	10–4	M	T	W	T	F	S	S
Open BH Mons. See noticeboard for shop/tea tent opening times									

The Church House

Widecombe in the Moor, Newton Abbot, Devon TQ13 7TA

🏠 ⬛ (†) ⬛ ⬛ 1933 **(1:F7)**

Fine two-storey granite building dating from c.1540

Originally a place where 'church ales' were held in the 16th and 17th centuries ('ales' being parish festivities raising funds for the church), the building later became almshouses, a school and a workhouse, before becoming the village school again in 1875. It is now the village hall and is used regularly for village events. The adjacent Sexton's Cottage is a NT shop and Dartmoor National Park information point.

⭐ No WC, nearest in public car park

ⓘ **T** 01364 621321
   E churchhouse@nationaltrust.org.uk

⬛ ⬛ ⬛ ⬛ Building ⬛ ⬛ Grounds ⬛

(†) Pushchairs admitted

→ [191:SX718768] In centre of Widecombe, N of Ashburton, W of Bovey Tracey. **Bus**: Country Bus/First 270/2 Newton Abbot–Totnes/Tavistock; Carmel/Country Bus 274 from ⊠ Okehampton. Every Sun only, June–Sept only, but 270 runs daily Aug only. **Road**: on B3387 approx 12ml from A38, Bovey Tracey

P Parking (not NT), 100yds (pay & display)

NT properties nearby
Hembury, Holne Woods, Parke Estate

Detail of a mosaic in the dining room of Chedworth Roman Villa, Gloucestershire

P Two car parks: villa car park, 15yds from entrance. Overflow car park, April–Sept, 250yds from entrance

NT properties nearby
Lodge Park and Sherborne Estate, Snowshill Manor and Garden

The Church House								
8 Feb–23 Dec	From 10:30*	M	T	W	T	F	S	S
Open to visitors when not in use as a village hall but closed on Tues all day and Wed and Fri mornings during school terms. *Closing time of shop/information centre is dependent on the weather but never before 4								

Dogs assisting visitors with disabilities are always welcome

Clevedon Court

Tickenham Road, Clevedon,
North Somerset BS21 6QU

🏠 ✿ 🍽 🚶 🎦 1961 (1:I4)

Outstanding 14th-century manor house and 18th-century terraced garden

Set in a beautifully landscaped terraced garden, the house was built by Sir John de Clevedon in c.1320, incorporating parts of a massive 13th-century tower and great hall. Much of the original building is still evident, although the Elizabethans made many alterations and additions. Home to the Elton family since 1709, visitors will see striking examples of Eltonware pottery and a fascinating collection of Nailsea glass.

★ The Elton family opens and manages the property for the NT

ℹ **T** 01275 872257
E clevedoncourt@nationaltrust.org.uk

♿ 🅿 Ⓓ ⦂ 🖼 🗖 📷 🔉 Building 🔔
Grounds 🔔 🔔

🍽 Tea-shop (not NT). Tel. property for opening dates

🚶 Children's guide. Children's quiz/trail

🎦 Suitable for school groups

➜ [172:ST423716] **Bus**: First 364 Bristol–Clevedon (passing ▣ Nailsea & Blackwell). **Station**: Yatton 3ml. **Road**: 1½ml E of Clevedon, on Bristol road (B3130), signposted from M5 exit 20

🅿 Free parking, 50yds. Unsuitable for trailer caravans or motor caravans. Some parking 100yds E of entrance in cul-de-sac

NT properties nearby
Blaise Hamlet, Brean Down, Dyrham Park, Leigh Woods, Tyntesfield, Westbury College Gatehouse

Clevedon Court									
1 Apr–30 Sep	2–5		M	T	**W**	**T**	F	S	**S**
Open BH Mons. Car park opens at 1:15. Entry to house by timed ticket, on a first-come, first-served basis									

Clouds Hill

Wareham, Dorset BH20 7NQ

🏠 🗖 🪑 🎦 🚶 1937 (1:J7)

The rural retreat of T. E. Lawrence

This tiny isolated brick and tile cottage in the heart of Dorset was the peaceful retreat of T. E. Lawrence ('Lawrence of Arabia'). The austere rooms are much as he left them and reflect his complex personality and close links with the Middle East, as detailed in a fascinating exhibition.

What's new in 2009 Free children's hidden nature trail

★ No WC

ℹ **T** 01929 405616
E cloudshill@nationaltrust.org.uk

🚶 Trail to picnic spot on top of the hill. 'On Lawrence Trail', 3ml circular walk

♿ ⦂ Building 🔔 Grounds 🔔

🗖 T. E. Lawrence books on sale

🎦 Suitable for school groups

🐕 In the grounds on leads only

➜ [194:SY824909] **Station**: Wool 3½ml; Moreton (U) 3½ml. **Road**: 1ml N of Bovington Tank Museum, 9ml E of Dorchester, 1½ml E of Waddock crossroads (B3390), 4ml S of A35 Poole–Dorchester

🅿 Free parking, 30yds. No coaches (only minibuses). No trailer caravans

Clouds Hill: T. E. Lawrence's rural retreat

NT properties nearby
Brownsea Island, Corfe Castle, Hardy Monument, Hardy's Cottage, Kingston Lacy, Max Gate

Clouds Hill									
14 Mar–1 Nov		12–5	M	T	W	**T**	**F**	**S**	**S**
Open BH Mons. Closes at dusk if earlier; no electric light									

Coleridge Cottage

35 Lime Street, Nether Stowey, Bridgwater, Somerset TA5 1NQ

 1909   **(1:H5)**

Home of the poet Samuel Taylor Coleridge

Discover the former home of Coleridge, who lived in the cottage for three years from 1797. It was here that he wrote *The Rime of the Ancient Mariner*, part of *Christabel, Frost at Midnight* and *Kubla Khan*. Mementoes of the poet can be seen here.

What's new in 2009 2009 marks 100 years of National Trust ownership of Coleridge Cottage. Special events are planned to celebrate

★ No WC, nearest WC at village library 500yds. The property is managed by Dunster Castle (01643 821314)

ℹ **T** 01278 732662
E coleridgecottage@nationaltrust.org.uk

🏃 Coleridge Way starts at Coleridge Cottage

♿ 🔷 🅰 **Building** 🔷

🎒 Suitable for school groups

➡ [181:ST191399] **Bus**: First 14 Bridgwater–Williton (passing close ⊟ Bridgwater). **Station**: Bridgwater 8ml. **Road**: at W end of Lime Street, opposite Ancient Mariner pub, 8ml W of Bridgwater

🅿 Parking (not NT), 500yds. Coach parking available by arrangement

NT properties nearby
Dunster Castle, Fyne Court, Holnicote Estate

Coleridge Cottage									
2 Apr–27 Sep		2–5	M	T	W	**T**	**F**	**S**	**S**
Open BH Mons & Easter									

Coleton Fishacre

Brownstone Road, Kingswear, Devon TQ6 0EQ

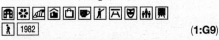
🏃 1982   **(1:G9)**

A luxuriant garden by the sea, with an Arts & Crafts-style house, featuring Art Deco-influenced interiors

In this enchanting corner of South Devon, house, garden and sea meet in perfect harmony. Lose yourself in the magical garden, where viewpoints allow frequent enticing glimpses out over the sea and where tender plants from the Mediterranean, South Africa and New Zealand thrive. In this most evocative of holiday homes, built for Rupert D'Oyly Carte, there is true 1920s elegance. A light, joyful atmosphere fills the rooms and music plays, echoing the family's Gilbert and Sullivan connections.

★ The lane leading to Coleton Fishacre is narrow and can be busy. Use of passing places and reversing may be necessary. Members may prefer to visit on Friday or Saturday or from 2:30, when the property is quieter. Visitors wishing to walk the coast path are requested to park in Coleton Camp or Brownstone car parks

ℹ **T** 01803 752466
E coletonfishacre@nationaltrust.org.uk

🏃 Guided walk 2:15–3:15 every Fri (free). Other garden and house tours by arrangement or as advertised

🎨 Exhibition of local artwork in house. Music events in house and garden

🏃 Coastal walks on the surrounding Dart and Start Bay Estate. Please park in Coleton Camp or Brownstone car parks

♿ 🔷 🔷 🔷 🔷 🔷 🔷 🔷 🔷
Building 🔷 🔷 🔷 **Grounds** 🔷 ▶

🎁 Selection of gifts, postcards and books. Plant sales: unusual shrubs and herbaceous plants

☕ Licensed tea-room (NT-approved concession). Specialising in local produce. Tel. 01803 752984. Children's menu

👪 Baby-changing facilities. Hip-carrying infant seats for loan. Quiz/trail. Family activity packs

For public transport details, see page 377

🎨 Hands-on activities

🐕 On leads only on surrounding NT land.
Dog crèche

➡️ [202:SX910508] **Foot**: South West Coast
Path within ⅖ml. **Bus**: Stagecoach in Devon
120 Paignton–Kingswear; otherwise
Stagecoach in Devon 22/4 Brixham–
Kingswear (with connections from Paignton).
On all, alight ¾ml SW of Hillhead, 1½ml walk to
garden. **Station**: Paignton 8ml; Kingswear
(Paignton & Dartmouth Rly) 2¼ml by footpath,
2¾ml by road. **Road**: 3ml from Kingswear;
take Lower Ferry road, turn off at toll house
(take care in narrow lanes). 6ml from Brixham,
take A3022 to Kingwear, turn left at toll
house. Narrow entrance and drive

🅿️ Free parking, 20yds. For visitors to house and
garden only. Coaches must book

NT properties nearby
Bradley, Compton Castle, Dart Estuary, Greenway,
Salcombe: Thurlestone to Torcross

Coleton Fishacre								
28 Feb–8 Mar	10:30–5	M	T	W	T	F	**S**	**S**
14 Mar–1 Nov	10:30–5	M	T	**W**	**T**	**F**	**S**	**S**
Open BH Mons								

Coleton Fishacre, Devon, is set in a magical garden

Compton Castle

Marldon, Paignton, Devon TQ3 1TA

🎨✝️❄️🏠🏛️🏯🎭👫🏭🚶 1951 **(1:G8)**

Dramatic fortified manor house and small formal garden

Home for most of the past 600 years to the Gilbert
family, including Sir Humphrey Gilbert, half-brother
to Sir Walter Raleigh, this imposing castle set
against a backdrop of rolling hills and orchards
evokes a bewitching mixture of romance and
history. This is the last truly fortified dwelling to be
built in Devon, and its extremely high curtain walls,
symmetrical towers and portcullis create an
unforgettable approach. Machicolations, spiral
staircases and squints make Compton a place of
discovery and adventure for imaginative children
and adults alike.

⭐ Credit cards not accepted. Few rooms open.
Restricted access to those with limited mobility

ℹ️ **T** 01803 661906
E comptoncastle@nationaltrust.org.uk

🎭 NGS garden day in June

🚶 NGS garden day in June to include walks
with the gardener

♿ 🔣 ⠿ 📷 🔧 💻 🎵 Building 🔩🔩
Grounds 🔩🔩➡️

🏠 Table-top shop only – guidebooks
and postcards

☕ Refreshments at Castle Barton restaurant (not
NT) from 10 (tel. 01803 873314). No credit cards

👫 Baby-changing and feeding facilities. Baby
back-carriers admitted. Hip-carrying infant
seats for loan. Family guide. Children's
quiz/trail. Unpacked Tracker Packs

🎨 Suitable for school groups. Hands-on
activities. 3D model

➡️ [202:SX865648] **Bus**: Stagecoach in Devon 7
🚉 Paignton–Marldon; 111 Dartmouth–
Torquay (passing 🚉 Totnes). On both alight
Marldon, 1½ml. **Station**: Torquay 3ml. Newton
Abbot 6ml. **Road**: at Compton, 5ml W of
Torquay, 1½ml N of Marldon. Signposted off
A380 to Marldon (not suitable for coaches) or
turn south from A381 Totnes road at Ipplepen
– 2ml to Compton

P Free parking, 30yds. Additional parking at Castle Barton opposite entrance, 100yds. Access for coaches via Ipplepen, not Marldon. Coaches may park at bus turning area opposite, 125yds

NT properties nearby
Bradley, Coleton Fishacre, Greenway

Compton Castle									
30 Mar–29 Oct	11–5	**M**	T	**W**	**T**	F	S	S
Open BH Mons								

Compton Castle, Devon: a place of discovery and adventure

Corfe Castle

The Square, Corfe Castle, Wareham, Dorset BH20 5EZ

🏰 🏠 🏛 💺 🚶 🎒 🛡 👪 📦 👤 1982   (1:K7)

Thousand-year-old castle, an iconic survivor of the English Civil War, rising above the Isle of Purbeck

One of Britain's most majestic ruins and once a controlling gateway through the Purbeck Hills, the castle boasts breathtaking views and several waymarked walks. Steeped in history, an interactive exhibition uncovers many stories of treachery and treason. Defended during the Civil War by the prudent and virtuous Lady Bankes, the castle fell, due to betrayal from within, and was subsequently partially destroyed by the Parliamentarians. Many fine Norman and early English features remain.

Corfe Castle									
Castle/shop									
1 Feb–28 Feb	10–4	**M**	**T**	**W**	**T**	**F**	**S**	**S**
1 Mar–31 Mar	10–5	**M**	**T**	**W**	**T**	**F**	**S**	**S**
1 Apr–30 Sep	10–6*	**M**	**T**	**W**	**T**	**F**	**S**	**S**
1 Oct–31 Oct	10–5	**M**	**T**	**W**	**T**	**F**	**S**	**S**
1 Nov–31 Jan 10	10–4	**M**	**T**	**W**	**T**	**F**	**S**	**S**
Tea-room									
1 Feb–28 Feb	10–4	**M**	**T**	**W**	**T**	**F**	**S**	**S**
1 Mar–31 Mar	10–5	**M**	**T**	**W**	**T**	**F**	**S**	**S**
1 Apr–30 Sep	10–5:30	**M**	**T**	**W**	**T**	**F**	**S**	**S**
1 Oct–31 Oct	10–5	**M**	**T**	**W**	**T**	**F**	**S**	**S**
1 Nov–31 Jan 10*	10–4	**M**	**T**	W	T	**F**	**S**	**S**

*Shop closes 5:30 April–Sept. The whole property is closed 25/26 Dec. High winds can cause closure of all or parts of the castle. Tea-room: open daily during winter local school holidays; *closed for refurbishment 4 Jan–29 Jan 10 (tel. 01929 481332)

What's new in 2009 After two years of an exciting programme of essential conservation work, full access is now available to all parts of the castle previously closed to visitors

i **T** 01929 481294 (Infoline), 01929 480921 (shop), 01929 480609 (Learning)
E corfecastle@nationaltrust.org.uk

🚶 Guided tours of castle often available, April–Oct

🛡 Living history, archaeology week, open-air theatre and cinema, school holiday activities, including family trails

🚶 Corfe Common walks leaflet from NT shop

♿ 🅿 🚗 🚻 ⦿ 📷 🎧 🔤 🔤 Grounds 🚶 ♿

🏠 In village square

💺 Traditional tea-room (licensed) by castle entrance in village square. Children's menu

👪 Baby-changing facilities. Pushchairs and baby back-carriers admitted. Family guide. Children's guide. Children's quiz/trail. School holiday activities inc. family treasure trails. Baby back-carriers for loan (small donation requested). Children must be accompanied by an adult within the castle

📦 Suitable for school groups. Education room/centre. Hands-on activities. Interactive exhibition at Castle View

🐕 On leads only

For general and membership enquiries, please telephone 0844 800 1895

→ [195:SY959824] **Bus**: Wilts & Dorset 40 Poole–Swanage (passing ✠ Wareham). **Station**: Wareham 4½ml. Corfe Castle (Swanage Steam Railway) a few mins walk (park & ride from Norden Station). **Road**: on A351 Wareham–Swanage road

P Parking (pay & display) at Castle View, off A351 (800yds walk uphill to castle). NT members free. Norden park & ride (all-day parking, ½ml walk to castle) and West St (in village). Pay & display (neither NT)

NT properties nearby
Brownsea Island, Clouds Hill, Studland Beach

The 1,000-year-old Corfe Castle in Dorset

Cornish Mines and Engines

Pool, nr Redruth, Cornwall TR15 3NP

🔧 🏠 🚶 🎫 🎭 👪 🖼 🚶 1967　　(1:C9)

Impressive Cornish beam engines and industrial heritage discovery centre

At the very centre of the Cornish Mining World Heritage Site, these two great beam engines sit preserved in their towering engine houses – a reminder of Cornwall's days as a world-famous centre of industry, engineering and innovation. Both engines were originally powered by high-pressure steam, introduced by local hero Richard Trevithick. One can still be seen in action, rotated by electricity, with the great beam rising and falling. The Discovery Centre gives you the whole dramatic story of Cornish mining, with an atmospheric film and static displays. Don't miss the experience of walking through the flue tunnel and the dizzying view up inside the 36m chimney stack.

What's new in 2009 Newly created seating area to enjoy your picnic, designed and made by two local schools

⭐ Trevithick Cottage, once home to Richard Trevithick, is nearby at Penponds and open April to Oct, Wed 2–5, free (donations welcome)

ℹ **T** 01209 315027
　E cornishmines@nationaltrust.org.uk

👪 Family fun and steam day in the summer. Talks and film shows

🚶 Self-guided site leaflet

♿ 🅿 ♿ •• 🔍 📷 📋 🔊 **Building** 🔊 ♿ ⬍ **Grounds** 🔊 ♿ ➡

🛍 Large range of mining and industrial heritage books

👪 Baby-changing facilities. Pushchairs and baby back-carriers admitted. Children/family activity packs. Family fun and steam day in the summer

🖼 Suitable for school groups

→ [203:SW672415] at Pool, 2ml W of Redruth on either side of A3047 midway between Redruth and Camborne. **Cycle**: NCN3, ½ml. **Bus**: First 14/18 Penzance/St Ives–Truro (passing ✠ Camborne and Redruth). **Station**: Redruth 2ml; Camborne 2ml. **Road**: site is signposted from A30 'Camborne East' and 'Redruth' junctions. Industrial Discovery Centre and Taylor's engine house reached through Morrisons' car park

P Free parking (not NT), 25yds. Main car park is shared with Morrisons' superstore. Secondary car park (not NT) outside Michell's engine house off A3047

NT properties nearby
Glendurgan Garden, Godolphin, Godrevy, Trelissick Garden

Cornish Mines and Engines								
Centre/shop								
29 Mar–30 Jun	11–5	**M**	T	**W**	**T**	**F**	S	S
1 Jul–31 Aug	11–5	**M**	T	**W**	**T**	**F**	S	S
1 Sep–1 Nov	11–5	**M**	T	**W**	**T**	**F**	S	S

Nov to end Jan 10 by arrangement only; please tel. for details or to arrange group visits at any time of year

Unless indicated, last admission is always 30mins before closing time

Cotehele

St Dominick, nr Saltash, Cornwall PL12 6TA

(1:E8)

Tudor house with superb collections of textiles, armour and furniture, set in extensive grounds

In the woods above the tidal River Tamar nestles Cotehele, built by the Edgcumbes in Tudor times. It is a house of many stories, myths and legends. King George III and Queen Charlotte came to see Cotehele's ancient and romantic interior in 1789, and found it festooned with tapestries and adorned with textiles, arms and armour, pewter, brass and old oak furniture. Little has changed, and a visit to the old house is a magical experience. Outside, the terraces are formally planted, then beyond you can lose yourself in the jungle plantation of the valley garden, which includes a medieval stewpond and dovecote (complete with doves – a children's favourite). Climb to the top of the Prospect Tower, a three-sided 18th-century folly high above the house, and enjoy fantastic views, or seek out the tranquillity of the Upper Garden. Cotehele Quay on the river is home to the restored Tamar sailing barge, *Shamrock*, and gateway to the wider estate, with its abundant wildlife and evocative industrial ruins – all that remains of a rich industrial past.

What's new in 2009 New Discovery Centre on Cotehele Quay. Second-hand bookshop. Shuttle bus

ℹ️ **T** 01579 351346, 01579 352711 (restaurant), 01579 352717 (tea-room), 01579 352713 (shop/plant sales)
E cotehele@nationaltrust.org.uk

Full winter events programme

Estate walks leaflet available

Building **Grounds**

Shop and plant sales. Gallery selling contemporary arts and crafts

Barn Restaurant (licensed). Children's menu. Edgcumbe Arms tea-room (licensed) on Cotehele Quay. Children's menu

Baby-changing and feeding facilities. Hip-carrying infant seats for loan. Children's guide. Children's quiz/trail. Tracker Packs

Suitable for school groups. Education room/centre

Under close control on woodland walks

→ [201:SX422685] **Cycle**: NCN27, 8ml. Hilly route from Tavistock to Cotehele.
Ferry: Calstock can be reached from Plymouth by water (contact Plymouth Boat Cruises Ltd, tel. 01752 822797) and from Calstock local river passenger ferry operates during summer subject to tides (tel. 01822 833331). **Bus**: First 190 Gunnislake–Callington (Sun, June–Sept only); DAC 79 Tavistock–Callington (passes ➡ Gunnislake) to within 1¼ml. **Station**: Calstock (U), 1½ml (signposted from station). **Road**: on W bank of the Tamar, 1ml W of Calstock by steep footpath (6ml by road), 8ml SW of Tavistock, 14ml from Plymouth via Saltash Bridge; 2ml E of St Dominick, 4ml from Gunnislake (turn at St Ann's Chapel). Coaches only by prior arrangement

P Free parking. Parking charge on quay

NT properties nearby

Antony, Buckland Abbey, Lanhydrock, Lydford Gorge, Saltram

Tudor Cotehele nestles in the woods above the River Tamar in Cornwall

Cotehele									
House									
28 Feb–8 Mar	11–4	M	T	W	T	F	**S**	**S**	
14 Mar–1 Nov	11–4:30	**M**	**T**	**W**	**T**	F	**S**	**S**	
Hall of House with garland									
9 Nov–24 Dec	11–4	**M**	**T**	**W**	**T**	**F**	**S**	**S**	
Garden									
All year	10–dusk	**M**	**T**	**W**	**T**	**F**	**S**	**S**	
Restaurant/shop/plants/gallery									
14 Feb–13 Mar	11–4	**M**	**T**	**W**	**T**	**F**	**S**	**S**	
14 Mar–1 Nov	10:30–5	**M**	**T**	**W**	**T**	**F**	**S**	**S**	
2 Nov–24 Dec	11–4	**M**	**T**	**W**	**T**	**F**	**S**	**S**	
Edgcumbe Arms									
14 Feb–1 Nov	11–5	**M**	**T**	**W**	**T**	**F**	**S**	**S**	
7 Nov–20 Dec	11–4	M	T	W	T	F	**S**	**S**	

Open Good Fri. Hall of House with garland closed weekend 14/15 Nov. Barn Restaurant closed Fridays 21 March–31 Oct. Edgcumbe Arms closes at dusk if earlier than 5. Limited opening in Nov/Dec, tel. for details

The cider press in one of the outbuildings at Cotehele Mill, near Saltash, Cornwall

Cotehele Mill

St Dominick, nr Saltash, Cornwall PL12 6TA

 1947 (1:E8)

Working watermill and workshops

A short level walk from Cotehele Quay, tucked away in the Morden Valley, the old mill is an atmospheric reminder of the recent past when corn was ground here for the local community. Flour is still produced in the traditional way and is on sale at the mill, and on Tuesdays and Thursdays you can see milling in action. A range of outbuildings containing a collection of blacksmiths', carpenters', wheelwrights' and saddlers' tools is presented as workshops, giving an insight into the working lives of local craftsmen.

What's new in 2009 Shuttle bus. Traditional furniture-maker working on site

ℹ️ **T** 01579 350606, 01579 351346 (property office) **E** cotehele@nationaltrust.org.uk

🎫 Guided tours at 3

♿ Building Grounds

👪 Pushchairs and baby back-carriers admitted. Children's quiz/trail

🏫 Suitable for school groups

🐕 Under close control on woodland walk to mill. Not in mill buildings

➡️ [201:SX417682] **Cycle**: NCN27, 8ml. Hilly route from Tavistock to Cotehele.
Ferry: Calstock can be reached from Plymouth by water (contact Plymouth Boat Cruises Ltd, tel. 01752 822797) and from Calstock local river passenger ferry operates during summer subject to tides (tel. 01822 833331). **Bus**: First 190 Gunnislake–Callington (Sun, June–Sept only); DAC 79 Tavistock–Callington (passes ⮊ Gunnislake) to within 1¼ml. **Station**: Calstock (U), 1½ml (signposted from station). **Road**: on W bank of the Tamar, 1ml W of Calstock by steep footpath (6ml by road), 8ml SW of Tavistock, 14ml from Plymouth via Saltash Bridge; 2ml E of St Dominick, 4ml from Gunnislake (turn at St Ann's Chapel). Coaches by prior arrangement only

🅿️ There is no parking at the mill except by prior arrangement for visitors with disabilities. All other visitors must park at Cotehele Quay and walk ½ml through the woods. Do not forget your membership card!

NT properties nearby
Antony, Buckland Abbey, Lanhydrock, Lydford Gorge, Saltram

Cotehele Mill									
14 Mar–30 Sep	11–5	**M**	**T**	**W**	**T**	**F**	**S**	**S**	
1 Oct–1 Nov	11–4:30	**M**	**T**	**W**	**T**	**F**	**S**	**S**	

The Courts Garden

Holt, nr Bradford-on-Avon, Wiltshire BA14 6RR

[icons] 1943   (1:J4)

Delightful English country garden

One of Wiltshire's best-kept secrets, this charming garden is full of variety and shows English country style at its best. The peaceful water gardens, with irises and lilies, and the beautiful herbaceous borders, complemented with surrounding topiary and ornaments, demonstrate an imaginative use of colour and planting. Stroll through the arboretum and enjoy the many wonderful species of tree and natural planting of spring bulbs.

★ Please, no tripods or easels without prior consent. No ball games or picnics

i **T** 01225 782875
E courtsgarden@nationaltrust.org.uk

[icon] By appointment at an additional charge

[icon] See website for details

[icon] Walks leaflet available showing cross-country route to Great Chalfield Manor and Garden

[icons] Grounds [icons]

[icon] Plant sales – small area at entrance

[icon] Tea-room (NT-approved concession) on ground floor of house

[icon] Pushchairs and baby back-carriers admitted. Children's quiz/trail

[icon] Suitable for school groups

→ [173:ST861618] **Cycle**: NCN4, 1¼ml.
Bus: First 237 Trowbridge–Melksham (passing close ≋ Trowbridge).
Station: Bradford-on-Avon 2½ml; Trowbridge 3ml. **Road**: 3ml SW of Melksham, 2½ml E of Bradford-on-Avon, on S side of B3107. Follow signs to Holt

P Free parking (not NT), 80yds. Parking in village hall car park opposite, on N side of B3107 (not for coaches)

NT properties nearby
Dyrham Park, Great Chalfield Manor and Garden, Lacock Abbey, Westwood Manor

The Courts Garden								
14 Mar–1 Nov	11–5	**M**	**T**	W	**T**	**F**	**S**	**S**
Tea-room open as garden. Out of season by appointment only								

Dunster Castle, Somerset, has had a turbulent history

Dunster Castle

Dunster, nr Minehead, Somerset TA24 6SL

[icons]
[icon] 1976   (1:G5)

Ancient castle with fine interiors and subtropical gardens

Dramatically sited on a wooded hill, a castle has existed here since at least Norman times, with an impressive medieval gatehouse and ruined tower giving a reminder of its turbulent history. Home of the Luttrell family for more than 600 years, the present building was remodelled in 1868–72 by Antony Salvin. The fine oak staircase and plasterwork ceiling he adapted can still be seen. Visitors can relax on the sunny sheltered terrace, which is home to a variety of subtropical plants and the National Collection of Strawberry Trees. Magnificent views over the Bristol Channel and a pleasant walk beside the River Avill add to the ambience.

What's new in 2009 Major roof project now complete, enabling the exceptional 17th-century leather hangings to be re-displayed in the Leather Gallery. Complemented by newly displayed contemporary artwork by Hannah Firmin

Charges for National Trust members apply on some special event days

i **T** 01643 823004 (Infoline), 01643 821314
E dunstercastle@nationaltrust.org.uk

X 'Attic and Basement' tours to areas not normally on public view (charge inc. NT members). Rooms are unfurnished. Tel. to book

Y Family events

[icons] Building **[icons]**
Grounds **[icons]**

[icon] NT shop

[icon] Baby-changing facilities. Baby back-carriers admitted. Front-carrying baby slings for loan. Family guide. Children's guide. Children's quiz/trail. Wheel-friendly route in gardens. Buggy park. Colouring sheets. Activity days. Ghostbusters' trail. Family events

[icon] Suitable for school groups. Live costumed interpretation. Adult study days

[icon] In park only on lead

→ [181:SS995435] **Bus**: First 398 Tiverton–Minehead; also 28 Taunton–Minehead (passing **[icon]** Taunton), alight Dunster Steep, ½ml. **Station**: Dunster (W Somerset Rly) 1ml. **Road**: in Dunster, 3ml SE of Minehead. NT car park approached direct from A39

P Parking, 300yds

NT properties nearby
Arlington Court, Coleridge Cottage, Dunster Working Watermill, Holnicote Estate, Knightshayes Court, West Exmoor Coast

Dunster Castle										
Castle										
14 Mar–22 Jul	11–5*	M	T	W	T		F	S	S
24 Jul–2 Sep	11–5	M	T	W	T		F	S	S
4 Sep–1 Nov	11–5*	M	T	W	T		F	S	S
Garden/park										
1 Feb–13 Mar	11–4	M	T	W	T	F	S	S
14 Mar–1 Nov	10–5	M	T	W	T	F	S	S
2 Nov–31 Dec	11–4	M	T	W	T	F	S	S
1 Jan–31 Jan 10	11–4	M	T	W	T	F	S	S
Shop										
2 Feb–13 Mar	11–4	M	T	W	T	F	S	S
14 Mar–1 Nov	10–5	M	T	W	T	F	S	S
2 Nov–3 Jan 10	11–4	M	T	W	T	F	S	S
Open Good Fri. Garden, park & shop closed 25, 26 & 27 Dec. Shop closed Jan 10. *Last entry to castle 4, 14 Mar–22 Jul & 4 Sept–1 Nov										

Show your card and display sticker for free parking

Dunster Working Watermill

Mill Lane, Dunster, nr Minehead, Somerset TA24 6SW

[icons] 1976 **(1:G5)**

Fully restored watermill

A restored 18th-century watermill in a tranquil riverside setting built on the site of a mill mentioned in the Domesday Survey of 1086.

★ The mill is a private business and all visitors inc. NT members pay the admission charge

i **T** 01643 821759
E dunstermill@nationaltrust.org.uk

[icons] Building **[icons]**

[icon] Selling mill flour, muesli and souvenirs (not NT)

[icon] Riverside tea-room (not NT)

[icon] Baby back-carriers admitted

[icon] Suitable for school groups

→ [181:SS995435] On River Avill, beneath Castle Tor. **Foot**: approach via Mill Lane or Castle Gardens. **Bus**: First 398 Tiverton–Minehead; also 28 Taunton–Minehead (passing **[icon]** Taunton), alight Dunster Steep, ½ml. **Station**: Dunster (W Somerset Rly) 1ml. **Road**: in Dunster, 3ml SE of Minehead. NT car park approached direct from A39

P Parking (not NT), 500yds. Alternative parking in Dunster Castle NT car park, £2

NT properties nearby
Arlington Court, Coleridge Cottage, Dunster Castle, Holnicote Estate

Dunster Working Watermill								
Mill								
1 Apr–31 Oct	11–4:45	M	T	W	T	F	S	S
Tea-room*								
1 Apr–31 Oct	10:30–4:45	M	T	W	T	F	S	S
Open Good Fri:10.30–4.45. *Tea-room hours may vary, please contact direct to confirm times								

Dunster Working Watermill, fully restored

Dyrham Park

Dyrham, nr Bath, Gloucestershire SN14 8ER

🎴✚🕸🐦🏠💺🏇🎧🎭💂👫🏛
🧍 1961 (1:J4)

Spectacular late 17th-century mansion, garden and deer park

Set in a beautiful Gloucestershire valley and surrounded by 110 hectares (274 acres) of garden and rolling parkland, this grand baroque house with spectacular sweeping views towards Bristol, was designed by Talman for William Blathwayt, Secretary at War during the reign of William III. Lavish 17th-century collections reflect the fashion for all things Dutch, including paintings and furniture. Later 18th-century additions include furniture by Gillow and Linnell, and the Victorian domestic quarters provide visitors with an intriguing insight into life below stairs.

What's new in 2009 Ongoing West Garden development – 'a contemporary garden with echoes of the past'

⭐ Due to the fragile nature of their contents, some rooms have very low light levels

ℹ️ **T** 0117 937 2501
E dyrhampark@nationaltrust.org.uk

🏇 Park, garden and house walks and talks held on weekdays during the season (not Good Fri or BH Mons)

🎧 Audio guides available for house

💂 Family activity days, winter lectures and workshops

🧍 Parkland walks available with map

♿ 🅿️🚉♿ ⋮⋮ 📷🖥️📺🎹🎺🎻
Building 📖♿ **Grounds** ♿▶️

🏠 NT shop. Plant sales

💺 Courtyard tea-room (licensed) at main house. Children's menu. Kiosk in tea-garden, serving hot drinks, sandwiches, ice-creams and snacks. Car park kiosk (NT-approved concession) for snacks and ice-creams

👫 Baby-changing facilities. Front-carrying baby slings and hip-carrying infant seats for loan. Children's guide. Children's quiz/trail. Children's activity packs. Family activity days

The east front of Dyrham: a grand baroque house

🏛 Suitable for school groups. Hands-on activities. Adult study days. Guide leaflets to the house in several languages

🦌 Dog walking area close to main car park

➡️ [172:ST743757] **Foot**: Cotswold Way passes property. **Cycle**: Avon and Wiltshire cycleways. **Bus**: special link from Queen's Square, ½ml 🚉 Bath Spa (tel. 0117 937 2501 for times). **Station**: Bath Spa 8ml. **Road**: 8ml N of Bath, 12ml E of Bristol; approached from Bath–Stroud road (A46), 2ml S of Tormarton interchange with M4, exit 18

🅿️ Free parking, 500yds

NT properties nearby
Bath Assembly Rooms, Clevedon Court, Lacock Abbey, Leigh Woods, Newark Park, Prior Park Landscape Garden, Tyntesfield

Dyrham Park									
House									
14 Mar–1 Nov	11–5*		M	T	W	T	F	S	S
Garden/shop/tea-room									
28 Feb–8 Mar	11–5		M	T	W	T	F	**S**	**S**
14 Mar–30 Jun	11–5		**M**	T	W	T	F	**S**	**S**
1 Jul–30 Aug	11–5		**M**	**T**	**W**	**T**	**F**	**S**	**S**
31 Aug–1 Nov	11–4		**M**	T	W	T	F	**S**	**S**
7 Nov–20 Dec	11–4		M	T	W	T	F	**S**	**S**
Park									
All year	11–5:30		**M**	**T**	**W**	**T**	**F**	**S**	**S**

Open BH Mons and Good Fri: 11–5. Last admission 1hr before closing. Park closed 25 Dec. *Between 11–12 access to the house will be by guided tour only

Dogs assisting visitors with disabilities are always welcome

Finch Foundry

Sticklepath, Okehampton, Devon EX20 2NW

 1994   (1:F7)

The last working water-powered forge in England

In the village of Sticklepath on the edge of Dartmoor you can discover the evocative sights and sounds of a 19th-century water-powered forge. See the three large waterwheels driving the huge tilt hammer and grindstone, and enjoy demonstrations throughout the day. The foundry used to make sickles, scythes and shovels for West Country farmers and miners. You will find a fascinating display of tools in the old grinding shop, and in the garden is a summerhouse that once belonged to Tom Pearse (of Widecombe Fair fame). Starting from the foundry there are waymarked walks along the River Taw and up on to Dartmoor.

[i] **T** 01837 840046
E finchfoundry@nationaltrust.org.uk

[K] Machinery demonstrations and talks throughout the day at quarter past each hour from 11:15–4:15

[icons] Building [icon]
Grounds [icons]

[icon] NT shop. Plant sales

[icon] Tea-room. Children's menu

[icon] Baby back-carriers admitted. Children's quiz/trail

[icon] Suitable for school groups. Teacher's resource pack available

[icon] Dogs welcome in all areas except tea-room, shop and foundry during demonstrations

[→] [191:SX641940] In the centre of Sticklepath village. **Foot**: on the 180ml Tarka Trail. **Cycle**: on West Devon Cycle Route. **Bus**: Western Greyhound 510 Exeter–Okehampton (passing ≍ Exeter Central), Carmel Coaches 179 Okehampton–Moretonhampstead. **Station**: Okehampton (Sun, June–Sept only) 4½ml. **Road**: 4ml E of Okehampton off A30

[P] Free parking. Not suitable for coaches and high vehicles. Access is narrow and low

NT properties nearby
Castle Drogo, Lydford Gorge

Finch Foundry									
21 Mar–1 Nov	11–5	**M**	T	**W**	**T**	**F**	**S**	**S**	

Fyne Court

Broomfield, Bridgwater, Somerset TA5 2EQ

 1967   (1:H5)

Nature reserve and visitor centre

The former pleasure grounds of the partly demolished home of the Crosse family, this nature reserve is leased by the Somerset Wildlife Trust and is the headquarters for the Quantock Hills Area of Outstanding Natural Beauty. It is ideal for walks and discovering a wide variety of habitats.

[★] Only visitor centre and grounds open to visitors; buildings contain an education base for the Wildlife Trust. The 8-hectare (20-acre) reserve is managed by Somerset Wildlife Trust, remainder of estate by NT

[i] **T** 01823 652400 (Somerset Wildlife Trust)
E fynecourt@nationaltrust.org.uk

[K] Contact property for details

[icons] Grounds [icons]

[icon] Baby-changing facilities. Pushchairs and baby back-carriers admitted

[icon] Suitable for school groups. Education centre. Booking essential

[→] [182:ST222321] 6ml N of Taunton; 6ml SW of Bridgwater. **Station**: Taunton 6ml; Bridgwater 6ml

[P] Parking (not NT), 150yds

NT properties nearby
Beacon and Bicknoller Hills, Coleridge Cottage, Dunster Castle, Holnicote Estate

Fyne Court									
1 Apr–31 Oct	9–6	**M**	**T**	**W**	**T**	**F**	**S**	**S**	
1 Nov–31 Jan 10	9–5	**M**	**T**	**W**	**T**	**F**	**S**	**S**	
Opens 10 Sat and Sun. Closes dusk if earlier									

Glastonbury Tor

nr Glastonbury, Somerset

[symbols] 1933 **(1:I5)**

Prominent hill overlooking the Isle of Avalon, Glastonbury and the Somerset Levels

The dramatic and evocative Tor dominates the surrounding countryside and offers spectacular views over Somerset, Dorset and Wiltshire. At the summit of this very steep hill an excavation has revealed the plans of two superimposed churches of St Michael, of which only a 15th-century tower remains.

[star] No WC

[i] **T** 01934 844518
E glastonburytor@nationaltrust.org.uk

[symbol] Easter trail and Apple Day

[symbol] Public footpaths across the Tor

[symbols] Grounds [symbol]

[symbol] On leads only

[symbol] [182/183:ST512386] **Foot**: short walk from the town centre, eastwards along A361. **Cycle**: NCN3. **Bus**: 376/377 Bristol–Yeovil (passing [rail] Bristol Temple Meads) within ½ml of the Tor. **Road**: signposted from Glastonbury town centre, from where seasonal park & ride (not NT) operates

[P] No parking on site (except for orange or blue badge holders). Please use council-run park & ride from centre of Glastonbury from April to Sept, or park in free car park at Somerset Rural Life Museum, Abbey Farm, Glastonbury. Tel. 01458 831197 to confirm times available. Lower entrance to the Tor is approx. ½ml from museum car park

NT properties nearby
Collard Hill, Lytes Cary Manor, Polden Hills, Stourhead

Glastonbury Tor							
All year	M	T	W	T	F	S	S

The Somerset Levels with Glastonbury Tor glimpsed in the distance

For public transport details, see page 377

Glendurgan Garden

Mawnan Smith, nr Falmouth, Cornwall TR11 5JZ

❄ 🏰 🏠 🛍 💷 😋 👭 🚩 🚶 1962   **(1:C9)**

Glendurgan Garden									
14 Feb–31 Jul	10:30–5:30	M		T	W	T	F	S	S
1 Aug–31 Aug	10:30–5:30	M	T	W	T	F	S	S	
1 Sep–31 Oct	10:30–5:30	M		T	W	T	F	S	S
Open BH Mons. Closed Good Fri									

Superb subtropical garden, with special interest for families

Described by the Fox family, who gave Glendurgan to the Trust, as 'a little peace [sic] of heaven on earth', the garden is a place of great beauty and tranquillity. Three valleys converge and drop towards the sparkling waters of the Helford River and the hamlet and beach at Durgan. The garden has many fine trees, rare and exotic plants from the four corners of the globe, outstanding spring displays of magnolias and camellias, plus carpets of wild flowers. Glendurgan has always been a magical place for children, with the baffling laurel maze, the Giant's Stride (rope swing), the beach and the recreated school house. It is an informal garden that all ages can enjoy. The house is privately occupied.

⭐ Ferry link to Durgan beach, from Helford Village, Helford Passage and Trebah Garden

ℹ️ **T** 01326 250906 (during opening hours), 01872 862090 (out of hours), 01326 250247 (tea-room) **E** glendurgan@nationaltrust.org.uk

😋 Series of garden events

🚶 *Coast of Cornwall* leaflet 16 (Helford River)

♿ 🅿️ 🚾 ⋯ 🔧 ⬆️ ⬇️

🛍 NT shop. Plant sales

💷 Tea-room (NT-approved concession). Serving beverages, light lunches, snacks, cakes and ice-cream

👭 Baby-changing facilities. Pushchairs and baby back-carriers admitted. Giant's Stride (a pole with ropes to swing from) and maze

🚩 Suitable for school groups

➜ [204:SW772277] **Foot**: South West Coast Path within ⅜ml. **Ferry**: service links Helford village, Helford Passage, Trebah beach and Durgan beach (for Glendurgan). Tel. 01326 250770. **Bus**: First T4 Falmouth–Helston/Helford. **Station**: Penmere (U) 4ml. **Road**: 4ml SW of Falmouth, ½ml SW of Mawnan Smith, on road to Helford Passage

🅿 Free parking. Car park gates locked at 5:30

NT properties nearby

Trelissick Garden

Glendurgan's baffling laurel maze in mid-summer

Godolphin

Godolphin Cross, Helston, Cornwall TR13 9RE

🏰 🏠 🏛 🔧 📷 ❄ 🚜 💷 🍴 🏕 😋 👭 🚩

🚶 2000   **(1:B9)**

Ancient and atmospheric house and garden set within an historic estate

At the heart of an historic estate, owned by the National Trust since 2000, lies one of Cornwall's most beautiful and romantic old houses. Newly acquired by the Trust, Godolphin was considered in the 17th century to be the most fashionable

---

Please remember – your membership card is *always* needed for free admission

house in Cornwall. It was the springboard for the political ambitions of the illustrious Godolphin family, who had made their fortune from the rich mineral deposits on the estate. However, after 1710 no Godolphin lived here, and the house and estate were left to settle gently into the landscape. Centuries of benign neglect have given the house and garden and surrounding estate buildings an extraordinarily haunting air of antiquity and peace, a fragile atmosphere that has been protected and nurtured through the 20th century by the Schofield family. Miraculously the garden has barely changed since the 14th and 16th centuries, with the latest fashions passing it by. It is so rare to discover a garden such as this, which has not been radically altered through the ages, and this is why it is considered to be one of the most important historic gardens in Europe. This garden is not about plants and flowers but about the unique remains of a medieval pattern. There are many fascinating walks on the estate, which includes Godolphin Hill and more than 400 recorded archaeological features – from Bronze Age enclosures to dramatic 19th-century mining remains. Godolphin is a distinct area within the Cornish Mining World Heritage Site.

What's new in 2009 New visitor reception area. Work starts on repairs to outbuildings

⭐ Restoration work may mean part-closure of house at short notice

ℹ️ **T** 01736 763194
  E godolphin@nationaltrust.org.uk

🚶 Occasional guided walks

🛡️ Including four weekend-long events in May (spring food fair), June, Aug and Sept (autumn food fair). Small admission fee for admission to the whole property (including NT members). See events leaflet or website for details

🚶 Estate walks leaflet available

♿ **House** 🏛️ **Estate** 🏛️

🍵 Tea and coffee only

👪 Pushchairs admitted to estate and garden

🏫 House, garden and estate suitable for school groups. Education room/centre. Some art/craft workshops for adult learners (booked groups only)

🐕 On estate only

➡️ [203:SW599321] **Bus**: First T20 Camborne–Helston (passing close ⊞ Camborne). **Station**: Camborne 9ml. **Road**: from Helston take A394 to Sithney Common, turn right on to B3302 and follow signs. From Hayle take B3302 through Leedstown. From W, take B3280 through Goldsithney

P Free parking. Coach access from Townshend

NT properties nearby
Glendurgan Garden, The Lizard, Penrose Estate, St Michael's Mount, Trelissick Garden, Trengwainton Garden

Godolphin									
House									
26 Apr–9 May	11–5	M	T	W	T	F	S	S
14 Jun–27 Jun	11–5	M	T	W	T	F	S	S
26 Jul–8 Aug	11–5	M	T	W	T	F	S	S
13 Sep–26 Sep	11–5	M	T	W	T	F	S	S
Garden									
29 Mar–1 Nov	10–5	M	T	W	T	F	S	S
Estate									
All year		M	T	W	T	F	S	S
A small charge will apply to members on event weekends									

Godolphin from the south-east, showing the ruined Great Hall wall, with the old Cider House beyond

Godrevy

Gwithian, nr Hayle, Cornwall

⛱ 🍴 🏠 🏛 🚶 1939   **(1:B9)**

High cliffs and sheltered coves with sandy beaches

The Trust owns all the coastline from Godrevy to Navax Point. The main beach below the summer car park connects to Gwithian Beach, forming an impressive sweep of unbroken sand around the edge of St Ives Bay. Away from the bustle of the beach, the coastal grasslands and heathland are rich with wild flowers and provide open access for miles of walking. Seals are a common sight, and guillemots, razorbills, fulmars and cormorants breed on the cliffs.

⭐ Please be aware of cliff edges, unstable cliffs and the state of the tide, and keep children supervised. WC not always available

ℹ️ **T** 01872 552412 (Area Warden)

🚶 NT *Coast of Cornwall* leaflet 9 includes details of walks

♿ 🚻 **Grounds** 🅿️

🍴 Ice-cream van. Godrevy Café (NT-approved concession) (licensed). Open main season and weekends/holidays all year. Tel. 01736 757999

🏛 Suitable for school groups

🐕 Seasonal restriction on beach, Easter to end Sept

➡️ [203:SW582430] **Bus:** Western Greyhound 501 (summer only) St Ives–Newquay (passing ≋ Hayle). **Station:** Hayle 5ml. **Road:** just off the B3301 N of Gwithian village

🅿️ Charge for parking. Limited parking Nov–April

NT properties nearby
Cornish Mines and Engines, Godolphin, St Michael's Mount, Trengwainton Garden

Godrevy							
All year	M	T	W	T	F	S	S

If you were fascinated by the medieval manor at Great Chalfield, why not take a trip to Lytes Cary too?

Great Chalfield Manor and Garden

nr Melksham, Wiltshire SN12 8NH

🏠 ✚ ❀ 🚶 🛡 👪 🏛 🚶 1943   **(1:J4)**

Charming 15th-century manor house with Arts & Crafts garden

A fine example of a medieval manor, complete with an upper moat, gatehouse and small parish church. Beautiful oriel windows and rooftop soldiers (*c*.1480) adorn the house, restored between 1905 and 1911 by Major R. Fuller – whose family still live here and manage the property on behalf of the Trust. The delightful gardens were designed by Alfred Parsons and feature terraces, gazebo and lily pond. Grass paths offer visitors romantic views across the spring-fed fishpond. The house and gardens have featured in many tv and film productions, including *Persuasion* and *The Other Boleyn Girl*.

⭐ Great Chalfield Manor and Garden is administered for the NT by the tenant

ℹ️ **T** 01225 782239
E greatchalfieldmanor@nationaltrust.org.uk

🚶 Access to house is by guided tour only (numbers limited)

🛡 Garden open outside normal times for spring flowers, under NGS. Charity spring plant fair in May. Charge inc. NT members

🚶 Walks leaflet showing cross-country route to The Courts Garden

♿ 🅿️ 🚹 🚻 ⦂ 🎞 📖 📖 **Building** 🔊 ♿ **Grounds** 🅿️

👪 Hip-carrying infant seats for loan

🏛 Suitable for school groups

➡️ [173:ST860631] **Foot:** pleasant 1ml walk by public footpath from The Courts Garden (NT), Holt. **Cycle:** NCN4. On the Wiltshire Cycleway. **Bus:** First 237 Trowbridge–Melksham (passing close ≋ Trowbridge), alight Holt, 1ml. **Station:** Bradford-on-Avon, 3ml. **Road:** 3ml SW of Melksham off B3107 via Broughton Gifford Common (follow sign for Broughton Gifford, take care in narrow lane). Coaches must approach from N (via Broughton Gifford); lanes from S too narrow

The west wing of the 15th-century Great Chalfield Manor, Wiltshire, seen from across the garden

P Free parking, 100yds on grass verge outside manor gates

NT properties nearby
The Courts Garden, Dyrham Park, Lacock Abbey, Westwood Manor

Great Chalfield Manor and Garden									
Manor house									
1 Apr–1 Nov	*		M	**T**	**W**	**T**	F	S	**S**
Garden									
1 Apr–1 Nov	11–5		M	**T**	**W**	**T**	F	S	S
1 Apr–1 Nov	2–5		M	T	W	T	F	S	**S**

*Admission to manor house by guided tour. Tue–Thur: tours at 11, 12, 2, 3, 4. Sun: tours at 2, 3, 4. No booking for tours. Tours take 45mins and numbers are limited to 25. Visitors arriving during a tour can visit the adjoining parish church and garden first. Group visits are welcome on Fri & Sat (not BHols) by written arrangement with the tenant, Mrs Robert Floyd. Charge applies

Greenway

Greenway Road, Galmpton, nr Brixham, Devon TQ5 0ES

2000   **(1:G8)**

Greenway house and garden on the River Dart: 'the loveliest place in the world'

The many collections, including archaeology, Tunbridgeware, silver, botanical china and books, the atmospheric house set in the 1950s, and the glorious woodland garden with its wild edges and rare plantings, all allow a glimpse into the private holiday home of the famous and well-loved author, Agatha Christie, and her family. Enjoy the adventure of arriving here by ferry and alighting at Greenway Quay, with dramatic views of the house from the river.

What's new in 2009 Greenway House will open after our major restoration project: 'Another Chapter'. For the first few months of the season we will gradually be opening the house for timed, limited-access visits while we continue to reinstate the collection. Advance booking for car parking is essential; those arriving by 'green' means will have slots made available to see this unique and magical property

⭐ Visitors wishing to come to Greenway must book their parking in advance. Failure to do so will regrettably result in being turned away. Tel. 01803 842382 to book; slots may be booked in advance or up to one hour prior to arrival. We do encourage visitors to travel by 'green ways' to Greenway. Ferries available from Dartmouth, Brixham and Torquay. Visitors travelling from Dittisham are encouraged to park in the Ham car park; however, we strongly recommend not using this route in July and August to avoid congestion

ℹ️ **T** 01803 842382
E greenway@nationaltrust.org.uk

🚶 Guided tours of the house, tours of the holiday apartment and 'Meet the Gardener' guided walks. Details at reception

🎭 Lectures and workshops in the Barn Gallery. Garden days, plant fairs. Spring and autumn walks with lunch. Open-air theatre

Walks through the estate link with the Dart Valley Trail, John Musgrave Trail, Greenway walk and Galmpton Village Walk. Details in reception. Please note that there is no parking for these walks at Greenway

Building **Grounds**

NT shop with local crafts and produce, books and themed games. Plant sales

Barn café (licensed) serving home-made light meals, locally produced seasonal and vegetarian food. Children's menu. Tack Room kiosk serving takeaway drinks, sandwiches and ice-creams. Greenway House kitchen serving lunches and set afternoon teas (booking recommended)

Baby-changing facilities. Pushchairs and baby back-carriers admitted. Children's quiz/trail. Children's activity packs. Tracker Packs

Adult study days

On leads on main drive and café courtyard only. Not in garden or house. Walks on the estate, on leads near livestock

→ [202:SX876548] **Foot**: Dart Valley Trail from Kingswear or Dartmouth. Greenway Walk from Brixham. Village Walk from Galmpton. **Ferry**: enjoy a cruise on the River Dart from Dartmouth (use Dartmouth park & ride, bus service every 15mins, please allow at least 4hrs parking) and Dittisham. Sea/river link from Torquay and Brixham. Tel. Greenway Ferry and Quay Services (licensed operators to the NT) 01803 844010, www.greenwayferry.co.uk and www.rivierabelle.co.uk. Ferries available for individuals, groups and charters. NB: there is a steep walk uphill (800yds) from Greenway Quay to the garden. **Station**: Paignton 4½ml, Churston (Paignton & Dartmouth Steam Rly) 2ml. **Road**: there are no parking spaces on the narrow country lanes leading to Greenway. No brown signs; follow signs for Greenway Ferry/YHA

P Free parking, 550yds. Time limited on busy days. All cars and midi-coaches (25-seat max.) only, by prior arrangement. Greenway Quay: limited parking (not NT). Charges apply

NT properties nearby
Bradley, Coleton Fishacre, Compton Castle, Dart Estuary, Overbeck's, Salcombe: Thurlestone to Torcross

Greenway			M	T	W	T	F	S	S
28 Feb–19 Jul	10:30–5		M	T	**W**	**T**	**F**	**S**	**S**
21 Jul–30 Aug	10:30–5		M	**T**	**W**	**T**	**F**	**S**	**S**
2 Sep–25 Oct	10:30–5		M	T	**W**	**T**	**F**	**S**	**S**

Timed tickets to the house only. Barn Gallery: open as garden, showing modern contemporary art by local artists

View over the River Dart from Greenway, Devon: Agatha Christie's holiday home

Hailes Abbey

nr Winchcombe, Cheltenham,
Gloucestershire GL54 5PB

 1937 **(1:K1)**

13th-century Cistercian abbey

Founded in 1246 and once a celebrated
pilgrimage site, the abbey now lies in ruins.
Remains of the dramatic cloister arches survive,
along with artefacts displayed in the museum.

⭐ Hailes Abbey is financed, managed and
maintained by English Heritage.
For further information tel. 0117 975 0700
(EH regional office) or visit
www.english-heritage.org.uk/hailes

ℹ️ **T** 01242 602398
E hailesabbey@nationaltrust.org.uk

📷 ⠿ **Building** 🏛

🏪 EH shop in museum. Plant sales

🍦 Ice-cream and soft drinks

🚼 Baby-changing facilities

🪑 Suitable for school groups

🐕 On leads and only in grounds

➡️ [150:SP050300] **Foot**: Cotswold Way within
⅔ml. **Bus**: Castleways 606 Cheltenham–
Willersey, alight Greet, 1¾ml by footpath.
Station: Cheltenham 10ml. **Road**: 2ml NE of
Winchcombe, 1ml E of Broadway road
(B4632, originally A46)

🅿️ Free parking (not NT)

NT properties nearby
Hidcote Manor Garden, Snowshill Manor and
Garden

Hailes Abbey									
Site/museum									
23 Mar–30 Jun	10–5	M	T	W	T	F	S	S
1 Jul–31 Aug	10–6	M	T	W	T	F	S	S
1 Sep–30 Sep	10–5	M	T	W	T	F	S	S
1 Oct–31 Oct	10–4	M	T	W	T	F	S	S
Please confirm times with property									

**Inspired by Hardy's Cottage?
Then visit Branscombe and
stir your imagination further**

Hardy Monument

Black Down, Portesham, Dorset

🏠 ♿ 1938 **(1:J7)**

Monument to Vice-Admiral Hardy

⭐ No WC. Car park not NT

ℹ️ **T** 01297 561900
E hardymonument@nationaltrust.org.uk

➡️ From the B3157 Weymouth–Bridport road,
turn off at Portesham; the road climbs steeply
to a car park signposted 'Hardy Monument'

Hardy Monument									
4 Apr–27 Sep		11–5	M	T	W	T	F	**S**	**S**

Open BH Mons. May close in bad weather. Staffed by
volunteers. Numbers at the top of the monument are
limited. Children must be accompanied by an adult

Hardy's Cottage

Higher Bockhampton, nr Dorchester,
Dorset DT2 8QJ

🏠 ❀ 📷 1948 **(1:J7)**

Birthplace of novelist and poet Thomas Hardy

Thomas Hardy was born in 1840 in this small cob
and thatch cottage, and from here he would walk
to school every day in Dorchester, three miles
away. It was built by his great-grandfather and is
little altered since the family left. The interior has
been furnished by the NT (see also Max Gate).
His early novels *Under the Greenwood Tree* and
Far from the Madding Crowd were written here. It
has a charming cottage garden.

Hardy's Cottage, near Dorchester, Dorset, dates from
1800, and was the birthplace of Thomas Hardy in 1840

⭐ No WC

ℹ️ **T** 01305 262366
E hardyscottage@nationaltrust.org.uk

♿ 🈯️ ⭐️ Ⓐ 🎴 Building ⓛ
Grounds 🈯️ ➡️

📷 Thomas Hardy's books, postcards and other items for sale

➡️ [194:SY728925] **Station**: Dorchester South 4ml; Dorchester West (U) 4ml. **Road**: 3ml NE of Dorchester, $\frac{1}{2}$ml S of A35. From Kingston Maurward roundabout follow signs to Stinsford and Higher Bockhampton

🅿️ Free parking (not NT). Cottage is 600yds walk through woods or lane from car park. Drop-off point by prior arrangement with Custodian

NT properties nearby
Clouds Hill, Hardy Monument, Max Gate

Hardy's Cottage							
15 Mar–29 Oct	11–5	**M**	**T**	**W**	**T**	F	S	S

Heelis

Kemble Drive, Swindon, Wiltshire SN2 2NA

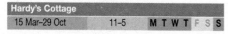 (1:K3)

Central office for the National Trust

An architectural gem, designed by Feilden Clegg Bradley Architects in 2005, the Trust's award-winning central office is a remarkable example of innovative and sustainable building construction. Timber from our woodlands and wool from Herdwick sheep grazed on Trust farmlands, help make Heelis a unique working environment.

⭐ Heelis operates a green travel policy and, therefore, visitor parking facilities are limited and must be booked with reception. Admission to offices by booked guided tour only

ℹ️ **T** 01793 817400
E heelisreception@nationaltrust.org.uk

🎴 Every Fri at 12:30, book with reception

♿ 🅿️ 🈯️ 🈵️ Building 🈯️ ↕️

📷 Heelis café (licensed). Children's menu

Heelis, the National Trust's award-winning central office in Swindon, was designed be Feilden Clegg Bradley Architects in 2005

🚼 Baby-changing facilities. Pushchairs and baby back-carriers admitted

➡️ [173:SU141850] **Bus**: Thamesdown Transport and Stagecoach, 13 & 14, alight Rodbourne Road, then 200yds.
Station: Swindon, $\frac{3}{4}$ml. **Road**: off B4289. Follow signs for Swindon Designer Outlet Centre. Park & ride from the Copse and Wroughton

🅿️ Parking (not NT), 100yds (pay & display). Additional car and coach parking at Outlet Centre north car park

NT properties nearby
Avebury, The Buscot and Coleshill Estates, Great Coxwell Barn, Lacock Abbey, Uffington White Horse and Wayland Smithy

Heelis							
All year	10–4	**M**	**T**	**W**	**T**	**F**	**S**	**S**

Admission to offices by booked guided tour only. Shop/café open 11–4 Sun & BHols. Facilities may also be open later at certain times of the year. Closed 25/26 Dec & 1 Jan 10

Dogs assisting visitors with disabilities are always welcome

Hidcote Manor Garden

Hidcote Bartrim, nr Chipping Campden,
Gloucestershire GL55 6LR

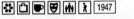 1947 **(1:L1)**

Celebrated 20th-century garden in the beautiful north Cotswolds

Hidcote is one of England's great gardens. Designed and created by the horticulturist Major Lawrence Johnston in the Arts & Crafts style, it is made up of exquisite garden rooms, each possessing its own special character. Visitors will discover rare shrubs and trees, outstanding herbaceous borders and unusual plant species. The garden changes in harmony with the seasons, from vibrant spring bulbs to autumn's glorious Red Border. Nestled in the Cotswolds with sweeping views across the Vale of Evesham, Hidcote is appealing all year round.

What's new in 2009 Lawrence Johnston's all-weather court has been restored and is open to players. The Theatre Lawn is open for croquet. The orchard is being transformed into a working kitchen garden

⭐ As the number of coaches is limited per day, group leaders should check with property before booking transport. On BHols and fine weekends garden is least crowded after 3

The White Garden, Hidcote Manor, Gloucestershire

ℹ **T** 01386 438333
E hidcote@nationaltrust.org.uk

🎭 Private evening tours, lecture lunches, family trails, open-air theatre

🚶 Public footpaths leading from the car park, inc. the Monarch's Way and Cotswold Way

♿ Building 🔊♿ Grounds 🔊➡♿

📷 NT shop. Plant sales

☕ Garden Restaurant (licensed) close to visitor reception. Children's menu. Thatched Barn Café close to car park

👶 Baby-changing facilities. Hip-carrying infant seats for loan. Children's quiz/trail. Family trails. Limited access for pushchairs and prams

➡ [151:SP176429] **Cycle**: NCN5, 1¼ml. **Station**: Honeybourne (U) 4½ml. **Road**: close to village of Mickleton, 4ml NE of Chipping Campden, 1ml E of B4632 (originally A46), off B4081. Coaches are not permitted through Chipping Campden High Street

🅿 Free parking, 100yds. Coaches must book – space limited

NT properties nearby
Charlecote Park, Chastleton House, Dover's Hill, Snowshill Manor and Garden, Upton House and Gardens

Hidcote Manor Garden									
Garden									
28 Feb–8 Mar	11–4	M	T	W	T	F	S	S
14 Mar–28 Jun	10–6	M	T	W	T	F	S	S
29 Jun–30 Aug	10–6	M	T	W	T	F	S	S
31 Aug–30 Sep	10–6	M	T	W	T	F	S	S
3 Oct–1 Nov	10–5	M	T	W	T	F	S	S
7 Nov–20 Dec	12–4	M	T	W	T	F	S	S
Barn Café/plant sales/shop/restaurant									
28 Feb–8 Mar	11–4	M	T	W	T	F	S	S
14 Mar–28 Jun	10–5	M	T	W	T	F	S	S
29 Jun–30 Aug	10–5	M	T	W	T	F	S	S
31 Aug–30 Sep	10–5	M	T	W	T	F	S	S
3 Oct–1 Nov	10–4	M	T	W	T	F	S	S
Shop/plant sales									
7 Nov–20 Dec	12–4	M	T	W	T	F	S	S
Barn Café/plant sales additional opening									
16 Apr–26 Jun	11–4	M	T	W	T	F	S	S
Open good Fri. Last admission 1hr before closing									

Show your card and display sticker for free parking

Holnicote Estate

Selworthy, Minehead, Somerset TA24 8TJ

✝ 🐟 ⛰ 🐑 🏠 ☕ 🚶 ⛺ 🎭 🎒 🕴

🚲 | 1944 | **(1:G5)**

Varied landscape of moorland, woods, farms and coast, rich in wildlife

The beautiful Holnicote Estate encompasses a vast area of the Exmoor National Park, taking in the high tors of Dunkery and Selworthy Beacons, with breathtaking panoramic views. Its traditional cottages and farms are grouped in and around pretty villages and hamlets, including Selworthy, Allerford, Bossington, Horner and Luccombe. Offering four miles of spectacular coastline between Porlock Bay and Minehead and more than 100 miles of footpaths through enchanting rural landscapes, woods, moors, farmland and villages, the Estate is a peaceful escape from the hustle and bustle of everyday living. Noted for its diversity of wildlife, many rare species can be discovered in the Horner and Dunkery Nature Reserve.

⭐ WCs at Bossington, Allerford, Selworthy and Horner

ℹ **T** 01643 862452
  E holnicote@nationaltrust.org.uk

🚶 *Holnicote Walks* leaflets available from estate office, Porlock visitor centre and Selworthy Periwinkle tea-rooms

♿ 🚾 Grounds 🚶 ♿

☕ Tea-rooms (not NT) at Selworthy, Bossington, Allerford and Horner

🎒 Suitable for school groups. Education room/centre. Hands-on activities. Adult study days

🐕 Dogs on leads

🚲 On Porlock family cycle route

➡ [181:SS920469] **Foot**: 3¾ml of South West Coast Path on property; Coleridge Way; Macmillan Way. **Bus**: Quantock 39 Minehead–Porlock, 300 Minehead–Lynmouth, alight Holnicote, then ½ml. **Station**: Minehead (West Somerset Rly) 5ml. **Road**: off A39 Minehead–Porlock, 3ml W of Minehead

Farmland near Tivington, Holnicote Estate, Somerset

🅿 Free parking at Allerford, North Hill, Dunkery, Webbers Post and Selworthy (not NT). Parking (pay & display) at Horner and Bossington. NT members must display car sticker. Only Horner car park is suitable for coaches

NT properties nearby

Arlington Court, Beacon and Bicknoller Hills, Coleridge Cottage, Dunster Castle, Fyne Court, Knightshayes Court, Watersmeet

Holnicote Estate									
Estate									
All year			M	T	W	T	F	S	S
Estate office									
All year	8:30–5		M	T	W	T	F	S	S
Estate office closed BHols and public hols									

Horton Court

Horton, nr Chipping Sodbury, South Gloucestershire BS37 6QR   **(1:J3)**

Closed in 2009 due to refurbishment

Killerton

Broadclyst, Exeter, Devon EX5 3LE

🏠🏪✝🏛️♿👤🐾🏠🔒💷🎯🪑🛡️🚼
🖼️🚶♿🍷 1944   (1:G6)

Glorious landscape garden surrounded by parkland, fine 18th-century house with renowned historical fashion collection

Killerton house has a notably relaxed, welcoming and informal atmosphere. Visitors are often heard to remark that they could imagine living here: it feels so much like a real home. The house was built in 1778 for the Aclands, one of the oldest families in Devon, and you will find much here to bring generations of fascinating and dynamic Aclands to life. On the first floor, the Paulise de Bush collection of 18th- to 20th-century costume is displayed, with a different themed exhibition every year. Killerton house is beautifully positioned on the flanks of a hill, surrounded by its glorious garden and overlooking parkland. It also has an extensive agricultural and wooded estate. There are numerous waymarked circular walks, through a variety of habitats and landscapes. The garden is the great glory of Killerton. It was created in the 1770s by renowned nurseryman and landscape designer John Veitch, and features an abundance of rhododendrons, magnolias, herbaceous borders and rare trees, as well as an

Coade stone vase on the great terrace in the glorious 18th-century garden at Killerton, Devon

ice house and a rustic summerhouse (known as The Bear's Hut). There is a discovery centre near the stable courtyard and a packed programme of activities and events to enjoy all year round.

What's new in 2009 'Jobs for the Girls': fascinating exhibition of historical fashions worn in the world of work

⭐ Some areas of the house may be closed when building work on roof starts in the autumn

ℹ️ **T** 01392 881345, 01392 881912 (shop)
E killerton@nationaltrust.org.uk

🎫 Guided tours on request

🎭 Full events programme throughout year

🚶 Walks leaflet available for park and nearby Ashclyst Forest. Orienteering course

♿ 🅿️🚹♿🚾👁️📷🎧💻🔔
Building 🔍♿🅱️ **Grounds** 🅱️➡️

🏠 Quality plants grown on the property in peat-free compost

🍴 Garden Tea-room (licensed) in house (can be booked for special functions). Orchard Tea-room (licensed) in stable block (outside tariff area) with open-air seating. Locally produced home-made food. Children's menu

🚼 Baby-changing and feeding facilities. Pushchairs and baby back-carriers admitted to house. Hip-carrying infant seats for loan. Children's play area. Children's quiz/trail. Family activities and discovery centre open in school holidays

🖼️ Suitable for school groups. Education room/centre. Live interpretation. Award-winning Victorian programme. Orienteering courses. Learning Officer

🐕 On leads and only in park

🚲 On NCN52

➡️ [192:SS973001] **Cycle**: NCN52.
Bus: Stagecoach in Devon 1/A/B Exeter–≋ Tiverton Parkway (passing close ≋ Exeter Central), alight Killerton Turn ¾ml.
Station: Pinhoe (U), not Sun, 4½ml; Whimple (U), 6ml; Exeter Central & St David's, both 7ml.
Road: off Exeter–Cullompton road (B3181); from M5 northbound, exit 30 via Pinhoe and Broadclyst; from M5 southbound, exit 28

🅿️ Free parking, 280yds

For public transport details, see page 377

Library at Killerton, with Dining Room beyond

NT properties nearby

A La Ronde, Budlake Old Post Office Room, Clyston Mill, Marker's Cottage, Knightshayes Court

Killerton										
House		M	T	W	T	F	S	S		
28 Feb–8 Mar	2–4	M	T	W	T	F	**S**	**S**		
11 Mar–24 Jul	11–5	**M**	T	**W**	**T**	**F**	S	S		
25 Jul–31 Aug	11–5	**M**	**T**	**W**	**T**	**F**	S	S		
2 Sep–1 Nov	11–5	**M**	T	**W**	**T**	**F**	S	S		
5 Dec–23 Dec	2–4	**M**	**T**	**W**	**T**	**F**	S	S		
Park/garden										
All year	10:30–7	**M**	**T**	**W**	**T**	**F**	**S**	**S**		
Garden Tea-room										
As house	11–5									
Orchard Tea-room										
1 Feb–8 Feb	11–4:30	M	T	W	T	F	**S**	**S**		
14 Feb–10 Mar	11–5	**M**	**T**	**W**	**T**	**F**	S	S		
11 Mar–1 Nov	11–5:30	**M**	**T**	**W**	**T**	**F**	S	S		
2 Nov–24 Dec	11–5	**M**	**T**	**W**	**T**	**F**	S	S		
27 Dec–31 Dec	11–5	**M**	**T**	**W**	**T**	**F**	S	S		
2 Jan–31 Jan 10	11–5	M	T	W	T	F	**S**	**S**		
Shop/plant sales										
1 Feb–8 Feb	11–5	M	T	W	T	F	**S**	**S**		
14 Feb–10 Mar	11–5	**M**	**T**	**W**	**T**	**F**	S	S		
11 Mar–1 Nov	11–5:30	**M**	**T**	**W**	**T**	**F**	S	S		
2 Nov–24 Dec	11–5	**M**	**T**	**W**	**T**	**F**	S	S		
27 Dec–3 Jan 10	11–5	**M**	**T**	**W**	**T**	**F**	S	S		
9 Jan–31 Jan 10	11–5	M	T	W	T	F	**S**	**S**		

Tea-room closes 4:30 on Tues. Shop/plant sales close 5 when house closed, 3 on Christmas Eve. In winter shop and tea-room may not open in bad weather. Garden tea-room open daily in Aug and on BHol Mons and on selected dates in Dec for Christmas lunches

Killerton: Budlake Old Post Office Room

Broadclyst, Exeter, Devon EX5 3LW

⊞ ❀ 🕭 🕭 1944   (1:G7)

Charming example of a 1950s Post Office Room with cottage garden

This small thatched cottage housed the village Post Office. Outside are a wash house, double-seated privy, pigsty and chicken house, 0.25-hectare ($\frac{1}{2}$-acre) garden with vegetable plot, cottage garden, herb and rose borders.

★ No refreshments or WC. Nearest WCs at Killerton. Footpath to Killerton along old carriage drive

ⓘ **T** 01392 881690
   E budlakepostoffice@nationaltrust.org.uk

🕭 Follow the old carriage way between Budlake Post Office and Killerton and link up with a series of walks around the Killerton Estate

♿ 🖼 **Building** 🖼 **Grounds** 🖼

🕭 Pushchairs and baby back-carriers admitted

🐕 On leads only in garden

→ [192:SS973001] **Cycle**: NCN52.
   Bus: Stagecoach in Devon 1/A/B Exeter–🚉 Tiverton Parkway (passing close 🚉 Exeter Central), alight Killerton Turn $\frac{3}{4}$ml.
   Station: Pinhoe (U), not Sun, $4\frac{1}{2}$ml; Whimple (U), 6ml; Exeter Central & St David's, both 7ml.
   Road: off Exeter–Cullompton road (B3181); from M5 northbound, exit 30 via Pinhoe and Broadclyst; from M5 southbound, exit 28

P Limited parking on site, 10yds. Not suitable for coaches. Ample parking at Killerton 800yds

NT properties nearby
Killerton, Clyston Mill, Marker's Cottage, Knightshayes Court

Budlake Old Post Office Room								
5 Apr–1 Nov	2–5	**M**	**T**	W	T	F	S	**S**
Last admission 10mins before closing								

Killerton: Clyston Mill

Broadclyst, Exeter, Devon EX5 3EW

🖼 🎐 🏠 👁 🏢 🎯 👤 1944 **(1:G7)**

Historic working watermill in idyllic riverside setting

Dating back to the 19th century, Clyston Mill is in an idyllic setting by the River Clyst, surrounded by farmland and orchards. The mill is still in full working order, producing flour.

⭐ No refreshments or WC

ℹ **T** 01392 462425
E clystonmill@nationaltrust.org.uk

🚶 Tours by arrangement

👁 Milling afternoons

🚶 Short riverside walk plus walk to mill through Broadclyst village and churchyard

♿ **Building** 🏞 **Grounds** 🏞

👶 Pushchairs and baby back-carriers admitted. Children's quiz/trail. Children need to be supervised – mill on three floors, steep narrow stairs

🖼 Suitable for school groups

➔ [192:SX981973] **Cycle**: NCN52.
Bus: Stagecoach in Devon 1/A/B Exeter–🚆 Tiverton Parkway (passing close 🚆 Exeter Central), alight Killerton Turn ¾ml.
Station: Pinhoe (U), not Sun, 4½ml; Whimple (U), 6ml; Exeter Central & St David's, both 7ml. **Road**: off Exeter–Cullompton Road (B3181) in village of Broadclyst. Park in village car park, walk towards church and follow signs through churchyard

🅿 Free parking (not NT), 450yds

NT properties nearby
Killerton, Budlake Old Post Office Room, Marker's Cottage, Knightshayes Court

Clyston Mill								
5 Apr–1 Nov		2–5	M	T	W	T	F	S	S

If Clyston Mill captivated you, Cotehele Mill is sure to do the same

Killerton: Marker's Cottage

Townend, Broadclyst, Exeter, Devon EX5 3HR

🏠 🏠 1944 **(1:G7)**

Thatched medieval cob house with smoke-blackened timbers and painted wooden screen

Fascinating medieval cob cottage with a thatched roof and smoke-blackened timbers. The house contains an unusual painted decorative screen showing St Andrew. A passage opens out on to a garden with a cob summerhouse and blacksmith's workshop.

⭐ No WC

ℹ **T** 01392 461546
E markerscottage@nationaltrust.org.uk

♿ 📷 **Building** 🏞 **Grounds** 🏞

➔ [192:SX985973] **Cycle**: NCN52.
Bus: Stagecoach in Devon 1/A/B Exeter–🚆 Tiverton Parkway (passing close 🚆 Exeter Central). **Station**: Pinhoe (U), not Sun, 2½ml; Whimple (U), 4½ml; Exeter Central & St David's, both 6ml. **Road**: in village of Broadclyst. Park in village car park. Leaving car park by vehicle entrance, turn left, then right and turn right on to Townend. Marker's Cottage is second cottage on left

🅿 Free parking (not NT), 250yds

NT properties nearby
Killerton, Budlake Old Post Office Room, Clyston Mill, Knightshayes Court

Marker's Cottage								
5 Apr–1 Nov		2–5	M	T	W	T	F	S	S

Interior of the medieval thatched Marker's Cottage

King John's Hunting Lodge

The Square, Axbridge, Somerset BS26 2AP

 1968   (1:I4)

Wool-merchant's house of c.1500

The early Tudor timber-framed house provides a fascinating insight into local history.

⭐ The property is run as a local history museum by Axbridge and District Museum Trust, in co-operation with Sedgemoor District Council, Somerset County Museums Service and Axbridge Archaeological and Local History Society

ℹ️ **T** 01934 732012
E kingjohns@nationaltrust.org.uk

🚶 Occasional tours of historic Axbridge, starting from the museum

♿ 🏛 **Building** 🪜

📷 In museum (not NT)

🏫 Suitable for school groups

➡️ [182:ST431545] In the Square, on corner of High Street. **Bus:** First 126 Weston-super-Mare–Wells (passing close ➤ Weston-super-Mare). **Station:** Worle (U) 8ml

🅿️ Parking (not NT), 100yds

NT properties nearby
Cheddar Cliffs, Clevedon Court, Prior Park Landscape Garden, Tyntesfield

King John's Hunting Lodge									
1 Apr–30 Sep	1–4	**M**	**T**	**W**	**T**	**F**	**S**	**S**
Closed 1 Oct–31 Jan 10: open first Sat of month to coincide with farmers' market, 10–4									

Kingston Lacy in Dorset, contains an outstanding collection of paintings and other works of art

Kingston Lacy

Wimborne Minster, Dorset BH21 4EA

🏛🏛🔧🌳🍴🛍🏛🛒🚶🎧🅿️⚐🚻🏫 🚶♿🍴 1982   (1:K7)

Elegant country mansion with important collections, set in attractive formal gardens and extensive parkland

Home of the Bankes family for more than 300 years, this striking 17th-century house was radically altered in the 19th century by Sir Charles Barry. The house is noted for its lavish interiors, including William Bankes's dramatic Spanish Room, with its gilded leather walls. The family's collection of art is outstanding, with paintings by Rubens, Van Dyck, Titian and Brueghel as well as the largest private collection of Egyptian artefacts in the UK. This wonderfully eclectic experience continues outside. Take a stroll across the beautiful formal lawns towards the restored Japanese tea garden. There are several waymarked walks through the surrounding parkland, with its fine herd of North Devon cattle, and the 3,440-hectare (8,500-acre) estate – dominated by the botanically rich Iron Age hill fort of Badbury Rings, home to fourteen varieties of orchid.

⭐ Point-to-point races are held at Badbury Rings three days a year – on these days a charge is made for parking

ℹ️ **T** 01202 883402
E kingstonlacy@nationaltrust.org.uk

🚶 By arrangement outside normal hours

🎧 Virtual tour available with level access in the Egyptian Room

⚐ Garden and park events. Open-air theatre. Children's activity days. Carol concert. Farmers' markets

Waymarked park walks. Leaflet from reception

Building **Grounds**

NT shop. Plant sales

Stables Restaurant (licensed) includes courtyard. Limited menu on Mon and Tues when house closed. Sunday roast lunches (beef is from Estate herd). Christmas lunches. Children's menu

Baby-changing and feeding facilities. Children's/family guides. Children's trail. Children's Tracker Packs

Suitable for school groups. Study Centre. Live interpretation. Hands-on activities. Adult study days

On leads in park and woodland

22ml of public bridleway with shared access for cyclists on the Estate (but not the park)

[195:ST980019] **Bus**: Wilts & Dorset 13 from Bournemouth, 3 from Poole (passing ≋ Bournemouth and close ≋ Poole), alight Wimborne Square for NT path, 2½ml. Nordcat 28 Wimborne Town Square–Kingston Lacy (6 Feb–19 Dec). **Station**: Poole 8½ml. **Road**: on B3082 Blandford–Wimborne road, 1½ml W of Wimborne Minster

Free parking. Charge at Badbury Rings on point-to-point race days

NT properties nearby

Brownsea Island, Clouds Hill, Corfe Castle, Hardy's Cottage, Max Gate, Mompesson House, Studland Beach, White Mill

Kingston Lacy		
House		
14 Mar–1 Nov	11-5	M T **W T F S S**
Garden/park		
6 Feb–8 Mar	10:30–4	M T W T **F S S**
13 Mar–1 Nov	10:30–6	**M T W T F S S**
6 Nov–20 Dec	10:30–4	M T W T **F S S**
Shop/restaurant		
6 Feb–8 Mar	10:30–4	M T W T **F S S**
13 Mar–1 Nov	10:30–5:30	**M T W T F S S**
6 Nov–20 Dec	10:30–4	M T W T **F S S**
Admission by timed ticket to house may operate on BH Suns & Mons. Open BH Mons. Last admission to house 1hr before closing		

Knightshayes Court

Bolham, Tiverton, Devon EX16 7RQ

1973 **(1:G6)**

Victorian country house with richly decorated interiors and garden with outstanding plant collection

When pioneer lace-maker John Heathcoat was chased out of Loughborough by the Luddites in 1816, his relocation to Tiverton led eventually to one of the finest surviving Gothic Revival houses being built in the lush landscape of mid Devon. In 1869 his grandson employed the architect and decorator William Burges – a passionate Gothic enthusiast – to build Knightshayes Court. He was an eccentric but inspired choice, responsible for a truly remarkable house and some extraordinary 'medieval' romantic interiors. The vast garden was the Heathcoat Amory family's great passion. They packed it with rare trees and shrubs, creating the celebrated 'Garden in the Wood'. Other features include a waterlily pond, amusing topiary and plenty of seasonal colour. The newly restored kitchen garden, now fully productive, supplies fresh organic vegetables and fruit to the licensed restaurant.

What's new in 2009 Guided tours of the plant nursery

Access to some parts of the house and garden may be restricted during early spring and winter

T 01884 254665, 01884 257381 (reception), 01884 259010 (shop), 01884 259416 (restaurant) **E** knightshayes@nationaltrust.org.uk

Guided tours at weekends in Nov and Dec. Times and prices on request, inc. specialist plant nursery tours

The Billiard Room, Knightshayes Court, Devon

🎭 Send sae for events leaflet

🚶 Leaflet showing current flowers and plants of interest. Updated monthly

♿ 🅿 🄳 ♿ •• 🖼 🚼 🔊 🅿

Building 🔊🖼♿ Grounds ♿➡

🎁 Gift shop. Well-stocked plant centre with many unusual plants (tel. 01884 243464)

☕ Stables Restaurant (licensed). In Oct opening hours may vary, although light refreshments are always available during opening hours. Children's menu

👪 Baby-changing facilities. Pushchairs and baby back-carriers admitted. Pushchairs for loan. Front-carrying baby slings for loan. Children's guide. Children's quiz/trail. Tracker Packs

🏫 Suitable for school groups. Education room/centre. Hands-on activities

🐕 On leads and only in facilities areas, woodland and park

➡ [181:SS960151] **Cycle**: NCN3. **Bus**: First 398 Tiverton–Minehead, alight Bolham, then ¾ml. Otherwise Stagecoach in Devon 1 from 🚉 Tiverton Parkway; 55/A/B Exeter–Tiverton (passing close 🚉 Exeter Central), alighting Tiverton 1¾ml. **Station**: Tiverton Parkway 8ml. **Road**: 7ml from M5 exit 27 (A361); 2ml N of Tiverton; turn right off Tiverton–Bampton road (A396) at Bolham

🅿 Free parking

NT properties nearby
Killerton, Budlake Old Post Office Room, Clyston Mill, Marker's Cottage

Knightshayes Court										
House										
14 Feb–22 Feb	11–4		**M**	**T**	**W**	**T**		**S**	**S**
28 Feb–8 Mar	11–4		M	T	W	T		**S**	**S**
14 Mar–1 Nov	11–5		**M**	**T**	**W**	**T**		**S**	**S**
Garden										
As house			**M**	**T**	**W**	**T**	**F**	**S**	**S**
Shop/plant centre/restaurant										
As house	11–4		**M**	**T**	**W**	**T**	**F**	**S**	**S**
5 Nov–20 Dec	11–4		M	T	W	**T**	**F**	**S**	**S**
21 Dec–22 Dec	11–4		**M**	**T**	W	T	F	S	S
Open Good Fri										

Knightshayes Court, Devon: one of the finest surviving Gothic Revival houses in the country

Unless indicated, last admission is always 30mins before closing time

Lacock Abbey, Fox Talbot Museum and Village

Lacock, nr Chippenham, Wiltshire SN15 2LG

🏚️🏠✝️🔆🚂🏡🏯💺🎻🎭🚻🖼️

| 1944 | (1:K4)

Country house created out of a medieval abbey, former home of William Henry Fox Talbot, a pioneer of photography

The picturesque village, with its many lime-washed, half-timbered stone houses, dates from the 13th century and has been seen in many tv and film productions, including *Pride and Prejudice*, *Cranford* and *Wolfman*. The Abbey is at the heart of the village and was founded in 1232 and converted into a country house *c*.1540. The atmospheric monastic rooms include medieval cloisters, a sacristy and chapter house and have survived largely intact. They have featured in two Harry Potter films, plus the recent *The Other Boleyn Girl*. The handsome 16th-century stable courtyard houses a clockhouse, brewery and bakehouse. The pioneering photographic achievements of William Henry Fox Talbot (1800–77), who invented the negative/positive process, can be experienced in the Fox Talbot Museum. His descendants gave the Abbey and village to the Trust in 1944. A stroll through the Abbey's Victorian woodland grounds reveals a stunning display of flowers in spring and magnificent trees, while the Botanic Garden reflects the plant collections of Fox Talbot – for whom botany was a lifelong scientific interest.

What's new in 2009 Recently opened holiday cottage

⭐ Presentation of the Abbey rooms is being reviewed. Admission may be by a combination of guided tours and self-guided visits. Please tel. 01249 730227 or check the NT website when planning your visit. Children's playground opposite Fox Talbot Museum maintained by Lacock Parish Council, not by NT

ℹ️ **T** 01249 730459
   E lacockabbey@nationaltrust.org.uk

🚶 Abbey closed Wed other than for booked groups by appointment with House Manager (tel. 01249 730227). Charge inc. NT members

The fine medieval cloisters of Lacock Abbey

🎭 See website or ask at property for details of events. Garden open outside normal opening times for spring flowers under NGS

♿ 🅿️ ♿ 🚾 ⠿ 📷 🎨 💻 ♿
Building ♿♿♿ **Grounds** ♿➡️♿

🏠 In village. Also museum shop (open times as museum)

☕ Tea-rooms, pubs, restaurant and bakery in the village. (Most owned by NT but leased and managed by tenants.)

🚻 Baby-changing facilities: Baby back-carriers admitted. Children's quiz/trail. Hip-carrying infant seats for loan from the Abbey. Baby-changing facilities in Abbey WCs and Red Lion car park WCs. Children's play area (not NT) in village playing field (opposite visitor reception). No pushchairs in Abbey but can be left in hall

🖼️ Suitable for school groups. Education room/centre

Most Trust properties offer Gift Aid on Entry for non-members, see page 10

→ [173:ST919684] **Foot**: surrounding network of footpaths inc. route beside Wilts & Berks Canal. **Cycle**: NCN4, 1ml. **Bus**: Faresaver 73 Melksham–Corsham, First 234 Chippenham–Frome (passing ⊟ Melksham and close ⊟ Chippenham and close ⊟ Trowbridge). **Station**: Melksham 3ml, Chippenham 3½ml. **Road**: 3ml S of Chippenham. M4 exit 17, signposted to Chippenham (A350). Follow signs for Lacock, leading to main car park

P Parking, 220yds (pay & display). NT members must display car sticker. No visitor parking on village streets

NT properties nearby
Avebury, The Courts Garden, Dyrham Park, Great Chalfield Manor and Garden, Prior Park Landscape Garden, Westwood Manor

Lacock Abbey										
Museum										
23 Feb–1 Nov	11–5:30	**M**	**T**	**W**	**T**	**F**	**S**	**S**		
7 Nov–20 Dec	11–4	M	T	W	T	**F**	**S**	**S**		
2 Jan–31 Jan 10	11–4	M	T	W	T	**F**	**S**	**S**		
Grounds/cloisters										
28 Feb–1 Nov	11–5:30	**M**	**T**	**W**	**T**	**F**	**S**	**S**		
Abbey										
14 Mar–1 Nov*	11–5	**M**	T	W	**T**	**F**	**S**	**S**		
Shop										
1 Feb–13 Mar	11–4	**M**	**T**	**W**	**T**	**F**	**S**	**S**		
14 Mar–1 Nov	10–5:30	**M**	**T**	**W**	**T**	**F**	**S**	**S**		
2 Nov–31 Jan 10	11–4	**M**	**T**	**W**	**T**	**F**	**S**	**S**		

Museum, Abbey & grounds closed Good Fri, but High Street shop open. *Please see Important Note on previous page. High Street shop closed 25/26 Dec & 1 Jan 10. Admission to the Abbey by timed ticket may operate on BHol weekends and busy event days

Lanhydrock park seen from the higher garden, above the house

Lanhydrock
Bodmin, Cornwall PL30 5AD

Y [1953] **(1:D8)**

Magnificent late Victorian country house with extensive servants' quarters, gardens and wooded estate

Lanhydrock is the perfect historic country house and estate. Explore the high-Victorian interiors of this wealthy but unpretentious family home, and discover evidence of the Robartes family all around the house. Generations of the family have walked in the Long Gallery, contemplating historic events such as the English Civil War, Jacobite Rebellion or the First World War. The gatehouse and north wing (which houses the Long Gallery with its biblical plasterwork ceiling – chilldren enjoy spotting all the familiar stories and characters) are 17th-century, while the rest of the house was restored after a fire in 1881, to include the latest advances in design and technology. There are 50 rooms to explore, with the servants' quarters and 'below stairs' being particularly evocative. The garden is firmly Victorian, with a magnificent collection of magnolias, camellias and rhododendrons, and is full of colour all year. Beyond you can follow numerous paths through woods and parkland down to the banks of the River Fowey, haunt of otters and kingfishers.

★ 50 rooms are open to visitors, who should allow at least two hours to tour the house. Secure locker system for large bags. Church (adjacent to house): service every Sun 9:45

i **T** 01208 265950, 01208 265211 (estate) **E** lanhydrock@nationaltrust.org.uk

🏃 Guided garden tours on various days, weather permitting

🎭 Including open-air concert in July

🚶 Estate walks leaflet available

🏠 NT shop. Plant centre in car park

🍽 Servants' Hall restaurant (licensed) in main house. Children's menu. Stables snack bar in harness block

Charges for National Trust members apply on some special event days

[icon] Baby-changing and feeding facilities. Front-carrying baby slings and hip-carrying infant seats for loan. Children's play area. Children's guide. Children's quiz/trail. Pushchair for outdoor use for loan

[icon] Suitable for school groups. Education room/centre. Live interpretation. Hands-on activities

[icon] On leads and only in park and woods

[icon] [200:SX088636] **Cycle**: NCN3, runs past entrance. **Station**: Bodmin Parkway 1¾ml via original carriage-drive to house, signposted in station car park; 3ml by road. **Road**: 2½ml SE of Bodmin. Follow signposts from either A30, A38 Bodmin–Liskeard or take B3268 off A390 at Lostwithiel

[P] Free parking, 600yds

NT properties nearby
Trerice

Lanhydrock									
House									
28 Feb–31 Mar	11–5	M	T	W	T	F	S	S	
1 Apr–30 Sep	11–5:30	M	T	W	T	F	S	S	
1 Oct–1 Nov	11–5	M	T	W	T	F	S	S	
Garden									
All year	10–6	M	T	W	T	F	S	S	
Plant centre									
28 Feb–31 Mar	11–5	M	T	W	T	F	S	S	
1 Apr–30 Sep	11–5:30	M	T	W	T	F	S	S	
1 Oct–1 Nov	11–5	M	T	W	T	F	S	S	
Shop and refreshments									
14 Feb–27 Feb	11–4	M	T	W	T	F	S	S	
28 Feb–31 Mar	11–5	M	T	W	T	F	S	S	
1 Apr–30 Sep	11–5:30	M	T	W	T	F	S	S	
1 Oct–1 Nov	11–5	M	T	W	T	F	S	S	
2 Nov–24 Dec	11–4	M	T	W	T	F	S	S	
27 Dec–31 Dec	11–4	M	T	W	T	F	S	S	
2 Jan–31 Jan 10	11–4	M	T	W	T	F	S	S	

Open BH Mons & Mons in Aug. Refreshments: open 10:30 28 Feb–1 Nov. Closed 25, 26 Dec and 1 Jan 10. Shop and restaurant are inside the tariff area

If you enjoyed the Victorian grandeur of Lanhydrock, then you will love the lavish Gothic decor at Knightshayes Court

Lanhydrock, Cornwall, feels like a real family home

Lawrence House

9 Castle Street, Launceston, Cornwall PL15 8BA

 [icons] 1964   (1:E7)

Beautiful Georgian town house

Built in 1753, Lawrence House was given to the Trust to help preserve the character of the street. It is now leased to Launceston Town Council and in use as a local museum and civic centre.

What's new in 2009 Display on Launceston trade and industry

[icon] Museum website www.lawrencehousemuseum.org.uk

[icon] **T** 01566 773277
E lawrencehouse@nationaltrust.org.uk

[icon] By arrangement with the Curator

[icons] Building [icons]

[icon] Baby-changing and feeding facilities. Pushchairs and baby back-carriers admitted. Children's quiz/trail

[icon] Suitable for school groups. Education room/centre. Hands-on activities

[icon] [201:SX330848] **Bus**: 76/A from Plymouth (passing Plymouth)

[P] Parking (not NT) (pay & display)

NT properties nearby
Cotehele

Lawrence House								
30 Mar–30 Oct	10:30–4:30	M	T	W	T	F	S	S

Open evenings, weekends all year by appointment for groups or individuals for study

Levant Mine and Beam Engine

Trewellard, Pendeen, nr St Just, Cornwall TR19 7SX

⟨𝗍 ⚙ ⌂ 𝗂 ⚘ ⚹ ▦ 𝗂 ⚹⟩ 1967   **(1:A9)**

Unique steam-powered Cornish beam engine in action

Part of Cornwall and West Devon Mining World Heritage Site, this is the only Cornish beam engine anywhere in the world that is still in steam at a tin and copper mine. The famous Levant engine is housed in a small engine house on the edge of the cliffs. Restored after 60 idle years by a group of volunteers known as the 'Greasy Gang', it is a thrilling experience for young and old alike to see this old engine in action, with its evocative sounds and smells. You can take a short underground tour through the miners' dry tunnel, and the winding and pumping shafts are also on view, as is a restored electric winding engine. A film tells the story of Levant mine and the miners who worked here. A short walk along the cliffs will take you to Botallack Mine (NT), with its famous cliff-clinging engine houses and historical displays in the Count House Workshop; in the other direction is Geevor mine (not NT) and a mining museum.

ℹ️ **T** 01736 786156
E levant@nationaltrust.org.uk

🚶 Self-guided tour leaflet

♿ 🅿 ⦙⦙ 📷 ✏ **Building** ♿

Levant Mine's engine house is perched on a cliff

🛍 Small outlet for industrial/mining artefacts

☕ Nearest refreshments (not NT) at Geevor mine or Pendeen village

🚼 Baby-changing facilities. Pushchairs and baby back-carriers admitted. Family activity trail

🎒 Suitable for school groups. Live interpretation

➡️ [203:SW368346] **Foot**: South West Coast Path passes entrance. **Bus**: First 17/A from 🚆 Penzance. **Station**: Penzance 7ml. **Road**: 1ml W of Pendeen, on B3306 St Just–St Ives road

🅿 Free parking, 100yds. Not suitable for coaches. Limited parking for coaches at Geevor mine, ½ml walk to Levant mine

NT properties nearby
Botallack Count House, St Michael's Mount, Trengwainton Garden

Levant Beam Engine		M	T	W	T	F	S	S
Steaming								
6 Mar–27 Mar	11–5	M	T	W	T	**F**	S	S
1 Apr–29 May	11–5	M	T	**W**	T	**F**	S	S
3 Jun–28 Jun	11–5	M	T	**W**	**T**	**F**	S	S
1 Jul–30 Sep	11–5	M	**T**	**W**	**T**	**F**	**S**	S
2 Oct–30 Oct	11–5	M	**T**	**W**	**T**	F	S	S
Not steaming								
6 Feb–27 Feb	11–4	M	T	W	T	**F**	S	S
6 Nov–29 Jan 10	11–4	M	T	W	T	**F**	S	S
Open BH Suns & Mons								

Little Clarendon

Dinton, Salisbury, Wiltshire SP3 5DZ

🏠 1940   **(1:K5)**

Late 15th-century stone house

⭐ No WC

ℹ️ **T** 01985 843600
E littleclarendon@nationaltrust.org.uk

➡️ ¼ml E of Dinton church, close to post office; take B3089 from Salisbury to Dinton

Little Clarendon		M	T	W	T	F	S	S
13 April	2–5	**M**	T	W	T	F	S	S
4 May	2–5	**M**	T	W	T	F	S	S
25 May	2–5	**M**	T	W	T	F	S	S
31 Aug	2–5	**M**	T	W	T	F	S	S

Little Fleece Bookshop

Bisley Street, Painswick, Gloucestershire GL6 6QQ

🏠 📷 ♿ 1942 **(1:J2)**

Traditional Cotswold house in the beautiful village of Painswick

A 17th-century building, originally part of a former inn and restored in exemplary Arts & Crafts style in 1935. Although a private dwelling, Little Fleece trades as an antiquarian and second-hand bookshop, specialising in art, gardens, architecture and local interest; also sells antiquarian prints.

⭐ No WC, nearest in village

ℹ️ **T** 01452 812264
E littlefleece@nationaltrust.org.uk

♿ **Building** 🦽

♿ Pushchairs admitted

➡️ [162:SO868098] **Foot:** Cotswold Way within ⅞ml. **Bus:** Stagecoach in the Cotswolds 46 Nailsworth–Cheltenham Spa (passes close ⊠ Stroud). **Station:** Stroud 4ml. **Road:** 3ml N of Stroud A46, 6ml SE of Gloucester B4073. Off main High Street, Painswick

🅿️ Large car park in village (not NT)

NT properties nearby
Haresfield Estate, Minchinhampton and Rodborough Commons, Woodchester Park

Little Fleece Bookshop
Variable. Contact the tenant for details

The Lizard and Kynance Cove

Cornwall

🏠 ⚓ 🏖️ 🐕 ☕ 🎣 ♿ 🔫 🚶 1935 **(1:C10)**

Dramatic and historic stretch of Cornish coast

The Lizard is the most southerly point of mainland Britain and the turning point of one of the busiest shipping lanes in the world. The coastline on either side offers dramatic cliff walks, masses of rare wild flowers and fascinating geological features. The area played a key role in the history of modern communications. Marconi's historic wireless experiments on The Lizard in 1901 are celebrated at the restored **Lizard Wireless Station**, Bass Point, and the **Marconi Centre** at Poldhu. Two miles north of Lizard Point lies Kynance Cove – white sand, turquoise water and islands of multicoloured serpentine rock with stacks and arches hidden amongst the towering cliffs – long considered one of the most beautiful places in Cornwall.

ℹ️ **T** 01326 561407
E lizard@nationaltrust.org.uk

🚶 NT *Coast of Cornwall* leaflet 14 includes maps and details of circular walks and information on local history, geology and wildlife

♿ 🚾 **Grounds** 🦽

☕ Award-winning environmentally friendly café (NT-approved concession) at Kynance Cove beach. Ice-cream van at Kynance car park in July and Aug. Café on Lizard Point (not NT)

♿ Baby-changing facilities at Lizard Point car park WC and Kynance Cove WC

🔫 Suitable for school groups

🐕 Seasonal bans on some beaches, inc. Kynance

➡️ [203:SW688133] **Foot:** 3¾ml of South West Coast Path on property. **Bus:** First T34 ⊠ Redruth–Helston–Lizard, then to Kynance Cove 1½ml; to Lizard Point 1ml. **Road:** from Helston, A3083 to Lizard town

🅿️ NT car parks at Kynance and Lizard Point (charge Easter to Nov). Free parking in Lizard town, from where a footpath leads to Lizard Point. No caravans or trailers

NT properties nearby
Glendurgan Garden, Godolphin, St Michael's Mount

The Lizard							
All year	M	T	W	T	F	S	S
Tel. for opening times of Lizard Wireless Station and Marconi Centre							

If the Lizard's rare flora and fauna amazed you, then you will enjoy discovering the wildlife on the West Exmoor Coast

Lodge Park and Sherborne Estate

Lodge Park, Aldsworth, nr Cheltenham, Gloucestershire GL54 3PP

🏠🌳♿🏛️📷🍵🗡️🌲🛡️🚻🧍🔔

📶 1983 (1:K2/L2)

Rare 17th-century grandstand and Cotswold country estate

Lodge Park, situated on the picturesque Sherborne Estate in the Cotswolds, was created in 1634 by John 'Crump' Dutton and inspired by his passion for gambling, banqueting and entertaining. Until 1983 it was the home of Charles Dutton, 7th Lord Sherborne, and, when bequeathed, it was the first project undertaken by the Trust that relied totally on archaeological evidence. Visitors can now experience how the unique grandstand would have looked in the 17th century and enjoy the impressive views of the deer course and park, which was designed by Charles Bridgeman in the 1720s. Wonderful walks around the surrounding Sherborne Estate cover 1,650 hectares (4,000 acres) of beautiful rolling countryside, and include the restored and working water meadows and sweeping views of the River Windrush. The village of Sherborne is divided into two parts, with the East End exploiting the model village design of the mid 19th century, and the West End retaining many of the older buildings in the village.

What's new in 2009 Small National Trust shop, light refreshments and plant sales at Lodge Park

⭐ WC at Lodge Park only

ℹ️ **T** 01451 844130
E lodgepark@nationaltrust.org.uk

🛡️ 17th- and 18th-century Living History displays

♿ 🅿️ 🚻 📷 🔲 Building 🦽🪜

🛍️ Small shop and plant sales

🍵 Hot drinks available at Lodge Park

🚼 Pushchairs admitted to ground floor. Tracker Packs

🐕 Under close control

➡️ [163:SP146123] **Bus**: Swanbrook 853 Oxford–Gloucester (passing ⇌ Gloucester

and close ⇌ Oxford). 1½ml walk to Lodge Park from bus stop or 1ml Sherborne; also 833 Cheltenham–Northleach with booked connections for Sherborne (tel. 01452 423598). **Road**: 3ml E of Northleach; approach from A40 only

🅿️ Parking for estate walks at Ewe Pen Barn car park [163:SP158143] and water meadows [163:SP175154]. Donation of £1 welcome

NT properties nearby

Chastleton House, Chedworth Roman Villa, Hidcote Manor Garden, Snowshill Manor and Garden

Lodge Park and Sherborne Estate									
Grandstand/Deer Park									
13 Mar–1 Nov	11–4	M	T	W	T	**F**	**S**	**S**
Sherborne Estate									
All year		**M**	**T**	**W**	**T**	**F**	**S**	**S**

Grandstand open Easter Mon. Property occasionally closes for weddings. Please tel. to confirm opening times

The unique grandstand at Lodge Park in the snow in April

Loughwood Meeting House

Dalwood, Axminster, Devon EX13 7DU

➕ 🚼 1969 (1:H7)

17th-century thatched Baptist meeting house

Around 1653 the Baptist congregation of the nearby village of Kilmington constructed this simple building dug into the hillside. They attended services here at the risk of imprisonment or transportation. The interior was fitted in the early 18th century.

For events details, visit www.nationaltrust.org.uk/events

⭐ No WC

ℹ️ **T** 01392 881691
E loughwood@nationaltrust.org.uk

♿ Building 🔼 🔼

♿ Pushchairs and baby back-carriers admitted. Family guide

➡️ [192/193:SY253993] **Bus**: Stagecoach in Devon 380 Axminster–Exeter (passing close 🚉 Axminster). **Station**: Axminster 2½ml. **Road**: 4ml W of Axminster; turn right on Axminster–Honiton road (A35), 1ml S of Dalwood, 1ml NW of Kilmington

🅿️ Small free car park, 20yds. Not suitable for coaches. Very narrow country lanes

NT properties nearby
Branscombe, Shute Barton

Loughwood Meeting House							
All year	M	T	W	T	F	S	S
Services held twice yearly. Details at Meeting House							

Lundy

Bristol Channel, Devon EX39 2LY

[icons] 1969 (1:D5)

Unspoilt island, home to a fascinating array of wildlife amidst dramatic scenery

Undisturbed by cars, the island encompasses a small village with an inn and Victorian church, and the 13th-century Marisco Castle. Of interest to nature-lovers are the variety of migratory seabirds, heathland and grassland habitats and the Lundy ponies. Designated the first Marine Conservation Area, Lundy offers opportunities for diving and seal watching.

⭐ The island is financed, administered and maintained by the Landmark Trust. Holiday cottages available to rent

ℹ️ **T** 01271 863636 (Infoline)
E lundy@nationaltrust.org.uk

♿ [icons] Building 🔼 Grounds 🔼

🛍️ Shop selling the famous Lundy stamps, souvenirs and postcards, plus general supplies and groceries

Lundy, in the Bristol Channel, is a haven for wildlife

🍽️ Marisco Tavern (not NT) (licensed) in the village. Children's menu

♿ Baby-changing facilities. Pushchairs admitted. Family activity packs

🏫 Suitable for school groups. Education room/centre. Live interpretation. Hands-on activities

➡️ [180:SS130450] In the Bristol Channel 11ml N of Hartland Point, 25ml W of Ilfracombe, 30ml S of Tenby. **Cycle**: NCN31 (Bideford). **Ferry**: sea passages from Bideford or Ilfracombe according to tides up to four days a week, March to end Oct. **Bus**: First 3 Barnstaple–Ilfracombe, First 1, 2 (🚉) Barnstaple–Bideford. **Station**: Barnstaple: 8½ml to Bideford, 12ml to Ilfracombe

🅿️ Public parking at Bideford or Ilfracombe for ferries (pay & display)

NT properties nearby
Arlington Court, Bideford Bay and Hartland, Morte, Watersmeet, West Exmoor Coast

Lundy							
1 Apr–31 Oct	M	T	W	T	F	S	S
Helicopter service from Hartland Point Nov to mid March, Mon & Fri only, for visitors staying on the island							

For public transport details, see page 377

Lydford Gorge

The Stables, Lydford Gorge, Lydford,
nr Okehampton, Devon EX20 4BH

 1947   (1:F7)

The deepest gorge in the South West, with spectacular 30m waterfall

This lush oak-wooded steep-sided river gorge, with its fascinating history and many legends, can be explored through a variety of short or long walks. See the spectacular White Lady Waterfall, pass over the tumbling water at Tunnel Falls and watch the river bubble in the Devil's Cauldron. There's an abundance of wildlife to spot, including woodland birds, dragonflies darting above the river and trout swimming in the quieter stretches. A walk along a disused railway line will lead you to the bird hide; and you can enjoy a picnic in the orchard area or Pixie Glen.

What's new in 2009 New information at the bird hide about the Lyd Valley and its wildlife

⭐ Walking in the gorge is strenuous. It is extremely rugged, with uneven surfaces, slippery paths and vertical drops. Walking boots are essential. It is vital that children are supervised at all times. Unsuitable for visitors with heart complaints or walking difficulties and very young children

ℹ️ **T** 01822 820320, 01822 820441 (shop), 01822 822004 (tea-room)
E lydfordgorge@nationaltrust.org.uk

Lydford Gorge									
Gorge/shop/tea-room									
14 Feb–22 Feb	11–3:30	**M**	**T**	**W**	**T**	**F**	**S**	**S**
28 Feb–8 Mar	11–3:30	M	T	W	F		**S**	**S**
14 Mar–4 Oct	10–5	**M**	**T**	**W**	**T**	**F**	**S**	**S**
5 Oct–1 Nov	10–4	**M**	**T**	**W**	**T**	**F**	**S**	**S**
Gorge/tea-room									
7 Nov–20 Dec	11–3:30	M	T	W	T	F	**S**	**S**
Shop									
7 Nov–29 Nov	11–3:30	M	T	W	T	F	**S**	**S**
3 Dec–20 Dec	11–3:30	M	T	W	**T**	**F**	**S**	**S**
21 Dec–23 Dec	11–3:30	**M**	**T**	**W**	T	F	S	S
Gorge (waterfall entrance only)									
1 Feb–13 Feb	11–3:30	**M**	**T**	**W**	**T**	**F**	**S**	**S**
21 Dec–31 Jan 10	11–3:30	**M**	**T**	**W**	**T**	**F**	**S**	**S**

The main walk through Lambhole Wood, Lydford Gorge, Devon

😷 Seasonal and wildlife walks and events. Children's activity days. Trails

🚶 1½ml and 3ml routes. Seasonal guided walks

♿ 🅿️ 🚻 👓 🅰️ 🔄 ♿ 🔵 🔲 **Grounds** 🦮

🛍️ Shop and plant centre at main entrance. Small shop at waterfall entrance

🍴 Tea-rooms at both entrances to gorge, serving light lunches and delicious home-made cakes. Children's menu

🚼 Baby-changing and feeding facilities. Microwave at waterfall tea-room for heating baby food. Baby back-carriers admitted and for loan. Children's play area. Children's activity days. Unsuitable for pushchairs due to uneven terrain, narrow paths and long flights of steps

🎒 Suitable for school groups. Education resource book (£3)

🐕 On leads only

➡️ [191/201:SX509845] **Foot**: as road directions or via Blackdown Moor from Mary Tavy. **Cycle**: NCN27 & 31. Property is close to three cycle routes: Devon Coast to Coast, West Devon Way and Plym Valley. **Bus**: First 86, 87 Plymouth–Barnstaple (passing close ☒ Plymouth); 187 ☒ Gunnislake–☒ Okehampton, Sun, June to Sept only; bus stop at main entrance and waterfall entrance to gorge. **Road**: 7ml S of A30. Halfway between Okehampton and Tavistock, 1ml W off A386 opposite Dartmoor Inn; main entrance at W end of Lydford village; waterfall entrance near Manor Farm

🅿️ Free parking

NT properties nearby
Buckland Abbey, Castle Drogo, Cotehele, Finch Foundry

Please remember – your membership card is *always* needed for free admission

Lytes Cary Manor

nr Charlton Mackrell, Somerton, Somerset TA11 7HU

🏠✝🌸🏰🏡🛡🥀🎭🚻🖼

👤 1949 (1:15)

Intimate manor house with Arts & Crafts-style garden

This intimate manor house was the former home of medieval herbalist Henry Lyte; here visitors can learn about his famous 16th-century plant directory, *Lytes Herbal*. The manor spans many years with its 14th-century chapel and 15th-century Great Hall. In the 20th century it was rescued from dereliction by Sir Walter Jenner, who refurbished the interiors in period style. Its Arts & Crafts-style garden is a combination of outdoor rooms, topiary, statues and herbaceous borders. Explore the waymarked walks through the wider estate and riverside and discover many features typical of farmed lowland England, including ancient hedges, rare arable weeds and farmland birds.

What's new in 2009 New winter events programme

ℹ️ **T** 01458 224471
E lytescarymanor@nationaltrust.org.uk

🔑 Guided tours by arrangement, tel. to book

🎭 Family-themed events throughout summer. New winter events programme

👤 Guided walks. Details from property

♿ 🅿 ♿ 🚾 ⊙ 🎵 Building 🔼 🔽
Grounds ♿

☕ Kiosk serving light refreshments

🚼 Baby-changing facilities. Pushchairs admitted. Hip-carrying infant seats for loan. Children's quiz/trail. Family events in summer

🏫 Suitable for school groups

🐕 On leads, only in car park and on estate walks

➡️ [183:ST529269] **Bus**: First 376 Bristol–Yeovil (passing ☰ Bristol Temple Meads); 54/A/B/C Taunton–Yeovil (passing close ☰ Taunton). Both pass within ¾ml ☰ Yeovil Pen Mill. Alight Kingsdon, 1ml. **Station**: Yeovil Pen Mill 8½ml; Castle Cary 9ml; Yeovil Junction 10ml. **Road**: near village of Kingsdon, off A372. Signposted from Podimore Roundabout where A303 meets A37

🅿 Free parking, 40yds. Coaches by prior arrangement only

NT properties nearby
Barrington Court, Montacute House, Priest's House, Tintinhull Garden

Lytes Cary Manor									
14 Mar–1 Nov	11–5		M	T	W	T	F	S	S
Estate and river walks									
All year	Dawn–dusk		M	T	W	T	F	S	S
Open Good Fri, BH Mons. Closes dusk if earlier									

The manor house at Lytes Cary, Somerset, was rescued from dereliction by Sir Walter Jenner

Max Gate

Alington Avenue, Dorchester, Dorset DT1 2AB

🏠 ✳ 👤 📷 1940   (1:J7)

Home of novelist and poet Thomas Hardy

Thomas Hardy designed the house and lived there for 43 years, from 1885 until his death in 1928. Here he wrote *Tess of the d'Urbervilles*, *Jude the Obscure* and *The Mayor of Casterbridge*, as well as much of his poetry. Visitors can see several pieces of his furniture.

★ No WC

ℹ️ **T** 01305 262538
   E maxgate@nationaltrust.org.uk

♿ ⟨⟩ 📷 🖼 Building ⟨⟩

🏛 Suitable for school groups

➡️ [194:SY704899] **Bus**: Coach House Travel 4 from town centre. **Station**: Dorchester South 1ml; Dorchester West (U) 1ml. **Road**: 1ml E of Dorchester. From Dorchester follow A352 Wareham road to roundabout named Max Gate (at junction of A35 Dorchester bypass). Turn left and left again into cul-de-sac outside the house

🅿️ Free parking (not NT), 50yds

NT properties nearby
Cerne Abbas Giant, Clouds Hill, Golden Cap, Hardy Monument, Hardy's Cottage

Max Gate									
5 Apr–30 Sep	2–5	M	T	W	T	F	S	S

Only hall, dining and drawing rooms, and garden open. Private visits, tours and seminars for schools, colleges and literary societies, at other times, by appointment with the tenants, Mr and Mrs Andrew Leah

Mompesson House in the Cathedral Close, Salisbury

Mompesson House

The Close, Salisbury, Wiltshire SP1 2EL

🏠 ✳ 💻 👪 🖼 🍵 1952   (1:K5)

Elegant and spacious 18th-century house in the Cathedral Close

The house, featured in the award-winning film *Sense and Sensibility*, is a haven of peace in Salisbury's famous Cathedral Close. Its magnificent plasterwork, fine period furniture and graceful oak staircase are all part of the pleasure, and the Turnbull collection of 18th-century drinking glasses is of national importance. The delightful walled garden has a pergola and traditionally planted herbaceous borders.

What's new in 2009 A new exhibition – 'The Eye Deceived: Battersby and The Art of Illusion' at Mompesson House

ℹ️ **T** 01722 420980 (Infoline), 01722 335659
   E mompessonhouse@nationaltrust.org.uk

♿ 🖼 🖼 ⟨⟩ 📷 🎵 📖 ♿ Building ⟨⟩ ♿
Grounds ⟨⟩ ♿

🛍 NT shop in High Street, 60yds.
   Tel. 01722 331884

🍵 Tea-room

👪 Pushchairs and baby back-carriers admitted. Front-carrying baby slings and hip-carrying infant seats for loan. Children's guide. Children's quiz/trail

🏛 Suitable for school groups

➡️ [184:SU142297] On N side of Choristers' Green in the Cathedral Close, near High Street Gate. **Bus**: Wilts & Dorset buses from surrounding area. **Station**: Salisbury ½ml

🅿️ Parking (not NT), 260yds in city centre (pay & display). Coach parking in Central Car Park. Coach drop-off point 100yds at St Ann's Gate

NT properties nearby
Mottisfont Abbey, Pepperbox Hill, Philipps House and Dinton Park, Stonehenge Landscape, Stourhead

Mompesson House								
14 Mar–1 Nov	11–5	M	T	W	T	F	S	S
Open Good Fri								

Unless indicated, last admission is always 30mins before closing time

Montacute House

Montacute, Somerset TA15 6XP

🏠 ✳ 🏡 🏠 🛏 ♿ ☕ 🎨 🎭 🖼 👹 ♿ 🚶
🍷 | 1931 | (1:16)

Magnificent Elizabethan Ham-stone house, incorporating National Portrait Gallery exhibition, garden and park

Montacute House is a magnificent, glittering mansion, built in the late 16th century for Sir Edward Phelips. Renaissance highlights include elegant chimneys, carved parapets, contemporary plasterwork and heraldic glass. On walking through the grand Long Gallery, the longest of its kind in Europe, visitors can admire more than 50 of the finest Tudor and Elizabethan portraits from the National Portrait Gallery collection. The splendid staterooms display a fine range of 17th- and 18th-century furniture and textiles, including beautiful samplers from the Goodhart collection. The fine formal gardens are perfect for an afternoon stroll and include an interesting collection of roses, topiary and mixed borders. Waymarked walks lead around the wider estate, which encompasses St Michael's Hill, the site of a Norman castle, which is topped by an 18th-century lookout tower.

What's new in 2009 Exhibition highlighting the history and conservation on St Michael's Hill, an important feature of the estate

ℹ️ **T** 01935 823289
E montacute@nationaltrust.org.uk

🚶 Many walks in park and estate to enjoy. Leaflet available

♿ 🅿️ 🚾 ⬜ ⬜ ⬜ ⬜ ⬜ Building ⬜ ⬜ ⬜
Grounds ⬜ ➡️

📷 NT shop. Plant sales

🍷 Licensed restaurant available for private bookings. Christmas lunches served Suns in Dec, booking recommended. Open weekdays for corporate and private lunches during Nov & Dec (groups 25–50 only), booking essential. Café

👶 Baby-changing facilities. Pushchairs and baby back-carriers admitted. Children's play area. Children's guide. Family trail. Garden activity packs. Family picnic area where children can run and play ball games

A colourful border and pavilion at Montacute House

🖼 Suitable for school groups. Live interpretation

🐕 On leads and only in park

➡️ [183/193:ST499172] **Foot**: Leyland Trail and Monarch Trail both pass through Montacute Park. **Cycle**: NCN30, passes Montacute village. **Bus**: South West Coaches 81 Yeovil Bus Station–South Petherton (passing within ¾ml ⊠ Yeovil Pen Mill). **Station**: Yeovil Pen Mill 5½ml; Yeovil Junction 7ml (bus to Yeovil Bus Station); Crewkerne 7ml. **Road**: in Montacute village, 4ml W of Yeovil, on S side of A3088, 3ml E of A303; signposted

🅿️ Free parking. Limited parking for coaches

NT properties nearby
Barrington Court, Lytes Cary Manor, Priest's House, Stourhead, Tintinhull Garden, Treasurer's House

Montacute House								
House								
13 Mar–1 Nov	11–5	**M**	T	**W**	**T**	**F**	**S**	**S**
Garden/shop*								
28 Feb–12 Mar	11–4	M	T	**W**	**T**	**F**	**S**	**S**
13 Mar–1 Nov	11–5:30	**M**	T	**W**	**T**	**F**	**S**	**S**
4 Nov–20 Dec	11–4	M	T	**W**	**T**	**F**	**S**	**S**
Café								
28 Feb–8 Mar	11–4	M	T	W	T	F	**S**	**S**
13 Mar–1 Nov	11–5:30	**M**	T	**W**	**T**	**F**	**S**	**S**
4 Nov–20 Dec	11–4	M	T	W	T	F	**S**	**S**
Restaurant								
13 Mar–1 Nov	12–3	**M**	T	**W**	**T**	**F**	**S**	**S**
7 Nov–20 Dec	12–3	M	T	W	T	F	**S**	**S**
Park								
All year		**M**	**T**	**W**	**T**	**F**	**S**	**S**
*Shop closes 5:30 March–Nov. Closes dusk if earlier								

Newark Park, Gloucestershire

Newark Park

Ozleworth, Wotton-under-Edge,
Gloucestershire GL12 7PZ

🚶 1949   (1:J3)

Former Tudor hunting lodge later converted to fashionable home

An eclectic art collection can be enjoyed at this unusual and atmospheric house. It has a wild romantic garden with countryside walks and enjoys outstanding views.

What's new in 2009 Plant sales and second-hand bookstall

⭐ The property is lived in and has an interesting and warm atmosphere

ℹ️ **T** 01793 817666 (Infoline), 01453 842644
   E newarkpark@nationaltrust.org.uk

🎧 Audio guide for garden

📺 Open-air theatre production. Teddy Bears' picnic

🚶 Walks link with Cotswold Way

♿ 🚻 ⦂⦂ 🅰 🚻 🎵 Building 🔾🔾
Grounds 🔾

🛍️ Small gift shop

☕ Self-service machine and ice-creams

👶 Baby back-carriers admitted. Family guide. Children's quiz/trail. Pushchairs on ground floor only

🏫 Suitable for school groups

🐕 On leads, only in grounds

➡️ [172:ST786934] **Foot**: Cotswold Way passes property. **Bus**: First 309, 310 Bristol–Dursley, alight Wotton-under-Edge, 1¾ml. Frequent services link 🚋 Bristol Temple Meads with the bus station. **Station**: Stroud 10ml.
Road: 1½ml E of Wotton-under-Edge, 1¾ml S of junction of A4135 & B4058, follow signs for Ozleworth. House signposted from main road

🅿️ Free parking, 100yds. Coaches by prior arrangement only

NT properties nearby
Chedworth Roman Villa, Dyrham Park, Lodge Park and Sherborne Estate, Prior Park Landscape Garden, Woodchester Park

Newark Park			M	T	W	T	F	S	S
4 Mar–28 May	11–5		M	T	**W**	**T**	F	S	S
3 Jun–1 Nov	11–5		M	T	**W**	**T**	F	**S**	**S**
Open BH Mons and Good Fri: 11–5. Closes dusk if earlier. Also open Easter Sat & Sun 11–5									

The Old Mill

Wembury Beach, Wembury, Devon PL9 0HP

🏠 �︎ ☕ 🚶 👶 🚶 1939   (1:F9)

Former mill house

A café is housed in the building, which stands on a small beach near the Yealm estuary.

What's new in 2009 Improved public access around Wembury Point

ℹ️ **T** 01752 862314
   E oldmill@nationaltrust.org.uk

🚶 Regular guided rock-pool rambles and other marine-related events are led by Devon Wildlife Trust wardens from Wembury Marine Centre (open Easter to end Sept); for details tel. 01752 862538

🚶 South West Coast Path runs through property

☕ Café (NT-approved concession). Serving home-made cakes and light meals using local produce

For further information, visit www.nationaltrust.org.uk

🏃 Tracker Packs

🍴 On beach, 1 Oct–31 March only

➡ [201:SX517484] **Foot**: South West Coast Path within ⅜ml. **Bus**: First 48 Plymouth–Wembury, ½ml. **Station**: Plymouth 10ml. **Road**: at Wembury, off A379 E of Plymouth

🅿 Parking. Charge applies. NT members must display cards

NT properties nearby
Overbeck's, Saltram

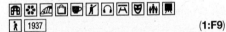

The Old Mill								
1 Apr–24 Jul	11:30–4:30	M	T	W	T	F	S	S
25 Jul–6 Sep	10:30–5	M	T	W	T	F	S	S
7 Sep–1 Nov	11:30–4:30	M	T	W	T	F	S	S
Also open BH Mons. Limited winter opening. May close early in bad weather								

Overbeck's

Sharpitor, Salcombe, Devon TQ8 8LW

🏠 ✶ 🖼 🏛 ☕ 🍴 🎧 🏺 🎭 🏃 🚩

🏃 1937   (1:F9)

Luxuriant coastal garden surrounding elegant Edwardian house with diverse collections

This beautiful garden offers spectacular views over the Salcombe estuary and surrounding coast. Run on organic principles, the 2.75-hectare (7-acre) garden has an intimate and informal atmosphere and is filled with rare and exotic plants, which flourish due to the sheltered microclimate. The inventor Otto Overbeck lived here until 1937, and the house contains his collections of curios, natural history and nautical artefacts, as well as his most peculiar invention, the 'Rejuvenator'.

What's new in 2009 Hidden Histories: display about Overbeck's during the First World War. Gateway to the Countryside: exhibition about the local wildlife and landscapes with suggested walks. Green initiative: visitors arriving by ferry from Salcombe or walking from other destinations receive a free cup of tea

⭐ Grounds very steep. Youth hostel on site (tel. 0870 770 6016)

ℹ **T** 01548 842893, 01548 845013 (shop), 01548 845014 (tea-room)
E overbecks@nationaltrust.org.uk

🏃 Out-of-hours tours on request. Garden tours all year

🎧 Audio tour (deposit required)

🎭 Family events all year: Easter Egg Hunt, Big Bug Weekend, Pirates at Overbeck's and storytelling. Garden tours and demonstrations all year

🏃 Circular coast, farmland and woodland walks (one to two hours). South West Coast Path adjacent

♿ 🅿️ 📷 🎨 💻 🔊 **Building** 🏛

Grounds 🌿

📷 NT shop

🍽 Tea-room. Freshly prepared sandwiches, soups, salads and ploughmans. Children's menu in school holidays

🏃 Baby-changing facilities. Pushchairs and baby back-carriers admitted. Family trails and hands-on activities. Single pushchairs only. Family events all year: Easter Egg Hunt, Big Bug Weekend, Pirates at Overbeck's and storytelling

▦ Suitable for school groups

Gardener working beneath a beautifully blooming magnolia in spring at Overbeck's, Devon

Charges for National Trust members apply on some special event days

[202:SX728374] **Foot**: South West Coast Path within ⅜ml. **Ferry**: from Salcombe to South Sands, then ½ml strenuous walk (uphill). **Bus**: Stagecoach in Devon X64, Sun & BHols only; Tally Ho! 164, 606 from ≢ Totnes. From all alight Salcombe, 1¼ml. **Road**: 1½ml SW of Salcombe, signposted from Malborough and Salcombe (narrow approach road). Roads leading to Overbeck's are steep and single track and not suitable for coaches over 25 seats or large vehicles

P Small car park reserved for visitors to garden and house, 150yds. Charge for non-members (refundable on paid admission). Limited parking on driveway. Care must be taken on steep narrow ascent to entrance. Not suitable for motorhomes/large vehicles (tel. for advice)

NT properties nearby
Coleton Fishacre, Greenway, Salcombe: Thurlestone to Torcross, Saltram

Overbeck's									
Garden only									
2 Feb–13 Feb	11–5	**M**	**T**	**W**	**T**	**F**	S	S	
14 Feb–13 Mar	11–5	**M**	**T**	**W**	**T**	**F**	**S**	**S**	
2 Nov–31 Jan 10	11–5	**M**	**T**	**W**	**T**	**F**	S	S	
Garden/house/shop/tea-room									
14 Mar–1 Jul	11–5	**M**	**T**	**W**	T	F	**S**	**S**	
2 Jul–2 Sep	11–5	**M**	**T**	**W**	**T**	**F**	**S**	**S**	
5 Sep–1 Nov	11–5	**M**	**T**	**W**	T	F	**S**	**S**	
Tea-room/shop									
14 Feb–8 Mar	11–4	M	T	W	T	F	**S**	**S**	

Tea-room open as house but 11–4:15, Garden closed 25, 26 Dec & 1 Jan 10. Garden closes at dusk if earlier than 5

Loe Pool, Cornwall, looking inland to a boathouse

Penrose Estate: Gunwalloe and Loe Pool

nr Helston, Cornwall TR13 0RD

 **1974**   **(1:B10)**

Wooded country around Cornwall's largest natural lake and dramatic coastal scenery

At the heart of the Penrose Estate lies Loe Pool, a freshwater lake which meets the sea at the dramatic shingle bank of Loe Bar. Surrounding the Pool is a mix of rich farmland and woodland through which there are many paths, including the five-mile circuit of the Pool itself. At Gunwalloe, two sandy coves lie either side of the 14th- and 15th-century church (not NT) and the valley reedbed provides a haven for birdlife.

i **T** 01326 561407
E southwestcornwall@nationaltrust.org.uk

🚶 Occasional guided walks

🚶 NT *Coast of Cornwall* leaflet 12 includes maps, details of walks and information on local history and wildlife

♿ **Grounds** 🖼

🍴 Gunwalloe Beach Café (not NT)

🏛 Suitable for school groups. Penrose education and activity pack available for teachers. Education room at Chyvarloe basecamp

🐕 On leads only in landscape park at Penrose. Seasonal bans on one beach at Gunwalloe

🚲 Rough track from Helston to Loe Bar

→ [203:SW639259] **Foot**: South West Coast Path goes through property. **Bus**: First 2/2A, ≢ Penzance–Falmouth to Porthleven. **Station**: Camborne 10ml to Porthleven. **Road**: Penrose Estate: 2ml SW of Helston on B3304 turn left, signposted Loe Bar, and left to car park. Gunwalloe: take A3083 from Helston and turn right 1ml past main RNAS Culdrose entrance

P Pay & display at Gunwalloe. Charge applies all year (NT members free). Free parking available at various sites around Penrose

NT properties nearby
Glendurgan Garden, Godolphin, The Lizard

Penrose Estate							
All year	M	W	T	W	T	F	S	S

Show your card and display sticker for free parking

Philipps House and Dinton Park

Dinton, Salisbury, Wiltshire SP3 5HH

🏠 ♣ 🚶 1943 **(1:K5)**

Early 19th-century neo-Grecian house

An impressive collection of fine Regency furniture is housed on the ground floor of this neo-Grecian house, which was designed by Jeffry Wyatville in 1820 for William Wyndham. A variety of parkland walks can be enjoyed throughout the year.

⭐ No WC

ℹ️ **T** 01722 716663
E philippshouse@nationaltrust.org.uk

🚶 Various walks around the park start from the car park; download from the website or tel. property office

♿ ⠿ Building 🏞️ Grounds 🏞️🏞️

🐕 In park only

➡️ [184:SU004319] **Bus**: Wilts & Dorset 25 from Salisbury (passing ➤ Salisbury). **Station**: Tisbury 5ml. **Road**: 9ml W of Salisbury, on N side of B3089; in Dinton take St Mary's Road at crossroads. Park in car park opposite cricket ground. House entrance 200yds further on left

🅿️ Free parking, 20yds. Visitors to house only should park at house. Visitors to park should at all times use St Mary's Road car park, from where walks begin

NT properties nearby

Little Clarendon, Mompesson House, Stonehenge Landscape, Stourhead

Philipps House and Dinton Park									
House									
4 Apr–31 Oct	10–1	M	T	W	T	F	**S**	S	
6 Apr–26 Oct	1–5	**M**	T	W	T	F	S	S	
Park									
All year		**M**	**T**	**W**	**T**	**F**	**S**	**S**	

If you enjoyed the walks at Dinton Park, why not discover the parkland at Stourhead?

Philipps House, near Salisbury, sits within Dinton Park

Priest's House

Muchelney, Langport, Somerset TA10 0DQ

🏠 🚶 🚲 1911 **(1:I6)**

Late medieval hall-house in a picturesque village

Set in the picturesque village of Muchelney and little altered since the early 17th century, the house was built by the nearby Abbey (now run by EH) in 1308 for the parish priest. Interesting features include the Gothic doorway, magnificent double-height tracery windows and a massive 15th-century stone fireplace. The house is occupied and furnished by tenants.

⭐ No WC

ℹ️ **T** 01458 253771
E priestshouse@nationaltrust.org.uk

♿ ⠿ 📷 Building 🏞️

➡️ [193:ST429250] **Cycle**: Muchelney is on the South Somerset Cycle Trail. **Bus**: First 54/A/B/C Yeovil Bus Station–Taunton (passing within ¾ml ➤ Yeovil Pen Mill), alight Huish Episcopi, 1ml. **Road**: 1ml S of Langport

🅿️ No parking on site

NT properties nearby

Barrington Court, Lytes Cary Manor, Montacute House, Stembridge Tower Mill, Tintinhull Garden, Treasurer's House

Priest's House									
15 Mar–27 Sep	2–5	**M**	T	W	T	F	S	**S**	
Admission by guided tour, last tour commences at 5									

Dogs assisting visitors with disabilities are always welcome

Prior Park Landscape Garden

Ralph Allen Drive, Bath, Somerset BA2 5AH

🎯 🍽 🚻 🎭 🎪 🚌 ⬆ ⬇ 📷 1993   (1:J4)

Beautiful and intimate 18th-century landscape garden

One of only four Palladian bridges in the world can be crossed at Prior Park, which was created in the 18th century by local entrepreneur Ralph Allen, with advice from 'Capability' Brown and the poet Alexander Pope. The garden is set in a sweeping valley where visitors can enjoy magnificent views of Bath. Recent restoration of the 'Wilderness' has reinstated the Serpentine Lake, Cascade and Cabinet. A five-minute walk leads to the Bath Skyline, a six-mile circular route encompassing beautiful woodlands and meadows, an Iron Age hill fort, Roman settlements, 18th-century follies and spectacular views.

What's new in 2009 Guided tours of the restored 'Wilderness'

⭐ Prior Park College, a school, operates from the mansion (not NT). Prior Park is a green tourism site; there is only disabled parking. Wilderness and view point fully accessible. There are steep slopes, steps and uneven paths in the garden

ℹ️ **T** 01225 833422
E priorpark@nationaltrust.org.uk

🎫 Guided tours of the Wilderness. Other tours by arrangement

🎭 Family trails and events throughout the year

🚶 Bath Skyline walk leaflet and map free from Prior Park visitor reception and NT website. No direct access from the Bath Skyline into the garden

♿ 🅿️ 📱 🚾 ⠿ 📷 🎨 **Grounds** 🐾 🏔️

🍽 Kiosk, Sat, Sun, school holidays, events and BHols, Feb–Oct

👶 Baby-changing facilities. Pushchairs and baby back-carriers admitted. Front-carrying baby slings and hip-carrying infant seats for loan. Children's quiz/trail. Family activity packs

🏫 Suitable for school groups. Live interpretation. Hands-on activities

The Palladian bridge at Prior Park, Somerset

🐕 Nov–31 Jan 10 only, on leads

➡️ [172:ST760633] Prior Park is a green tourism site; there is only disabled car parking (please tel. to book), but public transport runs regularly (every 30mins) to and from the park. Please tel. for leaflet or download from the website.
Foot: 1ml very steep uphill walk from railway station. To rear of railway station cross river, pass Widcombe shopping parade, turn right on to Prior Park Road at White Hart PH, proceed up steep hill, garden on left. Kennet & Avon canal path ¾ml. **Cycle**: NCN4, ¾ml. **Bus**: First 2, Bath–Combe Down. Pick up on Dorchester Street, nr railway station. City Sightseeing Skyline Tour open-top tour bus runs to the garden (last stop on tour) every 20mins in summer, every hour in winter (11–5). Pick up from railway station and Abbey. £1 off for NT members. Ticket valid for 24 hours.
Station: Bath Spa 1¼ml. **Road**: no brown signs

🅿️ Disabled parking only (please tel. to book)

NT properties nearby
Bath Assembly Rooms, Clevedon Court, The Courts Garden, Dyrham Park, Great Chalfield Manor and Garden, Lacock Abbey, Tyntesfield, Westwood Manor

Prior Park Landscape Garden		M	T	W	T	F	S	S
1 Feb–8 Feb	11–dusk	M	T	W	T	F	**S**	**S**
14 Feb–30 Oct	11–5:30	**M**	T	**W**	**T**	F	**S**	**S**
31 Oct–31 Jan 10	11–dusk	M	T	W	T	F	**S**	**S**
Kiosk								
14 Feb–1 Nov	11:30–4:30	M	T	W	T	F	**S**	**S**

Last admission 1hr before closing. Closed 25 Dec. Closes dusk if earlier than 5:30. Kiosk also open school hols, events & BHols

For events details, visit www.nationaltrust.org.uk/events

St Anthony Head

Cornwall

🔲 🔲 🔲 🔲 🔲 🔲 🔲 1959 (1:C9)

Headland with fine views over Falmouth Bay

At the southernmost tip of the Roseland peninsula, St Anthony Head overlooks the spectacular entrance to one of the world's largest natural harbours – Carrick Roads and the Fal estuary. The starting point for a number of excellent coastal and sheltered creekside walks, the Head also bears newly revealed remains of a century of defensive fortifications.

ℹ️ **T** 01872 862945
   E stanthonyhead@nationaltrust.org.uk

🚶 NT *Coast of Cornwall* leaflet 18/19 includes maps and details of circular walks and information about local history, geology and wildlife

♿ 🔲 Grounds 🔲

🔲 Suitable for school groups. Adult study days

➡️ [204:SW847313] **Ferry**: Falmouth to St Mawes foot ferry (all year, but no Sun service in winter); St Mawes to Place (1ml from St Anthony Head along coast path), daily in summer only. **Bus**: First 50 Truro–St Mawes, alight St Mawes for ferry to Place, or alight Portscatho, 3ml. **Station**: Penmere, via ferry to St Mawes then to Place, 6ml. **Road**: S of St Mawes off A3078

🅿️ Parking

NT properties nearby
Trelissick Garden

St Anthony Head							
All year	M	T	W	T	F	S	S

The iconic island of St Michael's Mount, Cornwall

St Michael's Mount

Marazion, nr Penzance, Cornwall TR17 0HS

🔲 🔲 ➕ 🔲 🔲 🔲 🔲 🔲 🔲 🔲 🔲 🔲
🔲 1954 (1:B9)

Rocky island crowned by medieval church and castle, home to a living community

This iconic island rises gracefully to the church and castle at its summit. Accessible on foot at low tide across a causeway, at other times it is reached by a short evocative boat trip. The oldest surviving buildings date from the 12th century, when a Benedictine priory was founded here. Following the English Civil War, the island was acquired by the St Aubyn family, who still live in the castle. In the intervening years many additions and alterations were made to convert it for use as a mansion house. Fascinating rooms from different eras include the mid 18th-century Gothick-style Blue Drawing Room.

⭐ Sensible shoes are advisable as causeway and paths are cobbled and uneven. Steep climb to castle. Unsuitable for prams and pushchairs. Passages in the castle are narrow, so some delays may occur in the height of the season. Dogs are not allowed in the castle or grounds and there are no facilities or grassed areas for dogs on the island. Access by boat or causeway and all visits to St Michael's Mount are subject to favourable weather conditions

ℹ️ **T** 01736 710507/01736 710265 (tide information/general enquiries), 01736 711067 (shop), 01736 710748 (restaurant)
   E stmichaelsmount@nationaltrust.org.uk

🔲 Tours available of gardens

🔲 Including church services at 11:15 Suns, Whitsun–end Sept, Good Fri, Easter Sun and Christmas Day. Local bands play beside harbour most Suns July & Aug. Check website and local press for details

♿ 🔲 🔲 🔲 🔲 Castle 🔲 Grounds 🔲

🔲 NT shop. Island shop (not NT). Plant sales

🔲 The Sail Loft Restaurant (licensed). Menu features local seafood dishes. Children's menu. Island Café (not NT) (licensed)

🔲 Baby-changing facilities. Hip-carrying infant seats for loan. Children's quiz/trail

For public transport details, see page 377

■ Suitable for school groups. Arrangements can be made for school or other groups during the winter months

→ [203:SW515298] **Foot**: South West Coast Path within ⅞ml. **Cycle**: NCN3, ¾ml. **Bus**: First 2/A/B Penzance–Helston; 17B Penzance–St Ives. All pass ⊟ Penzance.
Station: Penzance 3ml. **Road**: ½ml S of A394 at Marazion, from where there is access on foot over the causeway at low tide or, during summer months only, by ferry at high tide, if weather conditions favourable

P Public car parks on mainland at Marazion opposite St Michael's Mount 400yds and 800yds (not NT, fee payable)

NT properties nearby
Godolphin, Trengwainton Garden

St Michael's Mount		M	T	W	T	F	S	S
29 Mar–30 Jun	10:30–5	M	T	W	T	F	S	S
1 Jul–31 Aug	10:30–5:30	M	T	W	T	F	S	S
1 Sep–1 Nov	10:30–5	M	T	W	T	F	S	S

Last admission 45mins before castle closing time. Sufficient time should be allowed for travel from the mainland. Castle winter opening: Tues & Fri. Entry by guided tour only, 11 and 2, subject to weather conditions. Garden open weekdays in May & June; Thur & Fri July–Oct. Special garden tours some evenings – see local information or website

The creamy-grey west front of Saltram, Devon

Saltram

Plympton, Plymouth, Devon PL7 1UH

🎏 📷 ✂ ♣ 🔌 🔲 💷 🎭 🎧 🎪 🏴 👥 🔨 🎒 ☥ 🚲
🍸 1957   (1:F8)

Magnificent Georgian house with opulent Robert Adam interiors, gardens, follies and landscape parkland

Still a largely undiscovered treasure, and the result of centuries of sophistication and extravagance, Saltram is now the perfect family day out: close to Plymouth and yet in a world of its own. Home to the Parker family for nearly 300 years, the house with its original contents provides a fascinating insight into country estate life throughout the centuries. Fine Robert Adam interiors and beautiful collections bring the 'age of elegance' to life at Saltram. Learn about some of the fascinating characters and family stories, including the correspondence of Frances, the second Countess, with Jane Austen, and John, Lord Boringdon's, great friendship with Sir Joshua Reynolds. Explore the magnificent garden and romantic follies, and enjoy discovering many secluded spots throughout the landscape park and estate bordering the Plym estuary. For younger visitors there are children's activities rooms and a family trail to help you discover the secrets of Saltram, while the garden can be enjoyed with our family explorer packs.

What's new in 2009 Additional areas of the house open to the public for the first time

★ Occasional special events require NT members to pay for entry

i **T** 01752 333500
E saltram@nationaltrust.org.uk

🏃 Out-of-hours house tours available for groups, 10–11:30, Mon–Thurs inclusive. £10 (booking essential). Grounds: guided walks may be available by arrangement

🎧 Available on request. These are especially suitable for visitors with sight difficulties

🛡 Wide range of year-round events, including jazz picnic, open-air theatre, craft fairs, lecture lunches and Hallowe'en night

🧍 Extensive footpaths around the estate. Maps available from Visitor Reception

🚹 P♿ D♿ ⓦ🚻 ☕ 🅿 ♿ ♿ ♿

Building ♿♿♿ **Grounds** ♿➡

🏠 Gift and garden shops in stables. Chapel Gallery in garden selling local arts and crafts

🍴 Park Restaurant (licensed) in the stables. Occasional evening opening. Special events programme. Available for private hire/functions. Children's menu

👶 Baby-changing facilities. Pushchairs for loan in house. Children's play area. Children's guide. Family house trail. Family garden explorer packs. Children's events

📖 Suitable for school groups. Education room/centre. Hands-on activities. Adult study days

🐕 On leads on designated paths only, not in garden or grazed area of park

🚲 Many good cycle tracks in the parkland, part of NCN27

➡ [201:SX520557] **Foot**: South West Coast Path within 4ml. **Cycle**: NCN27. **Bus**: Plymouth Citybus 22 from Plymouth, alight Merafield Road, ½ml. **Station**: Plymouth 3½ml. **Road**: 3½ml E of Plymouth city centre. Travelling south (from Exeter): leave A38, 3ml N of Plymouth. Exit is signed Plymouth City Centre/Plympton/Kingsbridge. At roundabout take centre lane, then 3rd exit for Plympton. Take right-hand lane and follow brown signs.

Saltram								
Park								
All year	Dawn–dusk	**M**	**T**	**W**	**T**	**F**	**S**	**S**
House								
28 Feb–8 Mar	12–4:30	M	T	W	T	F	**S**	**S**
14 Mar–1 Nov	12–4:30	**M**	**T**	**W**	**T**	F	**S**	**S**
Catering								
1 Feb–12 Mar	11–4	**M**	**T**	**W**	**T**	F	**S**	**S**
14 Mar–1 Nov	11–5	**M**	**T**	**W**	**T**	**F**	**S**	**S**
2 Nov–31 Jan 10	11–4	**M**	**T**	**W**	**T**	F	**S**	**S**
Shop/garden/gallery								
1 Feb–12 Mar	11–4	**M**	**T**	**W**	**T**	F	**S**	**S**
14 Mar–1 Nov	11–5	**M**	**T**	**W**	**T**	F	**S**	**S**
2 Nov–31 Jan 10	11–4	**M**	**T**	**W**	**T**	F	**S**	**S**

Admission by timed ticket. Open Good Fri. Last admission to house 45mins before closing. Shop/gallery/garden closed 24–26 Dec & 1 Jan 10. Catering closed 25/26 Dec

Travelling north (from Liskeard): leave A38 at Plympton exit. At roundabout take first exit for Plympton, then as before

🅿 Free parking, 50yds

NT properties nearby
Antony, Buckland Abbey, Cotehele, Overbeck's, Salcombe: Thurlestone to Torcross

Saloon, Saltram: magnificent Georgian house with opulent Robert Adam interiors

Shute Barton

Shute, nr Axminster, Devon EX13 7PT

🏠 🦇 🛈 👶 1959 **(1:H7)**

Medieval manor house with later architectural features

⭐ Extensive building work will be carried out at Shute Barton in the early months of 2009. The property will not open until Saturday, 23 May. No WC

🛈 **T** 01392 883126
E shutebarton@nationaltrust.org.uk

➡ 3ml SW of Axminster, 2ml N of Colyton on Honiton–Colyton road (B3161)

Shute Barton								
23 May–30 Sep	2–5:30	M	T	**W**	T	F	**S**	**S**
3 Oct–31 Oct	2–5	M	T	**W**	T	F	**S**	**S**

Admission by guided tour. The house is tenanted; there is visitor access to most parts of the interior

Snowshill Manor and Garden

Snowshill, nr Broadway, Gloucestershire WR12 7JU

🏠 ❋ 🏡 🏠 ☕ 🚶 ⛱ 🛡 👫 1951   **(1:K1)**

Cotswold manor set in hillside gardens housing Charles Wade's collection of 'colour, craftsmanship and design'

A traditional golden-yellow manor house set in a delightful village high above the Vale of Evesham, Snowshill Manor is packed to the rafters with a spectacular collection of craftsmanship and design from across the globe. Charles Paget Wade amassed more than 22,000 items during his lifetime, creating an Aladdin's cave of unexpected delights. Experience his uniquely presented collection, which includes samurai armour, clocks, toys, bicycles, tools and musical instruments. Outside, wander through the numerous small 'outdoor rooms', with their terraces and ponds, and admire the views.

What's new in 2009 Children's manor trail

⭐ The Wade Costume Collection is housed at Berrington Hall in Herefordshire and can be viewed there, by appointment only. Photography inside the house by written arrangement only

ℹ **T** 01386 852410
E snowshillmanor@nationaltrust.org.uk

🚶 Explorer tours taking in parts of manor house and its collection not usually on display

🛡 Children's activity days. Seasonal garden trails. Winter weekend events

♿ 🅿 🚼 ⌨ ⠿ 🎧 🖥 ♿ 🦽 **Building** ♿
Grounds 👁 ♿

🛍 NT shop. Plant sales

🍽 Licensed restaurant. Children's menu

👫 Baby-changing and feeding facilities. Front-carrying baby slings and hip-carrying infant seats for loan. Children's play area and maze. Children's quiz/trail. Tracker Packs. Children's activity days

➡ [150:SP096339] **Foot**: Cotswold Way within ¾ml. **Bus**: Castleways, Evesham or Cheltenham–Broadway, then 2½ml uphill.

'Boneshaker' bicycles of 1870–85 at Snowshill Manor, Gloucestershire: an Aladdin's cave of delights

Station: Moreton-in-Marsh 7ml, Evesham 8ml. **Road**: 2½ml SW of Broadway; turn from A44 Broadway bypass into Broadway village; at green turn right uphill to Snowshill

🅿 Free parking, 500yds. Walk from car park to manor house and garden along undulating country path. Transfer available

NT properties nearby
Chastleton House, Chedworth Roman Villa, Coughton Court, Hidcote Manor Garden, Lodge Park and Sherborne Estate

Snowshill Manor and Garden										
Manor										
14 Mar–1 Nov	12–5	M	T	**W**	**T**	**F**	**S**	**S**
Priest's House										
14 Mar–1 Nov	11–5	M	T	**W**	**T**	**F**	**S**	**S**
Garden										
14 Mar–1 Nov	11–5:30	M	T	**W**	**T**	**F**	**S**	**S**
Shop/restaurant/grounds										
14 Mar–1 Nov	11–5:30	M	T	**W**	**T**	**F**	**S**	**S**
7 Nov–13 Dec	12–4	M	T	W	T	F	**S**	**S**

Admission by timed ticket at busy times. Tickets issued at reception on a first-come, first-served basis and cannot be booked in advance. Tickets often run out at peak times; please arrive early. Last admission: Manor 4:10; garden 5. Open BHols

Unless indicated, last admission is always 30mins before closing time

Stembridge Tower Mill

High Ham, Somerset TA10 9DJ

[✦] [🏠] 1969 (1:I5)

The last remaining thatched windmill in England

[★] Please respect the privacy of the cottage adjacent to the site and stay within the immediate vicinity of the mill and orchard. Please park outside on road, unless otherwise instructed. No WC

[i] **T** 01935 823289
E stembridgemill@nationaltrust.org.uk

[→] 2ml N of Langport, ½ml E of High Ham; take the Somerton road from Langport and follow High Ham signs. Take road opposite cemetery in High Ham. Mill is on right

Stembridge Tower Mill									
Outside viewing only*									
14 Mar–1 Nov		11–5	**M**	**T**	**W**	**T**	**F**	**S**	**S**

*Please respect privacy of holiday tenants in cottage. Possible to enter Mill Easter Mon, early May BH Mon and Aug BH Mon 11–5

Stoke-sub-Hamdon Priory

North Street, Stoke-sub-Hamdon, Somerset TA4 6QP

[🏠] 1946 (1:I6)

14th/15th-century farm buildings, formerly a priests' residence

The priests who lived here served the Chapel of St Nicholas (now destroyed). The Great Hall is open to visitors.

[★] No WC

[i] **T** 01935 823289
E stokehamdonpriory@nationaltrust.org.uk

[♿] Grounds [♿][♿]

[→] [193:ST473175] **Bus:** South West Coaches 81 Yeovil Bus Station–South Petherton (passing within ¾ml ⊞ Yeovil Pen Mill). **Station:** Crewkerne or Yeovil Pen Mill, both 7ml. **Road:** between A303 and A3088. 2ml W of Montacute between Yeovil and Ilminster

[P] No parking on site. Not suitable for coaches

NT properties nearby
Barrington Court, Lytes Cary Manor, Montacute House, Priest's House, Tintinhull Garden, Treasurer's House

Stoke-sub-Hamdon Priory									
16 Mar–1 Nov		10–6	**M**	**T**	**W**	**T**	**F**	**S**	**S**

Closes dusk if earlier. Only Great Hall open

Stonehenge Landscape

3/4 Stonehenge Cottages, King Barrows, Amesbury, Wiltshire SP4 7DD

[🏛][♿][👕][🎧][🏠][🍴][🚶][♿] 1927 (1:K5)

Ancient ceremonial landscape of great archaeological and wildlife interest

Within the Stonehenge World Heritage Site, the Trust owns and manages 850 hectares (2,100 acres) of downland surrounding the famous stone circle. Walking across the grassland visitors can discover other prehistoric monuments, including the Avenue, the King Barrows, Winterbourne Stoke Barrows, the great henge of Durrington Walls and the Cursus. There is also a great diversity of wildlife.

What's new in 2009 Improved landscape access

[★] The stone circle is managed by English Heritage (NT members admitted free). All grassland areas on the Stonehenge Landscape are designated NT open access and are open to everyone, but on foot only. Camping is not permitted. Please observe the NT byelaws. WC at the stone circle

[i] **T** 01980 664780
E stonehenge@nationaltrust.org.uk

[👕] Guided walks

[🎧] For the stone circle only. Available from the English Heritage kiosk

[🚶] The grassland is available for visitors to explore on foot. Maps of accessible areas and self-guided walks leaflets can be obtained by contacting the property office and from the NT website

[♿] [P♿] Grounds [♿]

[🏫] Suitable for school groups

🐕 Under close control at all times

🚵 On byways and bridleways only

→ [184:SU120420] **Bus**: Stonehenge Tour bus
🚆 Salisbury–Stonehenge. **Station**: Salisbury
9½ml. **Road**: Monument 2ml W of Amesbury,
at junction of A303 & A344

P Parking (not NT), 50yds. A charge may
apply over the peak period June–Oct.
NT members free

NT properties nearby
Avebury, Little Clarendon, Mompesson House,
Philipps House and Dinton Park, Stourhead

Stonehenge Landscape
Open access at all times

Stourhead

Stourhead Estate Office, Stourton, Warminster,
Wiltshire BA12 6QD

🏰➕🏛️🔣🌳🐾🏠🍷🏺☕🚶🎧📻♿ 👫🚃🚶🚵🔔☂ 1946   (1:J5)

**World-famous 18th-century landscape
garden, Palladian mansion, parkland,
woods and chalk downs**

Lying in secluded privacy in its own valley,
Stourhead features one of the finest landscape
gardens in the world. Designed by Henry Hoare II
as a place to entertain, the garden was laid out
between 1741 and 1780. The magnificent lake is
central to this iconic garden of classical temples
and follies. Its lakeside paths and backdrop of

The Bristol High Cross at Stourhead in Wiltshire: just
one of the many follies

colourful, rare and exotic trees reveal many
beautifully contrived vistas, capturing the
imagination of visitors for over two centuries.
While the garden seasons change in beautiful
succession, the majestic Palladian mansion,
originally home to the Hoare family, houses a
unique collection of Chippendale furniture,
magnificent paintings and an exquisite Regency
library. Waymarked walks can be enjoyed across
the chalk downland and woodland of the wider
estate, which is managed for nature conservation.
Two Iron Age hill forts can be discovered, and
from the top of King Alfred's Tower, a 50m-high
red brick triangular folly, visitors will experience
spectacular views across three counties.

What's new in 2009 Discover what it takes to
look after one of the Trust's busiest estates
during our behind the scenes weekend
'Stourhead Uncovered'. See our fascinating film
Servants. Opportunity to observe conservation
in action while the Temple of Apollo is
undergoing restoration

i **T** 01747 841152
E stourhead@nationaltrust.org.uk

🚶 Free daily volunteer-led garden tours. Tours
subject to availability. Stout footwear and
waterproof clothing advisable

🎧 Available for garden

♿ Programme of events throughout the year for
children, families and adults, including free
trails and drop-in activities

🚶 Walks leaflet available at Visitor Reception
and shop

♿ 🅿️ 🚃 🚾 ⠿ 📷 📻 📢 🖼️ Building 🔎 ♿
Grounds 🚶 ➡️ 🚵 ♿

🛍️ NT shop and plant centre. Farm shop and art
gallery (not NT)

☕ Restaurant (licensed) serving fresh seasonal
food. Private dining room, max. 50 (booking
required). Children's menu. Ice-cream parlour
and refreshments in Spread Eagle courtyard.
Spread Eagle Inn (not NT), open all year

👫 Baby-changing and feeding facilities.
Hip-carrying infant seats for loan in house.
Pushchairs admitted to garden only.
Children's guide. Children's activity area.
Family trails. Activity packs. Family events

Charges for National Trust members apply on some special event days

■ Suitable for school/higher education groups. Education room/centre. Hands-on activities. Adult study days

🐕 On short leads in landscape garden (1 Nov–31 Jan 10). Under close control all year on wider estate. Not admitted to house or King Alfred's Tower

🚲 Some access across estate on bridleways and Wiltshire Cycle Way

➔ [183:ST780340] **Cycle**: Wiltshire Cycle Way runs through estate. **Bus**: First 58 Shaftesbury–Wincanton (passing ☒ Gillingham), alight Zeals, 1¼ml. **Station**: Gillingham 6¾ml; Bruton (U) 7ml. **Road**: at Stourton, off B3092, 3ml NW of Mere (A303), 8ml S of Frome (A361). King Alfred's Tower: 3½ml by road from Stourhead House

P Free parking, 400yds. Transfer by shuttle, throughout main season only, to house and garden entrances. King Alfred's Tower: designated parking 50yds

NT properties nearby
Barrington Court, Bruton Dovecote, Lytes Cary Manor, Mompesson House, Montacute House, Stonehenge Landscape, Tintinhull Garden

Stourhead										
Garden										
All year	9–6	M	T	W	T	F	S	S
House										
14 Mar–1 Nov	11–5	M	T	W	T	F	S	S
Tower										
14 Mar–1 Nov	11–5	M	T	W	T	F	S	S
Restaurant										
1 Feb–28 Feb	10–4:30	M	T	W	T	F	S	S
1 Mar–31 Oct	10–5:30	M	T	W	T	F	S	S
1 Nov–31 Jan 10	10–4:30	M	T	W	T	F	S	S
Shop										
1 Feb–28 Feb	10–4	M	T	W	T	F	S	S
1 Mar–31 Mar	10–5	M	T	W	T	F	S	S
1 Apr–30 Sep	10–6	M	T	W	T	F	S	S
1 Oct–31 Oct	10–5	M	T	W	T	F	S	S
1 Nov–31 Jan 10	10–4	M	T	W	T	F	S	S
Farm shop										
1 Feb–28 Mar	10–4	M	T	W	T	F	S	S
29 Mar–24 Oct	10–6	M	T	W	T	F	S	S
25 Oct–23 Dec	10–5	M	T	W	T	F	S	S

Garden and tower close dusk if earlier. Farm shop closed 24 Dec–1 Jan 10. Garden, house, tower, shop and restaurant closed 25 Dec

Studland Beach and Nature Reserve

Purbeck Estate Office, Studland, Swanage, Dorset BH19 3AX

🏊🏕🐕🏠🏧💷🎭🚌🎪👫🏛🐕

🚲 | 1982 | **(1:K7)**

Vast area of sandy beaches and heathland

Glorious sandy beaches stretch continuously for three miles from South Haven Point to the chalk cliffs of Handfast Point and Old Harry Rocks, and include Shell Bay and a designated naturist area. The heathland behind the beach is a haven for many rare birds and native wildlife and is a designated National Nature Reserve. Studland is the richest 1,000 hectares (2,400 acres) for wild flowers in Britain. There are several trails through the sand dunes and woodlands, including bird hides at Little Sea. Studland Beach is just one highlight of the 3,200-hectare (8,000-acre) Purbeck Estate cared for by the National Trust.

★ WCs at Knoll Beach and Middle Beach. Shell Bay WCs are composting/low water flush

ℹ **T** 01929 450259
E studlandbeach@nationaltrust.org.uk

🎭 Bookable guided walks of nature reserve

🎪 Family, winter and evening events

🚶 Sand dunes trail and woodland walk leaflets available

♿ P♿🚾♿♿ **Grounds** ♿♿

🛍 Located at Knoll Beach Visitor Centre and seasonally at Middle Beach. NT range and beach products

☕ Beach café (licensed) at Knoll Beach Visitor Centre. Children's menu. Licensed café (not NT) at Middle Beach. Fish restaurant (not NT) (licensed) at Shell Bay. Mobile catering vans on the beach during the summer

👫 Baby-changing facilities at all beach WCs. Pushchairs for loan at Knoll Beach

■ Suitable for school groups. Education room/centre. Adult study days

🐕 No restrictions 1 Oct–30 April. Knoll Beach & Middle Beach: dogs on leads 1 May–30 June and 8 Sept–30 Sept. No dogs allowed

1 July–7 Sept. Shell Bay & South Beach: dogs on leads 1 May–30 Sept. Dogs permitted all year on nature reserve, estate footpaths and South West Coast Path (on a lead)

🚲 Cycling on bridleways across the Purbeck Estate. Route booklet available from Visitor Centre

➔ [195:SZ036835] **Foot**: 5ml of South West Coast Path on property. **Ferry**: car ferry from Sandbanks, Poole, to Shell Bay. **Bus**: Wilts & Dorset 50 Bournemouth–Swanage to Shell Bay and Studland. **Station**: Branksome or Parkstone, both 3½ml to Shell Bay or 6ml to Studland via vehicle ferry

P Car parks at Shell Bay & South Beach (open 9–11), Knoll Beach & Middle Beach (open 9–8). Prices vary through the season. NT members must show cards on entry. Some car parks are pay & display

NT properties nearby
Brownsea Island, Clouds Hill, Corfe Castle, Hardy's Cottage, Kingston Lacy, Max Gate

Studland Beach									
Beach									
All year		**M**	**T**	**W**	**T**	**F**	**S**	**S**	
Shop/café									
1 Feb–3 Apr	10–4*	**M**	**T**	**W**	**T**	**F**	**S**	**S**	
4 Apr–28 Jun	9:30–5*	**M**	**T**	**W**	**T**	**F**	**S**	**S**	
29 Jun–6 Sep	9:30–6	**M**	**T**	**W**	**T**	**F**	**S**	**S**	
7 Sep–1 Nov	9:30–5	**M**	**T**	**W**	**T**	**F**	**S**	**S**	
2 Nov–31 Jan 10	10–4*	**M**	**T**	**W**	**T**	**F**	**S**	**S**	

*Shop/café closes 1hr later at weekends. Shop and café open hours may be longer in fine weather and shorter in poor weather. Visitor Centre, shop and café closed 25/26 Dec. **Car parks can be very full in peak season**

Tintagel Old Post Office: this 14th-century building was originally a yeoman's farmhouse

Show your card and display sticker for free parking

Tintagel Old Post Office

Fore Street, Tintagel, Cornwall PL34 0DB

🏠 ❄ 🖥 🚻 🎦 [1903]　　　　　(1:D7)

One of the Trust's most delightful medieval buildings, enhanced by a cottage garden

Standing apart from its modern commercial neighbours on Tintagel's main street, this low-set 14th-century yeoman's farmhouse exudes charm and beckons the curious to explore. Inside, one room is restored to show how it looked when, for a brief time in the late 19th century, it was used as the local letter-receiving station. The remaining rooms are furnished with local oak pieces and a good collection of samplers from the same period. Outside, the small enclosed cottage garden offers a tranquil haven away from the hustle and bustle of the busy village street.

★ WC in Trevena Square (not NT)

ℹ **T** 01840 770024
　E tintageloldpo@nationaltrust.org.uk

♿ ⠿🖼🏞🚻🖼 Building 🖼🖼
Grounds 🖼🖼

🖥 NT shop

🚻 Hip-carrying infant seat for loan. Children's quiz/trail. Pushchairs and backpacks can be left at entrance

🎦 Suitable for school groups

➔ [200:SX056884] In centre of village.
Foot: South West Coast Path within ⅔ml.
Bus: Western Greyhound 594 St Columb Major–Boscastle via Wadebridge (connections with 555 at Wadebridge from 🚉 Bodmin Parkway)

P No parking on site. Numerous pay & display car parks in village (not NT)

NT properties nearby
Barras Nose, Boscastle

Tintagel Old Post Office									
14 Feb–1 Mar	11–4	**M**	**T**	**W**	**T**	**F**	**S**	**S**	
7 Mar–8 Mar	11–4	M	T	W	T	F	**S**	**S**	
14 Mar–30 Sep	11–5:30	**M**	**T**	**W**	**T**	**F**	**S**	**S**	
1 Oct–1 Nov	11–4	**M**	**T**	**W**	**T**	**F**	**S**	**S**	

Tintinhull Garden

Farm Street, Tintinhull, Yeovil, Somerset BA22 8PZ

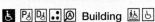 1953 (1:16)

Delightful formal garden

Created last century around a 17th-century manor house, this is one of the most harmonious small gardens in Britain. It features secluded lawns, small pools and colourful borders. There is also an attractive kitchen garden and orchard to explore.

ℹ️ **T** 01935 823289
   E tintinhull@nationaltrust.org.uk

♿ P 🅿 ∷ 🖼 Building 🏛 ♿

🏪 Plant sales and guidebooks

🍴 Tea-room in courtyard. Light refreshments only

👪 Pushchairs and baby back-carriers admitted. Family activities

🖼 Suitable for school groups. Hands-on activities

➔ [183:ST503198] **Bus**: First 52 Yeovil Bus Station–Martock (passing within ¾ml ☒ Yeovil Pen Mill). **Station**: Yeovil Pen Mill 5½ml; Yeovil Junction 7ml (bus to Yeovil Bus Station). **Road**: 5ml NW of Yeovil, ½ml S of A303, on E outskirts of Tintinhull. Follow road signs to Tintinhull village

🅿 Free parking, 150yds

NT properties nearby
Barrington Court, Lytes Cary Manor, Montacute House, Priest's House, Stembridge Tower Mill, Treasurer's House

Tintinhull Garden								
14 Mar–1 Nov	11–5	M	T	**W**	**T**	**F**	**S**	**S**
Closes dusk if earlier. Open BH Mons								

The formal garden at Tintinhull surrounds an elegant 17th-century manor house

Treasurer's House

Martock, Somerset TA12 6JL

🏛 1971 (1:16)

Small medieval house

Medieval house with Great Hall, completed in 1293, and Solar Block containing an unusual wall painting. There is also a kitchen, added in the 15th century.

⭐ The house is occupied by tenants. Only the medieval hall, wall painting and kitchen are shown to visitors. No WC

ℹ️ **T** 01935 825015
   E treasurersmartock@nationaltrust.org.uk

♿ Building 🏛 Grounds 🏛 🏛

➔ [193:ST462191] **Bus**: First 52 Yeovil Bus Station–Martock (passing within ¾ml ☒ Yeovil Pen Mill). **Station**: Crewkerne 7¼ml; Yeovil Pen Mill 8ml. **Road**: opposite church in middle of village; 1ml NW of A303 between Ilminster and Ilchester

🅿 Free parking (not NT), 400yds. Parking limited and unsuitable for trailer caravans

NT properties nearby
Barrington Court, Lytes Cary Manor, Montacute House, Priest's House, Stembridge Tower Mill, Tintinhull Garden

Treasurer's House								
15 Mar–27 Sep	2–5	**M**	**T**	W	T	F	S	**S**

If you enjoyed exploring Tintinhull Garden, you'll love Montacute House

Dogs assisting visitors with disabilities are always welcome

Trelissick Garden

Feock, nr Truro, Cornwall TR3 6QL

🟥 ♣ 🛋 🏛 🏠 🗄 🍷 🎧 🎭 🎭 👪 🚺 🧍

🍸 | 1955 | (1:C9)

Tranquil varied garden in fabulous position, with a superb collection of tender and exotic plants

This Cornish maritime garden is in an extraordinary position on a wooded peninsula. To the north it is embraced by Lamouth Creek, the winding estuary of the River Fal is to the east and to the south is Channels Creek and the great expanse of Carrick Roads. Trelissick is a magical place that will transport your imagination to days gone by. Throughout the year the 12-hectare (30-acre) garden is awash with colour, while the park has breathtaking views down towards the sea. There is a fine Georgian stable block, a shop, gallery and restaurant (the house is not open to the public), and the whole estate is encircled with woods full of wonderful walks.

⭐ Copeland China Collection, by courtesy of Mr and Mrs William Copeland, open Thur May and Sept, 2–4. Booking recommended, tel. 01872 864452. Joint ticket for garden and china collection £11, NT members £4. Fal River Links partnership ferries to Trelissick landing stage from Falmouth, Truro and St Mawes. Service operates May to Sept. Check with operators for times and disabled access. Art gallery closed occasionally for rehang

ℹ️ **T** 01872 862090, 01872 865515 (shop), 01872 863486 (catering)
E trelissick@nationaltrust.org.uk

🎭 Theatrical, musical and winter events

🧍 NT *Coast of Cornwall* leaflet 17 – Trelissick woodland walks

♿ 🅿️ 🚻 👓 📷 🎨 🦯 🔍

Grounds 🚶 🏞️ ➡️ ♿

🏠 Shop, art gallery, Cornwall Crafts gallery. Plant sales

🍷 Crofters restaurant (licensed). Last orders 30mins before closing. Children's menu. Ice-cream kiosk in car park, limited opening. Sunday lunches in Barn Function Room

Trelissick Garden: Ferris's Cottage appearing behind the trees, with deep pink and red rhododendrons in the foreground

(licensed). Booking required, tel. 01872 863486. Also available for conferences and banquets

👪 Baby-changing facilities. Pushchairs and baby back-carriers admitted

🖼️ Suitable for school groups. Education room/centre

🐕 Dogs on leads in the park and on woodland walks only; not allowed in the garden

➡️ [204:SW837396] **Cycle**: NCN3. **Ferry**: link from Falmouth, Truro and St Mawes (see www.falriverlinks.co.uk). Enterprise boats 01326 374241, K&S Cruisers 01326 211056, Newman's Cruises/Tolverne Ferries 01872 580309. **Bus**: First T16 Truro–Feock. **Station**: Truro 5ml; Perranwell (U), 4ml. **Road**: 4ml S of Truro, on B3289 above King Harry Ferry

🅿️ Parking, 50yds, £3.50 (refunded on admission to garden)

NT properties nearby
Glendurgan Garden, Trerice

Trelissick Garden									
1 Feb–13 Feb	11–4	M	T	W	T	F	S	S
14 Feb–1 Nov	10:30–5:30	M	T	W	T	F	S	S
2 Nov–23 Dec	11–4	M	T	W	T	F	S	S
27 Dec–31 Dec	11–4	M	T	W	T	F	S	S
2 Jan–31 Jan 10	11–4	M	T	W	T	F	S	S
Woodland walks									
All year		M	T	W	T	F	S	S
Garden closes dusk if earlier									

For events details, visit www.nationaltrust.org.uk/events

Trengwainton Garden

Madron, nr Penzance, Cornwall TR20 8RZ

❖ 🏠 🏛 💷 🎿 🌲 🛡 🚻 🎯 🐾 1961 (1:B9)

Sheltered garden with an abundance of exotic trees and shrubs

Intimately linked to the picturesque stream running the length of the garden, paths lead up to a terrace and summerhouses, from where there are splendid views across Mount's Bay to The Lizard. The walled gardens contain many rare and unusual species which are difficult to grow in the open anywhere else in the country. Kitchen garden crops are gradually being reintroduced into the productive area. Visitors can climb on to a raised platform to take in the scale of the walled gardens and their unique raised beds, built to the dimensions of Noah's Ark, as described in *The Bible*.

ℹ️ **T** 01736 363148, 01736 362297 (shop), 01736 331717 (tea-room)
E trengwainton@nationaltrust.org.uk

🎿 By arrangement

🛡 Series of garden events

🔋 📱 🎮 🔧 ⛱ 🚻 ♿ 🦽 Grounds 🏔 ➡️ ♿

🏪 NT shop. Plant sales

💷 Tea-room (NT-approved concession) plus 30 additional outdoor covers adjacent to car park. Range of non-allergenic products. Children's menu

🚻 Baby-changing facilities. Pushchairs and baby back-carriers admitted. Family quiz/trail. Tracker Packs

🖼 Suitable for school groups

🐾 On leads only in garden, not tea-room garden

➡️ [203:SW445315] **Foot**: footpath to the property from Penzance via Heamoor. **Cycle**: NCN3, 2½ml. **Bus**: First 17/A/B St Ives–St Just (passing ➡️ Penzance). **Station**: Penzance 2ml.
Road: 2ml NW of Penzance, ½ml W of Heamoor off Penzance–Morvah road (B3312), ½ml off St Just road (A3071)

🅿️ Free parking, 150yds

NT properties nearby
Godolphin, Levant Beam Engine, St Michael's Mount

Trengwainton Garden							
Garden/shop							
8 Feb–1 Nov	10:30–5	**M**	**T**	**W**	**T**	F	S	S

Open Good Fri. Tea-room opens 10, last admission 15mins before closing

Exotic tree ferns by the pond at Trengwainton Garden

Trerice

Kestle Mill, nr Newquay, Cornwall TR8 4PG

🏚 ❖ 🏠 🏛 💷 🌲 🛡 🚻 🖼 🔔
🍵 1953 (1:C8)

Elizabethan manor house with fine interiors and delightful garden

A grand Elizabethan manor on a Cornish scale, Trerice remains little changed by the advances in building fashions over the centuries, thanks to long periods under absentee owners. Today the renowned stillness and tranquillity of Trerice, much prized by visitors, is occasionally pierced by the curious lilts of Tudor music or shouts of excitement from the Bowling Green (surely you will want to try a game of Kayling or Slapcock?), bringing back some of the bustle and noise that must have typified its time as a busy manor house.

What's new in 2009 Now open Saturdays and closed Fridays

⭐ This year open Saturdays and closed Fridays. Restricted access to first floor to comply with fire regulations

ℹ️ **T** 01637 875404
E trerice@nationaltrust.org.uk

For public transport details, see page 377

🏺 Living history, children's craft activities, guided tours and lecture lunches

♿ 🅿️ 🇩 🕮 ∴ 🅾 🗺 ♨ ⬆️ 📠

Building 🅛 🅐 🅐 ♿ **Grounds** ♿ ➡️

🏠 NT shop. Plant sales

🍽 Tea-room (licensed) in Great Barn. Children's menu. Tea-garden (licensed)

♿ Baby-changing and feeding facilities. Hip-carrying infant seats for loan. Family trail. Children's craft activities

📖 Suitable for school groups. Indoor education area. Live interpretation. Hands-on activities

➜ [200:SW841585] **Cycle**: NCN32.
Bus: Western Greyhound 527 🚆 Newquay–🚆 St Austell, alight Kestle Mill, ¾ml.
Station: Quintrell Downs (U), 1½ml.
Road: 3ml SE of Newquay via A392 and A3058 signed from Quintrell Downs (turn right at Kestle Mill), or signed from A30 at Summercourt via A3058

🅿️ Free parking, 300yds. Coach access only via Kestle Mill 1ml

NT properties nearby
Carnewas and Bedruthan Steps, Cornish Mines and Engines, Lanhydrock, Trelissick Garden

Trerice								
House/shop								
28 Feb–1 Nov		11–5	**M**	**T**	**W T**	**F**	**S**	**S**

Tea-room & garden open 10:30. Tea-room last serving 4:30. Garden, tea-room, shop & Great Hall open 4–6, 11–13, 18–20 Dec, 11–3, Fri, Sat & Sun

The Great Chamber at Trerice, Cornwall

Tyntesfield

Wraxall, North Somerset BS48 1NX

🏠 🐾 ✝️ ✳️ 🍀 🏠 🗄 🍽 🎷 🎭 👪 📖

🚶 2002   (1:14)

Spectacular Victorian Gothic Revival country house with gardens, arboretum and rolling parkland

Tyntesfield, a glorious Victorian extravaganza, is a magical place, bristling with towers and turrets, created by four generations of the Gibbs family. Saved for the nation in 2002, with a dramatic fundraising campaign, Tyntesfield provides a unique opportunity to experience the work needed to conserve and restore a country estate. After six years of fundraising and planning while opening to 350,000 visitors, the essential work to re-roof, re-wire and re-plumb the house and chapel is now starting. During this conservation in action project, visitors will be treated to a fascinating insight into the technology of Tyntesfield and discover, with our Room Interpreters, how each generation of the Gibbs family influenced its architecture and collections. To find out more about the conservation project, visit the interactive exhibition in the beautiful stables. Make sure you take the opportunity to relax in the formal terraced gardens, then stroll through rolling parkland to the wonderful walled kitchen garden, where produce is available to visitors. Be amazed at the arboretum and track down the eight champion trees, before enjoying one of the new estate walks with stunning views of the Land Yeo valley.

What's new in 2009 Interactive exhibition exploring the conservation in action project. Sawmill restored into Learning Centre, offering facilities for schools, events, conferences and lifelong learning

⭐ As the conservation project progresses, the rooms open may vary. For up-to-date information about which areas of the house are open, please tel. the Infoline. At present facilities onsite are basic and temporary. Admission to the house is by timed ticket only (issued at Visitor Reception on arrival). Entry to the property and car park cannot be guaranteed on busy days

The east front of Tyntesfield, a house which bristles with towers and turrets

i **T** 0844 800 4966 (Infoline), 01275 461900
E tyntesfield@nationaltrust.org.uk

Regular guided tours of the house – check online for details. For garden and wider estate tours enquire at Visitor Reception

Extensive events programme, inc. open-air theatre, specialist tours and lectures. Family events in school holidays. Guided walks of the stunning gardens and the rare wildlife on the estate (email for more information)

New estate walks leaflet available from Visitor Reception

Building **Grounds**

Tyntesfield souvenirs, local Somerset produce and a plant centre with garden furniture

Kiosk serving light refreshments (no hot meals). Seating area in marquee or picnic benches

Baby-changing and feeding facilities. Front-carrying baby slings and hip-carrying infant seats for loan. Children's quiz/trail. Family activity packs. Bag and buggy store available

Suitable for school groups. Education room/centre

→ [172:ST506715] 7ml SW of Bristol.
Bus: Frequent bus services, inc. First X7 Bristol–Clevedon (drops on B3128 at main entrance, 765yds, level walk) First 354 Bristol–Nailsea (drops on B3130 at Wraxall, 765yds, walk inc. steep steps).
Station: Nailsea & Backwell 3½ml. **Road**: on B3128. 7ml SW of Bristol; M5 Southbound exit 19 via A369 (towards Bristol), B3129, B3128. M5 Northbound exit 20, B3130 (towards Bristol), B3128. Brown signs from exit 19 and 20 of M5. For a Tyntesfield Travel Map, please contact the property

P Free parking. Temporary car park, 1,000yds to house (vehicle transfer is available for those who prefer not to walk). Parking is limited and access to the car park cannot be guaranteed. Tight corners. One-way system

NT properties nearby
Blaise Hamlet, Clevedon Court, Dyrham Park, Leigh Woods, Prior Park Landscape Garden

Tyntesfield									
House/chapel									
4 Apr–1 Nov	11–5	**M**	**T**	W	T	F	**S**	**S**	
Gardens/visitor reception/shop/catering kiosk									
4 Apr–1 Nov	10:30–5:30	**M**	**T**	**W**	T	F	**S**	**S**	

New opening arrangements for 2009: Weds, only gardens open. Open Good Fri. Last admission to house 1hr before closing. Free flow entry by timed ticket. Entry cannot be guaranteed on busy days. Rooms may close for conservation work

Watersmeet

Watersmeet Road, Lynmouth, Devon EX35 6NT

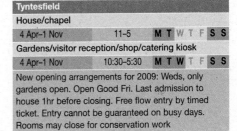 1996 **(1:F5)**

Dramatic river gorge and ancient woodlands near the rocky North Devon coast

A haven for wildlife, with waterfalls and excellent walking, where the lush valleys of the East Lyn and Hoar Oak Water tumble together. At the heart of this area sits Watersmeet House, a 19th-century fishing lodge, which is now a National Trust tea-room and tea-garden, shop and information point.

⭐ Property in deep gorge with steep walk down to house

Farmland above Myrtleberry Cleave, Watersmeet, Devon

ℹ️ **T** 01598 753348
E watersmeet@nationaltrust.org.uk

🚶 See local listings for guided walks on Watersmeet Estate

🚶 Walks leaflet from shop

♿ 🚻 ♿ Building 🏞️ Grounds ♿

🍽️ Tea-garden

🚼 Baby-changing facilities. Children's quiz/trail

🐕 Including in the tea-garden

➡️ [180:SS744487] **Foot**: South West Coast Path within ⅔ml. **Bus**: TW Coaches 309, 310 from Barnstaple (passing close ⊠ Barnstaple), Quantock 300 from Minehead; Filers 300 from Ilfracombe. On all, alight Lynmouth, then walk through NT gorge. **Road**: 1½ml E of Lynmouth, in valley on E side of Lynmouth–Barnstaple road (A39)

🅿️ Parking (not NT), 500yds (pay & display). Free NT car parks at Combepark, Hillsford Bridge and Countisbury

NT properties nearby
Arlington Court, Dunster Castle, Holnicote Estate, West Exmoor Coast

Watersmeet		M T W T F S S
Watersmeet		
All year		M T W T F S S
House		
14 Mar–28 Mar	10:30–4:30	M T W T F S S
29 Mar–24 May	10:30–5	M T W T F S S
25 May–3 Oct	10:30–5:30	M T W T F S S
4 Oct–1 Nov	10:30–4:30	M T W T F S S

West Exmoor Coast

Heddon Valley, Parracombe, Barnstaple, Devon EX31 4PY

🦌 🏛️ 🏠 📷 🍽️ 🚶 🏕️ 🎭 🚼 🏛️ 🚶
🐕 1963   (1:F5)

Towering cliffs, secluded coves and a beautiful wooded valley within Exmoor National Park

A favourite landscape of the Romantic poets and smugglers, with the Heddon Valley, Woody Bay and Hangman Hills to explore. This area offers spectacular coastal and woodland walks, as well as a NT information centre and gift shop in the Heddon Valley.

ℹ️ **T** 01598 763402
E heddonvalley@nationaltrust.org.uk

🚶 See local listings for guided walks on the local estate

🎭 See local listing for events throughout the year

🚶 Walks leaflet available from the National Trust shop and local tourist information centres

♿ 🚻 ♿ 🚽

🍽️ Ice-cream kiosk in shop

🚼 Children's activity packs. Tracker Packs. All-terrain pushchairs for loan

🏛️ Suitable for school groups

➡️ [180:SS655481] **Foot**: South West Coast Path within ⅔ml. **Bus**: TW Coaches 309, 310 Barnstaple–Lynton (passing close ⊠ Barnstaple), alight just N of Parracombe, then 2ml. **Road**: halfway between Combe Martin and Lynton, off A39 at Hunters Inn

🅿️ Parking, 50yds. Donations welcome

NT properties nearby
Arlington Court, Dunster Castle, Holnicote Estate, Watersmeet

West Exmoor Coast		M T W T F S S
West Exmoor Coast		
All year		M T W T F S S
Heddon Valley Shop		
14 Mar–3 Jul	11–5	M T W T F S S
4 Jul–30 Aug	10:30–5:30	M T W T F S S
31 Aug–1 Nov	11–5	M T W T F S S

Unless indicated, last admission is always 30mins before closing time

West Pennard Court Barn

West Pennard, nr Glastonbury, Somerset BA6 8LR

⌂ 1938 **(1:I5)**

15th-century barn with an unusual roof

★ Access by key only – see opening arrangements. Upper floor of the barn is of compacted earth. The surroundings are pastures grazed by cows. In winter the ground is wet and soft – suitable footwear advised. No WC

ℹ️ **T** 01985 843600 (Regional office), 01458 850212
E westpennardcourtbarn@nationaltrust.org.uk

➔ 3ml E of Glastonbury, 7ml S of Wells, 1½ml S of West Pennard (A361)

West Pennard Court Barn

Admission by appointment. Access by key, to be collected by arrangement with Mr P. H. Green, Court Barn Farm, West Bradley, Somerset. Tel. 01458 850212

Westbury College Gatehouse

College Road, Westbury-on-Trym, Bristol BS9 3EH

⌂ ⛶ 1907 **(1:I3)**

15th-century gatehouse

★ Access by key, Mon to Fri only – see opening arrangements. No WC

ℹ️ **T** 01934 844518
E westburycollege@nationaltrust.org.uk

➔ 3ml N of the centre of Bristol

Westbury College Gatehouse

Access (Mon–Fri) by key to be collected by appointment from the Parish Office, Church Road, Westbury-on-Trym, Bristol BS9 4AG. Tel 0117 950 8644 (am only)

Westbury Court Garden

Westbury-on-Severn, Gloucestershire GL14 1PD

✽ ☕ 🎫 🎪 ⛶ 1967 **(1:J2)**

Dutch water garden – a rare and beautiful survival

Originally laid out between 1696 and 1705, this is the only restored Dutch water garden in the country. Visitors can explore canals, clipped hedges and working 17th-century vegetable plots and discover many old varieties of fruit trees.

ℹ️ **T** 01452 760461
E westburycourt@nationaltrust.org.uk

🎫 Evening guided tours (book at garden): 13 May, 17 June, 15 July, 12 Aug

🎪 Easter Trail 10–13 April. Apple Day 17–18 Oct

♿ 🅳 ♿ ⠿ **Grounds** ♿ ♿

☕ Coffee machine. Hot and cold drinks

⛶ Pushchairs and baby back-carriers admitted. Family guide. Children's quiz/trail. Easter trail

➔ [162:SO718138] **Foot**: River Severn footpath runs from garden to river. **Bus**: Stagecoach in South Wales 73 🚆 Gloucester–Chepstow; Stagecoach in Wye & Dean 30/31 🚆 Gloucester–Coleford. **Station**: Gloucester 9ml. **Road**: 9ml SW of Gloucester on A48

🅿️ Free parking, 300yds

NT properties nearby
Ashleworth Tithe Barn, The Kymin, May Hill, The Weir

Westbury Court Garden									
11 Mar–28 Jun	10–5	M	T	**W**	**T**	**F**	**S**	**S**
1 Jul–31 Aug	10–5	**M**	**T**	**W**	**T**	**F**	**S**	**S**
2 Sep–25 Oct	10–5	M	T	**W**	**T**	**F**	**S**	**S**
Open BH Mons. Open other times of year by appointment									

Spring in the parterre of Westbury Court Garden: the only restored Dutch water garden in the country

Westwood Manor

Bradford-on-Avon, Wiltshire BA15 2AF

🏠 ✠ 🔆 👪 1960   (1:J4)

15th-century stone manor house

The manor house, altered in the 17th century, has splendid late Gothic and Jacobean windows and ornate plasterwork. It contains a fine collection of exceptional period furniture, 17th- and 18th-century tapestries and needlework, as well as a number of important stringed musical instruments. Attractive views can be enjoyed from the modern topiary garden.

⭐ Westwood Manor is administered for the NT by the tenant. No WC

ℹ **T** 01225 863374
   E westwoodmanor@nationaltrust.org.uk

♿ 🦽 ⠿ 🅰 Building 🦽🦽 Grounds 🦽

👪 Hip-carrying infant seats for loan. Children's quiz/trail. House unsuitable for under-fives

➜ [173:ST812590] **Cycle**: NCN4, ¾ml. **Bus**: Libra 94, Bodmans 96 ⇥ Bath–Trowbridge (passing close ⇥ Trowbridge). **Station**: Avoncliff (U), 1ml; Bradford-on-Avon 1½ml. **Road**: 1½ml SW of Bradford-on-Avon, in Westwood village, beside the church; village signposted off Bradford-on-Avon to Rode road (B3109)

🅿 Free parking, 90yds

NT properties nearby
The Courts Garden, Dyrham Park, Great Chalfield Manor and Garden, Lacock Abbey

Westwood Manor								
1 Apr–30 Sep	2–5	M	**T**	**W**	T	F	S	**S**
Small groups at other times by written application with sae to the tenant								

White Mill

Sturminster Marshall, nr Wimborne, Dorset BH21 4BX

🏠 👤 🎞 👪 🔲 1982   (1:K6)

Corn mill with original wooden machinery in a peaceful riverside setting

⭐ No WC, nearest at the Mill House

ℹ **T** 01258 858051 **E** whitemill@nationaltrust.org.uk

➜ On the River Stour in the parish of Shapwick, close to Sturminster Marshall

White Mill								
21 Mar–1 Nov	12–5	M	T	W	T	F	**S**	**S**
Admission by guided tour. Open BH Mons: 12–5, last tour 4								

Woodchester Park

Nympsfield, nr.Stroud, Gloucestershire GL10 3TS

📢 🐾 👤 🚶 1994   (1:J3)

Beautiful secluded wooded valley

The tranquil wooded valley contains a 'lost landscape' – the remains of an 18th- and 19th-century landscape park with a chain of five lakes. The restoration of this landscape is an on-going project. Waymarked trails (steep in places) lead through picturesque scenery, passing an unfinished Victorian mansion (not owned by the National Trust).

⭐ Address for correspondence: National Trust (Woodchester Park), The Ebworth Centre, The Camp, Stroud, Glos GL6 7ES. For details of Woodchester Mansion Open Days, contact the Woodchester Mansion Trust (tel. 01453 861541). WC not always available

ℹ **T** 01452 814213
   E woodchesterpark@nationaltrust.org.uk

👤 Tours by arrangement

🚶 Contact warden for details

♿ Grounds 🦽

🐕 Under close control, on leads where requested

➜ [162:SO797012] 4ml SW of Stroud.
   Foot: Cotswold Way within ⅔ml.
   Bus: Cotswold Green 35 Stroud–Nympsfield (passing close ⇥ Stroud). **Station**: Stroud 5ml. **Road**: off B4066 Stroud–Dursley road

🅿 Parking, £2 (pay & display). Accessible from Nympsfield road, 300yds from junction with B4066. Last admission to car park 1hr before dusk

NT properties nearby
Haresfield Estate, Minchinhampton and Rodborough Commons, Newark Park

Woodchester Park								
All year	9–dusk	M	T	W	T	F	S	S

For further information, visit www.nationaltrust.org.uk

While the South and South East is one of England's most densely populated and urbanised areas, it still boasts extensive and beautiful open spaces, as well as miles of dramatic coastline. The fact that so much has survived is due largely to the work of the National Trust.

National Trust countryside in Kent ranges from parts of the densely wooded Kentish Weald, to the world-famous White Cliffs of Dover. In Sussex the Trust cares for large areas of the South Downs, including Devil's Dyke, a magnificent ridge of chalk downland which is home to many associated plants and butterflies, Ditchling Beacon, the highest point in East Sussex commanding magnificent views of the Sussex Weald, and the dramatic coastline of the Seven Sisters.

Across the water on the Isle of Wight, the National Trust owns and maintains ten per cent of land, including seventeen miles of stunning unspoilt coastline.

In Surrey the scenery changes again, with vast areas of lowland heath at Hindhead and the Devil's Punch Bowl, ancient woodland at Leith Hill and flower-rich meadows at Denbies Hillside. On the border of Buckinghamshire and Hertfordshire, the Ashridge Estate is a huge area of stunning Chilterns countryside, featuring woodlands, commons and fine chalk downland.

Other much-loved beauty spots in the region – including Coombe Hill in Buckinghamshire and Finchampstead Ridges in Berkshire – are owned and protected by the Trust, as are many areas of common land, such as Cookham Dean Common in Berkshire, Passfield Common in Hampshire and parts of the New Forest.

Far left: **Ashridge Estate, bordering Buckinghamshire and Hertfordshire** Middle: **cycling at Devil's Dyke, West Sussex** Top right: **Slindon Estate, West Sussex** Above right: **the Seven Sisters, Sussex**

Previous page: **the Library door at Claydon House in Buckinghamshire**

There is so much to enjoy in the South East. Whether you relish a vigorous walk, prefer a gentle stroll, or simply want to find the perfect picnic spot, the National Trust will have the ideal place for you.

Bikes, boats and water

Why not enjoy a peaceful walk alongside a river or canal? The Trust

Top: **a New Forest pony on Hale Purlieu Common in Hampshire**

Above: **the River Wey, Surrey**

Left: **tower at Leith Hill, Surrey**

manages three miles of the Royal Military Canal between Appledore and Warehorne, at Romney Marsh in Kent, which was built as a defence against Napoleonic invasion. There are also nearly 20 miles of towpath to walk or cycle beside the River Wey in Surrey, while at Dapdune Wharf you can learn all about the history of the waterway, take part in fun family events or enjoy a boat ride.

Havens for wildlife

Enjoy wildlife in its natural habitat in the woods, heathland and countryside managed by the Trust across the region. At Toys Hill, near Westerham in Kent, there are large areas of woodland where you can observe birds and mammals and identify plants and trees. While in West Sussex, Devil's Dyke and Harting Down, near Petersfield, there are havens for downland flora and fauna. So take your binoculars and camera, venture away from the footpaths and go exploring.

Downs, cliffs and coast

Enjoy idyllic English scenery on a stroll through open downland along the Sussex coast. Birling Gap, near Eastbourne in East Sussex, is the perfect place to take in spectacular sea views of the South Coast's lesser-known white cliffs – the Seven Sisters. And for beautiful sandy dunes and an abundance of coastal wildlife, visit East Head, near Chichester Harbour in West Sussex.

Meanwhile, across the Solent, much of the most spectacular coastal scenery on the Isle of Wight, including Tennyson Down and Compton Bay, is owned and protected by the National Trust.

From cottages to mansions

As well as grand mansions, the National Trust protects many small gems tucked away in quiet corners of the countryside. The Slindon Estate, six miles north of Bognor Regis on the A29 in West Sussex, boasts a village of beautiful 17th-century flint cottages, as well as wonderful beech woodland – which is full of bluebells in spring. There is also a collection of National Trust properties in the pretty village of Chiddingstone, near Edenbridge in Kent. These include a row of timber houses that date from the 16th and 17th centuries, the post office and the Castle Inn.

In Oxfordshire, the attractive National Trust villages of Buscot and Coleshill, near Faringdon, with their traditional vernacular buildings, offer a glimpse into a bygone age.

Today the Trust manages these agricultural estates by supporting environmentally sustainable farming systems and improving their nature conservation. A leaflet can be obtained from the local shop and tea-room offering a series of pleasant circular walks around the area.

In the picturesque village of Long Crendon, near Aylesbury in Buckinghamshire, the old Courthouse is a fine example of an early timber-framed building where manorial courts were held from the time of King Henry VIII to the end of the 19th century. Nearby is the Boarstall Duck Decoy, a rare example of a once common device used to trap duck, and the intriguing Boarstall Tower, which has fascinating links with the English Civil War.

Saddlescombe Farm, near Devil's Dyke in Sussex, is open on certain days each year to give visitors the opportunity to discover a fascinating ancient downland farm with more than 1,000 years of history. The open days include tours of the 17th-century farm buildings, the surrounding downs and the walled garden. Interested groups can book a tour throughout the summer.

was intensive flint-mining here in the early Neolithic period, and there are also fascinating remains of an Iron Age hill fort and Roman fortifications to discover. While at Coldrum Long Barrow near Trottiscliffe in Kent, you can find out about ancient civilisations at the Neolithic burial chamber.

One of the most famous ancient landmarks in the country is at Uffington in Oxfordshire. The White Horse, which can be seen for miles

Part of the newly opened Reigate Fort in Surrey

In our ancestors' footsteps

Visitors now also have the opportunity to explore Reigate Fort, just off the M25 in Surrey. Newly opened, it was built in 1898 as one of thirteen military installations stretching from the North Downs to Essex. The fort is still intact today – with magazine rooms, a tool store, firing step and casemates. Visitors can see the exterior of the fort structures, while information boards show how the interiors looked. As well as a guidebook, there are guided tours inside the buildings, and groups can book special study days.

A very different site is Cissbury Ring, near Worthing in Sussex. There

around, has been the subject of discussion since the 17th century. Thought to date from the Bronze Age, it is referred to in 12th-century written records, however no one knows exactly why or when it was created.

■ For details of the open days at Saddlescombe Farm, see the regional newsletter events listings. For group tours, telephone 01273 857712.
■ For details of the guidebook, guided tours and study days at Reigate Fort, telephone 01342 843225.

Compton Bay, Isle of Wight

www.nationaltrust.org.uk/coastandcountryside

Alfriston Clergy House

The Tye, Alfriston, Polegate, East Sussex BN26 5TL

🏠 ✳️ 🏛 🗼 🌲 🦃 🏃 🧺 1896 (2:H8)

Medieval thatched cottage and picturesque garden

This rare 14th-century Wealden 'hall house' was the first building to be acquired by the National Trust in 1896. The thatched, timber-framed house is in an idyllic setting, with views across the River Cuckmere, and it is surrounded by a delightful, tranquil cottage garden featuring a magnificent Judas tree.

⭐ No WC. Nearest in village car park

ℹ️ **T** 01323 870001
E alfriston@nationaltrust.org.uk

🦃 Themed hunts held during school holidays. Themed family fun days throughout season

♿ ⁝⁝📷📱 Building 🔼 Grounds 🔼🔼

🏃 Pushchairs and baby back-carriers admitted. Children's quiz/trail

🧺 Suitable for school groups

➡️ [189:TQ521029] **Foot**: South Downs Way within ⅔ml. **Cycle**: NCN2. **Bus**: Countryliner 125 from Lewes, Renown 126 from Eastbourne and Seaford (pass close ➡ Lewes and ➡ Seaford). **Station**: Berwick (U) 2½ml. **Road**: 4ml NE of Seaford, just E of B2108, in Alfriston village, adjoining The Tye and St Andrew's Church

The herb garden, Alfriston Clergy House, East Sussex

🅿️ Parking (not NT), 500yds at other end of village

NT properties nearby
Bateman's, Frog Firle Farm, Monk's House, Sheffield Park Garden

Alfriston Clergy House									
28 Feb–12 Mar	11–4	M	T	W	T	F	S	S
14 Mar–1 Nov	10:30–5	M	T	W	T	F	S	S
2 Nov–20 Dec	11–4	M	T	W	T	F	S	S
Open Good Fri								

Ascott

Wing, nr Leighton Buzzard, Buckinghamshire LU7 0PS

🏠 ✳️ 1949 (2:E3)

Jacobean house remodelled in the 19th century, with superb collections and gardens

Originally a half-timbered farmhouse, Ascott was bought in 1876 by the de Rothschild family and considerably transformed and enlarged. It now houses a quite exceptional collection of fine paintings, Oriental porcelain and English and French furniture. The extensive gardens are a mixture of the formal and natural, containing specimen trees and shrubs, as well as a herbaceous walk, lily pond, Dutch garden and remarkable topiary sundial.

ℹ️ **T** 01296 688242 **E** ascott@nationaltrust.org.uk

♿ 🐕🧤⁝⁝📷🖼 Building 🔼🔼♿
Grounds 🔼🔼➡️

➡️ [165:SP891230] **Bus**: Arriva 100 Aylesbury–Milton Keynes (passing close ➡ Aylesbury and ➡ Leighton Buzzard). **Station**: Leighton Buzzard 2ml. **Road**: ½ml E of Wing, 2ml SW of Leighton Buzzard, on S side of A418

🅿️ Free parking, 220yds

NT properties nearby
Ashridge Estate, Claydon House

Ascott									
24 Mar–26 Apr	2–6	M	T	W	T	F	S	S
28 Apr–23 Jul	2–6	M	T	W	T	F	S	S
28 Jul–11 Sep	2–6	M	T	W	T	F	S	S
Open BH Mons. Last admission 1hr before closing.									
Garden open in aid of NGS on Mons 4 May and									
31 Aug (NT members pay on these days)									

Ashdown House

Lambourn, Newbury, Berkshire RG17 8RE

🏠 ✥ 🔌 🏃 🖼 🚶 1956 **(2:C5)**

Unusual Dutch-style house on the Berkshire Downs

This extraordinary house nestles in a beautiful valley in the Berkshire Downs. Visitors are allowed access to the magnificent staircase lined with paintings (once the property of the Queen of Bohemia, sister of King Charles I), and the roof, from which three counties can be seen. A series of beautiful walks criss-cross nearby Ashdown Woods.

⭐ Ashdown House is in the county of Oxfordshire. Postal address as above. No WC. The house is tenanted and access is limited to the staircase and roof (reached via 100 steps)

ℹ️ **T** 01494 755569 (Infoline), 01793 762209
  E ashdownhouse@nationaltrust.org.uk

🚶 Many walks in Ashdown Woods, Weathercock Down and Alfred's Castle

♿ 🅿️ 📷 🖼 🖥 Building 🏞 Grounds 🏃

🐕 On leads and only in woodland

➡️ [174:SU282820] **Bus**: Thamesdown 47 Swindon–Lambourn, with connections from Newbury (passing close ⭐ Swindon & Newbury). **Road**: 2½ml S of Ashbury, 3½ml N of Lambourn, on W side of B4000

🅿️ Free parking, 250yds. Not suitable for coaches

NT properties nearby
Avebury, Buscot Park, Great Coxwell Barn, Uffington White Horse and Wayland Smithy

Ashdown House									
House/garden									
1 Apr–31 Oct	2–5	M	T	**W**	T	F	**S**	S	
Woodland									
All year	Dawn–dusk	**M**	**T**	**W**	T	F	**S**	**S**	
Admission by guided tour to house at 2:15, 3:15 & 4:15. Numbers limited									

If you loved exploring the Ashridge Estate, why not discover Hatchlands Park?

Ashridge Estate

Visitor Centre, Moneybury Hill, Ringshall, Berkhamsted, Hertfordshire HP4 1LX

🏠 🔌 🏠 ☕ 🏃 🖼 🎭 🏙 🚌 🚶 🚲 1926 **(2:E3)**

Vast area of open downland and woods

This magnificent and varied estate runs across the borders of Herts and Bucks, along the main ridge of the Chiltern Hills. There are 2,000 hectares (5,000 acres) of woodlands, commons and chalk downland supporting a rich variety of wildlife and offering splendid walks through outstanding scenery. The area's focal point is the Monument, erected in 1832 to the Duke of Bridgewater. There are also spectacular views from Ivinghoe Beacon, accessible from Steps Hill. Don't miss the new Discovery Room in the Visitor Centre (next to the Bridgewater Monument), where there are hands-on activities and fascinating information about the history and wildlife of Ashridge.

What's new in 2009 Tea-room (not NT) under new management

⭐ WC not always available

ℹ️ **T** 01494 755557 (Infoline), 01442 851227
  E ashridge@nationaltrust.org.uk

🚶 Programme of guided walks all year

Ancient woodland on the Ashridge Estate

🎭 Children's workshops and activity days. Guided walks

🚶 Extensive network of paths. Information about self-guided walks available from the shop

♿ P♿ 🅿️ 📷 ✏️ 🍴 Building ♿

Grounds 🚶➡️🔍

🍴 Tea-room (NT-approved concession) in Visitor Centre. Children's menu

👶 Baby-changing facilities. Pushchairs and baby back-carriers admitted. Family activity packs. Children's workshops and activity days

🏫 Suitable for school groups. Education room/centre. Hands-on activities. Learn & Discover at the Ashridge Estate. Primary school programme

🐕 Under close control

🚲 Short stretch of permitted cycle path and 9ml of bridleways giving cyclists shared access

➡️ [181:SP970131] **Foot**: 2¾ml of The Ridgeway on property. **Bus**: Monument: Arriva 30/31 from 🚃 Tring, alight Aldbury, ½ml. Beacon: Arriva 61 Aylesbury–Luton (passing close 🚃 Aylesbury and 🚃 Luton). **Station**: Monument: Tring 1¾ml; Beacon: Cheddington 3½ml. **Road**: between Berkhamsted and Northchurch, and Ringshall and Dagnall, just off B4506

P Free parking, 50yds

NT properties nearby
Chilterns Gateway Centre, Pitstone Windmill, Shaw's Corner, Whipsnade Tree Cathedral

Ashridge Estate								
Estate								
All year		M	T	W	T	F	S	S
Visitor Centre/shop								
14 Mar–20 Dec	10–5	M	T	W	T	F	S	S
Monument								
14 Mar–1 Nov	12–5	M	T	W	T	F	S	S
Tea-room*								
1 Feb–13 Mar	10–4	M	T	W	T	F	S	S
14 Mar–20 Dec	10–5	M	T	W	T	F	S	S
31 Dec–31 Jan 10	10–4	M	T	W	T	F	S	S

*Tea-room opening hours may vary. Open BH Mons & Good Fri: 12–5. Monument also Mon–Fri by arrangement, weather permitting. Shop and tea-room close dusk if earlier than 5

Basildon Park

Lower Basildon, Reading, Berkshire RG8 9NR

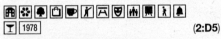

🍴 1978 (2:D5)

Elegant country house set in extensive parkland

This impressive Georgian mansion, surrounded by glorious parkland, was lovingly rescued from almost certain demolition by Lord and Lady Iliffe in the mid 1950s when they restored the elegant interior and scoured the country salvaging 18th-century architectural fixtures and fittings. They then filled their comfortable new home with fine paintings, fabrics and furniture which can still be enjoyed by visitors today. There are waymarked trails through the parkland and gardens including a new wildlife area, with a pond and picnic tables ideal for families. An exhibition reveals what went on behind the scenes when the mansion was featured in the recent film adaptation of Jane Austen's *Pride and Prejudice*.

What's new in 2009 Extensive stonework conservation to the exterior of the mansion. Activities throughout the year to celebrate 30 years of National Trust ownership. Winter opening of tea-room and grounds

⭐ The mansion is 400 yards from the main car park (transfer service available). There are numerous steps leading up the principal show rooms on the first and second floor

ℹ️ **T** 0118 984 3040
E basildonpark@nationaltrust.org.uk

🔎 Free introductory talks throughout day (booking not required)

🎭 Family-friendly events, lecture lunches, concerts, theatre

🚶 Leaflet with details of waymarked trails

♿ P♿ 🅿️ ✏️ .: 📷 🔄 📱 🪑 🍴 🍴
Building 🚶♿♿ Grounds 🚶

🛍️ NT merchandise, plus local and environmentally friendly products

🍴 Ground-floor tea-room (licensed) at mansion. Light refreshments available in stableyard. Children's menu

Unless indicated, last admission is always 30mins before closing time

The impressive Basildon Park, west front

Baby-changing facilities. Front-carrying baby slings and hip-carrying infant seats for loan. Family-friendly events, children's trails and learning activities

Suitable for school groups

On leads and only in park, woodland and grounds

[175:SU611782] **Bus**: Thames Travel 132 ⊠ Reading–⊠ Goring & Streatley, alight Lower Basildon (Park Wall Lane) then ½ml on foot. **Station**: Pangbourne 2½ml; Goring & Streatley 3ml. **Road**: between Pangbourne and Streatley, 7ml NW of Reading, on W side of A329; leave M4 at exit 12 and follow signs for Beale Park (not NT) through Pangbourne, then brown NT signs to Basildon Park

Free parking, 400yds

NT properties nearby
Greys Court, The Vyne

Basildon Park									
House (main show rooms)									
11 Mar–1 Nov	12–5	M	T	**W**	**T**	**F**	**S**	**S**	
5 Dec–13 Dec	12–4	M	T	**W**	**T**	**F**	**S**	**S**	
Ground floor exhibition area/tea-room/shop/grounds									
11 Feb–8 Mar	11–3	M	T	**W**	**T**	**F**	**S**	**S**	
11 Mar–1 Nov	11–5	M	T	**W**	**T**	**F**	**S**	**S**	
4 Nov–20 Dec	11–3	M	T	**W**	**T**	**F**	**S**	**S**	
5 Dec–13 Dec	11–4	M	T	**W**	**T**	**F**	**S**	**S**	
Open BH Mons. House and shop close at 7 on 11/12 Dec									

Bateman's

Burwash, Etchingham, East Sussex TN19 7DS

🏠 🏚 ✖ 🛠 ✿ 🗗 ☕ 🎪 🛡 👪 🚶 1940 (2:H7)

Jacobean house, home of Rudyard Kipling

The interior of this beautiful 17th-century house, Rudyard Kipling's home from 1902 to 1936, reflects the author's strong associations with the East. There are many oriental rugs and artefacts, and most of the rooms – including his book-lined study – are much as Kipling left them. The delightful grounds run down to the small River Dudwell with its watermill, and contain roses, wild flowers, fruit and herbs. Kipling's Rolls-Royce is also on display.

What's new in 2009 Improved trails and quizzes for children

⭐ The garden is open free of charge in November and December. Shop and tea-room are open the same time as the garden during these months

ℹ️ **T** 01435 882302
E batemans@nationaltrust.org.uk

🛡 Family Fun days, Kipling literary days, Paint the Garden. Easter Egg trails, Jungle Hunt trails, Hallowe'en trails. Traditional Edwardian Christmas decorations

🚶 Guided garden and estate walks (booking essential)

♿ 🅿 🅿 🔊 ⠿ ◎ ♿ 🚗 **Building** ♿ ♿ ♿ **Grounds** ♿ ▶

🗗 NT shop with largest collection of Kipling books for sale in the area

☕ Mulberry Tea-room (licensed). Children's menu

Baby-changing facilities. Front-carrying baby slings and hip-carrying infant seats for loan. Children's guide. Children's quiz/trail

On leads and only in car park; dog crèche

[199:TQ671238] **Bus**: Renown 318 Uckfield–⊠ Etchingham. **Station**: Etchingham 3ml. **Road**: ½ml S of Burwash. A265 W from Burwash, first turning on left

Free parking, 30yds. Coaches: tight left turn into first bay

NT properties nearby

Bodiam Castle, Scotney Castle, Sissinghurst Castle Garden

Bateman's									
House									
14 Mar–1 Nov	11–5	M	T	W	T	F	S	S	
Garden/tea-room/shop									
28 Feb–8 Mar	11–4	M	T	W	T	F	S	S	
14 Mar–1 Nov	11–5*	M	T	W	T	F	S	S	
4 Nov–23 Dec	11–4	M	T	W	T	F	S	S	
Open Good Fri: 11–5. The mill grinds corn most Weds and Sats at 2. *Shop closes 5:30 March–Oct. Shop, tea-room and garden open 21, 22 & 23 Dec. House: downstairs rooms decorated for a traditional Edwardian Christmas on 6/7, 13/14 & 20/21 Dec, 11:30–3:30									

Bembridge Windmill

High Street, Bembridge, Isle of Wight PO35 5SQ

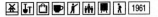 1961 **(2:D9)**

Grade I listed building – the only surviving windmill on the Isle of Wight

This picturesque 300-year-old windmill is one of the best-loved landmarks on the Isle of Wight. Although no longer working, most of its orginal machinery is still intact. Visitors can explore all four floors and enjoy glorious views across unspoilt countryside.

⭐ No WC

ℹ️ **T** 01983 873945
E bembridgemill@nationaltrust.org.uk

Conducted school groups and special visits March to end Oct (but not July or Aug), by written appointment

The Windmill is the starting point for the Culver trail

Building

Small shop in kiosk

Kiosk. Tea, coffee and ice-cream

Children's quiz/trail

Suitable for school groups

Bembridge Windmill									
14 Mar–1 Nov	11–5	M	T	W	T	F	S	S	
Closes dusk if earlier									

[196:SZ639874] **Cycle**: NCN67, ½ml.
Ferry: Ryde (Wightlink Ltd) 6ml (tel. 0871 376 1000); E Cowes (Red Funnel) 13ml (tel. 0844 844 9988). **Bus**: Southern Vectis 14 from Ryde Esplanade to within ½ml; 10 Newport–Sandown to within ¼ml. **Station**: Brading (U) 2ml by footpath. **Road**: ½ml S of Bembridge on B3395

P Free parking (not NT), 100yds in lay-by

NT properties nearby

Brighstone Shop and Museum, Mottistone Manor Garden, The Needles Old Battery and New Battery, Newtown Old Town Hall

Boarstall Duck Decoy

Boarstall, nr Aylesbury, Buckinghamshire HP18 9UX

1980 **(2:D3)**

Rare survival of a 17th-century duck decoy in working order, with a woodland nature trail and visitor centre

⭐ WC during opening hours

ℹ️ **T** 01280 822850
E boarstalldecoy@nationaltrust.org.uk

Midway between Bicester and Thame, 2ml W of Brill

Boarstall Duck Decoy									
4 Apr–30 Aug	10–4	M	T	W	T	F	S	S	
8 Apr–26 Aug	3:30–6	M	T	W	T	F	S	S	
Open BH Mons: 10–4									

The picturesque 300-year-old Bembridge Windmill

Boarstall Tower

Boarstall, nr Aylesbury, Buckinghamshire HP18 9UX

1943 **(2:D3)**

14th-century moated gatehouse and gardens

This property is tenanted and therefore only open to the public at special times, including Heritage Open Day

T 01280 822850 (Mon–Fri)
E boarstalltower@nationaltrust.org.uk

Midway between Bicester and Thame, 2ml W of Brill

Boarstall Tower
Open 11–5 on 11 Apr, 13 Apr, 4 May, 25 May, 12 Sep (Heritage Open Day)

Bodiam Castle

Bodiam, nr Robertsbridge, East Sussex TN32 5UA

1926 **(2:I7)**

Perfect example of a late medieval moated castle

One of the most famous and evocative castles in Britain, Bodiam was built in 1385, as both a defence and a comfortable home. The exterior is virtually complete and the ramparts rise dramatically above the moat. Enough of the interior survives to give an impression of castle life. There are spiral staircases and battlements to explore, and wonderful views of the Rother Valley from the top of the towers. In the impressive gatehouse is the castle's original wooden portcullis, an extremely rare example of its kind.

What's new in 2009 Opening some weekdays in November and December

Bodiam Castle is often used by education groups in term time. The only WC is located in the car park, 400yds from the castle entrance

T 01580 830196
E bodiamcastle@nationaltrust.org.uk

Introductory talks on selected days during the summer

For details send sae marked 'Events' or visit our website

Sussex Border Path runs through estate

Bodiam Castle, East Sussex: built 1385

Building **Grounds**

Wharf Tea-room (book for private room with waitress service). Children's menu. Ice-cream kiosk open near castle during summer weekends and throughout Aug

Baby-changing facilities. Pushchairs and baby back-carriers admitted. Family guide. Children's activity packs

Suitable for school groups. Education room/centre. Live interpretation. Hands-on activities. Adult study days

On leads and only in grounds

[199:TQ785256] **Foot**: on the Sussex Border path. **Ferry**: Bodiam Ferry from Newenden Bridge (A28). **Bus**: Stagecoach in Hastings 349 Hastings–Hawkhurst. **Station**: steam railway from Tenterden ¼ml; Robertsbridge 5ml. **Road**: 3ml S of Hawkhurst, 3ml E of A21 Hurst Green

Parking, 400yds, £2. Coaches £5

NT properties nearby

Bateman's, Scotney Castle, Sissinghurst Castle Garden, Smallhythe Place

Bodiam Castle		
Castle		
1 Feb–8 Feb	10:30–4	M T W T F **S S**
14 Feb–31 Oct	10:30–6	**M T W T F S S**
1 Nov–20 Dec	10:30–4	M T **W T F S S**
2 Jan–31 Jan 10	10:30–4	M T W T F **S S**
Shop/tea-room closes at 5 from 14 Feb–31 Oct. Last admission into castle 1hr before closing. Entrance to castle 400yds from car park. Castle closes dusk if earlier		

Charges for National Trust members apply on some special event days

Box Hill

The Old Fort, Box Hill Road, Box Hill, Tadworth, Surrey KT20 7LB

 1914 (2:F6)

Woodland and open down with wonderful views

An outstanding area of woodland and chalk downland, Box Hill has long been famous as a destination for day-trippers from London. Surprisingly extensive, it has much to offer the rambler and naturalist with many beautiful walks and views towards the South Downs. On the summit there is an information centre, shop, servery, ample car parking and a magnificent view.

What's new in 2009 Invasive scrub cleared to open up the views on the zig-zig road and northwards from the Broadwood Tower to Juniper Hall. Fort opened up and new interpretation board and leaflet

i T 01306 885502
E boxhill@nationaltrust.org.uk

Guided walks throughout the year

The romantic folly at Box Hill

Children's activities. Special Christmas shopping day 18 Dec

Short walk, nature walk, long walk, family fun trail, all with self-guided leaflets, 50p each

Building Grounds

NT shop. Information about Box Hill obtainable

Servery. For snacks, hot and cold drinks and ice-cream. Ice-cream kiosk (not NT) in east car park

Baby-changing facilities. Pushchairs admitted. Children's quiz/trail

Suitable for school groups. Education room/centre

Under close control (where sheep grazing)

→ [187:TQ171519] **Foot**: 1ml of North Downs Way from Stepping Stones to South Scarp; 1ml of Thames Down link footpath at Mickleham Downs; 1ml from Dorking station (½ml from Box Hill station). Many rights of way lead to Box Hill summit. **Bus**: Sunray Travel 516 ⊠ Leatherhead–Dorking to Box Hill east car park; Arriva 465 Kingston–Dorking to foot of Box Hill, 1½ml to summit. **Station**: Box Hill & Westhumble 1½ml. **Road**: 1ml N of Dorking, 2½ml S of Leatherhead on A24

P Parking, £3 (pay & display). Coaches must **not** use zig-zag road from Burford Bridge on W side of hill as weight restriction applies, but should approach from E side of hill B2032 or B2033; car/coach parks at summit

NT properties nearby
Headley Heath, Leith Hill, Polesden Lacey, Ranmore Common

Box Hill									
All year		M	T	W	T	F	S	S
Servery								
1 Feb–28 Mar	10–4	M	T	W	T	F	S	S
29 Mar–24 Oct	9–5	M	T	W	T	F	S	S
25 Oct–31 Oct	10–4	M	T	W	T	F	S	S
Shop/info centre								
1 Feb–28 Mar	11–4	M	T	W	T	F	S	S
29 Mar–24 Oct	11–5	M	T	W	T	F	S	S
25 Oct–31 Jan 10	11–4	M	T	W	T	F	S	S
Shop, information centre and servery closed 25 Dec									

Bradenham Village

nr High Wycombe, Buckinghamshire

🏠 🧺 🦌 🧍 🚲 1956   (2:E4)

Picturesque village in the Chiltern hills

The church and 17th-century manor house (not open) provide an impressive backdrop to the sloping village green. A network of paths provides easy access for walkers to explore the delightful surrounding countryside – which includes hills, farmland and classic Chilterns beech woods.

ℹ️ **T** 01494 755573
   E bradenham@nationaltrust.org.uk

🦌 Guided tours of manor garden

🔋 Grounds 🧗

🚲 Off-road cycling permitted on bridleways

➔ [165:SU825970] **Station**: Saunderton 1ml.
   Road: 4ml NW of High Wycombe, off A4010

🅿️ Designated parking at the village green above the cricket pavilion

NT properties nearby
Hughenden Manor, West Wycombe Park

Bradenham Village							
All year	**M**	**T**	**W**	**T**	**F**	**S**	**S**

Cottages in Bradenham Village, Buckinghamshire

Brighstone Shop and Museum

North Street, Brighstone, Isle of Wight PO30 4AX

🏠 🏢 👪 1989   (2:C9)

The Island's only National Trust gift shop

Situated within a row of traditional cottages is the National Trust shop and village museum (run by the Brighstone Museum Trust), which depicts village life in the 19th century. The shop has a wide range of gifts and cards, including many local items.

⭐ Nearest WC in public car park, 100yds

ℹ️ **T** 01983 740689
   E brighstone@nationaltrust.org.uk

🔋 🦽 ♿ Building 🧗

🏢 Wide range of gifts and cards

👪 Pushchairs admitted

➔ [196:SZ428828] **Cycle**: NCN67, 100yds.
   Ferry: Yarmouth (Wightlink Ltd) 8ml (tel. 0871 376 1000); E Cowes (Red Funnel) 12ml (tel. 0844 844 9988). **Bus**: Southern Vectis 7 Newport–Alum Bay. **Road**: next to post office, just off B3399 in Brighstone

🅿️ Free parking (not NT), 100yds

NT properties nearby
Bembridge Windmill, Mottistone Manor Garden, The Needles Old Battery and New Battery, Newtown Old Town Hall

Brighstone Shop and Museum								
2 Feb–9 Apr	10–1	**M**	**T**	**W**	**T**	**F**	**S**	S
10 Apr–22 May	10–4	**M**	**T**	**W**	**T**	**F**	**S**	S
23 May–26 Sep	10–5	**M**	**T**	**W**	**T**	**F**	**S**	S
24 May–27 Sep	12–5	M	T	W	T	F	S	**S**
28 Sep–24 Dec	10–4	**M**	**T**	**W**	**T**	**F**	**S**	S
29 Dec–31 Jan 10	10–1	**M**	**T**	**W**	**T**	**F**	**S**	S
Closed 25–28 Dec inc. and 1 Jan 10								

If you were attracted by the atmosphere of The Buscot and Coleshill Estates, be sure to visit the estate at Mottisfont too

Dogs assisting visitors with disabilities are always welcome

Buckingham Chantry Chapel

Market Hill, Buckingham, Buckinghamshire

✠ 💺 1912 **(2:D2)**

15th-century chapel, restored by Gilbert Scott in 1875. Now a second-hand bookshop

⭐ Available for hire. No WC

ℹ **T** 01280 822850
E buckinghamchantry@nationaltrust.org.uk

➔ On Market Hill

Buckingham Chantry Chapel
Open Tue & Sat 9:30–3 for second-hand bookshop. Available for private function hire evenings only

The Buscot and Coleshill Estates

Coleshill Estate Office, Coleshill, Swindon, Wiltshire SN6 7PT

🏨 🍴 ❄ 🛋 🏠 🚽 💺 🎿 🎪 🎭 🎵
🚶 1956 **(2:B4)**

Traditional agricultural estates with villages, farms and woodland

These estates on the western borders of Oxfordshire include the attractive, unspoilt villages of Buscot and Coleshill, each with a thriving village shop and tea-room. There are circular walks of differing lengths and a series of footpaths criss-crossing the estates.

⭐ Public WCs located in Coleshill estate office yard

ℹ **T** 01793 762209
E buscotandcoleshill@nationaltrust.org.uk

🏃 Regular series of guided estate walks throughout the year

🚶 Walks leaflet available, 50p from Coleshill estate office

💺 Tea-room (not NT) in Buscot village shop. Shop/café (not NT) in Coleshill village

🏫 Suitable for school groups. Education room/centre

🐕 On leads only

➔ [SU239973] **Cycle**: NCN45, 10ml. Regional Route 40: Oxfordshire Cycleway.
Bus: Stagecoach in Swindon 7 Swindon–Highworth (passing close ≏ Swindon), alight Highworth then 2ml walk. **Station**: Swindon 10ml. **Road**: Coleshill village on B4019 between Faringdon and Highworth. Buscot village on A417 between Faringdon and Lechlade

🅿 Free car parks at Buscot village and Badbury Clump

NT properties nearby
Buscot Park, Great Coxwell Barn, Uffington White Horse and Wayland Smithy

The Buscot and Coleshill Estates							
All year	M	T	W	T	F	S	S
Mill open 2nd Sun of the month: April to Oct, 2–5							

Swan with cygnets on the Coleshill Estate

Buscot Old Parsonage

Buscot, Faringdon, Oxfordshire SN7 8DQ

🏠 ❄ 1949 **(2:C4)**

Early 18th-century riverside house with small garden

⭐ No WC

ℹ **T** 01793 762209
E buscot@nationaltrust.org.uk

➔ 2ml from Lechlade, 4ml from Faringdon on A417

Buscot Old Parsonage							
1 Apr–28 Oct	2–6	M	T	**W**	T	F	S	S
Admission by written appointment with the tenant. Please mark envelope 'NT booking'							

Show your card and display sticker for free parking

Buscot Park

Estate Office, Buscot Park, Faringdon, Oxfordshire SN7 8BU

 1949   (2:C4)

Late 18th-century house, set in enchanting landscaped grounds, containing the Faringdon Collection of art

Palladian-style country house built 1780-3 and remodelled 1934-6 by the 2nd Lord Faringdon. Houses the Faringdon Collection of art established in the late 19th century by Alexander Henderson, later the 1st Lord Faringdon. This includes Old Master paintings by Rembrandt, Botticelli and Murillo, works by pre-Raphaelite artists, such as Burne-Jones and Rossetti, as well as furniture designed by Robert Adam and Thomas Hope. The beautiful landscaped gardens contain the famous water garden designed by Harold Peto.

What's new in 2009 Faux Fall (water feature) by David Harber. Contemporary glassware by Sally Fawkes and Gilles-Jones in house

★ This property is administered on behalf of the NT by Lord Faringdon, and the contents of the house are owned by The Faringdon Collection Trust. www.buscotpark.com

ℹ️ **T** 0845 345 3387 (Infoline), 01367 240786
E estbuscot@aol.com

Extensive walks in grounds

Building Grounds

Occasional sales of plants surplus to garden requirements; also garden fruit, vegetables and flowers when in season (not NT)

Licensed tea-room (not NT)

Buscot Park									
House/grounds/tea-room*									
1 Apr–30 Sep	2–6	M	T	**W**	**T**	**F**	S	S
See below	2–6	M	T	W	T	**F**	**S**	**S**
Grounds only									
6 Apr–29 Sep	2–6	**M**	**T**	W	T	F	S	S

Open BH Mons. Last admission to house 1hr before closing. House and grounds also open 2–6 (*tea-room 2–5:30) at weekends 11/12, 25/26 April; 2/3, 9/10, 23/24 May; 13/14, 27/28 June; 11/12, 25/26 July; 8/9, 22/23, 29/30 August; 12/13, 26/27 Sept

For public transport details, see page 377

Baby-changing facilities. Hip-carrying infant seats for loan

Only in the Paddock field

➡️ [163:SU239973] **Bus**: Stagecoach in Swindon 64, 74 Swindon–Fairford (both passing close ⊠ Swindon). On both, alight Lechlade, 2¾ml walk. **Road**: between Lechlade and Faringdon, on A417

P Free parking

NT properties nearby
The Buscot and Coleshill Estates, Great Coxwell Barn, Uffington White Horse and Wayland Smithy

The Peto-designed water garden, Buscot Park

Chartwell

Mapleton Road, Westerham, Kent TN16 1PS

1946   (2:G6)

Family home and garden of Sir Winston Churchill

Bought by Sir Winston for its magnificent views over the Weald of Kent to Sussex, Chartwell was his home and the place from which he drew inspiration from 1924 until the end of his life. The rooms and gardens remain much as they were when he lived here, with pictures, books, maps and personal mementoes strongly evoking the career and wide-ranging interests of this great statesman. The terraced hillside gardens reflect the importance to Churchill of the landscape and nature. They include the lakes he created, the water gardens where he fed his fish, Lady Churchill's Rose Garden and the

Golden Rose Avenue – a Golden Wedding anniversary gift from their children which runs down the centre of the productive kitchen garden. Many of Sir Winston's paintings can be seen in the garden studio, where talks are given most days about 'Painting as a Pastime'.

What's new in 2009 Newly reinstated displays in museum room, refurbished to the colourful 1960s design. Late afternoon house tours on Thursdays (not bookable)

⭐ Car park open for countryside access all year (not 25 Dec). House less busy weekday afternoons

ℹ️ **T** 01732 866368 (Infoline), 01732 868381 **E** chartwell@nationaltrust.org.uk

🛡️ Lecture lunches, special tours, book signings, guided walks. Themed restaurant events

🚶 Three waymarked walks

♿ 🅿️ 🅳 ⌨️ :: 📷 ✂️ 🖥️ 📺 🎵 🔔 🔊

Building ♿♿♿ Grounds ♿♿

Chartwell										
House										
14 Mar–28 Jun	11–5	M	T	**W**	**T**	**F**	**S**	**S**
1 Jul–30 Aug	11–5	M	**T**	**W**	**T**	**F**	**S**	**S**
2 Sep–1 Nov	11–5	M	T	**W**	**T**	**F**	**S**	**S**
Garden										
1 Feb–13 Mar	11–4	M	T	**W**	**T**	**F**	**S**	**S**
14 Mar–28 Jun	11–5	M	T	**W**	**T**	**F**	**S**	**S**
1 Jul–30 Aug	11–5	M	**T**	**W**	**T**	**F**	**S**	**S**
2 Sep–1 Nov	11–5	M	T	**W**	**T**	**F**	**S**	**S**
4 Nov–24 Dec	11–4	M	T	**W**	**T**	**F**	**S**	**S**
27 Dec–31 Jan 10	11–4	M	T	**W**	**T**	**F**	**S**	**S**
Shop/restaurant										
1 Feb–13 Mar	11–4	M	T	**W**	**T**	**F**	**S**	**S**
14 Mar–28 Jun	10:30–5	M	T	**W**	**T**	**F**	**S**	**S**
1 Jul–30 Aug	10:30–5	M	**T**	**W**	**T**	**F**	**S**	**S**
2 Sep–1 Nov	10:30–5	M	T	**W**	**T**	**F**	**S**	**S**
4 Nov–24 Dec	11–4	M	T	**W**	**T**	**F**	**S**	**S**
27 Dec–31 Jan 10	11–4	M	T	**W**	**T**	**F**	**S**	**S**
Car park										
All year	9–5:30*	**M**	**T**	**W**	**T**	**F**	**S**	**S**

Admission by timed ticket to house, which should be purchased immediately on arrival but cannot be booked. Open BH Mons. Last admission 45mins before house closing. *Car park closes 5:30 (4:30 from 2 Nov–31 Jan 10), or dusk if earlier, also closed 25 Dec. Garden open Nov–31 Jan 10, as above, weather and conditions permitting

🏪 NT shop with licence to sell alcohol. Plant sales

🍽️ Licensed restaurant adjacent to car park. Children's menu. Dispatch Box kiosk

👶 Baby-changing facilities. Hip-carrying infant seats for loan. Children's quiz/trail

🎒 Suitable for school groups

🐕 On short leads in gardens

➡️ [188:TQ455515] **Foot**: Greensand Way passes through car park. **Bus**: Surrey Connect 236 Westerham–East Grinstead (passing ≋ Edenbridge and ≋ Edenbridge Town), Mon–Fri only, to within ½ml. SelKent 246 from Bromley North (passing ≋ Bromley South); Arriva 401 from Tunbridge Wells (passing ≋ Sevenoaks). Both Suns & BHols only. Kent Passenger Services 238 ≋ Sevenoaks–Edenbridge (Wed only). **Station**: Edenbridge (U) 4ml, Edenbridge Town 4½ml, Oxted 5ml, Sevenoaks 6½ml. **Road**: 2ml S of Westerham, fork left off B2026 after 1½ml; leave M25 at exit 5 or 6

🅿️ Parking, 250yds (pay & display). Year-round opening (except 25 Dec) for countryside access; gates locked at 5:30 March–Oct, 4:30 Nov–31 Jan 10. Coach park and disabled parking adjacent to main car park

NT properties nearby
Emmetts Garden, Ightham Mote, Knole, Quebec House, Toys Hill

Winston Churchill's studio at Chartwell, Kent

Chastleton House

Chastleton, nr Moreton-in-Marsh,
Oxfordshire GL56 0SU

 1991   (2:C3)

**One of England's finest and most
complete Jacobean houses**

Chastleton House is filled not only with a
mixture of rare and everyday objects, furniture
and textiles collected since its completion in
1612, but also with the atmosphere of 400 years
of continuous occupation by one family. The
gardens have a typical Elizabethan and

**The south front and dovecote of Chastleton House,
Oxfordshire: a Jacobean gem**

Jacobean layout, with a ring of fascinating
topiary at their heart, and it was here in 1865
that the rules of modern croquet were codified.
Since acquiring the property, the Trust has
concentrated on conserving it rather than
restoring it to a pristine state.

What's new in 2009 Items from the costume
collection on display and being added to during
the season. New themed tours on last Saturday
morning of each month during open season

⭐ As Chastleton House is relatively fragile and
the access roads are narrow, the number of
visitors is restricted. Admission is by timed
ticket, which can be reserved by contacting
the property (Tues–Fri, 10–2) on 01608 674
981 (booking line). No same day bookings.
Visitors not booked are admitted on a first-
come, first-served basis. No shop or tea-room

ℹ️ **T** 01494 755560 (Infoline), 01608 674981
E chastleton@nationaltrust.org.uk

🚶 Out-of-hours guided 'Private View' Wed
mornings at 10. Charge inc. NT members

😊 Summer garden party and Christmas concert,
plus regular themed tours and activities

♿ Building

👪 Pushchairs and baby back-carriers admitted.
Hip-carrying infant seats for loan. Family
activity packs

➡️ [163:SP248291] **Cycle:** cycles can be hired
from Country Lanes at Moreton-in-Marsh
station, Easter to 30 Sept (tel. 01608
650065). **Station:** Moreton-in-Marsh 4ml.
Road: 6ml from Stow-on-the-Wold.
Approach only from A436 between A44 (W of
Chipping Norton) and Stow

🅿️ Free parking, 270yds. Return walk to car park
includes a short but steep hill. Sensible shoes
recommended

NT properties nearby
Hidcote Manor Garden, Snowshill Manor and
Garden, Stowe Landscape Gardens, Upton
House and Gardens

Chastleton House		M	T	W	T	F	S	S
1 Apr–30 Sep	1–5	M	T	**W**	T	**F**	**S**	S
1 Oct–31 Oct	1–4	M	T	**W**	T	**F**	**S**	S

Admission by timed ticket, tel. property to book. Last
admission 1hr before closing

For general and membership enquiries, please telephone 0844 800 1895

Clandon Park

West Clandon, Guildford, Surrey GU4 7RQ

🏛 🦇 ❖ 🏠 🍴 🌲 🛡 ♿ 🔔 🍷 1956 (2:F6)

Grand 18th-century Palladian mansion

Clandon Park was built c.1730 for the 2nd Lord Onslow by the Venetian architect Giacomo Leoni. It is the most complete example of Leoni's work to survive – the most impressive room being the magnificent two-storeyed, white Marble Hall. The house is filled with a superb collection of 18th-century furniture, porcelain and textiles, acquired in the 1920s by the connoisseur Mrs Gubbay. The attractive gardens contain a grotto and sunken Dutch garden, and Clandon also boasts a Maori meeting house, brought back from New Zealand in 1892 by the 4th Earl of Onslow, who was Governor there. The Onslow family is unique in that it has provided three Speakers of the House of Commons.

What's new in 2009 New collection of Meissen and other porcelain figures on display in the Gallery

⭐ The Queen's Royal Surrey Regiment Museum (tel. 01483 223419) is based at Clandon Park and open to visitors the same days as the house 12–5 (free entry)

ℹ️ **T** 01483 222482, 01483 222502 (Clandon Park Restaurant)
E clandonpark@nationaltrust.org.uk

🎬 Conservation demonstrations 1 & 8 March. Easter Egg Trails. 'Putting the House to Bed' days 8 & 15 Nov

♿ 🅿️ 🅿️ 🚾 ⠿ 📷 🎞 🖥 🔔 🔲
Building 🔲🔳🔲 Grounds 🔲🔳

🍽 Clandon Park Restaurant (NT-approved concession) (licensed). Booking essential for groups and during Dec. Children's menu

👪 Baby-changing facilities. Front-carrying baby slings and hip-carrying infant seats for loan. Children's quiz/trail. Pushchairs allowed in house Tues, Wed & Thur. Baby-feeding facilities; please ask staff

➡️ [186:TQ042512] **Bus:** Arriva 37 from close 🚉 Guildford; Countryliner 479 Guildford–Epsom (passing 🚉 Leatherhead, close 🚉 Guildford);

Father and daughter with a volunteer room steward in the Marble Hall at Clandon Park, Surrey

463 Guildford–🚉 Woking, alight Park Lane roundabout, ½ml walk to park west gate.
Station: Clandon 1ml. **Road:** at West Clandon on A247, 3ml E of Guildford; if using A3 follow signposts to Ripley to join A247 via B2215

🅿️ Free parking, 300yds

NT properties nearby
Box Hill, Claremont Landscape Garden, Hatchlands Park, Leith Hill, Polesden Lacey, River Wey and Dapdune Wharf, Shalford Mill

Clandon Park										
House										
15 Mar–1 Nov	11–5	M	**T**	**W**	**T**	F	S	**S**
Garden										
15 Mar–1 Nov	11–5	M	**T**	**W**	**T**	F	S	**S**
Shop/restaurant										
1 Mar–8 Mar	12–4	M	T	W	T	F	S	**S**
15 Mar–1 Nov	12–5*	M	**T**	**W**	**T**	F	S	**S**
3 Nov–29 Nov	12–4	M	**T**	**W**	**T**	F	S	**S**
1 Dec–23 Dec	12–4**	**M**	**T**	**W**	**T**	F	S	**S**

Open BH Mons, Good Fri and Easter Sat. *Restaurant opens at 11. **Restaurant open 12–10 in Dec (booking essential)

Unless indicated, last admission is always 30mins before closing time

Claremont Landscape Garden

Portsmouth Road, Esher, Surrey KT10 9JG

[icons] 1949   (2:F6)

One of the first and finest gardens of the English Landscape style

Claremont is a beautiful garden surrounding a small lake and featuring an unusual grass amphitheatre. The garden's creation and development has involved great names in garden history, including Sir John Vanbrugh, Charles Bridgeman, William Kent and 'Capability' Brown. In 1726 it was described as 'the noblest of any in Europe' and the garden today is of national importance. Visitors walking round the lake will see the island and pavilion, grotto and many viewpoints and vistas. There are hidden features to enjoy as well as wider estate walks and a new children's play area.

What's new in 2009 Children's play area and family guide

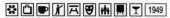

View across the lake at Claremont

⭐ No dogs April to Oct

ℹ️ **T** 01372 467806
E claremont@nationaltrust.org.uk

🏃 Tours 1st and 3rd Sat, 2nd Wed and last Sun of each month April to Oct. Starts 2 at entrance kiosk

🎭 Including children's activities during school holidays, lecture lunches and guided walks. Send sae for details

♿ [icons] **Grounds** [icons]

🍴 Licensed tea-room. Closed 17 & 18 Dec for Christmas lunches (booking essential). Children's menu

👪 Baby-changing facilities. Pushchairs admitted. Children's quiz/trail. Children's play area. Family guide. Children's activities during school holidays

🏫 Suitable for school groups

🐕 On short leads 1 Nov–31 March. No dogs April to Oct

➡️ [187:TQ128634] **Bus**: Travel London 515/A Kingston–Guildford (passing close ≋ Esher). **Station**: Esher 2ml; Hersham 2ml; Claygate 2ml. **Road**: 1ml S of centre of Esher, on E side of A307 (no access from Esher bypass)

🅿️ Free parking at entrance

NT properties nearby
Clandon Park, Ham House and Garden, Hatchlands Park, The Homewood, Polesden Lacey, River Wey and Dapdune Wharf

Claremont Landscape Garden			
Garden			
1 Feb–31 Mar	10–5		M **T W T F S S**
1 Apr–31 Oct	10–6		**M T W T F S S**
1 Nov–31 Jan 10	10–5		M **T W T F S S**
Shop/tea-room			
1 Feb–15 Feb	11–4		M T W T **F S S**
18 Feb–29 Mar	11–4		M T **W T F S S**
1 Apr–31 Oct	11–5		M T **W T F S S**
1 Nov–20 Dec	11–4		M T **W T F S S**
9 Jan–31 Jan 10	11–4		M T W T **F S S**

Open all year (closed Mons 1 Nov–31 March). Closes dusk if earlier. Closed 25 Dec. Open 1 Jan 10 10–4. Belvedere Tower open first weekend each month April–Oct & New Year's Day. Late night openings 6, 13, 20, 27 June until 9. Shop and tea-room close 1hr before garden, and may close early in bad weather

Claydon House

Middle Claydon, nr Buckingham,
Buckinghamshire MK18 2EY

🏠 ✝ ✜ ♦ 🐾 📷 🍴 🎭 👫 📖 🧍 🔔
🍷 | 1956 | (2:D3)

Splendid 18th-century English interiors in an idyllic country setting

Home of the Verney family for more than 400 years, the extraordinary interiors of Claydon House, built 1759-69, represent a veritable three-dimensional pattern book of 18th-century decorative styles. Outstanding features include the astonishingly lavish wood carving in the Chinese Room and the fine parquetry grand staircase. Claydon has strong associations with Florence Nightingale, who was the sister-in-law of Sir Harry Verney. She was a regular visitor to the house, which contains many of her personal belongings. Claydon House is set within 21 hectares (52 acres) of unspoilt parkland with far-reaching views and lakeside walks. The courtyard contains small workshops and galleries, as well as a popular restaurant and tea-room (not NT). The private gardens are open to visitors at an additional charge (inc. NT members).

What's new in 2009 'In Sickness and in Health', an exhibition from the Verney archives on family health, drawing heavily on the writings of Florence Nightingale. Tea-room now open from 11

⭐ All Saints' Church (not NT) in the grounds is also open to the public

ℹ️ **T** 01494 755561 (Infoline), 01296 730349 **E** claydon@nationaltrust.org.uk

🎫 Introductory talks and garden talks

🎭 Various events and family-friendly days

🧍 Permitted footpath (approx. 3ml) skirting lakes

♿ 🦽 📶 ⠿ 🔊 📷 ♿ 🔊 **Building** 🔊 🦽 ♿
Grounds 🔊 🦽 ➡️

📷 Art gallery, ceramics studio, seasonal plant sales (all non NT). Second-hand bookshop

🍴 Carriage House Restaurant (not NT) (licensed) **privately owned**. Tea-room (not NT) now open from 11 on open days. Open same days as house, 12–5:30. Tel. 01296 730004 for details

Claydon House, library door with ornate doorcase, c.1768

👫 Baby-changing facilities. Front-carrying baby slings and hip-carrying infant seats for loan. Family guide. Children's guide. Children's quiz/trail. Family-friendly days

📖 Suitable for school groups

🐕 On leads and only in park

➡️ [165:SP720253] **Foot**: Bernwood Jubilee Way. **Cycle**: NCN51. **Bus**: Arriva 17 from Aylesbury (passing close ≋ Aylesbury). **Road**: in Middle Claydon 13ml NW of Aylesbury, 4ml SW of Winslow; signposted from A413 & A41 (M40 exit 9 12ml); entrance by N drive only

🅿️ Free parking

NT properties nearby
King's Head, Stowe Landscape Gardens, Waddesdon Manor

Claydon House								
7 Mar–1 Nov	1–5*	**M**	**T**	**W**	T	F	**S**	**S**

Open Good Fri. *Closes dusk if earlier. Grounds, private garden (not NT – additional charge applies), shops & restaurants (not NT) 12–5. Special Christmas opening 5/6, 12/13, 19/20 Dec, 11–4

Cliveden

Taplow, Maidenhead, Buckinghamshire SL6 0JA

 1942 (2:E5)

Magnificent formal gardens overlooking the River Thames, once the exclusive haunt of the rich and famous

With splendid views across the River Thames, Cliveden was the glittering hub of society as the home of Waldorf and Nancy Astor in the early part of the 20th century. Later it was infamously associated with the 'Profumo Affair'. The spectacular estate, with a celebrated parterre, has a series of formal gardens, each with its own character, an outstanding collection of sculpture and statues from the ancient and modern worlds, as well as extensive woodland and riverside walks. The house is now let as a private hotel, part of which is open to visitors at limited times.

What's new in 2009 Major conservation works continue throughout the garden

★ No WC at woodlands

ℹ️ **T** 01494 755562 (Infoline), 01628 605069
E cliveden@nationaltrust.org.uk

🎭 Open-air theatre, children's theatre, seasonal guided walks

♿ 🅿️ 🅿️ 🏷️ ⠿ 🔍 🎧 ♿ 🔲
Building 🔲 🔲 🔲 **Grounds** ♿ ➡️

Detail of shell fountain at Cliveden, Buckinghamshire

Cliveden										
Estate/garden/shop										
28 Feb–25 Oct	11–6		M	T	W	T	F	S	S
26 Oct–23 Dec	11–4		M	T	W	T	F	S	S
House (part)/Octagon temple										
2 Apr–29 Oct	3–5:30		M	T	W	**T**	F	S	**S**
Restaurant										
28 Feb–25 Oct	11–5		M	T	W	T	F	S	S
26 Oct–1 Nov	11–4		M	T	W	T	F	S	S
7 Nov–20 Dec	11–3		M	T	W	T	F	**S**	**S**
Woodlands										
28 Feb–25 Oct	11–5:30		M	T	W	T	F	S	S
26 Oct–23 Dec	11–4		M	T	W	T	F	S	S
2 Jan–31 Jan 10	11–4		M	T	W	T	F	S	S

Admission to house is limited and by timed ticket only from Information Kiosk. Shop closes 5:30 28 Feb–25 Oct. Some areas of formal garden may be roped off when ground conditions are bad

🍽️ Licensed restaurant. Children's menu. Kiosk in main car park

👶 Baby-changing facilities. Children's guide. All-terrain buggies for hire. Family garden Explorer Packs. Children's theatre

📻 Audio-visual guide in Gas Yard

🐕 Under close control and only in specified woodlands

➡️ [175:SU915851] **Bus**: no bus service. **Station**: Taplow (not Sun) 2½ml; Burnham 3ml. **Road**: 2ml N of Taplow; leave M4 at exit 7 on to A4, or M40 at exit 4 on to A404 to Marlow and follow brown signs. Entrance by main gates opposite Feathers Inn

🅿️ Free parking

NT properties nearby
Greys Court, Hughenden Manor, West Wycombe Park

Dorneywood Garden

Dorneywood, Burnham, Buckinghamshire SL1 8PY

🔅 📭 👬 1942   **(2:E5)**

1930s-style garden, with herbaceous borders, rose garden, cottage garden and lily pond

⭐ The upkeep of Dorneywood is paid for by the Dorneywood Trust, at no cost to the NT or public. Garden open by written appointment only on four days a year. Charge inc. NT members (goes to NGS). Write or email for tickets, giving at least two weeks' notice, to the Secretary, Dorneywood Trust, at above address

ℹ️ **T** 01628 665361
   E dorneywood@nationaltrust.org.uk

➡️ On Dorneywood Road, SW of Burnham Beeches, 1½ml N of Burnham village, 2ml E of Cliveden

Dorneywood Garden		M	T	W	T	F	S	S
13 May	2–5	M	T	**W**	T	F	S	S
27 May	2–5	M	T	**W**	T	F	S	S
1 Jul	2–5	M	T	**W**	T	F	S	S
25 Jul	2–5	M	T	W	T	F	**S**	S
Admission by appointment								

Emmetts Garden

Ide Hill, Sevenoaks, Kent TN14 6AY

🔅 📷 📭 🧍 🎪 🛡️ 👬 🖼️ 🚶 1965   **(2:H6)**

Interesting hillside garden with year-round features

Influenced by William Robinson, this delightful plantsman's garden was laid out in the late 19th century and contains many exotic and rare trees and shrubs from across the world. Explore the rose and rock gardens, and enjoy glorious shows of spring flowers and shrubs, followed by vibrant autumn colours. Its dramatic hilltop location means there are spectacular views.

What's new in 2009 Restoration of the rose garden to reflect its heyday

ℹ️ **T** 01732 751509 (Infoline), 01732 868381
   E emmetts@nationaltrust.org.uk

🛡️ Family picnic day in Aug and talks with the Head Gardener throughout the season

Emmetts Garden								
Garden								
14 Mar–1 Nov	11–5	**M**	**T**	**W**	T	F	**S**	**S**
Shop/tea-room								
14 Mar–1 Nov	11–4:30	**M**	**T**	**W**	T	F	**S**	**S**
Open BH Mons & Good Fri. Last admission 45mins before closing								

🚶 Weardale walk to Chartwell

♿ 🅿️ 🚾 :: 📷 🦯 🔄 **Grounds** 🧑‍🦽 ➡️

📷 Tack Room shop. Plant sales

📭 Stable Tea-room in former stable block

👬 Baby-changing facilities. Pushchairs and baby back-carriers admitted. Children's quiz/trail. Family picnic day

🖼️ Suitable for school groups

🐕 On short leads only

➡️ [188:TQ477524] **Foot**: from Ide Hill (½ml). Weardale walk from Chartwell (3ml) – guide leaflet available. **Bus**: New Enterprise 404 from Sevenoaks, Mon–Fri only, alight Ide Hill, 1½ml. **Station**: Sevenoaks 4½ml; Penshurst (U) 5½ml. **Road**: 1½ml S of A25 on Sundridge to Ide Hill road, 1½ml N of Ide Hill off B2042, leave M25 exit 5, then 4ml

🅿️ Free parking, 100yds

NT properties nearby
Chartwell, Ightham Mote, Knole, Quebec House, Toys Hill

The 19th-century Emmetts Garden, Kent

Show your card and display sticker for free parking

Great Coxwell Barn

Great Coxwell, Faringdon, Oxfordshire SN7 7LZ

🏠 🎭 1956   (2:C4)

13th-century stone barn

This large monastic barn has a stone-tiled roof and interesting timber structure. Set in a wonderful former farmyard, this barn was a favourite of William Morris, who would regularly bring his guests to wonder at the structure.

⭐ No WC

ℹ️ **T** 01793 762209 (Coleshill Estate office)
  E greatcoxwellbarn@nationaltrust.org.uk

♿ P♿ ••

🎭 Suitable for school groups

🐕 On leads only

➔ [163:SU269940] **Bus**: Stagecoach in Swindon 65/6 Swindon–Oxford (passing close 🚃 Swindon & passing 🚃 Oxford), alight Great Coxwell Turn, ¾ml. **Station**: Swindon 10ml. **Road**: 2ml SW of Faringdon between A420 and B4019

🅿️ Limited parking in roadside lay-by

NT properties nearby
Ashdown House, Buscot Park, Coleshill Estate, including Badbury Hill, Uffington White Horse and Wayland Smithy

Great Coxwell Barn								
All year	Early–dusk	**M**	**T**	**W**	**T**	**F**	**S**	**S**

Greys Court

Rotherfield Greys, Henley-on-Thames, Oxfordshire RG9 4PG

🏠 ❀ ♠ 🏆 🏠 💷 𝑥 🎬 🎭 👪
🏃 1969   (2:D5)

A picturesque family home with delightful gardens in an idyllic setting

Set amid rolling countryside, this enchanting place dates back to medieval times and has a serene and tranquil atmosphere. The gardens are designed as an inspirational series of outdoor areas through which you can stroll at your leisure, before enjoying a treat in the tea-room. If you are feeling a little more energetic, you can follow 'the Gentle Walk', a 30-minute circuit around the estate, created by the former owner Lady Brunner, for her husband.

⭐ **Please note that the house is closed until April 2010 for important reservicing and conservation work.** Gardens and tea-room remain open

ℹ️ **T** 01494 755564 (Infoline), 01491 628529
  E greyscourt@nationaltrust.org.uk

🏃 Gardens only

🎭 Various events inc. guided walks, open-air theatre and music

🏃 Spectacular bluebells in the woods. Dogs welcome on the estate walk

♿ P♿ D♿ 👶 •• 📷 🔊 **Tea-room** 🦮
Grounds 🪜

📷 Book and card shop

☕ Tea-room in Cromwellian stables. Light lunches and teas

👪 Baby-changing facilities. Children's quiz/trail. Pushchairs in gardens only. Family explorer packs

🐕 In the car park and on the estate walk

➔ [175:SU725834] **Cycle**: on Oxfordshire cycleway. **Bus**: White's 145 from Henley-on-Thames town hall (½ml walk from 🚃 Henley-on-Thames). Alight Greys Green and follow signed footpath to Greys Court (approx ¼ml). **Station**: Henley-on-Thames 3ml. **Road**: W of Henley-on-Thames. From Nettlebed mini-roundabout on A4130 take B481 and property is signed to the left after approx. 3ml. There is also a direct (unsigned) route from Henley-on-Thames town centre. Follow signs to Badgemore Golf Club towards Peppard, approx 3ml out of Henley

🅿️ Free parking, 220yds

NT properties nearby
Basildon Park, Cliveden, Hughenden Manor

Greys Court								
Garden/tea-room								
1 Apr–27 Sep		12–5	**M**	T	**W**	**T**	**F**	**S** **S**

Open BH Mons. Closed Good Fri. Garden open in aid of NGS 16 May (charge inc. NT members). On village fête day, 6 September, special opening arrangements apply. Contact property for details (charge inc. NT members)

Chopin, Mahler and Elgar. Hatchlands is set in a beautiful 174-hectare (430-acre) park designed by Repton, with a variety of waymarked walks offering vistas of open parkland and views of the house. The woodlands are a haven for wildlife and there is a stunning wood, which is carpeted with bluebells from April to May.

T 01483 222482
E hatchlands@nationaltrust.org.uk

Audio guide allows visitors to hear the instruments (charge inc. NT members)

Inc. Cobbe Collection Trust concerts, tel. 01483 211474 or visit www.cobbecollection.co.uk. Easter trails on Easter Sunday and Easter Monday

Building **Grounds**

Licensed tea-room (NT-approved concession). Busy for lunch on Wed concert days. Children's menu

Baby-changing facilities. Hip-carrying infant seats for loan. Children's quiz/trail. Tracker Packs

Under close control in designated parkland areas

[187:TQ063516] **Bus**: Countryliner 478/9 Guildford–Epsom (passing ‌ Leatherhead and close ‌ Guildford). **Station**: Clandon 2ml, Horsley 2½ml. **Road**: E of East Clandon, N of A246 Guildford–Leatherhead road

P Free parking, 300yds

NT properties nearby
Box Hill, Clandon Park, Leith Hill, Polesden Lacey, River Wey and Dapdune Wharf, Shalford Mill

The park at Hatchlands, Surrey

Hatchlands Park

East Clandon, Guildford, Surrey GU4 7RT

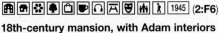 1945 (2:F6)

18th-century mansion, with Adam interiors and collection of keyboard instruments, set in parkland

Built in the 1750s for Admiral Boscawen, hero of the Battle of Louisburg, the house contains the earliest recorded decorations by Robert Adam in an English country house – whose ceilings here appropriately feature nautical motifs. On display is the Cobbe Collection, the world's largest group of keyboard instruments associated with famous composers such as Purcell, J. C. Bach,

Hatchlands Park									
Park walks									
1 Apr–31 Oct	11–6		M	T	W	T	F	S	S
House/garden									
1 Apr–30 Jul	2–5:30		M	T	W	T	F	S	S
1 Aug–31 Aug	2–5:30		M	T	W	T	F	S	S
1 Sep–29 Oct	2–5:30		M	T	W	T	F	S	S
Shop									
As house	1–5								
Restaurant									
As house	11–5								
Open BH Mons									

Hindhead Commons and The Devil's Punch Bowl Café

London Road, Hindhead, Surrey GU26 6AB

 1906   **(2:E7)**

The gateway to the Surrey Hills, with fine views

Take a walk through Hindhead Commons and see why this area of open heathland is classified as an Area of Outstanding Natural Beauty. Visitors can enjoy the stunning scenery of the Devil's Punch Bowl from a special viewpoint less than 50yds from the National Trust café, then continue for half a mile to enjoy the view from Highcombe Edge.

What's new in 2009 Construction of the A3 Hindhead by-pass is under way. There are viewing platforms at the north and south ends of the tunnel, a short walk from the café

★ Work on the A3 Hindhead Tunnel may affect access onto Hindhead Common

ℹ️ T 01428 683207 (Infoline), 01428 608771
E hindhead@nationaltrust.org.uk

🧍 Maps and local walks leaflets on sale

♿ 🅿️ 🚾 Grounds

🍽️ Devil's Punch Bowl Café. Hot and cold food available. Children's menu

👶 Baby-changing facilities

➡️ [133:SU895356] Beside A3, at Hindhead, near crossroads with A287. **Bus**: Stagecoach in South 18/19; 71 Haslemere Aldershot. **Station**: Haslemere 3ml

🅿️ Parking, £2 (pay & display). No lorries. Coach parties by arrangement

NT properties nearby
Ludshott Common, Oakhurst Cottage, Winkworth Arboretum, The Witley Centre

Hindhead Commons									
Commons									
All year		M	T	W	T	F	S	S	
Café									
1 Feb–31 Mar	9–4	M	T	W	T	F	S	S	
1 Apr–31 Oct	9–5	M	T	W	T	F	S	S	
1 Nov–31 Jan 10	9–4	M	T	W	T	F	S	S	
Closed 25/26 Dec & 1 Jan 10									

For public transport details, see page 377

Hinton Ampner

Bramdean, nr Alresford, Hampshire SO24 0LA

🏠 ✿ 🏛️ 🍽️ 🧍 🌳 👶 1986   **(2:D7)**

Elegant country house with highly distinctive gardens

Best known for its fine gardens, Hinton Ampner is an elegant country house with an outstanding collection of furniture, paintings and *objets d'art*. The house was extensively remodelled after a traumatic fire in 1960 by its final owner, Ralph Dutton, 8th and last Lord Sherborne, who also created the gardens – widely acknowledged to be a masterpiece of 20th-century garden design. With their crisply manicured lawns and fine topiary, the gardens cleverly combine formal design with informal planting, and the gardeners are always on hand to talk to visitors. The walled garden, currently being turned back into a productive area, is a popular attraction with a thriving and extensive vegetable plot. Produce from the garden, when available, is on sale along with a wide range of plants.

What's new in 2009 Part of the upstairs of the property opening (Tues and Wed only)

ℹ️ T 01962 771305
E hintonampner@nationaltrust.org.uk

♿ 🅿️ 🚾 Building
Grounds

🏛️ NT shop. Plant sales

🍽️ Small tea-room

The entrance hall at Hinton Ampner, Hampshire

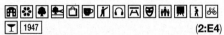

Baby-changing facilities. No baby-feeding facilities

→ [185:SU597275] **Bus**: Stagecoach in Hampshire 67 Winchester–Petersfield (passing close ⊠ Winchester & passing ⊠ Petersfield). **Station**: Winchester 9ml, Alresford (Mid-Hants Railway) 4ml. **Road**: on A272, 1ml W of Bramdean village, 8ml E of Winchester, leave M3 at exit 9 and follow signs to Petersfield

P Free parking. Special entrance for coaches. Map indicating where coaches can park sent with confirmation of booking

NT properties nearby
Mottisfont Abbey, Uppark House and Garden, The Vyne, Winchester City Mill

Hinton Ampner									
Garden									
15 Mar–2 Nov	11–5	**M**	**T**	**W**	T	F	**S**	**S**	
House*									
15 Mar–2 Nov	11:30–5	**M**	**T**	**W**	T	F	**S**	**S**	
Tea-room/shop									
28 Feb–14 Mar	11:30–4	M	T	W	T	F	**S**	**S**	
15 Mar–2 Nov	11:30–5	**M**	**T**	**W**	T	F	**S**	**S**	
7 Nov–20 Dec	11–4	M	T	W	T	F	**S**	**S**	
Christmas: house/garden/tea-room/shop									
5 Dec–20 Dec	11–4	M	T	W	T	F	**S**	**S**	

*Timed tickets on Mons. House open Good Fri 1–5

The Homewood

Portsmouth Road, Esher, Surrey KT10 9JL

🏠 ❄ 1999   (2:F6)

20th-century Modernist house and garden

⭐ Administered and maintained on the Trust's behalf by a tenant. Please tel. for opening arrangements and prices. **Access is via minibus from Claremont Landscape Garden only**. No WC

ℹ **T** 01372 476424
E thehomewood@nationaltrust.org.uk

→ **Access is via minibus from Claremont Landscape Garden only**

The Homewood
Contact property for details. Panoramic photographs are available to see on website

Hughenden Manor

High Wycombe, Buckinghamshire HP14 4LA

🏠 ❄ ♣ 🛋 📷 💷 🍴 🎧 🪑 🎭 👶 📷 🚶 🚲 🖼
☕ 1947   (2:E4)

Country home of the Victorian statesman Benjamin Disraeli

Recent enhancements at Hughenden Manor offer a vivid insight into the charismatic personality and colourful private life of the most unlikely Victorian Prime Minister, Benjamin Disraeli, who lived here from 1848 until his death in 1881. Much of his furniture, paintings and books remain and the new presentation of the Disraeli Room allows visitors to browse among an extraordinary collection of personal memorabilia, including cuttings of his hair, kept for posterity and labelled by his devoted wife, Mary Anne. Part of the cellars are now open to the public for a glimpse into life below stairs, and there are hands-on activities for children in the house to help them enjoy their visit. The formal gardens have been recreated, based on the original designs of Mary Anne Disraeli, and there are beautiful walks through the park and woodland surrounding this fascinating country home.

What's new in 2009 Extended opening of the walled garden from Wednesday to Friday

⭐ Certain rooms have little electric light. Visitors wishing to make a close study of the interior of the house should avoid dull days early and late in the season

ℹ **T** 01494 755565 (Infoline), 01494 755573
E hughenden@nationaltrust.org.uk

🏃 Manor tours at 11:30 (limited availability)

🎧 German Forest and Top Secret Hughenden (about the Second World War), £1

🎭 Programme of family-friendly events, including hands-on workshops and Discovery Days during school holidays

♿ 🅿 🅳 🅦 ⠿ 📷 🎨 💻 🎵 🦽 🛗
Building 🦽 🦽 ♿ Grounds 🦽 🦽

💷 The Stables Restaurant (licensed). Also available for winter events. Booked Christmas lunch available 10 & 11 Dec. Children's menu

---

Please remember – your membership card is *always* needed for free admission

🏼 Baby-changing facilities. Hip-carrying infant seats for loan. Family Tracker Packs. Family-friendly events, inc. hands-on workshops and Discovery Days during school holidays

🏛 Suitable for school groups. Education room/centre. Live interpretation. Hands-on activities. Adult study days

🐕 Under close control in park and woodland

🚲 Bridleways running through the woodlands to nearby villages

➔ [165:SU866955] **Foot**: 1½ml from High Wycombe. **Bus**: Arriva 300 High Wycombe–Aylesbury (passing close ⊠ High Wycombe). Note: long and steep walk to house entrance. **Station**: High Wycombe 2ml. **Road**: 1½ml N of High Wycombe; on W side of the Great Missenden road (A4128)

🅿 Free parking, 200yds. Some waiting possible at peak times; parking space for only one coach; overflow car park 400yds

NT properties nearby
Claydon House, Cliveden, Waddesdon Manor, West Wycombe Park

The façade of Hughenden Manor, Buckinghamshire

Hughenden Manor										
House										
4 Mar–1 Nov	1–5	M	T	**W**	**T**	**F**	**S**	**S**
12 Dec–20 Dec	11–3	**M**	**T**	**W**	**T**	**F**	**S**	**S**
Garden										
4 Mar–1 Nov	11–5	M	T	**W**	**T**	**F**	**S**	**S**
12 Dec–20 Dec	11–4	**M**	**T**	**W**	**T**	**F**	**S**	**S**
Park										
All year			**M**	**T**	**W**	**T**	**F**	**S**	**S**
Shop/restaurant										
4 Mar–1 Nov	11–5	M	T	**W**	**T**	**F**	**S**	**S**
Shop										
4 Nov–6 Dec	11–4	M	T	**W**	**T**	**F**	**S**	**S**
12 Dec–20 Dec	11–4	**M**	**T**	**W**	**T**	**F**	**S**	**S**
Restaurant										
4 Nov–6 Dec	11–4	M	T	W	**T**	**F**	**S**	**S**
12 Dec–20 Dec	11–4	**M**	**T**	**W**	**T**	**F**	**S**	**S**

Admission by timed ticket on Sun, BHols & other busy days. Open BH Mons. Last entry 4:30 or dusk if earlier. Occasional early closing for special events & weddings. Restaurant closed 19 Nov. Please note 1st floor closed during Dec opening

Ightham Mote

Mote Road, Ivy Hatch, Sevenoaks, Kent TN15 0NT

🏠 ✝ 🔆 🍴 📷 🏠 🍷 🦮 🎫 🍽 🏼 📷 🚶

🚲 1985   (2:H6)

Outstanding 14th-century moated manor house

Set in a Kentish sunken valley, Ightham Mote is a rare example of a moated medieval manor house, dating from 1320 with important later additions and alterations. It was the subject of the Trust's largest conservation project, begun in 1989 and completed in 2004 – an exhibition of which is in the visitor reception. Ightham Mote has many special features, including a Great Hall, Crypt, Tudor Chapel with a hand-painted ceiling and the private apartments of the American donor Charles Henry Robinson. However, one of its most enchanting features has to be the Grade I listed dog kennel, situated in the picturesque courtyard. Ightham Mote also offers some lovely gardens and water features, with lakeside and woodland walks.

ℹ **T** 01732 811145 (Infoline), 01732 810378
E ighthammote@nationaltrust.org.uk

Visitors enjoying Ightham Mote, Kent

🚶 Regular free introductory talks, garden and tower tours

🎭 Family activities and lecture lunches

🚶 Three waymarked self-guided walks on surrounding estate – leaflet obtainable from visitor reception. Regular guided walks

♿ 🅿 🚾 ⌨ 👁 📷 📹 🖥 📺 ♿ ♿ ♿

Building 🚶 🚶 🚶 ♿ **Grounds** ♿ ➡

📷 Plant sales

🍽 Mote Restaurant (licensed) adjacent to visitor reception. Children's menu. Refreshment kiosk in walled car park open on busy days

👶 Baby-changing and feeding facilities. Front-carrying baby slings and hip-carrying infant seats for loan. Children's quiz/trail. Family activity packs. Family activities

🏫 Suitable for school groups. Education room. Hands-on activities. Adult study days

🐴 On estate walks only

🚲 On surrounding bridleways and roads on 223-hectare (550-acre) estate

➡ [188:TQ584535] Between Sevenoaks and Borough Green 1¾ml S of A25. **Bus**: New Enterprise 404 from ⊠ Sevenoaks, calls Thu and Fri only, on other days alight Ivy Hatch, ¾ml. Autocar 222 Tonbridge–⊠ Borough Green, alight Fairlawne, ½ml by footpath. Arriva 306/8 ⊠ Sevenoaks–Gravesend (passing ⊠ Borough Green), alight Ightham Common, 1½ml. **Station**: Borough Green & Wrotham 3ml; Hildenborough 4ml; Sevenoaks 6ml. **Road**: 6ml N of Tonbridge on A227; 6ml S of Sevenoaks on A25; 16ml W of Maidstone on A20/A25

🅿 Free parking, 200yds

NT properties nearby
Chartwell, Emmetts Garden, Knole, Old Soar Manor, Quebec House, Toys Hill

Ightham Mote									
House									
14 Mar–1 Nov	11–5	M	T	W	T	F	S	S	
2 Nov–20 Dec*	11–3	M	T	W	T	F	S	S	
Estate									
All year	Dawn–dusk	M	T	W	T	F	S	S	
Shop/restaurant/garden**									
14 Mar–1 Nov	10:30–5	M	T	W	T	F	S	S	
5 Nov–20 Dec	11–3	M	T	W	T	F	S	S	
Restaurant									
20 Dec–30 Dec***	11–3	M	T	W	T	F	S	S	

Restaurant open for occasional themed evenings and for booked functions. Please tel. 01732 811314 for opening times of Mote Restaurant and 01732 811203 for shop opening times outside normal property hours. Booking at Mote Restaurant advised winter & evenings. *Partial gardens/courtyard & ground floor access Nov/Dec, 11–3. **Except when function ongoing. Closed Jan 10. ***Not 24/25 Dec. Great Hall dressed for Christmas during winter

King's Head

King's Head Passage, Market Square, Aylesbury, Buckinghamshire HP20 2RW

🎭 🍽 🍴 🚶 🎭 👶 🏫 📺 🍸 1925   (2:E3)

Historic ancient coaching inn in the heart of Aylesbury

Set in the heart of this historic market town, the King's Head is one of England's best preserved coaching inns. Dating back to 1455, the building has many fascinating architectural features – including stained-glass windows, exposed wattle and daub and the original stabling for the inn. Around the central cobbled courtyard there are the town's Tourist Information Centre, a thriving second-hand bookshop, coffee shop in the Great Hall and various small retail outlets. The award-winning Farmers' Bar is now run by the local Chiltern Brewery.

What's new in 2009 Exciting programme of events (see website)

⭐ The King's Head has full conference facilities

Unless indicated, last admission is always 30mins before closing time

[i] **T** 01296 381501
E kingshead@nationaltrust.org.uk

[🎭] History and Mystery tours, Wed, Fri, Sat at 2.
Ghost tours available by arrangement

[🎭] Festivals, exhibitions, family activities, musical
events, Christmas events. Check website for
more details

[♿][icons] Building [icon] Grounds [icon]

[🍴] Farmers' Bar (not NT) (licensed). Lunches
provided by the Chiltern Brewery. Coffee shop

[👪] Baby-changing facilities. Pushchairs and baby
back-carriers admitted. Family activities and
events

[🏫] Suitable for school groups. Hands-on
activities. Adult study days

[➔] [165:SP818137] At top of Market Square.
Access through cobbled lane. **Bus:** from
surrounding areas. **Station:** Aylesbury
400yds

[P] No parking on site. Car parks in town centre
(not NT)

NT properties nearby
Boarstall Duck Decoy, Boarstall Tower, Long
Crendon Courthouse

King's Head								
Visitor reception								
All year	9–4	M	T	W	T	F	S	S
Great Hall/bookshop								
All year	10:30–4	M	T	W	T	F	S	S
Farmers' Bar								
All year	Licensing hours	M	T	W	T	F	S	S
Closed BH Mons. Tours available Wed, Fri, Sat at 2 (tel. to check availability)								

Deer in front of Knole, Kent

Knole

Sevenoaks, Kent TN15 0RP

 **1946** (2:H6)

**History and grandeur in the heart of Kent.
Birthplace of novelist and poet Vita
Sackville-West**

Set within a glorious deer park, Knole appears
much like a small village when viewed from a
distance. It is a complex and beautiful house,
which has links with kings, queens and nobility,
as well as literary connections with Vita
Sackville-West and Virginia Woolf. Thirteen
superb staterooms are laid out much as they
were in the 18th century, to impress visitors with
the wealth and standing of the Sackville family
(who still live at Knole). The house boasts a
world-renowned collection of Royal Stuart
furniture, paintings by Gainsborough, Van Dyck
and Reynolds, as well as important 17th-century
tapestries. The 404-hectare (1,000-acre) deer
park surrounding the house is a Site of Special
Scientific Interest and is the only remaining
medieval deer park in Kent.

What's new in 2009 Extended opening hours
during school summer holidays. 'Speaking
Stones' – a family guide to Green Court and
Stone Court. In March some show rooms will
have their winter covers on with conservation
explanation

[★] Please do not feed the deer; they can be
dangerous. In order to protect Knole's fragile
and rare textiles, light of all kinds is carefully
controlled. This restricts opening hours of the
show rooms. **There is no wheelchair
access beyond the Great Hall.** Virtual
reality tour available

[i] **T** 01732 450608 (Infoline), 01732 462100
E knole@nationaltrust.org.uk

[🎭] Guided tours take place while house is closed
to the public (booking required)

[🎭] Educational family day in Aug. Exclusive
evening candlelit tours in summer and
autumn. Carol concerts in the Great Hall.
Lord Sackville's Christmas lecture. Putting the
House to Bed tour and lunch

[🚶] Deer park has pedestrian access all year round

Unless indicated, last admission is always 30mins before closing time

  ♿ 🅿️ 🅳 🚻 ⠿ 📷 🎧 💻 🔤 ♿

Building 🔵🔴🔵 **Grounds** 🔴🔵

🏠 NT shop. Christmas shop open Wed–Sun (Nov/Dec). Annual plant sale

🍽 Brewhouse Tea-room (licensed). Also open Nov and Dec (Wed–Sun). Children's menu

👶 Baby-changing and feeding facilities. Front-carrying baby slings and hip-carrying infant seats for loan. Children's house trail. Family Tracker Pack. Easter trail. Autumn trail

🎒 Suitable for school groups. Costume workshop. Teachers' resource book

🐕 On leads and in park only

🚲 Cycling permitted on roads and tracks

➡ [188:TQ532543] **Foot**: park entrance at south end of Sevenoaks town centre, opposite St Nicholas's church. **Bus**: from

Set in a magnificent deer park, Knole is one of England's greatest show houses

Knole									
House			M	T	W	T	F	S	S
7 Mar–29 Mar	12–4		M	T	W	T	F	**S**	**S**
1 Apr–19 Jul	12–4		M	T	**W**	**T**	**F**	**S**	**S**
21 Jul–31 Aug	11–4:30		M	**T**	**W**	**T**	**F**	**S**	**S**
2 Sep–1 Nov	12–4		M	T	**W**	**T**	**F**	**S**	**S**
Shop/tea-room									
7 Mar–29 Mar	11–4		M	T	W	T	F	**S**	**S**
1 Apr–19 Jul	10:30–5		M	T	**W**	**T**	**F**	**S**	**S**
21 Jul–31 Aug	10:30–5		M	**T**	**W**	**T**	**F**	**S**	**S**
2 Sep–1 Nov	10:30–5		M	T	**W**	**T**	**F**	**S**	**S**
Christmas shop/tea-room									
4 Nov–20 Dec	11–4		M	T	**W**	**T**	**F**	**S**	**S**
Garden									
1 Apr–30 Sep	11–4		M	T	**W**	T	F	S	S

Park open daily for pedestrians. Vehicles admitted only when house is open. Garden (by courtesy of Lord Sackville): please note limited opening

surrounding area to Sevenoaks, ¾ml walk. **Station**: Sevenoaks 1½ml. **Road**: leave M25 at exit 5 (A21). Park entrance in Sevenoaks town centre off A225 Tonbridge Road (opposite St Nicholas's church)

🅿 Parking, 60yds, £2.50. Park only open to vehicles from 10:30 when house open. When house closed parking available in nearby town centre. Park open to vehicles in winter when shop and tea-room open. Park gates locked at 6

NT properties nearby
Chartwell, Emmetts Garden, Ightham Mote, Toys Hill

Lamb House

West Street, Rye, East Sussex TN31 7ES

🏠 ✿ 1950   **(2:J8)**

Fine brick-fronted house with literary associations

⭐ Administered and largely maintained on the Trust's behalf by a tenant. No WC

ℹ️ **T** 01580 762334
E lambhouse@nationaltrust.org.uk

➡ In West Street, facing W end of church

Lamb House									
19 Mar–24 Oct	2–6		M	T	W	**T**	F	**S**	**S**

Leith Hill

Leith Hill Place Workshop, Leith Hill Lane, Dorking, Surrey RH5 6LY

 1923   **(2:F7)**

Woodland, parkland, farmland and open heath with Leith Hill Tower commanding extensive views

The highest point in south-east England, the hill is crowned by an 18th-century Gothic tower, with panoramic views north to London and south to the English Channel. There are colourful displays of rhododendrons and bluebells in May and June. Rugged countryside provides exhilarating walking in woodland and over heathland and farmland.

What's new in 2009 Grazing Sussex cattle on Dukes Warren

The Gothic tower at Leith Hill, Surrey

⊠ No WC. Henman base camp (hostel for recreational, corporate and conservation working groups). Etherley Farm Campsite. Tel. 01306 621423 for details

ⓘ **T** 01306 711777
  E leithhill@nationaltrust.org.uk

⚐ Guided walks throughout the year (tel. 01372 220644 for details)

⚐ Two circular trails – self-guided leaflet available from Tower when open, also noticeboard at Tower and Rhododendron Wood, £1 donation

♿ **Tower** ♿ **Grounds** ♿

⬛ Servery (not NT) at Leith Hill Tower. Light refreshments when tower open. May close early in bad weather

⬛ Suitable for school groups. Information room and telescope on top of tower

🐾 Under close control in Rhododendron Wood

➔ [187:TQ139432] **Foot**: comprehensive network of rights of way including the Greensand Way National Trail. **Cycle**: many rights of way lead to the tower. **Bus**: Arriva 21 Guildford–Dorking (passing close ⊠ Guildford and passing ⊠ Chilworth and Dorking), alight Holmbury St Mary, 2½ml. **Station**: Holmwood (U), not Sun, 2½ml; Dorking 5½ml. **Road**: 1ml SW of Coldharbour A29/B2126

Ⓟ Free parking in designated areas along road at foot of the hill, some steep gradients to the tower. No direct vehicle access to summit. Rhododendron Wood £2 per car.

NT properties nearby
Box Hill, Clandon Park, Hatchlands Park, Polesden Lacey, Ranmore Common

Leith Hill									
Tower									
1 Feb–28 Mar	10–3:30	M	T	W	T	F	**S**	**S**	
29 Mar–26 Jul	10–5	M	T	W	T	**F**	**S**	**S**	
2 Aug–31 Aug	10–5	M	T	**W**	T	**F**	**S**	**S**	
6 Sep–24 Oct	10–5	M	T	W	T	**F**	**S**	**S**	
25 Oct–31 Jan 10	10–3:30	M	T	W	T	F	**S**	**S**	
Wood/estate									
All year		**M**	**T**	**W**	**T**	**F**	**S**	**S**	

Open BHols. Closed 25 Dec (tower). Last tickets sold 30mins before closing time

Charges for National Trust members apply on some special event days

Long Crendon Courthouse

Long Crendon, Aylesbury,
Buckinghamshire HP18 9AN

 1900   (2:D4)

Early 15th-century building set in idyllic village

Set in an attractive and unspoilt village, this
building is a fine example of early timber-frame
construction. Manorial courts were held here
from the reign of Henry V until Victorian times.
The ground floor (now tenanted) was the village
poor house.

What's new in 2009 Exhibition of village history

⭐ The stairs at Long Crendon are extremely
steep. No WC

ℹ️ **T** 01280 822850
E longcrendon@nationaltrust.org.uk

♿ Building 🅰️

➡️ [165:SP698091] Next to the parish church at
the end of High Street. **Bus:** Arriva 261,
Aylesbury–Oxford (passing ➤ Haddenham &
Thame Parkway). **Station:** Haddenham &
Thame Parkway 2ml by footpath, 4ml by
road. **Road:** 2ml N of Thame, via B4011

🅿️ Limited on-street parking (not NT)

NT properties nearby
Boarstall Duck Decoy, Boarstall Tower, Claydon
House, King's Head, Stowe Landscape Gardens,
Waddesdon Manor

Long Crendon Courthouse									
Upper floor only									
4 Apr–27 Sep	11–6	M	T	W	T	F	**S**	**S**
8 Apr–30 Sep	2–6	M	T	**W**	T	F	S	S
Open BH Mons: 11–6									

Mottisfont, Hampshire, stands beside the River Test

Monk's House

Rodmell, Lewes, East Sussex BN7 3HF

🏠 ✳️ 🖼️ 1980   (2:G8)

Country retreat of the novelist Virginia Woolf

⭐ Administered and largely maintained on the
Trust's behalf by a tenant

ℹ️ **T** 01323 870001 (c/o Alfriston Clergy House)
E monkshouse@nationaltrust.org.uk

➡️ From A27 SW of Lewes, follow signs for
Kingston and then Rodmell village, where turn
left at Abergavenny Arms pub, then ½ml

Monk's House								
1 Apr–31 Oct	2–5:30	M	T	**W**	T	F	**S**	**S**

Mottisfont

Mottisfont, nr Romsey, Hampshire SO51 0LP

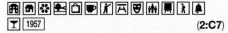
🍷 1957   (2:C7)

**Historic house set in atmospheric gardens
and grounds in the River Test Valley**

This handsome house, built on the 12th-century
remains of an Augustinian priory, stands amid
sweeping lawns next to the River Test,
immortalised by F. M. Halford, the father of
modern fly fishing. Plump brown trout wallow in
its fast-flowing, clear waters and the tranquil
lawns alongside are dotted with majestic plane
trees. Mottisfont's famous walled gardens –
home to the National Collection of Old-fashioned
Roses (at their best in June) – are a pleasure to
visit at any time of the year. The house contains a
stunning drawing room, decorated in the *trompe
l'oeil* style by Rex Whistler in 1938, as well as
Derek Hill's collection of early 20th-century art.
The wider estate includes much of Mottisfont
village and surrounding farmland and woods.

What's new in 2009 Tulip and species Narcissi
meadows in April–May. Continued restoration of
house with decoration and artefacts reminiscent
of the neo-classical style of the donor, Mrs Russell

⭐ From 5 June–20 June, when the old-
fashioned roses are in bloom, the gardens are
open every day and late Monday–Saturday
(Sundays close at 5). Weekends are

For public transport details, see page 377

extremely busy and weekday and/or evening visits are recommended (especially evenings to enjoy the scent of the roses)

i **T** 01794 340757
E mottisfont@nationaltrust.org.uk

Open-air theatre, art exhibitions, seasonal events and family activities

7ml estate path (leaflet £1), access from main car park (open 9–6)

Building **Grounds**

NT shop. Second-hand bookshop. Rare and unusual plant sales. Rose sales, May–June

Kitchen Café (licensed) at east entrance to house. Children's menu. Kiosk outside rose garden at selected times

Baby-changing facilities. Pushchairs admitted. Hip-carrying infant seats for loan. Children's quiz/trail. Family activity packs. Highchairs available in Kitchen Café

Live interpretation

Dogs in car park and on estate walk

Mottisfont			
Garden/shop/Kitchen Café			
1 Feb–8 Feb	11–4	M T W T F	S S
14 Feb–22 Feb	11–4	M T W T F S S	
28 Feb–2 Apr	11–5	M T W T F S S	
4 Apr–19 Apr	11–5	M T W T F S S	
20 Apr–24 May	11–5	M T W T F S S	
25 May–4 Jun	11–5	M T W T F S S	
5 Jun–20 Jun	11–8*	M T W T F S S	
21 Jun–1 Nov	11–5	M T W T F S S	
7 Nov–20 Dec	11–4**	M T W T F S S	
House			
14 Mar–2 Apr	11–5	M T W T F S S	
4 Apr–19 Apr	11–5	M T W T F S S	
20 Apr–24 May	11–5	M T W T F S S	
25 May–27 Jun	11–5	M T W T F S S	
28 Jun–1 Nov	11–5	M T W T F S S	

Open Good Fri & Hallowe'en. Café last orders 4:30. *Garden closes 5 on Suns in June. **Open until 5 in Dec. Car park gates close 6, and 8:30 in June (6 on Suns). Access to some rooms in house may occasionally be restricted due to functions. Please tel. in advance. Family Activity weekends in Nov, Christmas events and Fair during Dec weekends

[185:SU327270] In Test Valley between Romsey and Stockbridge. **Foot**: situated on Hampshire's long-distance path, Testway. Clarendon Way passes 2ml to the N. **Cycle**: on Testway. **Station**: Dunbridge (U) ¾ml. **Road**: signposted off A3057 Romsey to Stockbridge, 4½ml N of Romsey. Also signposted off B3087 Romsey to Broughton

P Free parking

NT properties nearby
Hinton Ampner, Mompesson House, Winchester City Mill

Mottistone Manor Garden is set in an idyllic valley

Mottistone Manor Garden

Mottistone, Isle of Wight PO30 4EA

1965　　(2:C9)

Enchanting garden set in a sheltered valley

This magical garden, with gentle grassy slopes and terraces affording distant views to the sea, is full of delights and surprises. Surrounding an attractive Elizabethan manor house (not open) and set in an idyllic sheltered valley, the 20th-century garden boasts colourful borders and an organic vegetable plot, as well as Mediterranean-style planting to take advantage of its extreme southerly location. Its many surprises include a young olive grove and a traditional tea garden set alongside The Shack, a unique cabin retreat designed as their summer drawing office by the architects John Seely (2nd Lord Mottistone) and Paul Paget. Visitors of all ages are enchanted by Mottistone's cast of Flowerpot characters, and there are delightful walks from the garden onto the downs across the adjoining Mottistone Estate.

What's new in 2009 Small exhibition in The Shack about the life and work of architects Seely & Paget

⭐ The manor house is only open one day a year

ℹ️ **T** 01983 741302
   E mottistonemanor@nationaltrust.org.uk

🚶 Many trails across surrounding estate

♿ 🅿️ 🎧 🖼️ 📷 💻 🎒 🛍️ **Grounds** ♿ 🦽 ♿

🛍️ Plant sales and gift shop

💷 Tea-garden (NT-approved concession) serving hot and cold snacks

👶 Baby-changing facilities. Pushchairs and baby back-carriers admitted. Children's quiz/trail. Family activity packs

🐕 On leads only

➡️ [196:SZ406838] **Foot**: 1ml N of coastal path; 1ml S of Tennyson Trail. **Cycle**: NCN67. On the 'Round the Island' cycle route. **Ferry**: Yarmouth (Wightlink Ltd) 6ml (tel. 0871 376 1000); E Cowes (Red Funnel) 12ml (tel. 0844 844 9988). **Bus**: Southern Vectis 7 Newport–Alum Bay. **Road**: at Mottistone, between Brighstone and Brook on B3399

🅿️ Free parking, 50yds

NT properties nearby
Bembridge Windmill, Brighstone Shop and Museum, The Needles Old Battery and New Battery, Newtown Old Town Hall

Mottistone Manor Garden								
15 Mar–1 Nov	11–5	**M**	**T**	**W**	**T**	F	S	S

Closes dusk if earlier. House open BH Mon 25 May only, 2–5. Additional charges apply. Guided tours for NT members on that day 10–12 by timed ticket available from visitor reception (advance booking not possible). Late night opening: garden open until 9 on Wed 24 June

The Needles Old Battery and New Battery

West High Down, Alum Bay, Isle of Wight PO39 0JH

🎧 🐕 🖼️ 🏠 🛍️ 💷 🚶 👶 🏫 | 1975 | **(2:C9)**

Victorian coastal defence and secret rocket testing site perched high above the Needles Rocks

The Old Battery, built in 1862 following the threat of a French invasion, is a spectacularly sited fort perched on the extreme westerly edge of the Island. It contains exhibitions about its involvement in both World Wars, plus two original gun barrels displayed in the parade ground. An underground tunnel leads to a searchlight emplacement overlooking the Needles Rocks. The New Battery is on a separate site further up the headland and contains an exhibition on Britain's secret rocket testing programme during the Cold War.

What's new in 2009 Updated family activity packs

⭐ No vehicular access to either Battery (visitors with disabilities by arrangement). The Old Battery has a number of steep paths and uneven surfaces. Access to the tunnel is via a narrow spiral staircase. WCs are available for visitors to the Old Battery. The New Battery has uneven surfaces and steps down to the exhibition rooms. There is no WC at the New Battery. The route from the Old Battery up to the New Battery is steep

ℹ️ **T** 01983 754772
   E needlesoldbattery@nationaltrust.org.uk

♿ 🅿️ 🎧 🦽 🛍️ 🎒 **Building** ♿ 🦽 ♿
Grounds ♿ 🦽

🛍️ Shop at Needles Old Battery

💷 Tea-room at Needles Old Battery serving home-made food. Kiosk at Needles New Battery serving hot and cold drinks, ice-cream and snacks

👶 Baby-changing and feeding facilities. Pushchairs and baby back-carriers admitted. Family activity packs

🏫 Suitable for school groups. Tours by NT guide (booking required, charge applies)

🐕 On leads only

Dogs assisting visitors with disabilities are always welcome

The Needles Old Battery and New Battery										
Tea-room										
1 Feb–8 Mar	11–3	M	T	W	T	F	**S**	**S**		
Battery/tea-room										
14 Mar–1 Nov	10:30–5	**M**	**T**	**W**	**T**	**F**	**S**	**S**		
Tea-room										
7 Nov–13 Dec	11–3	M	T	W	T	F	**S**	**S**		
9 Jan–31 Jan 10	11–3	M	T	W	T	F	**S**	**S**		
The Needles New Battery										
14 Mar–1 Nov	11–4	M	T	W	T	F	**S**	**S**		

Property closes in high winds: tel. on day of visit to check. New Battery also open school hols and other days where possible

➡ [196:SZ300848] **Foot**: access is on foot only from Alum Bay ¾ml along a well-surfaced private road, Highdown NT car park 2ml, Freshwater Bay 3½ml. **Cycle**: NCN67, ½ml. 'Round the Island' route. **Ferry**: Yarmouth (Wightlink Ltd) 5ml (tel. 0871 376 1000); E Cowes (Red Funnel) 16ml (tel. 0844 844 9988). **Bus**: Southern Vectis 7 Newport–Alum Bay, then ¾ml. Southern Vectis 'Needles Tour' from Yarmouth and Alum Bay (March–Nov). **Road**: Alum Bay W of Freshwater Bay (B3322)

🅿 No parking on site. Parking Alum Bay (not NT; minimum £3), or in Freshwater Bay (IOW Council) or Highdown car park SZ325856 (NT) and walk over Downs

NT properties nearby
Bembridge Windmill, Brighstone Shop and Museum, Mottistone Manor Garden, Newtown Old Town Hall, Tennyson Down

The searchlight in the Old Battery, looking out over the Needles Rocks

Newtown Old Town Hall

Newtown, Newport, Isle of Wight PO30 4PA

🏠 🚹 🚻 🏛 🚶 1933   (2:C9)

17th-century town hall with no town but a fascinating history

The small, tranquil village of Newtown once sent two members to Parliament and the Town Hall was the setting for often turbulent elections. This intriguing historic building is the only remaining evidence of the former importance of Newtown and contains local history and an exhibition depicting the exploits of 'Ferguson's Gang' – a mysterious group of anonymous benefactors.

What's new in 2009 Regular exhibitions

⭐ No WC, nearest WC in car park

ℹ️ **T** 01983 531785
   E oldtownhall@nationaltrust.org.uk

🚹 By written appointment

🚶 Footpaths lead to adjacent estuary and National Nature Reserve (tel. 01983 531622)

♿ 🔤 ⠿ 🅿 🎞 🖼 Building 🐕

🚻 Baby back-carriers admitted. Children's quiz/trail. Pushchairs admitted if visitor numbers allow

🏫 Suitable for school groups

➡ [196:SZ424905] **Cycle**: NCN67, ½ml. **Ferry**: Yarmouth (Wightlink Ltd) 5ml (tel. 0871 376 1000); E Cowes (Red Funnel) 11ml (tel. 0844 844 9988). **Bus**: Wightbus 35 from Newport; otherwise Southern Vectis 7 Newport–Yarmouth, alight Barton's Corner, 1ml. **Road**: Newtown is between Newport and Yarmouth, 1ml N of A3054

🅿 Free parking, 15yds. Not suitable for coaches

NT properties nearby
Bembridge Windmill, Brighstone Shop and Museum, Mottistone Manor Garden, The Needles Old Battery and New Battery

Newtown Old Town Hall								
15 Mar–29 Jun	2–5	M	**T**	**W**	T	F	S	**S**
1 Jul–31 Aug	2–5	**M**	**T**	**W**	T	F	S	**S**
2 Sep–21 Oct	2–5	M	**T**	**W**	T	F	S	**S**

Last admission 15mins before closing. Open Good Fri and Easter Sat. Closes dusk if earlier than 5

Nymans

Handcross, nr Haywards Heath,
West Sussex RH17 6EB

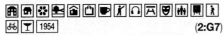

1954   (2:G7)

The forecourt at Nymans, West Sussex, in spring

Outstanding 20th-century garden, set around a romantic house and ruins, in beautiful woodland

Theatrically designed with plants from around the world, Nymans is internationally renowned for its garden design, rare plant collection and intimacy. Visit the Messel family rooms in the house and see the dramatic ruins, which form a magnificent backdrop to the main lawn. Enjoy wonderful views across the Sussex countryside and explore the wider estate with walks through ancient woodland, beside lakes and wildflowers. Nymans is one of the leading green gardens in the National Trust, actively engaging visitors with its methods of sustainable gardening. There is an extensive and varied events programme, including family activities, horticultural workshops and summer theatre.

What's new in 2009 Mobility buggy tours, family bamboo jungle, advanced community compost machine (first in the NT), restored Sunken Rock Garden, refurbished shop and restaurant, mobile refreshment buggy in garden. Family (one adult) ticket available

T 01444 405250
E nymans@nationaltrust.org.uk

Guided tours of the garden, 11 and 2

Audio guide available from reception or download from website

Summer theatre, gardening workshops, woodland events, Easter trail, themed family activity weeks, evening events, croquet

Woodland walks leaflet. Seasonal walks guides. Family trails

Building   Grounds

NT shop. Plant centre

Restaurant (licensed) serving home-cooked food made from local produce. Open-air seating. Christmas lunches Dec. Mobile refreshment buggy in garden

Baby-changing facilities. Pushchairs and baby back-carriers admitted to garden. Children's activity area in restaurant. Family Tracker Packs. Family trails. Family events

Suitable for education groups

In Nymans Woods only

On NCN20

[187:TQ265294] **Cycle**: NCN20.
Bus: Metrobus 273 Brighton–Crawley, 271 Haywards Heath–Crawley. Both stop outside Nymans. Both pass Crawley.
Station: Balcombe 4ml; Crawley 5ml.
Road: on B2114 at Handcross, just off London–Brighton M23/A23, 5ml S of Crawley

P Free parking. Designated coach bays

NT properties nearby
Devil's Dyke, Petworth House and Park, Sheffield Park Garden, Standen, Wakehurst Place

Nymans									
Garden/shop/restaurant									
All year	10–5	M	T	**W**	**T**	**F**	**S**	**S**	
House									
11 Mar–1 Nov	11–4	M	T	**W**	**T**	**F**	**S**	**S**	

Open BH Mons. Last admission to house, 3:45. Closed 25 Dec–1 Jan 10. Nymans closes 4, 5 Nov–31 Jan 10

Please remember – your membership card is *always* needed for free admission

Oakhurst Cottage

Hambledon, nr Godalming, Surrey GU8 4HF

🏠 📷 1952   (2:E7)

Small 16th-century timber-framed cottage

Restored and furnished as a labourer's simple dwelling, the cottage contains fascinating artefacts reflecting four centuries of continual occupation. The delightful garden contains typical Victorian plants.

⭐ No WC

ℹ T 01798 342207
   E oakhurstcottage@nationaltrust.org.uk

♿ 📠 📠 📠 🏢 Building 📠

➡ [186:SU965380] **Bus**: Stagecoach in Hants & Surrey 71 Guildford–Hindhead (passes close ☒ Goldalming), alight Lane End 1ml. **Station**: Witley 1½ml. **Road**: off A283 between Wormley and Chiddingfold

P Parking (not NT), 200yds, outside post office

NT properties nearby
Petworth House and Park, Winkworth Arboretum, The Witley Centre

Oakhurst Cottage			M	T	W	T	F	S	S
25 Mar–25 Oct	2–5		M	T	**W**	T	F	**S**	**S**

Admission by guided tour and appointment only. Open BH Mons: 2–5. Please book at least 3 days in advance

Old Soar Manor

Plaxtol, Borough Green, Kent TN15 0QX

🏠 1947   (2:H6)

Remains of a late 13th-century knight's dwelling

This is all that is left of the manor house of c.1290 which stood until the 18th century. The solar chamber over a barrel-vaulted undercroft was once inhabited by a medieval knight.

⭐ No WC

ℹ T 01732 810378
   E oldsoarmanor@nationaltrust.org.uk

♿ Building 📠

➡ [188:TQ619541] **Bus**: Autocar 222 ☒ Tonbridge–☒ Borough Green; New Enterprise 404 from ☒ Sevenoaks. On both alight E end of Plaxtol, then ¾ml by footpath.
Station: Borough Green & Wrotham 2½ml.
Road: 2ml S of Borough Green (A25); approached via A227 and Plaxtol; narrow lane

P No parking on site. Not suitable for coaches

NT properties nearby
Chartwell, Ightham Mote, Knole, Toys Hill

Old Soar Manor			M	T	W	T	F	S	S
1 Apr–30 Sep	10–6		**M**	**T**	**W**	**T**	F	**S**	**S**

Owletts

The Street, Cobham, Gravesend, Kent DA12 3AP

🏠 ❀ 1938   (2:H5)

Red-brick Charles II house with interesting garden

⭐ Owletts is occupied as a family home and is administered and maintained on the Trust's behalf by a descendant of the donor. No WC

ℹ T 01372 453401
   E owletts@nationaltrust.org.uk

➡ 1ml S of A2 at W end of village, at junction of roads from Dartford and Sole Street

Owletts			M	T	W	T	F	S	S
26 Mar–24 Oct	2–5:30		M	T	**W**	T	F	**S**	S

Petworth House and Park

Petworth, West Sussex GU28 0AE

🏠 ♨ 🏠 ☕ 📷 🎧 🎭 👪 🖼 🔥
☂ 1947   (2:E7)

Magnificent country house and park with an internationally important art collection

The vast late 17th-century mansion is set in a beautiful 283-hectare (700-acre) deer park, landscaped by 'Capability' Brown and immortalised in Turner's paintings. The house contains the Trust's finest collection of pictures, with numerous works by Turner, Van Dyck, Reynolds and Blake, as well as ancient and neo-classical sculpture, fine furniture and carvings by

Grinling Gibbons. The servants' quarters contain fascinating kitchens (including a splendid copper *batterie de cuisine* of more than 1,000 pieces) and other service rooms. On weekdays additional rooms in the house are open to visitors by kind permission of Lord and Lady Egremont.

i **T** 01798 343929 (Infoline), 01798 342207
E petworth@nationaltrust.org.uk

人 10-minute 'Welcome to Petworth' introductory talks on the house and grounds on weekdays when house is open (subject to availability)

∩ Available in English, German and French

♥ Concerts, open-air theatre, family events, living history events, lecture lunches and Christmas events. Send sae for details

人 Pleasure Grounds: spring and autumn guided walks

⟨icons⟩
Building ⟨icons⟩ **Park** ⟨icon⟩

⟨icon⟩ NT shop. Plant sales

⟨icon⟩ Licensed restaurant. Mother's Day & Christmas lunches by arrangement. Children's menu

⟨icon⟩ Baby-changing facilities. Pushchairs admitted. Children's quiz/trail. Children's Tracker Packs

Petworth House, West Sussex

Petworth House and Park								
House								
14 Mar–4 Nov	11–5	M	T	W	T	F	S	S
Shop/restaurant/Pleasure Grounds								
28 Feb–11 Mar	11–4	M	T	W	T	F	S	S
14 Mar–4 Nov	11–5	M	T	W	T	F	S	S
11 Nov–20 Dec	10–3:30	M	T	W	T	F	S	S

Open Good Fri. **Please note:** extra rooms shown weekdays from 1 as follows. Mon (not BH Mons): White and Gold Room and White Library. Tues/Wed: three bedrooms on first floor

⟨icon⟩ Suitable for school groups. Education room/ centre. Hands-on activities. Adult study days

⟨icon⟩ Under close control and only in park, not in Pleasure Grounds

→ [197:SU976218] **Bus:** Stagecoach in the South Downs 1 Worthing–Midhurst (passing ≋ Pulborough); Compass 76 Horsham– Petworth (passing ≋ Horsham).
Station: Pulborough 5¼ml. **Road:** in centre of Petworth (A272/A283); both house and park car parks on A283; pedestrian access from Petworth town and A272. No vehicles in park

P Parking, 700yds. Coaches can drop off at Church Lodge entrance and park in house car park. There is a £2 parking charge for Petworth Park car park for non-members

NT properties nearby
Black Down, Oakhurst Cottage, Uppark House and Garden, Winkworth Arboretum

Pitstone Windmill

Ivinghoe, Buckinghamshire

⟨icons⟩ 1937 **(2:E3)**

Example of the earliest form of windmill

★ No WC

i **T** 01442 851227
E pitstonemill@nationaltrust.org.uk

→ ½ml S of Ivinghoe, 3ml NE of Tring, just W of B488

Pitstone Windmill								
7 Jun–30 Aug	2:30–6	M	T	W	T	F	S	S

Open BHols. Due to staffing restrictions, property may not open as publicised. Please tel. in advance

Unless indicated, last admission is always 30mins before closing time

Polesden Lacey

Great Bookham, nr Dorking, Surrey RH5 6BD

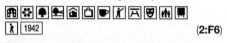

| 1942 | (2:F6)

Regency country house with renowned Edwardian interiors and gardens, set in beautiful downland countryside

Experience this beautiful Regency house, which is located in an exceptional setting and enjoys stunning views across the Surrey Hills. Once the home of poet and playwright Richard Brinsley Sheridan at the end of the 18th century, Polesden Lacey was remodelled in 1906-9 by the Hon. Mrs Ronald Greville, a well-known Edwardian hostess, and was the venue for the honeymoon of the future King George VI and Queen Elizabeth in 1923. Enjoy Mrs Greville's collections of fine paintings, furniture, porcelain and silver – which are displayed in the reception rooms and galleries, as they were at the time of her celebrated house parties. Then explore the beautiful walled rose garden, with its variety of scented plants, before strolling through the extensive grounds and lawns. There are also a number of landscape walks to try out.

What's new in 2009 Refurbished visitor facilities with the addition of a farm shop from March

⭐ Admission to house by timed tickets at busy times

Polesden Lacey								
House								
14 Mar–24 Oct	11–5	M	T	**W**	**T**	**F**	**S**	**S**
25 Oct–1 Nov	11–4	M	T	**W**	**T**	**F**	**S**	**S**
Garden/restaurant/garden shop/farm shop								
1 Feb–13 Feb	10–4	**M**	**T**	**W**	**T**	**F**	S	S
14 Feb–24 Oct	10–5	**M**	**T**	**W**	**T**	**F**	S	S
25 Oct–31 Jan 10*	10–4	**M**	**T**	**W**	**T**	**F**	S	S

Open BH Mons. Admission to house by timed ticket at busy times. Tickets issued at reception on a first-come, first-served basis and cannot be booked in advance. Tickets may run out at peak times – please arrive early. *Garden, restaurant, garden shop, farm shop closed 24/25 Dec. Gift shop closed 24–26 Dec

ℹ️ **T** 01372 458203 (Infoline), 01372 452048
E polesdenlacey@nationaltrust.org.uk

🚶 Free garden tours by volunteer guides on most days when the house is open. Special tours of the house for booked groups only at an additional charge

🎭 Events include the Polesden Lacey Festival: an open-air theatre and music festival. House open for special events on selected dates during Mar, Nov & Dec

🚶 Self-guided walks on the estate (free leaflet available)

Polesden Lacey: extensively remodelled in 1906-9, this Regency house enjoys an exceptional setting

Most Trust properties offer Gift Aid on Entry for non-members, see page 10

[icons row]
Building [icons] **Grounds** [icons]

🏠 NT gift shop, garden shop and farm shop

🍴 Licensed restaurant. Booked Christmas lunches throughout Dec

👶 Baby-changing facilities. Baby feeding facilities. Hip-carrying infant seats for loan. Children's play area. Children's quiz/trail. Family activity packs. Tracker Packs

📖 Suitable for school groups. Learning Officer

🐕 On leads in designated parts of the grounds and car park. Under close control on landscape walks, estate and farmland

➡️ [187:TQ136522] **Foot**: North Downs Way within ⅔ml. **Bus**: Countryliner 479 ≋ Leatherhead–Little Bookham, alight Great Bookham 1½ml. **Station**: Boxhill & Westhumble 2ml; Dorking 4ml. **Road**: 5ml NW of Dorking, 2ml S of Great Bookham, off A246 Leatherhead–Guildford road

🅿️ Parking, 200yds (pay & display), 7:30–dusk, £2.50. Fee redeemable against purchases over £10 off a single transaction in shops or tea-room or NT membership taken out at Polesden Lacey. Car parking free 1–23 Dec

NT properties nearby
Box Hill, Clandon Park, Claremont Landscape Garden, Hatchlands Park, River Wey and Dapdune Wharf

Priory Cottages

1 Mill Street, Steventon, Abingdon, Oxfordshire OX13 6SP

🏠 🚶 1939   (2:C5)

Former monastic buildings, now converted into two houses

⭐ Priory Cottage South only open. No WC

ℹ️ **T** 01793 762209
   E priorycottages@nationaltrust.org.uk

➡️ 4ml S of Abingdon

Priory Cottages									
2 Apr–24 Sep	2–6		M	T	W	**T**	F	S	S
Admission by written appointment with the tenant									

Quebec House

Quebec Square, Westerham, Kent TN16 1TD

🏠 🚶 🛈 👶 1918   (2:G6)

Childhood home of General James Wolfe, victor of the Battle of Quebec (1759)

This Grade I-listed gabled house in the beautiful village of Westerham has features of significant architectural and historical interest. It has 16th-century origins and was extended and changed in the 18th and 20th centuries. Quebec House was the childhood home of General James Wolfe and contains family and military memorabilia. The old coach house contains an exhibition about the Battle of Quebec (1759).

What's new in 2009 Room displays reminiscent of the 1720s

ℹ️ **T** 01732 866368 (Infoline), 01732 868381
   E quebechouse@nationaltrust.org.uk

🛈 Family activities

[icons] **Building** [icons]
Grounds [icon]

👶 Family trails and activities

➡️ [187:TQ449541] **Bus**: SelKent 246 from ≋ Bromley North (passing ≋ Bromley South); Arriva 401 from ≋ Sevenoaks (also ≋ Tunbridge Wells Suns). **Station**: Sevenoaks 4ml; Oxted 4ml. **Road**: at E end of village, on N side of A25, facing junction with B2026 Edenbridge road. M25 exit 5 or 6

🅿️ Parking (not NT), 200yds to E of Quebec House on A25. Visitors should then follow footpath beside A25 to house

NT properties nearby
Chartwell, Emmetts Garden, Ightham Mote, Knole, Toys Hill

Quebec House									
14 Mar–1 Nov	1–5		M	T	**W**	**T**	**F**	**S**	**S**
Garden/exhibition									
14 Mar–1 Nov	12–5		M	T	**W**	**T**	**F**	**S**	**S**
Open BH Mons									

If you enjoyed discovering Quebec House, then a visit to Knole will be sure to interest you

River Wey and Godalming Navigations and Dapdune Wharf

Navigations Office and Dapdune Wharf, Wharf Road, Guildford, Surrey GU1 4RR

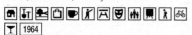

📅 1964 (2:F6)

Tranquil waterway running for nearly 20 miles through the heart of Surrey

The Wey was one of the first British rivers to be made navigable, and opened to barge traffic in 1653. This 15½-mile waterway linked Guildford to Weybridge on the Thames, and then to London. The Godalming Navigations, opened in 1764, enabled barges to work a further four miles upriver. The award-winning visitor centre at Dapdune Wharf in Guildford tells the story of the Navigations and the people who lived and worked on them through interactive exhibitions. Visitors can see where the huge Wey barges were built and climb aboard *Reliance*, one of the last surviving barges. Boat trips are available.

[i] T 01483 561389
E riverwey@nationaltrust.org.uk

Tours of Dapdune Wharf and guided walks along the towpath by arrangement

The River Wey on an autumn morning

Programme of events

Year-round guided walks programme

Building Grounds

Small shop at Dapdune Wharf

Small tea-room at Dapdune Wharf

Pushchairs admitted. Children's quiz/trail. Baby-changing facilities at Dapdune Wharf

Suitable for school groups. Education room/centre. Hands-on activities

On leads at Dapdune Wharf and lock areas; elsewhere under control

Cyclists welcome, but the towpath is very narrow and cyclists are asked to give way to other users and to dismount in lock areas

→ [186:SU993502] **River**: visiting craft can enter from the Thames at Shepperton or slipways at Guildford or Pyrford. Visitor moorings available at Dapdune Wharf and along towpath side of Navigations. **Foot**: North Downs Way crosses Navigations south of Guildford. Easy access from town centre on foot via towpath. **Bus**: Arriva 28 Guildford–Woking, Stagecoach Hants & Surrey 20 Guildford–Aldershot, Arriva 4 Guildford–Park Barn (cricket ground, 100yds). **Station**: Addlestone, Byfleet & New Haw, Guildford, Farncombe & Godalming all close to the Navigations. **Road**: Dapdune Wharf is on Wharf Road to rear of Surrey County Cricket Ground, off Woodbridge Rd (A322), Guildford. Access to rest of Navigations from A3 & M25

[P] Free parking, 10yds at Dapdune Wharf. Parking for the Navigations available in Godalming town centre, Catteshall Road bridge. Dapdune Wharf: Bowers Lane (Guildford), Send village, Newark Lane (B367) and New Haw Lock

NT properties nearby
Clandon Park, Claremont Landscape Garden, Hatchlands Park, Polesden Lacey, Shalford Mill, Winkworth Arboretum

River Wey and Dapdune Wharf			M	T	W	T	F	S	S
28 Mar–1 Nov	11–5		**M**	T	**W**	**T**	**F**	**S**	**S**

River trips 11–4 (conditions permitting). Access to towpath during daylight hours all year

For general and membership enquiries, please telephone 0844 800 1895

Runnymede

Runnymede Estate Office, North Lodge, Windsor Road, Old Windsor, Berkshire SL4 2JL

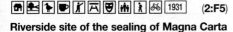 1931   (2:F5)

Riverside site of the sealing of Magna Carta

Runnymede is an attractive area of riverside meadows, grassland and broadleaved woodland, rich in flora and fauna, and with a network of pleasant footpaths. It was on this site, in 1215, that King John sealed Magna Carta, an event commemorated by the American Bar Association Memorial. The John F. Kennedy Memorial and various memorial trees are indicative of the area's importance in world history. Also here are the Fairhaven Lodges and Kiosks, designed by Lutyens, one of which is now an art gallery.

What's new in 2009 Art gallery with exhibitions and art courses throughout the year. Tel. 0845 200 8453 or visit www.1215art.com

★ (Runnymede is in the county of Surrey. Postal address as above.) The information given below relates to the Runnymede side of the river. WC only available when tea-room is open, tel. 01784 477110. No barbecues

ℹ **T** 01784 432891
   E runnymede@nationaltrust.org.uk

𝕏 Guided walks throughout the year

🏃 Three waymarked paths and network of footpaths; information/map guide available

♿ 🚻 👓 📷 **Building** 📖 **Grounds** 📖 📖

🍽 Magna Carta Tea-room (not NT)

👶 Pushchairs admitted

🐕 On leads near livestock

🚲 Cycling permitted on Thames Path. NCN4 nearby

➔ [176:TQ007720] **Foot**: 1¼ml of Thames Path on property. **Bus**: Runnymede, 1¼ml from

Runnymede							
All year	**M**	**T**	**W**	**T**	**F**	**S**	**S**

Memorials car park (hard-standing): 15 April–15 Sept, 8:30–7. 16 Sept–14 April, 8:30–5. Car parks close at dusk if earlier. Closed 25/26 December. Riverside car park (seasonal): 15 April–15 Sept, 10–7. When ground conditions allow

Memorials: First 71 🚉 Egham–Old Windsor, alight 'Bells of Ouzeley'. **Station**: Egham ½ml from Runnymede, 1½ml from Memorials; Wraysbury 1ml from Ankerwycke.
Road: Runnymede: on the Thames, 2ml W of Runnymede Bridge, on S side of A308 (M25, exit 13), 6ml E of Windsor

🅿 Parking (pay & display). Limited space for coaches on hard-standing, grass surface car park closed when wet

NT properties nearby
Cliveden, Osterley Park and House, River Wey and Dapdune Wharf

The river meadows at Runnymede, Surrey

St John's Jerusalem

Sutton-at-Hone, Dartford, Kent DA4 9HQ

✚ ❀ 1943   (2:H5)

Tranquil garden and 13th-century chapel

★ Occupied as a private residence, maintained and managed by a tenant on the Trust's behalf. Access is to the chapel and garden only

ℹ **T** 01732 810378 (c/o Ightham Mote)
   E stjohnsjerusalem@nationaltrust.org.uk

➔ 3ml S of Dartford at Sutton-at-Hone

St John's Jerusalem								
1 Apr–30 Sep	2–6	M	T	**W**	T	F	S	S
7 Oct–28 Oct	2–4	M	T	**W**	T	F	S	S

Show your card and display sticker for free parking

Sandham Memorial Chapel

Harts Lane, Burghclere, nr Newbury,
Hampshire RG20 9JT

 1947 (2:C6)

**Chapel containing Stanley Spencer's
visionary paintings**

Set amid pleasant countryside, this modest red-brick building houses an unexpected treasure – an outstanding series of wall paintings by Stanley Spencer. Inspired by his experiences during the First World War, and influenced by Giotto's Arena Chapel in Padua, the remarkable paintings are peppered with highly personal and unexpected detail. The work, which took six years to complete, is one of Spencer's finest achievements and an internationally recognised monument of British art.

⭐ As there is no lighting in the chapel it is best to view the paintings on a bright day. Groups by arrangement only to avoid delay. No WC (contact property for details of nearby facilities)

ℹ️ **T** 01635 278394
E sandham@nationaltrust.org.uk

🔵 Building 🔵
Grounds 🔵

📕 Books on Stanley Spencer and related subjects on sale

👪 Pushchairs and baby back-carriers admitted. Children's quiz/trail

🔲 Suitable for school groups. Talks available. Out-of-hours visits available on request

🐕 In grounds on leads only

➡️ [174:SU463608] **Bus**: Cango C21/2 'demand-responsive' service from Newbury. Book on 0845 602 4135. **Station**: Newbury 4ml. **Road**: 4ml S of Newbury, ½ml E of A34. From M4, follow A34, then brown signs. From A339 (Basingstoke to Newbury) follow brown signs and white NT signs

🅿️ No parking on site. Parking in lay-by opposite chapel and village car park, ½ml

NT properties nearby
Basildon Park, The Vyne

Sandham Memorial Chapel										
28 Feb–29 Mar	11–3	M	T	W	T	F	**S**	**S**
1 Apr–27 Sep	11–5	M	T	**W**	**T**	**F**	**S**	**S**
30 Sep–31 Oct	11–3	M	T	**W**	**T**	**F**	**S**	**S**
1 Nov–20 Dec	11–3	M	T	W	T	F	**S**	**S**
Open BH Mons: 11–5. Open other times by appointment								

Scotney Castle

Lamberhurst, Tunbridge Wells, Kent TN3 8JN

1970 (2:17)

Victorian country house and 14th-century ruined castle with romantic garden in a wooded estate

Sandham Memorial Chapel was built in the 1920s to house paintings by Stanley Spencer

Dogs assisting visitors with disabilities are always welcome

Scotney Castle was home to the Hussey family from the late 18th century and in 1835 Edward Hussey III, who took the 'Picturesque' style as his inspiration, commissioned eminent architect Anthony Salvin to design a new country house in an Elizabethan style. The celebrated gardens, designed around the ruins of a 14th-century moated castle, feature spectacular displays of rhododendrons, azaleas and kalmia in May and June, wisteria and roses ramble over the ruins in summer, and trees and shrubs provide rich colour in autumn. There are fine walks through the estate, with its parkland, woodland, hop farm and wonderful vistas and views. The country house is opening in stages over the next few years, with selected rooms open at the moment. The different styles of each room show visitors how a house can be changed to accommodate three generations of a family alongside modern living.

⭐ Designated one of the 'Seven Wonders of the Weald'

ℹ️ **T** 01892 893820 (Infoline), 01892 893868
E scotneycastle@nationaltrust.org.uk

🏃 By arrangement and subject to availability

♿ Throughout the season

🚶 Estate walks guide on sale at visitor reception and shop. Self-guided estate walks are also available to download from the NT website

♿ 🅿️ 🅿️ 🚻 ·· 💿 📷 House 🐾 Grounds 💺 ➡️ ♿

🛍️ NT shop. Plant sales

☕ Tea-room

🚼 Baby-changing facilities. Pushchairs admitted to garden. Baby carriers available for loan. Children's quiz/trail

🐕 On leads and on estate walks only

➡️ [188:TQ688353] **Foot:** links to local footpath network. **Cycle:** NCN18, 3ml. **Bus:** Arriva 256 Tunbridge Wells–Wadhurst (passing 🚃 Tunbridge Wells), alight Lamberhurst Green, 1ml. **Station:** Wadhurst 5½ml. **Road:** 1ml S of Lamberhurst off A21

🅿️ Parking, 130yds

NT properties nearby
Bateman's, Bodiam Castle, Sissinghurst Castle Garden

Scotney Castle									
House/garden*									
28 Feb–1 Nov	11–5	M	T	**W**	**T**	**F**	**S**	**S**
7 Nov–20 Dec	11–4	M	T	W	T	F	**S**	**S**
Shop/catering**									
28 Feb–1 Nov	11–5	M	T	**W**	**T**	**F**	**S**	**S**
7 Nov–20 Dec	11–4	M	T	**W**	**T**	**F**	**S**	**S**
Estate walks									
All year		**M**	**T**	**W**	**T**	**F**	**S**	**S**

*Garden closes 5:30, 28 Feb–1 Nov. **Shop closes 5:30, 28 Feb–1 Nov. Open BH Mons & Good Fri. Last admission 1hr before closing. Closes dusk if earlier. House timed tickets

Scotney Castle, with the Victorian country house beyond

Shalford Mill

Shalford, nr Guildford, Surrey GU4 8BS

❌ 🚻 🏃 🖼️ 1932   **(2:E6)**

18th-century watermill with well-preserved machinery

⭐ No WC. Regular guided tours. No parking at Mill

ℹ️ **T** 01483 561389
E shalfordmill@nationaltrust.org.uk

➡️ 1½ml S of Guildford on A281 opposite Seahorse Inn

Shalford Mill									
29 Mar–1 Nov	11–5	M	T	**W**	T	F	S	**S**

Guided tours for groups by prior arrangement, except Wed & Sun

Sheffield Park Garden

Sheffield Park, East Sussex TN22 3QX

 (2:G7)

Internationally renowned landscape garden and parkland

This magnificent informal landscape garden was laid out in the 18th century by 'Capability' Brown and further developed in the early years of the 20th century by its owner, Arthur G. Soames. The original four lakes form the centrepiece. There are dramatic shows of daffodils and bluebells in spring, and the rhododendrons and azaleas are spectacular in early summer. Autumn brings stunning colours from the many rare trees and shrubs, and winter walks can be enjoyed in this garden for all seasons. Visitors can now explore South Park, a recent acquisition of 107 hectares (265 acres) of historic parkland, with stunning views.

What's new in 2009 South Park open for the first time. Historic cricket pitch restored with matches planned for summer

Autumn at Sheffield Park Garden, East Sussex

⭐ Closed Sunday 28 June for 'Old England v Old Australia' cricket match (contact property for details)

ℹ **T** 01825 790231
E sheffieldpark@nationaltrust.org.uk

📅 Events programme throughout the year, inc. 'Old England v Old Australia' cricket match, 28 June. Contact property for details and tickets

🚶 Waymarked routes across the new parkland

♿ 🅿️ 🚻 ⋯ 📷 🔧 🔩 🔲 Building 🏠 ♿ Grounds 🏠 ➡️ 🔲

🏪 Shop selling NT products, plants & outdoor gifts

🍴 Tea-room (not NT) adjoins car park

🚼 Baby-changing facilities. Pushchairs and baby back-carriers admitted. Children's quiz/trail. Family activity packs. All-terrain pushchair and back-carriers available

🏫 Suitable for school groups

🐕 On leads in parkland only. Restrictions apply when livestock grazing

➔ [198:TQ415240] **Bus**: Bluebell Railway link (Metrobus 473) from near ☒ East Grinstead–Kingscote station, Countryliner 121 from close ☒ Lewes (Sat only), 246 from Uckfield (Mon, Wed, Fri only). **Station**: Sheffield Park (Bluebell Rly) ¾ml; Uckfield 6ml; Haywards Heath 7ml. **Road**: midway between East Grinstead and Lewes, 5ml NW of Uckfield, on E side of A275 (between A272 & A22)

🅿️ Free parking

NT properties nearby
Alfriston Clergy House, Devil's Dyke , Nymans, Standen, Wakehurst Place

Sheffield Park Garden									
7 Feb–1 Mar	10:30–4	M	T	W	T	F	**S**	**S**
4 Mar–3 May	10:30–5:30	M	**T**	**W**	**T**	**F**	**S**	**S**
5 May–1 Jun	10:30–5:30	**M**	**T**	**W**	**T**	**F**	**S**	**S**
3 Jun–4 Oct	10:30–5:30	M	**T**	**W**	**T**	**F**	**S**	**S**
6 Oct–2 Nov	10:30–5:30	**M**	**T**	**W**	**T**	**F**	**S**	**S**
4 Nov–3 Jan 10	10:30–4	M	**T**	**W**	**T**	**F**	**S**	**S**
9 Jan–31 Jan 10	10:30–4	M	T	W	T	F	**S**	**S**
South Park									
2 Feb–31 Jan 10	Dawn–dusk	**M**	**T**	**W**	**T**	**F**	**S**	**S**

Open BH Mons. Closed 28 June, 21–27 Dec. Last admission 1hr before closing time or dusk if earlier

Sissinghurst Castle Garden

Sissinghurst, nr Cranbrook, Kent TN17 2AB

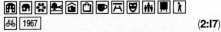

🚲 1967 (2:I7)

Garden in a ruin in a farm, created by Vita Sackville-West and Harold Nicolson

This internationally renowned garden was developed by Vita Sackville-West and Sir Harold Nicolson around the surviving parts of an Elizabethan mansion. It comprises small enclosed compartments, with colour throughout the season, resulting in an intimate and romantic atmosphere. The surrounding Wealden landscape and farm were central to Vita and Harold's love and overall vision for Sissinghurst. The new vegetable garden, now fully productive, supplies fresh vegetables and fruit to the licensed restaurant. The garden is more peaceful after three.

What's new in 2009 Vegetable garden open May to September, 12–4

⭐ The library and Vita Sackville-West's study are open 14 March–1 November, until 4

ℹ️ **T** 01580 710701 (Infoline), 01580 710700
E sissinghurst@nationaltrust.org.uk

🎭 Garden supper evenings, lecture lunches, estate walks, local food events and literary festival, monthly farmers' market

🚶 Woodland & lake walks open all year. Free. Leaflet available

♿ 🅿️ 🐕 ♿ ⠿ 📷 🔄 📖 🔔 🏛️
Building ♿♿♿ **Grounds** ♿♿➡️

🏠 NT shop. Plant sales

☕ Restaurant (licensed) serving fresh produce from the farm. Coffee shop near car park, serving light refreshments and ice-cream

Sissinghurst Castle Garden, Kent

👶 Baby-changing facilities. Baby back-carriers for loan. Children's quiz/trail. Children's activity packs. No pushchairs admitted in the garden as paths are narrow and uneven. Ball games etc not allowed in garden. Pond dipping. Family events throughout season

🏫 Suitable for school groups. Hands-on activities. Adult study days. Adult education in association with University of Kent

🚴 Cycling on local lanes and bridlepaths

➔ [188:TQ810380] **Foot**: from Sissinghurst village, past church to footpath on left, signposted to garden. Path can get muddy. **Cycle**: NCN18, 8ml. **Bus**: special link from Staplehurst to garden, Tues, Fri, Sun & BHols only (tel. property), otherwise Arriva 5 Maidstone–Hawkhurst (passing ≅ Staplehurst), alight Sissinghurst, 1¼ml. **Station**: Staplehurst 5½ml. **Road**: 2ml NE of Cranbrook, 1ml E of Sissinghurst village on Biddenden Road, off A262

🅿️ Parking, 315yds, £2

NT properties nearby
Bateman's, Bodiam Castle, Scotney Castle, Smallhythe Place, Stoneacre

Sissinghurst Castle Garden										
Garden*										
15 Mar–2 Nov	11–6:30		**M**	**T**	W	T	**F**	**S**	**S**	
27 Oct–1 Nov	11–4		**M**	**T**	W	T	**F**	**S**	**S**	
Vegetable garden										
2 May–27 Sep	12–4		**M**	**T**	W	T	**F**	**S**	**S**	
Shop/restaurant										
28 Feb–8 Mar	11–4		M	T	W	T	F	**S**	**S**	
14 Mar–26 Oct	10:30–5:30		**M**	**T**	W	T	**F**	**S**	**S**	
14 Mar–24 Mar	10–5:30		**M**	**T**	W	T	**F**	**S**	**S**	
27 Oct–1 Nov**	11–4		**M**	**T**	W	T	**F**	S	S	
2 Nov–22 Dec	11–4		**M**	**T**	W	T	**F**	**S**	**S**	
Coffee shop/garden shop										
1 Feb–8 Mar	11–4		M	T	W	T	F	**S**	**S**	
14 Mar–10 Apr	11–5:30		**M**	**T**	W	T	**F**	**S**	**S**	
16 May–31 Aug	11–5:30		**M**	**T**	**W**	**T**	**F**	**S**	**S**	
1 Sep–27 Oct	11–5:30		**M**	**T**	W	T	**F**	**S**	**S**	
Tower/library										
14 Mar–26 Oct	11–5		**M**	**T**	W	T	**F**	**S**	**S**	
27 Oct–1 Nov	11–4		**M**	**T**	W	T	**F**	**S**	**S**	

*Garden opens at 10 on weekends. Closes dusk if earlier. Restrictions on entry into the garden may apply.
**Shop/restaurant opens 10 on weekends 27 Oct–1 Nov

For public transport details, see page 377

Smallhythe Place

Smallhythe, Tenterden, Kent TN30 7NG

🏠 ❀ 🏛 🍽 🎬 ♿ 👪 🎭 1939   **(2:I7)**

Smallhythe Place								
28 Feb–22 Mar	11–5	M	T	W	T	F	**S**	**S**
28 Mar–1 Nov	11–5	**M**	**T**	**W**	T	F	**S**	**S**
Café								
As house	12–4							

Open Good Fri. Last admission 4:30 or dusk if earlier

Ellen Terry's early 16th-century house and cottage gardens

The half-timbered house, built in the early 16th century when Smallhythe was a thriving shipbuilding yard, was the home of the Victorian actress Ellen Terry from 1899 to 1928 and contains her fascinating theatre collection. The cottage grounds include her rose garden, orchard, nuttery, a wonderful display of wild flowers and the Barn Theatre, which holds exhibitions and regular performances of plays, music and talks.

What's new in 2009 Exciting programme of events in the Barn Theatre

ℹ️ **T** 01580 762334
   E smallhytheplace@nationaltrust.org.uk

🎭 Including indoor and open-air theatre. Music and beer festival

♿ ⋯ 🅿️ 🎧 📖 🎵 Building 🏢 🏛
Grounds 🏛 ➡️

🏠 Small collection of souvenirs. Occasional sales of plants from the garden

🍽 Small café (licensed) serving hot and cold drinks, alcoholic drinks and small snacks including ice-cream. Refreshments, including full meals, also available at Chapel Down Winery (not NT), 500yds from property

👪 Children's quiz/trail. Children's activity packs. Tracker Packs. Children must be accompanied by an adult

🎭 Suitable for school groups

🐾 In the grounds

➡️ [189:TQ893300] **Bus**: Coastal Coaches 312 🚃 Rye–Tenterden. **Station**: Rye 8ml; Appledore 8ml; Headcorn 10ml. **Road**: 2ml S of Tenterden, on E side of Rye road (B2082)

🅿️ Free parking (not NT), 50yds. Coaches park at Chapel Down Winery, 500yds

NT properties nearby
Bodiam Castle, Lamb House, Scotney Castle, Sissinghurst Castle Garden

Roses at Smallhythe Place, Kent

South Foreland Lighthouse

The Front, St Margaret's Bay, Dover, Kent CT15 6HP

🏠 🌊 🏰 🏛 🏠 🎣 🎬 🎭 👪 🎭
🚶 1989   **(2:K6)**

Fascinating and distinctive Victorian lighthouse

A striking landmark on the White Cliffs of Dover, this beautiful and historic building was the first to have an electrically powered signal and was used in experiments by Faraday and Marconi. Today, visitors can climb to the top of the lighthouse and enjoy views across east Kent and the Channel.

For general and membership enquiries, please telephone 0844 800 1895

i **T** 01304 852463
E southforeland@nationaltrust.org.uk

All visitors guided or accompanied in the tower. Out-of-hours tours by arrangement; guided walks to the lighthouse from the White Cliffs Visitor Centre, April–October

Children's activities

On Saxon Shore Way. Public footpaths in all directions. See White Cliffs of Dover

Building Grounds

Basic shop on ground floor

Bottled water and confectionery available from shop

Pushchairs and baby back-carriers admitted. Children's quiz/trail. Children's events. Pushchairs on ground floor (reception) only due to stairs

Suitable for school groups. Group activity pack

In the grounds

➔ [179:TR359433] **No vehicular access**. **Foot**: on public footpaths 2½ml from Dover, 1ml from St Margaret's. **Cycle**: NCN1, ½ml. **Bus**: Stagecoach in E Kent Diamond 15; Canterbury–Dover–Deal, alight Bay Hill 1ml (via Lighthouse Road). **Station**: Martin Mill 2½ml; Dover Priory 3½ml by footpath

P **No parking on site**. Drivers should park at White Cliffs of Dover (NT) and walk along clifftops to lighthouse (approx. 2ml) or park at St Margaret's village/bay and walk from there (approx. 1ml). Visitors with walking difficulties should tel. the property

NT properties nearby
The White Cliffs of Dover

South Foreland Lighthouse										
27 Mar–5 Apr	11–5:30	M	T	W	T		F	S	S
6 Apr–19 Apr	11–5:30	M	T	W	T		F	S	S
20 Apr–24 May	11–5:30	M	T	W	T		F	S	S
25 May–31 May	11–5:30	M	T	W	T		F	S	S
1 Jun–19 Jul	11–5:30	M	T	W	T		F	S	S
20 Jul–6 Sep	11–5:30	M	T	W	T		F	S	S
7 Sep–25 Oct	11–5:30	M	T	W	T		F	S	S
26 Oct–1 Nov	11–5:30	M	T	W	T		F	S	S

Admission by guided tour, last tour 5. Open by arrangement during closed period for booked groups only

Sprivers Garden

Horsmonden, Kent TN12 8DR

1966   (2:H7)

Small 18th-century style formal garden with nearby woodland walk

⭐ Occupied as a private residence, administered and maintained on the Trust's behalf by a tenant. No access to the house. No parking on site. No WC

i **T** 01892 893868
E sprivers@nationaltrust.org.uk

➔ 3ml N of Lamberhurst on B2162

Sprivers Garden									
7 June	2–5	M	T	W	T	F	S	**S**
10 June	2–5	M	T	**W**	T	F	S	S
13 June	2–5	M	T	W	T	F	**S**	S

Woodland walk (outside garden) open all year

South Foreland Lighthouse, Kent: a striking landmark

Standen

West Hoathly Road, East Grinstead,
West Sussex RH19 4NE

[icons] 📺 1973 (2:G7)

Arts & Crafts family home with Morris & Co. interiors, set in a beautiful hillside garden

Life in a Victorian family home is brought vividly to life in this gem of the Arts & Crafts Movement. Standen is hidden at the end of a quiet Sussex lane with breathtaking views over the High Weald and Weir Wood Reservoir. The design of the house, inspired by the original medieval farmhouse, is a monument to the combined genius of architect Philip Webb and his friend William Morris. All the big names of the Arts & Crafts period are represented, including ceramics by William De Morgan, furniture by George Jack and metalwork by W. A. S. Benson. The beautiful five-hectare (twelve-acre) hillside gardens provide year-round interest and the woodlands now offer a number of easily accessible and picturesque walks.

⭐ Some exterior decoration may take place during 2009. Access to parts of the garden may be restricted during periods of bad weather. Only selected show rooms in house will be open outside the main visiting season and conservation work may be taking place

ℹ️ T 01342 323029
E standen@nationaltrust.org.uk

Standen, West Sussex: Arts & Crafts family home

🎭 Study days & demonstrations. Exhibitions. Craft workshops. Guided walks. Family activities

🚶 Nature walks through the Standen Estate: leaflets available from ticket office

[accessibility icons]
Building [icons] Grounds [icons]

🏬 Shop specialises in Arts & Crafts Movement merchandise. Plant sales and garden accessories area. Licensed, selling local beers and wines

🍴 The Barn Restaurant (licensed) serving variety of hot and cold dishes. Reservations not possible. Children's menu

👶 Baby-changing facilities. Front-carrying baby slings and hip-carrying infant seats for loan. Family activities. Family activity packs. Children's quiz/trails

🏫 Suitable for school groups. Hands-on activities. Adult study days. Arts & Crafts resource room

🐕 On leads and only in designated areas; under close control on woodland walks

➡️ [187:TQ389356] **Cycle**: NCN21, 1¼ml. **Bus**: Bluebell Railway link 473 from ☒ East Grinstead; Metrobus 84 ☒ East Grinstead–Crawley (passing ☒ Three Bridges), alight at approach road just north of Saint Hill, ½ml, or at Saint Hill, then ¾ml by footpath. **Station**: East Grinstead 2ml; Kingscote (Bluebell Railway) 2ml. **Road**: 2ml S of East Grinstead, signposted from town centre and B2110 (Turners Hill Road)

🅿️ Free parking, 200yds

NT properties nearby
Nymans, Sheffield Park Garden, Toys Hill, Wakehurst Place

Standen								
28 Feb–8 Mar*	11–4:30	M	T	W	T	F	**S**	**S**
14 Mar–26 Jul*	11–4:30	M	T	**W**	**T**	**F**	**S**	**S**
27 Jul–31 Aug*	11–4:30	**M**	T	**W**	**T**	**F**	**S**	**S**
2 Sep–1 Nov*	11–4:30	M	T	**W**	**T**	**F**	**S**	**S**
7 Nov–20 Dec	11–3	M	T	W	T	F	**S**	**S**

Open BH Mons. Some queueing on approach to property may occur on BHols. *Shop/restaurant close at 5, garden at 5:30

Most Trust properties offer Gift Aid on Entry for non-members, see page 10

Stoneacre

Otham, Maidstone, Kent ME15 8RS

🏠 😊 1928 ~ **(2:I6)**

15th-century half-timbered yeoman's house and harmonious garden

⭐ Occupied as a private residence, administered and maintained on the Trust's behalf by a tenant. Not suitable for coaches. No WC

ℹ️ **T** 01892 893842
   E stoneacre@nationaltrust.org.uk

➡️ At N end of Otham village, 3ml SE of Maidstone, 1ml S of A20

Stoneacre									
21 Mar–3 Oct	11–5:30	M	T	W	T	F	**S**	**S**
Open BH Mons								

Stowe Landscape Gardens

Buckingham, Buckinghamshire MK18 5DQ

📶 1990 **(2:D2)**

Breathtakingly beautiful landscape gardens

A beautiful creation of the 18th century, Stowe is one of Europe's foremost landscape gardens. Nestling among spectacular vistas and vast open spaces are more than 40 monuments and temples, each with its own special significance. Stowe is the perfect setting for a family picnic or for those seeking peace and tranquillity, with walks and trails for all to enjoy. With the changing seasons, continuing restoration and a calendar of events for all the family, each visit provides something new. Visitors can also take a tour of Stowe House (not NT) or explore the 300 hectares (750 acres) of surrounding historic parkland.

What's new in 2009 Newly opened interpretation centre with jigsaws, timeline and comment board. Restoration of Sleeping Parlour and Sleeping Wood now complete

⭐ House (not NT), charge inc. NT members. Visitors to the gardens should allow plenty of time because of the extensive areas. Stowe House is used by Stowe School and opened to the public by Stowe House Preservation Trust. Tel. 01280 818166 for details or visit www.shpt.org for opening times

ℹ️ **T** 01494 755568 (Infoline), 01280 822850, 01280 818166 (House – not NT)
   E stowegarden@nationaltrust.org.uk

🚶 Guided tours in gardens at 11 & 2 most days

😀 Wide range of family events and activities. For details see website

🚶 Series of garden trails explore different areas and the stories behind Stowe Landscape Gardens

♿ 🅿️ 📠 🚾 📷 🔄 🔋 📺 Building 📶 ⬆️
Grounds 🔄 ➡️ 🔄

🛍️ Well-stocked shop offers variety of NT products as well as plants and outdoor garden gifts

☕ Tea-room 200yds from visitor reception

👶 Baby-changing and feeding facilities. Pushchairs and baby back-carriers admitted. Children's quiz/trail. Children's activity packs

🎭 Suitable for school groups. Live interpretation. Hands-on activities

🐕 On leads only

Stowe Landscape Gardens								
1 Feb–1 Mar	10:30–4	M	T	W	T	F	**S**	**S**
4 Mar–1 Nov	10:30–5:30	M	T	**W**	**T**	**F**	**S**	**S**
7 Nov–31 Jan 10	10:30–4	M	T	W	T	F	**S**	**S**
Shop								
1 Feb–1 Mar	10:30–4	M	T	W	T	F	**S**	**S**
4 Mar–1 Nov	10:30–5:30	M	T	**W**	**T**	**F**	**S**	**S**
4 Nov–18 Dec	11–3	M	T	**W**	**T**	**F**	S	S
7 Nov–31 Jan 10	10:30–4	M	T	W	T	F	**S**	**S**
Tea-room								
1 Feb–1 Mar	10:30–3:30	M	T	W	T	F	**S**	**S**
4 Mar–1 Nov	10:30–5	M	T	**W**	**T**	**F**	**S**	**S**
7 Nov–31 Jan 10	10:30–3:30	M	T	W	T	F	**S**	**S**
Parkland								
All year	Dawn–dusk	**M**	**T**	**W**	**T**	**F**	**S**	**S**

Open BH Mons. Last admission 1½hr before closing. Gardens closed Sat 23 May. Please note gardens may close early towards end of Oct due to shorter daylight hours. May close in severe weather

Unless indicated, last admission is always 30mins before closing time

→ [152:SP665366] **Foot**: 3ml from Buckingham along Stowe Avenue and through park. **Bus**: nearest buses serve Buckingham (3ml), then taxi. **Station**: Bicester North 9ml. **Road**: 3ml NW of Buckingham via Stowe Avenue, off A422 Buckingham–Banbury road. Motorway access from M40 (exits 9 to 11) and M1 (exits 13 or 15a)

P Free parking, 200yds

NT properties nearby
Canons Ashby House, Claydon House, King's Head, Waddesdon Manor

The Palladian bridge, Cobham monument and Gothic Temple at Stowe Landscape Gardens, Buckinghamshire

Uppark House and Garden

South Harting, Petersfield,
West Sussex GU31 5QR

T 1954   **(2:E8)**

Uppark: a tranquil and intimate 18th-century house

This gem on the South Downs, rescued after a major fire in 1989, houses an elegant Georgian interior with a famous Grand Tour collection which includes paintings, furniture and ceramics. An 18th-century dolls' house, with original contents, is one of the highlights. The complete servants' quarters in the basement are shown as they were in Victorian days when H. G. Wells's mother was housekeeper. The

beautiful and peaceful garden is now fully restored in the early 19th-century Picturesque style, in a downland and woodland setting.

What's new in 2009 Virtual tour of the show rooms and changing Fire Exhibition

⭐ Open on Good Friday

ℹ **T** 01730 825857 (Infoline), 01730 825415 **E** uppark@nationaltrust.org.uk

🎫 Free garden history tour at 2:30, first Thur of month (April–Oct) and every Thur in July and Aug

😃 School holiday trails and activities. Spring and autumn lecture lunches. Christmas events

🚶 Woodland walk

♿ P♿ D♿ ♿ •• 📷 ♿ ♿
Building ♿♿♿ **Grounds** ♿♿♿➡

🏠 NT shop. Plant sales

🍴 Licensed restaurant. Children's menu

👪 Baby-changing facilities. Hip-carrying infant seats for loan. Children's quiz/trail. Children's activity packs. Children's ball games area

🐕 On leads and only on Woodland Walk

→ [197:SU775177] **Foot**: South Downs Way within ⅔ml. **Bus**: Countryliner 54 ⚇ Petersfield–⚇ Chichester (bus stop is 500yds from property, via a steep hill). **Station**: Petersfield 5½ml. **Road**: 5ml SE of Petersfield on B2146, 1½ml S of South Harting

P Free parking, 300yds

NT properties nearby
Harting Down and Beacon Hill, Hinton Ampner, Petworth House and Park

Uppark House and Garden							
House							
29 Mar–29 Oct	12:30–4:30	**M**	**T**	**W**	**T**	F	S	S
Part of house							
5 Dec–10 Dec	11–3	**M**	**T**	**W**	**T**	F	S	S
Garden/shop/restaurant							
29 Mar–29 Oct	11:30–5	**M**	**T**	**W**	**T**	F	S	S
29 Nov–20 Dec	11–3:30	**M**	**T**	**W**	**T**	F	S	S

Open Good Fri. BH Mons & BH Suns: garden/shop/restaurant open 11–5 & house 11:30–4:30. Garden tours 1st Thur of each month and every Thur in July/Aug. Print Room open 1st Mon of each month, times as house

Charges for National Trust members apply on some special event days

The Vyne

Sherborne St John, Basingstoke,
Hampshire RG24 9HL

| 1956 | (2:D6) |

**A 16th-century house and estate and a
treasure trove of history**

Originally built as a great Tudor 'power house',
The Vyne was visited by King Henry VIII on at
least three occasions and was later home to the
Chute family for more than 350 years. Dramatic
improvements and changes over the centuries
have made The Vyne a fascinating microcosm of
changing fads and fashions over five centuries.
The house is filled with the original family
collection – an eclectic mix of fine furniture,
portraits, textiles and sculpture. The attractive
gardens and grounds feature an ornamental lake,
one of the earliest summerhouses in England and
woodland walks. A flourishing wetlands area,
with bird hide, attracts a wide diversity of wildlife.

What's new in 2009 The restoration of The
Vyne's Walled Garden into a working kitchen
garden continues with the new Glasshouse and
reinstated vegetable plots. Vegetables from the
Walled Garden and lamb from our local tenant
farmer are featured on the menu in the
Brewhouse restaurant, when available

⭐ Ball games and picnics only allowed in the
field before car park

ℹ️ **T** 01256 883858
E thevyne@nationaltrust.org.uk

🚶 Guided tours of house arranged for groups
(25–50) by appointment only 16 March–28
Oct: Mon, Tues & Wed 11–12

🎭 Open-air theatre, family events, Christmas
and lecture lunches. Extra value days – 1st &
2nd Mon of each month, excl. BHols

🚶 Woodland, parkland and wetland walks and
trails

♿ 🅿️ 🏛️ ⛪ ∴ 📷 ✂️ 💻 🎵 📶 🔲
Building 📶📶🦽 Grounds ♿

🏠 NT shop. Plant sales

🍴 Brewhouse (licensed) adjacent to house.
Kiosk in tea-garden open at busy times

The Oak Gallery at The Vyne, Hampshire

👶 Baby-changing facilities. High chairs and
colouring table. Hip-carrying infant seats for
loan. Children's quiz/trail. Tracker Packs

📕 Suitable for school groups

➡️ [175/186:SU639576] **Cycle**: NCN23, 1ml.
Bus: Stagecoach in Hampshire 45 from
Basingstoke (passing ≅ Basingstoke). No
Sun service. **Station**: Bramley 2½ml;
Basingstoke 4ml. **Road**: 4ml N of
Basingstoke between Bramley and Sherborne
St John. From Basingstoke Ring Road A339,
follow North Hampshire Hospital signs until
property signs. Follow A340 Aldermaston
Road towards Tadley. Right turn into
Morgaston Road. Right turn into car park

🅿️ Free parking, 40yds. ⅓ml walk through gardens
from visitor reception to house entrance

NT properties nearby
Basildon Park, Sandham Memorial Chapel

The Vyne			
House			
14 Mar–1 Nov	1–5*		**M T W** T F **S S**
House, Christmas opening			
12 Dec–20 Dec	11–3		**M T W** T F **S S**
Grounds/shop/restaurant			
1 Feb–8 Mar	11–5		M T W T F **S S**
14 Mar–1 Nov	11–5		**M T W** T F **S S**
7 Nov–29 Nov	11–3		M T W T F **S S**
30 Nov–23 Dec	11–3		**M T W** T F **S S**

*Open 11–5 at weekends. Open Good Fri & BHol
Mons: 11–5 (inc. house). Guided tours of house for
groups (25–50) by appointment only 16 March–28 Oct:
Mon, Tues & Wed 11–12. During busy periods timed
tickets may be issued for entry to house

Show your card and display sticker for free parking

Waddesdon Manor

Waddesdon, nr Aylesbury,
Buckinghamshire HP18 0JH

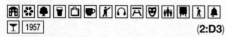

(2:D3)

**Magnificent house and grounds in the
style of a 19th-century French château**

Waddesdon Manor was built (1874-89) by Baron
Ferdinand de Rothschild to entertain his guests
and display his vast collection of 18th-century
French decorative arts. The furniture, Savonnerie
carpets and Sèvres porcelain rank in importance
with those in the Louvre in Paris and the Royal
and Wallace Collections in London. There is also
a fine collection of portraits by Gainsborough
and Reynolds, and works by Dutch and Flemish
Masters of the 17th century. The Victorian
gardens are considered one of the finest in
Britain and famous for the parterre, seasonal
displays, shady walks and views, fountains and
statuary. At its heart lies the aviary, stocked with
species that were once part of Baron Ferdinand's
collection. The Wine Cellars, modelled on the
private cellars at Château Lafite-Rothschild,
contain thousands of bottles of Rothschild wines
dating back to 1868. Look out for changing
displays in the refurbished Coach House and the
Woodland Playground.

What's new in 2009 House exhibitions of porcelain
and drawings

⭐ All visitors (inc. NT members) require timed
tickets to enter the house, available from the
ticket office. Last recommended admission to
house 2:30. 27/28 June 'MAD about
Waddesdon' festival, special admission prices
apply (inc. NT members). Admission free for
children in August. To visit the house, a gardens
ticket must be purchased. There are a limited
number of house tickets and they sell out
quickly on busy days (especially Bank Holidays
and Christmas). Timed tickets to the house can
be bought at least 24 hours in advance (booking
charge £3 per transaction). Tel. Monday to
Friday, 10–4 (not Bank Holidays). Groups must
book and pay in advance

The colourful parterre at the south front of Waddesdon Manor, Buckinghamshire

Dogs assisting visitors with disabilities are always welcome

ℹ️ **T** 01296 653211 (Infoline), 01296 653226
E waddesdonmanor@nationaltrust.org.uk

🚶 Free daily guided walks around garden, 11:30. Free wine cellar tour, 3, Wed

🎧 Adult and family audio tours of the house, £2. Includes free child audio tour

🎭 Special interest days, children's activities, wine tastings, music evenings, garden workshops, Christmas opening and events. Manor Restaurant monthly evening openings

🚶 Wildlife interpretation trail

♿ 🅿 🅿 💺 👁 🔄 🚶 🔼 🔄

Building ♿ 🔼 ♿ **Grounds** ♿ ➡️

🛍️ Gift, food and wine and new toy shops (not NT). Plant centre

🍽️ Manor Restaurant (not NT) (licensed). Open for breakfast, lunch and tea. Full Rothschild wine list. Children's menu. Stables Restaurant and Coffee Bar (not NT) (licensed) 800yds downhill from Manor. Land train transfer available. Simple fresh food. Children's menu. Summerhouse kiosk in the gardens and coffee bar kiosk in shop courtyard. Both open in good weather for alfresco snacks

👶 Baby-changing and feeding facilities. Front-carrying baby slings and hip-carrying infant seats for loan. Woodland playground and wildlife interpretation trail. Children's quiz/trail. Aviary. Children welcome in house under supervision. House tours for children during the school hols. Admission free for children in Aug in house

🎦 Live interpretation. Adult study days. Audio-visual presentations

➡️ [165:SP740169] **Bus**: Arriva 16 from Aylesbury (passing close ➤ Aylesbury). **Station**: Aylesbury 6ml; Haddenham & Thame Parkway 9ml. **Road**: access via Waddesdon village, 6ml NW of Aylesbury on A41; M40 (westbound) exit 6 or 7 via Thame & Long Crendon or M40 (eastbound) exit 9 via Bicester

🅿 Free parking

NT properties nearby
Claydon House, Cliveden, Hughenden Manor, King's Head, Stowe Landscape Gardens

Waddesdon Manor										
Gardens/shops/restaurants										
1 Feb–29 Mar	10–5	M	T	W	T	**F**	**S**	**S**		
1 Apr–23 Dec	10–5	M	T	**W**	**T**	**F**	**S**	**S**		
27 Dec–31 Dec	10–5	**M**	**T**	**W**	**T**	F	S	S		
House										
1 Apr–1 Nov	12–4*	M	T	**W**	**T**	**F**	**S**	**S**		
Christmas season in house										
11 Nov–23 Dec	12–4*	M	T	**W**	**T**	**F**	**S**	**S**		
21 Dec–22 Dec	12–4	**M**	**T**	W	T	F	S	S		
Bachelors' wing										
1 Apr–30 Oct	12–4	M	T	**W**	**T**	**F**	S	S		
Coffee bar										
1 Apr–23 Dec	11–5	M	T	**W**	**T**	**F**	**S**	**S**		
Summerhouse										
1 Apr–1 Nov	11–5	M	T	**W**	**T**	**F**	**S**	**S**		

*Opens 11 at weekends. Admission by timed ticket only, inc. NT members. Open BH Mons. Last admission 1hr before closing. Sculpture in garden uncovered week before Easter, weather permitting. Bachelors' Wing: space limited and entry cannot be guaranteed. Coffee bar & summerhouse open weather permitting

Wakehurst Place

Ardingly, nr Haywards Heath, West Sussex RH17 6TN

🏠 ❄️ 🌳 ♿ 🐕 🛍️ 🍽️ 🚶 🏞️ 🎭 👶 🎦 🚶 🔔
☂️ 1964   **(2:G7)**

Outstanding botanical garden with world's largest seed conservation project, leased and run by RBG, Kew

A vast and varied garden with plants from around the world, Wakehurst Place is internationally renowned for its combination of formal botanic gardens, extensive tree collections and its vital plant conservation work. Enjoy wonderful views across the woodland and lakes, and explore the wider estate with walks through the Loder Valley nature reserve, wetlands conservation area and sweeping woodland valleys. Wakehurst Place is a globally important site for plant conservation and research, with more than a billion seeds collected so far for future preservation. Visit the Millennium Seed Bank to see this project in action at the laboratory viewing area and interactive, touch-screen exhibition. There is a varied events calendar throughout the year and a formal learning programme for schools and education groups with an engaging Learning Centre in the house.

For events details, visit www.nationaltrust.org.uk/events

What's new in 2009 Enhanced schools' and adult learning programmes. New home-cooked dishes. Wider range at plant centre

⭐ **Wakehurst Place is funded and run by the Royal Botanical Gardens, Kew**. Free entry applies to National Trust and National Trust for Scotland members only. Reciprocal international organisation members do not receive free entry

ℹ️ **T** 01444 894066 (Infoline), 01444 894000
E wakehurst@kew.org

🚶 Guided tours daily

📅 Bluebell weekends, autumn colour festival, Christmas festivities, inc. regular family events all year round

🚶 Numerous signed walks

♿ 🅿️🚻🚻🚻🚻 **Building** ♿🚻
Grounds ♿➡️♿🚻

🛍️ Shop and plant centre (run by Royal Botanical Gardens Kew)

Wakehurst Place, West Sussex

💬 The Stables & Tack Room Restaurant (not NT) (licensed) adjacent to house. Children's menu. Seed Café (not NT) at Visitor Centre, with tables on veranda

🚼 Baby-changing facilities. Pushchairs and baby back-carriers admitted. Family guide. Children's quiz/trail

📖 Suitable for school groups. Education room/centre. Live interpretation. Hands-on activities. Adult study days

➡️ [187:TQ339314] **Foot**: footpath from Balcombe (4ml). **Bus**: Metrobus 81/82 Haywards Heath–Crawley, passing ≋ Haywards Heath and Three Bridges. **Station**: Haywards Heath 6ml; East Grinstead 6ml; Horsted Keynes (Bluebell Rly) 4ml. **Road**: on B2028, 1ml N of Ardingly; 3ml S of Turners Hill. From M23 exit 10, take A264 towards East Grinstead

🅿️ Free parking near Visitor Centre

NT properties nearby
Alfriston Clergy House, Bateman's, Chartwell, Emmetts Garden, Nymans, Sheffield Park Garden, Standen

Wakehurst Place								
Garden/shop/restaurant/house								
All year	10–6*	M	T	W	T	F	S	S

*Closes 4:30 1 Nov–31 Jan 10. Last admission to Seed Bank and house 1½hr before closing. Closed 24/25 Dec. Shop closed Easter Sun

West Green House Garden

West Green, Hartley Wintney, Hampshire RG27 8JB

❄️ 🛍️ 💬 1957   (2:D6)

Celebrated garden with an intriguing collection of follies

The delightful series of walled gardens surrounds a charming 18th-century house.

What's new in 2009 The garden is now only open for booked groups

⭐ The property is let by the NT and the house is not open to visitors. The lessee has kindly agreed to open the gardens **for booked groups only** and is responsible for all arrangements and facilities. There are limited visitor facilities. Entry free to NT members within

For public transport details, see page 377

West Wycombe Park, Hampshire

groups. Contact property for group prices (NT members pay group price less £8 entry)

i **T** 01252 844611
E westgreenhouse@nationaltrust.org.uk

Grounds

Shop (not NT). Plant sales (not NT)

Tea-room (not NT). Lunches and teas as arranged with group organisers

→ [175:SU745564] **Bus**: Stagecoach in Hampshire 200 Basingstoke–Camberley (passing Winchfield, Blackwater and Camberley), alight Phoenix Green, 1ml. **Station**: Winchfield 2ml. **Road**: 1ml W of Hartley Wintney, 10ml NE of Basingstoke, 1ml N of A30

P Coaches must park on the gravel car park before the gates and must not let passengers alight in the lane

NT properties nearby
Basildon Park, Sandham Memorial Chapel, The Vyne

West Green House Garden								
1 May–31 Jul	11–4	**M**	**T**	**W**	**T**	**F**	S	S
Open for booked groups only								

West Wycombe Park

West Wycombe, Buckinghamshire HP14 3AJ

1943 **(2:E4)**

Perfectly preserved rococo landscape garden, surrounding a neo-classical mansion

The fine landscape garden was created in the mid 18th century by Sir Francis Dashwood, founder of the Dilettanti Society and the Hellfire Club. The house is among the most theatrical and Italianate in England, its façades formed as classical temples. The interior has Palmyrene ceilings and decoration, with pictures, furniture and sculpture dating from the time of Sir Francis. The lavishly decorated house has featured in many films and television series, including *The Importance of Being Earnest*, *Vanity Fair*, *Little Dorrit* and the award-winning *Cranford Chronicles*.

What's new in 2009 Audio guides to the Park and its Temples, with an introduction by Sir Edward Dashwood, available for hire (additional charge)

★ No picnics or dogs in the park. West Wycombe Caves and café are privately owned and NT members must pay admission fees

Please remember – your membership card is *always* needed for free admission

i T 01494 755571 (Infoline), 01494 513569
E westwycombe@nationaltrust.org.uk

🏃 Tours of house on weekdays

🎧 Audio guides to the Park and its Temples, with
an introduction by Sir Edward Dashwoood,
available for hire (additional charge)

🚶 Circular walks leaflet available from post
office, newsagent and Hughenden Estate
Office. Architectural guide to village (£1)
available from property and post office

♿ 🅿 ⦂ 🔅 🔆 Building 🚶 🔆
Grounds 🔆

→ [175:SU828947] **Foot**: circular walk links
West Wycombe with Bradenham and
Hughenden Manor. **Bus**: Arriva 40 High
Wycombe–Stokenchurch; Magpie Travel 321
High Wycombe–Princess Risborough; Red
Rose 275 High Wycombe–Oxford.
Station: High Wycombe 2½ml. **Road**: 2ml W
of High Wycombe. At W end of West
Wycombe, S of the Oxford road (A40)

P Free parking, 250yds

NT properties nearby
Cliveden, Hughenden Manor, West Wycombe Village

West Wycombe Park								
Grounds only								
1 Apr–31 May	2–6	**M**	**T**	**W**	**T**	F	S	S
House/grounds								
1 Jun–31 Aug	2–6	**M**	**T**	**W**	**T**	F	S	S

Admission by guided tour only on weekdays, tours every
20mins (approx). Last admission 45mins before closing

West Wycombe Village and Hill

West Wycombe, Buckinghamshire

🏠 ✝ 🏛 🍴 🍽 🚻 🚽 🏕 🎒 🏃 🐾 1934   **(2:E4)**

**Chilterns village with buildings spanning
several hundred years**

The village is rare in its architecture, with
cottages and inns dating from the 16th to 18th
centuries. The hill, with its fine views, is
surmounted by an Iron Age hill fort and is part of
the original landscape design of West Wycombe
Park. It is now the site of a church and the
Dashwood Mausoleum.

★ The church, mausoleum and caves do not
belong to the NT. WCs in village

i T 01494 755573
E westwycombe@nationaltrust.org.uk

🚶 Leaflets obtainable from village store (50/51
High St) and newsagent (36/37 High St):
Village architectural trail and West Wycombe,
Bradenham & Hughenden circular walks

♿ Grounds 🔆

🍽 Refreshments at garden centre and village
pubs (not NT)

🔳 Suitable for school groups

→ [175:SU828946] 2ml W of High Wycombe,
on both sides of A40. **Bus**: Arriva 40 High
Wycombe–Stokenchurch; Magpie Travel 321
High Wycombe–Princess Risborough; Red
Rose 275 High Wycombe–Oxford.
Station: High Wycombe 2½ml. **Road**: 2ml W
of High Wycombe. At W end of West
Wycombe, S of the Oxford road (A40)

P Free parking at top of hill and in village. Single
track lane to top of hill. Height restrictions
apply in village car park. Car park on hill
locked at dusk

NT properties nearby
Cliveden, Hughenden Manor, West Wycombe Park

West Wycombe Village							
All year	**M**	**T**	**W**	**T**	**F**	**S**	**S**

A view of a row of houses at West Wycombe Village,
Buckinghamshire

The White Cliffs of Dover

Langdon Cliffs, Upper Road, Dover, Kent CT16 1HJ

[T] 1968   (2:K7)

Magnificent coastal site overlooking the English Channel

The White Cliffs of Dover are internationally famous as an icon of Britain. The Visitor Centre has spectacular views and introduces the visitor to five miles of coast and countryside through imaginative displays and interpretation. Much of the chalk downland along the clifftops is a Site of Special Scientific Interest, Area of Outstanding Natural Beauty and Heritage Coast, with interesting flora and fauna, and the Visitor Centre is an excellent place for watching the world's busiest shipping lanes.

What's new in 2009 Site history interpretation panels and colour souvenir guide

⭐ WC only available when centre is open. Car parking fee applies

[i] **T** 01304 202756
E whitecliffs@nationaltrust.org.uk

[✗] Guided walks from White Cliffs, including to South Foreland Lighthouse (2ml), April–Oct

[♥] Plant Fair, children's activities and Apple Fayre

[🚶] On public footpaths, towards St Margaret's and Deal. Self-guided and guided walks around property, and long distance footpath – Saxon Shore Way

The White Cliffs of Dover Visitor Centre with Dover Castle in the background

⬅ [icons] Building 🏛♿

Grounds 🏛

[🏠] NT shop and items of local interest

[☕] Coffee shop in Visitor Centre. Range of drinks, ice-cream, snacks and light lunches to eat in or take away. Children's menu

[👶] Baby-changing facilities. Pushchairs and baby back-carriers admitted. Baby back-carriers for loan. Children's quiz/trail. Children's activity packs. Tracker Packs

[🎒] Suitable for school groups

[🐕] Under close control at all times (stock grazing)

[🚲] Cycling strictly prohibited along the White Cliffs but NCN1 crosses property

→ [138:TR336422] **Foot**: signed pathways from the port, station and town centre. Located on the Saxon Shore Way path. **Cycle**: NCN1. **Ferry**: signed route from Dover ferry terminal. **Bus**: Stagecoach in E Kent Diamond 15 Canterbury–Dover–Deal, alight Castle Hill then 1ml (via Upper Road). **Station**: Dover Priory 2½ml. **Road**: from A2/A258 Duke of York roundabout, take A258 towards Dover town centre, 1ml turn left into Upper Road, ¾ml turn right into entrance. From A20 straight ahead at first four roundabouts and left at second set of lights. Turn right at next lights. After ½ml turn right into Upper Road, follow for ¾ml turn right into entrance

[P] Car £3, disabled badge holders £2, motorhomes £4, coaches £7, annual season ticket £30

NT properties nearby
Bockhill Farm, Kingsdown Leas, St Margaret's Leas, South Foreland Lighthouse

The White Cliffs of Dover									
Visitor Centre									
1 Feb–28 Feb	11–4	**M**	**T**	**W**	**T**	**F**	S	S	
1 Mar–31 Oct	10–5	**M**	**T**	**W**	**T**	**F**	S	S	
1 Nov–31 Jan 10	11–4	**M**	**T**	**W**	**T**	**F**	S	S	
Car park									
1 Feb–28 Feb	8–5	**M**	**T**	**W**	**T**	**F**	S	S	
1 Mar–31 Oct	8–6	**M**	**T**	**W**	**T**	**F**	S	S	
1 Nov–31 Jan 10	8–5	**M**	**T**	**W**	**T**	**F**	S	S	

Car park closed 24/25 Dec. Visitor Centre open July & Aug until 6 at weekends, closed 24/26 Dec

Show your card and display sticker for free parking

Winchester City Mill

Bridge Street, Winchester, Hampshire SO23 0EJ

 **1929** (2:D7)

Working watermill in the heart of Winchester

Spanning the River Itchen, this water-powered corn mill was first recorded in the Domesday survey of 1086. Rebuilt in 1744, it remained in use until the turn of the last century and has now been restored to full working order. The waterwheel and machinery turn daily throughout the season and there is something to interest everyone, including awe-inspiring mill races, hands-on activities for children, a video presentation and displays about the river and its wildlife – including CCTV footage of otters. There are also regular flour milling demonstrations and the flour is on sale in the gift shop.

What's new in 2009 Displays and events celebrating the Mill's 80th anniversary of ownership by the National Trust

★ No WC available for public use at the Mill

ℹ️ **T** 01962 870057
   E winchestercitymill@nationaltrust.org.uk

🎟️ Tours by arrangement

😊 Holiday activities for children. Regular flour milling demonstrations

🚶 Winnall Moors walks leaflet

♿ 🅿️ ⠿ 📷 🔊 💻 🎵 🅱️ **Building** 🔧

🎁 Well-stocked gift shop

👪 Pushchairs and baby back-carriers admitted. Children's quiz/trail. Holiday activities for children

🏫 Suitable for school groups. Education room/centre. Hands-on activities. Partnership with Hampshire & Isle of Wight Wildlife Trust with displays about the River Itchen

➡️ [185:SU487294] At foot of High Street, beside City Bridge. **Foot**: South Downs Way, King's Way, Itchen Way, Three Castles Path, Clarendon Way – all pass through or terminate at Winchester. **Bus**: from surrounding areas. **Station**: Winchester 1ml

🅿️ No parking on site. Parking at Chesil car park. Park & ride to Winchester from M3, exit 10

NT properties nearby
Hinton Ampner, Mottisfont Abbey, Sandham Memorial Chapel, The Vyne

Winchester City Mill								
14 Feb–22 Feb	11–5	M	T	W	T	F	S	S
4 Mar–5 Apr	11–5	M	T	W	T	F	S	S
6 Apr–19 Apr	11–5	M	T	W	T	F	S	S
22 Apr–24 May	11–5	M	T	W	T	F	S	S
25 May–31 May	11–5	M	T	W	T	F	S	S
3 Jun–12 Jul	11–5	M	T	W	T	F	S	S
13 Jul–6 Sep	11–5	M	T	W	T	F	S	S
9 Sep–25 Oct	11–5	M	T	W	T	F	S	S
26 Oct–24 Dec	11–4:30	M	T	W	T	F	S	S
1 Jan 10	11–4	M	T	W	T	F	S	S
Open BH Mons								

Winchester City Mill, Hampshire: the water powers the waterwheel which turns the mill's machinery

Bluebells at Winkworth Arboretum, Surrey

Winkworth Arboretum

Hascombe Road, Godalming, Surrey GU8 4AD

 1952   (2:F7)

Tranquil hillside woodland with sweeping views

Established in the 20th century, this hillside arboretum now contains more than 1,000 different shrubs and trees, many of them rare. The most impressive displays are in spring, with magnolias, bluebells and azaleas, and autumn, when the colour of the foliage is stunning. In the summer it is an ideal place for family days out and picnics.

Winkworth Arboretum								
Arboretum								
All year	Dawn–dusk	**M**	**T**	**W**	**T**	**F**	**S**	**S**
Shop/tea-room								
1 Feb–1 Mar	11–4	M	T	W	T	F	**S**	**S**
4 Mar–29 Mar	11–4	M	T	**W**	**T**	**F**	**S**	**S**
1 Apr–22 Nov	11–5	M	T	**W**	**T**	**F**	**S**	**S**
28 Nov–20 Dec	11–4	M	T	W	T	F	**S**	**S**
9 Jan–31 Jan 10	11–4	M	T	W	T	F	**S**	**S**

Shop & tea-room open BH Mons 11–5. Arboretum may be closed in bad weather (especially in high winds)

What's new in 2009 150 late-flowering rhododendrons have been planted in the past two years

i **T** 01483 208477
E winkwortharboretum@nationaltrust.org.uk

'Plant of the month', Family Fun Day and other seasonal events

Walks leaflet available. Tree guide listing 200 species

Grounds

Tea-room. Children's menu

Baby-changing facilities. Pushchairs and baby back-carriers admitted. Children's quiz/trail. Family Fun Day

Suitable for school groups. Tree guide available

On leads only

→ [169/170/186:SU990412] **Bus**: Arriva 42/44 Guildford–Cranleigh (passing close ≷ Godalming). **Station**: Godalming 2ml. **Road**: near Hascombe, 2ml SE of Godalming on E side of B2130

P Free parking, 100yds

NT properties nearby
Clandon Park, Hindhead Commons, Oakhurst Cottage, River Wey and Dapdune Wharf, The Witley Centre

Amazed by the variety at Winkworth Arboretum? Then don't miss the unique gardens at Hinton Ampner

The Witley Centre

Witley, Godalming, Surrey GU8 5QA

🏊 🐾 📷 🍴 🏕 🎭 🚻 🚆 🚶 ⛸ 1921 **(2:E7)**

Countryside visitor and education centre

At the heart of Witley Common, a fascinating mix of woodland and heath, the purpose-built centre houses a countryside exhibition and provides a venue for school groups and children's holiday activities.

What's new in 2009 See pond life close at hand though the lens of the pond camera

ℹ️ **T** 01428 683207
E witleycentre@nationaltrust.org.uk

🎭 Fun days and children's holiday events

🚶 Selection of walks leaflets available at shop

♿ 🚾 👓 🎵 📶 **Building** ♿ ♿
Grounds ♿

📷 Small shop with limited range of souvenirs

🍦 Ice-cream and soft drinks

👪 Pushchairs admitted. Children's quiz/trail. Fun days and children's holiday events

🚆 Suitable for school groups. Education room/centre

🐕 Under close control

⛸ Cycling on bridleway around commons

➡️ [186:SU930410] 7ml SW of Guildford. **Bus**: Stagecoach in Hants & Surrey 70 Guildford–Midhurst, 71 Guildford–Haslemere (both passing close 🚉 Godalming & passing 🚉 Haslemere). **Station**: Milford 2ml. **Road**: between London–Portsmouth A3 and A286 roads, 1ml SW of Milford

🅿️ Free parking, 100yds

NT properties nearby

Black Down, Frensham Common, Hindhead Commons, Ludshott Common, Oakhurst Cottage, Winkworth Arboretum

The Witley Centre									
Centre									
2 Mar–30 Oct	11–4		M	T	W	T	F	S	S
Common									
All year			M	T	W	T	F	S	S

Explore the woodland and heath that makes up Witley Common in Surrey

Charges for National Trust members apply on some special event days

London

London is fortunate that, despite being one of the world's major conurbations, it still contains many green and relatively tranquil areas. The National Trust has played an important role in saving several fragments of the city's once extensive common land for present and future generations to enjoy.

London has grown so enormously over the centuries that several Trust properties, which would once have stood in the midst of open countryside, now fall within the Greater London area. The large estate of Osterley Park, for example, was originally created as a retreat, where wealthy guests could be entertained away from the hustle and bustle of the city. Since then, of course, the city has crept up on it, and it now provides a welcome green haven in the midst of suburbia.

Working with the community
Sutton House in Hackney is another property which has long since been surrounded by encroaching development. Originally part of a small village, it is now in the heart of a densely populated urban area – making it ideally placed for carrying out the Trust's work with local communities and inner city schools.

Valuable tranquil places
An unexpected jewel in Middlesex is Osterley Park and House, which is surrounded by 145 hectares (359 acres) of park and farmland. The 18th-century mansion was designed in 1761 by Robert Adam, the leading architect and interior designer of his day, and the interiors are dazzling and impressive. The park surrounding the mansion is a much-loved local amenity, and the Trust is in the midst of a major project which will restore the gardens to their former 18th-century splendour.

South West London is very built up, yet even here there is an unexpected oasis. Morden Hall Park is a picturesque and historic park with meadows, waterways and lovely old buildings. It has an impressive rose garden with more than 2,000 rose bushes, and is the perfect safe haven, whether you want to go for a stroll or a jog, or take the family for a picnic or a pleasant day out.

Accessible to all
Visitors with walking difficulties will find a trip to Morden Hall Park and Osterley Park particularly rewarding. Both places have extremely accessible paths – Morden Hall Park's run through the rose garden and along the River Wandle, while Osterley Park boasts numerous routes suitable for wheelchair users – encircling the lake as well as through the wider parkland.

Above left: **Osterley House**
Above: **the bridge over the River Wandle** (top) and **children in a meadow at Morden Hall Park**

Blewcoat School Gift Shop

23 Caxton Street, Westminster, London SW1H 0PY

🏠 🗂 1954 (2:G5)

Early 18th-century school for the poor, now the National Trust's London shop

Celebrating its 300th anniversary in 2009, this small and elegant building was originally built at the expense of a local brewer as a school for poor children. Used as a school until 1926 and now dwarfed by its surroundings, it is a tiny and evocative architectural gem in central London. Today it houses a National Trust shop with an extensive range of attractive gifts.

⭐ No WC

ℹ️ **T** 020 7222 2877
  E blewcoat@nationaltrust.org.uk

♿ 🏛 Building 🔼

➡️ [176:TQ295794] Near the junction of Caxton Street and Buckingham Gate. **Foot**: Thames Path within ⅔ml. **Cycle**: NCN4, ¾ml.
Bus: frequent local services (tel. 020 7222 1234). **Station**: Victoria ¼ml.
Underground: St James's Park (District & Circle lines) 100yds

🅿️ No parking on site

NT properties nearby
Carlyle's House

Blewcoat School Gift Shop		M	T	W	T	F	S	S
All year	10–5:30	**M**	**T**	**W**	**T**	**F**	S	S
7 Nov–19 Dec	10–4	M	T	W	T	F	**S**	**S**
Closed BH Mons and Good Fri								

Carlyle's House, Chelsea: London's first literary shrine

Carlyle's House

24 Cheyne Row, Chelsea, London SW3 5HL

🏛 ❄️ 🗝 👺 🏯 1936 (2:F5)

The home of a Victorian celebrity couple

In 1834 Thomas Carlyle, a struggling Scottish writer, and Jane, his clever ambitious wife, rented this modest but roomy terraced house in the then unfashionable village of Chelsea. Within a few years the house had become a favourite gathering place of the literary world, including Dickens, Tennyson and Browning. Explore the Carlyles' home – preserved in 1895 as London's first literary shrine – and see the kitchen, dining room, drawing room, bedroom and Carlyle's intriguing soundproofed study, all with original contents. There is also a small garden. Then explore the surrounding streets and discover where many other famous writers, artists and composers lived.

ℹ️ **T** 020 7352 7087
  E carlyleshouse@nationaltrust.org.uk

👺 Talks

♿ 📷 🏛 Building 🔼 Grounds 🔼

🏯 Suitable for school groups. Booked school groups welcome: Wed, Thur & Fri between 10 and 1. Max 15

➡️ [176:TQ272777] Off Chelsea Embankment between Albert and Battersea Bridges. NT sign on corner of Cheyne Row. Or via Kings Rd and Oakley St. NT sign on corner of Upper Cheyne Row. **Foot**: Thames Path within ⅜ml. **Cycle**: NCN4. **Bus**: frequent local services (tel. 020 7222 1234). **Station**: Victoria 1½ml.
Underground: Sloane Square (District & Circle lines) or South Kensington (Piccadilly, District & Circle lines) 1ml

🅿️ No parking on site. Very limited street parking at pay & display meters nearby

NT properties nearby
Fenton House, Ham House and Garden, Morden Hall Park, Osterley Park and House, Sutton House, 2 Willow Road

Carlyle's House		M	T	W	T	F	S	S
18 Mar–30 Oct	2–5	M	T	**W**	**T**	**F**	S	S
21 Mar–1 Nov	11–5	M	T	W	T	F	**S**	**S**
Open BH Mons: 11–5								

Please remember – your membership card is *always* needed for free admission

Eastbury Manor House

Eastbury Square, Barking IG11 9SN

🏛️ ✷ 🏠 ☕ 🍴 🎋 🎭 👫 🎪 🔔 1918 (2:G5)

Elizabethan merchant's house and gardens

An important example of a medium-sized brick-built Elizabethan manor house, the building is architecturally distinguished and well preserved, with notable early 17th-century wall paintings. The house is rumoured to have connections with the Gunpowder Treason Plot. 'Bee boles' can be seen in the walled garden. The property is managed by the London Borough of Barking and Dagenham.

What's new in 2009 Renovations to building, improved access and opening of new permanent exhibition telling Eastbury's story

⭐ House open first and second Saturday of every month

ℹ️ **T** 020 8724 1002
E eastburymanor@nationaltrust.org.uk
W www.barking-dagenham.gov.uk

🎋 Guided tours available when open to the public on Mon and Tues and the first and second Sat of each month. Costumed guided tours on the first Sat of each month

🎭 Family days, heritage days, entertaining events programme

♿ 🅿️ 🚻 👓 📷 🔄 🔊 📱
Building 🔊🔄🔊🔄 **Grounds** 🔄

🏠 The Old Buttery gift shop (not NT) sells a variety of traditional gifts and souvenirs, as well as books and publications

☕ Garden tea-room (not NT) in house. In good weather, refreshments can be taken in kitchen garden. Hot and cold drinks, sandwiches and snacks

👫 Baby-changing facilities. Pushchairs admitted. Children's activities on family days and during school holidays

🎪 Suitable for school groups. Education room/centre

🐕 On leads and only in garden

➡️ [177:TQ457838] In Eastbury Square, 500yds walk S from Upney station (follow brown

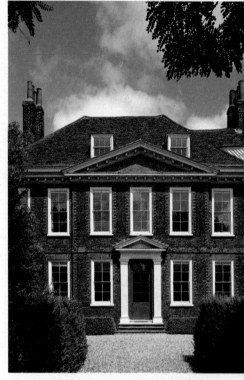

Fenton House, Hampstead, dates from the late 17th century

signs). **Cycle**: LCN15 ¾ml. Upney Lane local cycle route links LCN15 to property. **Bus**: TfL 62, 287, 368 ➤ Barking–Rainham/Chadwell Heath. **Station**: Barking, then one stop on District Line to Upney ¼ml.
Underground: Upney (District Line).
Road: ½ml N of A13, 2ml E of A406, just off A123 Ripple Road

🅿️ Free street parking for cars and coaches in Eastbury Square, adjacent

NT properties nearby
Rainham Hall, Sutton House

Eastbury Manor House								
House								
All year	10–4		**M**	**T**	W	T	F	S	S
Tea-room/shop								
As house	10–3:30								

Closed BH Mons. Last admission 1hr before closing. Closed 28/29 Dec. House open 1st & 2nd Sat of month all year

Fenton House

Hampstead Grove, Hampstead, London NW3 6SP

🏚 ⛲ 𝑖 ☻ 👫 🖼 𝑘 1952   **(2:G4)**

Handsome 17th-century merchant's house with walled garden

Set in the winding streets of Hampstead village, this charming late 17th-century house contains outstanding collections of porcelain, needlework, Georgian furniture, and paintings and drawings by the Camden Town Group, as well as the Benton Fletcher collection of early keyboard instruments – most of which are in working order. The delightful walled garden includes fine mixed borders, an orchard and a working kitchen garden.

What's new in 2009 Display of more than 3,000 snowdrops on the South Walk, visible from Windmill Hill. Newly refurbished entrance hall

George Inn: 17th-century coaching inn

George Inn

The George Inn Yard, 77 Borough High Street, Southwark, London SE1 1NH

🏚 🍺 🍽 👫 1937   **(2:G5)**

Last remaining galleried inn in London

Famous as a coaching inn during the 17th century and mentioned by Dickens in *Little Dorrit*, the George Inn is now leased to a private company and still used as a public house.

⭐ To book a table tel. 020 7407 2056

ℹ **T** 020 7407 2056
E georgeinn@nationaltrust.org.uk

🍽 Licensed restaurant (not NT)

👫 Children admitted subject to normal licensing regulations

🐕 On leads and only in courtyard

➡ [176:TQ326801] On E side of Borough High St, near London Bridge Station. **Cycle:** NCN4, ¼ml. **Bus:** frequent local services (tel. 020 7222 1234). **Station:** London Bridge ≋ & Underground (Northern & Jubilee lines)

NT properties nearby
Carlyle's House, Sutton House

⭐ For audition to use the early keyboard instruments, contact the Instrument Collection Manager, c/o fentonhouse@nationaltrust.org.uk

ℹ **T** 01494 755563 (Infoline), 020 7435 3471
E fentonhouse@nationaltrust.org.uk

𝑘 Demonstration tours (max. 20) of instruments by the Curator. Send sae or go to events website for details

☻ Garden Easter trail, summer concerts, costume exhibition and Apple Day

𝑘 Self-guided walks leaflet 50p

♿ ⠿ 📷 🖼 ⌨ ♨ Building 🪜 🪜
Grounds 🪜 🪜

👫 Baby-changing facilities. Front-carrying baby slings for loan. Children's quiz/trail

🖼 Suitable for school groups

➡ [176:TQ262860] Visitors' entrance on W side of Hampstead Grove. **Bus:** frequent local services (tel. 020 7222 1234).
Station: Hampstead Heath 1ml.
Underground: Hampstead (Northern Line) 300yds

🅿 No parking on site

NT properties nearby
Sutton House, 2 Willow Road

Unless indicated, last admission is always 30mins before closing time

Ham House and Garden

Ham Street, Ham,
Richmond-upon-Thames TW10 7RS

🏠 ✳️ 🏠 📷 🍴 🎭 💺 🧒 🖼️ 🚶 🔔
🍷 1948   (2:F5)

Unique 17th-century house with sumptuous interiors, original collections and restored formal gardens

One of a series of grand houses and palaces alongside the River Thames, Ham House and Garden is an unusually complete survival of the 17th century, where time appears to have stood still. Rich in history and atmosphere, Ham House was largely created by the charismatic Duchess of Lauderdale, who was deeply embroiled in the politics of the English Civil War and subsequent restoration of the monarchy. As a sumptuous statement of wealth and power, Ham was built to impress in its day and continues to do so today. With lavish interiors, unique historical features and unusual 17th-century gardens, Ham is a treasure trove waiting to be discovered. Its collections of art, textiles and furniture are outstanding, while its outbuildings – including an ice house, a dairy, with unusual cast-iron 'cows' legs', and the earliest known purpose-built still house (the 17th-century equivalent of an in-house pharmacy) – are intriguing. The gardens are a rare example of 17th-century formal garden design.

What's new in 2009 Eye-opener guided tours during February half-term

⭐ No barbecues

ℹ️ **T** 020 8940 1950
   E hamhouse@nationaltrust.org.uk

🍴 Guided garden tours Weds 1 & 2 (dates as house, no booking necessary). Ghost tours and selection of themed tours throughout the year (booking essential). Contact property or website for details

🎭 Open-air theatre, themed guided tours, Christmas events and special openings

🚶 Local walks leaflet available from property

♿ 🅿️ 🚾 ⚫ 🔍 ✏️ ♿ 🔧 🔩 **Building** ♿ ♿
↕️ ♿ **Grounds** ♿ ➡️ ♿ ♿

🎁 NT gifts, local arts and crafts, wide selection of books and plants grown in peat-free compost

🍽️ Orangery Café (licensed). Children's menu

👨‍👧 Baby-changing facilities. Front-carrying baby slings and hip-carrying infant seats for loan. Children's trails. Children's activity packs. Tracker Packs. Self-service toy box in garden

The south front of Ham House, a property rich in history and atmosphere, seen from the Wilderness

▥ Suitable for school groups. Education room/centre. Hands-on activities

➡ [176:TQ172732] On S bank of Thames, W of A307, between Richmond and Kingston; Ham gate exit of Richmond Park. **Foot**: Thames Path passes main entrance. 1½ml from Richmond, 3ml from Kingston. **Cycle**: NCN4. Ferry access from Twickenham.
Ferry: seasonal foot/bike ferry across River Thames from Twickenham towpath (by Marble Hill House–EH) to Ham House. **Bus**: TfL 371 Richmond–Kingston, alight Ham Street by Royal Oak pub, then ½ml walk. 65 Ealing Broadway–Kingston, alight Petersham Rd by Ham Polo Ground, ¾ml walk along historic avenues (both pass ⮽ Richmond and Kingston). Also K5 Morden–Ham, alight Dukes Avenue, then 1ml walk (tel. 020 7222 1234). **Station**: Richmond 1½ml by footpath, 2ml by road. **Underground**: Richmond 1½ml by footpath, 2ml by road. **Road**: on S bank of the Thames, W of A307, between Richmond and Kingston; Ham gate exit of Richmond Park, readily accessible from M3, M4 and M25

🅿 Free parking (not NT), 400yds

NT properties nearby
Carlyle's House, Claremont Landscape Garden, Morden Hall Park, Osterley Park and House

Ham House and Garden									
House									
14 Feb–25 Feb	12–4	M	T	W	T	F	S	S	
28 Feb–8 Mar	12–4	M	T	W	T	F	S	S	
14 Mar–1 Nov	12–4	M	T	W	T	F	S	S	
Garden									
1 Feb–11 Feb	11–4	M	T	W	T	F	S	S	
14 Feb–20 Dec	11–5	M	T	W	T	F	S	S	
21 Dec–31 Jan 10	11–4	M	T	W	T	F	S	S	
Shop/café									
1 Feb–8 Feb	11–4	M	T	W	T	F	S	S	
14 Feb–25 Feb	11–5	M	T	W	T	F	S	S	
28 Feb–8 Mar	11–5	M	T	W	T	F	S	S	
14 Mar–1 Nov	11–5	M	T	W	T	F	S	S	
7 Nov–20 Dec	11–5	M	T	W	T	F	S	S	
2 Jan–31 Jan 10	11–4	M	T	W	T	F	S	S	

Open Good Fri: house 12–4; garden 11–5. From 14 Feb–8 March only timed 'Eye-opener' tours of the house at 12:15, 1:15, 2:15 & 3:15, normal admission charges (bookable on day, max. 25). Special Christmas house openings

Lindsey House

99/100 Cheyne Walk, Chelsea, London SW10 0DQ

🏠 ✳ 1951   **(2:G5)**

Elegant 17th-century town house

⭐ The house is occupied by a tenant and is only open to the public on the Saturday of London Open House weekend. Only the ground floor entrance hall with staircase and the garden is accessible to visitors

ℹ **T** 020 7799 4553
  E lindseyhouse@nationaltrust.org.uk

➡ On Cheyne Walk, W of Battersea Bridge near junction with Milman Street on Chelsea Embankment

Morden Hall Park

Morden Hall Road, Morden SM4 5JD

🏠 🚻 🔲 ✳ 🍴 🐕 🐾 🎁 💷 𝕏 🎪 🛡 🏫 🎭
🚶 🚲 1942   **(2:G5)**

Green oasis in the heart of suburbia

With its refreshing wide open spaces and tranquil, meandering river, Morden Hall Park is a rare public commodity in south-west London. The attractive rose gardens, wild meadows and wetlands rich in wildlife, add up to a delightful haven in the midst of a densely built-up area. Visitors can stroll along the river to the site of two watermills which were used until 1913 to grind snuff, and explore other historic estate buildings now used by a range of local artisans. The original walled kitchen garden now houses the Riverside Café and gift shop, as well as a large, independently run garden centre. There is a refreshment kiosk in the rose garden and a second-hand bookshop.

What's new in 2009 Snuff Mill Centre with new features, information and interactive displays

⭐ No fires or BBQs in the park

ℹ **T** 020 8545 6850
  E mordenhallpark@nationaltrust.org.uk

𝕏 Guided tours by arrangement

🛡 Snuff Mill Exhibition open first Sunday each month. Discovery days third Sunday each month from April–October and family activities every Thursday during school holidays. Programme of walks and workshops for adults

🏃 Various walks throughout the year

♿ 🅿️ 🖼️ ⠿ 📷 🎨 🔊 📖 Building 🪜🖼️♿
Grounds 🖼️ ➡️

📷 NT shop. Garden centre run by Capital Gardens plc as NT tenants (tel. 020 8646 3002). Second-hand bookshop

🍽️ Riverside café. Children's menu. Refreshment kiosk in rose garden (open weekends and school hols)

🚼 Baby-changing facilities

🎒 Suitable for school groups. Education room/centre

🐕 On leads around buildings and rose garden; under close control elsewhere

🚲 Wandle Trail, from Croydon or Carshalton to Wandsworth, runs through the park

➡️ [176:TQ261684] Near Morden town centre. **Foot**: Wandle Trail from Croydon or Carshalton to Wandsworth. **Cycle**: NCN22, route passes through park. **Bus**: frequent from surrounding areas (tel. 020 7222 1234). **Station**: Tramlink to Phipps Bridge stop, on park boundary ½ml. **Underground**: Morden (Northern Line) 500yds to park, 800yds to café & shop. **Road**: off A24, and A297 S of Wimbledon, N of Sutton

🅿️ Free parking, 25yds

NT properties nearby
Claremont Landscape Garden, Ham House and Garden

The entrance façade of Osterley Park

Show your card and display sticker for free parking

Morden Hall Park									
Park									
All year	8–6	**M**	**T**	**W**	**T**	**F**	**S**	**S**
Shop/café									
All year	10–5	**M**	**T**	**W**	**T**	**F**	**S**	**S**
Kiosk									
4 Apr–25 Oct	11–5	M	T	W	T	F	**S**	**S**
Second-hand bookshop									
All year	12–4	M	T	W	T	F	**S**	**S**
1 Apr–30 Oct	11–3	**M**	**T**	**W**	**T**	**F**	S	S

Car park by café, shop and garden centre closes at 6. Shop and café closed 11 Feb, 25, 26 Dec & 1 Jan 10. Rose garden and estate buildings area open 8–6. Snuff Mill Environmental Education Centre open first Sun of April–Oct, 12–4. Kiosk also open every day during school hols, April–Oct 11–5 (unless the weather is bad)

Osterley Park and House

Jersey Road, Isleworth, Middlesex TW7 4RB

🏠 ❇️ 🍴 📷 🍽️ 🔊 🪑 🎭 🚼 🎒 🏃 🚲 🔔
🍸 1949 (2:F5)

Magnificent neo-classical house with fine Adam interiors, landscape park and 18th-century gardens

This extravagant mansion with its surrounding gardens, park and farmland is one of the last surviving country estates in London. Transformed in the late 18th century for a wealthy banking family by renowned architect and designer, Robert Adam, the house and surrounding gardens were created to entertain and dazzle their friends and clients. With a series of stunning show rooms affording glorious views over extensive parkland, Osterley continues to impress visitors today. The gardens are currently being restored to their former 18th-century splendour and there are pleasant walks around the park as well as wide open green spaces for families to enjoy.

What's new in 2009 Introductory film and interactive audio-visual guide to house

⭐ Please contact property to check operating times of mobility vehicles and transfer service. No barbecues, fires or gazebos

ℹ️ **T** 01494 755566 (Infoline), 020 8232 5050
E osterley@nationaltrust.org.uk

Osterley Park and House

House

4 Mar–1 Nov	1–4:30	M	T	**W**	**T**	**F**	**S**	**S**
5 Dec–20 Dec	12:30–3:30	M	T	W	T	F	**S**	**S**

Tea-room/shop*

4 Mar–1 Nov	11–5	M	T	**W**	**T**	**F**	**S**	**S**
4 Nov–20 Dec	12–4	M	T	**W**	**T**	**F**	**S**	**S**

Park

1 Feb–28 Mar	8–6	**M**	**T**	**W**	**T**	**F**	**S**	**S**
29 Mar–24 Oct	8–7:30	**M**	**T**	**W**	**T**	**F**	**S**	**S**
25 Oct–31 Jan 10	8–6	**M**	**T**	**W**	**T**	**F**	**S**	**S**

Garden

4 Mar–1 Nov	11–5	M	T	**W**	**T**	**F**	**S**	**S**

Open Good Fri & BH Mons. *Shop opens 12:30,
4 Mar–1 Nov. Car park closed 25/26 Dec & 1 Jan 10

Interactive audio-visual guide to house

Including guided walks, tours and family activities

Free leaflet features a map of walks in the park. Estate guide (£1) features walks around the park and garden

Building **Grounds**

NT gift shop

The Stables Tea-room and Garden (licensed). Children's menu

Baby-changing facilities. Front-carrying baby slings and hip-carrying infant seats for loan. Children's guide. Activity packs for house and garden. Pushchairs admitted when visitor numbers allow. Family events

Suitable for school groups. Education room/centre. Hands-on activities

On leads only in park, unless indicated

Cycling in park only with shared access

[176:TQ146780] **Cycle**: links to London cycle network. **Bus**: TfL H28 Hayes–Hounslow–Osterley, H91 Hounslow–Hammersmith to within ½ml. **Station**: Isleworth 1½ml. **Underground**: Osterley (Piccadilly Line), turn left on leaving station, ½ml. **Road**: on A4 between Hammersmith and Hounslow. Follow brown tourist signs on A4 between Gillette

Corner and Osterley underground station; from W M4, exit 3 then follow A312/A4 towards central London. Main gates at junction with Thornbury and Jersey roads

Parking, 400yds, £3.50. Coach-parking free. Car park open as park

NT properties nearby
Ham House and Garden

Rainham Hall

The Broadway, Rainham, Havering RM13 9YN

1949   (2:H5)

A charming and peaceful Georgian house and simple garden

Built in 1729 by Captain John Harle, the house was a showcase for the high-quality building materials which he sold. Currently sparsely furnished and awaiting conservation work, there is extensive panelling, an elegant carved staircase, plasterwork, original *trompe l'oeil* decoration, fine ironwork gates and railings, and much more. Set in a peaceful, simple garden with some surprising features.

No WC

T 020 7799 4552
E rainhamhall@nationaltrust.org.uk

Short guided tours

Open day events to coincide with the Rainham Christmas Fair and May Day activities. Occasional garden activities, such as open-air theatre

[177:TQ521821] **Bus**: frequent local services (tel. 020 7222 1234). **Station**: Rainham, 200yds. **Road**: 5ml E of Barking. Just S of the church

Limited parking (disabled only) on site. Free parking (not NT-Tesco), 300yds

NT properties nearby
Eastbury Manor House, Red House, Sutton House

Rainham Hall

4 Apr–31 Oct	2–5	M	T	W	T	F	**S**	**S**

Open BH Mons. Open early Dec for Rainham
Christmas Fair

Charges for National Trust members apply on some special event days

Red House

Red House Lane, Bexleyheath DA6 8JF

🏛 📷 ✳ 🗄 🍽 🏋 🎠 🎭 🏃 🚂 2003 **(2:H5)**

Iconic Art & Crafts home of William Morris – writer, artist, craftsman and socialist

Red House is of enormous international significance in the history of domestic architecture and garden design. The only house commissioned by William Morris, it was designed and built in 1859 by his friend and colleague, architect Philip Webb. It was Webb's first house and was strongly influenced by Gothic medieval architecture. It is constructed with the emphasis on natural materials – warm red brick is set under a steep red-tiled roof – and there are numerous original features, including items of fixed furniture designed by Morris and Webb, as well as wall paintings and stained glass by Edward Burne-Jones. Originally surrounded by orchards and countryside, Red House is now in suburbia, although visitors can still enjoy the peaceful garden which inspired some of Morris's later work.

What's new in 2009 New additions to the documents exhibition room as well as the letter from Webb to Morris found under the floorboards. Embroidered panel of Aphrodite, specially designed for Red House by William Morris. Daily unguided visits after 2 (no booking required)

⭐ When the property was acquired by the NT from private owners in 2003 it was opened for visitors to see it as it was. Research has now begun to reveal more about the house as originally created by Webb and Morris and, as time goes on, more features and items are displayed. WC now available. Nearest accessible WC at Danson Park

Red House									
4 Mar–22 Nov	11–4:45	M	T	**W**	**T**	F	S	S
27 Nov–20 Dec	11–4:45	M	T	W	T	**F**	**S**	**S**
Admission by booked guided tour from 11 and unguided viewing after 2									

ℹ **T** 020 8304 9878 (bookings 9:30–1:30, Tues–Sun) **E** redhouse@nationaltrust.org.uk

🏋 Daily tours. Special tours by arrangement

🎭 Easter trail. Autumn Apple Day. Christmas event and house dressed for Christmas

♿ 🅿 🚻 ⬛ ⬛ ⬛ Building 🦽 Grounds 🦽 ➡

📷 Small shop selling gifts, including books and items related to the Arts & Crafts Movement and the house. Second-hand books and plant sales when available

🍽 Tea-room serving light refreshments

🏃 Children's quiz

🚂 Suitable for school groups

➡ [177:TQ481750] **Bus**: frequent local services. **Station**: 🚉 Bexleyheath, ¾ml. **Road**: off A221 Bexleyheath. Visitors will be advised how to reach the property when booking

🅿 No parking at property except disabled parking space, which must be booked. Parking is at Danson Park (approx. 1ml). Parking charge at weekends and BHols

NT properties nearby
Ightham Mote, Knole, Rainham Hall

The bay window in the drawing room at Red House, Bexleyheath: an iconic Arts & Crafts home

Dogs assisting visitors with disabilities are always welcome

'Roman' Bath

5 Strand Lane, London WC2

🏛 1948 (2:G5)

Remains of a bath – possibly Roman

⭐ The Bath is administered and maintained by Westminster City Council. No WC

ℹ️ **T** 020 8232 5050
E romanbath@nationaltrust.org.uk

➡️ Just W of Aldwych station (now closed), approach via Surrey Street

'Roman' Bath										
1 Apr–30 Sep	1–5	M	T	**W**	T	F	S	S

Admission by appointment only with Westminster CC, 020 7641 5264 (24hrs notice) during office hours. Bath visible through window from pathway all year, 9–dusk

Sutton House

2 & 4 Homerton High Street, Hackney, London E9 6JQ

🏠 📷 💻 🎭 👺 👫 🏛 🔔 1938 (2:G4)

Tudor house surviving in the heart of a thriving East London community

Sutton House was built in 1535 by a prominent courtier of Henry VIII, Sir Ralph Sadleir. The house retains much of the atmosphere and character of a Tudor house despite some alterations by later occupants, who included a succession of merchants, Huguenot silkweavers and Victorian schoolmistresses. Visitors will see oak-panelled rooms, original carved fireplaces, wall decorations and the charming internal courtyard, as well as a Tudor kitchen and intimate Georgian and Victorian rooms. An attractive exhibition tells the history of the house and its many occupants.

ℹ️ **T** 020 8986 2264
E suttonhouse@nationaltrust.org.uk

🎭 Tours 1st Sun of each month at 3

👺 Including free monthly Family Days, Hallowe'en and Christmas events, regular exhibitions of work by local artists in the Gallery, and Black History Month activities. Guided walks

Sutton House: a unique survival in London's East End

♿ 📷 🚻 👓 📷 🎒 🖥 🎨 🔦 📷

Building 📷 📷 📷 ♿

🛍 NT shop. Good selection of inexpensive gifts and local history books

☕ Brick Place Café (licensed) serving light lunches, teas & snacks

👫 Baby-changing facilities. Children's quiz/trail. Family activity packs. Monthly free family days

🏛 Suitable for school groups. Live interpretation. Hands-on activities. Adult study days

➡️ [176:TQ352851] At the corner of Isabella Road and Homerton High Street. **Cycle**: NCN1, 1¼ml. **Bus**: frequent local services (tel. 020 7222 1234). **Station**: Hackney Central ¼ml; Hackney Downs ½ml

🅿️ No parking on site. Metered parking on adjacent streets

NT properties nearby
Fenton House, 2 Willow Road

Sutton House								
Historic rooms								
1 Feb–20 Dec	12:30–4:30	M	T	W	**T**	**F**	**S**	**S**
Art gallery/shop/café-bar								
1 Feb–20 Dec	12–4:30	M	T	W	**T**	**F**	**S**	**S**

Open BH Mons. Closed Good Fri. Sutton House is a lively property in regular use by local community groups. The rooms will always be open as advertised, but please tel. in advance if you would like to visit the property during a quiet time

2 Willow Road

Hampstead, London NW3 1TH

🏠 🎭 💷 ♿ 1994   (2:G5)

Unique and influential Modernist home from 1939

Located in one of London's most attractive areas on the edge of Hampstead Heath, this fascinating house was designed by Modernist architect Ernö Goldfinger for himself and his family. Alongside the impressive collection of modern art – which includes works by Henry Moore, Max Ernst and Bridget Riley – are personal possessions and highly innovative furniture designed by Goldfinger. The attention to detail and design in this intimate home are both surprising and enlightening and it still looks modern today.

What's new in 2009 Conservation in Action: work to document the archive collections will be taking place in view of visitors on some open days throughout the season

⭐ No WC, local pub allows visitors to use facilities

ℹ️ **T** 01494 755570 (Infoline), 020 7435 6166
E 2willowroad@nationaltrust.org.uk

🎭 Tours at 12, 1 & 2 (plus 11 on Sat)

🎭 Guided walks, evening events, British Sign Language-interpreted walks and tours, please contact the house

🔋 📷 ♿ 🎨 🖼️ 📷 ♿ Building ♿ ♿

👨‍👩‍👧 Children's quiz/trail

➡️ [176:TQ270858] On corner of Willow Road and Downshire Hill. **Foot**: from Hampstead underground, left down High Street and first left down Flask Walk (pedestrianised). Turn right at the end into Willow Road.
Bus: frequent local services (tel. 020 7222 1234). **Station**: Hampstead Heath ¼ml.
Underground: Hampstead (Northern Line) ½ml

🅿️ No parking on site. Limited on-street parking. East Heath Road municipal car park, 100yds, open intermittently

NT properties nearby
Fenton House

2 Willow Road									
7 Mar–28 Nov	11–5		M	T	W	T	F	**S**	S
2 Apr–30 Oct	12–5		M	T	W	**T**	**F**	S	S

Entry by timed tour only at 12, 1 & 2 (plus 11 on Sats). Places on tours limited and available on a first-come first-served basis on the day. Non-guided viewing 3–5 with timed entry when busy. Introductory film shown at regular intervals

As well as innovative furniture, 2 Willow Road contains many of Ernö Goldfinger's personal possessions

The East of England is a region characterised by wide expanses of open countryside, huge skies and sweeping views, supporting a rich diversity of flora and fauna.

Within this spectacular landscape the Trust cares for 11,000 hectares (27,000 acres) of land, almost half of which are designated Sites of Special Scientific Interest.

In Norfolk, Trust land includes the highest point in the county at West Runton, as well as the inspiring historic landscape and woodland at Sheringham Park.

In Suffolk, you can explore one of the most fascinating archaeological sites in this country at Sutton Hoo, or walk over rare lowland heath alongside the picturesque River Deben. There are also numerous wonderful walks on the Essex-Suffolk border, including through the beautiful Dedham Vale.

Or why not stride out on Dunstable Downs in Bedfordshire? These command outstanding views over the Vale of Aylesbury and along the Chiltern Ridge. A great starting point is the new Gateway Centre, high up on the Downs.

Strong culinary traditions

If you want to really get to know an area, then what better way than through its food? We have an extremely strong culinary tradition in the East of England, so come and visit one of the Trust's excellent restaurants and tea-rooms and enjoy home-cooked regional recipes.

We try, wherever possible, to serve local seasonal produce. This ensures you will enjoy the very finest ingredients while the local economy also receives a boost.

At Wimpole Hall, the restaurant serves rare-breed meat from Home Farm and crops from the Walled Garden. While at Felbrigg Hall, visitors can savour fruit from the Walled Garden, which every year is made into 4,000-plus desserts.

Elsewhere, herbs and flowers from the garden flavour and decorate meals at Oxburgh Hall and Peckover House, while Anglesey Abbey and Houghton Mill grind their own flour.

Top left: **Blakeney Point in Norfolk**
Top right: **exploring Dedham Vale on the Essex-Suffolk border by boat**
Above: **flour at 18th-century Houghton Mill in Cambridgeshire**

Previous page: **riding in Hatfield Forest, Hertfordshire**

Abundant wildlife

Throughout the East of England the National Trust works hard to maintain delicate natural habitats for the benefit of future generations, successfully balancing access with conservation.

Above: **having fun at Sutton Hoo, Suffolk**

Below: **an oystercatcher nest with eggs at Orford Ness in Suffolk**

This ensures there are splendid birdwatching opportunities throughout the region.

The North Norfolk coast, for example, as well as being home to several major colonies of common and grey seals, hosts more than 3,000 pairs of breeding Sandwich terns in the summer, while in the autumn and winter thousands of waders and waterfowl descend upon the marshes of Blakeney Freshes.

Wicken Fen National Nature Reserve in Cambridgeshire is a haven for rare wildlife and virtually the last remnant of the extensive fenland that once covered much of the East of England.

Further down the coast in Suffolk is Orford Ness. This was once a secret military test site, but is now an internationally important nature reserve and vital habitat for rare species, such as the little tern.

Rich habitats in this area include Dunwich Heath, a surviving fragment of the sandy heaths locally known as

the Sandlings. While adjacent to the RSPB's reserve at Minsmere, there is a heath where the rare Dartford warbler returned to this part of the country. It is now home to a strong breeding population.

The Essex coast also provides many good birdwatching opportunities, especially on the reserve of Northey Island in the Blackwater Estuary and at Copt Hall Marshes (visitors require a permit to visit Northey Island. Tel. the Warden on 01621 853142).

Treats for all the family

In the south of the region the Trust cares for an outstanding Arts & Crafts house – home to one of the greatest literary figures of the 20th century. Shaw's Corner in Hertfordshire offers a rare glimpse into the life and work of George Bernard Shaw, and if you have never seen a real Oscar before, this is the place to go.

Over in Suffolk, you can find out more about the exceptional children's author Beatrix Potter, who was a regular visitor to Melford Hall; and the original sketches and curiosities displayed there are guaranteed to enthral children of all ages.

Children will also enjoy the special play areas at many of our properties, including Blickling, Ickworth, Sutton Hoo and Wimpole Home Farm. Indeed, a visit to the Home Farm – with its rare-breed animals, goats, rabbits, pigs and special lambing days – is a must for every family.

At Wicken Fen children can take part in hands-on learning at one of Britain's oldest nature reserves. Or, for some serious family excitement, visit Brancaster Millennium Activity Centre, which runs activity weeks throughout the year. Whether they are keen on kayaking and sailing, or prefer a spot of orienteering, there's plenty to keep the children occupied.

www.nationaltrust.org.uk/coastandcountryside

A vision for Wicken Fen

When I arrived at Wicken Fen in 1995 I was fulfilling a career-long ambition to manage one of the most important nature conservation sites in Europe.

Yet Wicken Fen is so much more than just a nature reserve. Ask the thousands of people who visit each year, whether local residents or those from further afield, and they will tell you of the 'specialness' of the Fen.

I also think of Wicken Fen as a very special place. Not only is it one of the few remaining fragments of the once vast 'Great Fen' of East Anglia, it is also a cradle of ecology and modern day nature conservation. If that were not enough, it is in the vanguard of 'naturalistic' lowland landscape creation, in the form of the Wicken Fen Vision – the Trust's long-term project to increase the size of the reserve by up to 22 square miles. Its aim is to provide space to breathe for people and wildlife, space for us to explore and contemplate our environment.

The 'new' land, currently arable farmland, is gradually being converted into something more reminiscent of landscapes our ancestors would recognise. One of the exhilarating aspects of the project is that we are using drivers such as characteristic vegetation regeneration, hydrology and free-ranging large herbivores (cattle and ponies to you and me) to allow the habitats to develop in a more natural way. This, I believe, will create a landscape more pleasing to the senses and beneficial to wildlife.

Wicken Fen has it all: history – scientific, social and natural – groundbreaking and innovative work, wide open spaces that can offer a great sense of solitude, and all this under the huge, sometimes bright, sometimes very moody, fenland skies.

Martin Lester
Head Warden

Wicken Fen in Cambridgeshire is the National Trust's oldest nature reserve

www.nationaltrust.org.uk/coastandcountryside

Anglesey Abbey, Gardens and Lode Mill

Quy Road, Lode, Cambridge,
Cambridgeshire CB25 9EJ

🏠🍴❖🏛💷🔑🌿♿🔨⌕ 1966 (3:G7)

Glorious Jacobean-style house with an eclectic collection, within outstanding gardens with a working watermill

Behind its Jacobean-style exterior Anglesey Abbey is a vision of the golden age of English country house living, created by the first Lord Fairhaven and his brother from 1926 to 1966. It is a treasure trove of sumptuous furnishings, fine books and works of art, as well as a collection of French and English clocks. Life revolved around horse racing and shooting, and weekend guests enjoyed the height of 1930s luxury. As you move outside, examine the 12th-century gargoyles of the original priory and see if you can find the 20th-century additions added by Lord Fairhaven and his brother in 1939. This is a mere taste of Anglesey's statuary – there are more than 100 pieces of classical sculpture in the formal and landscape gardens. Be sure to explore the wildflower meadows and the Hoe Fen Wildlife Discovery area as well as the attractive Winter Garden, with its stunning year-round displays of colour. A mill at Anglesey was listed in the Domesday Book and the present watermill, Lode Mill, dates from the 18th century. Restored in 1982, it is in full working order. Come and feel the power of water in action on the first and third Saturdays of every month (subject to water levels).

What's new in 2009 Hoe Fen Wildlife Discovery Area now accessible all year via new woodland paths. RHS recommended garden

⭐ Snowdrop seasons 21 Jan–22 Feb 09 and 19 Jan–21 Feb 10 (closed Mons). The 'snowdrop line' is updated weekly; please call 01223 810080 and choose the option 1 'opening times and snowdrop update'. If you are able to visit on a weekday we strongly suggest that you do so, as you will have more space to enjoy the gardens and gardeners will be about to share their knowledge with you

ℹ **T** 01223 810080
E angleseyabbey@nationaltrust.org.uk

The Long Gallery at Anglesey Abbey

🔑 New programme of tours

🌿 Send sae for details

♿ 🅿♿📶 ::♿ 🔊 🔉 📖 VT ♿ ♿ ♿
Building 🔨♿ 🔨 **Grounds** ♿ ➡ ♿

🛍 NT shop with many local goods. Plant sales. Second-hand bookshop

☕ Redwoods restaurant (licensed). Serving traditional Cambridgeshire dishes, using locally sourced and seasonal produce. Children's menu

👶 Baby-changing facilities. Hip-carrying infant seats for loan. Children's quiz/trail. Tracker Packs. Pushchairs admitted to gardens only

🔨 Suitable for school groups. Education room/centre

➜ [154:TL533622] **Foot**: Harcamlow Way from Cambridge. **Cycle**: NCN51, 1¼ml. **Bus**: Stagecoach in Cambridge 10 from Cambridge (frequent services link 🚆 Cambridge and bus station). **Station**: Cambridge 6ml. **Road**: 6ml NE of Cambridge on B1102. Signposted from A14, junction 35

🅿 Free parking, 50yds

NT properties nearby
Houghton Mill, Ickworth House, Park and Gardens, Wicken Fen National Nature Reserve, Wimpole Hall, Wimpole Home Farm

Please remember – your membership card is *always* needed for free admission

Blakeney Point, Norfolk: home to many seals

Anglesey Abbey										
Winter Garden		M	T	W	T	F	S	S
1 Feb–15 Mar	10:30–4:30	M	T	**W**	**T**	**F**	**S**	**S**
4 Nov–23 Dec	10:30–4:30	M	T	**W**	**T**	**F**	**S**	**S**
30 Dec–31 Jan 10	10:30–4:30	M	T	**W**	**T**	**F**	**S**	**S**
House								
8 Apr–1 Nov	11–5	M	T	**W**	**T**	**F**	**S**	**S**
Galleries								
8 Apr–1 Nov	11–5	M	T	**W**	**T**	**F**	**S**	**S**
18 Nov–17 Jan 10	11–3:30	M	T	**W**	**T**	**F**	**S**	**S**
Lode Mill								
As Winter Garden	11–3:30	M	T	**W**	**T**	**F**	**S**	**S**
18 Mar–1 Nov	1–5	M	T	**W**	**T**	**F**	**S**	**S**
Garden								
18 Mar–1 Nov	10:30–5:30	M	T	**W**	**T**	**F**	**S**	**S**
Restaurant/shop/plants								
As gardens*		M	T	**W**	**T**	**F**	**S**	**S**

Open BHol Mons and Good Fri. Snowdrop seasons: 21 Jan–22 Feb 09 & 19 Jan–21 Feb 10 (gardens open on Tues during 09, from 27 Jan, & during 2010 snowdrop seasons). *Winter Garden/garden

Blakeney National Nature Reserve

Norfolk Coast Office, Friary Farm, Cley Road, Blakeney, Norfolk NR25 7NW

 1912   **(3:13)**

An extensive area of saltmarsh, vegetated shingle, dunes and grazing marsh

Blakeney National Nature Reserve is an iconic coastal reserve, well known for its internationally important seabirds and overwintering wildfowl and waders. It is also home to an increasing number of seals (both Common and Grey), at Blakeney Point. The reserve is an amazing place to see a huge range of important coastal habitats and species. It covers an area of 1,097 hectares (2,711 acres) at Blakeney Point, Blakeney Freshes, Blakeney Marshes, Morston Marshes and Stiffkey Marshes. The information centre at Morston Quay gives visitors the opportunity to understand more about this dynamic coastal environment.

What's new in 2009 New interpretation boards at Stiffkey, Morston and Blakeney on marine awareness and Blakeney Harbour, funded in part by the Crown Estate. New replacement boardwalk installed on Blakeney Point

WCs at Blakeney Point closed Oct–April. Local authority maintained WCs at Morston Quay and Blakeney Quay

T 01263 740241
E blakeneypoint@nationaltrust.org.uk

For school and special interest groups (small charge) by arrangement

The Peddars Way and Norfolk Coast Path passes through the reserve

Tea-room (NT-approved concession) at Morston Quay. No tea-room at Blakeney Point

Suitable for school groups

Please visit website, check signage or tel. for details

Regional route 30 runs along ridge above the coast

→ [133:TG000460] **Foot**: Norfolk Coast Path passes property. **Cycle**: regional route 30 runs along ridge above the coast. **Ferry**: ferries (not NT) to Blakeney Point. **Bus**: Norfolk Green Coast Hopper 36 ▣ Sheringham–Hunstanton. **Station**: Sheringham (U) 8ml. **Road**: Morston Quay, Blakeney and Cley are all off A149 Cromer–Hunstanton road

P Parking (pay & display) at Morston Quay. Car £3 all day (50p after 6), car with trailer £4, coach £10. Parking also at Blakeney Quay (administered by Blakeney Parish Council). All quayside car parks are liable to tidal flooding

NT properties nearby
Brancaster, Felbrigg Hall, Garden and Park, Sheringham Park

Blakeney National Nature Reserve							
All year	M	T	W	T	F	S	S

Tea-room (not NT) and Information Centre at Morston Quay open according to tides and weather

For general and membership enquiries, please telephone 0844 800 1895

Blickling Hall, Gardens and Park

Blickling, Norwich, Norfolk NR11 6NF

(3:J4)

Magnificent Jacobean house with gardens and park

Built in the early 17th century, Blickling is one of England's great Jacobean houses. The spectacular Long Gallery houses one of the finest private collections of rare books in England, and you can view fine Mortlake tapestries, intricate plasterwork ceilings, an excellent collection of furniture and paintings, as well as the newly restored 19th-century Hungerford Pollen painted ceiling. The glorious gardens are beautiful all year round – with thousands of spring bulbs, swathes of bluebells, vibrant summer borders and rich autumn colours. It really is a garden for all seasons and, with its 18th-century Orangery, secret garden and woodland dell, there is plenty to discover. The Hall is set in an historic park with miles of beautiful woodland and lakeside walks – it even has a pyramid-shaped Mausoleum.

What's new in 2009 Live costumed interpretation in house and gardens on selected days. Family Tracker Packs. Wilderness replanting scheme taking shape in the gardens

★ RAF Museum in Harness Room. Croquet available. Coarse fishing on lake (July–Feb), day tickets available

ℹ️ **T** 01263 738030
E blickling@nationaltrust.org.uk

🏃 Highlight tours of house available on selected days (additional charge, inc. NT members). Garden tours at 2 on most garden open days (additional charge, inc. NT members). Guided estate walks (approx. 3ml), twice a month: free

🎭 Including open-air concerts and theatre, guided walks, themed family and restaurant events. Leaflet available

🚶 Extensive network of footpaths around the estate, including three waymarked walks. Links to Weavers' Way and Marriott's Way (long-distance paths)

Building | **Grounds**

📷 NT shop and plant sales. Second-hand bookshop in Lothian Barn

Blickling Hall, Norfolk, is surrounded by glorious gardens and set in an historic park

Unless indicated, last admission is always 30mins before closing time

📷 Restaurant and courtyard café serving local seasonal produce (licensed). Children's menu. Functions and weddings catered for in private suite of rooms

👪 Baby-changing facilities. Front-carrying baby slings and hip-carrying infant seats for loan. Children's play area. Family guide. Children's quiz/trail. Family activity packs

▥ Suitable for school groups

🐕 On leads and only in park and woods

🚲 Cycle hire centre in orchard picnic area. Map available of routes. Bridleways on property give shared use for cyclists

➔ [133:TG178286] **Foot**: Weavers' Way from Great Yarmouth & Cromer (Aylsham, 2ml). **Cycle**: permitted path alongside Bure Valley Rly, 🚆 Wroxham–Aylsham. **Bus**: Sanders 4, 41/43/44, First 50, Norfolk Green X5 Norwich–Holt/Sheringham (passing close 🚆 Norwich), alight Aylsham 1½ml. **Station**: Aylsham (Bure Valley Rly from 🚆 Hoveton & Wroxham) 1¾ml; N Walsham (U) 8ml. **Road**: 1½ml NW of Aylsham on B1354. Signposted off A140 Norwich (15ml N) to Cromer (10ml S) road

P Parking, 400yds, £2.50

NT properties nearby
Felbrigg Hall, Garden and Park, Sheringham Park

Blickling Hall, Gardens and Park									
House									
28 Feb–12 Jul	11–5	M	T	**W**	**T**	**F**	**S**	**S**
15 Jul–6 Sep	11–5	**M**	T	**W**	**T**	**F**	**S**	**S**
9 Sep–1 Nov	11–5	M	T	**W**	**T**	**F**	**S**	**S**
Garden/shop/restaurant/bookshop									
1 Feb–27 Feb	11–4	M	T	W	**T**	**F**	**S**	**S**
28 Feb–12 Jul	10:15–5:15	M	T	**W**	**T**	**F**	**S**	**S**
15 Jul–6 Sep	10:15–5:15	**M**	T	**W**	**T**	**F**	**S**	**S**
9 Sep–1 Nov	10:15–5:15	M	T	**W**	**T**	**F**	**S**	**S**
5 Nov–31 Jan 10	11–4	M	T	W	**T**	**F**	**S**	**S**
Park									
All year	Dawn–dusk	**M**	**T**	**W**	**T**	**F**	**S**	**S**
Plant centre									
28 Feb–1 Nov	10:15–5:15	M	T	**W**	**T**	**F**	**S**	**S**
Cycle hire									
4 Apr–1 Nov	10:15–5	M	T	W	T	F	**S**	**S**

Open BH Mons: Easter–Aug inc. During school hols (Easter Sun–Oct inc.), all facilities (inc. cycle hire) open Wed–Mon inc. Closed 24–26 Dec & 1 Jan 10. Courtyard café open at selected times

Bourne Mill

Bourne Road, Colchester, Essex CO2 8RT

❌ 👪 1936 (3:I8)

Picturesque watermill with working waterwheel

⭐ Parking limited. No WC

ℹ **T** 01206 572422
E bournemill@nationaltrust.org.uk

➔ 1ml S of centre of Colchester, in Bourne Road, off the Mersea Road (B1025)

Bourne Mill									
7 Jun–28 Jun	2–5	M	T	W	T	F	S	**S**
5 Jul–30 Aug	2–5	M	**T**	W	T	F	S	**S**

Open Easter, May & Aug BH Suns & Mons

Brancaster

Brancaster Millennium Activity Centre, Dial House, Brancaster Staithe, King's Lynn, Norfolk PE31 8BW

🏛 🎣 ♿ 🦮 ⌂ ♻ 👪 ▥ 🚲 1923 (3:H3)

Extensive coastal area famous for wild birds

Extensive coastal area around the fishing village of Brancaster Staithe. As well as the site of the Roman fort of Branodunum and Scolt Head Island (to which there is a private ferry service), there are tidal mud and sandflats and saltmarshes to explore. For those who prefer a more structured visit, there is the well-resourced Brancaster Millennium Activity Centre, which offers residential and day courses for families, adults and school groups. The centre also delivers its innovative Energy Busters Outreach Programme, exploring ways to reduce carbon footprints with schools and colleges in Norfolk.

What's new in 2009 New fishing quay at Brancaster Staithe with interpretation on the local fishing industry (funded by the Marine and Fisheries Agency, East of England Development Agency and King's Lynn and West Norfolk Borough Council)

⭐ Scolt Head Island National Nature Reserve is managed by Natural England (tel. 01328 711183) and is an important breeding site for four species of tern, oystercatcher and ringed plover. Please note that it can be dangerous to walk over the saltmarsh and sandflats, especially at low tide. Local authority maintained WC at Beach Road, Brancaster

[i] **T** 01485 210719
E brancaster@nationaltrust.org.uk

[🏆] Family fun weeks and activity days at Brancaster Millennium Activity Centre for children in school holidays

[🔥] **Grounds** [🏛]

[👪] Family fun weeks and activity days at Brancaster Millennium Activity Centre for children in school hols

[🏛] Suitable for school groups. Education room/centre. Brancaster Millennium Activity Centre is suitable for residential school groups. Adult study days

[🐕] On leads or under control at all times. Dog-free area on Brancaster Beach, W of golf clubhouse May–Sept. No dogs on Scolt Head Island NNR (not NT) April–mid Aug

[🚲] Activity centre offers group cycling activities; all staff trained in cycle group leadership. 'Start Cycling' scheme organised for groups

[→] [132:TF800450] **Foot**: Norfolk Coast Path passes property. **Cycle**: NCN1, runs along ridge above the coast. **Bus**: Norfolk Green Coast Hopper 36 ᕦ Sheringham–Hunstanton. **Road**: Brancaster Staithe is halfway between Wells and Hunstanton on A149 coast road

[P] Parking (not NT) at public car park at Beach Road, Brancaster (charge inc. NT members). Limited parking at the Staithe

NT properties nearby
Blakeney National Nature Reserve

Brancaster							
All year	**M**	**T**	**W**	**T**	**F**	**S**	**S**

The fishing village of Brancaster Staithe, Norfolk

Chilterns Gateway Centre, Dunstable Downs and Whipsnade Estate

Dunstable Road, Whipsnade, Bedfordshire LU6 2GY

[🏠][🏛][🏊][🍴][💷][🍽][🎧][🏞][🏆][👪][🏛][🐕][🚲]

[🍷] 1928   (3:E8)

Extensive chalk and grassland Area of Outstanding Natural Beauty

Commanding outstanding views over the Vale of Aylesbury and along the Chiltern Ridge, this is a kite-flying hotspot and the ideal place to watch gliders soar over the glorious landscape. Set within 206 hectares (510 acres) of grassland and farmland, this prime walking country is home to a wealth of wildlife. Plan your route in the comfort of our visitor centre, then visit our family-friendly café before exploring the gift shop, which sells an excellent range of kites.

What's new in 2009 New car parking areas

[⭐] The Centre is owned by Bedfordshire County Council and managed by the NT. Open daily (except 24/25 Dec) 10–5 (later, locally advertised times may apply in the summer)

[i] **T** 01582 500920
E dunstabledowns@nationaltrust.org.uk

[🎦] By appointment (if staffing availability permits)

[🎧] Fixed point audio description of views and Downs available in Chilterns Gateway Centre

[🏆] Family-focused events throughout year, including annual kite festival. See website for details

[🏃] Large selection of Downs-based circular walks leaflets available from Centre. OS maps available in shop

[♿][P][🚾][♿][♿][♿] **Building** [🏛] **Grounds** [🏛]

[🛍] NT gift shop with large range of kites

[💷] Café serving refreshments and range of local produce, including the famous Bedfordshire Clanger. Concession serving ice-cream in good weather

[👪] Baby-changing and feeding facilities. Pushchairs and baby back-carriers admitted. Activity packs. Family trails. Family-focused events throughout year, including annual kite festival

For public transport details, see page 377

▓ Suitable for school groups. Education room/centre (subject to booking fees)

☒ Under close control, on leads near livestock

☒ Public bridleway giving cyclists shared access. Route is part of Icknield Way Trail

→ [165/166:TL002189] **Foot**: footpaths from West Street and Tring Road, Dunstable.
Cycle: bridleway from West Street, Dunstable, and Whipsnade. **Bus**: Arriva 60 from Luton, Centrebus 327 from ▇ Hemel Hempstead and Red Rose 343 from ▇ St Albans, all Suns only; otherwise Arriva 61 Aylesbury–▇ Luton to within 1½ml. **Station**: Luton 7ml. Luton Airport Parkway 7ml. **Road**: Dunstable Downs & car parks: on B4541 W of Dunstable. Whipsnade Estate: car parks at Whipsnade crossroads (Whipsnade Heath)–junction of B4541 & B4540. Whipsnade Tree Cathedral B4540 (off village green)

P Parking off B4540, Bison Hill and B4541 Dunstable Downs, and at Whipsnade Tree Cathedral and Crossroads. £1 charge on Dunstable Downs. Space for 3 coaches only at Dunstable (no other coach facilities, booking essential). Car park adjacent to the Gateway Centre open 8–6 all year, or dusk if earlier

NT properties nearby
Ascott, Ashridge Estate, Shaw's Corner, Whipsnade Tree Cathedral

Gateway Centre at Dunstable Downs, Bedfordshire

Chilterns Gateway Centre								
Downs								
All year		M	T	W	T	F	S	S
Centre								
2 Feb–13 Mar	10–4	M	T	W	T	F	S	S
14 Mar–30 Oct	10–5	M	T	W	T	F	S	S
31 Oct–31 Jan 10	10–4	M	T	W	T	F	S	S

Chilterns Gateway Centre closed 24/25 Dec. Centre closes dusk if earlier. Car park adjacent to Centre locked dusk in winter and 6 in summer

Coggeshall Grange Barn

Grange Hill, Coggeshall, Colchester, Essex CO6 1RE

🏠 ⌂ ☻ ♿ 1989   (3:18)

13th-century monastic barn

With a beautiful cathedral-like interior, majestic Coggeshall Grange Barn was originally part of a Cistercian monastery and is one of the oldest surviving timber-framed buildings in Europe. After years of agricultural use, the barn fell into disrepair but was saved from demolition and lovingly restored in the 1980s. It now houses a small collection of farm carts and local historic exhibits. Prior to its restoration, the barn was used as a film set for Southwark's Tabard Inn in Pier Paolo Pasolini's 1972 film version of Chaucer's *The Canterbury Tales*.

What's new in 2009 New display on the history and restoration of the barn

ℹ **T** 01376 562226
E coggeshall@nationaltrust.org.uk

☻ Craft fairs, theatre

♿ 🅿 ♿ ♿ ⓐ Building ♿ Grounds ♿

♿ Pushchairs and baby back-carriers admitted. Children's quiz/trail

→ [168:TL848223] **Foot**: Essex Way long-distance footpath passes the barn. **Bus**: First 70 Colchester–Braintree (passing close ▇ Marks Tey). **Station**: Kelvedon 2¼ml.
Road: signposted off A120 Coggeshall bypass; ¼ml S from centre of Coggeshall, on B1024

P Parking, 20yds. Only available during barn opening times

NT properties nearby
Bourne Mill, Hatfield Forest, Paycocke's

Coggeshall Grange Barn									
5 Apr–11 Oct	2–5		M	**T**	W	**T**	F	**S**	**S**
Open BH Mons									

If you like kite flying on Dunstable Downs, you will love bike riding at Hatfield Forest

Charges for National Trust members apply on some special event days

Dunwich Heath: Coastal Centre and Beach

Dunwich, Saxmundham, Suffolk IP17 3DJ

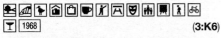

🍸 1968   (3:K6)

Coastal lowland heath, sandy cliffs and beach rich in wildlife, offering tranquillity and excellent views

Within an AONB and offering many excellent walks, the area is a remnant of the once extensive Sandlings heaths, with open tracts of heather and gorse, shady woods, sandy cliffs and beach. It is an important nature conservation area and home to scarce species such as the Dartford warbler and ant-lion.

★ Kite-flying restricted to beach only. Parking restrictions may operate at times of extreme fire risk. Cycling and horse riding on bridleways only

ℹ️ **T** 01728 648501
E dunwichheath@nationaltrust.org.uk

🎋 Details posted on property information boards and in events leaflet

♨ Annual events programme. Details posted on property information boards and in events leaflet (available from March)

🚶 Good network of walks along coast and around heath. Three waymarked trails on Dunwich Heath with map and information in guidebook. Circular walks taking in Mount Pleasant Farm and further afield RSPB Minsmere, Dunwich Forest and Westleton NNR

♿ 🅿 🚾 🛗 🄰 Building ♿♿♿

Grounds ♿➡♿

🏠 Gift shop in Coastguard Cottages

🍴 Tea-room (licensed) in Coastguard Cottages. Children's menu. Kiosk (seasonal)

👪 Pushchairs and baby back-carriers admitted. Front-carrying baby slings for loan

🎒 Suitable for school groups. Education room/centre. Hands-on activities. Specialising in coastal processes and issues

🐕 Open access area restrictions apply (please see notices)

There are many excellent walks at Dunwich Heath

🚲 Only on bridleways

➡ [156:TM476685] **Foot**: Suffolk Coast and Heaths Path and Sandlings Walk. Detailed maps on sale. **Cycle**: on Suffolk coastal cycle route. **Bus**: Coastlink from ≋ Darsham & Saxmundham. Book only on 01728 833526. **Station**: Darsham (U) 6ml. **Road**: 1ml S of Dunwich, signposted from A12. From Westledon/Dunwich road, 1ml before Dunwich village turn right into Minsmere road. Then 1ml to Dunwich Heath

🅿 Parking, 150yds (pay & display). Cars £4.20, caravans, large vans and motorhomes £12, motorcycles £3.20, coaches £32 (unless booked to use tea-room), limited to three coaches

NT properties nearby
Flatford: Bridge Cottage, Orford Ness National Nature Reserve, Sutton Hoo

Dunwich Heath		M	T	W	T	F	S	S
1 Feb–8 Mar	Dawn–dusk	M	T	W	T	F	**S**	**S**
11 Mar–12 Apr		M	T	**W**	**T**	**F**	**S**	**S**
13 Apr–19 Apr		**M**	**T**	**W**	**T**	**F**	**S**	**S**
22 Apr–24 May		M	T	**W**	**T**	**F**	**S**	**S**
25 May–31 May		**M**	**T**	**W**	**T**	**F**	**S**	**S**
3 Jun–12 Jul		M	T	**W**	**T**	**F**	**S**	**S**
13 Jul–13 Sep		**M**	**T**	**W**	**T**	**F**	**S**	**S**
16 Sep–25 Oct		M	T	**W**	**T**	**F**	**S**	**S**
26 Oct–1 Nov		**M**	**T**	**W**	**T**	**F**	**S**	**S**
4 Nov–20 Dec		M	T	**W**	**T**	**F**	**S**	**S**
27 Dec–28 Dec		**M**	T	W	T	F	S	**S**
1 Jan–3 Jan 10		M	T	W	T	**F**	**S**	**S**
9 Jan–31 Jan 10		M	T	W	T	**F**	**S**	**S**

Open BH Mons. Coastguard Cottages: shop & tea-room open from 10. Closing times vary

Elizabethan House Museum

4 South Quay, Great Yarmouth, Norfolk NR30 2QH

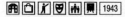 1943   (3:K5)

Delightful treasury of 16th-century domestic history

Step back in time at this beautiful 16th-century quayside house. Experience the lives of the people who lived here from Tudor to Victorian times. Find out what it was like to work in the kitchen and scullery through hands-on activities, and explore the differences between 'upstairs and downstairs' in Victorian life. There are Tudor costumes to try on, an activity-packed toy room and you can investigate the Conspiracy Room, where the execution of Charles I is said to have been planned. After the hive of activity inside this beautiful merchant's house, you can pause for a moment of peace in the small but delightful walled garden.

What's new in 2009 Civil War display featuring locally excavated coin hoard

⭐ The house is leased to Norfolk Museums and Archaeology Service

ℹ️ **T** 01493 855746
E elizabethanhouse@nationaltrust.org.uk

🎫 Guided tours for booked groups. Details of charges on application

🎭 Free family events and craft activities throughout the season

♿ ⠿ 🖼️ 🖥️ 📄 📑 **Building** 🔄 ♿

🎁 Gifts and cards

👪 Pushchairs and baby back-carriers admitted

🚌 Suitable for school groups. Guide available in French and German

➡️ [134:TG523073] On Great Yarmouth's historic South Quay. **Foot**: level walk from railway station along North Quay on to South Quay. **Cycle**: Regional Route 30 Great Yarmouth–Cromer. **Bus**: local services, plus services from surrounding areas. **Station**: Great Yarmouth ½ml. **Road**: from A47 take town centre signs, then follow brown Historic South Quay signs. From A12 follow brown signs

🅿️ Pay & display car park to the rear of the museum operated by Borough Council. Other parking available in close proximity to the museum near the town centre and historic quayside

NT properties nearby
Horsey Windpump

Elizabethan House Museum								
23 Mar–30 Oct	10–5	**M**	**T**	**W**	**T**	**F**	S	S
21 Mar–31 Oct	1:15–5	M	T	W	T	**F**	**S**	**S**

Felbrigg Hall, Garden and Park

Felbrigg, Norwich, Norfolk NR11 8PR

1969   (3:J4)

One of the most elegant country houses in East Anglia

A house of surprising contrasts, Felbrigg was built both before and after the English Civil War, and behind the sumptuous Stuart architecture lies a fascinating history. In the 19th century Felbrigg was almost lost to the shopping sprees of rackety 'Mad Windham', but was rescued when it passed to the Ketton-Cremer family in 1923, who restored it to its former glory. Explore the imposing Georgian Drawing Room and Gothic-style library, then investigate the kitchen, with its collection of beautiful kitchen implements and shining array of copperware. Outside, Felbrigg is a gardener's delight, with a decorative and productive walled garden, Victorian pleasure garden and rolling landscape park – with a lake and 200 hectares (520 acres) of woods to walk through on waymarked trails.

What's new in 2009 New displays from our vast unseen collection

ℹ️ **T** 01263 837444 **E** felbrigg@nationaltrust.org.uk

🎫 Occasional attics and cellars tours

🎭 Send sae for events leaflet

🚶 Waymarked walks to church, lake and woods

♿ 📱 📱 🏷️ ⠿ 📷 🖼️ 🖥️ 📑
Building 🔄 ♿ 🔄 **Grounds** ♿ ➡️ 📄

🎁 NT shop. Second-hand bookshop. Plant sales

🍽️ Carriage restaurant (licensed). Children's menu. Turret tea-room (licensed). Occasionally only

Dogs assisting visitors with disabilities are always welcome

Felbrigg Hall, Garden and Park

House		M T W T F S S
4 Apr–1 Nov	11–5	M T W T F S S

Gardens		
28 Feb–1 Apr	11–5	M T W T F S S
4 Apr–17 Apr	11–5	M T W T F S S
18 Apr–20 May	11–5	M T W T F S S
23 May–29 May	11–5	M T W T F S S
30 May–15 Jul	11–5	M T W T F S S
18 Jul–4 Sep	11–5	M T W T F S S
5 Sep–21 Oct	11–5	M T W T F S S
24 Oct–1 Nov	11–5	M T W T F S S
28 Dec–3 Jan 10	11–5	M T W T F S S

Shop/refreshments/plant sales		
28 Feb–1 Nov	As gardens	M T W T F S S
5 Nov–20 Dec	11–4	M T W T F S S
28 Dec–3 Jan 10	11–4	M T W T F S S
9 Jan–31 Jan 10	11–3	M T W T F S S

Bookshop		
4 Apr–1 Nov	11–5	M T W T F S S
5 Nov–20 Dec	11–4	M T W T F S S
9 Jan–31 Jan 10	11–4	M T W T F S S

Estate walks		
All year	Dawn–dusk	M T W T F S S

Open BH Mons and Good Fri

Carriage restaurant or Turret tea-room may be open. Booking advisable for restaurant

Baby-changing facilities. Front-carrying baby slings and hip-carrying infant seats for loan. Children's guide

Suitable for school groups

On leads in parkland when stock grazing. Under close control in woodland

Regional route 30 runs through the park

→ [133:TG193394] **Foot**: Weavers' Way runs through property. **Cycle**: Regional Route 30, Great Yarmouth–Wells. **Station**: Cromer (U) or Roughton Road (U), both 2½ml. **Road**: nr Felbrigg village, 2ml SW of Cromer; entrance off B1436, signposted from A148 and A140

P Parking, 100yds, £2

NT properties nearby
Blakeney National Nature Reserve, Blickling Hall, Gardens and Park, Horsey Windpump, Sheringham Park

Flatford: Bridge Cottage

Flatford, East Bergholt, Suffolk CO7 6UL

1943 (3:18)

Beautiful 16th-century thatched cottage by the River Stour

In the heart of the beautiful Dedham Vale, the charming hamlet of Flatford is the location for some of John Constable's most famous pastoral paintings. You can find out more about Constable from the exhibition in the thatched cottage. Just upstream from Flatford Mill there is a beautiful riverside tea-garden and a shop at Bridge Cottage, as well as boats available for hire to explore the River Stour.

What's new in 2009 Flatford Family Trail (leaflet available). New waymarked walks (up to two miles)

★ Car park is not NT. Flatford Mill, Valley Farm and Willy Lott's House are leased to the Field Studies Council, which runs arts-based

Waymarked trails help you explore the woods at Felbrigg Hall, Garden and Park

courses for all age groups. For information on courses tel. 01206 298283. There is no general public access to these buildings, but the Field Studies Council will arrange tours for groups

[i] **T** 01206 298260
E flatfordbridgecottage@nationaltrust.org.uk

[🚶] Short tours of the major Constable painting sites at Flatford. Longer guided walks visit the site of paintings in the wider Vale

[🎭] Annual open day for Valley Farmhouse in Sept

[🚶] Two waymarked walks at Flatford

[♿] [Pⓖ] [wc] [∷] [@] [🖼] [🎿] [⬆] [📱] **Building** [♿] [🔼]
Grounds [♿] [✂]

[🏪] NT shop with a range of Constable-related books and gifts

[☕] Riverside tea-room next to Bridge Cottage serving teas, light lunches and home-made cakes. Kiosk open during busy periods for ice-cream and snacks

[👪] Pushchairs and baby back-carriers admitted

[🏫] Suitable for school groups. Tours for school groups can be arranged on a theme of Constable's paintings at Flatford

[➜] [168:TM075333] ½ml S of East Bergholt. **Foot**: accessible from East Bergholt, Dedham and Manningtree. **Bus**: Network Colchester 93 Ipswich–Colchester (passing ▣ Ipswich and close ▣ Colchester Town), Mon–Sat alight E Bergholt, ¾ml. **Station**: Manningtree 1¾ml by footpath, 3½ml by road. **Road**: on N bank of Stour, 1ml S of East Bergholt (B1070)

[P] Parking (not NT), 200yds (pay & display), charge inc. NT members

NT properties nearby
Bourne Mill, Dedham Vale, The Suffolk Estuaries: Pin Mill and Kyson Hill, Thorington Hall

Flatford: Bridge Cottage								
1 Feb–28 Feb	11–3:30	M	T	W	T	F	**S**	**S**
1 Mar–30 Apr	11–5	M	T	**W**	**T**	**F**	**S**	**S**
1 May–30 Sep	10:30–5:30	**M**	**T**	**W**	**T**	**F**	**S**	**S**
1 Oct–31 Oct	11–4	**M**	**T**	**W**	**T**	**F**	**S**	**S**
1 Nov–20 Dec	11–3:30	M	T	**W**	**T**	**F**	**S**	**S**
2 Jan–31 Jan 10	11–3:30	M	T	W	T	F	**S**	**S**

Open BH Mons. Property may close early in winter if weather is bad (Oct–Jan 10 inc.)

For public transport details, see page 377

Hatfield Forest

nr Bishop's Stortford, Essex

 [1924] **(3:G8)**

Ancient royal hunting forest

Step back into the Middle Ages in the unique area of ancient coppiced and pollarded trees that is Hatfield Forest. Very little has changed since Henry I claimed this forested landscape in the early 12th century. This is a place of great historical and ecological importance, supporting rare and specialised wildlife – from deer to the smallest minibeast. Learn about the countryside, wildlife, art and history of this very special landscape in the Discovery Room. There are miles of excellent walks and nature trails to explore and fishing in the lake; there are even traditional woodland products for sale.

What's new in 2009 Oak stump interpretation outside Shell House. Spy cameras in bird nest and bat roost. Tracker Packs. New shop in lake area selling a variety of exciting products

[★] There are no admission charges for this property, although a car park charge does apply. Postal address: Hatfield Forest Estate Office, Takeley, Bishop's Stortford, Hertfordshire CM22 6NE. Dogs that may chase wildlife or livestock must be kept on leads at all times

[i] **T** 01279 874040 (Infoline), 01279 870678
E hatfieldforest@nationaltrust.org.uk

[🎭] Open-air theatre and concerts, including Woodfest (yearly celebration of woodland and associated activities). Many family events including Father Christmas trails. Wildlife-associated activities and walks. Send sae or visit NT website for details

[🚶] Three trail guides

[♿] [Pⓖ] [wc] [@] [⬆] **Grounds** [♿] [➡] [✂] [🔼]

[🏪] Guides and postcards available from the entrance kiosk, Shell House and Discovery Room. Annual book sale. Shop in lake area selling Discover Nature and Country Explorer range products, as well as books, trails, guides, postcards, local products and plants

[☕] Lakeside Café (not NT) (licensed) in lake area within forest. Serving home-made cakes pastries, baked potatoes and sandwiches. Local produce. Seasonal menu. Children's menu

Hatfield Forest									
All Year	Dawn–dusk	**M**	**T**	**W**	**T**	**F**	**S**	**S**	
Refreshments									
24 Mar–31 Oct	10–5	**M**	**T**	**W**	**T**	**F**	**S**	**S**	
1 Nov–31 Jan 10	10–3:30	M	T	**W**	**T**	**F**	**S**	**S**	
Shop									
24 Mar–31 Oct	10–5	**M**	**T**	**W**	**T**	**F**	**S**	**S**	
1 Nov–31 Jan 10	10–3:30	M	T	W	T	F	**S**	**S**	

Refreshments and shop available daily in school hols.
Refreshments: summer 10–6; winter 10–3:30

All-terrain pushchairs for loan. Children's quiz/trail. Wildlife and environment groups for young children. Tracker Packs. Family events, including Father Christmas trails

Suitable for school groups. Adult study days. Hands-on activities. Learning Officer

On leads near livestock and around lake. Dog-free area near lake. Dog training workshops available through property

Several miles of grass track suitable for cycling. Cyclists excluded from area of lake, gravel pit and on boardwalk

→ [167:TL547203] 4ml east of Bishop's Stortford. **Foot**: Flitch Way from Braintree. Three Forests Way and Forest Way pass through the forest. **Cycle**: Flitch Way. **Bus**: Stanstead Transit 7 Bishop's Stortford–Elsenham, alight Takeley Street (Green Man), then ½ml. **Station**: Stansted Airport 3ml. **Road**: from M11 exit 8, take B1256 towards Takeley. Signposted from B1256

P Parking. 24 March–31 Oct & Suns all year. 10–5 or dusk if earlier. Cars £4.50, minibuses £6.50, coaches £25, school coaches £10

NT properties nearby
Blakes Wood, Bourne Mill, Coggeshall Grange Barn, Danbury and Lingwood Commons, Paycocke's, Wimpole Hall, Wimpole Home Farm

Elgin's Coppice, Hatfield Forest, at sunset

Horsey Windpump

Horsey, Great Yarmouth, Norfolk NR29 4EF

1948 (3:K4)

Imposing five-storey drainage windpump

Striking windpump surrounded by internationally important wildlife habitats in the Broads National Park. The windpump offers stunning views of Horsey Mere and across the broadland landscape to the coast. The Horsey Estate is of exceptional nature conservation interest, notably for breeding birds and wintering wildfowl.

What's new in 2009 Wheelchair-accessible nature garden, including raised ponds for pond dipping, wildflower meadow and local varieties of fruit trees

★ The Horsey Estate was acquired by the NT in 1948 from the Buxton family, who continue to manage the Horsey Estate with nature conservation as a priority. NT WCs open March–Oct, as shop/tea-room. Correspondence to Norfolk Coast Office, Friary Farm, Cley Road, Blakeney, Norfolk, NR25 7NW

i **T** 01263 740241
E horseywindpump@nationaltrust.org.uk

For school groups and special interest groups (small charge)

Waymarked circular walks, leaflet available

Building Grounds

Small NT shop at the Staithe Stores, close to windpump

Light refreshments and ice-creams available at the Staithe Stores, close to windpump

Baby-changing facilities

Suitable for school groups

On leads only

→ [134:TG457223] **Cycle**: Regional Route 30, Great Yarmouth–Wells. **Bus**: First 1/A/B Lowestoft–Martham (passing close Great Yarmouth), alight W Somerton School, 1¾ml. **Station**: Acle (U) 10ml. **Road**: 15ml N of Great Yarmouth on B1159; 4ml NE of Martham

Please remember – your membership card is *always* needed for free admission

P Parking, 50yds. 50p up to 1 hour, £1.50 for 4 hours or £2.50 all day (pay & display). Open dawn to dusk. Access difficult for coaches

NT properties nearby
Elizabethan House Museum

Horsey Windpump									
28 Feb–29 Mar	10–5	M	T	W	T	F	S	S	
1 Apr–6 Sep	10–5	M	T	W	T	F	S	S	
9 Sep–18 Oct	10–5	M–T		W	T	F	S	S	
19 Oct–25 Oct	10–5	M	T	W	T	F	S	S	
28 Oct–1 Nov	10–5	M	T	W	T	F	S	S	
Open Good Fri & BH Mons									

Houghton Mill

Houghton, nr Huntingdon, Cambridgeshire PE28 2AZ

[icons] 1939   (3:F6)

Impressive working 18th-century watermill

Full of excellent hand-on activities for all the family and with most of its machinery still intact, this five-storey weatherboarded building is the last working watermill on the Great Ouse. Flour is for sale, ground in the traditional way by water-powered mill stones on Sundays and Bank Holiday Mondays. The mill stands on an island on the edge of the attractive village of Houghton and is an ideal starting point for a walk through the water meadows. The National Trust tea-room offers delicious food and drink to refresh you after your stroll.

What's new in 2009 Virtual tour. Hydro power display and improved tea-room with additional riverside seating

★ Milling demonstrations subject to river level

i T 01480 301494
   E houghtonmill@nationaltrust.org.uk

🎭 Open-air theatre and family events

🏃 Starting point for circular walks; maps available to buy

[icons] Building [icons]
Grounds ➡

🍽 Tea-room. Delightful riverside setting

👶 Baby-changing facilities. Children's quiz/trail. Family events

Houghton Mill is still operational today

🏫 Suitable for school groups. Hands-on activities

🐕 On leads and only in grounds

🚲 Through riverside meadows close to NCN51

➔ [153:TL282720] **Foot**: Ouse Valley Way from Huntingdon and St Ives. **Cycle**: NCN51 from Huntingdon. **Bus**: Huntingdon & District 555, Whippet 1A, from Huntingdon (passing close 🚉 Huntingdon). **Station**: Huntingdon 3½ml. **Road**: in village of Houghton, signposted off A1123 Huntingdon to St Ives

P Parking, 20yds, £1.50 (pay & display). No access for large coaches (drop off in village square)

NT properties nearby
Anglesey Abbey, Peckover House and Garden, Ramsey Abbey Gatehouse, Wicken Fen National Nature Reserve, Willington Dovecote and Stables, Wimpole Hall

Houghton Mill								
Mill/bookshop								
21 Mar–25 Oct	11–5	M	T	W	T	F	S	S
27 Apr–27 Sep	1–5	M	T	W	T	F	S	S
Tea-room								
As mill	11–5							
Walks/car park								
All year	9–6	M	T	W	T	F	S	S
Open BH Mons & Good Fri: mill 11–5; tea-room 11–5. Caravan and campsite open March–Oct. Groups and school parties at other times by arrangement with Property Manager. Milling demonstrations on Sun afternoons								

Ickworth House, Park and Gardens

The Rotunda, Horringer, Bury St Edmunds, Suffolk IP29 5QE

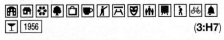

▼ 1956 (3:H7)

A Georgian Italianate palace in an idyllic English landscape

Ickworth's huge central Rotunda, flanked by two massive wings, dominates this eccentric house built by the equally eccentric 4th Earl of Bristol, who dreamed of creating an Italianate palace within an English landscape. It houses important collections of paintings (including work by Velázquez and Titian) and fine family portraits (several by Gainsborough), as well as Huguenot and ambassadorial silver and Regency furniture. The fabulous State Rooms were only used by the family on special occasions, and are as pristine and awe-inspiring today as they were when orginally created. Today, the West Wing contains visitor, conference, banqueting and wedding facilities, while the East Wing is now The Ickworth Hotel. Wooded Pleasure Grounds provide a shady and delightful contrast to the formality of the Italianate Garden. Beyond there are 729 hectares (1,800 acres) of idyllic parkland, including a vineyard and dense woodland offering miles of walks. For the more adventurous, a family cycle route, 'trim trail' and challenging play area offer opportunities to burn off some more energy.

The central rotunda at Ickworth: an eccentric house

What's new in 2009 House now opening two hours earlier, at 11

★ Ickworth offers conference, banqueting and wedding facilities in the West Wing (Sodexo Prestige) tel. 01284 735957 (ickworth.house@sodexo.com). For The Ickworth Hotel tel. 01284 735350. If you visit the house between 11 and 1 please be aware that booked learning activities may be taking place

ℹ **T** 01284 735270
E ickworth@nationaltrust.org.uk

🍴 Themed restaurant events/meals, concerts, plays, school holiday and family activities, country life events. Event hamper service available. Please tel. Sodexo Prestige

🚶 Waymarked walks in park and woodland. Lengths vary from 1¼ml to 7ml. All terrains

♿ P D WC ⛽ 🔍 👁 🔊 ⌨ ♿ House 🚻♿ 🔊 ♿ West Wing 🚻♿ 🔊 Grounds 🚻♿ ➡ ♿

🏪 Shop and plant centre (plant sales and garden products)

🍽 West Wing Restaurant (NT-approved concession) (licensed) serving Ickworth Estate wines. Morning, lunchtime and afternoon menus, hot and cold meals, drinks. Kiosk (NT-approved concession) in visitor car park. Hot and cold drinks, ice-cream, snacks

🚼 Baby-changing facilities. Front-carrying baby slings and hip-carrying infant seats for loan. Children's play area. Children's guide. Children's quiz/trail. Family activity packs. Family events and activities. All-terrain pushchair available for outdoor use. Family 'Trim Trail' in woods. Family cycle route

▣ Suitable for school groups. Education room/centre. Hands-on activities. Live interpretation. Learning Officer. Adult study days

🐕 On leads

🚲 Family cycle route (2½ml), various surfaces with some steep gradients; helmets and adult supervision advised

➔ [155:TL810610] **Foot**: 4½ml via footpaths from Bury St Edmunds. **Bus**: Burtons 344/5 Bury St Edmunds–Haverhill (passing close ≊ Bury St Edmunds). **Station**: Bury St

Unless indicated, last admission is always 30mins before closing time

Edmunds 3ml. **Road**: in Horringer, 3ml SW of Bury St Edmunds on W side of A143

P Free parking, 200yds

NT properties nearby

Anglesey Abbey, Lavenham Guildhall, Melford Hall, Theatre Royal, Bury St Edmunds

Ickworth House, Park and Gardens									
House									
14 Mar–1 Nov	11–5	M	T	W	T	F	S	S
Park									
All year	8–8	M	T	W	T	F	S	S
Italianate Garden									
1 Feb–13 Mar	11–4	M	T	W	T	F	S	S
14 Mar–1 Nov	10–5	M	T	W	T	F	S	S
2 Nov–31 Jan 10	11–4	M	T	W	T	F	S	S
Shop/restaurant									
1 Feb–13 Mar	11–4	M	T	W	T	F	S	S
14 Mar–1 Nov	10–5	M	T	W	T	F	S	S
2 Nov–31 Jan 10	11–4	M	T	W	T	F	S	S

Park, gardens, shop and restaurant open daily during Suffolk CC school hols. Open all BH Mons, Good Fri and 1 Jan 10. Property closed 24, 25, 26 Dec. Park closes dusk if earlier than 8

Lavenham: The Guildhall of Corpus Christi, this Tudor building contains fascinating exhibitions

Lavenham: The Guildhall of Corpus Christi

Market Place, Lavenham, Sudbury, Suffolk CO10 9QZ

🏠 ❄ 🗁 🍽 🎭 👪 🎦 1951 (3:17)

Tudor building in the heart of the remarkably preserved medieval village of Lavenham

One of the finest timber-framed buildings in Britain, the Guildhall is at the centre of what was once the fourteenth richest town in England. Built c.1530 by the religious Corpus Christi guild, it now contains fascinating exhibitions on local history and traditional farming practices, as well as the area's medieval cloth industry, while the dressing-up boxes and trailbooks will delight all children! Be sure to explore the tranquil courtyard garden, where there are traditional dye plants which produce colours that are bright even for today.

What's new in 2009 New timeline of Lavenham's history in the cellar. New programme of events

ℹ️ **T** 01787 247646
   E lavenhamguildhall@nationaltrust.org.uk

🎭 Talks, lecture lunches and craft demonstrations. Family fun days

♿ 🦽 ⠿ 🔘 ♿ 🖥 🚪 👜 📷
Building 🦽 🦽 🦽 **Grounds** 🦽 🦽

🗁 Gift shop with range of local products

🍽 Tea-room serving light lunches and home-made produce. Children's menu

👪 Baby back-carriers admitted. Hip-carrying infant seats for loan. Children's quiz/trail. Dressing-up clothes. Family fun days

🎦 Suitable for school groups

➡️ [155:TL916493] **Foot**: 'railway walk' links Lavenham with Long Melford. **Cycle**: South Suffolk Cycle Route A1. **Bus**: Chambers 753 Bury St Edmunds–Colchester (passes close ⊠ Bury St Edmunds and ⊠ Sudbury). **Station**: Sudbury (U) 7ml. **Road**: A1141 and B1071

P Free parking (not NT), 10yds

NT properties nearby
Flatford: Bridge Cottage, Ickworth House, Park and Gardens, Melford Hall, Theatre Royal, Bury St Edmunds

Lavenham Guildhall									
Guildhall									
7 Mar–29 Mar	11–4	M	T	**W**	**T**	**F**	**S**	**S**	
1 Apr–1 Nov	11–5	**M**	**T**	**W**	**T**	**F**	**S**	**S**	
7 Nov–29 Nov	11–4	M	T	W	T	F	**S**	**S**	
Shop									
7 Mar–1 Nov	As Guildhall								
5 Nov–20 Dec	11–4	M	T	W	**T**	**F**	**S**	**S**	
9 Jan–31 Jan 10	11–4	M	T	W	T	F	**S**	**S**	
Tea-room									
7 Mar–1 Nov	As Guildhall								
5 Nov–20 Dec	11–4	M	T	W	T	F	**S**	**S**	

Open BH Mons. Closed Good Fri. Parts of the building may be closed occasionally for community use. Tea-room open BH Mons

Melford Hall

Long Melford, Sudbury, Suffolk CO10 9AA

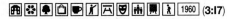 1960 (3:17)

Follow in Beatrix Potter's footsteps at this beautiful Tudor family home

At first sight, the thrusting turrrets of Melford Hall look very much as they did when Elizabeth I visited with her 2,000 courtiers in 1578. Inside the Hall, there is a fine panelled banqueting hall, as well as Regency, Georgian and Victorian rooms charting the tastes of the Hyde Parkers – who have lived here since 1786. The house is filled with reminders of the family's history and, as they were a naval family, this includes fine nautical paintings and even plunder looted from a Spanish ship in 1762. As well as being one of the earliest country houses in Britain to have central heating, Melford also boasts a family connection with Beatrix Potter, who sketched here on her visits, and the house is home to the original Jemima Puddleduck doll. Outside, a rare and beautiful 17th-century banqueting house, probably built by the Savage family, sits in Edwardian-style gardens that are surrounded by the remains of an ancient deer park, forming 52 hectares (130 acres) of parkland.

What's new in 2009 New interpretation displays

i T 01787 376395 (Infoline), 01787 379228
E melford@nationaltrust.org.uk

Programme of events throughout the season for all ages

1ml circular walk through park. 4ml walk linking Lavenham and Long Melford close to the property

Building L Grounds

NT gifts, second-hand books and plant sales at South Gatelodge

Light refreshments only

Baby-changing facilities. Hip-carrying infant seats and baby sling for loan. Family trail

Suitable for school groups

On leads and only in car park and park walk

→ [155:TL867462] **Foot**: 'railway walk' linking Long Melford with Lavenham, 4ml.
Bus: Beestons/Chambers/Felix various services, Mon–Sat from Sudbury; Chambers 753, Mon–Sat Bury St Edmunds–Colchester; Network Colchester 90C, Sun Haverhill–Ipswich (passes ⊠ Ipswich). All pass close ⊠ Sudbury. **Station**: Sudbury (U) 4ml. **Road**: in Long Melford off A134, 14ml S of Bury St Edmunds, 3ml N of Sudbury

P Free parking, 200yds. Access for coaches and other large vehicles by gated entrance 100yds north of main entrance (signed)

NT properties nearby
Flatford: Bridge Cottage, Ickworth House, Park and Gardens, Lavenham Guildhall, Theatre Royal, Bury St Edmunds

Melford Hall									
4 Apr–5 Apr	1:30–5	M	T	W	T	F	**S**	**S**	
11 Apr–19 Apr	1:30–5	**M**	T	**W**	**T**	**F**	**S**	**S**	
25 Apr–26 Apr	1:30–5	M	T	W	T	F	**S**	**S**	
1 May–30 Sep	1:30–5	M	T	**W**	**T**	**F**	**S**	**S**	
3 Oct–1 Nov	1:30–5	M	T	W	T	F	**S**	**S**	

Open BH Mons

If you felt inspired by local history at Melford Hall, then you'll settle in at Felbrigg Hall

Orford Ness National Nature Reserve

Quay Office, Orford Quay, Orford, Woodbridge, Suffolk IP12 2NU

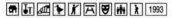 1993 (3:K7)

Internationally important nature reserve, with a fascinating 20th-century military history

The largest vegetated shingle spit in Europe, the Reserve contains a variety of habitats including shingle, saltmarsh, mudflat, brackish lagoons and grazing marsh. It provides an important location for breeding and passage birds as well as for the coastal shingle flora and wildlife, including a large number of nationally rare species. The Ness was a secret military test site from 1913 until the mid 1980s. Visitors follow a $5\frac{1}{2}$ml route, which can be walked in total or in part (the full walk involves walking on shingle). Other walks (approx. three miles) are open seasonally.

The military Pagodas at Orford Ness, Suffolk

⭐ Charge for ferry (inc. NT members). Access around the site is on foot only, but a trailer bus operates first Sat of the month July–Sept, booking essential (not a guided tour). Numbers limited. Some military buildings (eg 'pagodas') accessible only on guided events. No dogs or cycles

ℹ️ **T** 01728 648024 (Infoline), 01394 450900
E orfordness@nationaltrust.org.uk

🎒 Natural history, military history and general interest

🎭 Working lighthouse visit – joint NT and Trinity House event. Wildtrack Working Holidays. Tel. 0870 429 2429 for details. Marine Conservation Society Beachwatch – coastal survey and clean up. Tel. 01394 450900 after July for details

🚶 Illustrated trail guide covering three available walks and children's quiz/trail for sale

♿ D♿ ♿ Building 🏞️ Grounds 🏞️ ➡️ ♿

👫 Pushchairs and baby back-carriers admitted. Access involves a boat crossing. All pushchairs etc must be suitable for lifting on to a boat and up and down steep steps

➡️ [169:TM425495] **Foot**: Suffolk Coast Path runs nearby on mainland via Orford Quay. **Cycle**: NCN1, 1ml. No cycle parking. **Ferry**: access only via ferry *Octavia*. See 'opening arrangements'. **Bus**: Far East Travel 71 from Woodbridge (passing ≋ Melton). **Station**: Wickham Market 8ml. **Road**: access from Orford Quay, Orford town 10ml E of A12 (B1094/1095), 12ml NE of Woodbridge B1152/1084

🅿️ Parking (not NT), 150yds (pay & display), charge inc. NT members. Located in Quay Street

NT properties nearby
Dunwich Heath, The Suffolk Estuaries: Pin Mill and Kyson Hill, Sutton Hoo

Orford Ness National Nature Reserve							
11 Apr–27 Jun	M	T	W	T	F	**S**	S
30 Jun–26 Sep	M	**T**	**W**	**T**	**F**	**S**	S
3 Oct–31 Oct	M	T	W	T	F	**S**	S

The only access is by NT ferry from Orford Quay, with boats crossing regularly to the Ness between 10 & 2 only, the last ferry leaving the Ness at 5

Charges for National Trust members apply on some special event days

Oxburgh Hall

Oxborough, Norfolk PE33 9PS

🏠 ✝ 🎴 📷 ☕ 🍴 🎡 🛡 👪 🎦 🧍

🍷 | 1952 | (3:H5)

15th-century moated manor house

Oxburgh's secret doors and priest's hole make this a house of mystery and history. Step back in time through the magnificent Tudor gatehouse into the dangerous world of Tudor politics. Home to the Bedingfeld family since 1482, this stunning red-brick house charts their history from medieval austerity to neo-Gothic Victorian comfort. As well as early Mortlake tapestries in the Queen's Room, Oxburgh houses beautiful embroidered hangings by Mary, Queen of Scots, and Bess of Hardwick. Panoramic views from the roof look out over the Victorian French parterre, walled orchard, kitchen garden and a Catholic chapel. There are quizzes, trails and dressing-up clothes to try on, and charming woodland walks.

What's new in 2009 Two ancestral portraits on display in the house for the first time since 1951

ℹ️ **T** 01366 328258
E oxburghhall@nationaltrust.org.uk

🎡 Regular garden tours and winter woodland tours

🛡 Open-air theatre. Children's events. Musical events. Living history. Lecture lunches. Christmas events

🧍 Woodland Explorer trail

♿ 🅿️ ♿ 🚻 ♿ 📖 📺 ♿ 🔊 🔡

Building ♿♿♿ **Grounds** ♿ ➡️

📷 NT shop. Plant sales. Second-hand bookshop during season

☕ Tea-room (licensed) in Old Kitchen. Children's menu. The Pantry (kiosk) serving light snacks

👪 Baby-changing facilities. Front-carrying baby slings and hip-carrying infant seats for loan. Children's guide. Children's quiz/trail. Dressing-up clothes to try on

🎦 Suitable for school groups. Live interpretation and hands-on activities

➡️ [143:TF742012] **Station**: Downham Market 10ml. **Road**: at Oxborough, 7ml SW of

Oxburgh Hall: visit this 15th-century manor house and find out what it was like to be a priest on the run in the 16th century

Swaffham on S side of Stoke Ferry road; 3ml from A134 at Stoke Ferry

🅿️ Free parking

NT properties nearby
Peckover House and Garden, St George's Guildhall

Oxburgh Hall										
House			M	T	W	T	F	S	S
28 Feb–8 Mar	11–5		M	T	W	T	F	**S**	**S**
14 Mar–29 Jul	11–5		**M**	**T**	**W**	T	F	**S**	**S**
1 Aug–31 Aug	11–5		**M**	**T**	**W**	**T**	F-S	**S**	**S**
1 Sep–1 Nov	11–5		**M**	**T**	**W**	T	F	**S**	**S**
Garden/tea-room/shop									
1 Feb–8 Mar	11–4		M	T	W	T	F	**S**	**S**
14 Mar–29 Jul	11–5		**M**	**T**	**W**	T	F	**S**	**S**
1 Aug–31 Aug	11–5		**M**	**T**	**W**	**T**	**F**	**S**	**S**
1 Sep–1 Nov	11–5		**M**	**T**	**W**	T	F	**S**	**S**
7 Nov–20 Dec	11–4		M	T	W	T	F	**S**	**S**
2 Jan–31 Jan 10	11–4		M	T	W	T	F	**S**	**S**

Open BH Mons and Good Fri: 11–5 (inc. house).
Gatehouse open Sat & Sun 10–31 Jan 10, 12–3

Show your card and display sticker for free parking

Paycocke's

West Street, Coggeshall, Colchester,
Essex CO6 1NS

 1924 (3:18)

Fine late Gothic merchant's house

With its unusually intricate panelling and woodcarving, Paycocke's shows the wealth of the area generated by the 15th- and 16th-century wool trade. Examine the examples of the famous Coggeshall lace displayed in the house and explore the peaceful cottage garden.

⭐ Groups (10+) must book in advance with the tenant. Children must be accompanied by an adult. No WC, nearest WC at Grange Barn, ½ml

ℹ️ T 01376 561305
E paycockes@nationaltrust.org.uk

♿ Building ⬇️ Grounds

👶 Pushchairs admitted

➡️ [168:TL848225] **Foot**: close to Essex Way. **Bus**: First 70 Colchester–Braintree (passing ≋ Marks Tey). **Station**: Kelvedon 2½ml. **Road**: 5½ml E of Braintree. Signposted off A120. On S side of West Street, 400yds from centre of Coggeshall, on road to Braintree next to the Fleece Inn

🅿️ Parking at Grange Barn (½ml) until 5

NT properties nearby

Bourne Mill, Coggeshall Grange Barn, Flatford: Bridge Cottage, Hatfield Forest

Paycocke's								
5 Apr–11 Oct	2–5	M	T	W	T	F	S	S
Open BH Mons								

The street façade of Paycocke's in Coggeshall, Essex

Peckover House and Garden

North Brink, Wisbech, Cambridgeshire PE13 1JR

 1943 (3:G5)

Elegant Georgian town house with wonderful walled garden

Explore the fascinating home of the Peckovers, the Quaker banking family who lived here for 150 years. This is a hands-on house with a 'Cabinet of Curiosities', dressing-up clothes for children of all ages, and three floors revealing the lives of both the family and their servants. Built c.1722, this is one of England's finest town houses with superb rococo plaster and wood decorations. Outside, discover the hidden wonders of the 0.8 hectares (two acres) of beautiful Victorian garden, with its orangery, summerhouse, roses and manicured croquet lawn, as well as a 17th-century thatched barn and Georgian stables. There are stunning displays of daffodils, narcissi and tulips in spring and roses in summer.

What's new in 2009 Rear Hall now open

⭐ For car parking follow signs to Chapel Road car park and walk from there (250yds). Note: the birthplace of Octavia Hill, who co-founded the NT in 1895, is within walking distance (not NT). Open at the same times as Peckover House

ℹ️ T 01945 583463
E peckover@nationaltrust.org.uk

🎭 'Behind the Scenes' special guided tour one weekend a month (charge inc. NT members). Free garden tours most weekends

🎭 Garden talks, open-air theatre, Easter and Christmas events

♿ Building ⬇️ Grounds

🛍️ NT shop. Plant sales. Second-hand bookshop

🍴 Licensed tea-room in Reed Barn

👶 Baby-changing facilities. Hip-carrying infant seats for loan. Handling collection, including 'Cabinet of Curiosities'

🏫 Suitable for school groups. Hands-on activities. 'Upstairs downstairs' education package

Dogs assisting visitors with disabilities are always welcome

The orangery at Peckover House, Wisbech

Peckover House and Garden								
House/shop/bookshop*								
14 Mar–1 Nov	1–4:30	**M**	**T**	**W**	T	F	**S**	**S**
Garden/restaurant								
14 Mar–1 Nov	12–5	**M**	**T**	**W**	T	F	**S**	**S**
Open Good Fri & for Wisbech Rose Fair, 2/3 July.								
*Shop/bookshop open 12:30								

→ [143:TF458097] **Foot**: from Chapel Road car park walk up passageway to left of Wisbech Arms public house, turn right by river. Peckover House is 100yds on right. **Cycle**: NCN1, ¼ml. **Bus**: First X1 ⊞ Peterborough–Lowestoft; X1 and Norfolk Green 46 from King's Lynn (passing close ⊞ King's Lynn). **Station**: March 9½ml. **Road**: W of Wisbech town centre on N bank of River Nene (B1441)

P Free parking (not NT), 250yds

NT properties nearby
Houghton Mill, Oxburgh Hall, St George's Guildhall

Ramsey Abbey Gatehouse

Abbey School, Ramsey, Huntingdon, Cambridgeshire PE17 1DH

🏠 👥 1952 (3:F6)

Remains of a former Benedictine abbey

⭐ Property is on school grounds – please respect school security arrangements. Exterior can be seen all year, but interior open on selected days only. No WC

ℹ️ **T** 01480 301494
E ramseyabbey@nationaltrust.org.uk

→ At SE edge of Ramsey, at point where Chatteris road leaves B1096, 10ml SE of Peterborough

Ramsey Abbey Gatehouse
Open 1–5 first Sun of month, April–Sept inc. Group visits by appointment on other weekends

Rayleigh Mount

Rayleigh, Essex

🚶 🏕 🐕 🦮 1923 (3:I10)

Norman motte and bailey remains

Dating from the earliest days after the Norman Conquest, Rayleigh Mount still commands sweeping views across the Crouch Valley, just as it did when Sweyn of Essex built the first defences. Display boards explain the main points of interest and many kinds of wildlife can be seen in this haven in the middle of Rayleigh town centre. There are views over the mount and an exhibition on the history of Rayleigh in the adjacent windmill (not NT).

What's new in 2009 New model of the castle on display in the adjacent windmill

⭐ The windmill is owned and operated by Rochford District Council (tel. 01702 318120 for opening times). No WC, nearest WC in Mill Hall

ℹ️ **T** 01284 747500
E rayleighmount@nationaltrust.org.uk

🚶 Guided tours most summer Sat afternoons

🎭 Open-air theatre in July

♿ 🅿 Grounds 🦽

For events details, visit www.nationaltrust.org.uk/events

➡ [178:TQ805909] 100yds from High Street, next to Mill Hall car park. **Bus**: from surrounding areas. **Station**: Rayleigh 200yds. **Road**: 6ml NW of Southend (A129)

🅿 Parking (not NT) (pay & display), charge inc. NT members

NT properties nearby
Blakes Wood, Danbury and Lingwood Commons, Northey Island

Rayleigh Mount									
Summer	7–6	M	T	W	T	F	S	S	
Winter	7–5	M	T	W	T	F	S	S	

The Mount closes 2 Sats and other opening times may vary. Tel. 01284 747500 for details

St George's Guildhall

29 King Street, King's Lynn, Norfolk PE30 1HA

🏠 🗂 💻 🎭 🎬 [1951] (3:H5)

England's largest surviving medieval Guildhall

The building is now converted into a theatre and arthouse cinema and also houses several art galleries. Many interesting features survive.

ℹ **T** 01553 765565
   E stgeorgesguildhall@nationaltrust.org.uk

🎭 Theatre, film, music, comedy and King's Lynn Festival, performances, workshops and art exhibitions

♿ Building 🅰 Grounds 🦽

🗂 Crafts, Christmas shop from mid Nov (not NT)

🍽 Riverside restaurant (not NT) serves lunch and dinner Mon–Sat. Crofters Café (not NT). 9:30–5 Mon–Sat

🏫 Suitable for school groups

➡ [132:TF616202] On W side of King Street close to the Tuesday Market Place. **Cycle**: NCN1, ¼ml. **Bus**: from surrounding area. **Station**: King's Lynn ½ml

🅿 Parking (not NT) (pay & display)

NT properties nearby
Oxburgh Hall, Peckover House and Garden

St George's Guildhall							
All year	M	T	W	T	F	S	S

Closed Good Fri, BH Mons, 24 Dec to 1st Mon in Jan 10. Tel. for opening dates and times for Guildhall. The Guildhall is not usually open on days when there are performances in the theatre. Tel. box office, open Mon–Fri 10–2, for details

Shaw's Corner

Ayot St Lawrence, nr Welwyn, Hertfordshire AL6 9BX

🏠 ✳ 🗂 🚪 🎭 🏃 🏫 [1944] (3:F9)

Home of famous Irish playwright G. B. Shaw

Built in 1902 and home to George Bernard Shaw for more than 40 years, Shaw's Corner is an Arts & Crafts house which is much as he left it. The clothes in Shaw's wardrobe, the typewriter, glasses and dictionary in his study and the collection of hats in the hall, as well as the 1938 Oscar for *Pygmalion*, give you the sense Shaw has just left the room. Hidden away in the

George Bernard Shaw's desk in the study remains exactly as he left it

garden is the hut in which Shaw wrote his best known works. The hut revolved to catch the sun, and the electric heater and telephone meant that Shaw could work here in all weathers. Surrounding it the orchard, flower meadow, rose dell and densely planted herbaceous beds create a vigorous, quintessentially English garden, richly stocked with pre-1950s plants.

What's new in 2009 Information Room

⭐ Access roads very narrow

ℹ️ **T** 01438 829221 (Infoline), 01438 820307
E shawscorner@nationaltrust.org.uk

🎭 Events throughout the season, inc. open-air theatre during the summer

🅿️ Building Grounds

🍦 Ice-cream, cold drinks, plants and second-hand books on sale

🚼 Front-carrying baby slings and hip-carrying infant seats for loan. Family activity booklet

🏫 Suitable for school groups

🐕 On leads and only in car park

➡️ [166:TL194167] **Cycle**: NCN12, 1ml.
Bus: Centrebus 304/Harpenden Taxis 904 from ⊠ St Albans, Suns April–Oct only; otherwise Centrebus 304 ⊠ St Albans–Hitchin, alight Gustardwood, 1¼ml.
Station: Welwyn North 4½ml; Harpenden 5ml.
Road: in the village of Ayot St Lawrence. A1(M) exit 4 or M1 exit 10. Signposted from B653 Welwyn Garden City–Luton road near Wheathampstead. Also from B656 at Codicote

🅿️ Free parking, 30yds. Small car park not suitable for very large vehicles

NT properties nearby
Ashridge Estate, Chilterns Gateway Centre, Pitstone Windmill, Wimpole Hall, Wimpole Home Farm

Shaw's Corner									
House									
14 Mar–1 Nov	1–5	M	T	**W**	**T**	**F**	**S**	**S**	
Garden									
14 Mar–1 Nov	12–5:30	M	T	**W**	**T**	**F**	**S**	**S**	
Open BH Mons and Good Fri. May close earlier when evening events occur									

Sheringham Park

Visitor Centre, Wood Farm, Upper Sheringham, Norfolk NR26 8TL

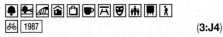

🚴 1987   (3:J4)

Spectacular landscape park and woodland garden with miles of footpaths and stunning coastal views

With fabulous displays of rhododendrons and azaleas from mid May to June and viewing towers providing amazing views, Sheringham Park is one of the finest examples of the work of Humphry Repton. Discover more about this famous landscape gardener in the exhibition, look around the shop and sample local, seasonal food from the courtyard kiosk. Stroll along the paths through woodland and parkland or follow the 'Tree Trail' to discover some rare and unusual trees. You could also take part in one of the organised events aimed at making the most of your visit.

What's new in 2009 New additions to the exhibition, including more information about Humphry Repton

ℹ️ **T** 01263 820550
E sheringhampark@nationaltrust.org.uk

🎭 Programme of events, including guided walks and tours, shows and fairs, plus special events for children and families

🚶 Tree Trail guide and waymarked walks

🅿️ Building Grounds

🍦 Small shop selling gifts and local goods. Plant sales in courtyard

🍴 Refreshment kiosk with outdoor seating (some under cover)

🚼 Baby-changing and feeding facilities. Pushchairs and baby back-carriers admitted. Special events for children and families

🏫 Suitable for school groups. Education room/centre. Learning Officer

🐕 On leads near livestock and visitor facilities

🚴 Cycle friendly. Some restrictions during rhododendron season (May–June)

Please remember – your membership card is *always* needed for free admission

→ [133:TG135420] **Foot**: Norfolk Coast Path passes through property. **Cycle**: Regional Route 30 1½ml S of property. **Bus**: First 50 from Norwich, Norfolk Green X6 from Norwich (passing close ⊠ Norwich), alight main entrance. Both pass ⊠ Sheringham. **Station**: Sheringham (U) 2ml. **Road**: 2ml SW of Sheringham, 5ml W of Cromer, 6ml E of Holt. Main entrance at junction A148/B1157

P Parking, 60yds, £4 (pay & display). Coaches free (please book in advance)

NT properties nearby
Beeston Regis Heath, Blickling Hall, Gardens and Park, Felbrigg Hall, Garden and Park, West Runton

Sheringham Park								
Park								
All year	Dawn–dusk	**M**	**T**	**W**	**T**	**F**	**S**	**S**
Visitor Centre								
1 Feb–14 Mar	11–4	M	T	W	T	F	**S**	**S**
15 Mar–30 Sep	10–5	**M**	**T**	**W**	**T**	**F**	**S**	**S**
1 Oct–31 Oct	10–5	M	T	**W**	**T**	**F**	**S**	**S**
1 Nov–31 Jan 10	11–4	M	T	W	T	F	**S**	**S**

Refreshment kiosk opens at 11 (except 9 May–28 June opens 10). Sheringham Hall is privately occupied. April–Sept: limited access by written appointment with the leaseholder. Visitor Centre & kiosk open every day in local Oct half-term hol

Sutton Hoo

Tranmer House, Sutton Hoo, Woodbridge, Suffolk IP12 3DJ

1998   (3:J7)

Awe-inspiring Anglo-Saxon royal burial site

Amazingly missed by grave robbers and left undisturbed for 1,300 years, Sutton Hoo provides clues to what has been called 'page one of English history'. Excavations in 1939 uncovered the incredible ship-burial of an Anglo-Saxon warrior king, including the iconic Sutton Hoo helmet, weapons and priceless royal treasure – all discovered when Edith Pretty hired Basil Brown to investigate some mysterious mounds of earth on her land! Incredible insights into Britain's history are offered by the fascinating Sutton Hoo exhibition, where a full-size reconstruction of the burial chamber and grave goods reveal the importance of the great Anglo-Saxon king buried here. One of Britain's most important and atmospheric archaeological sites, Sutton Hoo is set in a 99-hectare (245-acre) estate which offers estuary views and winding walks. There are beautiful displays of snowdrops, bluebells and daffodils in spring, and breathtaking rhododendrons in early summer.

The view looking over Hall Farm at Sheringham Park towards the coast, showing pasture and cultivated fields

What's new in 2009 Exhibition on Anglo-Saxon feasting, featuring artefacts loaned from the British Museum (14 March–1 November). This year marks the 70th anniversary of the excavation of the buried ship

i T 01394 389700
E suttonhoo@nationaltrust.org.uk

Guided tours of the Anglo-Saxon royal burial site. Plus 'Amazing Artefacts' exhibition mini-talks (seasonal)

Anglo-Saxon themed events. Wildlife/nature walks. Exclusive behind-the-scenes tours. Open-air theatre. Family events, children's activities and trails. Living history on special event days

Varied woodland and heathland walks, with estuary views. Beautiful displays of snowdrops, bluebells and daffodils in spring, rhododendrons in early summer. Rare Suffolk Sandlings heathland

Building Grounds

Gift shop selling locally produced ranges as well as exclusive ceramics, jewellery and children's gifts inspired by the Sutton Hoo artefacts

Restaurant (licensed) serving local, seasonal food. Open-air area. Hot lunches 11:30–2:30. Hot snacks and cakes available all day. Children's menu

Baby-changing and feeding facilities. Pushchairs and baby back-carriers admitted. Children's play area. Children's quiz/trail. Dressing-up box in exhibition hall. Family events. Children's activities

Suitable for school groups. Education room/centre. Hands-on activities. Learning Officer. Adult study days

On leads only. No entry to buildings or burial ground. Dogs welcome in restaurant terrace area

[169:TM288487] **Foot**: entrance to Sutton Hoo 1¼ml from Melton station. **Bus**: Ipswich Buses 71, 72, 72A. **Station**: Melton 1¼ml, Woodbridge 3ml. **Road**: on B1083 Melton–Bawdsey. Follow signs from A12 N of Woodbridge

Examining the iconic Sutton Hoo helmet

P Parking, 30yds. Car park (pay & display when exhibition closed). Motorcycle parking area, cycle racks and free pannier lockers

NT properties nearby
Dunwich Heath, Flatford: Bridge Cottage, Kyson Hill, Orford Ness National Nature Reserve

Sutton Hoo		M	T	W	T	F	S	S
1 Feb–8 Feb	11–4						S	S
14 Feb–22 Feb	11–4	M	T	W	T	F	S	S
28 Feb–8 Mar	11–4					F	S	S
14 Mar–5 Apr	10:30–5			W	T	F	S	S
6 Apr–19 Apr	10:30–5	M	T	W	T	F	S	S
22 Apr–24 May	10:30–5			W	T	F	S	S
25 May–31 May	10:30–5	M	T	W	T	F	S	S
3 Jun–28 Jun	10:30–5			W	T	F	S	S
29 Jun–6 Sep	10:30–5	M	T	W	T	F	S	S
9 Sep–25 Oct	10:30–5			W	T	F	S	S
26 Oct–1 Nov	11–4	M	T	W	T	F	S	S
7 Nov–20 Dec	11–4						S	S
27 Dec–3 Jan 10	11–4	M	T	W	T	F	S	S
9 Jan–31 Jan 10	11–4						S	S

Open BH Mons. Estate walks open daily all year 9–6 (except for some Thur, Nov–Jan 10)

Unless indicated, last admission is always 30mins before closing time

Theatre Royal, Bury St Edmunds

Westgate Street, Bury St Edmunds,
Suffolk IP33 1QR

🔲 🔲  1974 (3:17)

The only surviving Regency playhouse in Britain

Built in 1819 by architect William Wilkins, the Theatre Royal in Bury St Edmunds was one of the most sophisticated, elegant and modern playhouses of its age. Following a two-year programme of restoration and development, it reopened in September 2007. The painted 'sky' ceiling, intimate auditorium and handsome façade make this a beautiful little theatre in which to imagine yourself back in the pre-Victorian era. A favourite venue for audiences and performers alike, with year-round drama, music, dance and comedy.

What's new in 2009 Major summer heritage programme planned, featuring period performances, guided tours, demonstrations, talks and workshops

⭐ For full Theatre Royal information please visit www.theatreroyal.org

ℹ️ **T** 01284 769505
E theatreroyal@nationaltrust.org.uk

🏃 Tours available throughout the year. Booking strongly advised. Please note that due to the demands of the Theatre's performance schedule, it is not always possible for tours to take place. You are strongly advised to check in advance with the box office

🎭 Year-round programme of drama, music, comedy and dance. Fully staged productions and rehearsed readings of Georgian plays are regularly presented

♿ Dⱼ ♿ **Building** ♿ ♿

🍽️ Restaurant and bar facilities available two hours before most performances

🏫 Suitable for school groups

➡️ [155:TL856637] **Bus**: from surrounding areas. **Station**: Bury St Edmunds ¾ml. **Road**: on Westgate Street on S side of A134 from Sudbury (one-way system)

P Limited parking in Westgate Street. Nearest car park in Swan Lane (546yds)

NT properties nearby
Ickworth House, Park and Gardens, Lavenham Guildhall, Melford Hall

Theatre Royal, Bury St Edmunds
Open (apart from during performances) for visitors wishing to view the building. You are strongly advised to contact property for details

Ropes used for hauling sets and curtains backstage at the Theatre Royal, Suffolk

Thorington Hall

Stoke by Nayland, Suffolk CO6 4SS

🏠 1940 (3:18)

Rambling Suffolk farmhouse built around 1600

⭐ Open day in September, please tel. Regional Office (01284 747500) for other opening arrangements

ℹ️ **T** 01284 747500
E thoringtonhall@nationaltrust.org.uk

➡️ 2ml SE of Stoke by Nayland

Thorington Hall
Open on Sat during Heritage Open Day in Sept. Tel. Regional Office (01284 747500) for other opening arrangements

Most Trust properties offer Gift Aid on Entry for non-members, see page 10

Whipsnade Tree Cathedral

Trustees c/o Chapel Farm, Whipsnade, Dunstable, Bedfordshire LU6 2LL

 🏊 🏃 😷 🏚 🧍 1960　　　　　　　　　　　　**(3:E8)**

Trees, hedges and shrubs planted in the form of a medieval cathedral

Surrounded by grassland and wild flowers, this incredible place was created after the First World War in a spirit of 'faith, hope and reconciliation'. Take your time wandering the grass avenues between the trees and hedges that form the chancel, nave, transepts, chapels and cloisters. Covering an area of 3.82 hectares (9.5 acres), the Tree Cathedral is not consecrated ground but welcomes everyone to discover its special sense of peace.

★ The property is owned by the NT and administered by the Trustees of Whipsnade Tree Cathedral Fund. No WC, nearest at Dunstable Downs 1½ml, not always open

ℹ️ **T** 01582 872406
E whipsnadetc@nationaltrust.org.uk

🏃 Tours by arrangement

😷 The annual interdenominational service is held on 14 June at 3

🧍 Whipsnade circular walk – information from the Chilterns Gateway Centre. Icknield Way footpath passes the Tree Cathedral

♿ Grounds 🧗

🏠 Suitable for school groups

Wicken Fen is a nature-lovers' paradise

🐕 Under close control

➡️ [165/166:TL008180] **Foot**: on Icknield Way & Chiltern Way. **Bus**: Arriva 60 from Luton, Centrebus 327 from ➡ Hemel Hempstead, Red Rose 343 from ➡ St Albans, all Suns only. Otherwise Arriva 61 Aylesbury–➡ Luton to within 1½ml. **Station**: Cheddington 6ml; Luton 8ml. Hemel Hempstead 10ml. **Road**: 4ml S of Dunstable, off B4540

🅿️ Free parking (spaces limited). Signposted off B4540

NT properties nearby
Ascott, Ashridge Estate, Chilterns Gateway Centre, Shaw's Corner

Whipsnade Tree Cathedral							
All year	**M**	**T**	**W**	**T**	**F**	**S**	**S**
Car park locked at 7, April–end Oct; 5, Nov–31 Jan 10							

Wicken Fen National Nature Reserve

Lode Lane, Wicken, Ely, Cambridgeshire CB7 5XP

🏠 🍴 🏊 🚶 📷 🛒 🏃 🎡 😷 🏚 🚻 🏠 🧍 🚲
🍷 1899　　　　　　　　　　　　**(3:G6)**

The National Trust's oldest nature reserve, and England's most famous fen

Wicken Fen is one of Europe's most important wetland sites, supporting an amazing abundance of wildlife. There are more than 1,000 species of moth and butterfly, more than 200 species of birds and a spectacular array of dragonflies. The raised boardwalk and lush grass droves allow easy access to a lost landscape of flowering meadows, sedge and reedbeds, where you can encounter rarities such as hen harriers, water voles and bitterns. The Wicken Fen Vision, an ambitious landscape-scale conservation project, is opening up new areas of land to explore. Our grazing herds of Highland cattle and Konik ponies are helping to create a diverse range of new habitats for wildlife and visitors to enjoy.

What's new in 2009 Newly restored fenman's cottage providing a permanent home for the 'Dragonfly Project' – with experts on hand to answer questions. Newly extended waymarked trails

Wicken Fen National Nature Reserve

Wicken Fen National Nature Reserve									
1 Feb–15 Feb*	10–5	M	T	W	T	F	S	S
16 Feb–22 Feb	10–5	M	T	W	T	F	S	S
24 Feb–5 Apr	10–5	M	T	W	T	F	S	S
6 Apr–1 Nov	10–5	M	T	W	T	F	S	S
3 Nov–31 Dec*	10–4:30	M	T	W	T	F	S	S
Fen Cottage								
29 Mar–25 Oct	2–5	M	T	W	T	F	S	S

*Café closed on Tues. Reserve: closed 25 Dec. Some paths closed in very wet weather. Fen Cottage (showing the way of life c.1900) open BH Mons

i T 01353 720274
E wickenfen@nationaltrust.org.uk

✗ Tours by arrangement. See events leaflet for details

♘ Including walks and talks, family events, craft workshops and boat trips

↟ Fully accessible circular boardwalk from Visitor Centre. Nature trails. Trail guide on sale. Waymarked trails

♿ P ⌨ ☷ ∷ ◎ ⬚ ⌨ ⌨ **Building** ♿ ♿
Grounds ♿ ♿

□ Books and gifts in Visitor Centre. Binoculars for hire

☕ Café overlooking the ancient Fen serving home-made cakes, light lunches and hot soup. Children's menu

♀ Baby-changing facilities. Pushchairs and baby back-carriers admitted. Children's quiz/trail. Children's activities in Visitor Centre. Family events throughout year. Birthday packages. Boardwalk suitable for pushchairs

▦ Suitable for school groups. Education room/centre. Learning Officer. Wren Building available for hire (suitable for training courses)

☗ On leads only

⚲ Cycle routes are being developed across the Wicken Vision project area

→ [154:TL563705] **Cycle**: NCN11 from Ely.
Bus: Stagecoach in Cambridge 12 from Cambridge, Ely & Newmarket, alight Soham High Street, 3ml, or X9, 9 Cambridge–Ely, alight Stretham, 6ml. All pass ▆ Ely.
Station: Ely 9ml. **Road**: S of Wicken (A1123), 3ml W of Soham (A142), 9ml S of Ely, 17ml NE of Cambridge via A10

P Parking, 120yds, £2 (pay & display)

NT properties nearby
Anglesey Abbey, Houghton Mill, Ickworth House, Park and Gardens, Wimpole Hall, Wimpole Home Farm

Willington Dovecote and Stables

Willington, nr Bedford, Bedfordshire

⌂ ✗ ♀ 1914 (3:F7)
Outstanding 16th-century stone dovecote and stable building

★ No WC

i T 01480 301494
E willingtondovecote@nationaltrust.org.uk

→ 4ml E of Bedford, just N of the Sandy road (A603)

Willington Dovecote and Stables							
1 Apr–30 Sep	M	T	W	T	F	S	S

Open on the last Sun afternoon of the month (April–Sept inc.), 1–5, **otherwise** admission by telephone appointment with the Voluntary Custodian, Mrs J. Endersby, 21 Chapel Lane, Willington MK44 3QG. Tel. 01234 838278

The impressive parterre at Wimpole Hall: part of the grandest working estate in Cambridgeshire

Wimpole Hall

Arrington, Royston, Cambridgeshire SG8 0BW

⛲ 1976   **(3:G7)**

Magnificent country house, part of the grandest working estate in Cambridgeshire – also includes Home Farm

Wimpole Hall is a magnificent country house, part of the grandest working estate in Cambridgeshire. This country house, gardens, landscaped park and Home Farm were created by the greatest names of their day in architecture and landscape design. Discover the beautiful and unexpected Georgian interiors of Gibbs, Thornhill and Soane, contrasting with the more intimate rooms of the last owner, Elsie Bambridge, and the intriguing insight into life below stairs. Stroll around the colourful parterre garden and wander through the Pleasure Grounds to the walled kitchen garden, abundant with fruit and vegetables, which will eventually be served as part of a delicious menu in the restaurant. Stride out across the landscape park, among the gently grazing cattle and sheep and imagine the previous owners planning their visions of grand avenues, spectacular vistas, sweeping serpentine lakes and the dramatic Gothic tower with their landscape designers, such as Bridgeman, Brown and Repton.

What's new in 2009 Newly decorated Red Room open. New espalier fruit trees and summer herbaceous border in the walled kitchen garden. New information panels in the woodland belts

⭐ Wimpole Home Farm is part of the same Estate. It is made up of a working farm with rare breeds, a children's play area and adventure woodland (see following entry)

ℹ **T** 01223 206000
   E wimpolehall@nationaltrust.org.uk

🏃 Out-of-hours tours by arrangement. Free garden tours on selected weekdays, June and Sept (subject to availability)

👹 Family activity days, living history events, Easter Egg Trail, Tomato Festival, concerts, open-air theatre, Discovery Walks, lecture lunches and workshops, Hallowe'en, Christmas craft fair, Victorian Christmas

🚶 Walks leaflet available, £1

Building ♿ **Grounds** ♿➡♿

📷 NT shop, farm shop, toyshop, second-hand bookshop. Plant sales

🍴 Old Rectory Restaurant (licensed). Children's menu. Stable Kitchen in stable block

👶 Baby-changing facilities. Front-carrying baby slings and hip-carrying infant seats for loan. Children's guide. Children's quiz/trail

🏫 Extensive schools programme. Live interpretation. Hands-on activities. Lecture Lunches. Discovery Walks

🐕 On leads and only in park

➡ [154:TL336510] **Foot**: Wimpole Way from Cambridge, Harcamlow Way. **Cycle**: NT-permitted cycle path to main entrance from Orwell junction on A603. **Bus**: Whippet 75 from Cambridge (frequent services link 🚉 Cambridge and bus station). Alight Arrington, then a 1ml walk. **Station**: Shepreth 5ml. Taxi rank at Royston station 8ml. No services at Shepreth. **Road**: 8ml SW of Cambridge (A603), 6ml N of Royston (A1198)

🅿 Parking, 200yds, £2

NT properties nearby
Anglesey Abbey, Houghton Mill, Wicken Fen National Nature Reserve, Wimpole Home Farm

Wimpole Hall		M	T	W	T	F	S	S
Park								
All year	Dawn–dusk	M	T	W	T	F	S	S
Hall/bookshop								
28 Feb–15 Jul	10:30–5	M	T	W	T	F	S	S
18 Jul–27 Aug	10:30–5	M	T	W	T	F	S	S
29 Aug–1 Nov	10:30–5	M	T	W	T	F	S	S
Garden/shop/restaurant								
1 Feb–25 Feb	11–4	M	T	W	T	F	S	S
28 Feb–15 Jul	10:30–5	M	T	W	T	F	S	S
18 Jul–27 Aug	10:30–5	M	T	W	T	F	S	S
29 Aug–1 Nov	10:30–5	M	T	W	T	F	S	S
2 Nov–23 Dec	11–4	M	T	W	T	F	S	S
27 Dec–31 Dec	11–4	M	T	W	T	F	S	S
2 Jan–31 Jan 10	11–4	M	T	W	T	F	S	S

Open BH Mons 10:30–5 (Hall 11–5) & Good Fri 10:30–5 (Hall 11–5). Closed every Fri except Good Fri. Hall, farm & garden open Sat–Thur during local school hols (Hall closed in Feb half-term). Gallery open on selected dates throughout the year. Timed guided tours may be in operation 10:30–1

Show your card and display sticker for free parking

Wimpole Home Farm

Wimpole Hall, Arrington, Royston,
Cambridgeshire SG8 0BW

 1976 (3:G7)

Working farm with rare farm breeds, part of the grandest working estate in Cambridgeshire

A great day out for the whole family at Wimpole Home Farm

Wimpole Home Farm is a working farm set amidst historical thatched farm buildings and a modern farmyard. Designed and built in 1794 by Sir John Soane for 3rd Earl of Hardwicke, Home Farm was a sophisticated model farm of its time, in an age of great agricultural improvement. Retrace the footsteps of the gentry 200 years ago and wander through the Pleasure Grounds to visit the Farm. Alternatively take a ride in the wagon, pulled by Shire horses Captain and Reggie, straight to the farmyard to discover the traditional and rare breeds of sheep, cattle, pigs, poultry, goats and horses. Youngsters can join in a variety of fun farm activities: grooming the donkeys Daisy and Clementine; collecting eggs; feeding goats and learn about the traditional methods of farming from exhibits under the rafters of the Great Barn and the old Dairy. Hidden among the trees, the adventure playground is a popular spot with those who love to climb, slide, scramble and swing, while tiny tots enjoy their own play area with Kidbine Harvester and mini pedal tractors. The Farm Kitchen offers a range of tasty snacks and meals for all the family.

⭐ Members pay half price to enter the farm in support of the rare breeds conservation programme

ℹ️ **T** 01223 206000
E wimpolefarm@nationaltrust.org.uk

👤 Stockman tours, Sats in June and Sept (limited availability)

🎭 Lambing time, Easter Egg Trail, Family Activity Days, Tractormania, shearing and woolcraft. Father Christmas. Plus all the daily events: grooming donkeys, egg collecting, Shire horse wagon rides

♿ 🅿️ 🚻 🚼 🔄 ↔️ 👐 **Building** 🏛️♿ **Grounds** 🏛️📷

🍽️ Farm Kitchen serving light refreshments and hot meals. Children's menu. Groups can be accepted at the Old Rectory Restaurant

🚼 Baby-changing and feeding facilities. Pushchairs and baby back-carriers admitted. Children's play area. Children's guide. Children's quiz/trail. Special children's corner. Lambing time, Easter Egg Trail, Family Activity Days, Tractormania. Father Christmas

📖 Suitable for school groups. Live interpretation. Hands-on activities. Heavy horse driving courses

➡️ [154:TL336510] **Foot**: Wimpole Way from Cambridge, Harcamlow Way. **Cycle**: NT-permitted cycle path to main entrance from Orwell junction on A603. **Bus**: Whippet 75 from Cambridge (frequent services link 🚉 Cambridge and bus station). Alight Arrington, then a 1ml walk. **Station**: Shepreth 5ml. Taxi rank at Royston station 8ml. No services at Shepreth. **Road**: 8ml SW of Cambridge (A603), 6ml N of Royston (A1198)

🅿️ Parking, 500yds

NT properties nearby
Anglesey Abbey, Houghton Mill, Wicken Fen National Nature Reserve, Wimpole Hall

Wimpole Home Farm		M	T	W	T	F	S	S
1 Feb–22 Feb	11–4	M	T	W	T	F	S	S
28 Feb–15 Jul	10:30–5	M	T	W	T	F	S	S
18 Jul–27 Aug	10:30–5	M	T	W	T	F	S	S
29 Aug–1 Nov	10:30–5	M	T	W	T	F	S	S
7 Nov–20 Dec	11–4	M	T	W	T	F	S	S
27 Dec–31 Dec	11–4	M	T	W	T	F	S	S
2 Jan–31 Jan 10	11–4	M	T	W	T	F	S	S

Open BH Mons & Good Fri: 10:30–5. Closed every Fri except Good Fri. Open Sat–Thur during local school hols

Dogs assisting visitors with disabilities are always welcome

East Midlands

The East Midlands is rightly renowned for its scenery. This is astonishingly diverse – ranging from the breathtaking landscape of the Peak District, to the peaceful woods and open heath of Clumber Park in Nottinghamshire and the historic parklands of our mansion properties.

We care for two National Nature Reserves, including the iconic Dovedale in the Peak District and Calke Park in Derbyshire.

Within the Peak District National Park the Trust cares for such landmark features as Kinder Scout and Dovedale, as well as the moorland of the High Peak, the heather moors on the Longshaw Estate and the dales of the South Peak.

Natural drama abounds, from the hidden limestone dales, rock features and disappearing rivers of the South Peak to Winnats Pass – a mile-long gorge in the High Peak.

Exploring the Peaks

There is plenty of space to roam in the Peak District, and the National Trust owns 14,946 hectares (36,931 acres) of land, with numerous walks and trails suitable for every ability. Enjoy a leisurely walk around Ilam Park or, for something more challenging, try to reach the top of Mam Tor, where you will be rewarded with amazing views.

Alternatively, why not follow one of our guided walks and find out more about the area from our knowledgeable guides?

If a member of your party uses a wheelchair, then the Manifold Track in the South Peak is accessible and there is an excellent pathway in Dovedale up to the Stepping Stones.

To make the most of your visit, call in at one of our Information Shelters at Milldale, Dalehead, Lee Farm, Edale End, South Head or Grindle Barns.

Above left: **evening light on the peaks of the Longshaw Estate, Derbyshire**
Above right: **Ilam Park, Derbyshire**
Below: **Mam Tor, Derbyshire**

Previous page: **glorious view across the moat towards Lyveden New Bield, Northamptonshire**

Geology, archaeology and hidden nature

The Peak District has some truly dramatic geological features. Besides the imposing crags, rock cliffs and caves, there are gorges which are a mosaic of grasslands, ancient woodlands and meadows, supporting numerous plants, birds and butterflies.

Left: sheep on the tussocky hillside at Mam Tor, Derbyshire
Below left: Winnats Pass in Edale, Derbyshire

Year-round pleasure

Whatever the time of year, there's always something to do in the countryside. The *Discover Your Peak District* leaflet suggests walks and events – you can hunt for butterflies or listen to fantastical tales! In the autumn and winter many National Trust houses close their doors, yet the parks and countryside are always open for you to enjoy and explore.

As a complete contrast, the moors, incised by spectacular valleys and wooded cloughs, are important for upland breeding birds, such as the golden plover and short-eared owl. In addition these impressive moors are home to fascinating archaeological remains.

Stately parkland

Our historic houses are set among stately parkland, with numerous historic features and wildlife to spot, as well as trails to explore. Among the most notable is the park at Calke Abbey, which is a National Nature Reserve.

Above: rock formations at Kinder Low, on Kinder Scout, Derbyshire

www.nationaltrust.org.uk/coastandcountryside

Calke Abbey is just the place to go on a mini adventure. You can look out for deer or find the tree that is an incredible 1,000 years old. There are many paths around the park to enjoy, including three suggested walks in our Park Guide, as well as Tracker Pack activities to keep younger visitors happy and occupied.

In Lincolnshire, at Belton House, visitors can enjoy the magnificent landscaped park with its majestic deer herd. Within the park you can also see Bellmount Tower and the restored boathouse and enjoy the River Witham, home to otters, water voles and native crayfish, as it lazily meanders along the western edge of the park.

With picturesque parkland, peaceful woodlands, open heath and a serpentine lake at its heart, Clumber Park has more than enough space for you to explore and relax with family and friends. There are more than twenty miles of open tracks and footpaths on the 1,500-hectare (3,800-acre) estate – ideal for a gentle stroll, a more vigorous hike, or you could even decide to explore by bicycle. There are even pathways suitable for wheelchair users.

My favourite walk

Standing on the moor above Longshaw reminds me why the Peak District is so special. From here you can see the distant moors of Kinder Scout and Bleaklow and the wonderful wooded Derwent Valley. In the foreground the parkland stretches out below, with its old majestic trees surrounding the Lodge that was once the escape of the Duke of Rutland.

There is a fantastic walk around the Longshaw Estate, starting at the Visitor Centre and taking you over the meadow and along Burbage Brook. You will see an abundance of wildlife along the way, including badgers and breeding birds – ranging from spotted woodpeckers to pied flycatchers. Be sure to keep an eye out for grey wagtails and dippers along the brook.

Mike Innerdale
Property Manager of the High Peak and Longshaw Estate

Top: the spire of the Gothic chapel beside the serpentine lake at Clumber Park in Nottinghamshire

Above: two views of moorland on the Longshaw Estate, Derbyshire

www.nationaltrust.org.uk/coastandcountryside

Belton House

Grantham, Lincolnshire NG32 2LS

🏠 🏡 ✝ ❖ ♣ ♿ 🖬 ➡ 🎿 🎧 🎭 😊 👫 📷 🔔

📺 1984 (3:E4)

17th-century country house with magnificent interiors, beautiful gardens and extensive parkland

This fine example of Restoration architecture was built in 1685-8 for 'Young' Sir John Brownlow and featured in the BBC's adaptation of *Pride and Prejudice*. Enjoy stunning rooms displayed in 17th-century, Regency, Victorian and 1930s style, with fine furnishings, tapestries, paintings and Grinling Glbbons' wood carvings. Outside, the tranquil gardens, richly planted Orangery and wonderful lakeside walks are a delight to explore.

What's new in 2009 Discovery Centre (wildlife-themed activities)

ℹ️ **T** 01476 566116
E belton@nationaltrust.org.uk

🎿 Guided tours in house 1st Wed in month (excluding school holidays). Attic and basement tours

😊 Horse trials, anniversary Spitfire prom, Easter and Hallowe'en trails, behind-the-scenes tours, Family Fun Weekends and Christmas Craft Fayre

♿ 🅿️ 🅳 🏢 📟 ⁝⁝ 🔴 🔵 💻 🚾 ♨️ ⬆️ ♨️
Building 🔼 🔽 **Grounds** ♿ ➡️ ⛷️

🛍️ Plant and garden shop. Gift shop

🖬 The Stables Restaurant (licensed). Main meals 12–2. Children's menu. Ice-cream available. Coffee shop open weekends and peak periods for snacks and ice-creams

👫 Baby-changing facilities. Pushchairs admitted. Front-carrying baby slings and hip-carrying infant seats for loan. Children's play area. Children's quiz/trails. Activity room in house; Belton Discovery Centre. Extensive outdoor adventure playground with under-6s 'corral'; miniature train rides in summer

📷 Suitable for school groups. Hands-on activities. Adult study days

🐾 On leads and only in parkland

Belton House		
House		
28 Feb–8 Mar	12:30–4	M T W T **F** **S** **S**
14 Mar–1 Nov	11–5*	M T **W** **T** **F** **S** **S**
Garden/park/shop/restaurant		
7 Feb–8 Mar	12–4	M T W T **F** **S** **S**
14 Mar–28 Jun	10:30–5:30	M T **W** **T** **F** **S** **S**
1 Jul–6 Sep	10:30–5:30	**M** **T** **W** **T** **F** **S** **S**
9 Sep–1 Nov	10:30–5:30	M T **W** **T** **F** **S** **S**
6 Nov–20 Dec	12–4	M T W T **F** **S** **S**
26 Dec–3 Jan 10	12–4	**M** **T** **W** **T** **F** **S** **S**
Adventure playground		
14 Mar–28 Jun	10:30–5:30	M T **W** **T** **F** **S** **S**
1 Jul–6 Sep	10:30–5:30	**M** **T** **W** **T** **F** **S** **S**
9 Sep–1 Nov	10:30–5:30	M T **W** **T** **F** **S** **S**

*House: open for guided tours from 11–12:30 (free flow from 12:30, although guided tours may replace free flow on some days). Tours content may change. Basement: open 11–12:30. Also open BH Mons. Shop/restaurant: open 10:30 14 March–1 Nov. Adventure playground, parkland, garden, shop & restaurant: open all week in school hols (1 March–2 Nov). Bellmount Woods: open daily, access from separate car park. Bellmount Tower and boat house: open occasionally (contact property for details). House and/or adventure playground likely to close early in poor weather/light conditions

➡️ [130:SK930395] **Bus**: Stagecoach in Lincolnshire 1 Grantham–Lincoln; Centrebus 609 Grantham–Sleaford (both pass close 🚂 Grantham). **Station**: Grantham 3ml. **Road**: 3ml NE of Grantham on A607 Grantham–Lincoln road, easily reached and signposted from A1

🅿️ Free parking, 250yds

NT properties nearby
Grantham House, Tattershall Castle, Woolsthorpe Manor, The Workhouse, Southwell

Enjoying the tranquil gardens at Belton House

Calke Abbey

Ticknall, Derby, Derbyshire DE73 7LE

🏠 🐈 ✚ 🍴 ✿ 🌳 🛴 🏡 🏛 💷 🎿 🎭 🎭

🖼 🧍 🍴 1985   (3:C4)

A country house, park and garden where time has stood still

Calke Abbey is a unique house, completed in 1704. The house has been preserved as it was found in the 1980s, giving visitors a chance to explore a period when great country houses struggled to survive. It tells the story of an eccentric family who amassed a huge collection of hidden treasures, including an 18th-century silk bed. Why not end your visit along the cellars and servants' tunnel and then explore the stableyards? In the walled gardens, explore the Orangery, the flower and kitchen gardens and the unique Auricula Theatre. Take a walk around Calke Park, a National Nature Reserve, where you can see roaming deer and a 1,000-year-old oak tree.

What's new in 2009 New children's play area. House conservation tours. Riding school open for public viewing, functions and events

⭐ All visitors (inc. NT members) require a house and garden (or garden only) ticket from visitor reception. At busy times these will be timed tickets. Delays in entry to the house are possible at BHols. One-way system operates in the park; access only via Ticknall entrance

ℹ️ **T** 01332 863822
E calkeabbey@nationaltrust.org.uk

🎿 Daily short conservation tours of the house, 11–12. Private guided tours available on request

🎭 Numerous events, including Family Fun days, lecture lunches and guided walks

🧍 Park guide available showing different circular walks

♿ 🅿️ ♿ ⋯ 📷 🔲 📺 🔊 ⬜
Building ♿ ♿ ♿ **Grounds** ♿ ♿ ➡️

🏛 NT shop. Plant sales

💷 Licensed restaurant. Children's menu. Coffee shop kiosk open during peak periods

🎭 Baby-changing facilities. Front-carrying baby slings and hip-carrying infant seats for loan. Children's quiz/trail. Family activity packs.

Calke Abbey								
House*								
28 Feb–1 Nov	11–5	M	T	W	T	F	S	S
Garden/stables								
28 Feb–1 Nov	11–5	M	T	W	T	F	S	S
2 Jul–4 Sep	11–5	M	T	W	T	F	S	S
Restaurant/shop								
28 Feb–1 Nov	10:30–5	M	T	W	T	F	S	S
2 Nov–23 Dec	10:30–4	M	T	W	T	F	S	S
2 Jan–31 Jan 10	10:30–4	M	T	W	T	F	S	S
Coffee shop kiosk								
26 Dec–1 Jan 10	10:30–3	M	T	W	T	F	S	S
Calke Park/National Nature Reserve								
All year	Dawn–dusk	M	T	W	T	F	S	S

House & garden open Good Fri. *House conservation tours 11–12:30

Children's play area. Family activities and events. Family Tracker Packs

🖼 Suitable for school groups. Live interpretation. Education room/centre. Learning and Events Officer

🐕 On leads in park and stables area only

➡️ [128:SK367226] **Bus**: Arriva 69 East Midlands Airport–Swadlincote (with connections from 🚆 Derby on Arriva 68A/B at Melbourne), alight Ticknall, then 1½ml walk through park to house. **Station**: Derby 9½ml; Burton-on-Trent 10ml. **Road**: 10ml S of Derby, on A514 at Ticknall between Swadlincote and Melbourne. Access from M42/A42 exit 13 and A50 Derby South

🅿️ Height of arch at Middle Lodge 3.6m

NT properties nearby
Kedleston Hall, Staunton Harold Church, Sudbury Hall and the National Trust Museum of Childhood

Time has stood still at Calke Abbey in Derbyshire

The Elizabethan Canons Ashby House, Northamptonshire

Canons Ashby House

Canons Ashby, Daventry,
Northamptonshire NN11 3SD

🏠 ✝ ❄ ♣ 🏛 🍽 🎿 🎭 🛡 👫 🎨
🏃 | 1981 | (3:D7)

**Tranquil Elizabethan manor house set in
beautiful gardens**

Canons Ashby has been the home of the Dryden
family since it was first built, and has survived
almost unaltered since c.1710. It is a romantic
property, with every inch – from the stone-
flagged kitchen and dairy to the intimate
interiors with their fascinating wall paintings and
delicate Jacobean plasterwork – steeped in
atmosphere. The house sits among beautiful
gardens, where you can enjoy colourful
herbaceous borders, an orchard featuring
varieties of fruit tree from the 16th century and a
surprisingly grand church – all that remains of
the 12th-century Augustinian priory from which
the house takes its name.

What's new in 2009 See the start of work on
the gardens to restore their Victorian splendour

ℹ️ **T** 01327 860044 (Infoline), 01327 861900
   E canonsashby@nationaltrust.org.uk

🎿 Monthly behind-the-scenes tours

🛡 Step Back in Time weekend, Christmas
   market, Shakespeare in the Park

🏃 Self-guided trail through historic parkland

♿ 🅿 📱 ∴ 📷 🎿 🖥 🎵 🔦 🏠
Building 🔦🔦 **Grounds** 🔦🔦

🏠 Gift shop and large second-hand bookshop

🍽 Cottage Garden tea-room. Light lunches.
   Children's menu

👶 Baby-changing facilities. Pushchairs and baby
   back-carriers admitted (except on busy days).
   Front-carrying baby slings for loan. Children's
   quizzes. Family Tracker Pack

🏫 Suitable for school groups. Live interpretation.
   Teachers' Resource book

🐕 On leads and only in Home Paddock and
   car park

➡️ [152:SP577506] **Cycle**: NCN70.
   Bus: occasional service from Banbury, taxi
   bus from Weedon Lois (not Sun).
   Station: Banbury 10ml. **Road**: easy access
   from either M40 exit 11, or M1 exit 16. From
   M1 take A45 (Daventry) and at Weedon
   crossroads turn left on to A5; 3ml S turn right
   on to unclassified road through Litchborough
   and Adstone. From M40 at Banbury take
   A422 (Brackley) and after 2ml turn left on to
   B4525; after 3ml turn left on to unclassified
   road signposted to property

🅿 Free parking, 200yds

NT properties nearby
Farnborough Hall, Stowe Landscape Gardens,
Upton House and Gardens

Canons Ashby House									
House/shop/tea-room		M	T	W	T	F	S	S	
28 Feb–8 Mar	11–5	M	T	W	T	F	**S**	**S**	
14 Mar–1 Nov	11–5	**M**	**T**	**W**	T	F	**S**	**S**	
7 Nov–20 Dec	12–4	M	T	W	T	F	**S**	**S**	
Park/church									
28 Feb–8 Mar	11–5:30	M	T	W	T	F	**S**	**S**	
15 Mar–30 Sep	11–5:30	**M**	**T**	**W**	T	F	**S**	**S**	
7 Nov–20 Dec	12–4	M	T	W	T	F	**S**	**S**	

Open Good Fri: 11-5. Closes dusk if earlier. Garden
closes 5:30 28 Feb–1 Nov. Grounds, shop tea-room &
church open all week in Aug. House entry before 1 by
timed tickets only

Unless indicated, last admission is always 30mins before closing time

Clumber Park

The Estate Office, Clumber Park, Worksop,
Nottinghamshire S80 3AZ

🏠✝🍀🌲🎣🏛💷🎿🎧🏞🛡👫📷🚶

🚲☕ 1946   (3:D2)

**Extensive area of parkland, including
peaceful woods, open heath and farmland**

Covering 1,537.5 hectares (3,800 acres),
Clumber Park was once the country estate of
the Dukes of Newcastle. Although the house
was demolished in 1938, the Gothic Revival
Chapel, the immense Lime Tree Avenue and the
spectacular glasshouses all remain to give clues
to its past. Why not experience a taste of the
past in our organically managed Walled Kitchen
Garden or hire a cycle to explore Clumber's
mosaic of habitats, have a picnic by the lake or
watch a game of cricket?

What's new in 2009 Restaurant refurbished and
new menus

⭐ Park closed 25 Dec

ℹ️ **T** 01909 544917
    E clumberpark@nationaltrust.org.uk

🎧 Chapel guided tours

🎧 Walled Kitchen Garden

🎪 Open-air concerts, theatre and special events
    throughout the year. Leaflet from Estate Office

🚶 Held throughout the year. Leaflet from Estate
Office

♿ 🅿️🚻∶◉🔁🚼🦽🔁 Chapel 🦽♿
Glasshouse 🦽♿
Grounds 🦽➡️🦽♿

📷 NT shop. Plant sales

☕ Licensed restaurant. Children's menu during
school holidays. Muniment Room and Duke's
Study within restaurant available for private
hire. Kiosk serving simple food during peak
periods

👫 Baby-changing and feeding facilities. Cycles
with child seats, trailers and trailer bikes
available. Gardens and Second World War
family Tracker Packs. Hands-on wildlife activities

📷 Suitable for school groups. Education room.
Adult learning days. Teachers' Resource
Pack. Hands-on activities. Learning Officer

🐕 Welcome in park. Must be on leads in Walled
Kitchen Garden, Pleasure Ground and
grazing areas

Geraniums in a glasshouse in the Walled Kitchen
Garden at Clumber Park, Nottinghamshire

Clumber Park								
Park								
All year	Dawn–dusk	M	T	W	T	F	S	S
Restaurant/shop/plant sales/chapel								
1 Feb–28 Mar	10–4	M	T	W	T	F	S	S
29 Mar–24 Oct	10–5*	M	T	W	T	F	S	S
25 Oct–31 Jan 10	10–4	M	T	W	T	F	S	S
Walled Kitchen Garden								
14 Mar–28 Mar	11–4	M	T	W	T	F	S	S
29 Mar–27 Sep	10–5*	M	T	W	T	F	S	S
28 Sep–1 Nov	11–4	M	T	W	T	F	S	S
Conservation Centre								
4 Apr–27 Sep	10:30–4:30	M	T	W	T	F	S	S

*Closes at 6 on Sat/Sun. BHol opening times as
Sat/Sun. Chapel: as visitor facilities (except 12–31 Jan
10, when closed for conservation cleaning). Cycle hire:
last hiring 2hrs before closing time

Most Trust properties offer Gift Aid on Entry for non-members, see page 10

The spectacular glasshouses at Clumber Park, Nottinghamshire, hint at the grandeur of the demolished house

🚲 Cycle hire available April–Sept, daily; Oct–March, Sat, Sun and school holidays. Opens 10, last hiring 2hrs before closing. £6.30 for 2hrs. ID essential. Free helmet hire. Tandems, child seats, trailer bikes and trikes available. Waymarked cycle routes and route guide available from cycle hire and visitor enquiries point. Cycle orienteering

➔ [120:SK629752] **Cycle**: NCN6. **Bus**: Stagecoach East Midlands 33 Nottingham–Worksop (First 25 from Rotherham, Suns only), alight Carburton, ½ml. **Station**: Worksop 4½ml; Retford 6½ml. **Road**: 4½ml SE of Worksop, 6½ml SW of Retford, 1ml from A1/A57, 11ml from M1 exit 30

🅿 Throughout park. Main parking 200yds from visitor facilities and 250yds from Walled Kitchen Garden

NT properties nearby
Hardwick Hall, Mr Straw's House, The Workhouse, Southwell

Grantham House

Castlegate, Grantham, Lincolnshire NG31 6SS

🏠 ✂ 💼 🍴 🛡 👪 🍷 1944 (3:E4)

Handsome town house, with architectural features from various eras and riverside walled garden

⭐ The property has been leased by the National Trust and the house and garden are open to visitors at various times, as advertised (see opening arrangements). The lessee is responsible for all arrangements and facilities. Entrance via 44 Castlegate – the stable block opposite St Wulfram's Church

ℹ **T** 01909 486411
E granthamhouse@nationaltrust.org.uk

➔ Immediately E of St Wulfram's church, Grantham

Grantham House
Please contact the Regional Office tel. 01909 511041 or see website for details

For further information, visit www.nationaltrust.org.uk

The Blue Bedroom at Hardwick Hall, Derbyshire

Gunby Hall

Gunby, nr Spilsby, Lincolnshire PE23 5SS

🏛 🏠 ⚥ 🐾 ♿ [1944]   (3:G3)

Fine red-brick house, dating from 1700, with Victorian walled gardens

ℹ️ T 07870 758876
   E gunbyhall@nationaltrust.org.uk

➡️ 2½ml NW of Burgh le Marsh, 7ml W of Skegness on S side of A158 (access off roundabout)

Gunby Hall								
House/garden								
3 Jun–23 Sep	2–5	M	T	**W**	T	F	S	S
Garden only								
1 Apr–27 May	2–5	M	T	**W**	T	F	S	S
2 Jun–27 Aug	2–5	M	**T**	**W**	**T**	F	S	S
2 Sep–24 Sep	2–5	M	T	**W**	T	F	S	S

Garden also open Tues/Thurs in April/May, by written appointment only to Mrs C. Ayres, Gunby Hall, Gunby, nr Spilsby, Lincolnshire PE23 5SS

Gunby Hall Estate: Monksthorpe Chapel

Monksthorpe, nr Spilsby, Lincolnshire PE23 5PP

✝️ 🏠 ⚥ 🐾 ♿ [2000]   (3:G3)

Remote late 17th-century Baptist chapel

ℹ️ T 01526 342543
   E monksthorpe@nationaltrust.org.uk

➡️ From A158 in Candlesby, turn off main road opposite Royal Oak pub, following signs to Monksthorpe. Follow road for about 1½ml and turn left. After 50yds turn left at dead end sign. Parking is on the left at entrance to avenue

Monksthorpe Chapel								
1 Apr–30 Sep	2–5	M	T	**W**	T	F	S	S

Chapel open and stewarded on some Sats: 2 May, 6 June, 4 July, 1 Aug, 5 Sept. Services on Sats at 3: 18 April, 16 May, 20 June, 18 July, 15 Aug, 19 Sept, 10 Oct (Harvest Service), 12 Dec (2, Carol Service). Flower Festival 14/15 Aug. Admission by key, obtained from Gunby (£10 deposit required)

Hardwick Hall

Doe Lea, Chesterfield, Derbyshire S44 5QJ

🏛 🔊 ✳️ 🐶 🐾 🏠 🍽 🏺 ♿ 🎯 🎧 🏞 ⚥ 🐾
🪑 🚶 ♿ 🔔 ⏱ [1959]   (3:D3)

One of Britain's greatest and most complete Elizabethan houses

Spectacular Hardwick Hall was built by Bess of Hardwick, Elizabethan England's second richest woman, and has survived almost unchanged. Inside the atmospheric Hall you can see Europe's finest collection of 16th- and 17th-century embroideries and tapestries. The award-winning 'Threads of Time' exhibition tells visitors the story of Bess and the collections in the Hall. Tranquil walled courtyards enclose the fragrant restored herb garden, orchards and lawns. In the historic parkland you can explore the Stone Centre and learn about the traditional craft of stonemasonry, enjoy the walks and trails and see rare breeds of cattle and sheep. In the grounds you can also visit the remains of Hardwick Old Hall, which Bess continued to use after her new house was built.

What's new in 2009 To celebrate 50 years in the National Trust's ownership, a series of special events will take place thoughout the year. Conservation tours of the Hall on Wednesday, Thursday, Friday, Saturday and Sunday (£2 donation towards conservation work)

The ruins of Hardwick Old Hall in the grounds are owned by the NT and administered by English Heritage (01246 850431)

T 01246 850430
E hardwickhall@nationaltrust.org.uk

Conservation tours of Hall Wed to Sun 11. Starting at the Gatehouse on the day. Limited availability. £2 donation for conservation projects

For Tobit Table Carpet Room

Activities to celebrate 50 years of ownership by the National Trust

Guided walks through park and at Park Farm throughout the year

Building **Grounds**

Hardwick souvenirs

Licensed restaurant serving hot food until 2:30. Menu includes meat reared on estate. Children's menu. Kiosk in main car park serving light refreshments

Baby-changing and feeding facilities. Front-carrying baby slings and hip-carrying infant seats for loan. Children's quiz/trail. Reins for loan

Suitable for school groups

On leads and only in park and car park

Cycles permitted on parkland roads

[120:SK463638] **Foot**: Rowthorne Trail; Teversal Trail. **Bus**: Stagecoach East Midlands 'Pronto' Chesterfield–Nottingham, alight Glapwell 'Young Vanish', 1½ml.
Station: Chesterfield 8ml. **Road**: Road: 6½ml W of Mansfield, 9½ml SE of Chesterfield; approach from M1 (exit 29) via A6175. Note: a one-way traffic system operates in the park; access only via Stainsby Mill entrance (leave M1 exit 29, follow brown signs), exit only via Hardwick Inn

Parking, 100yds, £2. Ponds parking, £2 (pay & display)

NT properties nearby
Clumber Park, Kedleston Hall, Stainsby Mill, Mr Straw's House, The Workhouse, Southwell

Hardwick Hall								
Hall tours								
18 Feb–22 Feb	12–4	M	T	**W**	**T**	**F**	**S**	**S**
28 Feb–8 Mar	12–4	M	T	W	T	F	**S**	**S**
14 Mar–1 Nov	11–12	M	T	**W**	**T**	**F**	**S**	**S**
Hall								
14 Mar–1 Nov	12–4:30	M	T	**W**	**T**	**F**	**S**	**S**
5 Dec–20 Dec	11–3	M	T	W	T	F	**S**	**S**
Garden								
18 Feb–22 Feb	12–4	M	T	**W**	**T**	**F**	**S**	**S**
28 Feb–8 Mar	12–4	M	T	W	T	F	**S**	**S**
14 Mar–1 Nov	11–5	M	T	**W**	**T**	**F**	**S**	**S**
5 Dec–20 Dec	11–3	M	T	W	T	F	**S**	**S**
Parkland gates								
All year	8:30–5:30	**M**	**T**	**W**	**T**	**F**	**S**	**S**
Shop/restaurant								
18 Feb–22 Feb	12–4	M	T	**W**	**T**	**F**	**S**	**S**
28 Feb–8 Mar	12–4	M	T	W	T	F	**S**	**S**
14 Mar–1 Nov	11–5	M	T	**W**	**T**	**F**	**S**	**S**
5 Dec–20 Dec	11–3	M	T	W	T	F	**S**	**S**
Stone Centre								
18 Feb–1 Nov	11–4:30	**M**	**T**	**W**	**T**	**F**	**S**	**S**
5 Dec–20 Dec	11–3	M	T	W	T	F	**S**	**S**
Kiosk								
14 Mar–1 Nov	10:30–4	**M**	**T**	**W**	**T**	**F**	**S**	**S**
5 Dec–20 Dec	11–3	M	T	W	T	F	**S**	**S**
26 Dec–1 Jan 10	11–3	**M**	**T**	**W**	**T**	**F**	**S**	S
Old Hall (EH)								
14 Mar–1 Nov	10–5	M	T	**W**	**T**	**F**	**S**	**S**
5 Dec–20 Dec	10–4	M	T	W	T	F	**S**	**S**
Open BH Mons and Good Fri: 12–4:30. Kiosk open between Christmas and New Year. Park gates shut 6 in summer, at dusk in winter								

Children in the garden at Hardwick Hall, Derbyshire

Show your card and display sticker for free parking

High Peak Estate

High Peak Estate Office, Edale End, Hope Valley,
Derbyshire S33 6RF

🏛️🛠️🎣🌳🏠💭🎧🎭👫🖼️🚶
🚲 1936   (3:B2)

Vast area of outstanding walking country

The High Peak stretches from the heather-clad
moors of Park Hall to the gritstone of Derwent
Edge, and from the peat bogs of Bleaklow to the
limestone crags of Winnats Pass. The wild
Pennine moorlands are of international
importance for their populations of breeding
birds, including golden plover, merlin and red
grouse. Sites of particular interest include Mam
Tor, with its spectacular views, landslip and
prehistoric settlement; Odin Mine, one of the
oldest lead mines in Derbyshire; and the
unspoilt valley of Snake Pass. Kinder Scout,
where the Mass Trespass of 1932 took place, is
the highest point for 50 miles. The Trust also
owns several farms in the beautiful Edale Valley.
A major woodland restoration project (in
partnership with the Forestry Commission) is
under way in the recently acquired Alport Valley.

What's new in 2009 New audio trail and family
trail at Mam Tor (see website for details)

⭐ No WC, available in adjacent villages:
Hayfield, Castleton, Edale, Hope. Also at
visitor centres/car parks at Heatherdene and
Fairholmes nr Ladybower, Edale, Castleton

Kinder Scout in the High Peak Estate, Derbyshire

High Peak Estate

All year	M T W T F S S

Open and unrestricted access for walkers all year to
moorland, subject to occasional management closures
(advertised locally). Access to farmland is via public
rights of way and permitted paths. Five information
shelters open all year: Lee Barn (110:SK096855) on
Pennine Way near Jacob's Ladder; Dalehead (110:
SK101843) in Edale; South Head Farm (SK060854) at
Kinder; Edale End (SK161864) between Edale and
Hope; Grindle Barns above Ladybower Reservoir
(SK189895)

ℹ️ **T** 01433 670368
   E highpeakestate@nationaltrust.org.uk

🎧 Downloadable audio tour of Mam Tor – also
   available at Castleton Visitor Centre

💭 Contact the property for a free leaflet

🚶 Walks leaflets available

🍦 Ice-cream concession at Mam Tor car park

👫 Children's guide. Family trail at Mam Tor

🖼️ Suitable for school groups. Live interpretation.
   Hands-on activities. Teachers' Pack

🐕 Please keep dogs on leads March–July

🚲 Circular cycle path at Upper Derwent Valley
   (Fairholmes). Many bridleways

➡️ [110:SK100855] **Foot**: Pennine Way passes
   through property. **Bus**: frequent from
   surrounding areas to Castleton.
   Station: Edale is 1½ml from Dale Head, 2ml
   from Lee Barn and 3ml from Edale End;
   Chinley is 3ml from South Head Farm; Hope
   is 3ml from Edale End. Bamford 3ml from
   Upper Derwent Valley – linked by cycle route.
   Road: estate covers area N & S of A57 on
   Sheffield side of Snake Top, E of Hayfield and
   W of Castleton

🅿️ Many free car parks (not NT) in area. Also pay
   & display (not NT) at Edale, Castleton,
   Bowden Bridge and Hayfield. NT pay &
   display at Mam Nick (SK123833). Upper
   Derwent Valley (not NT)

NT properties nearby
Ilam Park and South Peak Estate, Longshaw
Estate, Lyme Park, Marsden Moor Estate

Dogs assisting visitors with disabilities are always welcome

Ilam Park, Peak District

Ilam Park and South Peak Estate

Ilam, Ashbourne, Derbyshire DE6 2AZ

[icon] 1934   **(3:B3)**

South Peak Estate, including Ilam Park, Dovedale and Hamps and Manifold valleys

Set beside the River Manifold, Ilam Park's spectacular setting offers a chance to explore the limestone area of the Peak District. Enjoy the outstanding views towards Dovedale National Nature Reserve, part of the South Peak Estate, or use it as a base to explore the beautiful White Peak area. It's also a great place to while away an afternoon relaxing in the tea-room or browsing in the shop. Explore the National Trust's visitor centre and see changing exhibitions and an interactive display about the geology of the area. Enjoy the wonderful limestone scenery, rich daleside grasslands and important ash woodlands of the South Peak Estate. There are lovely walks around Ilam Park, through Dovedale and around Wetton Mill in the Manifold Valley.

What's new in 2009 The tea-room now serves dishes using meat from estate's tenant farmers who have been awarded the National Trust Fine Farm Produce Award. This is also now for sale from a freezer in the tea-room

---

⭐ Postal address: South Peak Estate Office, Home Farm, Ilam, Ashbourne, Derbyshire DE6 2AZ

ℹ️ **T** 01335 350503
E southpeakestate@nationaltrust.org.uk

😊 Including guided walks with wildlife and history themes

🚶 Walks information available from visitor centre/shop

♿ [icons] **Building** [icons]
Grounds [icons]

🛍️ NT shop and plant sales. Meat from estate's tenant farmers on sale in tea-room

☕ Manifold Tea-room. Children's menu

👪 Baby-changing and feeding facilities. Push-chairs and baby back-carriers admitted. Family and children's guides. Children's quiz/trail

🏫 Suitable for school groups. Education room/centre. Hands-on activities. Adult study days. Learning Officer

🐕 On leads only

➡️ [119:SK132507] 4½ml NW of Ashbourne.
Cycle: NCN68, 2ml. **Bus**: Bowers 442 🚌 Buxton–Ashbourne, alight Thorpe, 2ml

🅿️ Parking, 75yds (pay & display). Coaches by prior arrangement only

NT properties nearby
Biddulph Grange Garden, Kedleston Hall, Longshaw Estate, South Peak Estate, inc. Dovedale & Hamps & Manifold Valleys, Sudbury Hall and the National Trust Museum of Childhood

Ilam Park and South Peak Estate								
Park								
All year		M	T	W	T	F	S	S
Shop/tea-room								
1 Feb–27 Feb	11–4	M	T	W	T	F	**S**	**S**
28 Feb–28 Jun	11–5	**M**	**T**	W	T	**F**	**S**	**S**
29 Jun–30 Aug	11–5	**M**	**T**	**W**	**T**	**F**	**S**	**S**
31 Aug–1 Nov	11–5	**M**	**T**	W	T	**F**	**S**	**S**
2 Nov–20 Dec	11–4	M	T	W	T	F	**S**	**S**
3 Jan–31 Jan 10	11–4	M	T	W	T	F	**S**	**S**

Hall is let to YHA and not open. Note: small caravan site run by NT (basic facilities) open Mar–Oct (for bookings tel. caravan site office in season on 01335 350310 or estate office out of season)

Kedleston Hall

Derby, nr Quarndon, Derbyshire DE22 5JH

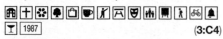

🍽 1987   (3:C4)

Spectacular 18th-century mansion with Adam interiors, pleasure ground and parkland

Take a trip back to the 1760s, when wealth and power enabled the creation of this outstanding house and beautiful landscape park. Designed to impress and amaze visitors, Kedleston was built between 1759 and 1765 for the Curzon family, who have lived in the area since the 12th century. Experience the most complete and least-altered sequence of Robert Adam interiors in England, with magnificent State Rooms and a fine collection of paintings and sculpture. The Eastern Museum is full of fascinating objects collected by Lord Curzon when he was Viceroy of India (1899-1905). Four different walks allow you to explore the 330 hectares (820 acres) of historic parkland, with a beautiful series of lakes and cascades. Enjoy the garden, which has been restored to an 18th-century Pleasure Ground, and visit All Saints' Church (owned by the Churches Conservation Trust) which is all

that remains of the medieval village of Kedleston. Visit during 2009 and find out more about how the property was used as a location for the new British film *The Duchess*, starring Keira Knightley, and see costumes from the film.

What's new in 2009 Exhibition showing how the interiors were transformed and cared for during the filming of *The Duchess*. Housekeeping-themed events to celebrate 200 years since long-serving housekeeper, Mrs Garnett, passed away

⭐ See conservation in action as we continue the work started in the late 1980s to ensure Kedleston is presented as it was when it was first built in the late 18th century

ℹ️ **T** 01332 842191
   E kedlestonhall@nationaltrust.org.uk

🔧 Talks available in Hall prior to opening most days. Complimentary tours of either garden, great west stable or fishing pavilion most days. Welcome by 18th-century costumed housekeeper in Hall at 1, 2 and 3

🎭 Throughout the year, leaflets available from visitor reception

🚶 New park guide including all walks and background information on the park and pleasure ground available from visitor reception

North front, Kedleston Hall, Derbyshire

For public transport details, see page 377

♿ 🅿️ 🄳 ♿ 🔛 📷 🚗 💻 📺 ♨️ ♿ 🔲
Building 🔛🔛 **Grounds** 🔛🔛➡️

🏠 NT shop. Plant sales

🍴 Licensed restaurant. Hot food served until 2:30. Children's menu

👶 Baby-changing facilities. Pushchairs admitted. Hip-carrying infant seats for loan. Children's guide. Children's quiz/trail. Tracker Pack

🔲 Suitable for school groups

🐕 On leads and only in park. Allowed on Wilderness and Lakeside walks, not on Long/Short walks

🚲 Cycling permitted on parkland roads

➡️ [128:SK312403] **Bus**: Arriva 109 🚉 Derby–Ashbourne, calls at the Hall summer Sats only, otherwise alight the Smithy, 1ml. **Station**: Duffield (U) 3½ml; Derby 5½ml. **Road**: all traffic should aim for Markeaton roundabout where A52 intersects with A38 (do NOT follow A52). Follow brown signs on A38, take exit from A38 (N) and then along Kedleston Road

🅿️ Free parking, 200yds. Non-members must pay admission fee to property to use car park

NT properties nearby
Calke Abbey, Ilam Park and South Peak Estate, Sudbury Hall and the National Trust Museum of Childhood

Kedleston Hall									
Hall									
28 Feb–1 Nov	12-5	M	T	W	T	F	S	S	
Pleasure grounds									
28 Feb–1 Nov	10-6	M	T	W	T	F	S	S	
Park									
28 Feb–1 Nov	10-6	M	T	W	T	F	S	S	
2 Nov–31 Jan 10	10-4	M	T	W	T	F	S	S	
Shop/restaurant									
14 Feb–22 Feb	11-5	M	T	W	T	F	S	S	
28 Feb–1 Nov	11-5	M	T	W	T	F	S	S	
23 Jul–28 Aug	12-4	M	T	W	T	F	S	S	
7 Nov–31 Jan 10	11-3	M	T	W	T	F	S	S	
Church*									
28 Feb–1 Nov	11-5	M	T	W	T	F	S	S	

Open Good Fri. Park: closed occasionally Nov–31 Jan 10. Last entry into Hall 4:15. *Church (not NT) times may change. Closed 25 Dec

Heather blooming on the Longshaw Estate, Derbyshire

Longshaw Estate

Sheffield, Derbyshire S11 7TZ

🔲 🏊 🐕 🏠 🏠 🍴 🚻 🎢 🛡️ 👶 🔲
🚶 1931   (3:C2)

Excellent walking country with ancient woods and tumbling streams

Use the maze of quiet paths to discover spectacular views of the Peak District, ancient woods, parkland and heather moorland. Or why not hunt out some of the unusual sites of Longshaw's industrial past, from millstone quarries to packhorse routes. The Visitor Centre, housed in the Duke of Rutland's Shooting Lodge, is the ideal starting point for your visit to Longshaw and as a gateway to the wider Peak District. Alternatively end your day here, with delicious home-baked local food and a visit to the shop.

What's new in 2009 New visitor guide and family trail. Wildlife-themed events and webcams at the Visitor Centre. New information and interpretation barn at Padley Gorge. Plants now on sale

⭐ Moorland Discovery Centre: 01433 637907

ℹ️ **T** 01433 637904
   E longshaw@nationaltrust.org.uk

Show your card and display sticker for free parking

👹 School holiday family activities and other seasonal events throughout the year, including Christmas celebrations

🚶 Walks leaflet and guidebook available from shop

♿ 🅿 🅳 ♿ 🔊 ♿ **Building** 🏛 **Grounds** 🦽 🏛 ➡

📷 NT shop in Visitor Centre. Christmas tree sales in main car park in Dec. Plant sales

🍵 Tea-room in Visitor Centre serving home-cooked food. Children's menu. Seasonal refreshments van at Padley Gorge

👶 Baby-changing facilities. Pushchairs and baby back-carriers admitted. Children's quiz/trail. Family trail. Family activities in school holidays

🎒 Suitable for school groups. Education room/centre

🐕 On leads only, not in Visitor Centre

➔ [110/119:SK266800] **Bus**: First 272 Sheffield–Castleton (passing 🚃 Hathersage), TM Travel 214 Sheffield–Matlock. Both pass close 🚃 Sheffield. **Station**: Grindleford (U) 2ml (1ml to Visitor Centre, 100yds to Padley Gorge). **Road**: 7½ml from Sheffield, next to A625 Sheffield–Hathersage road; Woodcroft car park is off B6055, 200yds S of junction with A625

🅿 Parking (pay & display). Car parks for estate at Haywood [110/119: SK256778], Wooden Pole [110/119: SK267790] and Woodcroft [110/119: SK267802]. Car parks not accessible to coaches, which should park on roadsides

NT properties nearby
Hardwick Hall, High Peak Estate, Ilam Park and South Peak Estate, Stainsby Mill

Longshaw Estate									
Estate									
All year		**M**	**T**	**W**	**T**	**F**	**S**	**S**	
Visitor Centre/shop									
1 Feb–5 Apr	10:30–4	M	T	W	T	F	**S**	**S**	
6 Apr–19 Apr	10:30–5	**M**	**T**	**W**	**T**	**F**	**S**	**S**	
22 Apr–26 Jul	10:30–5	M	T	**W**	**T**	**F**	**S**	**S**	
27 Jul–6 Sep	10:30–5	**M**	**T**	**W**	**T**	**F**	**S**	**S**	
9 Sep–25 Oct	10:30–5	M	T	**W**	**T**	**F**	**S**	**S**	
31 Oct–31 Jan 10	10:30–4	M	T	W	T	F	**S**	**S**	

Open BH Mons. Lodge is not open. Extended opening 18–30 Dec, tel. 01433 637904 for details

Lyveden New Bield

nr Oundle, Peterborough,
Northamptonshire PE8 5AT

🏠 ✝ 🌼 🚳 📷 🍵 🚶 🌳 🎗 👶 🎒 🚶 🚲 🍴

`1922`   **(3:E6)**

Intriguing Elizabethan lodge and moated garden

Set in the heart of rural Northamptonshire, Lyveden is a remarkable survival of the Elizabethan age. Begun by Sir Thomas Tresham to symbolise his Catholic faith, Lyveden remains

The intriguing Lyveden New Bield, Northamptonshire

incomplete and virtually unaltered since work stopped on his death in 1605. Discover the mysterious garden lodge and explore the Elizabethan garden with spiral mounts, terracing and moats. Wander through the new orchard, containing many old varieties of apples and pears, or explore the Lyveden Way, a circular path through beautiful meadows, woodland and villages.

What's new in 2009 New car parking facility and walks leaflet

⭐ As featured in BBC series *Hidden Gardens*. Accompanied children free

ℹ️ **T** 01832 205358
E lyvedennewbield@nationaltrust.org.uk

🚶 Free garden tours, Suns May–Sept, 2

🚶 Lyveden Way: 9ml circular walk between Lyveden and Wadenhoe. New walks leaflet

♿ P♿ 🚾 ∷ **Building** 🏠 **Grounds** 🏞️

🎁 Small selection of gifts

🍽️ Ice-cream, confectionery, hot and cold drinks sold in shop

👶 Baby-changing facilities. Pushchairs and baby back-carriers admitted. Family guide

🏫 Suitable for school groups

🐕 On leads only

🚲 Lyveden to Wadenhoe is a bridleway suitable for cycles

➡️ [141:SP983853] **Bus**: Stagecoach in Northants X4 ➡ Northampton– ➡ Peterborough, alight Lower Benefield, 2ml by bridlepath; Judges minicoaches 8 Kettering– Corby, alight Brigstock, 2½ml. Both pass close ➡ Kettering. **Station**: Kettering 10ml. **Road**: 4ml SW of Oundle via A427, 3ml E of Brigstock, leading off A6116

P Free parking, 100yds

NT properties nearby
Canons Ashby House, Houghton Mill

Lyveden New Bield		M	T	W	T	F	S	S
1 Feb–29 Nov	11–4	M	T	W	T	F	**S**	**S**
18 Mar–31 Oct	10:30–5	M	**T**	**W**	**T**	F	S	S
1 Aug–30 Aug	10:30–5	**M**	**T**	**W**	**T**	**F**	S	S
Open BH Mons. Good Fri: 10:30–5								

The Old Manor

Norbury, Ashbourne, Derbyshire DE6 2ED

🏠 ✳️ 🚶 👶 1987   (3:B4)

Low, stone-built medieval hall

Built between the 13th and 15th centuries, the hall's architectural features include a rare king post, medieval fireplace, a Tudor door and some 17th-century Flemish glass. The delightful gardens include a parterre herb garden.

What's new in 2009 Try our Detective Trail to explore more of this unique property

⭐ Limited parking for cars only

ℹ️ **T** 01283 585337
E oldmanor@nationaltrust.org.uk

♿ P♿ 🚾 ∷ ∅ 🏠 **Building** 🏠
Grounds 🏞️ 🏞️

👶 Baby back-carriers admitted

➡️ [128:SK125424] 4ml from Ashbourne; 9ml from Sudbury Hall. **Foot**: Norbury village is clearly signposted from A515. 2½ml walk to Norbury Church. **Bus**: Arriva Midlands 409 Uttoxeter–Ashbourne, alight Ellastone, ¾ml. **Station**: Uttoxeter (U) 7½ml

P No designated car park or facility for coach parking. Coaches must drop passengers at top of drive

NT properties nearby
Ilam Park and South Peak Estate, Kedleston Hall, Sudbury Hall and the National Trust Museum of Childhood

The Old Manor		M	T	W	T	F	S	S
3 Apr–23 Oct	10–12	M	T	W	T	**F**	S	S
4 Apr–24 Oct	2–4	M	T	W	T	F	**S**	**S**
Property is tenanted and visits are only available during opening hours. Groups must book. Visitors will be guided around the hall and gardens								

If Lyveden New Bield captured your imagination, then so will Oxburgh Hall

Unless indicated, last admission is always 30mins before closing time

Find out what life was like for a 19th-century miller at Stainsby Mill on the Hardwick Estate

Priest's House

Easton on the Hill, nr Stamford,
Northamptonshire PE9 3LS

🏠 1966   (3:E5)

Small pre-Reformation stone building

Of interest for its architecture, the house also contains a small museum exploring Easton's important industrial past.

What's new in 2009 New exhibition exploring Easton's important industrial past. Exhibitions on collyweston stone and slate industries

i **T** 01780 762619
  E priestshouse2@nationaltrust.org.uk

🔥 Building 🔥🔥

➡ [141:TF009045] **Bus**: Blands 180 from Stamford (passing close ≋ Stamford), alight Easton, ½ml. **Station**: Stamford 2ml. **Road**: approx. 2ml SW of Stamford off A43

P Ample roadside parking (not NT)

NT properties nearby
Lyveden New Bield, Woolsthorpe Manor

Priest's House								
5 Jul–30 Aug	2:30–4:30	M	T	W	T	F	S	**S**

Unmanned. Also open by appointment daily throughout the year. Names of keyholders on property noticeboard. Appointments for groups may be made through local representative Mr Paul Way, 39 Church St, Easton on the Hill, Stamford PE9 3LL

Stainsby Mill: Hardwick Estate

Doe Lea, Chesterfield, Derbyshire S44 5QJ

🔧🚶🌳🛡🚻🎒🚶 1976   (3:D3)

Impressive fully functioning water-powered flour mill

With newly reconstructed 1849–50 machinery, the mill is in full working order and gives a vivid evocation of the workplace of a 19th-century miller. Flour is ground regularly and is for sale throughout the season.

⭐ No WC, nearest at Hardwick Hall car park

i **T** 01246 850430 (Hardwick Hall)
  E stainsbymill@nationaltrust.org.uk

🚶 On request at the mill. Out-of-hours tours, contact Hardwick Hall

🛡 National Mills Day

🚶 Contact Hardwick Hall for details of estate walks

🔥 🚻🔆📷📹 Building 🔥
Grounds 🔥🔥

🛍 NT shop at Hardwick Hall. Flour and souvenirs sold at mill

🍴 Refreshments available at Hardwick Hall

🎒 Baby back-carriers admitted. Front-carrying baby slings available for loan. Children's quiz

Most Trust properties offer Gift Aid on Entry for non-members, see page 10

■ Suitable for school groups. Live interpretation. Learning Officer

🦮 On leads and only in park

➔ [120:SK455653] **Foot**: Rowthorne Trail and Teversal Trail nearby. **Bus**: Stagecoach East Midlands 'Pronto' Chesterfield–Nottingham, alight Glapwell 'Young Vanish', 1½ml. **Station**: Chesterfield 7ml. **Road**: from M1 exit 29 take A6175 signposted to Clay Cross, then first left and left again to Stainsby Mill

P Free parking (not NT). Limited car/coach parking area

NT properties nearby
Clumber Park, Hardwick Hall, Kedleston Hall, Mr Straw's House, The Workhouse, Southwell

Stainsby Mill								
18 Feb–22 Feb	12–4	M	T	**W**	**T**	**F**	**S**	**S**
28 Feb–8 Mar	12–4	M	T	W	T	F	**S**	**S**
14 Mar–1 Nov	10–4	M	T	**W**	**T**	**F**	**S**	**S**
5 Dec–20 Dec	11–3	M	T	W	T	**F**	**S**	**S**
Open BH Mons and Good Fri. Open 26 Dec & 1 Jan 10								

Restored machinery inside Stainsby Mill, a working, water-powered flour mill on the Hardwick Estate in Derbyshire

Staunton Harold Church

Staunton Harold, Ashby-de-la-Zouch,
Leicestershire LE65 1RW

 1954   **(3:C4)**

Imposing church built in 1653, with fine panelled interior

Set in attractive parkland, this is one of the few churches built between the outbreak of the English Civil War and the restoration of the monarchy, representing an open act of defiance to Cromwell's Puritan regime by its creator, Sir Robert Shirley. The interior retains its original 17th-century cushions, carved woodwork and painted ceilings.

What's new in 2009 Guided tours

⭐ No NT signage. Follow tourist signs to Ferrers Centre indicated by brown signs – anvil symbol. WCs (not NT) 500yds

ℹ️ **T** 01332 863822 (Calke Abbey)
   E calkeabbey@nationaltrust.org.uk

𝕂 Available on request (booking essential)

♿ P 🅙 Building 🦼 🏛️

🍽️ Refreshments available at Ferrers Centre and garden centre nearby (not NT)

🚼 Pushchairs admitted

■ Suitable for school groups

➔ [128:SK380209] **Cycle**: NCN6, 2½ml.
   Bus: Arriva Midlands 155 Coalville–Castle Donnington, alight Newbold, 1ml. **Road**: 5ml NE of Ashby-de-la-Zouch, W of B587. Access from M42/A42 exit 13, follow brown signs – anvil symbol

P Free parking (not NT), 400yds next to rear of the garden centre (by courtesy of the owner). Entrance indicated by brown signs – anvil symbol

NT properties nearby
Calke Abbey, Kedleston Hall, Sudbury Hall and the National Trust Museum of Childhood

Staunton Harold Church								
4 Apr–1 Nov	1–4:30	M	T	W	T	F	**S**	**S**
3 Jun–28 Aug	1–4:30	M	T	**W**	**T**	**F**	**S**	**S**
Open BH Mons & Good Fri								

Mr Straw's House

5–7 Blyth Grove, Worksop,
Nottinghamshire S81 0JG

🏠 ✣ ⬛ 🔲 ♥ ⍟ ▥ 1990   **(3:D2)**

A 1920s house captured in time

Step back in time to the 1920s and find out how a grocer's family lived. This ordinary semi-detached house was the home of the Straw family, who threw nothing away for more than 60 years and lived without many of the modern comforts we take for granted. Photos, letters, Victorian furniture and household objects can still be seen exactly where their owners left them. Explore all three floors of this award-winning visitor attraction with our room guides and find out more about the Straw family from the introductory video and annual exhibition and displays.

What's new in 2009 Annual exhibition, including a display of items not normally on view to the public

Mr Straw's House									
14 Mar–31 Oct	11–5	M	**T**	**W**	**T**	**F**	**S**	S

Admission by timed ticket only for all visitors (inc. NT members), which must be booked in advance. All bookings by tel. or letter (with sae), not email, to Custodian. On quiet days a same-day tel. call is often sufficient. Last admission 4. Closed Good Fri. Due to its location in residential area, the house is closed on BHols as a courtesy to neighbours

⭐ Blyth Grove is a private road; there is no access without advance booking. There is a car park with picnic area for visitors opposite the house. Please come to reception at 5 Blyth Grove just before your allotted visit time, if early visit rear gardens (with WCs)

ℹ️ **T** 01909 482380
E mrstrawshouse@nationaltrust.org.uk

♥ Easter fun. Behind-the-scenes tours. Rag rug days. Tasting-the-past days. The Friends group provides tea and cakes in the orchard 1st Sat of the month

♿ 🅿️ 👓 🄰 **Building** 🐾

🏠 NT shop. Plant sales

⍟ Children's quiz/trail

▥ Suitable for school groups. Hands-on activities. Teachers' resource pack

➡️ [120:SK592802] **Cycle**: NCN6, ¾ml.
Bus: from surrounding areas.
Station: Worksop ½ml. **Road**: follow signs for Bassetlaw Hospital and Blyth Road (B6045). Blyth Grove is a small private road off B6045, just S of Bassetlaw Hospital A&E entrance. House signposted with black and white signs at the bottom of Blyth Grove

🅿️ Free parking, 30yds

NT properties nearby
Clumber Park, Hardwick Hall, Stainsby Mill, The Workhouse, Southwell

The cosy family living room in Mr Straw's House, Worksop in Nottinghamshire

Sudbury Hall and the National Trust Museum of Childhood

Sudbury, Ashbourne, Derbyshire DE6 5HT

[T] 1967 (3:B4)

Late 17th-century house with sumptuous interiors and the Museum of Childhood, where you can take a fresh look at childhood

Sudbury Hall, which featured in the BBC's *Pride and Prejudice* and *Jane Eyre*, is a grand 17th-century family home. Experience the richly decorated interiors, including wood carving by Grinling Gibbons, and the Great Staircase, which is one of the most elaborate of its kind in any English house. There's also another world to discover below stairs in the 1930s kitchen, before you enjoy a walk around the naturalised garden, by the lake and boathouse. Housed in the 19th-century service wing of Sudbury Hall, the Museum contains fascinating displays and a fine collection of toys, games and dolls. Find something for everyone in the eight themed galleries, from Adventure to Toys. Come and hunt for the toys, games and activities from your childhood, share your childhood stories with others and create new stories and adventures. You can be a chimney sweep, a scullion or a Victorian pupil, and enjoy our captivating archive film, interactives and displays.

What's new in 2009 The Museum of Childhood's season now starts earlier – from 14 February. Curl up in the Story gallery and explore the delights of our 'Story Sacs'. New Sudbury Stories in the Hall's Porch Room. 'Why? cards' will help you understand how we care for this property

[i] **T** 01283 585305 (Infoline), 01283 585337
E sudburyhall@nationaltrust.org.uk

[X] Guided and specialist tours of Hall. Behind-the-scenes tours. Evening and morning tours by arrangement

[∩] Museum of Childhood – various audio visual and audio experiences

[♥] Family activities during school holidays

Sudbury Hall and the NT Museum of Childhood

Hall								
14 Feb–1 Nov	1–5	M	T	**W**	**T**	**F**	**S**	**S**

Museum/tea-room/shop								
14 Feb–29 Mar	11–5	M	T	**W**	**T**	**F**	**S**	**S**
30 Mar–1 Nov	11–5	**M**	**T**	**W**	**T**	**F**	**S**	**S**
7 Nov–20 Dec	11–5	M	T	W	T	F	**S**	**S**

Christmas event in the Museum								
5 Dec–20 Dec	10:30–3:30	M	T	W	T	F	**S**	**S**

Grounds								
14 Feb–20 Dec	10–5	**M**	**T**	**W**	**T**	**F**	**S**	**S**

Open BH Mons & Good Fri. Hall may have to close early if light is poor. Schools & tours 11–12

Building [↕][♿] Museum of Childhood [♿][↕] Grounds [↕][♿]

[□] Museum shop in stableyard, with toys, children's goods and home-made fudge. Gift shop selling wide range of products

[♥] The Coach House tea-room (licensed). Children's menu

[♦♦] Baby-changing and feeding facilities. Front-carrying baby slings and hip-carrying infant seats, reins and indoor buggies for loan. Children's guide. Children's quiz/trail. Children's activity packs. Family activities

[♦] Suitable for school groups. Live interpretation. Hands-on activities. Adult study days

[→] [128:SK158322] **Cycle:** cycleway from Uttoxeter to Doveridge, then road to property. **Bus:** Arriva 1 Burton on Trent–Uttoxeter (passing ≥ Tutbury & Hatton and close ≥ Burton on Trent). **Station:** Tutbury & Hatton (U) 5ml. **Road:** 6ml E of Uttoxeter at junction of A50 Derby–Stoke and A515 Ashbourne

[P] Free parking, 500yds

NT properties nearby
Calke Abbey, Ilam Park and South Peak Estate, Kedleston Hall, The Old Manor

If you and your family enjoyed exploring the Museum of Childhood, you will find lots to do at Belton House

Show your card and display sticker for free parking

Tattershall Castle

Sleaford Road, Tattershall, Lincolnshire LN4 4LR

🛎 1925   **(3:F3)**

Medieval brick castle rising dramatically above the Lincolnshire countryside

Explore the six floors of this red-brick medieval castle built by Ralph Cromwell, Lord Treasurer of England and one of the most powerful men in the country. Let the audio guide create a picture of what life was like at Tattershall Castle in the 15th century. Climb the 150 steps from the basement to the battlements and enjoy the magnificent views of the Lincolnshire countryside, then explore the grounds, moats and bridges.

ℹ️ **T** 01526 342543
   E tattershallcastle@nationaltrust.org.uk

Including family days and concerts

Leaflet on walk around Tattershall village available from shop

Building   Grounds

Hot and cold drinks and ice-cream available in shop. Seating area in exhibition room above shop

Baby-changing facilities. Pushchairs and baby back-carriers admitted. Children's guide. Children's quiz/trail. Family days

Suitable for school groups. Live interpretation. Hands-on activities

➔ [122:TF211575] **Cycle**: Hull to Harwich cycle route passes within 1ml. **Bus**: Brylaine 5 Lincoln–Boston (passing close ≷ Lincoln and Boston). **Station**: Ruskington (U) 10ml. **Road**: on S side of A153, 15ml NE of Sleaford; 10ml SW of Horncastle

Tattershall Castle									
28 Feb–8 Mar	11–4	M	T	W	T	F	S	S
14 Mar–4 Oct	11–5	M	T	W	T	F	S	S
5 Oct–1 Nov	11–4	M	T	W	T	F	S	S
7 Nov–20 Dec	11–4	M	T	W	T	F	S	S

Open Good Fri: 11–5. Last audio guide issued 1¼hrs before closing. NB: castle opens 1 on Sats when weddings except July & Aug

🅿 Free parking, 150yds. Coaches must reverse into parking area

NT properties nearby
Belton House, Grantham House, Gunby Hall, Monksthorpe Chapel

Children on the battlements at Tattershall Castle

Ulverscroft Nature Reserve

nr Loughborough, Leicestershire

🐾 1945   **(3:D5)**

Reserve in the care of the Leicestershire and Rutland Wildlife Trust

Part of the ancient forest of Charnwood, Ulverscroft is especially beautiful in spring during the bluebell season.

⭐ No WC. Access by appointment and permit only issued by Leicestershire & Rutland Wildlife Trust 0116 272 0444

ℹ️ **T** 01909 486411
   E ulverscroft@nationaltrust.org.uk

Grounds

Dogs assisting visitors with disabilities are always welcome

➔ [129:SK493118] 6ml SW of Loughborough.
Bus: Arriva X2, 28A/B, 217/8 Leicester–
Swadlincote (passing close ✉ Leicester), to
within 1ml. **Station**: Barrow upon Soar 7ml,
Loughborough 7½ml

🅿 Roadside parking only

NT properties nearby
Calke Abbey, Staunton Harold Church

Ulverscroft Nature Reserve

Access by permit only from The Secretary,
Leicestershire & Rutland Wildlife Trust, Brocks Hill
Environment Centre, Washbrook Lane, Oadby, Leics
LE2 5JJ. Tel. 0116 272 0444

Winster Market House

Main Street, Winster, nr Matlock, Derbyshire DE4 2DJ

🏠 🎦 │1906│ **(3:C3)**

Late 17th- or early 18th-century
market house

The restored building is a reminder of when
cheese and cattle fairs were prominent features
of local life. The Trust's first acquisition in the
Peak District, it now houses an information
room, with interpretation panels and scale
model of Winster village.

⭐ No WC, public WC in side street nearby.
Postal address: Home Farm, Ilam,
Ashbourne, Derbyshire DE6 2AZ

ℹ **T** 01335 350503
E winstermarkethouse@nationaltrust.org.uk

♿ ·: Building 🅛

🎦 Suitable for school groups

➔ [119:SK241606] 4ml W of Matlock.
Cycle: NCN67, 3ml. **Bus**: Hulley's 172
Matlock–Bakewell (passing close ✉ Matlock).
Station: Matlock (U) 4ml. **Road**: on S side of
B5057 in main street of Winster

🅿 Parking (not NT) in village

NT properties nearby
Hardwick Hall, Ilam Park and South Peak Estate,
Kedleston Hall, Longshaw Estate, South Peak
Estate, inc. Dovedale & Hamps & Manifold Valleys

Winster Market House								
1 Mar–31 Oct	Times vary	**M**	**T**	**W**	**T**	**F**	**S**	**S**

Woolsthorpe Manor

Water Lane, Woolsthorpe by Colsterworth,
nr Grantham, Lincolnshire NG33 5PD

🏠 🎦 ✳ ◻ ☕ 🚹 🏕 🔰 ♿ 🎦
│🚶│ │1943│ **(3:E4)**

Birthplace and family home of
Sir Isaac Newton

This modest 17th-century Lincolnshire manor
house was the birthplace and family home of
one of the world's most famous scientists.
Instead of running the family sheep farm as a
young man, Newton developed his remarkable
work about light and gravity here. Visit the
famous apple tree and discover Newton's ideas
in the hands-on Science Discovery Centre.
Enjoy The Byre activity room, short film and
explore the orchards and farmyard.

What's new in 2009 New furnishings and
setting in the historic Hall

⭐ Postal address: Woolsthorpe Manor, 23
Newton Way, Woolsthorpe by Colsterworth,
nr Grantham NG33 5NR

ℹ **T** 01476 860338
E woolsthorpemanor@nationaltrust.org.uk

🔰 Summer exhibition, family events, talks,
workshops and children's activities

🚶 Village walk from property. Leaflets available
at ticket desk

♿ 🅳 🅴 ·: ◎ ▣ 🅹 🅺 Building 🅛 🅜 🅤
Grounds 🅛 🅜

🛍 Small shop

☕ Drinks and snacks in the Science Centre

🚼 Baby-changing facilities. Baby back-carriers
available for loan. Children's activities and
quiz. Children's costumes. Family events

🎦 Suitable for school groups. Activity room.
Hands-on activities. Live interpretation (please
ask when booking). Short film. Hands-on
interactive Science Centre

➔ [130:SK924244] 8ml S of Grantham, ½ml NW
of Colsterworth. **Bus**: Centrebus 608
Grantham–South Witham (passes close ✉
Grantham). **Station**: Grantham 8ml.
Road: 1ml W of A1 (not to be confused with

Woolsthorpe near Belvoir). Leave A1 at Colsterworth roundabout via B676, at second crossroads turn right, then first left into Water Lane for car park

🅿 Free parking, 50yds. Groups must book in advance as parking for coaches is limited

NT properties nearby
Belton House, Grantham House, Tattershall Castle

Woolsthorpe Manor									
27 Feb–29 Mar	1–5	M	T	W	T	**F**	**S**	**S**	
1 Apr–28 Jun	1–5	M	T	**W**	**T**	**F**	**S**	**S**	
1 Jul–30 Aug	1–5*	M	T	**W**	**T**	**F**	**S**	**S**	
2 Sep–27 Sep	1–5	M	T	**W**	**T**	**F**	**S**	**S**	
2 Oct–1 Nov	1–5	M	T	W	T	**F**	**S**	**S**	

*Open 11–5 at weekends. Open BH Mons & Good Fri

The Workhouse, Southwell

Upton Road, Southwell, Nottinghamshire NG25 0PT

🏠 🚶 🎧 🎭 👪 🖼 2002   **(3:D3)**

Atmospheric 19th-century workhouse

Explore the most complete workhouse in existence and immerse yourself in the unique atmosphere as the audio guide (based on archive records) brings the 19th-century inhabitants back to life. Find out about poverty through the years with the help of the interactive displays, then meet the Reverend Becher, the founder of The Workhouse, in the introductory film. Discover the segregated work yards, day rooms, dormitories, master's quarters and cellars, then see the recreated working 19th-century garden and food the paupers would have eaten.

What's new in 2009 Time Travel Tour and storytelling club

⭐ Groups welcome but please book in advance. Limited refreshments on site; food available in local villages

ℹ️ **T** 01636 817250 (Infoline), 01636 817260
E theworkhouse@nationaltrust.org.uk

🚶 Tours run on selected summer evenings and throughout the open season

🎧 Included in the admission

🎭 Arts and social exhibitions. Special events programme throughout the season

The Workhouse, Southwell									
28 Feb–15 Mar	11–5	M	T	W	T	F	**S**	**S**	
18 Mar–1 Nov	12–5*	M	T	**W**	**T**	**F**	**S**	**S**	

*Only open for guided tours from 11–12. Booking is advisable at peak times as numbers on tours are limited. Open BH Mons & Good Fri. Last admission 1hr before closing. Normal house admission from 12

♿ 🅿 🚻 ♿ 🔊 📷 🎨 📷 🖼 📹 🍴 🎧

Building 🪑🪑🪑 Grounds 🪑▶

👶 Baby-changing facilities. Pushchairs admitted. Hip-carrying infant seats for loan. Children's quiz/trail. 'Master's Punishment' game to play. Regular family events

🖼 Suitable for school groups. Live interpretation. Hands-on activities. Adult study days. Resource centre

🐕 On leads only in grounds

➔ [120:SK712543] **Foot**: Robin Hood Trail goes past The Workhouse. **Cycle**: National Byway (Heritage Cycle Route). **Bus**: Nottingham City Transport 100 🚌 Newark–Nottingham, Stagecoach East Midlands 29A Newark–Southwell–Mansfield. Both pass 🚌 Newark Castle. **Station**: Fiskerton (U) 2ml, Newark Castle 7ml, Newark North Gate 7½ml. **Road**: 13ml from Nottingham on A612 and 8ml from Newark on A617 and A612

🅿 Free parking, 200yds

NT properties nearby
Belton House, Clumber Park, Hardwick Hall, Mr Straw's House, Tattershall Castle, Woolsthorpe Manor

The stark interior of The Workhouse at Southwell

The history of the West Midlands has shaped the countryside, which in turn has provided generations of people with endless inspiration and relaxation.

In Shropshire, the National Trust owns more than 2,800 hectares (7,000 acres) of some of the most breathtaking countryside in England, while in Herefordshire, the Trust protects nearly 2,000 hectares (5,000 acres) of parkland and countryside.

This countryside is amazingly diverse; in fact the variety of landscapes is unbeatable. They range from the rugged uplands of the Long Mynd in the Shropshire Hills, and the wild moorlands of Staffordshire, to the pure beauty of the rolling shires of Shakespeare Country and the North Cotswolds.

Savour the views from some of the most iconic landscapes in the region. From Kinver Edge and the Clent Hills, enjoy the miles of walks and many vistas across to the Malvern Hills and rolling Worcestershire countryside. Only twelve miles from Birmingham – these properties provide a startling contrasting landscape to the city and a welcome respite from the pressures and bustle of urban life.

Walk, ramble or stroll

Whether you like a long ramble, a brisk walk or a gentle stroll, there are endless opportunities in the West Midlands. The Long Mynd, or 'Long Mountain', for example, is a Site of Special Scientific Interest which offers excellent walking.

An ancient track, the Portway, runs along the top of the great ridge, which extends for ten miles and is home to a wide range of upland flora and fauna. Savour the stunning views across the Shropshire and Cheshire plains, and the Black Mountains, or try to spot some of the wide range of upland flora and fauna which make their home there.

Wenlock Edge is another rare and special landscape. Stretching for nineteen miles through Shropshire, its thickly wooded limestone escarpment offers dramatic views. There are also meandering paths to explore, historic quarries and limekilns, as well as rare flowers, mammals, birds and insects.

Above left: **spring water flowing down towards Carding Mill Valley reservoir in Shropshire**
Above right: **farmland at Wilderhope Manor, Shropshire**

Below: **children enjoying a walk on the Brockhampton Estate in Herefordshire**

Previous page: **diamond-paned window at Lower Brockhampton in Herefordshire**

Look out for our leaflets and information boards at the properties or visit www.nationaltrust.org.uk

Park life

Nearly eighteen per cent of the Trust's holding of parkland is in the West Midlands region, so you are spoilt for choice. They range from 'Capability' Brown's first commissioned landscape at Croome Park, near Worcester, to one of his final landscapes at Berrington Hall, near Leominster. There are plenty of activities. Choose from guided walks, talks and trails, to general and specialist events, such as the Ugly Bug Safari, Deer Park Safari and the Dawn Chorus Walks.

Stroll through the dappled woodland at Attingham Park and the Dudmaston Estate (both in Shropshire), enjoy a picnic while watching the deer at Charlecote Park, or simply tuck into some of the award-winning local produce at the traditionally managed Brockhampton Estate after enjoying a walk through the ancient farmland and woods.

Travel north-east to Staffordshire and you will find some of the finest scenery in the county, including lowland heath at Downs Banks, near Stone, and ancient woodland at Hawksmoor Nature Reserve, in the Churnet Valley.

Above: **Dudmaston Estate, Shropshire**
Below: **damsons ripening at Hill House Farm on the Brockhampton Estate, Herefordshire**

www.nationaltrust.org.uk/coastandcountryside

My favourite countryside

There is an abundance of wildlife at Croft Castle and Parkland, and you can also 'walk' through thousands of years of history. Climb to the Iron Age hill fort at Croft Ambrey, wander through the picturesque landscape of the Fishpool Valley, marvel at the extraordinary forms of the many ancient oak and sweet chestnut trees, or simply enjoy the views that overlook the Herefordshire countryside to the Black Mountains beyond.

Simon Barker
Regional Nature Conservation Adviser

Attingham Park

Shrewsbury, Shropshire SY4 4TP

[1947]   (4:H4)

Elegant 18th-century mansion with Regency interiors, set in extensive Repton landscape with deer park

Attingham Park, built in 1785 to the design of George Steuart with alterations by John Nash, was in continuous ownership by eight generations of the Berwick family and exemplifies the changing fortunes of the English country-house estate. One of the greatest country houses in Shropshire, it contains important collections of Regency furniture, Grand Tour paintings and ambassadorial silver. The large working estate and deer park, landscaped by Humphry Repton, is an area of great natural beauty. Set alongside the rivers Severn and Tern, there are numerous attractive walks and views over to the Shropshire Hills.

What's new in 2009 Attingham Re-discovered, the major interiors restoration project, continues with the Dining Room and Picture Gallery re-presented, plus a newly restored decorative

The elegant dining table at Attingham Park laid for a formal dinner

scheme in the Octagon Room and ongoing works throughout the house. Extended and improved Carriage House catering kiosk providing year-round catering. Major modern art exhibition in the parkland until September

⭐ In situ restoration and conservation in action ongoing in various parts of the mansion

ℹ️ **T** 01743 708123 (Infoline), 01743 708162
E attingham@nationaltrust.org.uk

🚶 Free costumed, Re-discovered and taster tours of the house from 11, except BHols

🛡️ Family events, trails and Trusty's Tuesday and Thursday Club throughout local school holidays. Diverse range of events including plant, food, Frost fairs and Regency weekends. Send sae for events leaflet

🚶 Walks of varying length. Programme of guided walks

Building 🏷️ 🔄 ♿ **Grounds** 🏷️ ➡️ 🐾

🛍️ NT shop. Plant sales

🍽️ Licensed tea-room catering for specialist diets. Children's menu. Kiosk in stableyard open all year round

👶 Baby-changing facilities. Front-carrying baby slings and hip-carrying infant seats for loan. Children's play area. Family games. Children's quiz/trail. Mansion family activity room

🏛️ Suitable for school groups. Guided and self-guided indoor and open-air programmes complement National Curriculum. Education room/centre. Live interpretation. Hands-on activities

🐕 On leads in vicinity of mansion and facilities. Clearly identified off-lead areas

➡️ [126:SJ550099] **Bus**: Arriva 96 Shrewsbury–Telford (passing close ⊟ Shrewsbury and Telford Central). **Station**: Shrewsbury 5ml. **Road**: 4ml SE of Shrewsbury, on N side of B4380 in Atcham village

🅿️ Free parking, 25yds

NT properties nearby
Attingham Park Estate: Cronkhill, Benthall Hall, Carding Mill Valley and the Shropshire Hills, Dudmaston Estate, Moseley Old Hall, Powis Castle, Sunnycroft

Please remember – your membership card is *always* needed for free admission

Attingham Park

Park/shop/reception										
1 Feb–13 Feb	9–5	M	T	W	T	F	S	S
14 Feb–1 Nov	9–6	M	T	W	T	F	S	S
2 Nov–31 Jan 10	9–5	M	T	W	T	F	S	S
House tours								
1 Feb–1 Mar	11:30–2:30	M	T	W	T	F	S	S
7 Mar–8 Mar	11–1	M	T	W	T	F	S	S
14 Mar–1 Nov	11–1	M	T	W	T	F	S	S
7 Nov–29 Nov	11:30–2:30	M	T	W	T	F	S	S
9 Jan–31 Jan 10	11:30–2:30	M	T	W	T	F	S	S
House								
7 Mar–8 Mar	1–4	M	T	W	T	F	S	S
14 Mar–1 Nov	1–5:30	M	T	W	T	F	S	S
Mansion Tea-room								
1 Feb–8 Mar	10:30–4:30	M	T	W	T	F	S	S
14 Mar–1 Nov	10:30–5	M	T	W	T	F	S	S
7 Nov–20 Dec	10:30–4:30	M	T	W	T	F	S	S
27 Dec–3 Jan 10	10:30–4:30	M	T	W	T	F	S	S
9 Jan–31 Jan 10	10:30–4:30	M	T	W	T	F	S	S
Carriage House Kiosk*								
14 Mar–1 Nov	9–5:30	M	T	W	T	F	S	S

Open BH Mons & Good Fri 11–5:30. House last admission 1hr before closing. Park, shop & visitor reception close dusk if earlier. **Mansion tea-room open every day Feb half-term. *Carriage House Kiosk also open Mon–Fri, 11:30–2 & Sat–Sun, 9–4 Feb/Mar, Nov/Dec & Jan 10 and every day in main season school hols.** House Special Christmas opening 12/13 & 19–21 Dec inc., 1–4. Whole site closed 25 Dec

Attingham Park Estate: Cronkhill

Atcham, Shrewsbury, Shropshire SY5 6JP

🏠 👫 1947   (4:H5)

First and best-known example of John Nash's Italianate villa designs, built in 1805

⭐ Visitors are reminded that the contents of the property belong to the tenants and should not be touched

ℹ️ **T** 01743 708123 (Infoline), 01743 708162
E cronkhill@nationaltrust.org.uk

➜ From Attingham take road to Cross Houses; Cronkhill is on the right

Attingham Park Estate: Cronkhill

Open Wed 22 & Sun 26 Apr, Wed 29 Jul & Sun 2 Aug, Wed 2 & Sun 6 Sept 11–4

The kitchen at Baddesley Clinton, Warwickshire

Baddesley Clinton

Rising Lane, Baddesley Clinton, Warwickshire B93 0DQ

🏠 ✝️ ❄️ 🍴 📷 🎁 🔪 🎭 👫 🚩 🚶 🚲 🍽️
1980   (4:K6)

Picturesque medieval moated manor house and garden

This atmospheric house dates from the 15th century and was the home of the Ferrers family for 500 years. The house and interiors reflect its heyday in the Elizabethan era, when it was a haven for persecuted Catholics – there are three priest's holes. There is a delightful garden with stewponds and a romantic lake and nature walk.

What's new in 2009 Camellia border between the moat and stewponds

⭐ Property postal address: Rising Lane, Baddesley Clinton Village, Knowle, Solihull, West Midlands B93 0DQ

ℹ️ **T** 01564 783294
E baddesleyclinton@nationaltrust.org.uk

🔪 Wed, Thur evenings by appointment. Supper can be included

🎭 Easter trail for families. 'Hands on the Past' living history. Brunch lectures in spring and autumn

Baddesley Clinton									
House									
11 Feb–1 Nov	11–5	M	T	**W**	**T**	**F**	**S**	**S**	
Grounds/shop/restaurant									
11 Feb–1 Nov	11–5	M	T	**W**	**T**	**F**	**S**	**S**	
4 Nov–20 Dec	11–4	M	T	**W**	**T**	**F**	**S**	**S**	

Admission by timed ticket to house; visitors may then stay until house closes. Open BH Mons

🚫 Pᴅ ᴡᴄ .. 🎨 📷 🎵 Building 🏠 🏛 ♿
Grounds 🏠 🏛 ➡ ♿

🏪 NT shop. Second-hand bookshop. Plant sales

🍽 The Barn Restaurant (licensed). Children's menu

👪 Baby-changing facilities. Front-carrying baby slings and hip-carrying infant seats for loan. Children's guide. House trail for younger children. Family activities

🎒 Suitable for school groups. Teachers' resource book. Live interpretation. Hands-on activities

🚴 1½ml public bridleway giving shared access for cyclists

➡ [139:SP199723] **Foot**: Heart of England Way passes close. **Station**: Lapworth (U), 2ml; Birmingham International 9ml. **Road**: ¾ml W of A4141 Warwick–Birmingham road, at Chadwick End, 7½ml NW of Warwick, 6ml S of M42 exit 5; 15ml SE of central Birmingham

P Free parking, 50yds

NT properties nearby
Birmingham Back to Backs, Charlecote Park, Clent Hills, Hanbury Hall, Packwood House

Benthall Hall

Broseley, Shropshire TF12 5RX

🏠 ✝ 🎨 🎒 👪 🚶 | 1958 | (4:15)

Handsome 16th-century house and restored garden

Situated on a plateau above the gorge of the River Severn, this fine stone house has mullioned and transomed windows and a stunning interior with carved oak staircase, decorated plaster ceilings and oak panelling. There is an intimate and carefully restored plantsman's garden, old kitchen garden and interesting Restoration church.

⭐ Benthall Hall is the home of Edward and Sally Benthall

ℹ **T** 01952 882159
E benthall@nationaltrust.org.uk

🚶 Walks around parkland and woodland

♿ Pᴅ ᴡᴄ .. 📷 Building 🏠 🏛
Grounds 🏛

👪 Pushchairs admitted. Children's quiz/trail

➡ [127:SJ658025] **Bus**: Arriva 9, 39, 99 Telford/ Wellington–Bridgnorth, alight Broseley, 1ml (passing close ⭑ Telford Central).
Station: Telford Central 7½ml. **Road**: 1ml NW of Broseley (B4375), 4ml NE of Much Wenlock, 1ml SW of Ironbridge

P Free parking, 100yds. Only one coach at a time

NT properties nearby
Attingham Park, Dudmaston Estate, Kinver Edge and the Rock Houses, Morville Hall, Moseley Old Hall, Sunnycroft, Wightwick Manor and Gardens

Benthall Hall									
1 Apr–30 Jun	2–5:30	M	**T**	**W**	T	F	S	S	
1 Jul–30 Sep	2–5:30	M	**T**	**W**	T	F	S	**S**	
Open BH Suns and Mons. Gardens open 1:30									

Yew trees in the garden at Benthall Hall, Shropshire

Berrington Hall

nr Leominster, Herefordshire HR6 0DW

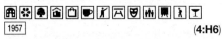

1957   **(4:H6)**

Neo-classical mansion with fine interiors, set in landscape grounds

Beautifully sited above a wide valley with sweeping views to the Brecon Beacons, this elegant Henry Holland house was built in the late 18th century and is set in parkland designed by 'Capability' Brown. The house displays delicate interiors with fine furniture and beautifully decorated ceilings along with a display of costumes from the Charles Wade collection of Snowshill Manor. Experience some of the fascinating servants' quarters and visit the walled garden and its collection of historic local apple trees. The waymarked trails in our parkland include one which takes in a Site of Special Scientific Interest because of its heronry.

What's new in 2009 New visitor route taking in the Servants' staircase and Butler's Bedroom

⭐ Not all the costume collection is displayed, but can be viewed by appointment

ℹ️ **T** 01568 615721
   E berrington@nationaltrust.org.uk

🎭 Daily taster tours of the house 11:30–1. Daily below-stairs tours. Regular garden and park tours during the summer

The drawing room, Berrington Hall, Herefordshire

♥ Including family activities, specialist days, popular events including Second World War and apple weekend

🚶 Park walks open Feb to Dec. Access to parkland restricted 28 Feb–15 June (due to nesting birds)

♿ 🅿️ 🚾 ⠿ 🖥️ 📺 ♿ ♿   Building 🔆 ♿
Grounds 🏞️ ➡️ ♿

🛍️ NT shop. Plant sales

🍴 Licensed tea-room

👪 Family activities. Baby-changing facilities. Front-carrying baby slings and hip-carrying infant seats for loan. Children's play area. Children's guide

🏫 Suitable for school groups. Hands-on activities. Adult study days

🐕 On leads in dog walking area

➡️ [137:SO510637] **Bus**: Lugg Valley 492 Ludlow–Hereford (passing close ➤ Ludlow and Leominster), alight Luston, 2ml. **Station**: Leominster (U) 4ml. **Road**: 3ml N of Leominster, 7ml S of Ludlow on W side of A49

🅿️ Free parking, 30yds. Coaches: entry and exit via Luston/Eye Lane only (the B4361 off the A49). Tight turn into drive. No entry or exit for coaches directly from/to A49. Local area map on request

NT properties nearby
Brockhampton Estate, Croft Castle and Parkland, The Weir

Berrington Hall									
*Below stairs/park walks/garden/shop/tea-room									
1 Feb–8 Mar	11–4	M	T	W	T	F		S	S
9 Mar–19 Jul	11–5	M	T	W		F		S	S
20 Jul–31 Aug	11–5	M	T	W	T	F		S	S
1 Sep–1 Nov	11–5	M	T	W		F		S	S
7 Nov–20 Dec	11–4	M	T	W	T	F		S	S
House									
7 Mar–1 Nov	1–5	M	T	W		F		S	S
House tours									
7 Mar–1 Nov	11–1	M	T	W		F		S	S

Open Good Fri. Parkland: restricted 28 Feb–15 Jun (due to nesting birds). Park Walk: closed 1/2 Aug. House ground floor only open 5/6 Dec. *Below stairs, park walks, garden, shop & tea-room open all week 16–22 Feb, 4–19 Apr, 25–31 May, 24–30 Oct, 11–5. Open 30/31 Jan 10

Tiers of colourful dahlias at Biddulph Grange Garden in Staffordshire

Biddulph Grange Garden

Grange Road, Biddulph, Staffordshire ST8 7SD

 1988 **(4:J2)**

Delightful high Victorian garden – an extraordinary survival from the 19th century

Designed in the mid 19th century by James Bateman to display specimens from his extensive and wide-ranging plant collection, the garden is set out in a series of connected 'compartments'. Visitors are taken on a sensory journey of discovery through tunnels and pathways to individual gardens inspired by countries around the world – from the tranquillity of a Chinese garden or an Egyptian Court to a formal Italian garden.

What's new in 2009 Refurbished woodland terrace area and joint ticket with Little Moreton Hall

⭐ There are many steps throughout the garden, tea-room, WCs and buildings

ℹ️ **T** 01782 517999
E biddulphgrange@nationaltrust.org.uk

🎭 Booked guided tours in groups of 10+, at 10 on Wed, Thur & Fri. A charge will apply (inc. NT members)

Biddulph Grange Garden									
28 Feb–8 Mar	11–3	M	T	W	T	F	**S**	**S**
14 Mar–28 Jun	11–5	M	T	**W**	**T**	**F**	**S**	**S**
1 Jul–31 Aug	11–5	**M**	**T**	**W**	**T**	**F**	**S**	**S**
2 Sep–1 Nov	11–5	M	T	**W**	**T**	**F**	**S**	**S**
7 Nov–20 Dec	11–3	M	T	W	T	F	**S**	**S**

Open BH Mons. Closes dusk if earlier. Tea-room last orders 4:30; winter menu in Nov/Dec

🎭 Lunchtime talks, walks and themed events

♿ 🅿️ 🚾 ⣿ 🖼️ Building 🏞️ Grounds 🏞️

🏪 NT shop. Plant sales

☕ Tea-room. Children's menu. Ice-cream kiosk

👶 Baby-changing facilities. Pushchairs admitted. Children's quiz/trail. Access for pushchairs is difficult

➡️ [118:SJ895591] **Bus**: Bakers 99 from Congleton (passing 🚆 Congleton). **Station**: Congleton 2½ml. **Road**: ½ml N of Biddulph, 3½ml SE of Congleton, 7ml N of Stoke-on-Trent. Access from A527 (Tunstall–Congleton road). Entrance on Grange Road

🅿️ Free parking, 50yds

NT properties nearby
Little Moreton Hall

For further information, visit www.nationaltrust.org.uk

Birmingham Back to Backs

50-54 Inge Street/55-63 Hurst Street,
Birmingham, West Midlands B5 4TE

 2004   **(4:J5)**

Carefully restored, atmospheric 19th-century courtyard of working people's houses

Birmingham's last surviving court of back-to-back housing has now been fully restored by the Birmingham Conservation Trust and the National Trust. Thousands of houses like these were built, literally back to back, around courtyards, for the rapidly increasing population of Britain's expanding industrial towns. The story of the site is told through the experiences of the people who lived and worked here. Visitors move through four different periods, from 1840 to the 1970s. The design of each interior reflects the varied cultures, religions and professions of the families who made their homes here.

What's new in 2009 New interpretation and events promoting the culturally related histories and stories of the Back to Backs (part of the Whose Story? project)

⭐ **Visiting the Back to Backs is by guided tour only**. Advance booking is strongly advised. Booking line open Tuesday–Friday 10–4, Saturday and Sunday 10–12. Bookings by email not accepted

ℹ️ **T** 0121 666 7671 (booking line),
0121 622 2442 (office)
E backtobacks@nationaltrust.org.uk

🚹 Full guided tour

📷 Whose Story? project events throughout the year. Easter and Hallowe'en activities. VE Day celebration week. Christmas celebrations. Family learning activities

♿

Building

📷 Sweet shop (not NT) selling traditional sweets and toffees

🚻 Family learning events

🎭 Suitable for school groups. Live interpretation. Hands-on activities

Courtyard at the Birmingham Back to Backs

➡️ [139:SP071861] **Foot**: in the centre of Birmingham next to the Hippodrome Theatre, within easy walking distance of bus and railway stations. Follow signs for Hippodrome Theatre. **Cycle**: NCN5. **Bus**: from surrounding areas. **Station**: Birmingham New Street ¼ml

🅿️ No parking on site. Nearest parking in Arcadian Centre, Bromsgrove Street

NT properties nearby
Baddesley Clinton, Charlecote Park, Clent Hills, Hanbury Hall, Kinver Edge and the Rock Houses, Moseley Old Hall, Packwood House, Wightwick Manor and Gardens

Birmingham Back to Backs									
3 Feb–23 Dec	10–5	M	T	W	T	F	S	S

Admission by timed ticket and guided tour only, advance booking advised. Open BH Mons but closed on Tues following BH Mons. Please note: during term time property will normally be closed for use by school groups on Tues, Wed and Thur mornings. Last tour times vary due to light levels, please check with the property. **Closed 1–6 Sept**

Charges for National Trust members apply on some special event days

Brockhampton Estate

Greenfields, Bringsty, nr Bromyard,
Herefordshire WR6 5TB

1946   **(4:17)**

Traditionally farmed estate and medieval manor house

At the heart of the Estate lies Lower Brockhampton, a romantic timber-framed manor house dating back to the late 14th century. The house is surrounded by a moat and is entered via a charming timber-framed gatehouse. Brockhampton was bequeathed to the National Trust in 1946 and is made up of 400 hectares (1,000 acres) of farmland and 280 hectares (700 acres) of mixed woodland. The Estate is home to a rich variety of wildlife, including dormice, buzzards and ravens. There are miles of meandering walks through the park and woodland, featuring ancient oaks, beech and fascinating sculptures. There is also an interesting ruined chapel.

What's new in 2009 Extended family room

i **T** 01885 488099 (Infoline), 01885 482077
E brockhampton@nationaltrust.org.uk

Guided tour of orchards, courtyard and chapel at Lower Brockhampton, 11:30–12:30 (dates as house opening)

Easter trails, moat dipping and bug hunts, bat walks, guided walks, re-enactment weekends, Hallowe'en events

Woodland and park walks from estate car park. Accessible all year. Nature walk and Nursery Rhyme Trail accessible only when Lower Brockhampton open

Building Grounds

Local produce and crafts in the Granary Shop at Lower Brockhampton. Plant sales

Old Apple Store tea-room in estate car park. Light lunches and cream teas using local produce. Cakes are baked by farm tenants

Baby-changing facilities. Pushchairs and baby back-carriers admitted. Family room. Children's quiz/trail. Children's activity packs. Easter trails. Moat dipping and bug hunts. Nursery Rhyme Trail, nature trail with bird hide

Brockhampton Estate							
Estate parkland & woodland							
All year	Dawn–dusk	**M**	**T**	**W**	**T**	**F**	**S** **S**
Tea-room							
4 Mar–28 Jun	10–5	M	T	**W**	**T**	**F**	**S** **S**
1 Jul–31 Aug	10–5	**M**	**T**	**W**	**T**	**F**	**S** **S**
2 Sep–1 Nov	10–5	M	T	**W**	**T**	**F**	**S** **S**
7 Nov–20 Dec	10–4	M	T	W	T	F	**S** **S**
2 Jan–31 Jan 10	10–4	M	T	W	T	F	**S** **S**
House							
4 Mar–29 Mar	12–4	M	T	**W**	**T**	**F**	**S** **S**
1 Apr–30 Sep	12–5	M	T	**W**	**T**	**F**	**S** **S**
1 Oct–1 Nov	12–4	M	T	**W**	**T**	**F**	**S** **S**
Guided tour							
As house	11:30–12:30						

Open BH Mons. Good Fri: 12–5. Tea-room closes 4 in Mar, Oct & Nov. Last orders in tea-room 30mins before house closes. Lower Brockhampton grounds open at 11 on open days

Suitable for school groups. Education room/centre. Hands-on activities

In woods and parkland, on leads

[149:SO682546] **Bus**: First/Bromyard Omnibus 420 Worcester–Hereford (passing Worcester Foregate Street and close Hereford). **Road**: 2ml E of Bromyard on Worcester road (A44); house reached by a narrow road through 1½ml of woods & park

P Parking, 50yds & 1½ml

NT properties nearby
Berrington Hall, Croft Castle and Parkland, Croome Park, The Greyfriars, The Weir

Learning about vegetables and sustainability at the Brockhampton Estate, Herefordshire

Show your card and display sticker for free parking

Carding Mill Valley and the Shropshire Hills

Chalet Pavilion, Carding Mill Valley, Church Stretton, Shropshire SY6 6JG

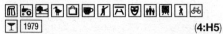

The head of Carding Mill Valley, on the Long Mynd in Shropshire

[Y] [1979]   (4:H5)

Extensive and beautiful area of upland heath

This popular area, with excellent facilities for all, includes part of the Long Mynd, with stunning views across the Shropshire and Cheshire plains and Black Mountains. This is excellent walking country with much to interest the naturalist; the Chalet Pavilion in Carding Mill Valley offers information about the area, as well as a tea-room and shop.

What's new in 2009 Many events of interest to walkers, families and others

★ For further information visit www.shropshirehills.info or www.cardingmillvalley.co.uk

[i] **T** 01694 723068
E cardingmill@nationaltrust.org.uk

🎭 Holiday activities

🚶 Sensible footwear required

[♿] [P] [D] [WC] [♪] [⬆] [⬇] **Building** [♿]
Grounds [♿]

[🛍] NT shop

🍽 Chalet Pavilion Carding Mill Valley. Can be booked for functions. Children's menu

👶 Baby-changing facilities. Pushchairs and baby back-carriers admitted. Children's quiz/trail. Family activity packs. Family room with activities for children in Pavilion

🏫 Suitable for school groups. Education room/centre. Live interpretation. Hands-on activities. Adult study days. Details on www.cardingmillvalley.org.uk

🐕 Must be under control

🚲 On waymarked bridlepaths only

→ [137:SO443945] **Foot:** Jack Mytton Way; Shropshire Way. **Bus:** Minsterley Motors 435 Shrewsbury–Ludlow, alight Church Stretton, ½ml. NT shuttle bus weekends & BHols

(Easter–Oct) connects Carding Mill Valley with ⮽ Church Stretton and other shuttles to Stiperstones, Discovery Centre and Bishop's Castle. **Station:** Church Stretton (U) 1m. **Road:** 15ml S of Shrewsbury, W of Church Stretton Valley and A49; approached from Church Stretton and, on W side, from Ratlinghope or Asterton

[P] Parking, 50yds (pay & display). Open daily all year. Parking £4 (March–Oct), £2.50 (Nov–Feb), 1 hr £2. Minibus £8, coach £10. Top car park closes at 7 (April–Oct), 4:15 (Nov–March). Opens at 9

NT properties nearby
Attingham Park, Berrington Hall, Croft Castle and Parkland, Powis Castle, Wenlock Edge, Wilderhope Manor

Carding Mill Valley and the Shropshire Hills								
Heathland								
All year		M	T	W	T	F	S	S
Tea-room/shop								
1 Feb–15 Feb	11–4	M	T	W	T	F	S	S
16 Feb–29 Mar	11–4	M	T	W	T	F	S	S
30 Mar–1 Nov	11–5	M	T	W	T	F	S	S
2 Nov–24 Nov	11–4	M	T	W	T	F	S	S
28 Nov–31 Jan 10	11–4	M	T	W	T	F	S	S

WC & Information open 9–7 summer; 9–4 winter. Tea-room and shop: closed 17 June and 26 Dec.
Christmas Opening 27 Dec–3 Jan 10

Dogs assisting visitors with disabilities are always welcome

Charlecote Park

Warwick, Warwickshire CV35 9ER

🏠 ♿ ❀ 🍴 🏡 🏛 ☕ 🎿 🎭 🖼 🚶 ☂ 1946 **(4:K7)**

Superb Tudor house and landscape deer park

The Tudor home of the Lucy family for more than 700 years, the mellow stonework and ornate chimneys of Charlecote sum up the very essence of Tudor England. There are strong associations with both Queen Elizabeth I and Shakespeare, who knew the house well – he is alleged to have been caught poaching the estate deer. The rich, early Victorian interior contains some important objects from Beckford's Fonthill Abbey. Landscaped by 'Capability' Brown, the balustraded formal garden opens on to a fine deer park on the River Avon.

What's new in 2009 Whose Story? project, using special events and interpretation to encourage visitors to get involved and experience the hidden history of Charlecote Park. Local walks. Extended opening of park and garden. New children's guide

ℹ **T** 01789 470277
  E charlecotepark@nationaltrust.org.uk

The chimneypiece in the Drawing Room at Charlecote Park, Warwickshire

Charlecote Park			M	T	W	T	F	S	S
Park/gardens/outbuildings*									
1 Feb–1 Nov	10:30–6		**M**	**T**	**W**	**T**	**F**	**S**	**S**
2 Nov–31 Jan 10	10:30–4		**M**	**T**	W	**T**	**F**	**S**	**S**
Restaurant/shop									
1 Feb–22 Feb	11–4		M	T	W	T	F	**S**	**S**
28 Feb–1 Nov	10:30–5		**M**	**T**	W	T	**F**	**S**	**S**
7 Nov–20 Dec	11–4		M	T	W	T	F	**S**	**S**
Conservation tours									
28 Feb–1 Nov	11–12		**M**	**T**	W	T	**F**	**S**	**S**
House									
28 Feb–1 Nov	12–5		**M**	**T**	W	T	**F**	**S**	**S**
7 Nov–20 Dec	12–4		M	T	W	T	F	**S**	**S**

Park, garden & outbuildings: close 4 in Feb. Shop closes 5:30 28 Feb–1 Nov. Restaurant/shop: open all week 14–22 Feb, 8–16 Apr, 25–31 May, 22 July–3 Sept, 26 Oct–1 Nov. *Park/gardens: some restricted access on Weds/Thurs. Closed 24/25 Dec. Parts of house only open in Nov/Dec

🎿 House conservation tours 28 Feb–1 Nov, 11–12 on house open days

🎭 Full programme of events throughout year

🚶 Park walks

♿ 🅿 🚻 ♿ 🚽 ⚫⚫ 📷 🎞 💻 🔨 🔊 🔡
Building ♿♿♿ **Grounds** ♿ ➡

🏠 Shop located in house beyond Victorian Kitchen (opposite stable block)

☕ The Orangery (licensed). Hot meals 12–2:30. Children's menu

🚼 Baby-changing facilities. Hip-carrying infant seats for loan. Children's quiz/trail

🖼 Suitable for school groups. Education room/centre. Live interpretation

➡ [151:SP263564] **Bus**: Stagecoach in Warwickshire 18/A 🚉 Leamington Spa–Stratford-upon-Avon. **Station**: Stratford-upon-Avon, 5½ml; Warwick 6ml; Leamington Spa 8ml. **Road**: 1ml W of Wellesbourne, 5ml E of Stratford-upon-Avon, 6ml S of Warwick on N side of B4086

🅿 Free parking, 300yds

NT properties nearby
Baddesley Clinton, Coughton Court, Hidcote Manor Garden, Packwood House, Upton House and Gardens

Coughton Court

nr Alcester, Warwickshire B49 5JA

🍽 ⊤ 1946 (4:K6)

Imposing Tudor house set in beautiful gardens with a fascinating collection of Catholic treasures

One of England's finest Tudor houses, Coughton Court has been the home of the Throckmorton family for 600 years. The house has fine collections of furniture, porcelain and family portraits, and fascinating connections with the Gunpowder Plot. The family has created and developed the award-winning gardens. Highlights include the walled garden with its spectacular displays of roses, hot and cool herbaceous borders, the bog garden and walks beside the river and lake. There are two churches, the 19th-century Catholic church and the pre-Reformation parish church of St Peter's.

What's new in 2009 Gunpowder Plot children's trail. Top Ten Highlights trail for adults. Special events programme celebrating 600 years of the Throckmorton family at Coughton Court

⭐ The Throckmorton family manages the gardens and plant sales. A charge applies for entrance to the walled garden (inc. NT members). Admission to house by timed ticket at weekends and on busy days. Property closed 13 June & 11 July

ℹ️ **T** 01789 762435 (Infoline), 01789 400777
E coughtoncourt@nationaltrust.org.uk

Coughton Court		M	T	W	T	F	S	S
House								
21 Mar–29 Mar	11–5	M	T	W	T	F	**S**	**S**
1 Apr–28 Jun	11–5	M	T	**W**	**T**	F	**S**	**S**
1 Jul–31 Aug	11–5	M	**T**	**W**	**T**	F	**S**	**S**
2 Sep–30 Sep	11–5	M	T	**W**	**T**	F	**S**	**S**
1 Oct–1 Nov	11–5	M	T	W	**T**	**F**	**S**	**S**
Garden/shop/restaurant								
As house	11–5:30							
Walled garden*								
As house	11:30–4:45							

Open BH Mons. **Closed Good Fri & Tues following a BH & 13 June & 11 July.** Admission by timed ticket at weekends and busy days. ***Walled garden closed Thurs/Fri in Oct/Nov**

The imposing façade of Coughton Court, Warwickshire

🏃 Free introductory talks

🎭 Full programme of events and activities, including children's crafts, open-air theatre, lectures and Christmas events

🏃 Riverside walk and bluebell wood in season

♿ 🅿️ 🚹 ♿ 👓 🔊 💻 🪑 🗺️
Building 🔊🔊♿ Grounds ♿➡️

🛍️ NT shop selling wide range of gifts and local produce. Second-hand bookshop. Plants, cultivated by the family's gardeners, for sale in the Throckmorton family's plant centre

🍽 Licensed restaurant. Hot meals 12–12:30, homebaked cakes, cold snacks and light refreshments available. No hot food on Tuesdays

👨‍👩‍👧 Baby-changing and feeding facilities. Front-carrying baby slings and hip-carrying infant seats for loan. Children's play area. Adults' and children's house trails

🏫 Suitable for school groups. Tudor connections, priest holes and interesting links with the Gunpowder Plot

➡️ [150:SP080604] **Cycle**: NCN5, ½ml.
Bus: First 247 Redditch–Evesham (passing ▇ Redditch and close ▇ Evesham), Stagecoach in Warwickshire 26 Redditch–Stratford-upon-Avon (passing close ▇ Stratford-upon-Avon). **Station**: Redditch 6ml. **Road**: 2ml N of Alcester on A435

🅿️ Free parking, 150yds

NT properties nearby
Baddesley Clinton, Birmingham Back to Backs, Charlecote Park, Hanbury Hall, Hidcote Manor Garden, Kinwarton Dovecote, Packwood House, Upton House and Gardens

For public transport details, see page 377

Croft Castle and Parkland

Yarpole, nr Leominster, Herefordshire HR6 9PW

[icons] [icons]

🏃 ⊤ 1957 (4:H6)

Castellated manor house set in stunning countryside with panoramic views

Croft Castle is a late 17th-century house with fine Georgian interiors and a family connection dating back more than 1,000 years. There are restored walled gardens, stunning views over the Welsh Marches and miles of marked walks. It is renowned for its fine parkland, which contains more than 300 veteran trees – including a magnificent avenue of Spanish chestnuts. A walk through the woodlands reveals the Iron Age hill fort at Croft Ambrey, which commands views over fourteen of the old counties.

What's new in 2009 Agents of Decay tour in house. Children's play area and new family trail

⭐ In high winds parts of the property may be closed

ℹ️ **T** 01568 780141 (Infoline), 01568 780246
E croftcastle@nationaltrust.org.uk

🎭 Taster tours on open days, March–Dec

🎭 Country fairs, open-air theatre, spooky Hallowe'en, family nature days, guided walks

🚶 Guided walks programme to discover wildlife, fungi, gardens and archaeology

Just one of the fine interiors at Croft Castle

♿ [icons]
Building [icons] **Grounds** [icons]

🛍 Shop. Plant sales. Second-hand bookshop

🍵 Carpenter's Shop tea-room serving local home-made food. Open weekends during winter. Children's menu

👪 Hip-carrying infant seats for loan. Children's quiz/trail. Family activity packs. All-terrain pushchairs on loan. Children's play area. Dressing-up clothes

🏫 Suitable for school groups

🐕 On leads and only in parkland

➡️ [137:SO455655] **Bus:** Lugg Valley 492 Ludlow–Hereford (passing close ≋ Ludlow and Leominster), alight Gorbett Bank, 2¼ml. **Station:** Leominster (U) 7ml. **Road:** 5ml NW of Leominster, 9ml SW of Ludlow; approach from B4362, turning N at Cock Gate between Bircher and Mortimer's Cross; signposted from Ludlow–Leominster road (A49) and from A4110 at Mortimer's Cross

🅿️ Parking, 100yds

NT properties nearby
Berrington Hall, Brockhampton Estate, The Weir

Croft Castle and Parkland		M	T	W	T	F	S	S
Parkland								
All year	8–9	**M**	**T**	**W**	**T**	**F**	**S**	**S**
Tea-room/picnic area/play area								
1 Feb–1 Mar	11–3:30	M	T	W	T	F	**S**	**S**
7 Mar–31 Jul	11–5	M	T	**W**	**T**	**F**	**S**	**S**
1 Aug–31 Aug	11–5	**M**	**T**	**W**	**T**	**F**	**S**	**S**
2 Sep–1 Nov	11–5	M	T	**W**	**T**	**F**	**S**	**S**
7 Nov–31 Jan 10	11–4	M	T	W	T	F	**S**	**S**
Castle								
7 Mar–31 Jul	1–5	M	T	**W**	**T**	**F**	**S**	**S**
1 Aug–31 Aug	1–5	**M**	**T**	**W**	**T**	**F**	**S**	**S**
2 Sep–1 Nov	1–5	M	T	**W**	**T**	**F**	**S**	**S**
7 Nov–20 Dec	1–4	M	T	W	T	F	**S**	**S**
Castle tours								
As castle	11–1							
Garden/shop								
As castle	11–5							

Open BH Mons. **Tea-room, garden & play area: open all week 23–31 May & 24 Oct–1 Nov.** Tea-room: closes 4 in Nov/Dec & closed 26/27 Dec. Park closes dusk if earlier

Please remember – your membership card is *always* needed for free admission

Croome Park

Croome D'Abitot, Worcestershire WR8 9DW

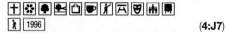

[x] [1996]   **(4:J7)**

Magnificent landscape park restored to its former glory

Croome was 'Capability' Brown's first complete landscape, making his reputation and establishing a new style of garden design which became universally adopted over the next 50 years. The elegant park buildings and other structures are mostly by Robert Adam and James Wyatt. Enjoy walks in the garden or wider estate, join in one of our many events, or simply relax with a cup of tea in our 1940s-style canteen.

What's new in 2009 A nature conservation corridor, with 'batcam' in our newly restored Second World War building. Recently restored ice-house and ongoing restoration planting

⭐ Postal address: NT Estate Office, The Builders' Yard, High Green, Severn Stoke, Worcestershire WR8 9JS. The Trust acquired 270ha (670 acres) of the park in 1996 with substantial grant aid from the Heritage Lottery Fund and a generous donation from Royal & SunAlliance. For information about the opening of Croome Court please tel. the property

[i] **T** 01905 371006
   E croomepark@nationaltrust.org.uk

🛡 Contact property for details

🚶 Walks booklet available. £1 from reception

♿ ▣▣▣ ▣▣▣▣▣▣ **Grounds** ▣▣▣▣

📷 NT shop. Plant sales

🍴 1940s-style canteen in restored wartime buildings. Open to general public (not restricted to visitors to Croome Park)

👶 Baby-changing facilities. Pushchairs admitted. Family trail

🖐 Hands-on activities

🐕 On leads in garden. Close control in park

→ [150:SO878448] **Bus**: Aston's 382 Worcester–Pershore, alight Ladywood Rd/Rebecca Rd crossroads, 2ml. **Station**: Pershore 7ml. **Road**: 9ml S of Worcester and E of M5. Signposted from A38 and B4084

[P] Free parking, 200yds

NT properties nearby
Brockhampton Estate, The Fleece Inn, The Greyfriars, Hanbury Hall, Middle Littleton Tithe Barn, Snowshill Manor and Garden

Croome Park			M	T	W	T	F	S	S
1 Feb–1 Mar	10–4		M	T	W	T	F	**S**	**S**
4 Mar–29 Mar	10–5:30		M	T	**W**	**T**	F	**S**	**S**
30 Mar–31 Aug	10–5:30		**M**	**T**	**W**	**T**	F	**S**	**S**
2 Sep–1 Nov	10–5:30		M	T	**W**	**T**	F	**S**	**S**
7 Nov–20 Dec	10–4		M	T	W	T	F	**S**	**S**
26 Dec–3 Jan 10	10–4		**M**	**T**	**W**	**T**	**F**	**S**	**S**
9 Jan–31 Jan 10	10–4		M	T	W	T	F	**S**	**S**
Tea-room/shop									
As park									

Open BH Mons. Open all week local school Feb half-term hols. Croome church open in association with The Churches Conservation Trust (which owns it). Last admission 45mins before closing

Cwmmau Farmhouse

Brilley, Whitney-on-Wye, Herefordshire HR3 6JP

🏠🏚📷🚶🖼🖐 [1965]   **(4:G7)**

Superb early 17th-century 'black and white' farmhouse with stone-tiled roof and vernacular buildings

⭐ Open eight afternoons a year. At other times the farmhouse is available as holiday accommodation (tel: 0844 800 2070 for NT Holiday Cottages information)

[i] **T** 01981 590509
   E cwmmaufarmhouse@nationaltrust.org.uk

→ 4ml SW of Kington between A4111 and A438. From Kington take Brilley road at junction opposite church, 4ml. Turn left at NT signpost. From A438 between Rhydspence and Whitney on Wye take Brilley road at junction, 2ml. Turn right at NT signpost. Farmhouse is approx. 1ml down a 'no through road'

Cwmmau Farmhouse			M	T	W	T	F	S	S
16 May–17 May	2–5		M	T	W	T	F	**S**	**S**
13 Jun–14 Jun	2–5		M	T	W	T	F	**S**	**S**
26 Sep–27 Sep	2–5		M	T	W	T	F	**S**	**S**
19 Dec–20 Dec	1–4		M	T	W	T	F	**S**	**S**

Dudmaston Estate

Quatt, nr Bridgnorth, Shropshire WV15 6QN

| 🏠 | 1978 | (4:l5) |

Late 17th-century mansion with art collection, lakeside garden, dingle, woodland, lakes, River Severn and estate

The house, with its intimate family rooms, contains fine furniture and Dutch flower paintings, as well as one of Britain's most important public collections of modern art in a classic country-house setting. The lakeside gardens are a mass of colour in spring and visitors can enjoy walks in the dingle, a wooded valley, or the popular 'Big Pool' walk. There are also estate walks to and from Hampton Loade. Dudmaston is the home of Colonel and Mrs Hamilton-Russell.

What's new in 2009 New shop and interpretation room

ℹ️ **T** 01746 780866
E dudmaston@nationaltrust.org.uk

🗝️ Guided tours of the house, garden and wider estate available throughout the season. See the board at the property for details

🎭 Wide range of events, inc. snowdrop walks (7, 8, 14 & 15 Feb), Christmas and children's activities. Please send sae for full programme

🚶 Walks leaflet available. Please send sae and £1

♿ 🅿️ 🚻 ⋯ 🎨 🚗 📷 🚽 🔔 🔊

Building 👣👣👣 Grounds 👣➡️🎨

📦 NT shop. Plant sales

🍽️ Tea-room in Orchard car park. Light lunches. Children's menu. Ice-cream kiosk

👶 Baby-changing facilities. Baby food heating facilities. Front-carrying baby slings, hip-carrying infant seats and small buggy for loan. Children's quiz/trails. Family activity room in house

🏫 Suitable for school groups. Hands-on activities. Adult study days. Conference facilities

🐕 On leads only and keep to footpaths. Not in gardens immediately surrounding house

➡️ [138:SO746887] **Foot**: NT walks from Hampton Loade car park to the property. **Ferry**: from Severn Valley Railway via river ferry and walk from Hampton Loade. **Bus**: Arriva Midlands 297

Bridgnorth–Kidderminster (passing close ⊠ Kidderminster). **Station**: Hampton Loade (Severn Valley Rly) 1½ml; Kidderminster 10ml. **Road**: 4ml SE of Bridgnorth on A442

🅿️ Free parking (100yds) in Orchard car park and parkland. Also parking at Hampton Loade and The Holt, both pay & display

NT properties nearby
Attingham Park, Benthall Hall, Berrington Hall, Kinver Edge and the Rock Houses, Sunnycroft, Wightwick Manor and Gardens

Dudmaston Estate								
House								
1 Apr–30 Sep	2–5:30	M	**T**	**W**	T	F	S	**S**
Garden								
1 Apr–30 Sep	12–6	**M**	**T**	**W**	T	F	S	**S**
Shop								
1 Apr–30 Sep	12–5:30	**M**	**T**	**W**	T	F	S	
Tea-room								
1 Apr–30 Sep	11:30–5:30	**M**	**T**	**W**	T	F	S	

Open BH Mons. St Andrew's Church, Quatt, open as house. Snowdrop walks 7, 8, 14 & 15 Feb

Dudmaston, near Bridgnorth

Farnborough Hall

Farnborough, nr Banbury, Oxfordshire OX17 1DU

🏠 ⋯ 🎨 🚻 🚶 | 1960 | (4:L7)

Honey-coloured stone house with exquisite plasterwork and fine landscaped garden

⭐ Farnborough Hall is occupied and administered by the Holbech family

ℹ️ **T** 01295 690002 (Infoline)
E farnboroughhall@nationaltrust.org.uk

➡️ 6ml N of Banbury, ½ml W of A423

Farnborough Hall								
1 Apr–30 Sep	2–5:30	M	T	**W**	T	F	**S**	S
3 May–4 May	2–5:30	**M**	T	W	T	F	**S**	S
Terrace walk open as house								

Unless indicated, last admission is always 30mins before closing time

The Fleece Inn

Bretforton, nr Evesham,
Worcestershire WR11 7JE

 1978   **(4:K7)**

A traditional English pub

The Fleece Inn is a half-timbered medieval farmhouse which originally sheltered a farmer and his stock. The Inn first became a licensed house in 1848. Fully restored to its former glory, with the witch circles and precious pewter collection, it has developed a reputation for traditional folk music and morris dancing. The Fleece provides top-quality cask ales, ciders, wines and a mouth-watering menu using local produce.

What's new in 2009 Thatched Barn is available for hire for functions, and has a civil-ceremony wedding licence. Hosts the Vale of Evesham Asparagus Festival

⭐ For further information visit www.thefleeceinn.co.uk

ℹ️ **T** 01386 831173
   E fleeceinn@nationaltrust.org.uk

🖐 Vale of Evesham Asparagus Festival, May BHol. Music and morris dancing throughout the year. Vintage and classic car events during the summer

♿ 🚻 🔍 **Building** 🚶 ♿

🍽 Top quality cask ales, ciders, wines and home-cooked food using local produce. Special asparagus menu in May/June

➡️ [150:SP093437] At the village square in the heart of Bretforton. **Bus**: Henshaws 554 from Evesham–Chipping Campden. **Station**: Evesham 2½ml. **Road**: 4ml E of Evesham, on B4035

🅿️ Parking (not NT) in village square only

NT properties nearby
Croome Park, Dover's Hill, Hidcote Manor Garden, Middle Littleton Tithe Barn, Snowshill Manor and Garden

The Fleece Inn									
All year	11–11	**M**	**T**	**W**	**T**	**F**	**S**	S
All year	12–10:30	M	T	W	T	F	S	**S**
Closed Mon–Thurs, 3–6, 1 Feb-May & Sept-Jan 10									

The Greyfriars

Friar Street, Worcester, Worcestershire WR1 2LZ

🏠 ❄ 🏠 🍽 🧑 🖐 👪 🏛 🔔 1966   **(4:J7)**

15th-century merchant's house in Worcester city centre

Built in 1480, with early 17th- and 18th-century additions, this fine timber-framed house was rescued from demolition after the Second World War and has been carefully restored and refurbished. An archway leads through to a delightful walled garden.

What's new in 2009 Conservation tours in February

⭐ No WC, nearest at Corn Market 200yds

ℹ️ **T** 01905 23571
   E greyfriars@nationaltrust.org.uk

🧑 Guided tours by appointment

🖐 Send sae for details

♿ 🔍 🏛 **Building** 🚶 **Grounds** ♿

🏠 Plants grown at nearby Hanbury Hall

🍽 Tea-shop only open weekends in fine weather

👪 Children's guide

🏛 Suitable for school groups. Hands-on activities

➡️ [150:SO852546] In centre of Worcester on Friar Street. **Bus**: from surrounding areas. **Station**: Worcester Foregate Street ½ml

🅿️ No parking on site. Pay & display car parks at Corn Market and St Martin's Gate

NT properties nearby
Brockhampton Estate, Croome Park, Hanbury Hall

The Greyfriars			M	T	W	T	F	S	S
4 Mar–27 Jun	1–5		M	T	**W**	**T**	**F**	**S**	S
1 Jul–30 Aug	1–5		M	T	**W**	**T**	**F**	**S**	**S**
2 Sep–12 Dec	1–5		M	T	**W**	**T**	**F**	**S**	S
Admission by timed ticket on Sats & BHols. Open BH Mons. Garden: opens 12, July/Aug. Closes dusk if earlier									

After enjoying a meal at The Fleece Inn, why not take a walk at nearby Croome Park?

Hanbury Hall

School Road, Hanbury, Droitwich Spa, Worcestershire WR9 7EA

[T] [1953] (4:J6)

Early 18th-century country house, garden and park

Completed in 1701, this homely William and Mary-style house is famed for its fine painted ceilings and staircase by Sir James Thornhill. The stunning eight-hectare (20-acre) garden, recreated in keeping with the period of the house, is surrounded by 160 hectares (395 acres) of park, with beautiful views over the surrounding countryside. Fascinating features within the garden include an orangery, ice house, 18th-century bowling green and working mushroom house.

What's new in 2009 Newly redecorated parlour. New walks booklet. Restoration of George London's early 18th-century park features

⭐ Garden, park, café, shop and children's play area open every day during school holidays. Please note house is closed on Thursdays and Fridays during local school holidays

[i] **T** 01527 821214
E hanburyhall@nationaltrust.org.uk

🛈 Guided tours 11–1, Sat–Wed when house open

🛈 Send sae for details

🛈 Walks booklet available, inc. information on park features

Building 🛈 🛈 🛈 **Grounds** 🛈 🛈 🛈 🛈

🛈 NT shop. Plant sales

🛈 Licensed tea-room in the Hall, serving light lunches and refreshments. Group bookings by arrangement. Children's menu. Stables Café serving drinks and snacks

🛈 Baby-changing facilities. Hip-carrying infant seats for loan. Children's play area. Children's quiz/trail

🛈 Suitable for school groups. Live interpretation. Hands-on activities

🛈 On leads in park on footpaths, not in garden. Dog-friendly circular walk

The front of Hanbury Hall, Worcestershire

→ [150:SO943637] **Foot**: a number of public footpaths cross the park. **Bus**: First 144 Worcester–Birmingham (passing close ≊ Droitwich Spa), alight Wychbold, 2½ml. **Station**: Droitwich Spa 4ml. **Road**: from M5 exit 5 follow A38 to Droitwich. From Droitwich 4½ml along B4090

[P] Free parking, 150yds

NT properties nearby

Clent Hills, Coughton Court, Croome Park, The Greyfriars, Rosedene

Hanbury Hall									
Garden/park/shop/Stables Café*		M	T	W	T	F	S	S
1 Feb–15 Mar	11–5	M	T	W	T	F	**S**	**S**
16 Mar–1 Jul	11–5	**M**	**T**	**W**	T	F	**S**	**S**
2 Jul–30 Aug	11–5	**M**	**T**	**W**	**T**	**F**	**S**	**S**
31 Aug–1 Nov	11–5	**M**	**T**	**W**	T	F	**S**	**S**
7 Nov–20 Dec	11–4	M	T	W	T	F	**S**	**S**
27 Dec–3 Jan 10	11–4	**M**	**T**	**W**	**T**	**F**	**S**	**S**
9 Jan–31 Jan 10	11–4	M	T	W	T	F	**S**	**S**
Tea-room								
28 Feb–15 Mar	11–5	M	T	W	T	F	**S**	**S**
16 Mar–1 Nov	11–5	**M**	**T**	W	T	F	**S**	**S**
House								
28 Feb–15 Mar	1–5	M	T	W	T	F	**S**	**S**
16 Mar–1 Nov	1–5	**M**	**T**	W	T	F	**S**	**S**
7 Nov–20 Dec	12–4	M	T	W	T	F	**S**	**S**
House tours								
28 Feb–15 Mar	11–1	M	T	W	T	F	**S**	**S**
16 Mar–1 Nov	11–1	**M**	**T**	W	T	F	**S**	**S**

Admission by timed ticket on very busy days. Open Good Fri. Closes dusk if earlier. **Garden, park, shop & Stables Café open seven days a week during local school holidays 14–22 Feb, 6–19 Apr, 25–31 May, 26–31 Oct. Please note house closed on Thu & Fri during local school hols**. Ground floor of house only in Nov & Dec. *Shop and Stables Café close 5 Feb–Nov. Garden and park close 5:30 Feb–Nov

Hawford Dovecote

Hawford, Worcestershire WR3 7SG

[符] | 1973 | (4:J6)

16th-century half-timbered dovecote

The recently restored half-timbered dovecote is
what remains of a former monastic grange.

[★] No WC

[i] **T** 01527 821214
   E hawforddovecote@nationaltrust.org.uk

[♿] Building [♿]

[→] [150:SO846607] **Bus**: First 303 Worcester–
   Kidderminster (passing [≋] Worcester Foregate
   Street & Kidderminster), alight Hawford Lodge,
   ¼ml. **Station**: Worcester Foregate Street 3ml;
   Worcester Shrub Hill 3½ml. **Road**: 3ml N of
   Worcester, ½ml E of A449

[P] Parking, 50yds. Access is on foot via the
   drive of the adjoining house

NT properties nearby
The Greyfriars, Hanbury Hall, Wichenford Dovecote

Hawford Dovecote									
28 Feb–1 Nov	9–6	M	T	W	T	F	S	S
Closes dusk if earlier. Other times by appointment									

The Holy Austin Rock Houses at Kinver Edge looking south,
showing the regular dwellings adjacent to the caves

Kinver Edge and the Rock Houses

The Warden's Lodge, Comber Road, Kinver, nr
Stourbridge, Staffordshire DY7 6HU

[符][⊥⊤][⚲][↟][♿][♿♿][▦][↟] | 1917 | (4:I5)

**High sandstone ridge and hill fort overlooking
dramatic red sandstone rock houses**

Kinver's woodland sandstone ridge offers
dramatic views across surrounding counties and
miles of heathland walking country. The famous
Holy Austin Rock Houses, which were inhabited
until the 1950s, have now been restored and are
open to visitors at selected times.

[★] Postal address: Holy Austin Rock Houses,
   Compton Road, Kinver, Staffordshire DY7 6DL.
   No WC

[i] **T** 01384 872553
   E kinveredge@nationaltrust.org.uk

[↟] Lower rock houses: out-of-hours tours by
   arrangement

[♥] Easter Egg trail on Easter Monday

[↟] Walks leaflet for sale at lower rock houses

[♿] [P.][D.][∴][◉][♿][↗] Building [♿] Grounds [♿]

[♿♿] Easter Egg trail on Easter Monday

[▦] Suitable for school groups

[🐾] On leads within grounds of rock houses

[→] [138:SO836836] **Bus**: Hansons 228 [≋]
   Stourbridge–Kinver. **Station**: Stourbridge
   Town 5ml. **Road**: 4ml W of Stourbridge, 4ml
   N of Kidderminster. 1½ml W of A449

[P] Free parking at Warden's lodge and on
   Compton Road for rock houses

NT properties nearby
Clent Hills, Dudmaston Estate

Kinver Edge and the Rock Houses									
Kinver Edge									
All year		M	T	W	T	F	S	S
House grounds									
1 Feb–31 Jan 10	10–4	M	T	W	T	F	S	S
Lower rock houses, upper terrace									
28 Feb–29 Nov	2–4	M	T	W	T	F	S	S
Open BH Mons. Rock houses will be closed on Kinver Fête day (date in May to be confirmed). Lower rock houses open for guided tours at other times (Mar–Nov), by arrangement									

Charges for National Trust members apply on some special event days

Kinwarton Dovecote

Kinwarton, nr Alcester, Warwickshire B49 6HB

🏠 🎫 1958   **(4:K7)**

Circular 14th-century dovecote

The building is a fine example of a 14th-century circular stone dovecote – one of the few in this country. It is the only relic of a moated grange belonging to the Abbey of Evesham, situated to the north-west of the dovecote. The walls are more than a metre thick and inside are hundreds of nesting holes, which would have been reached by the potence (ladder) rotating around a central pivot.

⭐ Farm stock may be grazing in field. No WC

ℹ️ **T** 01789 400777
   E kinwartondovecote@nationaltrust.org.uk

♿ Building 🔷

➡️ [150:SP106585] **Cycle**: NCN5. **Bus**: Stagecoach in Warwickshire 25/6 from Stratford-upon-Avon; otherwise as for Coughton Court, but alight Alcester, 1½ml. **Station**: Wilmcote (U), 5ml; Wootton Wawen (U), not Sun, 5ml. **Road**: 1½ml NE of Alcester, just S of B4089

🅿️ Limited parking (not NT)

NT properties nearby
Charlecote Park, Coughton Court, Hanbury Hall

Kinwarton Dovecote									
1 Mar–31 Oct	9–6	**M**	**T**	**W**	**T**	**F**	**S**	**S**	
Closes dusk if earlier. Other times by appointment									

Letocetum Roman Baths and Museum

Watling Street, Wall, nr Lichfield, Staffordshire WS14 0AW

🏠 🏛️ 👪 🏫 1934   **(4:K5)**

Excavated Roman bathhouse, other remains and museum

Letocetum was an important staging post on the Roman military road to North Wales. Foundations of a *mansio* (Roman inn) and bathhouse can be seen.

What's new in 2009 Volunteer guides on duty as detailed under the opening arrangements

⭐ Letocetum is in the guardianship of English Heritage. No WC

ℹ️ **T** 0121 625 6820
   E letocetum@nationaltrust.org.uk

♿ Building 🔷 Grounds 🔷

👪 Pushchairs and baby back-carriers admitted

🏫 Suitable for school groups

🐕 On leads only

➡️ [139:SK099067] **Cycle**: NCN5, 2¼ml.
Station: Shenstone 1¼ml. **Road**: on N side of A5 at Wall, near Lichfield

🅿️ Free parking (not NT), 50yds. Limited spaces

NT properties nearby
Moseley Old Hall, Shugborough Estate

Letocetum Roman Baths and Museum
Manned by volunteers on the last Sat/Sun of the month & BH Mons & Suns March–Oct

Middle Littleton Tithe Barn

Middle Littleton, Evesham, Worcestershire WR11 5LN

🏠 🏛️ 👪 1975   **(4:K7)**

13th-century tithe barn, one of the largest and finest in the country

⭐ No WC

ℹ️ **T** 01905 371006
   E middlelittleton@nationaltrust.org.uk

♿ Building 🔷

👪 Pushchairs and baby back-carriers admitted

🐕 On leads only

➡️ [150:SP080471] **Bus**: First 247 Evesham–Redditch (passing close ≋ Evesham), alight Middle Littleton School Lane, ½ml.
Station: Honeybourne (U) 3½ml; Evesham 4½ml.
Road: 3ml NE of Evesham, E of B4085

🅿️ Parking

NT properties nearby
Charlecote Park, Croome Park, The Fleece Inn, Hidcote Manor Garden, Snowshill Manor and Garden

Middle Littleton Tithe Barn									
1 Apr–2 Nov	2–5	**M**	**T**	**W**	**T**	**F**	**S**	**S**	
Directions for access on barn door									

Show your card and display sticker for free parking

Morville Hall

nr Bridgnorth, Shropshire WV16 5NB

🏠 ✳️ ♿ 🎭 [1965]   (4:I5)

Stone-built house of Elizabethan origin

⭐ All visits by guided tour. No WC

ℹ️ **T** 01746 780838
   E morvillehall@nationaltrust.org.uk

Morville Hall
Admission by guided tour. By written appointment only with the tenants, Dr & Mrs C. Douglas

Moseley Old Hall

Moseley Old Hall Lane, Fordhouses,
Wolverhampton, Staffordshire WV10 7HY

🏠 🏠 ➕ ✳️ 📷 🎭 🎭 🏠 🎭 🎭 🎭
🔔 [1962]   (4:J5)

Elizabethan house, famous for its association with Charles II

The richly panelled walls of Moseley Old Hall conceal ingenious secret hiding places designed for Catholic priests. One of these cramped priest holes saved Charles II when he hid here after the Battle of Worcester in 1651, and the bed where he slept is on view. An exhibition in the barn tells the story of the King's dramatic escape from Cromwell's troops. The house underwent various alterations in the 19th century. The garden has a good variety of herbs and plants and was recreated in 17th-century style with a formal knot garden, arbour and nut walk.

ℹ️ **T** 01902 782808
   E moseleyoldhall@nationaltrust.org.uk

🎭 Entry 12–1, by guided tour only. Free-flow through house from 1 (optional tours available). Last guided tour 3:30. Out-of-hours tours

📧 Send sae for details

♿ 🅿️ 📷 ♿ ⋮⋮ 📷 🖥️ 🎭 🎭 🎭
Building 🔤 🔤 🔤 **Grounds** 🔤

🛍️ NT shop. Plant sales

☕ Tea-room on first floor of 18th-century coach house. Two tables at ground floor level. Children's menu

The intricate 17th-century style knot garden at Moseley Old Hall, Staffordshire

👶 Baby-changing facilities. Baby back-carriers admitted. Front-carrying baby slings and hip-carrying infant seats for loan. Children's quiz/trail

🖥️ Suitable for school groups. Live interpretation. Hands-on activities

🐕 On leads only in grounds

➡️ [127:SJ932044] **Bus**: Travel West Midlands 503 from Wolverhampton, Arriva Midlands 7 from Cannock, both ½ml.
Station: Wolverhampton 4ml. **Road**: 4ml N of Wolverhampton; S of M54 between A449 and A460; traffic from N on M6 leave at exit 11, then A460; traffic from S on M6 & M54 take exit 1; coaches must approach via A460 to avoid low bridge

🅿️ Free parking, 50yds. Dropping-off place for coaches, but no on-site parking. Narrow lanes and tight corners

NT properties nearby
Attingham Park, Benthall Hall, Letocetum Roman Baths and Museum, Shugborough Estate, Sunnycroft, Wightwick Manor and Gardens

Moseley Old Hall									
1 Mar–1 Nov	12–5	M	T	**W**	T	F	**S**	**S**	
21 Jul–9 Sep	12–5	M	**T**	**W**	T	F	**S**	**S**	
8 Nov–20 Dec	12–4	M	T	W	T	F	S	**S**	

Open BH Mons (11–5) and following Tues (except 5 May). Entry, 12–1, by guided tour only (free-flow or conducted tours from 1). 8 Nov–20 Dec: guided tour only. Christmas events 29 Nov, 6/13 Dec

Dogs assisting visitors with disabilities are always welcome

Packwood House

Packwood Lane, Lapworth, Warwickshire B94 6AT

🏠 ❄ ♠ 🗇 🎇 🎋 🐚 🎎 🎏 🔥 [1941] (4:K6)

Much-restored Tudor house, park and garden with notable topiary

The house is originally 16th-century, yet its interiors were extensively restored between the World Wars by Graham Baron Ash to create a fascinating 20th-century evocation of domestic Tudor architecture. Packwood contains a fine collection of 16th-century textiles and furniture and the gardens have renowned herbaceous borders and a famous collection of yews.

⭐ Property postal address: Lapworth, Solihull, West Midlands B94 6AT

ℹ **T** 01564 783294
   E packwood@nationaltrust.org.uk

🎇 Out-of-hours tours by written arrangement

🐚 Easter trail for families. Meet the gardener. Open-air theatre

🚶 Lakeside walk

♿ 🅿 🅳 ♿ ‥ 🖵 Building 🦽 🦽
Grounds 🦽 🦽 🦽

🗇 NT shop. Plant sales

🍹 Cold drinks and ice-cream sold in the shop. Vending machine for hot drinks and soup

👪 Baby-changing facilities. Front-carrying baby slings and hip-carrying infant seats for loan. Children's guide. Children's quiz/trail. Family Easter trail

🎏 Suitable for school groups. Live interpretation

➡ [139:SP174723] **Bus**: Stagecoach in Warwickshire X20 Birmingham–Stratford-upon-Avon, alight Hockley Heath, 1¾ml. **Station**: Lapworth (U) 1½ml; Birmingham International 8ml. **Road**: 2ml E of Hockley Heath (on A3400), 11ml SE of central Birmingham

🅿 Free parking, 70yds

NT properties nearby
Baddesley Clinton, Birmingham Back to Backs, Charlecote Park, Clent Hills, Hanbury Hall

Packwood House							
Park							
All year		M	T	W	T	F	S S
House/garden/shop							
11 Feb–1 Nov	11–5	M	T	W	T	F	S S

Admission by timed ticket to house at busy times. Open BH Mons

Rosedene

Victoria Road, Dodford, nr Bromsgrove, Worcestershire B61 9BU

🏠 ❄ 🎇 🎏 [1997] (4:J6)

Mid 19th-century Chartist cottage

ℹ **T** 01527 821214

➡ Follow signs for Dodford off A448, left into Priory Road, left into Church Road, then left into Victoria Road

Rosedene
Admission by guided tours Suns only 5 April–27 Sept, Booking essential. Limited group visits at other times by arrangement

Shugborough Estate

Milford, nr Stafford, Staffordshire ST17 0XB

🏠 🏠 🍴 🔑 ❄ ♠ 🧺 🗇 🍹 🎇 🎋 🐚 🎎 🎏
🚶 🔔 🍸 [1966] (4:J4)

Rare survival of a complete estate, with all major buildings including mansion house, servants' quarters, model farm and walled garden

This historic estate is the home of the Earls of Lichfield. Visitors can view the entire estate, including all its major working historic buildings, set in their original parkland with several historic landscape monuments. Follow the story of food production at Shugborough – from its cultivation in the 1805 walled garden, its processing in the 1805 farm, its preparation in the multi-period servants' quarters, and finally its consumption in the fine dining room of the house. Some of the rooms contain artefacts from Admiral Anson's epic circumnavigation of the globe in the 1740s. Each part of this story is told by 'first person' guides, who work on a range of tasks using original equipment. Each day, visitors can see traditional methods being used – whether it is in the walled garden, at the mill, cheese-making in the dairy, cooking and baking, washing and ironing or even brewing (and you can sample the brewer's work). After all that, there are the beautiful riverside gardens to enjoy.

What's new in 2009 New Staffordshire Arts and Museum Service exhibition within the Servants' Quarters

★ Shugborough is wholly financed, administered and maintained by Staffordshire County Council. Access to the house and gardens is free to NT members: to experience the whole estate a greatly reduced price all-sites ticket is available. Admission charges apply when special events are held. Please tel. or visit www.shugborough.org.uk

i **T** 01889 881388
E shugborough.promotions@staffordshire.gov.uk

🏃 Wide range of tours and activities

♥ Easter and BHol events. Open-air concerts, craft fairs and spectacular Christmas evenings

🚶 Walks and trails suitable for all abilities

♿ 🅿♿🚻♿⊙🔄🔊🔉🔈
Building 🔊L🔊 Grounds 🔊➡🔊

☕ Lady Walk Tea-room (not NT) (licensed) in the Midden Courtyard. Menus based on Mrs Stearn's historically inspired recipes using local, organic ingredients. Hot meals 12–2:30, light refreshments 11–4:45. Children's menu. Garden room available for parties and group lunches

🚼 Baby-changing and feeding facilities. Hip-carrying infant seats for loan. Children's play area with adapted equipment to make it accessible for all. Children's guide. Children's quiz/trail. Farm gives children chance to see domestic and rare breeds of animals. Games gallery in corn mill. Pushchairs admitted to farm

▦ Suitable for school groups. Education room/centre. Live interpretation. Hands-on activities

🐕 On leads and only in parkland and gardens

➡ [127:SJ992225] **Foot**: pedestrian access from E, from the canal/Great Haywood side of the estate. Estate walks link to towpaths along Trent & Mersey Canal and Staffs &

Worcs Canal and to Cannock Chase trails. Lies on Staffordshire Way. **Bus**: Arriva 825 🚇 Stafford–Lichfield (passing close 🚇 Lichfield City). **Station**: Rugeley Town 5ml; Rugeley Trent Valley 5ml; Stafford 6ml.
Road: signposted from M6 exit 13; 6ml E of Stafford on A513; entrance at Milford.

🅿 Parking, £3 (pay & display). Refunded on purchase of an all-sites ticket

NT properties nearby
Attingham Park, Biddulph Grange Garden, Little Moreton Hall, Moseley Old Hall

Shugborough Estate									
House/farm/servants' quarters/grounds/tea-room									
20 Mar–29 Oct	11–5	M	T	W	T	F	S	S	
Shop									
20 Mar–29 Oct	11–5	M	T	W	T	F	S	S	
30 Oct–23 Dec	11–4	M	T	W	T	F	S	S	

Open BH Mons. Opening times and admission prices may vary when special events held. Tel. or see website

Sunnycroft

200 Holyhead Road, Wellington, Telford, Shropshire TF1 2DR

🏠 🐾 ❄ 🏛 💺 🏃 🎋 ♥ 🚻 ▦ 1999   (4:14)

Edwardian gentleman's suburban villa

The house is typical of the many thousands that were built for prosperous business and professional people on the fringes of Victorian towns and cities. Sunnycroft is one of the very few – perhaps the only one – to have survived largely unaltered and with a remarkable range of its contents remaining. The grounds amount to a 'mini-estate', with pigsties, stables, kitchen garden, orchards, conservatory, flower garden and superb Wellingtonia avenue.

What's new in 2009 Tea-room, serving cakes, ice-cream and drinks open as house

i **T** 01952 242884
E sunnycroft@nationaltrust.org.uk

🏃 Volunteer guided tours focusing on the history of the Landers, the family who built and lived in the house

♥ Including annual garden fête, Michaelmas Fayre and Christmas opening 18–21 Dec

Charges for National Trust members apply on some special event days

♿ 🅿️ 🅳 🚻 Building ⛰️ Grounds 🎫 ➡️
📖 Second-hand bookshop
🍴 Tea, coffee, cakes and ice-cream
👪 Children's quiz/trail
🏫 Suitable for school groups
🐕 In grounds only
➡️ [127:SJ652109] **Cycle**: NCN81, 1ml.
Bus: Arriva 66 from Telford (passing ⇄ Wellington Telford West). **Station**: Wellington Telford West ½ml. **Road**: M54 exit 7, follow B5061 towards Wellington

🅿️ Free parking, 150yds in orchard. Not suitable for coaches. Additional free parking (not NT) in Wrekin Road car park

NT properties nearby
Attingham Park, Attingham Park Estate: Cronkhill, Benthall Hall, Carding Mill Valley and the Shropshire Hills, Dudmaston Estate, Morville Hall, Moseley Old Hall, Wenlock Edge

Sunnycroft		M	T	W	T	F	S	S
20 Mar–1 Nov	1–5	M	T	W	T	F	S	S
18 Dec–21 Dec	1–4	M	T	W	T	F	S	S

Open Good Fri and BH Mons (free-flow through house). Admission by timed ticket (advanced booking not possible) and guided tour only. Last admission 1hr before closing

Sunnycroft: late-Victorian gentleman's surburban villa

Town Walls Tower

Shrewsbury, Shropshire SY1 1TN

🏠 1930   **(4:H4)**
Shrewsbury's last remaining watchtower
⭐ No WC
ℹ️ **T** 01743 708162
E townwallstower@nationaltrust.org.uk
➡️ Close to town centre near Welsh bridge, on S of town wall

Town Walls Tower
By written appointment only with the tenant, Mr A. A. Hector, Tower House, 26a Town Walls, Shrewsbury SY1 1TN

Upton House and Gardens

nr Banbury, Warwickshire OX15 6HT

🏠 ❄️ 🏠 🏠 🍴 🎿 🏯 🛡️ 👪 🖼️ 🔔
🍷 1948   **(4:L7)**

Presented in its 1930s heyday, mansion and terraced gardens with outstanding art and porcelain collection

Get a taste of country house life as you step into the home of a 1930s' millionaire. Walter Samuel, 2nd Viscount Bearsted, was Chairman of Shell and son of the company's founder. He was a passionate art collector, and visitors can enjoy internationally important works by artists such as Hogarth, Stubbs, Canaletto, Brueghel and El Greco. Lord Bearsted's extensive porcelain collection includes 18th-century Sèvres porcelain, Chelsea and Derby figures. Upton has all the elements of a millionaire's country home – with swimming pool, squash court and a glamourous Art Deco interior in Lady Bearsted's bathroom. The garden planting was principally designed by Kitty Lloyd-Jones with Lady Bearsted in the 1930s. The sweeping lawn gives way to a dramatic series of terraces and herbaceous borders, which descend to a kitchen garden and tranquil water garden. Upton is also home to the National Collection of Asters.

What's new in 2009 Newly refurbished 1930s squash court: venue for a summer film show and winter art exhibition. New winter walk through garden and woodland. Exhibition, 'Picture in Focus: Master of the Magdalen Legend'

Please remember – your membership card is *always* needed for free admission

Upton House and Gardens

Garden*/restaurant/shop/plant centre

		M	T	W	T	F	S	S
28 Feb–1 Nov	11–5	M	T	W	T	F	S	S
4 Apr–22 Apr	11–5	M	T	W	T	F	S	S
25 Jul–2 Sep	11–5	M	T	W	T	F	S	S
2 Nov–20 Dec	12–4	M	T	W	T	F	S	S
26 Dec–3 Jan 10	12–4	M	T	W	T	F	S	S

House tours

		M	T	W	T	F	S	S
28 Feb–1 Nov	11–1	M	T	W	T	F	S	S
4 Apr–22 Apr	11–1	M	T	W	T	F	S	S
25 Jul–2 Sep	11–1	M	T	W	T	F	S	S

House

		M	T	W	T	F	S	S
28 Feb–1 Nov	1–5	M	T	W	T	F	S	S
4 Apr–22 Apr	1–5	M	T	W	T	F	S	S
25 Jul–2 Sep	1–5	M	T	W	T	F	S	S
7 Nov–20 Dec	12–4	M	T	W	T	F	S	S

House admission from 11 on BHols by timed ticket, but visitors may stay until 5. Ground floor open only in house 7 Nov–20 Dec. *Garden winter route only Nov–Jan 10

⭐ For safety some areas of the gardens may be closed during bad weather

ℹ️ **T** 01295 670266
E uptonhouse@nationaltrust.org.uk

🎭 Free house taster tours, conservation tours, garden tours and introductory talks when available

🎭 Family activities, fine art study tours, 1930s days, jazz concerts, Civil War re-enactments and lecture lunches

♿ 🅿️ 📠 ♨️ 💺 ⠿ 🔊 📖 🎧 🖼️
Building 🔎🔎🔎 **Grounds** 🔎🔎 ➡️

Colourful borders at Upton House and Gardens

🛍️ NT shop. Plant sales. Kitchen garden produce for sale when in season

🍽️ Pavilion Restaurant (licensed). Open-air seating available. Children's menu

👪 Baby-changing and feeding facilities. Front-carrying baby slings and hip-carrying infant seats for loan. Children's quiz/trail

🏫 Suitable for school groups. Adult study days

➡️ [151:SP371461] On the edge of the Cotswolds, between Banbury and Stratford-upon-Avon. **Foot**: footpath SM177 runs adjacent to property, Centenary Way $\frac{1}{2}$ml, Macmillan Way 1ml. **Cycle**: NCN5, 5ml. Oxfordshire Cycle Way 1$\frac{1}{2}$ml. **Station**: Banbury 7ml. **Road**: on A422, 7ml N of Banbury, 12ml SE of Stratford-upon-Avon. Signed from exit 12 of M40

🅿️ Free parking, 300yds. Parking is on grass with hard-standing for coaches

NT properties nearby
Canons Ashby House, Charlecote Park, Chastleton House, Dover's Hill, Farnborough Hall, Hidcote Manor Garden

The Weir

Swainshill, Hereford HR4 7QF

🏛️ 🎭 🎭 🅿️ 👪 🚻 🧍 1959 (4:H7)

Informal 1920s riverside garden with fine views

An unusual and dramatic garden of four hectares (ten acres) with stunning views along the River Wye and across the Herefordshire countryside. The Weir is managed to create a varied habitat for a wide range of wildlife and is spectacular all year round, with drifts of early spring bulbs giving way to a succession of wild flowers, followed by a final flourish of autumn colour – courtesy of the mature trees. The river provides a sense of movement and change and is the perfect backdrop for a tranquil walk.

What's new in 2009 Unique opportunity to view the restoration of the Estate's 1920s walled garden. Limited opening June, July and August only

⭐ Due to the nature of the paths and steps, sturdy footwear is recommended

ℹ️ **T** 01981 590509 **E** theweir@nationaltrust.org.uk

Unless indicated, last admission is always 30mins before closing time

[i] Tours by arrangement

[i] Including annual open-air concert. Children's activities during school holidays

[i] Conservation and archaeological interest walks

[i] [i] Grounds [i] [i]

[i] Baby-changing facilities. Pushchairs and baby back-carriers admitted. Children's activities during school holidays

[→] [149:SO438418] **Bus**: to Hereford and then taxi. **Station**: Hereford 5ml. **Road**: 5ml W of Hereford on A438

[P] Free parking

NT properties nearby
Berrington Hall, Brockhampton Estate, Croft Castle and Parkland, Cwmmau Farmhouse, The Kymin

The Weir									
1 Feb–28 Feb	11–4	M	T	**W**	**T**	**F**	**S**	**S**
1 Mar–3 May	11–5	**M**	**T**	**W**	**T**	**F**	**S**	**S**
6 May–1 Nov	11–5	M	T	**W**	**T**	**F**	**S**	**S**
23 Jan–31 Jan 10	11–4	M	T	W	T	F	**S**	**S**

Open BH Mons. Last admission 45mins before closing

Wichenford Dovecote

Wichenford, Worcestershire WR6 6XY

[i] 1965   (4:I7)

17th-century half-timbered dovecote

[★] No WC

[i] T 01527 821214
E wichenforddovecote@nationaltrust.org.uk

[i] Building [i]

[→] [150:SO788598] **Bus**: Bromyard 308, 310 from Worcester (passing close ⭾ Worcester Foregate Street), alight Wichenford, ½ml. **Station**: Worcester Foregate Street 7ml; Worcester Shrub Hill 7½ml. **Road**: 5½ml NW of Worcester, N of B4204

[P] Free parking, 50yds

NT properties nearby
The Greyfriars, Hanbury Hall, Hawford Dovecote

Wichenford Dovecote									
1 Mar–31 Oct	9–6	**M**	**T**	**W**	**T**	**F**	**S**	**S**

Open other times by appointment

The corner fireplace lined with Dutch 'Persian Flower' tiles in the Oak Room at Wightwick Manor, Wolverhampton

Wightwick Manor and Gardens

Wightwick Bank, Wolverhampton, West Midlands WV6 8EE

[icons] 1937   (4:J5)

Victorian manor house with William Morris interiors and colourful garden

Wightwick Manor is one of only a few surviving examples of a house built and furnished under the influence of the Arts & Crafts Movement. The many original William Morris wallpapers and fabrics, pre-Raphaelite paintings, Kempe glass and de Morgan ware help conjure up the spirit of the time. An attractive seven-hectare (seventeen-acre) Thomas Mawson garden reflects the style and character of the house.

What's new in 2009 Produce from the restored kitchen garden can be sampled in the tea-room. Extended events programme

For general and membership enquiries, please telephone 0844 800 1895

ℹ️ **T** 01902 761400
E wightwickmanor@nationaltrust.org.uk

🚶 Guided tours every open day. Taster tours 11–12:30. First Thur & Sat of each month free-flow through house

😀 Children's activity days and trails during Aug

🚶 Seven hectares (seventeen acres) of beautiful gardens provide the perfect setting for a picturesque afternoon stroll

♿ 📶 😀 ⸬ 🖊️ 📷 🚪 💻 🪜 Building 🚶🚶 Grounds 🚶🚶 ➡️

🛍️ William Morris shop and tea-room open to the public

☕ Tea-room. Limited seating. Children's menu

👶 Baby-changing facilities. Hip-carrying infant seats for loan. Children's quiz/trail. Children's activity days in Aug

📚 Suitable for education groups. Hands-on activities and guided tours

🐕 On leads and only in garden

➜ [139:SO869985] **Bus**: Travel West Midlands 543 from Wolverhampton (passing close ⇌ Wolverhampton). **Station**: Wolverhampton 3ml. **Road**: 3ml W of Wolverhampton, up Wightwick Bank (off A454 beside Mermaid Inn)

🅿️ Free parking, 120yds. Located at bottom of Wightwick Bank (please do not park in Elmsdale opposite the property)

NT properties nearby
Benthall Hall, Clent Hills, Dudmaston Estate, Moseley Old Hall

The entrance front of Wightwick Manor, Wolverhampton

Wightwick Manor and Gardens								
1 Mar–1 Nov	11–5*	M	T	**W**	**T**	**F**	**S**	**S**
7 Nov–20 Dec	11–5*	M	T	W	T	F	**S**	**S**

*House opens at 12:30. Garden closes at 6. Admission is by timed ticket and guided tour, only available from visitor reception on the day of your visit. Taster tours: 1 Mar–1 Nov, Wed–Sun inc., 11–12:30. No guided tours on first Thur & Sat of the month – free-flow through the house from 12:30. Property opens BH Mons (ground floor only). Many of the contents are fragile and some rooms cannot always be shown, so tours vary

Wilderhope Manor

Longville, Much Wenlock, Shropshire TF13 6EG

🏠 🐴 🛏️ 🛍️ ☕ 🚪 👶 📚 🚶 1971   **(4:H5)**

Elizabethan gabled manor house, unfurnished but with fine interior architectural features

⭐ The manor is used as a youth hostel so access to some occupied rooms may be restricted

ℹ️ **T** 0870 770 6090 (Hostel Warden YHA)
E wilderhope@nationaltrust.org.uk

➜ 7ml SW of Much Wenlock, 7ml E of Church Stretton, ½ml S of B4371

Wilderhope Manor								
1 Apr–27 Sep	2–4:30	M	T	**W**	T	F	S	**S**
4 Oct–31 Jan 10	2–4:30	M	T	W	T	F	S	**S**

Most Trust properties offer Gift Aid on Entry for non-members, see page 10

Home to some of Britain's finest landscapes, stunning houses, fascinating industrial heritage, not to mention delicious local food and fascinating wildlife, the North West is a truly rich region. Whether you want fun and adventure, or peace and tranquillity, there is something for everyone in this lovely corner of England.

To the north, the dramatic and internationally-renowned beauty of the Lake District proves irresistible to all those keen on physical, mental or spiritual refreshment. To the south, the urban centres of Manchester and Liverpool are surrounded by countryside and parkland, which offer a 'green lung' for their communities and visitors.

The National Trust looks after one quarter of the Lake District National Park, including 'Britain's Favourite View' – England's highest mountain, Scafell Pike; our deepest lake, Wastwater; and 90 tenanted farms. Almost all the central fell area and major valley heads are owned or leased by the Trust, together with 24 lakes and tarns.

The North West also contains one of the most important bequests the Trust has ever received. Beatrix Potter's love of the area is legend, and she left 1,600 hectares (4,000 acres) and fourteen farms to the Trust on her death in 1943. This great estate was purchased piece by piece – beginning in 1902 with Brandlehow Park on the shore of Derwentwater.

Culinary excellence

Here in the North West we believe our local food is second to none. Don't miss the Chorley cakes at Rufford Old Hall, made with fruit from their orchards. Also be sure to sample some of the meats of the region – such as venison from the

Above left: **bluebells in the garden at Dunham Massey, Cheshire**
Above: **fresh seasonal vegetables from Sizergh Castle, Cumbria**

Previous page: **part of the 'Secret Garden', Quarry Bank Mill and Styal Estate, Cheshire**

parks at Dunham and Lyme; Herdwick lamb from Trust farms in Cumbria; or organic beef from farms in Silverdale, Coniston or Cheshire.

We are also extremely proud of our cheeses. Low Sizergh Farm produces award-winning cheeses, including Kendal Organic Crumbly, and there are delicious blue and red cheeses at Little Moreton Hall. At Rufford, the Lancashire ploughman's lunches are made using local creamy Garstang Blue and other Lancashire cheeses.

Many Trust farms have B&Bs or tea-rooms serving delicious home-made and locally produced food. Taste Herdwick stew and other traditional Cumbrian fare at walkers' tea-rooms at our two Yew Tree Farms – one of which is in Borrowdale and the other at Coniston.

Ancient woodland and far-reaching views

In West Cheshire the Trust cares for part of the very special Sandstone Ridge. Enjoy extensive walks through this historic landscape, with splendid views of the Cheshire Plain and Welsh Mountains from Alderley Edge, Bickerton Hill and nearby Bulkeley Hill Wood; while Helsby Hill has views across the Mersey Estuary to Liverpool.

Both Bickerton and Helsby have Bronze Age forts at their summits, while Bulkeley, part of the Peckforton range of hills, has the Sandstone Trail running along its length and is home to five hectares (twelve acres) of semi-natural ancient woodland.

Views of the Peak District and Welsh Mountains, with wide expanses of the great Cheshire Plain stretching in between, can be seen from The Cloud, a great rocky heathland 343 metres high near Timbersbrook in Cheshire.

Romantic ruins

Further south lies the folly of Mow Cop; built in 1754 it is famed as the birthplace of Primitive Methodism and stands in romantic ruin, while to the west of the county is the site of Lewis Carroll's birthplace near Daresbury – kindly donated to the Trust by the Lewis Carroll Birthplace Trust. Here you can find the plot bearing the footprint of Daresbury Parsonage, in which Carroll was born

Cumbrian cheeses at Low Sizergh Barn

in 1832 and where he entertained his ten brothers and sisters with his stories. Nearby Daresbury Church features a memorial to Carroll and his Wonderland characters in a stained glass window.

Miles of unspoilt coastline

Arnside Knott in Cumbria and Eaves and Waterslack Woods in Lancashire are home to a fantastic variety of wild flowers and butterflies. Also important for wildlife are the Stubbins Estate and Holcombe Moor, north of Manchester.

Another wildlife habitat for many species is Formby Sands. Enjoy the wonderful nature reserve, which stretches for miles along unspoilt coastline and includes one of the

Above: **Wasdale Head, Cumbria**
Below: **examining prehistoric footprints at Formby, near Liverpool**

If you love camping, the Trust manages three Lake District sites – Wasdale, Great Langdale and Low Wray – all set in spectacular locations. There's even all-year-round camping for the really hardy among you. Visit www.ntlakescampsites.org.uk

country's largest areas of sand dunes, as well as one of the few remaining red squirrel colonies left in Britain. This is also home to natterjack toads, a nationally rare species.

Natterjacks have also made themselves at home in a specially constructed pool at Sandscale Haws, Cumbria, where visitors can hear their extraordinary mating calls on May and June evenings. Sandscale is also home to a rich variety of birds, including shelducks, eider ducks, goldeneyes and plovers, and the high, grass-covered sand dunes are perfect for a day's exploring.

Rugged crags and still waters

In Cumbria, Coniston Water is home to a wealth of flora and fauna, including wetland plants, meadow flowers and the rare small-leaved lime. Arthur Ransome got his inspiration here, as did Donald Campbell. At weekends *Gondola* sails to the north end of Coniston Water, from where you can walk up a newly opened footpath, through the beautiful Monk Coniston grounds, to the iconic landscape of Tarn Hows.

In Borrowdale, you are surrounded by a fascinating combination of rugged crags, dramatic fells, old mine workings and wooded valleys. Fine sessile oak woodlands and colonies of internationally important lichens, mosses and insects all thrive here.

Wildfowl and waders nest along the shores of Derwentwater, and Friar's Crag, one of the Lakes' most famous viewpoints, sits at the north end of the lake near the handsome town of Keswick. There is wheelchair access to the Crag; other sites with access include Tarn Hows and Harrowslack, near Hawkshead.

Scafell Pike, England's highest mountain, is one of a dramatic horseshoe of peaks rising around the head of Wasdale. This remote and quiet valley is one of the wildest areas of the Lake District. At the foot of the slopes lies Wastwater, the area's deepest lake, where Arctic char survive in the pure water. Traditional thick drystone walls make a striking pattern at Wasdale Head, while the impressive scree slopes of Whin Rigg and Illgill Head provide ideal conditions for rare mountain plants to thrive.

Top: the campsite at Wasdale Head, Cumbria
Above: gazebo at Monk Coniston, Cumbria

Car parks in the Lake District

The National Trust is an independent charity which protects about one quarter of the Lake District National Park. All income from National Trust pay & display car parks supports landscape conservation work in the valleys where the car parks are located.

Lanthwaite Wood	NY 149 215	Great Wood	NY 272 213	Ash Landing	SD 388 955
Buttermere	NY 172 173	Aira Force	NY 401 201	Sandscale Haws	SD 199 758
Honister Pass	NY 225 135	Glencoyne Bay	NY 387 188	Blea Tarn	NY 296 044
Seatoller	NY 246 137	Wasdale Head	NY 182 074	Harrowslack	SD 388 960
Rosthwaite	NY 257 148	Old Dungeon Ghyll	NY 285 062	Red Nab	SD 385 995
Bowderstone	NY 254 167	Stickle Ghyll	NY 295 064	Glen Mary	SD 321 998
Watendlath	NY 276 164	Elterwater	NY 329 047		
Kettlewell	NY 269 196	Tarn Hows	SD 326 995		

Acorn Bank Garden and Watermill

Temple Sowerby, nr Penrith, Cumbria CA10 1SP

[icons] 1950 (6:E7)

Delightful garden renowned for its herbs and old English fruit; with superb tea-room and woodland walks

This tranquil garden, sheltered by ancient oaks and soft terracotta brick walls, is a haven for wildlife. The herb garden is nationally renowned – with 250 medicinal and culinary herbs – and the orchards are packed with traditional fruit varieties. Wander along the Crowdundle Beck to the partially restored watermill, then enjoy the magnificent backdrop of the rose-pink sandstone house (which, although not open to the public, adds to the wonderful setting). Taste local produce at the tea-room or stay a while longer in a holiday cottage.

★ Access to fragile grass paths in the garden may be restricted after wet weather

ℹ **T** 017683 61893
E acornbank@nationaltrust.org.uk

🔖 Newt watching in early summer. Apple Day in mid Oct (charge inc. NT members)

🚶 Through woodland, beside beck and pond to the watermill

Acorn Bank Garden and Watermill									
Garden/watermill/woodland walks/shop		M	T	W	T	F	S	S
28 Feb–22 Mar	10–5	M	T	W	T	F	**S**	**S**
28 Mar–1 Nov	10–5	M	T	**W**	**T**	**F**	**S**	**S**
Tea-room								
28 Feb–22 Mar	11–4:30	M	T	W	T	F	**S**	**S**
28 Mar–1 Nov	11–4:30	M	T	**W**	**T**	**F**	**S**	**S**
Open BH Mons: 10–5								

[accessibility icons]
Building [icons] **Grounds** [icons]

🏪 NT shop. Plant sales

🍴 Restaurant. Children's menu

🚼 Baby-changing facilities. Pushchairs and baby back-carriers admitted. Children's guide

🏫 Suitable for school groups. Adult study days

🐕 On leads on woodland walk

➡ [91:NY612281] **Cycle**: NCN7, 6ml.
Bus: Grand Prix 563 Penrith–Kirkby Stephen, to within 1ml (passes close ⇌ Penrith & ⇌ Appleby). **Station**: Langwathby (U) 5ml; Penrith 6ml. **Road**: just N of Temple Sowerby, 6ml E of Penrith off A66

🅿 Free parking, 80yds. Tight access for coaches. Recommended route map available when booking

NT properties nearby
Ullswater and Aira Force, Wordsworth House and Garden

The peaceful herb garden at Acorn Bank Garden: a haven for wildlife

Alderley Edge

c/o Cheshire Countryside Office, Nether Alderley, Macclesfield, Cheshire SK10 4UB

 1946 **(5:D8)**

Dramatic red sandstone escarpment, with impressive views

Alderley Edge is designated an SSSI for its geological interest. It has a long history of copper mining, going back to Bronze Age and Roman times. The mines are open twice a year, organised by the Derbyshire Caving Club. There are views across Cheshire and the Peak District and numerous paths through the oak and beech woodlands, including a link to Hare Hill.

- **i** **T** 01625 584412
  E alderleyedge@nationaltrust.org.uk

- 🧗 Guided walks programme, April to Sept

- 🎭 National Archaeology Week activities

- 🧗 Hare Hill 2ml. Alderley Edge walks leaflet available

- ♿ P♿♿♿ **Grounds** ♿➡

- ☕ Tea-room (not NT)

- 👨‍👩‍👧 Children's quiz/trail. Tracker Pack

- 🏫 Suitable for school groups

- 🐕 Under close control; on leads in fields

Alderley Edge									
All year	8–5:30	**M**	**T**	**W**	**T**	**F**	**S**	**S**
1 Jun–30 Sep	8–6	**M**	**T**	**W**	**T**	**F**	**S**	**S**
1 Oct–31 Oct	8–5:30	**M**	**T**	**W**	**T**	**F**	**S**	**S**
1 Nov–28 Mar	8–5	**M**	**T**	**W**	**T**	**F**	**S**	**S**
Tea-room									
All year	10–5*	M	T	W	T	**F**	**S**	**S**

*Tea-room also open BHols but closed 24/25 Dec

➡ [118:SJ860776] **Station**: Alderley Edge 1½ml.
Road: 1½ml east of Alderley village on B5087 Macclesfield road

P Parking (pay & display). Closing time displayed at entrance

NT properties nearby
Dunham Massey, Hare Hill, Lyme Park, Quarry Bank Mill and Styal Estate, Tatton Park

Beatrix Potter Gallery

Main Street, Hawkshead, Cumbria LA22 0NS

🏠🏠🎭👨‍👩‍👧🏫 1944 **(6:D8)**

17th-century solicitor's office, now home to the original watercolours and sketches of Beatrix Potter

Enjoy a new exhibition of Beatrix Potter's original artworks in this charming 17th-century building (previously the office of her husband, William

A tempting path through woodland at Alderley Edge

Heelis). Many of these pictures are not displayed anywhere else. Learn more about Beatrix as a farmer and early supporter of the National Trust. Children's trail based on the display.

What's new in 2009 Exhibition 'Because I Never Grew Up', celebrating 100 years since the publication of *Ginger and Pickles* and featuring original watercolours from the story. See our new 'Conservation in Action' room and learn more about the work we do

⭐ No WC, public WC 200yds away in main village car park

ℹ️ **T** 015394 36355, 015394 36471 (shop)
E beatrixpottergallery@nationaltrust.org.uk

🎭 Easter trail, book fair, occasional storytelling

♿ 🅿️ 👓 📷 📝 🎵 🏛 **Building** 🔥 🏔

📷 50yds away in the square. Limited selection of books on sale in the gallery

🧑‍🍼 Hip-carrying infant seats for loan. Children's quiz/trail

🏫 Suitable for school groups

➡️ [96:SD352982] In Main Street, Hawkshead village, next to Red Lion pub.
Bus: Stagecoach in Cumbria 505 ⊠ Windermere–Coniston. **Station**: Windermere 6½ml via ferry. **Road**: B5286 from Ambleside (4ml); B5285 from Coniston (5ml)

🅿️ Parking (not NT), 200yds (pay & display)

NT properties nearby
Coniston and Tarn Hows, Fell Foot Park, *Gondola*, Hawkshead and Claife, Hill Top, Stagshaw Garden, Townend

Beatrix Potter Gallery									
Gallery									
14 Feb–12 Mar	11–3:30	M	T	W	T	F	S	S	
14 Mar–1 Nov	10:30–4:30	M	T	W	T	F	S	S	
Shop									
14 Feb–1 Mar	10–4	M	T	W	T	F	S	S	
4 Mar–13 Mar	10–4	M	T	W	T	F	S	S	
14 Mar–1 Nov	10–5	M	T	W	T	F	S	S	
4 Nov–20 Dec	10–4	M	T	W	T	F	S	S	
21 Dec–31 Dec	10–4	M	T	W	T	F	S	S	

Admission by timed ticket issued on arrival to all visitors. Open Good Fri & Fri 30 Oct. Shop is open occasional extra days in winter. Please enquire before making a special journey

Yew Tree Farm, Borrowdale

Borrowdale

Bowe Barn, Borrowdale Road, Keswick, Cumbria CA12 5UP

🏛 🔧 📷 🔌 🎒 🏠 🅿️ ☕ 🍴 🪑 🎭 🧑‍🍼 🍽 🚶
🚲 1902 **(6:D7)**

Spectacular and varied landscape around Derwentwater

This is the location of the National Trust's first acquisition in the Lake District – Brandelhow Woods, on the lakeshore. The Trust now protects 11,806 hectares (29,173 acres), including eleven farms, half of Derwentwater (including the main islands), the hamlet of Watendlath and sites with literary or historical interest such as the Bowder Stone, Friar's Crag, Ashness Bridge and Castlerigg Stone Circle, a free-standing megalithic monument of 38 stones near Keswick.

What's new in 2009 New 546-yard recycled plastic boardwalk at southern end of Derwentwater providing easy access to wetland habitat

⭐ At peak times roads around Cat Bells may be very congested. For walks to Cat Bells, park at Keswick and use launch or local bus services

ℹ️ **T** 017687 74649
E borrowdale@nationaltrust.org.uk

🎭 Programme of events, including Easter Egg trail

🚶 Popular walks from NT car parks. See local guides, maps and website

For further information, visit www.nationaltrust.org.uk

♿ ♿ **Grounds** ♿

🛒 Shop and information centre at Keswick lakeside

🚬 Tea-rooms at Caffle House, Watendlath; at the Flock-In, Rosthwaite; at Knotts View, Stonethwaite; and at Seathwaite – properties owned, but not managed, by NT

🚹 Baby-changing facilities (Watendlath WC)

🚩 Suitable for school groups. Farm tours by arrangement

🐾 Under close control. Stock grazing

🚲 Several cycle routes throughout the valley

➞ [90:NY266228] **Cycle**: NCN71 (C2C). **Ferry**: Derwentwater launch service to various NT properties around lake, tel. 017687 72263. **Bus**: to information centre: Stagecoach in Cumbria X4/5 ⏳ Penrith–Workington, 555/6 Lancaster–Keswick (pass close ⏳ Lancaster, Kendal & Windermere). **Road**: B5289 runs S from Keswick along Borrowdale

🕱 NT car parks at Great Wood, Watendlath, Kettlewell, Bowderstone, Rosthwaite, Seatoller and Honister (pay & display). Coach parking available by prior arrangement at Seatoller car park only

NT properties nearby
Acorn Bank Garden and Watermill, Borrowdale: Force Crag Mine, Derwent Island House, Wordsworth House and Garden

Borrowdale									
All year		M	T	W	T	F	S	S
Shop/info centre									
28 Feb–1 Nov	10–5	M	T	W	T	F	S	S
Shop/information centre closes later on summer evenings									

Fold Head Farm, Watendlath in Borrowdale, Cumbria

Crummock Water in Buttermere, Cumbria

Borrowdale: Force Crag Mine

Head of Coledale, above Braithwaite, Keswick, Cumbria

📝 👨 🚶 🚹 🚩 🚶 🚲 1979   **(6:D7)**

Last mineral mine processing mill to operate in the Lake District

⭐ Admission into mine building via booked tours only (charge inc. NT members). NB: no access to the mine itself. Not suitable for children under ten years. Tel. for booking and details. WC not always available. Portaloo only on public open days. Site accessible via public footpaths

ℹ **T** 017687 74649
E forcecragmine@nationaltrust.org.uk

➞ From Braithwaite west of Keswick off A66 walk or cycle approx. 2¾ml up to mine buildings or catch minibus from Noble Knott Forestry car park opposite the Bassenthwaite Lake viewpoint, which is approx. ½ml from Braithwaite climbing up Whinlatter Pass towards Lorton

Borrowdale: Force Crag Mine
Admission by hourly guided tour on five open days a year. Contact NT Borrowdale for dates

Buttermere and Ennerdale

Unit 16, Leconfield Industrial Estate, Cleator Moor,
Cumbria CA25 5QB

 1935 **(6:C7)**

Tranquil area of dramatic fells, farms and woodland, encompassing three lakes

This area of 3,588 hectares (8,866 acres) of fell and commonland includes the lakes of Buttermere, Crummock and Loweswater, seven farms and woodland, as well as lakeshore access to Ennerdale Water. The famous Pillar Rock can be found in the high fells to the south, and there are extensive prehistoric settlements on the fells south of Ennerdale. Fishing and boats are available on Crummock Water and Loweswater.

⭐ WC in Buttermere village (not NT)

ℹ️ **T** 01946 816940
   E buttermere@nationaltrust.org.uk

♿ Grounds 🏔️

➡️ [89:NY180150] 8ml S of Cockermouth.
   Bus: Stagecoach in Cumbria 77 'Honister Rambler' from Keswick and Ken Routledge 949 from Cockermouth

🅿️ Parking (pay & display) at Honister Pass, Buttermere village, Lanthwaite Wood (Crummock Water)

NT properties nearby
Wordsworth House and Garden

Buttermere and Ennerdale							
All year	M	T	W	T	F	S	S

Tarn Hows and Coniston Water

Cartmel Priory Gatehouse

The Square, Cartmel, Grange-over-Sands,
Cumbria LA11 6QB

🏠 1946 **(6:D9)**

14th-century gatehouse of medieval priory

⭐ Most of the Gatehouse and the adjoining cottage have been returned to private residential use. The Great Room is expected to be open to the public several days a year

ℹ️ **T** 01524 701178
   E cartpriorygatehouse@nationaltrust.org.uk

➡️ In the square in village centre

Cartmel Priory Gatehouse
Tel. property or visit NT website for information

Coniston and Tarn Hows

Boon Crag, Coniston, Cumbria LA21 8AQ

 1930 **(6:D8)**

Landscape of fell, meadow and woodland around Coniston Water

The area looked after by the National Trust covers some 2,695 hectares (6,660 acres), including eleven farms and the well-known Tarn Hows beauty spot, with its magnificent mountain views. There is access to the shore of Coniston Water. The valley of Little Langdale shows several signs of early settlement, including a Norse meeting place, Ting Mound. Blea Tarn, with spectacular views of the Langdale Pikes, is readily accessible and there are wonderful walks to be enjoyed throughout the area.

What's new in 2009 Family Tracker Packs available from Roving Recruiter at Tarn Hows

ℹ️ **T** 015394 41197
   E coniston@nationaltrust.org.uk

🎫 Guided tours by arrangement.
   Tel. 015394 41951

🎧 Audio guide to Tarn Hows

🚶 Popular walks for all abilities, see local guides and maps

♿ 🅿️ 🚻 Grounds 🏔️ ▶️

For further information, visit www.nationaltrust.org.uk

Walkers' tea-room at Yew Tree Farm, Coniston (NT but privately run)

Baby-changing facilities at Tarn Hows. Tracker Packs

Suitable for school groups

On leads

Cycle tracks along Coniston lakeshore (west), Yewdale and in woodland south of Tarn Hows. Many off-road routes

[SD325995] Tarn Hows 2ml NE of Coniston. Blea Tarn in Little Langdale, 5ml N of Coniston. **Bus**: Stagecoach in Cumbria 505 'Coniston Rambler' Windermere–Coniston

P Car parks, pay & display, not suitable for coaches. Located at Tarn Hows, Glen Mary and Blea Tarn

NT properties nearby
Beatrix Potter Gallery, *Gondola*, Hill Top

Coniston and Tarn Hows		
All year		M T W T F S S

Dalton Castle

Market Place, Dalton-in-Furness, Cumbria LA15 8AX

🏰 👪 🐕 1965 **(6:D9)**

14th-century tower built to assert the authority of the Abbot of Furness Abbey

⭐ Opened on behalf of the Trust by the Friends of Dalton Castle

i **T** 01524 701178
E daltoncastle@nationaltrust.org.uk

In market place at top of main street of Dalton

Dalton Castle		
11 Apr–26 Sep	2–5	M T W T F **S** S

If you enjoyed finding out about the collections at Dunham Massey, why not take a trip to see what Lyme Park has to offer?

Derwent Island House

Derwent Island, Lake Road, Keswick, Cumbria CA12 5DJ

🏰 ✥ 🗖 1951 **(6:D7)**

Intriguing 18th-century house on an idyllic wooded island in Derwentwater

⭐ Private residence, accessed by private boats, open to public subject to lake levels and weather conditions. No WC, nearest WC at lakeside car park (not NT)

i **T** 017687 73780
E borrowdale@nationaltrust.org.uk

In Derwentwater, Keswick

Derwent Island House
Admission by timed ticket. Tickets only bookable three days prior to open days being advertised – see website. Tel. Keswick shop/info centre to book tickets and check cancellations due to lake levels

Dunham Massey

Altrincham, Cheshire WA14 4SJ

🏰 🏠 ✚ ♿ ✥ ♣ 🗖 ♥ 🍴 🎡 🛡 👪 🚻 🐕 🍽 1976 **(5:D8)**

Mansion with important collections and fascinating 'below stairs' area, set in a large country estate and deer park, with a rich and varied garden

Visit this elegant Georgian mansion, filled with fabulous collections of paintings, furniture and Huguenot silver, and be captivated by tales of family scandal and romance in the sumptuously decorated hall. Go 'below stairs' to the service wing and discover how the running of a country house took place. Enjoy the great plantsman's garden full of native favourites and exotic treasures, then discover the rare Victorian bark house and Georgian orangery. Wander around the beautiful avenues and ponds in the ancient park and spot the fallow deer and many rare birds. Finally make your way to the sawmill, where the giant waterwheel has been restored to full working order, then treat yourself to one of Dunham's renowned cream teas and the generous range of dishes made from fresh, local ingredients.

Charges for National Trust members apply on some special event days

What's new in 2009 Britain's largest winter garden opens November 2009

★ Extensive building works to improve car parking facilities being undertaken. Parking may be restricted at times. We apologise for any inconvenience

ℹ️ **T** 0161 941 1025
E dunhammassey@nationaltrust.org.uk

🏃 House tours most days. Garden tours Mon and Wed. Free

🎭 Including open-air theatre, Boredom Busters and family activities

🚶 Guided deer park walks Mon, Wed, Fri throughout year at 1:30. Free walks leaflet

The Georgian mansion at Dunham Massey, Cheshire, glimpsed through the trees

🛒 NT shop. Plant sales in garden

🍽️ Stables Restaurant (licensed) on first floor of old stables. Open for corporate and private bookings outside normal hours, groups only. Children's menu. Kiosk in car park

👪 Baby-changing facilities. Pushchairs admitted. Front-carrying baby slings and hip-carrying infant seats for loan. Children's quiz/trail. Boredom Busters and family activities

🏫 Suitable for school groups. Education room/centre. Live interpretation. Hands-on activities. Adult study days

🐕 Walks around estate. On leads in deer park

➡️ [109:SJ735874] **Foot**: close to Trans-Pennine Trail and Bridgewater Canal. **Cycle**: NCN62, 1ml. **Bus**: Warrington Transport 5 � Altrincham Interchange–Warrington. **Station**: Altrincham 3ml; Hale 3ml. **Road**: 3ml SW of Altrincham off A56: M6 exit 19; M56 exit 7

P Parking 200yds. From March–Nov shuttle service operates most days between car park and visitor facilities

NT properties nearby
Hare Hill, Lyme Park, Quarry Bank Mill and Styal Estate, Tatton Park

Dunham Massey									
House									
28 Feb–1 Nov	11–5	**M**	**T**	**W**	T	F	**S**	**S**
Garden									
28 Feb–1 Nov	11–5:30	**M**	**T**	**W**	**T**	**F**	**S**	**S**
2 Nov–31 Jan 10	11–4	**M**	**T**	**W**	**T**	**F**	**S**	**S**
Park									
1 Feb–1 Nov	9–7:30*	**M**	**T**	**W**	**T**	**F**	**S**	**S**
2 Nov–31 Jan 10	9–5	**M**	**T**	**W**	**T**	**F**	**S**	**S**
Restaurant/shop									
1 Feb–1 Nov	10:30–5**	**M**	**T**	**W**	**T**	**F**	**S**	**S**
2 Nov–31 Jan 10	10:30–4	**M**	**T**	**W**	**T**	**F**	**S**	**S**
Mill									
28 Feb–1 Nov	12–4	**M**	**T**	**W**	T	F	**S**	**S**

House: open for taster tours only, 11–12 (restricted places, allocated upon arrival). Self-guided visits from 12. Property closed 11 Feb & 25 Nov for staff training. Also closed 25 Dec (inc. park). *Closes 5 in Feb. **Closes 4 in Feb

Show your card and display sticker for free parking

Dunham Massey: White Cottage

Park Lane, Little Bollington, Altrincham, Cheshire WA14 4TJ

🏠 🔫 1976   **(5:D8)**

Timber-framed cottage, built c.1500

⭐ All visits must be booked through the NT Altrincham office

ℹ️ **T** 0161 928 0075
   E dunmasswhite@nationaltrust.org.uk

➡️ 3ml SW of Altrincham off A56: M6 exit 19; M56 exit 7

White Cottage									
29 Mar–25 Oct	2–5	M	T	W	T	F	S	**S**
Open last Sun of each month only								

Fell Foot Park on Lake Windermere, Cumbria

Fell Foot Park

Newby Bridge, Ulverston, Cumbria LA12 8NN

🔫 🏠 💺 🌲 🚽 👪 🕭 ⚓ 1948   **(6:D9)**

Country park beside Lake Windermere

As you walk down from the car park the view of Lake Windermere below you is breathtaking. The Victorian lawns and garden sweep away to fine picnic areas and numerous waterside spots. The Victorian boathouses are now home to a

cosy tea-room, shop, ice-cream kiosk and rowing boat hire, and there are tables outside where you can enjoy the magnificent views of the lake and mountains beyond. In spring and early summer there are daffodils and rhododendrons in full bloom. Or visit in autumn or winter and enjoy the changing seasons.

What's new in 2009 New adventure playground

⭐ No launching or landing of speedboats or jet-skis

ℹ️ **T** 015395 31273
   E fellfootpark@nationaltrust.org.uk

♿ 🚽 🐕 🕭 ⚓ 👓 🕭 🕭 **Grounds** 🕭 🕭

🍴 Tea-room at lakeshore. Trusty the Hedgehog lunch boxes

👪 Pushchairs and baby back-carriers admitted. Children's play area. Children's quiz/trail and wildlife room. Family activity packs

🏫 Suitable for school groups. Hands-on activities. 100 bird and bat boxes around the park relay live pictures to wildlife room

🐕 On leads only

➡️ [96/97:SD381869] **Ferry**: seasonal ferry links Fell Foot to Lakeside (southern terminus of main Windermere cruise ferries). **Bus**: Stagecoach in Cumbria 618 Ambleside–Barrow-in-Furness (connections from ⊠ Windermere). **Station**: Grange-over-Sands 6ml; Windermere 8ml. **Road**: at the extreme S end of Lake Windermere on E shore, entrance from A592

🅿️ Parking (pay & display). Access difficult for coaches, which must book in advance

NT properties nearby
Sizergh Castle and Garden

Fell Foot Park								
Park								
All year	9–5	M	T	W	T	F	S	S
Tea-room								
14 Feb–1 Nov	11–5	M	T	W	T	F	S	S
Shop								
28 Feb–1 Nov	11–5	M	T	W	T	F	S	S
Site closed 25/26 Dec. Closes dusk if earlier. Facilities, eg rowing boat hire (buoyancy aids available), 1 April–28 Oct: daily 11–4 (last boat), must be returned by 4:30								

Dogs assisting visitors with disabilities are always welcome

Formby

Victoria Road, Freshfield, Formby, Liverpool L37 1LJ

 1967 **(5:B7)**

Large area of beach, sand dunes and pine woods

This ever-changing sandy coastline set between the sea and Formby town offers miles of walks through the woods and dunes. Visitors may still catch a glimpse of the increasingly rare red squirrel in the pine woods. The shoreline and dunes are rich in wildlife, and prehistoric animal and human footprints can sometimes be found in silt beds on the shoreline.

What's new in 2009 Formby Point audio guide trail

⭐ WCs close at 5:30 in summer, 4 in winter. Coach parking is restricted and must be booked. Address for correspondence: Countryside Office, Blundell Avenue, Freshfield, Formby L37 1PH

ⓘ **T** 01704 878591
E formby@nationaltrust.org.uk

🎧 Audio guides available from entrance kiosk, £2. Last issue 3 in summer, 1:30 in winter. Deposit and ID are required

🚶 Send sae or email for details

♿ 🅿 ♿ ⋯ ♿ Grounds ♿ ➡

🍦 Ice-cream and soft drinks available

👶 Baby-changing facilities. Children's quiz/trail

🏫 Suitable for school groups, booking essential. Environmental education activities

🐕 Under close control; on leads around the squirrel walk

➡ [108:SD275080] **Foot**: Sefton Coastal Footpath traverses the property. **Cycle**: NCN62, 3ml. **Bus**: 'Cumfybus 160/1/4, ⭤ Formby–⭤ Freshfield, to within ½ml. **Station**: Freshfield 1ml. **Road**: 15ml N of Liverpool, 2ml W of Formby, 2ml off A565. 6ml S of Southport. Follow brown signs from roundabout at N end of Formby bypass

🅿 Cars £4, minibuses £10, coaches £25 – booking essential. Dune car park closes 5:30 April–Oct and 4 Nov–March. Note width restriction 3yds

NT properties nearby

20 Forthlin Road, Mr Hardman's Photographic Studio, Mendips, Rufford Old Hall, Speke Hall, Garden and Estate

Formby								
All year	Dawn–dusk	**M**	**T**	**W**	**T**	**F**	**S**	**S**
Closed 25 Dec. Car parks may be very full in peak season								

Enjoy miles of walks along the wildlife-rich foreshore at Formby near Liverpool

20 Forthlin Road, Allerton

Allerton, Liverpool L24 1YP

🏠 💷 🎧 🚶 📷 1995   (5:B8)

20 Forthlin Road		M	T	W	T	F	S	S
28 Feb–15 Mar	10, 12:30 & 3	M	T	**W**	**T**	**F**	**S**	**S**
18 Mar–1 Nov	10,10:50,2:30,3:20	M	T	**W**	**T**	**F**	**S**	**S**
7 Nov–29 Nov	10, 12:30 & 3	M	T	**W**	**T**	**F**	**S**	**S**

Admission by guided tour only. Open BH Mons. 28 Feb–15 Mar & 7 Nov–29 Nov all tours depart from Liverpool city centre. 18 Mar–1 Nov, morning tours depart from Liverpool city centre, afternoon tours depart from Speke Hall. To guarantee a place on a tour visitors are advised to book in advance at www.nationaltrust.org.uk/beatles, or tel. Infoline

The childhood home of music icon Sir Paul McCartney

A little terrace house in Liverpool is where the Beatles met, rehearsed and wrote many of their songs. Join our characterful custodian on a trip around the McCartney family home, and hear stories from one of the most exciting times in music history. Enjoy contemporary photos by Michael McCartney and original early Beatles memorabilia. Hear Michael's and Paul's reminiscences on the audio tour.

What's new in 2009 Extended opening period. To reserve your place on the tour visit · www.nationaltrust.org.uk/beatles

⭐ **There is no direct access by car or on foot**. Visits are by combined minibus tour only with Mendips, the childhood home of John Lennon (charge inc. NT members). Any photography inside 20 Forthlin Road or duplication of audio tour material is strictly prohibited. You will be asked to deposit handbags, cameras and recording equipment at the entrance to the house

ℹ️ **T** 0844 800 4791 (Infoline)
E 20forthlinroad@nationaltrust.org.uk

🎧 Audio tour features contributions from both Michael and Sir Paul McCartney

♿ 🚻 ⦂ 🅿 🎭 💻 ℹ️ Building 🔾

🏠 At nearby Speke Hall

💷 At nearby Speke Hall

🚶 Pushchairs admitted. Children's quiz/trail

🎒 Suitable for school groups

➡️ [108:SJ403862] Access is via minibus from Liverpool city centre or Speke Hall

🅿 No parking on site. Nearest car park at Speke Hall

NT properties nearby
Formby, Mr Hardman's Photographic Studio, Mendips, Rufford Old Hall, Speke Hall, Garden and Estate

20 Forthlin Road, Allerton, Liverpool

Gawthorpe Hall

Padiham, nr Burnley, Lancashire BB12 8UA

🏠 ❄️ 💷 🍴 🎧 🛡️ 🚶 📷 🔔 🍵 1972   (5:D6)

Elizabethan house with rich interiors and an important textile collection

This imposing house, set in tranquil grounds in the heart of urban Lancashire, resembles the great Hardwick Hall and is very probably by the same architect, Robert Smythson. In the middle of the 19th century Sir Charles Barry was commissioned to restore the house, thereby creating the opulent interiors we see today. The

For public transport details, see page 377

Long Gallery is hung with portraits of society figures from the 17th century, some of which are on loan from the National Portrait Gallery, London. Several rooms display part of the international collection of needlework, lace and costume assembled by the last family member to live here, Rachel Kay-Shuttleworth. The wooded park and riverside location offer wonderful walks.

⭐ Gawthorpe Hall is financed and run by Lancashire County Council. The NT only maintains a small administration office and a tea-room/shop. Please note that opening times and prices are controlled by Lancashire County Council and subject to change. Please tel. to confirm

ℹ️ T 01282 771004
E gawthorpehall@nationaltrust.org.uk

♿ 🅳♿⋯🅰📖🔼 Building 🔼
Grounds 🔼

💷 Coach House tea-room in the courtyard

👨‍👩‍👧 Baby-changing facilities. Children's quiz/trail

🎭 Suitable for school groups. Live interpretation. Hands-on activities. Adult study days

🐕 In grounds only and under close control

➜ [103:SD806340] **Foot**: pleasant walk by the River Calder from Padiham, ½ml; on route of Brontë Way public footpath. **Bus**: frequent Transdev Lancashire United and Burnley & Pendle buses from Burnley. All pass close ⊞ Burnley Barracks and ⊞ Burnley Manchester Road. **Station**: Rose Grove (U) 2ml. **Road**: on E outskirts of Padiham; ¾ml drive to house on N of A671; M65 exit 8 towards Clitheroe, then signposted from second traffic light junction to Padiham

🅿️ Free parking, 150yds. Tight access to site. Tight turning facilities

NT properties nearby
East Riddlesden Hall, Rufford Old Hall, Stubbins Estate

Gawthorpe Hall								
Hall/tea-room								
1 Apr–1 Nov	1–5	M	T	W	T	F	S	S
Garden								
All year	10–6	M	T	W	T	F	S	S
Tea-room opens 12:30. Open BH Mons and Good Fri								

Gondola

Pier Cottage, Coniston, Cumbria LA21 8AJ

🏠 🅰 🎭 👨‍👩‍👧 🎟️ 🍽️ 1980   (6:D8)

Rebuilt Victorian steam-powered yacht on Coniston Water

The original steam yacht *Gondola* was first launched in 1859 and now, completely rebuilt by the Trust, gives passengers the chance to sail in her sumptuous, upholstered saloons. This is the perfect way to view Coniston's spectacular scenery.

What's new in 2009 See website for details of guided walks combined with a cruise on *Gondola* and special evening cruises

⭐ NT members charged admission as *Gondola* is an enterprise. All sailings are weather permitting. No WC on board, nearest WC at Coniston Pier (Sat Nav LA21 8AN)

ℹ️ T 015394 41288
E gondola@nationaltrust.org.uk

🎭 Cruising the route of the original *Gondola* to Lake Bank. Campbell/*Bluebird* talks. Cruise on *Gondola* and guided walk of Monk Coniston Estate

♿ 🅿♿ ⋯ 🅰 Gangway 🔼🔼

Gondola steams across Coniston Water

Guidebook and *Gondola* souvenirs available on board

Pushchairs and baby back-carriers admitted

Suitable for school groups

Dogs in outside areas only

[96:SD307970] Sails from Coniston Pier (½ml from Coniston village). **Cycle**: no cycle parking. **Bus**: Stagecoach in Cumbria 505 from Windermere. **Station**: Foxfield (U), not Sun, 10ml; Windermere 10ml via vehicle ferry. **Road**: A593 from Ambleside. Pier is at end of Lake Road, turn immediately left after petrol station if travelling S from centre of Coniston village

Parking (not NT), 50yds, £2.20 (pay & display) at Coniston Pier. Two free coach parking spaces for booked groups

NT properties nearby

Beatrix Potter Gallery, Coniston and Tarn Hows, Hill Top

Gondola	
1 Apr–31 Oct	M T W T F S S

Steam yacht *Gondola* sails from Coniston Pier daily, weather permitting. Last sailing at 4. The National Trust reserves the right to cancel sailings and special charters in the event of high winds. In the event of cancellation due to adverse weather conditions, private charters or unforeseen operational difficulties, every reasonable effort will be made to inform the public. Piers at Coniston, Monk Coniston and Brantwood (not NT)

Enjoy a guided walk and cruise on *Gondola*

Grasmere and Great Langdale

High Close, Loughrigg, Ambleside, Cumbria LA22 9HH

1925 **(6:D8)**

Picturesque and varied landscape with Wordsworth connections

The protected area of 4,925 hectares (12,170 acres) includes ten farms and the famous Langdale Pikes. It also encompasses the glaciated valley of Mickleden, a Victorian garden at High Close and dramatic Dungeon Ghyll, as well as the bed of Grasmere lake and part of Rydal Water.

There is a spectacularly located NT campsite at Great Langdale, open all year [NY288057], charge (inc. NT members): tel. 015394 37668 or visit **www.langdalecampsite.org.uk**

T 015394 37663
E grasmere@nationaltrust.org.uk

Grounds

Suitable for school groups

Cycling on quiet roads and bridleways

[89/90:NY290060] Great Langdale valley starts 4ml W of Ambleside. **Bus**: to Grasmere information centre: Stagecoach in Cumbria 555/6, 599 from Windermere. To Langdale Campsite: Stagecoach in Cumbria 516 from Ambleside. **Station**: Windermere 8ml

Parking (pay & display). Three car parks in the two valleys, but none in Grasmere village

NT properties nearby

Beatrix Potter Gallery, Hill Top, Stagshaw Garden, Townend

Grasmere and Great Langdale	
All year	M T W T F S S

If the views at Grasmere and Great Langdale took your breath away, then you must experience Ullswater and Aira Force

Mr Hardman's Photographic Studio

59 Rodney Street, Liverpool L1 9EX

🏠 🏚 💆 👪 🔊 2003   **(5:B8)**

Beautiful Georgian terraced house – the former studio and home of the renowned local photographer E. Chambré Hardman

Situated just below the Anglican Cathedral in the centre of Liverpool is this fascinating house, home between 1947 and 1988 of Edward Chambré Hardman and his wife Margaret. The house contains a selection of photographs, the studio where most were taken, the darkroom where they were developed and printed, the business records and the Hardmans' living quarters – complete with all the ephemera of post-war daily life. The subject matter of the photographs – portraits of the people in Liverpool, their city and the landscapes of the surrounding countryside – provide a record of a more prosperous time when Liverpool was the gateway to the British Empire and the world. Parallel to this is the quality of Hardman's work and his standing as a photographer.

What's new in 2009 Programme of lectures

⭐ Admission by guided tour (booking not required but advised). Group size restricted to avoid overcrowding and to preserve the fragile contents

ℹ️ **T** 0151 709 6261
     E 59rodneystreet@nationaltrust.org.uk

💆 Range of events, from family summer holiday activities to specialist evening tours

♿ 🅿️ ♿ ⋮⋮ 📷 🎞️ 📺 📱 **Building** 🏛️

🏚 Guidebooks, prints and postcards on sale

👪 Pushchairs admitted. Hip-carrying infant seats for loan. Children's quiz/trail. Family days

🔊 Suitable for school groups

➡️ [108:SJ355895] Short walk N of Liverpool city centre. Rodney St is off Hardman St and Upper Duke St. Follow fingerposts.
     Ferry: Mersey Ferry 1ml. **Bus**: frequent from surrounding areas. **Station**: Liverpool Lime St ½ml. **Underground**: Liverpool Central ½ml

🅿️ No parking on site. Off-site parking most days near Anglican Cathedral (pay & display). Slater St NCP. Limited parking Rodney St and Pilgrim St (pay & display)

NT properties nearby
Formby, 20 Forthlin Road, Mendips, Rufford Old Hall, Speke Hall, Garden and Estate

Mr Hardman's Photographic Studio							
18 Mar–1 Nov	11–3:30	M	T	**W**	**T**	**F**	**S**	**S**

Open BH Mons. Admission by timed ticket only, inc. NT members. Visitors are advised to book in advance by tel. or email to property. Tickets on the day subject to availability

Prints at Mr Hardman's Photographic Studio

Hare Hill

Over Alderley, Macclesfield, Cheshire SK10 4QB

❄️ 🌳 🏞️ 🚶 1978   **(5:D8)**

Charming wooded and walled garden

This tranquil woodland garden, especially spectacular in early summer, includes more than 70 varieties of rhododendrons, plus azaleas, hollies and hostas. At its heart is a delightful walled area with a pergola and wire sculptures. The surrounding parkland has an attractive permitted path to nearby Alderley Edge.

⭐ Car park closes at 5

ℹ️ **T** 01625 584412
     E harehill@nationaltrust.org.uk

🚶 To Alderley Edge 2ml

♿ ♿ ⋮⋮ 📷 **Grounds** 🏞️ 🏞️

Unless indicated, last admission is always 30mins before closing time

🐕 Under close control at all times on the estate. Not in garden

➔ [118:SJ873763] **Station**: Alderley Edge 2½ml; Prestbury 2½ml. **Road**: between Alderley Edge and Macclesfield (B5087). Turn off N on to Prestbury Road. Left at T junction after 200yds, continue ¾ml, entrance on left. From Prestbury take Chelford Road 1½ml, entrance on right

P Parking. Not suitable for coaches

NT properties nearby
Alderley Edge, Dunham Massey, Lyme Park, Nether Alderley Mill, Quarry Bank Mill and Styal Estate, Tatton Park

Hare Hill									
4 Apr–10 May	10–5	M	T	**W**	**T**	F	**S**	**S**
11 May–31 May	10–5	**M**	**T**	**W**	**T**	**F**	**S**	**S**
3 Jun–29 Oct	10–5	M	T	**W**	**T**	F	**S**	**S**

Open BH Mons and Good Fri. Last admission 1hr before closing

Hawkshead and Claife

c/o Hill Top, Near Sawrey, Ambleside, Cumbria LA22 0LF

 1929   (6:D8)

Classic south Lakeland countryside with views of the fells and lakes and picturesque buildings

Hawkshead village, home to the Beatrix Potter Gallery, is surrounded by beautiful scenery, much of which is owned by the National Trust, some bequeathed by Beatrix Potter. This includes four miles of access along Windermere lakeshore from Ash Landing to Low Wray Bay. Claife Woodlands and the low-lying small farms between Hawkshead and Lake Windermere are typical of the area. Just north of the village is the Courthouse, which dates from the 15th century and is all that remains of the village manorial buildings (once held by Furness Abbey). Claife Station, on the west bank of Windermere, is a late 18th-century viewing station with glimpses of the lake. At Wray Castle there is access to the grounds, especially via boat.

⭐ There is a NT campsite in a superb location on the lakeshore at Low Wray [NY372012], check website for opening times and prices

The lovely garden at Hill Top in Cumbria

i **T** 015394 47997
E hawkshead@nationaltrust.org.uk

🚶 Occasional warden-led walks

♿ **Grounds** 👨‍🦽

🛍 See Beatrix Potter Gallery or Hill Top

📷 Suitable for school groups

🚴 Lakeshore track for mountain bikes from Harrowslack (SD388960) to St Margaret's Church (NY374006) along Windermere lakeshore (west)

➔ [96/97:SD352982] Hawkshead is 6ml SW of Ambleside. **Foot**: off-road path from Windermere ferry to Sawrey; many footpaths in the area. **Ferry**: Windermere ferry. **Bus**: Stagecoach in Cumbria 505 🚌 Windermere–Coniston. **Station**: Windermere 6ml via vehicle ferry

P Pay & display car parks at Ash Landing (close to ferry) and Harrowslack; free car park at Red Nab. All close to Lake Windermere. Pay & display car parks (not NT) in Hawkshead village

NT properties nearby
Beatrix Potter Gallery, Coniston and Tarn Hows, Fell Foot Park, Gondola, Hill Top, Townend

Hawkshead and Claife							
Countryside							
All year		**M**	**T**	**W**	**T**	**F**	**S**	**S**
Courthouse							
14 Mar–1 Nov	11–4	**M**	**T**	**W**	**T**	**F**	**S**	**S**

Hawkshead Courthouse: access by key from NT shop, The Square, Hawkshead or Beatrix Potter Gallery ticket office; free admission, but no parking facilities. Approx. ½ml walk from village

Hill Top

Near Sawrey, Hawkshead, Ambleside,
Cumbria LA22 0LF

🏠 ✿ 🍴 📷 ♿ 🚶 1944   **(6:D8)**

Delightful small 17th-century farmhouse where Beatrix Potter wrote many of her famous children's stories

Enjoy the tale of Beatrix Potter – Hill Top is a time-capsule of this amazing woman's life. Packed full of her favourite things, the house appears as if Beatrix had just stepped out for a walk. Every room contains a reference to a picture in a 'tale', as do the garden, village and surrounding countryside. The lovely cottage garden is a haphazard mix of flowers, herbs, fruit and vegetables, just as Beatrix used to plant. Her original watercolours are on display at the nearby Beatrix Potter Gallery.

What's new in 2009 Come and visit the house which was recreated for the film *Miss Potter* and see how many of the illustrations from the books you can see in real life

⭐ Hill Top is a small house and a timed entry system is in operation to avoid overcrowding and to protect the fragile interior. As at other NT properties last entry is 30 minutes before closing. As this can be a very busy property, visitors may sometimes have to wait to enter the house and early sell-outs are possible, especially at holiday times. Tickets cannot be booked in advance. Access to the garden and shop is always possible during opening hours

Beatrix Potter's bedroom at Hill Top

ℹ️ **T** 015394 36269 **E** hilltop@nationaltrust.org.uk

🎮 Easter trail

🚶 Occasional Beatrix Potter-themed guided walks in surrounding countryside with NT Warden

♿ ⠿ 📷 🦽 📖 ♿ Building 🦽 ♿ Grounds 🦽 ♿

📷 Specialises in Beatrix Potter-related items; mail order available all year, tel. 015394 36801 for details

☕ Drinks and treats available from shop. The neighbouring Tower Bank Arms and Sawrey House Country Hotel (both NT-owned and let to tenants) serve a variety of lunches, light refreshments and evening meals

➡️ [96/97:SD370955] 2ml S of Hawkshead, in hamlet of Near Sawrey; 3ml from Bowness via ferry. **Foot**: off-road path from ferry (2ml), marked. **Bus**: Cross Lakes Experience from Bowness Pier 3 across Lake Windermere on to Stagecoach in Cumbria 525; also 505 from 🚉 Windermere changing at Hawkshead (April–Sept only, plus weekends in Oct). Tel. 01539 445161 for complete ferry & bus timetable. **Station**: Windermere 4½ml via vehicle ferry. **Road**: B5286 and B5285 from Ambleside (6ml), B5285 from Coniston (7ml)

🅿️ Limited free parking, 150yds. Coaches must be booked. Roads are narrow and can be very busy, please allow extra time to park during peak times such as summer hols – avoid coming by car if possible

NT properties nearby
Beatrix Potter Gallery, Coniston and Tarn Hows, Fell Foot Park, *Gondola*, Hawkshead and Claife, Townend

Hill Top										
House			M	T	W	T	F	S	S
14 Feb–12 Mar	11–3:30		M	T	W	T		S	S
14 Mar–1 Nov	10:30–4:30		M	T	W	T		S	S
Shop/garden									
14 Feb–1 Mar	11–4		M	T	W	T	F	S	S
2 Mar–13 Mar	10–4		M	T	W	T	F	S	S
14 Mar–1 Nov	10:30–5		M	T	W	T	F	S	S
2 Nov–24 Dec	10–4		M	T	W	T	F	S	S

Open Good Fri & Fri 30 Oct. Limited number of timed tickets available daily

Little Moreton Hall

Congleton, Cheshire CW12 4SD

🏠 ✝ ❖ 🏛 ☕ 🍴 🎭 ♿ 🚻 🏮 🍷 1938

(5:D9)

Cheshire's most iconic black-and-white house – Tudor skill and craftsmanship at its finest

Gaze at the drunkenly reeling South Range, cross the moat and marvel at the cobbled courtyard before you enter a Hall full of surprises. The skill of the craftsmen fascinates, as you climb the stairs to the Long Gallery – imagine life here in Tudor times. The various delights of wall paintings, WCs over the moat, the Knot Garden, as well as colourful tales of the Moreton family and this iconic building itself, are revealed to you by our guided tours. Delicious home-baked local food and a visit to the shop complete your day.

What's new in 2009 Virtual tour. Radio loop system for guided tours

⭐ Pushchair access limited

Little Moreton Hall									
28 Feb–15 Mar	11–4	M	T	W	T	F	S	S
18 Mar–1 Nov	11–5	M	T	**W**	**T**	**F**	**S**	**S**
7 Nov–20 Dec	11–4	M	T	W	T	F	S	S

Open BH Mons. Closes dusk if earlier. Access during Yuletide celebrations restricted to ground floor, garden, shop and restaurant. Special openings at other times for booked groups

ℹ️ **T** 01260 272018
E littlemoretonhall@nationaltrust.org.uk

🎟️ Free guided tours, 28 Feb–29 Nov

🎭 Open-air theatre and regular events, including live interpretation and music. Chapel service Suns in main season

♿ 🅿️ 🅿️ 🚻 ∷ 📷 🔦 🖥️ 📹 ♿ ♿ ♿

Building ♿ ♿ ♿ ♿ **Grounds** ♿ ♿ ➡️

🛍️ NT shop. Plant sales

🍽️ Licensed restaurant. Home-cooked food with a regional and historic theme, using local produce where possible. Children's menu. Kiosk serving ice-cream, cold drinks, cakes and biscuits. Cold drinks in shop

🚼 Baby-changing facilities. Front-carrying baby sling and hip-carrying infant seats for loan. Children's guide. Children's quiz/trail. Family trail

🏛️ Suitable for school groups. Education room/centre. Live interpretation. Hands-on activities

➡️ [118:SJ832589] **Bus**: Stanways 315 ➡️ Alsager–Congleton (passing close ➡️ Kidsgrove). **Station**: Kidsgrove 3ml; Congleton 4½ml. **Road**: 4ml SW of Congleton, on E side of A34. From M6 jnct 17 & 18 follow A34 S

🅿️ Parking, 100yds

NT properties nearby
Alderley Edge, Biddulph Grange Garden, Quarry Bank Mill and Styal Estate

Little Moreton Hall: Cheshire's most iconic black-and-white house shows Tudor skill at its finest

Lyme Park

Disley, Stockport, Cheshire SK12 2NR

🏠 🚂 ✝ ❄ 🌳 ⛵ 🏠 🛍 ☕ 🚶 🎭 👫 🎬
🚶 ♿ 🍽 1947 (5:E8)

Lyme Park: the Dutch Garden and mansion

Glorious mansion house, surrounded by stunning gardens, moorland and ancient deer park

The mile-long drive to Lyme Park creates a real sense of anticipation, which the house more than matches up to. Originally Tudor, it now resembles a fabulous Italianate palace. Inside there are incredible Mortlake tapestries, an important collection of clocks, beautifully furnished rooms, along with a colourful family history. Stroll through the opulent Victorian garden, with its sunken parterre, or the Edwardian rose garden. Enjoy the luxurious Jekyll-style borders and Wyatt-designed Orangery, sit on the grass, or wander lazily by the lake (where Darcy and Elizabeth meet at 'Pemberley'), then venture beyond the garden, where the medieval deer park stretches into the distance; the vast moors and parkland are home to fallow and red deer. Seek out The Cage, an 18th-century hunting tower, or explore the woods and discover the lantern folly, with its breathtaking views. Delicious food, including venison from the park, is prepared in the Lyme kitchens; and with retail therapy at hand, Lyme really is a glorious day out.

What's new in 2009 Interactive exhibition about living and working at Lyme. 15th-century Caxton *Lyme Missal* on display from August

⭐ Lyme Park is owned and managed by the NT and partly financed by Stockport Metropolitan Borough Council. From October restaurant service may be restricted due to conservation work in kitchen

ℹ️ **T** 01663 762023
E lymepark@nationaltrust.org.uk

🎭 Conservation in action tours, 28 Feb, 1, 7 & 8 Mar, 11–5 (restricted numbers); house tours, 14 March–1 Nov, 11–12 (restricted numbers). Out-of-hours tours (extra charge inc. NT members)

✉️ Send sae for details

🚶 Walks leaflets in information centre

♿ 🅿️ 🅳 🦽 👓 📷 🔍 📖 🔊 Building 🔆 🔲
Grounds 🦽

🛍 Shops in The Timber Yard and house courtyard

🍽 Restaurant (licensed) in house. Children's menu. Coffee shop in The Timber Yard. Children's menu. Refreshment kiosk in main car park

👫 Baby-changing facilities. Front-carrying baby slings and hip-carrying infant seats for loan. Children's play area. Children's quiz/trail. Children's activity packs. Bottle-warming facilities

Show your card and display sticker for free parking

■ Suitable for school groups. Education room/centre

🐕 Under close control and only in park (in areas where livestock present on leads only)

🚲 Off-road cycling on the Knott area and hard surface roads only

➔ [109:SJ965825] **Foot**: northern end of Gritstone Trail; paths to Macclesfield Canal, Poynton Marina 1ml and Peak Forest Canal 2½ml. **Bus**: TrentBarton 199 Buxton–Manchester Airport, to park entrance. **Station**: Disley, ½ml from park entrance. NT courtesy bus from park admission kiosk to house for pedestrians on days house is open. **Road**: entrance on A6, 6½ml SE of Stockport (M60 exit 1), 12ml NW of Buxton (house and car park 1ml from entrance)

P Parking, coaches bringing booked groups to house and garden admitted free

NT properties nearby
Alderley Edge, Dunham Massey, High Peak Estate, Quarry Bank Mill and Styal Estate

Lyme Park		M	T	W	T	F	S	S
House/restaurant/shop								
28 Feb–8 Mar	11–5	M	T	W	T	F	**S**	**S**
14 Mar–1 Nov	11–5	**M**	**T**	W	T	**F**	**S**	**S**
Park								
1 Feb–31 Mar	8–6	**M**	**T**	**W**	**T**	**F**	**S**	**S**
1 Apr–11 Oct	8–8:30	**M**	**T**	**W**	**T**	**F**	**S**	**S**
12 Oct–31 Jan 10	8–6	**M**	**T**	**W**	**T**	**F**	**S**	**S**
Garden								
28 Feb–8 Mar	11–5	M	T	W	T	F	**S**	**S**
14 Mar–1 Nov	11–5	**M**	**T**	**W**	**T**	**F**	**S**	**S**
7 Nov–20 Dec	12–3	M	T	W	T	F	**S**	**S**
Timber Yard plant sales/shop								
1 Feb–8 Mar	11–4	M	T	W	T	F	**S**	**S**
14 Mar–1 Nov	10:30–5	**M**	**T**	**W**	**T**	**F**	**S**	**S**
7 Nov–29 Nov	11–4	M	T	W	T	F	**S**	**S**
2 Dec–3 Jan 10	11–4	M	T	**W**	**T**	**F**	**S**	**S**
9 Jan–31 Jan 10	11–4	M	T	W	T	F	**S**	**S**
Timber Yard coffee shop								
1 Feb–13 Mar	11–4	**M**	**T**	**W**	**T**	**F**	**S**	**S**
14 Mar–1 Nov	10:30–5	**M**	**T**	**W**	**T**	**F**	**S**	**S**
2 Nov–31 Jan 10	11–4	**M**	**T**	**W**	**T**	**F**	**S**	**S**

11–12 visit to house by guided tour only, restricted numbers. 28 Feb, 1, 7, 8 Mar Conservation in Action tours only, restricted numbers 11–5. Timber Yard closed Christmas Day

Lyme Park: glimpsed beyond the Long Border

Mendips

Woolton, Liverpool L25 7SA

🏠 🍴 🎧 👫 ■ 2002   (5:C8)

Childhood home of 20th-century icon John Lennon

Imagine walking through the back door into the kitchen where John Lennon's Aunt Mimi would have cooked him his tea. Join our Custodian on a fascinating trip down memory lane to life here, where John's passion for music began and where many early songs were written. Original photographs and other memorabilia are also on display. John's bedroom is a very atmospheric place in which to take a moment with your own thoughts about this incredible individual.

What's new in 2009 Extended opening period. To reserve your place on the tour visit www.nationaltrust.org.uk/beatles

⭐ No WC. **There is no direct access by car or on foot**. Visits are by combined minibus tour only with 20 Forthlin Road, the childhood home of Paul McCartney (charge inc. NT members). Any photography inside Mendips or duplication of audio tour material is strictly prohibited. You will be asked to deposit all handbags, cameras and recording equipment at the entrance to the house

Dogs assisting visitors with disabilities are always welcome

i **T** 0844 800 4791 (Infoline)
E mendips@nationaltrust.org.uk

🎧 Listen to extracts from interviews of former student lodgers who lived at Mendips

♿ 🔣 ⠿ 🅿️ 📷 🖥️ 🎧 Building ℹ️

🏠 At nearby Speke Hall

☕ At nearby Speke Hall

👪 Pushchairs admitted. Children's quiz/trail

🚩 Suitable for school groups

➡️ [108:SJ422855] Access is via minibus from Liverpool city centre or Speke Hall

P No parking on site. Nearest car park at Speke Hall

NT properties nearby
Formby, 20 Forthlin Road, Mr Hardman's Photographic Studio, Rufford Old Hall, Speke Hall, Garden and Estate

Mendips								
28 Feb–15 Mar	10, 12:30 & 3	M	T	**W**	**T**	**F**	**S**	**S**
18 Mar–1 Nov	10, 10:50, 2:30, 3:20	M	T	**W**	**T**	**F**	**S**	**S**
7 Nov–29 Nov	10, 12:30 & 3	M	T	**W**	**T**	**F**	**S**	**S**

Open BH Mons. Admission by guided tour only; 28 Feb–15 Mar & 7 Nov–29 Nov all tours depart from Liverpool city centre. 18 Mar–1 Nov morning tours depart from Liverpool city centre, afternoon tours depart from Speke Hall. To guarantee a place visitors are advised to book. Tel. Infoline or visit www.nationaltrust.org.uk/beatles

Nether Alderley Mill

Congleton Road, Nether Alderley, Macclesfield, Cheshire SK10 4TW

🚫 🚽 🚶 🖼️ 1950   (5:D8)

15th-century mill beside a tranquil mill pool

With its heavy oak framework, low beams and floors connected by wooden ladders set beneath an enormous sloping stone roof, this charming rustic mill is one of only four virtually complete corn mills in Cheshire.

⭐ The property can only be visited by booked groups. No WC

i **T** 01625 527468
E quarrybankmill@nationaltrust.org.uk

♿ Building ℹ️

🚩 Suitable for school groups

➡️ [118:SJ844763] **Bus**: Arriva 130 Manchester–Macclesfield (passing ☒ Alderley Edge). **Station**: Alderley Edge 2ml. **Road**: 1½ml S of Alderley Edge, on E side of A34

P Free limited NT parking. Space for one coach at a time, booking essential

NT properties nearby
Alderley Edge, Dunham Massey, Hare Hill, Quarry Bank Mill and Styal Estate, Tatton Park

Nether Alderley Mill
Sun 14 Jun, Sun 12 Jul, Sun 9 Aug, Sun 13 Sept. Groups at other times by prior arrangement

Take a fascinating trip down memory lane at Mendips, John Lennon's childhood home

Quarry Bank Mill and Styal Estate

Styal, Wilmslow, Cheshire SK9 4LA

1939   (5:D8)

One of Britain's greatest industrial heritage sites, showing how a complete industrial community lived

Quarry Bank, lying in the Bollin Valley, overflows with the atmosphere of the Industrial Revolution. Experience life as a mill worker – a visit to the cotton mill, powered by Europe's most powerful working waterwheel, will certainly stimulate your senses. The clatter of machinery and hiss of steam engines are astonishing. Take a tour of the Apprentice House, led by a costumed guide, and discover how – for food, clothing and lodgings – pauper children were expected to work in the mill. See the traditional vegetables, fruit and herbs still grown in the Apprentice House garden using organic methods and visit the recently opened three-hectare (eight-acre) 'Secret Garden' – the Greg family's stunningly picturesque valley retreat adjoining the mill. Stroll to Styal village – built by the Greg family to house the mill workers and still a thriving community, with two chapels, allotments and cottages. Or walk through woods along the River Bollin. Finally enjoy delicious local produce in our restaurant.

What's new in 2009 Extended restoration of the 'Secret Garden', the Greg family's picturesque valley retreat adjoining the Mill

⭐ Allow 1¼hrs minimum to visit Mill, 3½hrs to visit Mill, Apprentice House and the Secret Garden. Pushchairs are not permitted in the Mill or Apprentice House

ℹ **T** 01625 445896 (Infoline), 01625 527468
E quarrybankmill@nationaltrust.org.uk

🧥 Apprentice House: timed tickets only (limited availability), available from Mill on early arrival. Mill: occasional Suns, 2. Garden: Suns and Weds, 2

📖 See website or tel. for leaflet

🚶 Guided walk of woodlands and village every second Sun in month at 2. Additional historical and nature walks, see website

For public transport details, see page 377

Building 🔤🔤🔤 **Grounds** 🔤➡🔤

🏠 Selling souvenirs unique to the Mill together with a wide range of other gifts

🍴 Mill Restaurant (licensed) off Mill yard. Children's menu during school holidays. Mill Pantry serves snacks and ice-cream

👶 Baby-changing facilities. Front-carrying baby slings and hip-carrying infant seats for loan. Children's play area. Family trails

🏫 Suitable for school groups. Live interpretation. Hands-on activities

🐕 Under close control on estate. On lead only in Mill yard

🚲 Cycle route around Southern Woods

➡ [109:SJ835835] **Cycle**: NCN6, 1½ml. RCR85 ½ml. **Bus**: Swans Travel 'Shuttle' 200 ▣ Manchester Airport–Wilmslow. **Station**: Styal, ½ml (not Sun); Manchester Airport 2ml; Wilmslow 2½ml. **Road**: 1½ml N of Wilmslow off B5166, 2ml from M56, exit 5, 10ml S of Manchester. Heritage signs from A34 and M56

🅿 Parking, 200yds. Coaches £15 unless booked

NT properties nearby
Alderley Edge, Dunham Massey, Lyme Park, Tatton Park

Quarry Bank Mill and Styal Estate									
Mill/Apprentice House*									
28 Feb–1 Nov	11–5	M	T	W	T	F	S	S
4 Nov–13 Dec	11–4	M	T	W	T	F	S	S
19 Dec–27 Dec	11–4	M	T	W	T	F	S	S
28 Dec–3 Jan 10	11–4	M	T	W	T	F	S	S
6 Jan–31 Jan 10	11–4	M	T	W	T	F	S	S
Garden									
28 Feb–1 Nov	11–5	M	T	W	T	F	S	S
26 Dec–3 Jan 10	11–3	M	T	W	T	F	S	S
Shop/restaurant									
28 Feb–1 Nov	11–5	M	T	W	T	F	S	S
4 Nov–27 Dec	11–4	M	T	W	T	F	S	S
28 Dec–31 Jan 10	11–4	M	T	W	T	F	S	S

Open BH Mons, Boxing Day & New Year's Day. Closed 24/25 Dec. Mill: last admission 1hr before closing. *Apprentice House: limited availability – timed tickets only, available from Mill on early arrival

Apprentice House at Quarry Bank Mill

Rufford Old Hall

200 Liverpool Road, Rufford, nr Ormskirk, Lancashire L40 1SG

[T] 1936 (5:C6)

One of Lancashire's finest 16th-century Tudor buildings

Step back in time at one of Lancashire's finest 16th-century Tudor buildings, where a young Will Shakespeare once performed. His stage, the Great Hall, is as spectacular today as when the Bard was performing for the owner, Sir Thomas Hesketh, and his raucous guests. Wander around the house and marvel over the fine collections of furniture, arms, armour and tapestries. Then step outside and enjoy the gardens, topiary and sculpture and a walk in the woodlands, alongside the canal. Complete your visit with some delicious, freshly prepared local food in the cosy tea-room.

★ Admission charge may apply to NT members for special events

i **T** 01704 821254
E ruffordoldhall@nationaltrust.org.uk

By arrangement

Indoor and open-air plays and concerts. Victorian Christmas fair. Children's activities, inc. crafts and world-famous gnome hunt

Short canal and woodland walk

Building 🔲🔲🔲 Grounds 🔲➡

The Old Kitchen Tea-room (licensed). Christmas dinners. Children's menu

Baby-changing facilities. Front-carrying baby slings for loan. Children's guide. Children's quiz/trail. Bottle-warming service. Early learning toys

Suitable for school groups. Education room/centre. Hands-on activities. Adult study days

On leads and only in grounds, not in formal gardens

➔ [108:SD462161] **Foot**: adjoins towpath of Rufford extension of Leeds–Liverpool Canal. **Bus**: J&S 347 Southport–Chorley, Stagecoach in Lancashire 101 Preston–Ormskirk, Suns only. **Station**: Rufford (U), not Sun, ½ml; Burscough Bridge 2¼ml. **Road**: 7ml N of Ormskirk, in village of Rufford on E side of A59. From M6 exit 27, follow signs for Parbold then Rufford

P Free parking, 10yds. Car park can be very busy on summer days. Limited coach parking

NT properties nearby
Formby, Gawthorpe Hall, Speke Hall, Garden and Estate

Rufford Old Hall									
House/garden/shop/tea-room									
28 Feb–8 Mar	11–5	M	T	W	T	F	S	S
House									
14 Mar–1 Nov	11–5	M	T	W	T	F	S	S
14 Mar–31 Oct	1–5	M	T	W	T	F	S	S
Garden/shop*/tea-room									
14 Mar–1 Nov	11–5**	M	T	W	T	F	S	S
6 Nov–20 Dec	12–4	M	T	W	T	F	S	S

Open Good Fri. House entry, 11–1, by free guided tour only. *Shop also open Weds/Thurs in Dec, 12–4. **Garden closes 5:30

Please remember – your membership card is *always* needed for free admission

Sizergh Castle and Garden

Sizergh, nr Kendal, Cumbria LA8 8AE

[1950]   (6:E8)

Beautiful medieval house, extended in Elizabethan times, surrounded by rich gardens and estate in Cumbria's special limestone country

This imposing house, at the gateway to the Lake District, stands proud in a rich and beautiful garden with ponds, lake, an important collection of hardy ferns and a superb limestone rock garden. The estate is crossed by footpaths, giving stunning views over Morecambe Bay and the Lakeland hills. Still lived in by the Strickland family, Sizergh has many tales to tell, showing centuries-old portraits and fine furniture alongside modern-day family photos – it certainly feels lived in! The exceptional wood panelling culminates in the Inlaid Chamber, previously at the Victoria & Albert Museum, and returned here in 1999. Take time to explore the house and garden, sample fine local produce in our contemporary café, then follow one of our trail leaflets around the estate.

What's new in 2009 The exterior of the house, including previously hidden architectural detail, has been restored to its former glory following a two-year building project. Limited guided tours

Tulips in the garden at Sizergh

[i] T 015395 60951
E sizergh@nationaltrust.org.uk

Tours daily between 12 & 1. Limited availability (booking advisable). Tours can be joined on the day if places available

See website for details

Country walks on estate. Leaflets available from reception and shop

Building 🔲🔲🔲 Grounds 🔲➡🔲

NT shop. Plant sales

Licensed café

Baby-changing facilities. Front-carrying baby slings and hip-carrying infant seats for loan. Children's information sheets. Children's quiz

Suitable for school groups. Adult study days

On public footpaths, not in garden

➡ [97:SD498878] 3½ml S of Kendal.
Foot: footpaths 530002 and 530003 pass by Sizergh Castle. **Cycle**: NCN6, 1½ml. RCR20 passes main gate. **Bus**: Stagecoach in Cumbria 555/6 Keswick–Lancaster (passing close ≋ Lancaster); 552/3 Kendal–Arnside (passing ≋ Arnside). All pass ≋ Kendal. **Station**: Oxenholme 3ml. **Road**: M6 exit 36 then A590 towards Kendal, take Barrow-in-Furness turning and follow brown signs. From Lake District take A591 S then A590 towards Barrow-in-Furness

[P] Parking, 250yds

NT properties nearby
Arnside and Silverdale, Fell Foot Park, Townend

Sizergh Castle and Garden								
Castle								
15 Mar–1 Nov	12–5*	**M**	**T**	**W**	**T**	F	S	**S**
Garden								
15 Mar–1 Nov	11–5	**M**	**T**	**W**	**T**	F	S	**S**
Café/shop								
1 Feb–8 Mar	11–4	M	T	W	T	F	**S**	**S**
16 Feb–20 Feb	11–4	**M**	**T**	**W**	**T**	**F**	S	S
15 Mar–1 Nov	11–5	**M**	**T**	**W**	**T**	F	S	**S**
7 Nov–31 Jan 10	11–4	M	T	W	T	F	**S**	**S**

*Access to house by guided tour only between 12 and 1. Free flow begins at 1. At very busy times admission may be by timed ticket

Speke Hall, Garden and Estate

The Walk, Liverpool L24 1XD

🔔 1944 (5:C8)

Superb Tudor house with rich interiors, along with fine gardens and estate. Close to Liverpool City Centre – but with room to breathe

This rambling, atmospheric house spans the centuries – with a fine Great Hall and priest hole from the 16th century and an Oak Parlour and smaller cosy rooms from the Victorian era. Jacobean plasterwork and intricately carved furniture complete the picture. The fully equipped Victorian kitchen and servants' hall give a fascinating 'below stairs' experience. A lively trail and Tracker Packs, along with objects from the Dairy to be picked up and wondered at, mean children will be entertained. While the 21st-century Podcast tours will delight you – and perhaps even your teenagers. Wander through the garden for all seasons and enjoy spring bulbs, roses, summer borders, a delightful stream and autumn colour. Woodland walks give fabulous views of the North Wales hills and Mersey basin, while Home Farm, a model Victorian farm building, houses our shop and restaurant serving local food. There is also an orchard and children's play area.

Speke Hall: this rambling Tudor house has a wonderfully atmospheric interior

What's new in 2009 Extended opening hours and house tours. 'Behind Closed Doors' displays open up areas of the house not previously accessible. Sensory trail

⭐ Speke Hall is administered and financed by the NT with the help of a grant from the National Museums Liverpool

ℹ **T** 0844 800 4799 (Infoline), 0151 427 7231
E spekehall@nationaltrust.org.uk

🧑 Tudor tours by costumed guide when house open, £1. Tours of the roof space, £2.50 (not suitable for children under 12)

🎧 Podcast tours, available on MP3 players

🎭 Including Easter trails, Hallowe'en and Christmas family events. Open-air theatre and living history

🚶 Walks on The Bund and elsewhere on the estate. Leaflet guide. Family estate trail available at reception

Building 🅿️🅿️♿ Grounds ♿➡️

🏠 At Home Farm

🍴 Home Farm Restaurant 500yds from house. Locally sourced produce. Children's menu

Speke Hall, Garden and Estate									
House			M	T	W	T	F	S	S
28 Feb–15 Mar	11–4:30							S	S
18 Mar–1 Nov	11–5				W	T	F	S	S
7 Nov–13 Dec	11–4:30							S	S
Grounds									
1 Feb–15 Mar	11–dusk			T	W	T	F	S	S
17 Mar–1 Nov	11–5:30			T	W	T	F	S	S
3 Nov–31 Jan 10	11–dusk			T	W	T	F	S	S
Home Farm/restaurant/shop									
28 Feb–15 Mar	11–4:30							S	S
18 Mar–12 Jul	11–5				W	T	F	S	S
14 Jul–13 Sep	11–5			T	W	T	F	S	S
16 Sep–1 Nov	11–5				W	T	F	S	S
7 Nov–13 Dec	11–4:30							S	S

Open BH Mons. Grounds (garden and estate) closed 24–26 Dec, 31 Dec, 1 Jan 10. 11–1, entry to house by guided tour only, restricted numbers

Unless indicated, last admission is always 30mins before closing time

Baby-changing and feeding facilities. Front-carrying baby slings and hip-carrying infant seats for loan. Children's play area. Children's guide. Children's quiz/trail. Tracker Packs and MP3 audio tours of the house for loan. Pushchairs and back-carriers admitted at the Home Farm centre only. Family estate trail

Suitable for school groups. Education room/centre. Live interpretation. Hands-on activities

On leads on woodland and signed estate walks

→ [108:SJ419825] **Cycle**: NCN62, 1¾ml. **Bus**: Arriva 80A, Liverpool Great Charlotte Street–Liverpool Airport (passing ☒ Liverpool South Parkway) and close Liverpool Lime Street); 500 ☒ Liverpool Lime Street–Liverpool Airport; Supertravel 886 ☒ Liverpool South Parkway–Liverpool Airport. All to within ½ml. **Station**: Liverpool South Parkway 2ml; Hunt's Cross 2ml. **Road**: on N bank of Mersey, 1ml off A561 on W Liverpool Airport. Follow airport signs from M62 exit 6, A5300; M56 exit 12

P Free parking, 100yds

NT properties nearby
Formby, 20 Forthlin Road, Mr Hardman's Photographic Studio, Mendips, Rufford Old Hall

Stagshaw Garden

Ambleside, Cumbria LA22 0HE

⚬ 🚻 1957 (6:D8)

Steep woodland garden, noted for its flowering shrubs

The garden was created by the late Cubby Acland, Regional Agent for the Trust. It contains a fine collection of shrubs, including rhododendrons, azaleas and camellias. Adjacent to the garden are Skelghyll Woods, which offer delightful walks and access to the fells beyond.

★ No WC

i **T** 015394 46027
E stagshaw@nationaltrust.org.uk

♿ Grounds ♿

🚻 Pushchairs admitted. Steep paths in places, with steps

→ [90:NY380029] **Ferry**: landing at Waterhead ½ml. **Bus**: Stagecoach in Cumbria 555/6, 599 from ☒ Windermere. **Station**: Windermere 4ml. **Road**: ½ml S of Ambleside on A591

P Free parking. Not suitable for coaches. Very limited; access dangerous due to poor visibility; further pay & display parking for cars and coaches (not NT) ½ml at Waterhead

NT properties nearby
Ambleside, Townend, Windermere and Troutbeck

Stagshaw Garden								
1 Apr–30 Jun		10–6:30	M	T	W	T	F	S S
July to end Oct: by appointment, send sae to Property Office, St Catherine's, Patterdale Road, Windermere LA23 1NH								

Tatton Park

Knutsford, Cheshire WA16 6QN

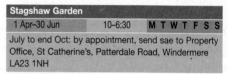

1960 (5:D8)

Estate with neo-classical mansion, extensive gardens, farm and medieval Old Hall, within large deer park

This is one of the most complete historic estates open to visitors. The early 19th-century Wyatt house sits amid a landscaped deer park and is opulently decorated, providing a fine setting for the Egerton family's collections of pictures, books, china, glass, silver and specially commissioned Gillows furniture. The theme of Victorian grandeur extends into the garden, with its Fernery, Orangery, Rose Garden, Tower Garden, Pinetum, and Italian and Japanese gardens. The restored Walled Garden includes a Kitchen Garden and magnificent glasshouses, where traditional methods of gardening are used. Other features include a 1930s working rare breeds farm, a children's play area, speciality shops and 400-hectare (1,000-acre) deer park.

What's new in 2009 Expanded and upgraded Housekeeper's Store. Land train takes families from the playground to the farm (weekends in high season and school holidays)

★ Tatton Park is financed, administered and maintained by Cheshire County Council. Without this commitment the Trust would not

The kitchen at Tatton Park, Cheshire

have been able to acquire this property. Members have free admission to the house and gardens only and pay half-price entry to the farm. Members must pay car entry charges each visit and supplementary charges for special events, eg RHS Flower Show or Christmas openings

[i] **T** 01625 374435 (Infoline), 01625 374400
E tatton@cheshire.gov.uk

[🚶] Guided tours of mansion at 12. Medieval Old Hall tours (special open days only). Garden tours on Fri. Japanese Garden tours, Wed and Sat

[♥] RHS Flower Show, 22–26 July. Hallé concert, Aug. Open-air theatre and concerts throughout the season. A Tour Through Time in the Old Hall. Antique fairs, car shows, family events at the farm and historical festivals. Christmas events. See website for details

[🚶] Some waymarked walks. Walks leaflets available

[♿] [Pd] [Dd] [WC] [:•] [⌀] [▭] [♪] [↟] [▥]
Building [♿][♿][♿] **Grounds** [♿][♿][➡][✧]

[🛍] Tatton Gifts (not NT). Award-winning, * expanded Housekeeper's Store selling estate and local food produce. Garden shop selling plants, gifts and seasonal produce from the Kitchen Garden

[🍴] Stables Restaurant (not NT) (licensed) in stableyard. Serves hot and cold food from quality local ingredients. Children's menu. Tuck shop adjacent to restaurant selling ice-creams and snacks in high season

[👪] Baby-changing facilities. Front-carrying baby slings for loan. Children's play area, quiz/trail

[🏫] Suitable for school groups. Education room/centre. Live interpretation. Hands-on activities. Adult study days

[🐕] On leads at farm and under close control in park. Not in gardens

[🚲] Cycle hire available from stableyard. Tel. 01827 284646

[→] [109/118:SJ745815] **Cycle**: Cheshire Cycleway passes property. **Bus**: Bakers 27 from Macclesfield (passing close [🚉] Macclesfield) Suns & BHols April–Sept; otherwise from surrounding areas to Knutsford, then 2ml. **Station**: Knutsford 2ml. **Road**: 2ml N of Knutsford, 4ml S of Altrincham, 5ml from M6, exit 19; 3ml from M56, exit 7, well signposted on A556; entrance on Ashley Road, 1½ml NE of junction A5034 with A50

[P] Parking charge inc. NT members

NT properties nearby
Alderley Edge, Dunham Massey, Little Moreton Hall, Lyme Park, Quarry Bank Mill and Styal Estate

Tatton Park										
House										
28 Mar–4 Oct	1–5	M	T	W	T	F	S	S		
Gardens										
28 Mar–4 Oct	10–6	M	T	W	T	F	S	S		
6 Oct–31 Jan 10	11–4	M	T	W	T	F	S	S		
Shops										
28 Mar–4 Oct	10:30–5	M	T	W	T	F	S	S		
6 Oct–31 Jan 10	11–4	M	T	W	T	F	S	S		
Restaurant										
28 Mar–4 Oct	10–6	**M**	**T**	**W**	**T**	**F**	**S**	**S**		
6 Oct–31 Jan 10	11–4	M	T	W	T	F	S	S		

Open BH Mons. Last admission 1hr before closing. House: special opening Oct half-term and Christmas events in Dec. Guided tours Tues–Sun 12 by timed ticket (available from garden entrance after 10:30) on first-come, first-served basis. Limited number of tickets. For prices and opening times for other attractions please contact Tatton Park. Tel. 01625 374400 or visit www.tattonpark.org.uk. Closed 25 Dec

Townend

Troutbeck, Windermere, Cumbria LA23 1LB

🏠 ⁑ 🛡 ♿ 🎒 1948   (6:D8)

17th-century Lake District stone and slate house, former home of a wealthy farming family

A real Lakeland hidden treasure set in the beautiful village of Troutbeck, this 17th-century solid stone and slate house sits imposingly on the hillside, its huge chimneys typical of the area. The Brownes lived here for generations, a wealthy, hardworking family, who loved wood carving, books and furniture, and collected them in this homely place. See fascinating kitchen and domestic tools, along with period clothing and the cosy servants' rooms. Our children's trail brings it all to life. A real fire in the 'down house' (the original kitchen) most days helps makes this a 'must do' visit when in the Lake District.

ℹ️ **T** 015394 32628
   E townend@nationaltrust.org.uk

🎭 Conservation demonstrations and living history

♿ 📖 📖 ⠿ 🖼 🖥 Building 🔦
Grounds 🔦 📷

👶 Hip-carrying infant seats for loan. Children's quiz/trail

🎒 Suitable for school groups. Live interpretation. Hands-on activities

➡️ [90:NY407023] 3ml SE of Ambleside at S end of Troutbeck village. **Bus**: Stagecoach in Cumbria 555, 559 from 🚆 Windermere, alight Troutbeck Bridge, 1½ml. **Station**: Windermere 2½ml. **Road**: off A591 or A592

🅿️ Free parking, 300yds. Not suitable for coaches

NT properties nearby
Fell Foot Park, Stagshaw Garden, Windermere and Troutbeck

Townend								
28 Feb–29 Mar*	11–3	M	T	W	T	F	**S**	**S**
1 Apr–1 Nov	11–5	M	T	**W**	**T**	**F**	**S**	**S**

Open BH Mons *Feb/March: entry by hourly guided tour only (due to conservation work). April–Nov: entry by guided tour, 11 & 12; free flow, 1–5. Places on guided tours are limited & available on a first-come first-served basis. May close early due to poor light

Ullswater and Aira Force

Tower Buildings, Watermillock, Penrith, Cumbria CA11 0JS

🌳 ⛵ 🛡 ♿ 🎒 🚶 🐕 1906   (6:D7)

Beautiful lake winding through a glaciated valley, and an impressive waterfall

Dramatic walks around Aira Force waterfall, renowned in Victorian times as a beauty spot, are among the highlights of the Trust's ownership in the valley. This totals 5,242 hectares (13,000 acres) of fell and woodland, and four farms (including Glencoyne, the largest). There is access to parts of Brotherswater and Ullswater, site of Wordsworth's famous daffodils.

ℹ️ **T** 017684 82067
   E ullswater@nationaltrust.org.uk

♿ 🚻 🔦 Grounds 📷 ➡️

🍽 Tea-room (not NT) at Aira Force. Tel. 017684 82881. Tea-room (not NT) at Side Farm, Patterdale. Tel. 017684 82337 (walkers only, no parking)

👶 Steps and slopes to waterfall at Aira Force, difficult for pushchairs

🎒 Suitable for school groups

➡️ [90:NY401203] 7ml S of Penrith. **Cycle**: NCN71, 2ml. **Bus**: Stagecoach in Cumbria 108 🚆 Penrith–Patterdale. **Station**: Penrith 10ml

🅿️ Parking. Two pay & display car parks at Aira Force and Glencoyne Bay. Coaches by arrangement

NT properties nearby
Acorn Bank Garden and Watermill, Townend

Ullswater and Aira Force							
All year	**M**	**T**	**W**	**T**	**F**	**S**	**S**

Townend: wonderfully homely interior

Most Trust properties offer Gift Aid on Entry for non-members, see page 10

Wasdale, Eskdale and Duddon

The Lodge, Wasdale Hall, Wasdale,
Cumbria CA20 1ET

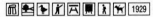 1929 **(6:C8)**

Vast area of open country – valleys, mountains, rivers and lake – from wild Wasdale to the Duddon Estuary

In Wasdale the Trust owns England's highest mountain, Scafell Pike (978m), and deepest lake, Wastwater, which has impressive scree slopes. The six valley farms are also owned by the Trust, as are the surrounding mountains – including Great Gable and the famous historic wall patterns at the valley head. Lower down the valley is the wooded and tranquil 600-hectare (1,482-acre) Nether Wasdale Estate with six farms. Over 5,000 hectares (12,300 acres) and eleven farms are protected in neighbouring Eskdale, with extensive areas of fell, six farms and Hardknott Roman Fort. In the beautiful and quiet Duddon Valley the Trust cares for 3,300 hectares (8,000 acres) and nine farms.

★ The stunningly located NT campsite at Wasdale Head (with accessible WC) and shop are open Easter to end Oct (and Nov to Easter 2010 with limited facilities) [NY183076]; charge (inc. NT members). Tel. 019467 26220 or visit www.wasdalecampsite.org.uk for details

ℹ️ T 019467 26064 E wasdale@nationaltrust.org.uk

♿ Grounds 🏔️

▣ Suitable for school groups

➔ [NY152055] Wasdale–Wastwater: 5ml E of A595 Cumbrian coast road from Barrow to Whitehaven, turning at Gosforth. Also from Santon Bridge. Eskdale [NY177013]–Boot: 6ml E of A595, turning at Eskdale Green. Also from Santon Bridge. Duddon [NY196932]–Ulpha: 3ml N of A595, turning at Duddon Bridge near Broughton-in-Furness.
Station: Drigg 8ml; Dalegarth (Ravenglass & Eskdale Rly) ¼ml from Eskdale; Foxfield 8ml from Duddon; Seascale 8ml from Wasdale

P Parking (NT pay & display) at Wasdale Head

NT properties nearby
Dalton Castle, Sandscale Haws

Wasdale, Eskdale and Duddon							
All year	M	T	W	T	F	S	S

Windermere and Troutbeck

St Catherine's, Patterdale Road, Windermere,
Cumbria LA23 1NH

▣ 1927 **(6:D8)**

Fine walking country around the shores of Windermere, including Bridge House and the Footprint Building

This property includes the beautiful and secluded head of the Troutbeck Valley, as well as several sites next to Windermere and eleven farms. One of these, Troutbeck Park, was once owned by Beatrix Potter and was her largest farm. Ambleside Roman Fort, tiny Bridge House in Ambleside and Cockshott Point on the lake at Bowness-on-Windermere are all popular places to visit. Footpaths lead from Ambleside over Wansfell to the Troutbeck Valley and offer high-level views and contrasting valley landscapes. A Community Learning Officer is based at the property and educational group visits and other activities can be arranged.

What's new in 2009 Exciting education programme for school groups

★ No WC

ℹ️ T 015394 46027
E windermere@nationaltrust.org.uk

🛡️ Annual out-and-about events

♿ Grounds 🏔️ ➡️

▣ Suitable for school groups. New 'Footprint' learning centre available by arrangement

➔ [90:NY407023] **Bus**: Stagecoach in Cumbria 555/6, 599 from ▆ Windermere, alight Troutbeck Bridge, then 1½ml walk.
Station: Windermere 2½ml. **Road**: Troutbeck is signposted E of A591 Windermere to Ambleside road

P Car parks (not NT)

NT properties nearby
Fell Foot Park, Stagshaw Garden, Townend

Windermere and Troutbeck							
All year	M	T	W	T	F	S	S

Wordsworth House and Garden

Main Street, Cockermouth, Cumbria CA13 9RX

🏠 ❀ ⬜ ⚒ 🗄 ♿ 👥 🖼 1938   (6:C7)

Birthplace and childhood home of William Wordsworth – a 'living' 1770s townhouse

The garden at Wordsworth House

Step back to the 1770s and experience life as William and his sister Dorothy might have done. Meet and talk to the household staff as you explore this award-winning property. Many of the rooms are there for you to enjoy as if you were a guest of the Wordsworth family – there are even toys for the children to play with and books to read. The maid will show you the Georgian kitchen and you can enjoy tastings of recipes popular at the time (18th-century Cumberland food is cooked in the kitchen daily). You may meet the clerk in the office used by William's father and test your writing skill with quill pen and ink; you may also hear music from the harpsichord drifting through the house. William loved his home, and refers to the views and the River Derwent in his poem The Prelude. The peaceful walled garden contains flowers, fruit, herbs and vegetables of the period – all of which are used in the house. The Discovery Room has interactive touch screens and fascinating research material. For a preview go to www.wordsworthhouse.org.uk then come and visit us in person.

What's new in 2009 Original Wordsworth manuscripts now on display. Wedding photography packages

ℹ️ **T** 01900 820884 (Infoline), 01900 824805
   E wordsworthhouse@nationaltrust.org.uk

👥 Family activities in school holidays: trails, art and craft activities and games. Talks in the garden and the house. Regular cooking and harpsichord demonstrations. Cockermouth festival in the summer. Evening events and study days

♿ 🅿♿ 🔊♿ 🔤 ♿ 📷 🎵 📖 📺 ♿ 🏷
Building ♿⬆♿ **Grounds** ♿

🍴 Refreshments available at nearby cafés

👥 Baby-changing facilities. Family activities in school holidays: trails, art and craft activities and games

🖼 Suitable for school groups. Education room/centre. Live interpretation. Hands-on activities. Adult study days, talks and harpsichord demonstrations

🐕 On leads in front garden only

➜ [89:NY118307] **Foot**: close to all town car parks and bus stop. **Cycle**: NCN71 (C2C), 7ml. NCN10 (Reivers) passes door. **Bus**: Stagecoach in Cumbria X4/5 🚉 Penrith–Workington; AA/Hoban/Reay's 35/6 Workington–Cockermouth. All pass close 🚉 Workington. **Station**: Workington 8ml, Maryport 6½ml. **Road**: just off A66, in Cockermouth town centre

🅿 No parking on site. Parking in town centre car parks. Long stay car park (not NT) 300yds on Wakefield Road, walk back over footbridge to house

NT properties nearby

Borrowdale: Force Crag Mine, Buttermere and Ennerdale, Derwent Island House

Wordsworth House and Garden									
House									
28 Feb–29 Mar	11–5*		M	T	W	T	F	**S**	**S**
1 Apr–31 Oct	11–5		**M**	**T**	**W**	**T**	**F**	**S**	**S**
Shop									
16 Feb–21 Feb	10–4		**M**	**T**	**W**	**T**	**F**	**S**	S
25 Feb–29 Mar	11–5		M	T	**W**	**T**	**F**	**S**	**S**
1 Apr–22 Dec	10–5		**M**	**T**	**W**	**T**	**F**	**S**	S

Last entry 4. Timed tickets may operate on busy days.
*For Waking-up the House events only (limited availability)

Dogs assisting visitors with disabilities are always welcome

Yorkshire

Yorkshire is famed for its acres of green fields and drystone walls. It is a haven for walkers and is a place where everyone can find peace, quiet and enjoyment.

In this spectacular region the National Trust owns nearly 5,400 hectares (13,343 acres) of land in the Yorkshire Dales and twelve miles of coastline, including part of the Cleveland Way.

A proud heritage

But as well as the rolling countryside, Yorkshire is proud of its industrial past. No better can this be seen than at Gibson Mill on the Hardcastle Crags Estate in West Yorkshire. This former cotton mill faced stiff competition from larger mills in Lancashire and, although it struggled through the 19th century, it was eventually forced to close. The mill was not left empty for very long, however, and soon found a new role – as an entertainments emporium. There was a roller skating rink inside, then, when the weather was cold, ice-skating could be enjoyed on the outer mill pond.

The top floor housed a café – with first and second-class dining – and in the evening the building was a

regular venue for dancing until as recently as the 1950s. In fact the mill was so popular that people would happily walk nearly twenty miles from Halifax and Huddersfield to enjoy the property. However, following the Second World War, the mill lay largely unused until 2005, when the National Trust was able to open it to the public again for the first time in 50 years.

Exhibitions at Gibson Mill

The mill offers visitors to Hardcastle Crags an opportunity to learn more about the crags and the mill itself. 'Hands-on' exhibitions inside Gibson Mill give visitors an exciting interactive experience. The exhibitions explore:

■ the industrial past of the mill;

■ the social heritage of the people who worked there, lived nearby and used the mill in their leisure time;

■ the natural beauty of Hardcastle Crags.

Above left:
Yockenthwaite Top Farm in the Yorkshire Dales
Above: **Hardcastle Crags**

Old toll road sign at Gibson Mill

Previous page: **the Peak Alum Works at Ravenscar in the north of the county**

Due to its location at the heart of a wooded valley, the building also gave the Trust the opportunity to look at ways to use green technology to keep the mill working and offer a

Works and absolutely unmissable. Here you can find out more about the twelve miles of spectacular coastline which is cared for by the National Trust.

Above: **Robin Hood's Bay**
Above right: **the Malham Tarn Estate**

The biomass boiler at Gibson Mill

sustainable way for it to run. This became a reality, and the mill's only connection with the outside world is now a telephone line! The mill's entire operation is maintained using sustainable technologies, including photo-voltaic and solar panels, water-powered turbines and a biomass boiler using locally harvested wood.

Industry, sea and green fields

There are many other opportunities to find out more about Yorkshire's industrial heritage. On the coast at Ravenscar, for example, you can visit the former site of the Peak Alum Works. This is a fascinating industrial archaeological site as well as a haven for wildlife, it is also hugely interesting for anyone with an interest in geology. Alum shale was quarried from the hillside and was used in liquor production at the site from 1650 to 1860, this was then used in dyeing and tanning leather. At Ravenscar village itself, there is the National Trust Coastal Centre. This is just a short walk from the Peak Alum

Meadows as far as the eye can see

No better can our heritage be seen than in the Yorkshire Dales, where centuries of farming have given us a landscape that is so familiar and yet so stunning. With drystone walls, green fields and meadows stretching as far as the eye can see, everyone should take the opportunity to discover the Yorkshire countryside. The Malham, Upper Wharfedale and Tarn Estates contain some of the finest upland landscapes in the Yorkshire Dales, with limestone pavements, waterfalls, and flower-rich hay meadows criss-crossed with stone walls and studded with traditional field barns. Caring for nearly 3,000 hectares (7,500 acres) in Malhamdale, the National Trust has waymarked walks and trails throughout the Dales, from Malham Cove to Fountains Fell. So go for a ramble, a circular walk or follow a trail across the ancient limestone pavements. Take a route around Malham Tarn, which with adjacent areas of raised bog, fen and woodland is protected as a National Nature Reserve. This special area is home to a unique community of rare plants and animals, as well as being the focal point of an outstanding industrial past. Come and stand high on the open moor, with the mist swirling round, and thoughts of man's first contact with the area thousands of years ago come flooding to mind.

region of classic upland limestone country. The limestone pavements in the Dales are a unique and irreplaceable habitat that has formed as a result of erosion by water over the centuries. Today it supports unusual and diverse plant communities. Visitors can discover more by joining one of the summer wildflower walks in Malhamdale or Upper Wharfedale hosted by the Trust.

Majestic Marsden Moor

If you love the outdoors and want to get out into the open countryside then take a walk on Marsden Moor. This windswept landscape appears bleak and inhospitable, but provides grazing for cattle and sheep and is home to numerous birds, such as golden plover, red grouse, curlew, snipe and the diminutive twite – in fact the estate is designated as an international Special Protection Area for birds. Footpaths across the moor sometimes follow ancient packhorse routes, from where it is possible to glimpse evidence of the estate's

It is easy to imagine Mesolithic hunters sitting around a campfire, or that you can hear the chink of Roman Centurions' armour as they march from Chester to York, or even – from our more recent industrial past – the rattle of pack horses' harnesses and clatter of workers' clogs. Walking at Marsden is not always for the faint-hearted – so why not join one of many guided walks with our volunteers and discover stunning views, inspiring history and a rich variety of moorland?

Above left: **limestone pavement on Malham Moor**
Above: **walking on Marsden Moor**

Spot a curlew on Marsden Moor

www.nationaltrust.org.uk/coastandcountryside

Beningbrough Hall and Gardens

Beningbrough, York, North Yorkshire YO30 1DD

1958 (5:G4)

18th-century house with interactive galleries and National Portrait Gallery paintings. Grounds and working walled garden

A grand 1716 Georgian mansion with an impressive baroque interior, set in a park and gardens. There are more than 100 18th-century portraits and seven interpretation galleries, designed in partnership with the National Portrait Gallery. There is a fully equipped Victorian laundry, with wet and dry rooms, and a delightful walled garden which supplies The Walled Garden Restaurant. There are many family facilities, including a wilderness play area.

What's new in 2009 House galleries, gardens, grounds, shop and restaurant are now open winter weekends. Georgian costumed interpretation on many days. Walled Garden Restaurant uses produce from the walled garden. New visiting exhibition of portraits from the National Portrait Gallery's collection, together with innovative hands-on activities in seven interpretation galleries

⭐ Some ground and first-floor rooms have no electric light. Visitors wishing to make a close study of the interior and portraits should avoid dull days early and late in the season

ℹ️ **T** 01904 472027
E beningbrough@nationaltrust.org.uk

🚶 Garden walks most weekends. 'Meet the Victorian laundry maid' (usually last Sat in month)

🎧 Free audio guides for the house, including programme for visually impaired people

🎭 Programme of events, summer concerts and themed restaurant evenings

🚶 Public footpath along the River Ouse. Permitted walk through the Pike Pond Woods

Building 🦽♿ Grounds 🦽♿

🛍️ NT shop and small plant centre, second-hand bookshop

🍴 Walled Garden Restaurant (licensed). Hot lunches 12–2:30. Gluten-free and vegetarian lunch options available. Children's menu. Kiosk in the garden open on busy days. Special themed evening functions. Restaurant uses produce from the walled garden and mainly local and organic suppliers

👪 Baby-changing facilities. Hip-carrying infant seats for loan. Wilderness play area, including large fort. Family art workshops linked to the portraits in the house

🏫 Suitable for school groups. Learning Centre. Live interpretation (Victorian below stairs and Georgian costumes). Making Faces art workshops. Hands-on interpretation. Outreach programme for rural schools. Community groups – tours and workshops available

🚲 2ml of NT-permitted cycle path through parkland. NT-Sustrans (65) leaflet available

The walled garden at Beningbrough Hall, North Yorkshire

→ [105:SE516586] **Foot**: footpath from York, along River Ouse, 10ml. **Cycle**: NCN65.
Bus: Stephensons 39 York–Easingwold.
Station: York 8ml. **Road**: 8ml NW of York, 2ml W of Shipton, 2ml SE of Linton-on-Ouse (A19)

P Free parking, 100yds. Coaches must come via A19 and use coach entrance. No coach access from the west via Aldwark toll bridge

NT properties nearby
Fountains Abbey and Studley Royal, Nunnington Hall, Rievaulx Terrace and Temples, Treasurer's House

Beningbrough Hall and Gardens									
Grounds/shop/restaurant									
1 Feb–8 Feb	11–3:30	M	T	W	T	F	**S**	**S**
14 Feb–22 Feb	11–3:30	**M**	**T**	**W**	T	F	**S**	**S**
1 Mar–8 Mar	11–3:30	M	T	W	T	F	**S**	**S**
14 Mar–30 Jun	11–5:30	**M**	**T**	**W**	T	F	**S**	**S**
1 Jul–31 Aug	11–5:30	**M**	**T**	**W**	**T**	**F**	**S**	**S**
1 Sep–1 Nov	11–5:30	**M**	**T**	**W**	T	F	**S**	**S**
7 Nov–31 Jan 10	11–3:30	M	T	W	T	F	**S**	**S**
House									
1 Mar–8 Mar	11–3:30	M	T	W	T	F	**S**	**S**
14 Mar–30 Jun	11–5	**M**	**T**	**W**	T	F	**S**	**S**
1 Jul–31 Aug	11–5	**M**	**T**	**W**	T	**F**	**S**	**S**
1 Sep–1 Nov	11–5	**M**	**T**	**W**	T	F	**S**	**S**
Galleries only									
1 Feb–8 Feb	11–3:30	M	T	W	T	F	**S**	**S**
14 Feb–28 Feb	11–3:30	**M**	**T**	**W**	T	F	**S**	**S**
1 Mar–8 Mar	11–3:30	M	T	W	T	F	**S**	**S**
7 Nov–31 Jan 10	11–3:30	M	T	W	T	F	**S**	**S**
Open Good Fri. Closed 27/28 Dec & 3/4 Jan 10									

Braithwaite Hall

East Witton, Leyburn, North Yorkshire DL8 4SY

🏠 1941   (5:E3)
17th-century farmhouse in beautiful Coverdale
⭐ No WC
ℹ **T** 01969 640287
  E braithwaitehall@nationaltrust.org.uk
→ 1½ml SW of Middleham, 2ml W of East Witton (A6108). Narrow approach road

Braithwaite Hall
May–Sept By arrangement in advance with the tenant, Mrs Duffus

Bridestones, Crosscliff and Blakey Topping

c/o Peakside, Ravenscar, Scarborough, North Yorkshire YO13 0NE

🏠👁🍴📷👁🚻♿🚶👤 1944   (5:I3)

Moorland nature reserve with peculiar rock formations

The Bridestones and Crosscliff Estate covers an area of 488 hectares (1,205 acres) and is a mixture of farmland, open moorland and woodland. Bridestones Moor – named after its peculiar rock formations created from sandstone laid down under the sea during the Jurassic period – is a SSSI and nature reserve with typical moorland vegetation, including three species of heather, an ancient woodland estimated to date from the end of the last Ice Age, and herb-rich meadows. The Bridestones Nature Trail is approximately 1½ miles long and leads visitors through a range of habitats. Blakey Topping at the northern end of Crosscliff Moor is the result of massive erosion by glacial meltwater and now gives a superb 360° view from its summit.

⭐ Access by car is via Forest Enterprise's Forest Drive: toll payable (inc. NT members). WC at Staindale Lake car park

ℹ **T** 01723 870423
  E bridestones@nationaltrust.org.uk

🎭 Children's events during summer hols

♿ P♿ 📷♿ Grounds ♿

🚻 Children's events during summer hols

📷 Suitable for school groups. Hands-on activities. Adult study days

🐕 On leads only

→ [94:SE877906] In North York Moors National Park. **Foot**: from Hole of Horcum via Old Wives' Way. **Cycle**: along Forest Drive.
Bus: to Bridestones: Moorsbus M6 from Thornton le Dale (connections from York and Scarborough), Sun, April–Oct and daily in Aug; otherwise Yorkshire Coastliner 840 Leeds–Whitby to within 2¼ml. To Blakey Topping: Yorkshire Coastliner 840 Leeds–Whitby, 1½ml. **Road**: 3½ml along Dalby Forest Drive (toll payable) which starts 2½ml N of Thornton-le-Dale NE of Pickering

---

For general and membership enquiries, please telephone 0844 800 1895

P Free parking (not NT), 100yds. Further parking at Staindale Lake, Crosscliff Viewpoint or Hole of Horcum (for Blakey Topping)

NT properties nearby
Nunnington Hall, Ormesby Hall, Rievaulx Terrace and Temples, Roseberry Topping, Scarthwood Moor, Yorkshire Coast

Bridestones			
All year			M T W T F S S

The Monster Rock at Brimham Rocks, North Yorkshire

Brimham Rocks

Summerbridge, Harrogate,
North Yorkshire HG3 4DW

🚲🏠🍽️🅿️👥🚻🏛️🚶 1970   (5:F4)

Dramatic moorland rock formations

Covering an area of 162 hectares (400 acres) and at a height of nearly 300 metres, Brimham Rocks enjoy spectacular views over the surrounding countryside. Set within the Nidderdale Area of Outstanding Natural Beauty, this fascinating moorland is filled with strange and fantastic rock formations and is rich in wildlife.

★ The property can be extremely busy on fine weekends, particularly from July to August, and Bank Holidays. Car parking is limited and queuing may be necessary. No barbecues

ℹ️ T 01423 780688
E brimhamrocks@nationaltrust.org.uk

👥 Family trails. Guided walks

🚶 Guided walks throughout year

♿ 🅿️🚻👓🔊🐕 Building 🏛️🏢 Grounds 🏢

☕ Kiosk near Brimham House. Serves light refreshments

🚼 Baby-changing facilities

🎒 Suitable for school groups

🐕 Under strict control at all times and on leads during April, May & June (ground-nesting birds)

➜ [99:SE206650] 10ml SW of Ripon.
Foot: Nidderdale Way passes through.
Bus: Harrogate & District 24 ⊠ Harrogate–Pateley Bridge, alight Summerbridge, 2ml. Suns & BHols 'Nidderdale Rambler' 26 Pateley Bridge–Brimham Rocks circular. **Road**: 11ml NW of Harrogate off B6165, 10ml SW of Ripon, 4ml E of Pateley Bridge off B6265

P Parking (pay & display). £4 up to 4hrs, £5 over 4hrs; motorcycles free; minibuses £8 all day; coaches £15 all day. Pay machines only take coins. Coaches/groups welcome but must book in advance

NT properties nearby
East Riddlesden Hall, Fountains Abbey and Studley Royal, Malham Tarn and Moor

Brimham Rocks			
All year	8–dusk		M T W T F S S
Shop/exhibition/kiosk			
14 Feb–22 Feb	11–5		M T W T F S S
28 Feb–5 Apr	11–5		M T W T F S S
6 Apr–19 Apr	11–5		M T W T F S S
25 Apr–24 May	11–5		M T W T F S S
25 May–4 Oct	11–5		M T W T F S S
10 Oct–25 Oct	11–dusk		M T W T F S S
26 Oct–1 Nov	11–dusk		M T W T F S S
7 Nov–27 Dec	11–dusk		M T W T F S S

Shop, kiosk and exhibition room also open BHol, 4 May & 1 Jan 10. Facilities may close in bad weather

For public transport details, see page 377

East Riddlesden Hall

Bradford Road, Keighley,
West Yorkshire BD20 5EL

1934   **(5:E5)**

**17th-century West Riding manor house
with formal and wild gardens, duckpond
and grounds**

Every time that you stand in the gardens of East
Riddlesden you will experience something new –
the pink cherry trees, clematis, borders, daffodils
and soothing lavender beds all create a sense of
tranquillity far removed from the bustle of
modern life. The house is a hidden gem above
the Aire Valley, where visitors can enjoy a picnic
and children play. This air of peace is far
removed from the Hall's tumultuous past, which
includes tales of dastardly deeds that the dark
sandstone of the Hall can only hint at. Going into
the Hall feels like walking through someone's
home, it has a cosy lived-in feel, and creates a
relaxing atmosphere where visitors can feel at
ease examining the exquisite embroideries and
blackwork, oak furniture and pewter.

What's new in 2009 Bird feeding area. Improved
Herb Garden with modern interpretation. New
Victorian session now available for schools

East Riddlesden Hall								
House/shop/tea-room								
28 Feb–1 Nov	11–4	**M**	**T**	**W**	T	F	**S**	**S**

House: entry 4–5 by free guided tour only. Shop and
tea-room: open as house; 7 Nov–20 Dec, open Sat &
Sun only, 12–4

ℹ️ **T** 01535 607075
    E eastriddlesden@nationaltrust.org.uk

🎭 Costumed tours, specialist tours, spooky
tours and evening tours for private groups,
subject to availability

🎭 Open-air theatre, children's events and open-
air concerts. Children's open-air trails and
school holiday programme

🚶 A permissive path runs alongside the river

♿ ... Building 🔵🔵🔵 Grounds 🔵

🛍️ NT shop. Plant sales

☕ Tea-room on first floor of bothy (no
pushchairs, space limited). Home-made
soups. Children's menu

👶 Baby-changing facilities. Hip-carrying infant
seats for loan. Children's play area. Grass
maze. Children's events. Outdoor Tracker
Packs

🏫 Suitable for school groups. Hands-on
activities. Live interpretation on various days
throughout the year. New Victorian session
now available

🐕 On leads and only in grounds, not garden

➡️ [104:SE079421] **Bus**: Keighley & District 662
   🚉 Bradford Interchange–Keighley, alight
Granby Lane. **Station**: Keighley 1½ml.
Road: 1ml NE of Keighley on S side of the
Bradford Road in Riddlesden, close to Leeds
& Liverpool Canal. A629 relief road from
Shipley and Skipton signed for East
Riddlesden Hall

🅿️ Free parking, 100yds. Parking for one coach.
Narrow entrance to property. No double-
decker coaches

NT properties nearby
Fountains Abbey and Studley Royal, Gawthorpe
Hall, Hardcastle Crags, Malham Tarn and Moor

East Riddlesden Hall, West Yorkshire: a hidden gem

Most Trust properties offer Gift Aid on Entry for non-members, see page 10

Fountains Abbey, North Yorkshire: these monastic ruins, the largest in the country, date from the 12th century

Fountains Abbey and Studley Royal Water Garden

Fountains, Ripon, North Yorkshire HG4 3DY

 1983 (5:F4)

Yorkshire's first World Heritage Site. Cistercian abbey, elegant Georgian water garden and medieval deer park

Set in the beautiful Skell Valley, this World Heritage Site offers a great day out for all the family. Lose yourself in the passages, staircases and towers of the largest monastic ruins in the country and marvel at a unique relic of ancient craftsmanship. Then explore the 12th-century abbey ruins, Elizabethan mansion (three rooms open to the public), medieval deer park and one of England's most spectacular Georgian water gardens – complete with neo-classical statues, follies and breathtaking surprise views. And, if this were not enough, there is also the only surviving 12th-century Cistercian corn mill in Britain, with interactive displays and an exhibition of artefacts from the abbey.

What's new in 2009 Major restoration of Studley Lake

★ The NT works in partnership with English Heritage to care for this site. EH maintains the Abbey (owned by the NT) and owns St Mary's Church (managed by the NT)

ℹ️ **T** 01765 608888
E fountainsenquiries@nationaltrust.org.uk

Free volunteer-led guided tours of abbey, deer park and water garden, April–Oct, plus extended tours of complete estate throughout the year. Special Christmas and winter tours

Available from admissions, £2

Open-air theatre, inc. Shakespeare and children's classics. Autumn concerts in abbey. Medieval re-enactments. Autumn drive through. Christmas entertainment. Religious services. Children's trails and craft workshops in school hols

Walking trails leaflet listing five walks, £1.50 from admissions and shops. Wildlife walks. Guided historical tours. Children's school holiday trails

Building 🔲🔲🔲 **Grounds** 🔲🔲🔲🔲

Two shops, at Visitor Centre and at entrance to water garden. Plant sales (herbs & flowers)

Fountains Restaurant (licensed) at Visitor Centre. Children's menu. Licensed tea-room

For further information, visit www.nationaltrust.org.uk

at entrance to water garden. Kiosk at Fountains Mill (ice-cream and beverages, limited opening)

👭 Baby-changing and feeding facilities. Pushchairs and baby back-carriers admitted. Children's activities and quiz/trail in school holidays. Play area near Visitor Centre. Open-air theatre, inc. children's classics

▊ Suitable for school groups. Education room/centre

🐕 On short leads only. Enclosed dog walk/WC at Visitor Centre

🚲 Cycling allowed through the deer park

➜ [99:SE271683] **Foot**: 4ml from Ripon via public footpaths and bridleways.
Cycle: signed on-road cycle loop.
Bus: Harrogate District Community Transport (Ripon Roweller 139) Ripon–Markington (connections with Harrogate & District 36 from Harrogate). **Road**: 4ml W of Ripon off B6265 to Pateley Bridge, signposted from A1, 12ml N of Harrogate (A61)

P Free parking at Visitor Centre car park. Parking at Studley Royal deer park £3 (pay & display). Coach parking at Visitor Centre only. Access off B6265

NT properties nearby
Beningbrough Hall and Gardens, Brimham Rocks, East Riddlesden Hall, Malham Tarn Estate

Fountains Abbey and Studley Royal									
Abbey/garden/Visitor Centre/mill									
1 Feb–28 Feb	10–4	M	T	W	T	F	S	S	
1 Mar–31 Oct	10–5	M	T	W	T	F	S	S	
1 Nov–31 Jan 10	10–4	M	T	W	T	F	S	S	
Restaurant									
1 Feb–30 Apr	10–4	M	T	W	T	F	S	S	
1 May–31 Oct	10–5	M	T	W	T	F	S	S	
1 Nov–31 Jan 10	10–4	M	T	W	T	F	S	S	
St Mary's									
1 Apr–30 Sep	12–4	M	T	W	T	F	S	S	
Deer park									
All year	Dawn–dusk	M	T	W	T	F	S	S	

Estate will close at dusk, if earlier than stated closing time. Whole estate closed 24/25 Dec & on Fri in Nov, Dec & Jan 10. Estate open on Fri in Feb. Studley Royal shop and tea-room opening times vary, check at property

Goddards Garden

27 Tadcaster Road, York, North Yorkshire YO24 1GG

✿ 𝙄 ⌂ 👭 1983   **(5:H5)**

Formal and informal gardens with a variety of features

The former home of Noel Goddard Terry of the famous York chocolate-making firm, the house was built in 1927 in the Arts & Crafts style and was designed by the firm of Brierley and Rutherford (it is now the Yorkshire office of the NT and not open to the public). The garden, designed by George Dillistone of Tunbridge Wells, complements the style of the house – with formal yew-hedged garden rooms, a bowling green, tennis court and herbaceous borders, plus wilderness gardens. There are plants of interest for every season and this tranquil garden is an oasis for wildlife and home to one of the few British colonies of midwife toads.

What's new in 2009 Plant-of-the-month information sheet and plant sales

⭐ House not open to public (used as office space)

i **T** 01904 702021
E goddardsgarden@nationaltrust.org.uk

𝙄 Tours by arrangement

♿ **Grounds** ♿ ➡

👭 Pushchairs admitted

🐕 On leads

➜ [105:SE884498] **Bus**: First York 4, 12, 13; Yorkshire Coastliner 840, 842, 843, 845, X44 from ➤ York. **Station**: ➤ York 1½ml.
Road: follow York outer ring road (A1237/A64), turn on to A1036 Tadcaster Road, signed to York racecourse, past York College, then turn right after St Edward's church, through brick gatehouse arch

P Free parking. Not suitable for coaches

NT properties nearby
Beningbrough Hall and Gardens, Treasurer's House

Goddards Garden								
16 Mar–30 Oct	11–4:30	M	T	W	T	F	S	S

Closed BHols. Last admission 1hr before closing

Charges for National Trust members apply on some special event days

Hardcastle Crags

Hollin Hall, Crimsworth Dean, Hebden Bridge,
West Yorkshire HX7 7AP

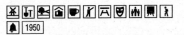

1950 (5:E6)

Beautiful wooded valley with 19th-century Gibson Mill at its heart, an exemplar of sustainable energy

A hidden beauty spot in the South Pennines with more than 160 hectares (400 acres) of unspoilt woodland. As well as being the home of the northern hairy wood ant, there are tumbling streams, glorious waterfalls and stacks of millstone grit, all crisscrossed by more than eighteen miles of footpaths. At its heart is Gibson Mill, a family-oriented visitor centre with hand-operated interactive displays, dressing up, dancing and exhibitions. With no link to the national grid, the mill is unique in the UK and is the National Trust's flagship sustainable building.

What's new in 2009 Civil ceremonies at Gibson Mill

⭐ Visitors are encouraged to come on foot, by cycle or public transport. Car parking and cycle racks available at Clough Hole car park on Widdop Road and Midgehole car park on Midgehole Road. During busy times limited car parking leads to heavy congestion. There are steep drops and water hazards throughout the property. Gibson Mill has narrow and low doorways and uneven floors. Gibson Mill may be closed if there is insufficient power. WC not always available, WCs at Gibson Mill (only when mill open)

ℹ️ **T** 01422 844518
E hardcastlecrags@nationaltrust.org.uk

The rock-strewn Hebden Water, Hardcastle Crags

Hardcastle Crags								
Hardcastle Crags								
All year		M	T	W	T	F	S	S
Gibson Mill as a minimum								
1 Feb–29 Mar	11–3	M	T	W	T	F	S	S
1 Apr–30 Apr	11–4	M	T	W	T	F	S	S
2 May–16 Jul	11–4	M	T	W	T	F	S	S
18 Jul–30 Aug	11–4	M	T	W	T	F	S	S
1 Sep–31 Oct	11–4	M	T	W	T	F	S	S
1 Nov–31 Jan 10	11–3	M	T	W	T	F	S	S
Muddy Boots Café								
1 Feb–29 Mar	11–3	M	T	W	T	F	S	S
1 Apr–30 Apr	11–4	M	T	W	T	F	S	S
2 May–16 Jul	11–4	M	T	W	T	F	S	S
18 Jul–30 Aug	11–5	M	T	W	T	F	S	S
1 Sep–30 Sep	11–4	M	T	W	T	F	S	S
1 Oct–31 Oct	11–4	M	T	W	T	F	S	S
1 Nov–31 Jan 10	11–3	M	T	W	T	F	S	S

Open Good Fri & BH Mons. Mill: open Mon–Thur: 14–22 Feb, 4–19 Apr, 23–31 May, 24 Oct–1 Nov & 19–31 Dec. Café: open 11–5 weekends in May–July and Sept. If limited power, café or parts of mill may close

🏃 Guided walks throughout the year. Send sae for details. Orienteering course, technical tours and members' tours of Gibson Mill by arrangement

🎭 Send sae for details

🚶 Four walks, in a figure of eight, with Gibson Mill in the middle

♿ Building Grounds

🍽️ Muddy Boots Café. Light refreshments and snacks only

† Baby-changing facilities. Pushchairs and baby back-carriers admitted

▮ Suitable for school groups. Education room/centre

🐾 Under control at all times

➔ [103:SD988291] **Foot**: access on foot via riverside walk from Hebden Bridge. Pennine Bridleway passes property. **Bus**: First 593 from ▤ Hebden Bridge to within 1ml. **Station**: Hebden Bridge 2ml. **Road**: at end of Midgehole Road, 1½ml NE of Hebden Bridge off the A6033 Keighley road

P Parking (pay & display). Midweek £3, weekend £4, weekend half day £2.50; motorcycle £1; minibus £5

NT properties nearby
East Riddlesden Hall, Gawthorpe Hall, Marsden Moor Estate

Maister House

· 160 High Street, Hull, East Yorkshire HU1 1NL

 1966   **(5:J6)**

18th-century merchant's house

Rebuilt in 1743 during Hull's heyday as an affluent trading centre, this house is a typical but rare survivor of a merchant's residence of that period. The restrained exterior belies the spectacular plasterwork staircase inside. The house is now let as offices.

★ Staircase and entrance hall only on show. No WC

i **T** 01723 870423
E maisterhouse@nationaltrust.org.uk

♿ Building 🔽

➔ [107:TA102287] In Hull city centre.
Cycle: NCN65. **Bus**: local services to within 100yds. **Station**: Hull ¾ml

P No parking on site

NT properties nearby
Treasurer's House, Yorkshire Coast

Maister House								
All year		10–4	**M**	**T**	**W**	**T**	**F**	S S
Closed BHols								

Dogs assisting visitors with disabilities are always welcome

Malham Tarn Estate

Yorkshire Dales Estate Office, Waterhouses, Settle, North Yorkshire BD24 9PT

⛺ ⛏ 🏠 ⚔ 😷 † ▮ ⚹ ♿ 1946   **(5:D4)**

High moorland landscape with dramatic limestone features

This outstanding area of 2,900 hectares (7,200 acres), consisting of upland hill farms, flower-rich hay meadows and characteristic limestone pavements, provides a marvellous setting for walking, cycling or just enjoying the great outdoors. The National Nature Reserve at Malham Tarn is home to a unique community of rare plants and animals; the bird hide provides excellent views of the Tarn's varied birdlife.

What's new in 2009 New windows in the bird hide provide clearer views across Malham Tarn and now also into the surrounding woodland

The rocky shoreline of Malham Tarn

★ WC available at the National Park car park in Malham

i **T** 01729 830416
E malhamtarn@nationaltrust.org.uk

⚔ Guided walks, inc. wild flower and bat walks

😷 Family events and guided walks

⚹ A selection of walks on the estate is included in walks leaflets, available from the National Park centre or Town Head Barn in Malham

♿ Grounds 🔽

[i] Family events inc. feeding the lambs at Easter

[i] Suitable for school groups. Farming exhibition in Town Head Barn, Malham. Farm visits by arrangement

[i] On leads only – stock grazing

[i] Off-road cycling permitted on bridleways

[→] [98:SD890660] Estate extends from Malham village, 19ml NW of Skipton, N past Malham Tarn. **Foot**: 6ml of Pennine Way & ⅔ml of Pennine Bridleway on property. **Bus**: Pennine 210 from Skipton–Malham (passing ≠ Skipton). **Station**: Settle 7ml

[P] Parking (not NT) in Malham village (pay & display). Free parking at Watersinks car park on south side of Malham Tarn

NT properties nearby
Brimham Rocks, East Riddlesden Hall, Fountains Abbey and Studley Royal, Upper Wharfedale

Malham Tarn Estate								
Estate								
All year		M	T	W	T	F	S	S
Town Head Barn								
1 Feb–29 Mar	10–4	M	T	W	T	F	S	**S**
31 Mar–1 Nov	10–4	M	**T**	**W**	**T**	**F**	**S**	**S**
8 Nov–13 Dec	10–4	M	T	W	T	F	**S**	**S**
3 Jan–31 Jan 10	10–4	M	T	W	T	F	**S**	**S**

Marsden Moor Estate

Estate Office, The Old Goods Yard, Station Road, Marsden, Huddersfield, West Yorkshire HD7 6DH

[🏛️][⚐][🍴][🚻][📷][🚌][😊][■][🚶][🚴] [1955] **(5:E7)**

Huge area of peak and moorland

The Estate, covering nearly 2,429 hectares (5,685 acres) of unenclosed common moorland and almost surrounding the village of Marsden, takes in the northern part of the Peak District National Park, with valleys, reservoirs, peaks and crags, as well as archaeological remains dating from pre-Roman times to the great engineering structures of the canal and railway ages. The landscape supports large numbers of moorland birds, such as golden plover, red grouse, curlew and diminutive twite. The Estate, a designated SSSI, forms part of an international Special Protection Area and is a candidate Special Area of Conservation.

[★] Public WC in Marsden village. The 'Welcome to Marsden' exhibition at the NT Estate Office gives a good insight into the area

[i] **T** 01484 847016
E marsdenmoor@nationaltrust.org.uk

[🚶] Send sae to Estate Office for events and guided walks leaflet – a pocket guide to Marsden, including six self-guided walks and a heritage trail covering Tunnel End and Marsden village

[♿] **Exhibition** [♿] **Grounds** [♿]

[🏪] Plant sales at events and some weekends at Estate Office

[■] Suitable for school groups

[i] On leads only

[🚴] Two bridleways cross the property. Also possible to undertake circular rides using these together with quiet roads

[→] [109:SE025100] **Foot**: Kirklees Way and Pennine Way pass through the property. Huddersfield Narrow Canal towpath nearby. **Bus**: First 183/4 from Huddersfield. **Station**: Marsden (adjacent to estate office). **Road**: estate covers area around Marsden village, between A640 and A635

[P] Free parking areas around the Estate, inc. in Marsden village (not NT) and at Buckstones and Wessenden Head (NT)

NT properties nearby
East Riddlesden Hall, Hardcastle Crags, High Peak Estate, Lyme Park, Nostell Priory and Parkland

Marsden Moor Estate								
Estate								
All year		M	T	W	T	F	S	S
Exhibition								
All year	9–5	M	T	W	T	F	S	S

Gritstone Edge on Marsden Moor

Moulton Hall

Moulton, Richmond, North Yorkshire DL10 6QH

🏠 🕴 1966   (5:F2)

17th-century manor house

ℹ️ **T** 01325 377227
  E moultonhall@nationaltrust.org.uk

➡️ 5ml E of Richmond; turn off A1, ½ml S of
  Scotch Corner

Moulton Hall
By arrangement with the tenant, Viscount Eccles

Mount Grace Priory

Staddle Bridge, Northallerton,
North Yorkshire DL6 3JG

✝️ 🏠 🎭 🎭 🚻 🏛️ 🕴 1953   (5:G3)

Ruin of a 14th-century Carthusian priory

This is England's most important Carthusian
ruin. The individual cells reflect the hermit-like
isolation of the monks; a reconstruction enables
visitors to see the austere and simple
furnishings. There is a small herb garden.

⭐ The priory is financed, administered and
  maintained by English Heritage. Please contact
  property to check details before your visit

ℹ️ **T** 01609 883494
  E mountgracepriory@nationaltrust.org.uk

♿ 🚻 Building 🏛️ Grounds 🏛️

🏪 Shop. Herbs for sale May–Aug

🥤 Hot drinks machine, cold drinks & snacks
  from shop (EH)

🚻 Baby-changing facilities. Pushchairs and baby
  back-carriers admitted. Children's quiz/trail.
  Family activity packs

🏛️ Suitable for school groups

➡️ [99:SE449985] **Foot**: Cleveland Way within
  ⅜ml. **Cycle**: NCN65, 2½ml. **Bus**: Abbott 80,
  89 ➡️ Northallerton–Stokesley, alight Priory
  Road End, ½ml. **Station**: Northallerton 6ml.
  Road: 6ml NE of Northallerton, ½ml E of A19
  and ½ml S of its junction with A172

🅿️ Free parking

For public transport details, see page 377

NT properties nearby
Fountains Abbey and Studley Royal, Nunnington
Hall, Ormesby Hall, Rievaulx Terrace and Temples

Mount Grace Priory									
21 Mar–28 Sep	10–6	**M**	T	**W**	T	**F**	**S**	**S**
2 Oct–31 Jan 10	10–4	**M**	T	**W**	T	**F**	**S**	**S**
Closed 24–26 Dec & 1 Jan 10								

The Billiard Room at Nostell Priory, West Yorkshire

Nostell Priory and Parkland

Doncaster Road, Nostell, nr Wakefield,
West Yorkshire WF4 1QE

🏠 ✝️ ❄️ 🍴 🏠 🍴 🕴 🎭 🚻 🏛️ 🕴 ♿ 🔔
🍴 1954   (5:G6)

**18th-century architectural masterpiece
with Adam interiors, Chippendale furniture,
fine collections and landscape park and
gardens**

Former home of the Winn family for 300 years,
Nostell Priory was built by James Paine on the
site of a medieval priory for Sir Rowland Winn,
4th Baronet, in 1733. Later Robert Adam was
commissioned to complete the state rooms,
which are among the finest examples of his
interiors. The Priory houses England's best
documented collections of Chippendale furniture,
designed especially for the house by the great
cabinetmaker. Other treasures include an
outstanding art collection, with works by Pieter
Brueghel the Younger and Angelica Kauffmann,

the remarkable 18th-century doll's-house (with its original fittings and Chippendale-style furniture), one of the finest libraries in the National Trust's portfolio and the John Harrison long-case clock with its extremely rare movement made of wood. In the grounds are wonderful lakeside walks with a stunning collection of rhododendrons, azaleas and a delightful magnolia avenue in spring. More than 121 hectares (300 acres) of parkland are open to the public.

What's new in 2009 Exhibitions and trails telling the story of the house and Winn family through the ages. Annually changing exhibitions in the museum room. New car park planned for spring

i **T** 01924 863892
E nostellpriory@nationaltrust.org.uk

ℹ Including free introductory talks in house. Occasional conservation tours (booking required). Upstairs Downstairs tours (booking required)

☺ Craft and country fairs, open-air theatre and jazz and other musical spectaculars. Children's events every Thurs in Aug. Licensed for civil weddings. One cabinet or commode open each day every week. Family croquet, giant chess set. Send sae for details

☾ Walks from the front of the house, alternate Weds evenings, 7, Thurs & Fri, 10:30

♿ Pₐ Dₐ ♿ ⚫ ◎ 🅰 ⚫ ⚫
Building **♿ ♿ ⬍ ♿** Grounds **♿ ➡ ♿**

🛍 NT shop and plant sales

☕ Stables tea-room. Serving lunches and refreshments. Children's menu

👪 Baby-changing and feeding facilities. Front-carrying baby slings and hip-carrying infant seats for loan. Children's play area. Children's quiz/trail. Family activity packs. Family area in tea-room. Children's events every Thurs in Aug. Family croquet

🏫 Suitable for school groups. Education room/centre. Adult study days

🐕 On leads only in park

🚲 Permitted in the park

➔ [111:SE407172] **Cycle:** NCN67, 3ml.
Bus: Arriva 496 Wakefield–Doncaster; also Arriva 485, B Line 123, 223, 244 from

Wakefield. **Station:** Fitzwilliam 1½ml.
Road: on A638 5ml SE of Wakefield towards Doncaster

P Parking, £2 (refunded on purchase of adult house or garden ticket)

NT properties nearby
Clumber Park, East Riddlesden Hall, Hardcastle Crags, Marsden Moor Estate, Mr Straw's House

Nostell Priory and Parkland

House*

		M	T	W	T	F	S	S
28 Feb–1 Nov	11–5	M	T	**W**	**T**	**F**	**S**	**S**
12 Dec–20 Dec	11–4	M	T	**W**	**T**	**F**	**S**	**S**

Grounds/shop/tea-room

		M	T	W	T	F	S	S
28 Feb–1 Nov	11–5:30	M	T	**W**	**T**	**F**	**S**	**S**
7 Nov–6 Dec	11–5	M	T	W	T	F	**S**	**S**
12 Dec–20 Dec	11–5	M	T	**W**	**T**	**F**	**S**	**S**
26 Dec–3 Jan 10	11–4	M	T	**W**	**T**	**F**	**S**	**S**
9 Jan–31 Jan 10	11–4	M	T	W	T	F	**S**	**S**

Parkland

		M	T	W	T	F	S	S
All year	9–7	**M**	**T**	**W**	**T**	**F**	**S**	**S**

*House open 11–1 for guided tours. Open 16 & 17 Dec, 5–8. Open BH Mons: house 11–5; gardens, shop & tea-room 11–5:30, parkland closes dusk if earlier. Rose garden may be closed on occasions for private functions

Detail of the Top Hall, Nostell Priory, West Yorkshire

Nunnington Hall

Nunnington, nr York, North Yorkshire YO62 5UY

🏠 ✿ 📷 🍽 🎋 🦚 👫 🏛 1953   **(5:H4)**

Picturesque Yorkshire manor house with organic garden and exciting programme of exhibitions

The sheltered walled garden, with spring-flowering organic meadows, orchards and flamboyant peacocks, complements this beautiful Yorkshire house, nestling on the quiet banks of the River Rye. Take the afternoon to enjoy and absorb the atmosphere of this former family home. Explore period rooms while hearing the Hall's many tales, and then discover one of the world's finest collections of miniature rooms in the attic. The Hall also holds a series of important art and photography exhibitions during the year. Why not make a day of it? Its close proximity to Rievaulx Terrace makes it an ideal afternoon visit after a walk at Rievaulx Terrace in the morning.

What's new in 2009 Now opening at 11

🛈 **T** 01439 748283
   E nunningtonhall@nationaltrust.org.uk

🎟 Full events list available

♿ 📖 🔊 👓 🖼 Building 🪜♿
Grounds 🪜

📷 NT shop. Plant sales

🍽 Restaurant within historic building. Children's menu

Ripening apples at Nunnington Hall

Nunnington Hall									
28 Feb–1 Nov	11–5	M	T	W	T	F	S	S
7 Nov–12 Dec	11–4	M	T	W	T	F	**S**	**S**
Open BH Mons									

👫 Baby-changing and feeding facilities. Hip-carrying infant seats for loan. Children's quiz/trail. Children's activity packs

🏛 Suitable for school groups

➔ [100:SE670795] **Bus**: Stephensons 196 Hovingham–Helmsley. **Road**: in Ryedale, 4½ml SE of Helmsley (A170) Helmsley–Pickering road; 1½ml N of B1257 Malton–Helmsley road; 21ml N of York, B1363. Nunnington Hall is 7½ml SE of the NT Rievaulx Terrace and Temples

🅿 Free parking, 50yds

NT properties nearby
Beningbrough Hall and Gardens, Bridestones, Ormesby Hall, Rievaulx Terrace and Temples, Treasurer's House

Ormesby Hall

Church Lane, Ormesby, nr Middlesbrough, Redcar & Cleveland TS7 9AS

🏠 🐕 ✿ 🍴 🍽 🎨 🎋 🦚 👫 🏛 🧍 🔔
🍽 1962   **(5:G2)**

The Pennyman family's intimate 18th-century mansion

Ormesby Hall is an intimate home lived in by the Pennyman family for more than 300 years, with fine plasterwork, carved wood decoration and fascinating portraits. The Victorian laundry and kitchen with scullery and game larder are worth exploring, and there is a beautiful stable block (let to the Cleveland Mounted Police) that can be seen from the Hall. Ormesby has the only National Trust model railway layouts on permanent display. There is also an attractive garden.

What's new in 2009 Expanded programme of events and activities, some on weekdays

⭐ Parts of the Hall may occasionally be closed for private functions

🛈 **T** 01642 324188
   E ormesbyhall@nationaltrust.org.uk

[:] Guided tours of Hall part of events programme

[:] Send sae or see website for details

[:] Orienteering route through estate and Park to Park walk – information available at property

[symbols] Building [symbols]
Grounds [symbols]

[:] Tea-room serving home-made scones and cakes

[:] Baby-changing facilities. Front-carrying baby slings for loan. Children's quiz/trail. Family activity packs

[:] Suitable for school groups. Education room/centre. Living history programmes. Community activities

[:] On leads only in park

[→] [93:NZ530167] **Cycle**: NCN65, 2¼ml.
Bus: Arriva 9, 63, 69 from Middlesbrough (passing close ≷ Middlesbrough).
Station: Marton (U) 1½ml; Middlesbrough 3ml.
Road: 3ml SE of Middlesbrough, W of A171. From A19 take A174 to A172. Follow signs for Ormesby Hall. Car entrance on Ladgate Lane (B1380)

[P] Free parking, 100yds

NT properties nearby
Mount Grace Priory, Nunnington Hall, Rievaulx Terrace and Temples, Roseberry Topping, Souter Lighthouse, Washington Old Hall

Ormesby Hall									
14 Mar–1 Nov	1:30–5	M	T	W	T	F	**S**	**S**
Open BH Mons and Good Fri. Closed 4/5 July for special event									

Rievaulx Terrace and Temples

Rievaulx, Helmsley, North Yorkshire YO62 5LJ

[symbols] 1972   (5:H3)

One of Yorkshire's finest 18th-century landscape gardens, containing two temples

Discover one of Ryedale's true gems – the 18th-century landscape of Rievaulx Terrace. Stroll through woods then out on to the grass terrace, with its stunning views down over the Cistercian ruin of Rievaulx Abbey. In spring the bank between the temples is awash with wild flowers, in summer the lawns are the perfect spot for a picnic, while in autumn the beech woods are a mass of rich hues. Step back into the 18th century as you gaze up at the wonderful painted ceiling of the Ionic Temple. Being so close to Nunnington Hall, the Terrace makes an ideal morning visit before discovering Nunnington in the afternoon.

[★] No access to Rievaulx Abbey from Terrace

[i] **T** 01439 798340 (summer), 01439 748283 (winter) **E** rievaulxterrace@nationaltrust.org.uk

[:] Tours throughout the day

[:] Rievaulx Terrace and Nunnington Hall's combined events list available from Nunnington Hall

[symbols] Building [symbol]
Grounds [symbols]

[□] NT shop

[:] Ice-cream, coffee/tea machine and cold drinks

[:] Baby-changing facilities. Pushchairs and baby back-carriers admitted. Children's quiz/trail. Children's activity packs

[:] Suitable for school groups

[:] On leads only

[→] [100:SE579848] **Foot**: Cleveland Way within ⅔ml. **Bus**: Moorsbus M8 from Helmsley Sun & BHols mid March–Oct, daily late July–Aug. Discounted entry for visitors using the Moorsbus. **Road**: 2½ml NW of Helmsley on B1257

[P] Free parking, 100yds. Unsuitable for trailer caravans. Cars park beside visitor centre, coaches a short walk away. Tight corners and no turning space beyond coach park

NT properties nearby
Beningbrough Hall and Gardens, Bridestones, Nunnington Hall, Ormesby Hall, Treasurer's House

Rievaulx Terrace and Temples									
28 Feb–1 Nov	11–5	M	T	W	T	F	S	S
Last admission 1hr before closing. Ionic Temple closed 1–2									

Roseberry Topping

Newton-under-Roseberry, North Yorkshire

 1985   (5:G2)

Distinctive hill with fine views across Yorkshire

The peculiar shape of this hill is due to a geological fault and a mining collapse early in the 20th century. From the summit at 320 metres there is a magnificent 360° view and, on a clear day, visitors can see as far as Teesside in one direction and the Yorkshire Dales in another. Newton and Cliff Ridge Woods skirt the northern edge of the property and Cliff Rigg quarry still retains evidence of the extraction of whinstone, once used for road-building. The area is rich in wildlife, particularly moorland birds. A spur of the Cleveland Way National Trail runs up to the summit.

★ Address for correspondence: Peakside, Ravenscar, Scarborough, North Yorkshire YO13 0NE. WC at Ayton car park

ℹ **T** 01642 328901
   E roseberrytopping@nationaltrust.org.uk

♿ 🚻

➔ [93:NZ575126] **Foot**: Cleveland Way passes property. **Bus**: Arriva North East 81 Redcar–Stokesley, alight Newton-under-Roseberry, then ½ml. **Station**: Great Ayton (U) 1½ml. **Road**: 1ml from Great Ayton next to Newton-under-Roseberry on A173 Great Ayton–Guisborough

P Parking (not NT), £2, at Newton-under-Roseberry

NT properties nearby
Bridestones, Nunnington Hall, Ormesby Hall, Rievaulx Terrace and Temples, Souter Lighthouse, Yorkshire Coast

Roseberry Topping							
All year	M	T	W	T	F	S	S

Looking towards Roseberry Topping, North Yorkshire

Treasurer's House, York: carefully restored 1897 to 1930

Treasurer's House

Minster Yard, York, North Yorkshire YO1 7JL

🏰 ❄ ♟ ☕ 🗝 ⌂ ♨ 👫 📷 🔔
⛲ 1930   (5:H5)

Elegant town house dating from medieval times

Originally home to the treasurers of York Minster and built over a Roman road, the house is not all that it seems. Nestled behind the Minster, its size, splendour and contents are a constant surprise to visitors – as are the famous ghost stories. The house was carefully restored between 1897 and 1930 by one remarkable man, wealthy local industrialist Frank Green, with thirteen rooms presented in a variety of historic styles. Outside is an attractive formal sunken garden and herb and produce garden.

What's new in 2009 Expanded organic herb and kitchen garden. Occasional attic tours

ℹ **T** 01904 624247
   E treasurershouse@nationaltrust.org.uk

𝑘 Occasional attic tours; ghost cellar tours daily except Fri. Themed guided tours in Nov (charge, inc. NT members)

♿ 🚻 ♟ 📷 🎧 💻 📋 Building ♿ ♿
Grounds ♿ ➡

📕 Small range of books, cards, souvenirs and original artwork on sale

☕ Licensed tea-room. All food freshly prepared and baked on premises inc. traditional Yorkshire recipes. Special dietary requirements catered for. Children's menu. Wedding breakfasts and corporate functions

[icon] Baby-changing and feeding facilities. Hip-carrying infant seats for loan. Children's guide. Children's quiz/trail. Interactive exhibition area for children

[icon] Suitable for school groups

[icon] On leads and only in formal garden

[icon] [105:SE604523] In city centre adjacent to Minster (N side, at rear). **Cycle**: NCN65, ⅓ml. Close to city cycle routes. **Bus**: from surrounding areas. **Station**: York ½ml

[icon] No parking on site. Public car park nearby in Lord Mayor's Walk. Park & ride service from city outskirts

NT properties nearby
Beningbrough Hall and Gardens, Nunnington Hall

Treasurer's House								
1 Mar–12 Mar	11–4:30	M	T	W	T	F	S	S
14 Mar–1 Nov	11–4:30	M	T	W	T	F	S	S
2 Nov–30 Nov	11–3	M	T	W	T	F	S	S

1 Mar–12 Mar: access by guided tour or free flow, tbc. 14 Mar–1 Nov: free flow access. Nov: access by Ghostly Myths guided tour to selected rooms of house. Herb garden access limited, check before visiting

Upper Wharfedale

Yorkshire Dales Estate Office, Waterhouses, Settle, North Yorkshire BD24 9PT

[icons] 1989   (5:E4)

Area of classic Yorkshire Dales countryside

Amongst the 2,470 hectares (6,100 acres) of the Upper Wharfe Valley north of Kettlewell, the Trust owns nine farms as well as the hamlets of Yockenthwaite and Cray. The landscape features the characteristic drystone walls and barns of the Dales, important flower-rich hay meadows and valleyside woodland. It is a wonderful place to enjoy the great outdoors.

What's new in 2009 Exhibition in Town Head Barn, Buckden, focusing on the River Wharfe and climate change

[icon] No WC, nearest at National Park car park in Buckden

[icon] **T** 01729 830416
E upperwharfedale@nationaltrust.org.uk

Upper Wharfedale								
Estate								
All year		M	T	W	T	F	S	S
Upper Wharfedale – Town Head Barn								
1 Feb–29 Mar	10–4	M	T	W	T	F	S	S
4 Apr–1 Oct	10–4	M	T	W	T	F	S	S
4 Oct–13 Dec	10–4	M	T	W	T	F	S	S
3 Jan–31 Jan 10	10–4	M	T	W	T	F	S	S

[icon] Guided walks throughout year, inc. meadow and woodland walks

[icon] A selection of the many walks in Upper Wharfedale are included in walks leaflets, available from the National Park centre or Town Head Barn, Buckden

[icon] **Grounds** [icon]

[icon] Exhibition in Town Head Barn, Buckden. Suitable for school groups. Farm visits by arrangement

[icon] On leads only – stock grazing

[icon] Off-road cycling permitted on bridleways

[icon] [98:SD935765] Upper Wharfedale extends from Kettlewell village (12ml N of Skipton) N to Beckermonds and Cray. **Bus**: Pride of the Dales 72 [icon] Skipton–Buckden

[icon] Parking (not NT) in Kettlewell and Buckden (pay & display)

NT properties nearby
Brimham Rocks, East Riddlesden Hall, Fountains Abbey and Studley Royal, Malham Tarn Estate

Upper Wharfedale, North Yorkshire

Yorkshire Coast

Peakside, Ravenscar, Scarborough,
North Yorkshire YO13 0NE

[icons] 1976 (5:12)

Varied coastal area with natural history and industrial archaeology interest

This group of coastal properties extends more than 40 miles from Saltburn in the north to Filey in the south, centred on Robin Hood's Bay. The Cleveland Way National Trail follows the clifftop and gives splendid views. A wide range of habitats – meadow, woodland, coastal heath and cliff grassland – provides sanctuary to many forms of wildlife, from orchids to nesting birds. The area is rich in industrial archaeology, and the remains of the alum industry and jet and ironstone mining can be seen. The Old Coastguard Station in Robin Hood's Bay, an exciting exhibition and education centre, is run in partnership with the North York Moors National Park Authority. It shows how the elements have shaped this part of the coastline. At Ravenscar Coastal Centre an exhibition covers local history, including the story of alum production – Britain's first chemical industry.

i **T** 01723 870423, 01947 885900 (Old Coastguard Station)
E yorkshirecoast@nationaltrust.org.uk

Guided walks

Cowbar Nab at Staithes, North Yorkshire

Old Coastguard Station Ravenscar Coastal Centre Grounds

Shops in Old Coastguard Station and Ravenscar Coastal Centre

Suitable for school groups. Education room/centre. Hand-on activities (at Old Coastguard Station)

→ [94:NZ980025] **Foot**: Cleveland Way passes through property. **Cycle**: NCN1.
Bus: Scarborough & District 115 from Scarborough Mon–Sat.
Station: Scarborough 10ml. **Road**: Coastal Centre in Ravenscar village, signposted off A171 Scarborough–Whitby. Old Coastguard Station in Robin Hood's Bay

P Parking (not NT) (pay & display), charge inc. NT members at Old Coastguard Station. Free roadside parking at Ravenscar

NT properties nearby
Bridestones, Nunnington Hall, Ormesby Hall, Rievaulx Terrace and Temples

Yorkshire Coast		M	T	W	T	F	S	S
All year		M	T	W	T	F	S	S
Coastguard Station								
1 Feb–8 Feb	10–4	M	T	W	T	F	**S**	**S**
14 Feb–22 Feb	10–4	**M**	**T**	**W**	**T**	**F**	**S**	**S**
28 Feb–29 Mar	10–4	M	T	W	T	F	**S**	**S**
4 Apr–19 Apr	10–5	**M**	**T**	**W**	**T**	**F**	**S**	**S**
21 Apr–1 Nov	10–5	M	**T**	**W**	**T**	**F**	**S**	**S**
8 Nov–31 Jan 10	11–4	M	T	W	T	F	**S**	**S**
Coastal Centre								
4 Apr–19 Apr	10–4:30	**M**	**T**	**W**	**T**	**F**	**S**	**S**
25 Apr–31 May	10–4:30	M	T	W	T	F	**S**	**S**
1 Jun–30 Sep	10–4:30	**M**	**T**	**W**	**T**	**F**	**S**	**S**
3 Oct–31 Oct	10–4:30	M	T	W	T	F	**S**	**S**
Open BH Mons. Closed 26/27 Dec								

Charges for National Trust members apply on some special event days

North East

England's far north-eastern counties of Northumberland, Durham and Tyne & Wear offer magnificent scenery, with wide stretches of unspoilt moorland and upland pasture, plus a long and dramatic coastline – arguably one of the finest in Britain.

Dunes, beaches and rock pools

In the North East the National Trust cares for sixteen miles of dunes, sandy beaches and tidal rock pools along the Northumberland coast, and five miles of the Durham coast. For many years, the Durham beaches were a dumping ground for the local collieries, but this unexpectedly beautiful area of coast now has Heritage Coast status.

In the south of the region, near Horden in County Durham, a piece of coast marks the 500th mile acquired through the Trust's Neptune Coastline Campaign. Once an industrial mining hotspot, this stretch of coastline has since been dramatically restored, and while even today it may be some time before the beaches return to golden sands, the seeds have been sown for the future.

Moving north, the spectacular coastline takes in the dramatic Souter Lighthouse and The Leas, with its famous seabird colony on Marsden Rock. Further north of the River Tyne and up the Northumberland coast is Druridge Bay, where the Trust owns a mile of coast backed by golden sand dunes. From Craster, Trust ownership runs for five miles, including the brooding ruins of Dunstanburgh Castle (managed by English Heritage). Boats cross to the Farne Islands from Seahouses, giving visitors the chance to see the homes of thousands of seabirds – including puffins, terns, kittiwakes and guillemots.

A haven for wildlife

The North East is a haven for wildlife, offering one of the few sanctuaries in England for our threatened native red squirrels. If you are out walking, keep your eyes peeled for a rare sighting. Red squirrels live in wooded areas and can be seen in the region at Allen Banks, Cragside and Wallington – the latter of which has a wildlife hide that is perfect for spotting these special

Above left: Souter Lighthouse, Tyne & Wear

Above: view of Dunstanburgh Castle, Northumberland

Red squirrel: under threat

Previous page: **Horden Beach on the Durham coast**

animals. As well as squirrels, there is an abundance of birdlife. The Farne Islands, for example, are home to more than 100,000 nesting birds and their chicks during the breeding season (May to July). Lying just off the north-east coast from Seahouses, the Farnes offer one of the most exciting

Hadrian's Wall and Housesteads Fort, Northumberland

wildlife experiences in the world. Accessible by boat only, both Inner Farne and Staple Island can be landed on when the weather permits, and their inhabitants include puffins, terns, guillemots, eider ducks and a colony of grey seals. St Cuthbert died on Inner Farne in 687, and the chapel built in his memory can be visited today.

Birdwatching at Inner Farne on the Farne Islands

Woodland walks and breathtaking views

Inland Northumberland offers the natural beauty and tranquillity of Allen Banks and Staward Gorge – a walking haven with many miles of footpaths – while both Ros Castle and the World Heritage Site of Hadrian's Wall boast breathtaking views. There are also numerous beautiful woodland walks, including one along the banks of the River Wear at Moorhouse Woods, north of Durham City, and another beside the Derwent at Ebchester.

An island retreat

Accessible by a causeway at low tide, Holy Island is an island treasure that has as its centrepiece Lindisfarne Castle. Once a Tudor fort, the castle sits on a rocky crag that can be seen for miles along the sweeping coastline. Converted into a holiday home in 1903, this enchanting place, with its small rooms full of intimate decoration and design, is totally charming. Just below the castle is the lovely walled garden planned by Gertrude Jekyll and dating back to 1922. Be sure also to stroll along the headland and explore the village – just remember to keep an eye on the tides which cover the causeway.

Climb 76 steps for a stunning view

Along the Marsden coastline, just to the north of Sunderland, is Souter Lighthouse. Once a beacon that warned boats of the lethal rocks below for more than 100 years, it was the most technologically advanced lighthouse in the world and the first to be powered by electricity. Now visitors can climb the 76 steps to the top of the tower and, on a clear day, see for miles out to sea. While at Souter, discover The Leas, a haven for flora and fauna, and enjoy a bracing walk along the clifftops.

Our most impressive ruin

One of the most rugged stretches of countryside in the North East is home to Hadrian's Wall. Snaking across the landscape, the wall was built around AD122 when the Roman Empire was at its height. A World Heritage Site, it remains one of Britain's most impressive ruins. The Trust protects six miles of Hadrian's Wall, including Housesteads Fort, one of the best preserved sections of the ramparts and a place which conjures an evocative picture of Roman military life.

Allen Banks and Staward Gorge

Estate Office, Bardon Mill, Hexham,
Northumberland NE47 7BU

 1942   (6:F5)

Gorge of the River Allen with ornamental and ancient woodland

This extensive area of gorge and river scenery, including the 41-hectare (101-acre) Stawardpeel Site of Special Scientific Interest, has many miles of waymarked walks through ornamental and ancient woods. On a high promontory within Staward Wood are the remains of a medieval pele tower and at Allen Banks is a reconstructed Victorian summerhouse.

⭐ If using Satnav to visit the property, please use grid reference for the car park (NY7996401)

ℹ **T** 01434 344218
   E allenbanks@nationaltrust.org.uk

🏃 Guided walks

🛡 Guided walks and workshops covering a range of subjects, such as tree identification, fungi and woodland birds

🏃 Free map and guide to four waymarked routes, available at the property

♿ 🚻 **Grounds** 🚶

🚼 Baby-changing facilities. Family tree trail

🏫 Suitable for school groups. Visitor map and guides

🐾 Under close control

➡ [86:NY799640] **Foot**: numerous public and permitted rights of way give access to walkers. **Cycle**: NCN72, 2½ml. **Bus**: Arriva/Stagecoach in Cumbria 685 Carlisle–Newcastle upon Tyne, to within ½ml. **Station**: Bardon Mill 1½ml. **Road**: 5½ml E of Haltwhistle, 3ml W of Haydon Bridge, ½ml S of A69, near meeting point of Tyne and Allen rivers

If your family enjoyed Cherryburn, they will love exploring Souter Lighthouse too

🅿 Parking (pay & display) at Allen Banks. Cars £2 half day, £4 full day. Can accommodate two coaches at a time (all coaches must book). 3.3m (11ft) height restriction on approach road. Coaches £5 half day, £10 full day. NT members/Educational Group members free

NT properties nearby
Hadrian's Wall and Housesteads Fort

Allen Banks and Staward Gorge							
All year	Open all hours	M	T	W	T	F	S	S

Cherryburn

Station Bank, Mickley, Stocksfield,
Northumberland NE43 7DD

 1991   (6:G5)

Cottage and farmhouse, the birthplace of Thomas Bewick

Thomas Bewick (1753–1828), Northumberland's greatest artist, wood engraver and naturalist, was born in the cottage here. The nearby 19th-century farmhouse, the later home of the Bewick family, houses an exhibition on Bewick's life and work and a small shop selling books, gifts and prints from his original wood engravings. Occasional printing demonstrations take place in the adjoining barn. There are splendid views over the Tyne Valley. The south bank of the River Tyne, where Bewick spent much of his childhood, is a short walk away.

What's new in 2009 Short Paddock walk

ℹ **T** 01661 843276
   E cherryburn@nationaltrust.org.uk

🛡 Easter trail, Teddy Bears' Picnic. Folk in the Farmyard: traditional Northumbrian music, song or dance first Sun of every month. The 'Big Draw' in Oct. Concerts, lecture evenings and press room demonstrations

♿ 🅿 🚻 🚻 ⠿ 🔊 🎵 **Building** 🚶 ♿
Grounds 🚶

🏠 Shop in farmhouse. Send sae for mail order Bewick print price list. Small selection of plants grown by Cherryburn volunteers, summer months only

📺 Tea, coffee, soft drinks and snacks available

👪 Baby-changing facilities. Family guide. Children's quiz/trail. Children's toy corner. Farmyard animals usually include donkeys, poultry, rabbits and lambs. Teddy Bears' Picnic

▓ Suitable for school groups. Hands-on activities

➔ [88:NZ075627] Close to S bank of River Tyne. **Bus**: Arriva Northumbria 602 Newcastle–Hexham (passes ⊞ Newcastle), alight Mickley Square $\frac{1}{4}$ml. **Station**: Stocksfield (U) $1\frac{1}{2}$ml or Prudhoe (U) $1\frac{1}{2}$ml. **Road**: 11ml W of Newcastle, 11ml E of Hexham; $\frac{1}{4}$ml N of Mickley Square (leave A695 at Mickley Square on to Riding Terrace leading to Station Bank)

P Free parking, 100yds

NT properties nearby
George Stephenson's Birthplace, Gibside

Cherryburn								
Public opening								
14 Mar–1 Nov	11–5	M	T	W	T	F	S	S
Booked groups								
16 Mar–30 Oct	11–4	M	T	W	T	F	S	S
2 Nov–31 Jan 10	11–3	M	T	W	T	F	S	S
Shop open at other times by arrangement								

Cragside

Rothbury, Morpeth, Northumberland NE65 7PX

🏠🏚🔧❄🔌🏡📷📺🎪🎭👪🏭
🏃 1977   (6:G3)

Extraordinary Victorian house, gardens and estate – the wonder of its age

The revolutionary home of Lord Armstrong, Victorian inventor and landscape genius, was a wonder of its age. Built on a rocky crag high above the Debdon Burn, Cragside is crammed with ingenious gadgets and was the first house in the world lit by hydroelectricity. Even the variety and scale of Cragside's gardens are incredible. Surrounding the house on all sides is one of the largest 'hand-made' rock gardens in Europe. In the Pinetum below, England's tallest Douglas fir soars above other woodland giants. Across the valley, the Orchard House still produces fresh fruit of all varieties, from nectarines and apricots to grapes and strawberries. Today, Armstrong's amazing creation can be explored on foot and by car and provides one of the last shelters for the endangered red squirrel. The lakeside walks, adventure play area and labyrinth are all good reasons for children to visit Cragside again and again.

What's new in 2009 Newly restored Iron Bridge open for first time in 30 years

⭐ Visitors may find the uneven ground, steep and slippery footpaths and distances between various parts of the property difficult. Stout footwear advisable. Pedestrians and vehicles share the same route in places, so please be vigilant. Estate will temporarily close when car parks are full. We do not have facilities to take credit/debit card payments at the admission point

ℹ️ **T** 01669 620333
E cragside@nationaltrust.org.uk

Cragside is crammed with ingenious gadgets and was the first house in the world to be lit by hydroelectricity

🎭 Send sae for details

🏃 Leaflets for self-guided walks available

♿ 🅿 🚻 🦽 🚾 👓 📷 🎨 📺 🔔 📠
Building ♿🔼♿ **Visitor Centre** ♿♿
Grounds 🦽

🏠 NT shop. Plant sales

📺 Stables Restaurant (licensed) in visitor centre. Hot meals served 12–2. Children's menu. Kiosk in Crozier car park – mainly weekends and school hols (weather permitting)

[mother & baby icon] Baby-changing facilities. Front-carrying baby slings and hip-carrying infant seats for loan. Children's adventure play areas. Tracker Packs available during school holidays. Children's guide

[icon] Suitable for school groups. Education room/centre

[dog icon] On leads and only on estate

→ [81:NU073022] **Bus**: Arriva 508 from Gateshead and [rail] Newcastle (passing [rail] Morpeth), Sun only, June–Oct. Northumbria Coaches 516 Morpeth–Thropton with connections from Newcastle. **Road**: 13ml SW of Alnwick (B6341) and 15ml NW of Morpeth on Wooler road (A697), turn left on to B6341 at Moorhouse Crossroads, entrance 1ml N of Rothbury

[P] Free parking in nine car parks throughout the estate. Coach parking 350yds from house, 150yds from visitor centre. Coaches cannot proceed beyond the coach park or tour estate as drive is too narrow in places

NT properties nearby
Druridge Bay, Embleton and Newton Links, Lindisfarne Castle, Wallington

Cragside										
House										
28 Feb–8 Mar	11–5	M	T	W	T	F	**S**	**S**
14 Mar–3 Apr	1–5*	M	**T**	**W**	**T**	**F**	**S**	**S**
4 Apr–19 Apr	11–5	M	**T**	**W**	**T**	**F**	**S**	**S**
21 Apr–22 May	1–5*	M	**T**	**W**	**T**	**F**	**S**	**S**
23 May–31 May	11–5	M	**T**	**W**	**T**	**F**	**S**	**S**
2 Jun–24 Jul	1–5*	M	**T**	**W**	**T**	**F**	**S**	**S**
25 Jul–6 Sep	11–5	M	**T**	**W**	**T**	**F**	**S**	**S**
8 Sep–23 Oct	1–5*	M	**T**	**W**	**T**	**F**	**S**	**S**
24 Oct–1 Nov	11–5	M	**T**	**W**	**T**	**F**	**S**	**S**
Gardens/estate/shop/restaurant										
28 Feb–8 Mar	10:30–5	M	T	W	T	F	**S**	**S**
14 Mar–1 Nov	10:30–5	M	**T**	**W**	**T**	**F**	**S**	**S**
4 Nov–20 Dec	11–4	M	T	**W**	**T**	**F**	**S**	**S**

*House open 11–5 on Sat/Sun. Open BH Mons. On BHol weekends, the property is often very crowded. Last admission to house 1hr before closing. House may have to open late or close early if light or temperature levels are too low. Occasionally entry to house from 11–1 may be by guided tour only, on a first-come, first-served basis (places limited)

Dunstanburgh Castle

Craster, Alnwick, Northumberland NE66 3TT

[icons] 1961   **(6:H3)**

Massive ruined castle in an impressive coastal setting

A magnificent ruin dominating a lonely stretch of Northumberland's beautiful coastline, Dunstanburgh must be reached on foot along paths following the rocky shore.

★ The castle is managed by English Heritage

[i] **T** 01665 576231
E dunstanburghcastle@nationaltrust.org.uk

[shop icon] Small shop for postcards and souvenirs

[cup icon] Hot drinks and snacks

[icon] Suitable for school groups. Free school visits; book through EH

[dog icon] On leads only

→ [75:NU258220] 9ml NE of Alnwick, approached from Craster to the S or Embleton to the N (on foot only). **Cycle**: NCN1, ¾ml. **Bus**: Arriva 501 [rail] Newcastle–[rail] Alnwick–Berwick, alight Craster, 1½ml. **Station**: Chathill (U), not Sun, 5ml from Embleton, 7ml from castle; Alnmouth, 7ml from Craster, 8¼ml from castle

[P] Parking (not NT). Car parks at Craster and Embleton, 1½ml (no coaches at Embleton)

NT properties nearby
Cragside, Farne Islands, Lindisfarne Castle

Dunstanburgh Castle									
1 Feb–30 Mar	10–4	**M**	T	**W**		**T**	**F**	**S**	**S**
1 Apr–30 Sep	10–5	**M**	**T**	**W**		**T**	**F**	**S**	**S**
1 Oct–31 Oct	10–4	**M**	**T**	**W**		**T**	**F**	**S**	**S**
1 Nov–31 Jan 10	10–4	**M**	T	W		**T**	**F**	**S**	**S**
Closed 24–26 Dec & 1 Jan 10									

Farne Islands

Northumberland

[icons] 1925   **(6:H2)**

Rocky islands, habitat for seals and many species of seabird

'Home' for more than 100,000 pairs of breeding seabirds, including 55,000 pairs of puffins, the Islands make up one of Europe's most important

---

Unless indicated, last admission is always 30mins before closing time

seabird reserves. Up to 23 species nest annually and many of the birds are very confiding, allowing excellent opportunities for study and photography. There is also a large grey seal colony, and the islands are interesting historically, having strong links with Celtic Christianity and, in particular, St Cuthbert.

⭐ Access by ferry (charge inc. NT members). WC on Inner Farne only

ℹ️ **T** 01665 721099 (Infoline), 01665 720651
E farneislands@nationaltrust.org.uk

♿ 🚻 :: 🔧 **Grounds** ♿

📷 Information centre and shop at 16 Main Street, Seahouses

🎒 Suitable for school groups

➡️ [75:NU230370] 2–5ml off the Northumberland coast, opposite Bamburgh. Trips every day from Seahouses harbour, weather permitting.
Cycle: NCN1, ¾ml. From Seahouses harbour.
Bus: Arriva 501 🚋 Newcastle–🚋 Alnwick–Berwick, alight Seahouses, 1½ml.
Station: Chathill (U), not Sun, 4ml

🅿️ Parking (not NT) in Seahouses, opposite harbour (pay & display)

NT properties nearby
Beadnell Bay, Dunstanburgh Castle, Lindisfarne Castle, Northumberland Coast, St Aidan's and Shoreston Dunes, St Cuthbert's Cave

Farne Islands									
Both islands									
1 Apr–30 Apr	10:30–6	M	T	W	T	F	S	S	
Staple									
1 May–31 Jul	10:30–1:30	M	T	W	T	F	S	S	
Inner Farne									
1 May–31 Jul	1:30–5	M	T	W	T	F	S	S	
Both islands									
1 Aug–30 Sep	10:30–6	M	T	W	T	F	S	S	
Centre/shop									
22 Mar–30 Jun	10–5	M	T	W	T	F	S	S	
1 Jul–31 Aug	10–5:30	M	T	W	T	F	S	S	
1 Sep–30 Sep	10–5	M	T	W	T	F	S	S	
1 Oct–31 Oct	11–4	M	T	W	T	F	S	S	
1 Nov–24 Dec	11–4	M	T	W	T	F	S	S	
3 Jan–31 Jan 10	11–4	M	T	W	T	F	S	S	

Only Inner Farne and Staple Islands can be visited.
Visitors to Inner Farne in May–July should wear hats!
Information centre/shop open half-term hols 10–5

George Stephenson's Birthplace

Wylam, Northumberland NE41 8BP

🏠 🛠️ ♿🚻 👶 🎍 🏚️ 🛡️ 👫 🎒 🚲 1949 **(6:G5)**

Birthplace of the world-famous railway engineer

This small stone tenement was built c.1760 to accommodate mining families. The furnishings reflect the year of Stephenson's birth here (1781), his whole family living in the one room.

What's new in 2009 Fully accessible WC

ℹ️ **T** 01661 853457
E georgestephensons@nationaltrust.org.uk

🛡️ Geordie Food Day – June

♿ 🅿️ :: 🔧 🎍 ♿ **Building** ♿

☕ Tea-room serving light refreshments

👫 Pushchairs admitted. Children's quiz/trail

🎒 Suitable for school groups

➡️ [88:NZ126650] **Foot**: access on foot (and cycle) through country park, ½ml E of Wylam.
Cycle: NCN72. Easy (flat) ride beside River Tyne (approx. 5ml). **Bus**: Arriva 684 Newcastle–Ovington, alight Wylam, 1ml.
Station: Wylam (U) ½ml. **Road**: 8ml W of Newcastle, 1½ml S of A69 at Wylam

🅿️ Parking (not NT) by war memorial in Wylam village, ½ml (pay & display).

NT properties nearby Cherryburn, Gibside

George Stephenson's Birthplace									
19 Mar–1 Nov	12–5	M	T	W	T	F	S	S	
Open BH Mons									

Visitors exploring the Farne Islands, Northumberland

Gibside

nr Rowlands Gill, Burnopfield,
Newcastle upon Tyne NE16 6BG

[icons] 1974

(6:H5)

Stunning 18th-century landscape garden

The Column of Liberty, rising dramatically high above the treetops, is the first sight visitors have of this impressive landscape garden created by the Bowes family in the 18th century. Spanning 160 hectares (400 acres), Gibside is a 'grand design' of spectacular vistas, winding paths and grassy open spaces. At key points there are decorative garden buildings, such as the Palladian chapel, Georgian stables, greenhouse and the ruins of a bathhouse and hall. There is a wonderfully tranquil atmosphere, and visitors will feel themselves very close to nature. Much of Gibside is a Site of Special Scientific Interest and wildlife, such as red kites, can be seen.

What's new in 2009 Victorian shrubbery

⭐ Chapel access restricted during weddings

ℹ️ **T** 01207 541820
E gibside@nationaltrust.org.uk

🎫 Guided tours of the stable block. Introductory talks on arrival and at chapel

🎧 Audio guide available from Visitor Reception

📺 Open-air concerts and theatre. Seasonal events, including Easter Egg trails and Christmas concerts. Family events. Food events. Wildlife events

🚶 Network of footpaths, including waymarked routes of 2½ml–4ml

♿ [icons] **Chapel** [icons] **Grounds** [icons]

🏪 Gibside Larder and gift shop selling regional products and award-winning local meat

🍴 Tea-room serving home-made soups, cakes and cream teas. Produce from walled garden, when in season. Children's menu. Kiosk serves ice-cream and snacks

👶 Baby-changing facilities. Pushchairs and baby back-carriers admitted. All-terrain baby buggies for loan. Trusty Club. Family outdoor activity packs. Family activity days

Strolling along the Avenue towards the Chapel at Gibside, Newcastle upon Tyne

🏫 Suitable for school groups. Education room/centre. Hands-on activities

🐕 On leads on the walks and in the stables courtyard

➡️ [88:NZ172583] **Foot**: ½ml from Derwent Walk, footpath/cycle track linking Swalwell and Consett. **Cycle**: NCN14, ½ml. **Bus**: Go North East 'The Red Kite' 45, 46/A from Newcastle (passing ⊟ Newcastle and Metrocentre), alight Rowlands Gill, ½ml. **Station**: Blaydon (U) 5ml; Metrocentre 5ml. **Road**: 6ml SW of Gateshead, 20ml NW of Durham; entrance on B6314 between Burnopfield and Rowlands Gill; from A1 take exit north of Metrocentre and follow brown signs

🅿️ Free parking, 100yds. Limited coach parking

NT properties nearby
Cherryburn, George Stephenson's Birthplace, Souter Lighthouse, Washington Old Hall

Gibside			
Grounds			
1 Feb–8 Mar	10–4		M T W T F S S
9 Mar–1 Nov	10–6		M T W T F S S
2 Nov–31 Jan 10	10–4		M T W T F S S
Chapel			
14 Mar–1 Nov	11–4:30		M T W T F S S
Stables/shop/tea-room			
1 Feb–8 Mar	11–3:30		M T W T F S S
9 Mar–1 Nov	11–4:30		M T W T F S S
2 Nov–31 Jan 10	11–3:30		M T W T F S S

Shop/tea-room close 30mins after Stables. Closed 21–26 Dec & 31 Dec–1 Jan 10. Last admission: 1 Feb–8 Mar 3:30, 9 Mar–1 Nov 4:30, 2 Nov–31 Jan 10 3:30. Shop/tea-room opens 10 weekends. Last entry to tea-room 15mins before closing

Hadrian's Wall and Housesteads Fort

Bardon Mill, Hexham, Northumberland NE47 6NN

 (6:F5)

Roman wall snaking across dramatic countryside

Running through an often wild landscape with vast panoramic views, the Wall was, for a long period, the Roman Empire's most northerly outpost. Built around AD122, it has sixteen permanent bases, of which Housesteads Fort is one of the best preserved, conjuring up an evocative picture of Roman military life.

What's new in 2009 Guided tours conducted by English Heritage guides

⭐ The Trust owns approx. six miles of the Wall, running west from Housesteads Fort to Cawfields Quarry, and over 1,000 hectares (2,471 acres) of farmland. Access to the Wall and the public rights of way is from car parks operated by the Northumberland National Park Authority at Housesteads, Steel Rigg and Cawfields. Housesteads Fort is owned by the NT, and maintained and managed by English Heritage

ℹ **T** 01434 344363 (EH site staff), 01434 344314 (NT warden)

🏃 Programme of guided tours at Housesteads run by English Heritage

🚶 Hadrian's Wall Path National Trail provides a series of circular walks on the estate and surrounding area suitable for all abilities. Details available at Visitor Centre

♿ 🅿🚾👓💧🔲 Building 🐾 Grounds ♿🐾

Hadrian's Wall, Northumberland

🛍 Shop/information centre at Housesteads car park

☕ Kiosk. Picnic tables outside information centre; seating inside. Children's lunch pack

👶 Baby-changing facilities. Children's guide. Play area

🎒 Suitable for school groups. Education room/centre. Free school visits; book through EH at Housesteads. Visits to wider estate booked through Warden's office

🐕 On leads only (sheep and ground-nesting birds)

➡ [87:NY790688] **Foot**: 6ml of Hadrian's Wall Path & Pennine Way on property. **Bus**: Stagecoach in Cumbria AD122 Hadrian's Wall service, June–Sept & Suns in April & Oct, ☒ Hexham–Carlisle (passing ☒ Haltwhistle). Check before journey. **Station**: Bardon Mill (U) 4ml. **Road**: 6ml NE of Haltwhistle, ½ml N of B6318; best access from car parks at Housesteads, Cawfields and Steel Rigg

🅿 Parking (not NT) (pay & display), charge inc. NT members. Car and coach parks (operated by National Park Authority) at Housesteads (½ml walk to the Fort), Steel Rigg and at Cawfields at the western end

NT properties nearby
Allen Banks and Staward Gorge, Bellister

Hadrian's Wall and Housesteads Fort								
1 Feb–31 Mar	10–4	M	T	W	T	F	S	S
1 Apr–30 Sep	10–6	M	T	W	T	F	S	S
1 Oct–31 Jan	10–4	M	T	W	T	F	S	S

Closed 24–26 Dec & 1 Jan 10. Opening times subject to confirmation by EH. Tel. for details or visit www.english-heritage.org.uk

Holy Jesus Hospital

City Road, Newcastle upon Tyne NE1 2AS

(6:H5)

An extraordinary mix of architecture from over seven centuries of Newcastle upon Tyne's history

The Holy Jesus Hospital survives amid 1960s city-centre developments, displaying features from all periods of its 700-year existence. There are remains of the 14th-century Augustinian friary, 16th-century fortifications connected with the Council of the North, a 17th-century almshouse built for the Freemen of the City and a 19th-century soup kitchen. The National Trust's Inner City Project is now based here, working to provide opportunities for modern inner-city dwellers to gain access to and enjoy the countryside on their doorstep. An exhibition room is open to visitors and guided tours of the whole site are offered once a month.

⭐ Holy Jesus Hospital is owned by Newcastle City Council and leased to the NT as the base for its Inner City Project. The building and arrangements for visiting are managed by the NT

ℹ️ **T** 0191 255 7610
   E innercityproject@nationaltrust.org.uk

🗝️ 1st Sat of every month (except Jan) or by arrangement

♿ 🅿️ 🔋 ♿ 📷 📶 **Building** ♿ ♿ ♿

👫 Pushchairs and baby back-carriers admitted

➡️ [88:NZ253642] In centre of Newcastle upon Tyne. **Cycle**: close to riverside routes. **Bus**: from surrounding areas. **Station**: Newcastle ¼ml. **Underground**: Tyne & Wear Metro-Manors, ¼ml. **Road**: close to Tyne Bridge and A167

🅿️ No parking on site. City centre car parks nearby; pay & display 30yds

NT properties nearby
Cherryburn, George Stephenson's Birthplace, Gibside, Souter Lighthouse, Washington Old Hall

Holy Jesus Hospital								
3 Feb–2 Jul	12–4	M	**T**	**W**	**T**	F	S	S
6 Jul–28 Aug	12–4	**M**	**T**	**W**	**T**	**F**	S	S
1 Sep–10 Dec	12–4	M	**T**	**W**	**T**	F	S	S
12 Jan–28 Jan 10	12–4	M	**T**	**W**	**T**	F	S	S

Closed BH Mons and Good Fri. Guided tours first Sat of every month except Jan 10, 9–4

Lindisfarne Castle

Holy Island, Berwick-upon-Tweed, Northumberland TD15 2SH

🏰 🏠 ♿ ✳️ ✈️ 🛎️ 🏠 📷 🗝️ 😊 👫 🎥 🚶

🚲 🔔 1944

(6:G1)

Romantic 16th-century castle with spectacular views, transformed by Lutyens into an Edwardian holiday home

Dramatically perched on a rocky crag and accessible over a causeway at low tide only, the island castle presents an exciting and alluring aspect. Originally a Tudor fort, it was converted into a private house in 1903 by the young Edwin Lutyens. The small rooms are full of intimate decoration and design, with windows looking down upon the charming walled garden planned by Gertrude Jekyll. The property also has several extremely well-preserved 19th-century lime kilns.

What's new in 2009 New green garden interpretation, explaining composting and record of climate conditions

⭐ Holy Island can only be reached by vehicle or on foot via a 3ml causeway, which is closed from two hours before high tide until three hours after. Tide tables are listed in local newspapers, on Northumberland County Council website and displayed at the causeway. To avoid disappointment check safe crossing and castle times before making a long/special journey. No large bags, pushchairs or rucksacks in castle. Emergency WC only; otherwise nearest WC in village 1ml from castle

Lindisfarne Castle								
14 Feb–22 Feb	10–3	**M**	**T**	**W**	**T**	**F**	**S**	**S**
14 Mar–1 Nov	Times vary	M	**T**	**W**	**T**	**F**	**S**	**S**
27 Dec–29 Dec	10–3	**M**	**T**	W	T	F	**S**	**S**
Garden								
All year	10–dusk	**M**	**T**	**W**	**T**	**F**	**S**	**S**

Open BH Mons (inc. Scottish BHols). Lindisfarne is a tidal island accessed via a 3ml causeway at low tide. Therefore the castle opening times vary depending on the tides. On open days the castle will open for 5hrs, which will always include 12–3. It will open either 10–3 or 12–5. The NT flag will fly only when the castle is open. To obtain a copy of the tide tables and detailed opening times send sae to Lindisfarne Castle stating which month you wish to visit or refer to www.lindisfarne.org.uk

For public transport details, see page 377

T 01289 389244
E lindisfarne@nationaltrust.org.uk

Guided tours by arrangement outside normal opening times

Gertrude Jekyll garden talks. Weddings

Headland walk around the castle

Building Grounds

In main street on Holy Island showing a virtual tour of the castle

Baby-changing and feeding facilities. Front-carrying baby slings for loan. Children's quiz/trail

Suitable for school groups. Hands-on activities

Castle field is part of an island cycle route

→ [75:NU136417] **Foot**: castle is approached on foot from main Holy Island village and car park, 1ml from entrance. **Cycle**: NCN1. Coast & Castles cycle route. **Bus**: Travelsure 477 from ⬛ Berwick-upon-Tweed, with connecting buses at Beal to and from Newcastle. Times vary with season and tides. Also private island minibus service from Holy Island car park to castle. **Station**: Berwick-upon-Tweed 10ml from causeway. **Road**: on Holy Island, 5ml E of A1 across causeway

The dining room at Lindisfarne Castle, Northumberland

P Parking (not NT), 1ml (pay & display), charge inc. NT members

NT properties nearby
Dunstanburgh Castle, Farne Islands, Ros Castle, St Aidan's and Shoreston Dunes, St Cuthbert's Cave

Lindisfarne Castle, Northumberland, was converted into a private house by Edwin Lutyens

Dogs assisting visitors with disabilities are always welcome

Souter Lighthouse

Coast Road, Whitburn, Sunderland,
Tyne & Wear SR6 7NH

Y 1990 (6:15)

Striking Victorian lighthouse above 2½ miles of beach, cliff and grasslands with spectacular views

Now boldly painted in red and white hoops, Souter Lighthouse opened in 1871 and was the first to use alternating electric current, the most advanced lighthouse technology of its day. The engine room, light tower and keeper's living quarters are all on view, and there is a DVD, model and information display. A ground-floor closed-circuit TV shows views from the top for those unable to climb. The Compass Room contains hands-on exhibits for all visitors, covering storms at sea, communication from ship to shore, pirates and smugglers, lighthouse life, lighting the seas and shipwreck. Immediately to the north is The Leas, 2½ miles of beach, cliff and grassland with spectacular views, flora and fauna, and to the south, Whitburn Coastal Park, with coastal walks to the Whitburn Point Local Nature Reserve.

[i] **T** 0191 529 3161
E souter@nationaltrust.org.uk

Countryside festival, talks and family events and activities

Rockpool rambles and coastal walks

Building 🔹🔹🔹 **Grounds** 🔹

NT shop

Tea-room. Home-made food (special dietary requirements catered for), inc. seasonal vegetables and fruit grown in lighthouse grounds. Children's menu. Paint Store Pantry in Foghorn Field, within lighthouse grounds. Open weekends throughout season and other days, weather permitting. Children's menu. Coffee shop by shop

Baby-changing facilities. Hip-carrying infant seats for loan. Children's play area. Family guide. Children's quiz/trail. Family activity packs. Family events and activities. Families

The fascinating Souter Lighthouse, opened in 1871

welcome but for safety reasons back-carriers are not permitted inside. At busy times it may not be possible to allow small children up steep staircase

Suitable for school groups. Education room/centre. Hands-on activities. Interpretation panels along coastal path

On leads and only in grounds

[88:NZ408641] **Foot**: South Tyneside Heritage Trail; 'Walking Works Wonders' local trail. **Cycle**: NCN1, adjacent to property. **Bus**: Stagecoach North East E1 ⊠ Sunderland–South Shields (passing ⊠ Sunderland and Tyne & Wear Metro South Shields). **Station**: East Boldon (Tyne & Wear Metro) 3ml. **Road**: 2½ml S of South Shields and 5ml N of Sunderland on A183 coast road

[P] Free parking, 100yds. Car-park barrier locked at set times in the evening – please see notices at entrance

NT properties nearby
Gibside, Ormesby Hall, Penshaw Monument, Washington Old Hall

Souter Lighthouse									
14 Mar–1 Nov	11–5	M	T	W	T	F	S	S
Open Good Fri								

For public transport details, see page 377

Wallington

Cambo, Morpeth, Northumberland NE61 4AR

🎴🎴🎴🎴🎴🎴🎴🎴🎴🎴🎴🎴🎴🎴
🎴🎴 1941   **(6:G4)**

Magnificent mansion with fine interiors and collections, set in an extensive garden and parkland

Dating from 1688, the house was home to many generations of the Blackett and Trevelyan families, who all left their mark. The restrained Palladian exterior gives way to the magnificent rococo plasterwork of the interior, which houses fine ceramics, paintings, needlework and a collection of dolls' houses. The Central Hall was decorated to look like an Italian courtyard, heavily influenced by the Pre-Raphaelites, with a series of scenes of Northumbrian history by William Bell Scott. The original formality of Sir Walter Blackett's 18th-century landscape, influenced by 'Capability' Brown, who went to school in the estate village, underlies the present surroundings. There are walks through a variety of lawns, shrubberies and woodland, enlivened with water features, lakes, buildings, sculpture and a wildlife hide. The beautiful walled garden has varied collections of plants and a well-stocked conservatory. Longer estate walks encompass wooded valleys and high moorland, including land around the recently reacquired Folly at Rothley Castle.

What's new in 2009 A new exhibition space has been created in the house to showcase the quality of the reserve collections. It will allow for a changing programme of exhibits associated with Wallington, offering visitors a chance to see items not normally on display

⭐ The walled garden, grounds and farm shop are open all year, in support of the estate's farm tenants and other regional suppliers

ℹ️ **T** 01670 773967 (Infoline), 01670 773600
E wallington@nationaltrust.org.uk

🎫 Out-of-hours house and garden tours by arrangement

🎭 Year-round programme for all ages and interests, including open-air theatre, tours and talks, music and concerts, dancing, Family Fun Day, food and craft festival

🚶 Leaflets for self-guided walks available

Wallington									
House									
28 Feb–27 Sep	11–1* & 1–5	**M**	T	**W**	**T**	**F**	**S**	**S**	
28 Sep–1 Nov	11–1* & 1–4:30	**M**	T	**W**	**T**	**F**	**S**	**S**	
Walled garden									
1 Mar–31 Mar	10–6	**M**	**T**	**W**	**T**	**F**	**S**	**S**	
1 Apr–30 Sep	10–7	**M**	**T**	**W**	**T**	**F**	**S**	**S**	
1 Oct–31 Oct	10–6	**M**	**T**	**W**	**T**	**F**	**S**	**S**	
1 Nov–31 Jan 10	10–4	**M**	**T**	**W**	**T**	**F**	**S**	**S**	
Gift shop/restaurant									
16 Feb–24 May	10:30–5:30	**M**	T	**W**	**T**	**F**	**S**	**S**	
25 May–27 Sep	10:30–5:30	**M**	**T**	**W**	**T**	**F**	**S**	**S**	
28 Sep–1 Nov	10:30–4:30	**M**	T	**W**	**T**	**F**	**S**	**S**	
4 Nov–31 Jan 10	10:30–4:30	M	T	**W**	**T**	**F**	**S**	**S**	
Farm Shop outside turnstile									
16 Feb–27 Sep	10:30–5	**M**	**T**	**W**	**T**	**F**	**S**	**S**	
28 Sep–31 Jan 10	10:30–4	**M**	T	**W**	**T**	**F**	**S**	**S**	

*House: open Fri–Mon during these times for booked tours only, & Wed/Thurs during school hols; fully open 1–19 Apr & 11 Jul–30 Aug (free flow operating). House closed Tues. Last admission to house 1hr before closing. Farm shop: open Tues in Dec.
Garden/grounds open all year

♿ 🅿️ 🅳 🔤 ⋮ 🎧 🚹 🔲
Building 🔣🔣⬍🔲 **Grounds** 🔣➡️🔣

📷 NT shop. Plant sales and farm shop

☕ Restaurant (upstairs, downstairs seating available on request). May be limited off-season. Children's menu

🚼 Baby-changing facilities. Front-carrying baby slings and hip-carrying infant seats for loan around house. Children's play area. Children's quiz/trail. Tracker Packs (on prior request). Family Fun Day

The east front of Wallington, Northumberland

🪑 Suitable for school groups. Hands-on activities

🐕 On leads only in grounds and walled garden

➜ [81:NZ030843] **Foot**: Public transport limited, contact property for details.
Bus: Northumbria Minicoaches 419 from Morpeth, Wed, Fri only (passing close ☒ Morpeth). **Road**: A1 N to Newcastle then 20ml NW (A696, airport/ Ponteland road), and turn off on B6342 to Cambo. A1 S to Morpeth (A192) then 12ml W (B6343)

P Free parking, 200yds

NT properties nearby
Cragside, Gibside

Washington Old Hall: the Lower Garden

Washington Old Hall

The Avenue, Washington Village, Washington, Tyne & Wear NE38 7LE

 1956   (6:H5)

Manor house associated with the family of George Washington

Washington Old Hall is a delightful stone-built 17th-century manor house, which incorporates parts of the original medieval home of George Washington's direct ancestors. It is from here that the family took their surname of 'Washington'. There are displays on George Washington, and the recent history of the Hall. There is also a fine collection of oil paintings, delftware and heavily carved oak furniture, giving an authentic impression of gentry life following the turbulence of the English Civil War. The tranquil Jacobean garden leads to the Nuttery, a wildflower nut orchard.

⭐ Improvements to provide level access to all garden areas

ℹ **T** 0191 416 6879
E washingtonoldhall@nationaltrust.org.uk

🎪 4 July Independence Day celebrations. Good Food event

♿ 🅿 🚻 ⠿ 🅰 🎨 🖥 📑 **Building** 🔥 ♿
Grounds 🔥

🛍 Souvenir desk in entrance hall

🍴 Tea-room (not NT) on first floor. Serving light refreshments (run by Friends of Washington Old Hall)

👶 Hip-carrying infant seats for loan. Children's quiz/ trail. Pushchairs admitted (ground floor only)

🪑 Suitable for school groups. Education room/centre

🐕 On leads only in garden

➜ [88:NZ312566] In Washington Village next to church on the hill. **Cycle**: NCN7, 1ml.
Bus: Go North East W6 from Washington Galleries bus station to Hall; connections on M1–M3 from Heworth Metro, X2, 56 from ☒ Sunderland. **Station**: Heworth (Tyne & Wear Metro) 4ml; Newcastle 7ml. **Road**: 7ml S of Newcastle, 5ml from The Angel of the North. From A1 exit Jct 64 and follow brown signs. From A19 join A1231 and follow brown signs. From all other routes, join A1231 and follow brown signs

P Free parking in small car park beside Old Hall. Otherwise unrestricted parking on The Avenue. Coaches must park on The Avenue

NT properties nearby
Gibside, Ormesby Hall, Penshaw Monument, Souter Lighthouse

Washington Old Hall								
House								
16 Mar–1 Nov	11–5	M	T	W	T	F	S	S
Garden								
As house	10–5	M	T	W	T	F	S	S
Tea-room								
As house	11–4	M	T	W	T	F	S	S
Open Good Fri and Easter Sat								

Please remember – your membership card is *always* needed for free admission

Wales

Wales is a land of myth and legend, and the National Trust is responsible for protecting large swathes of it for this and future generations to enjoy.

A sixth of the coastline, a total of 137 miles, is owned and managed by the Trust – including many popular beaches on Gower, Pembrokeshire, Llŷn, Anglesey and Ceredigion.

The Trust also cares for 45,000 hectares (111,200 acres) of land, much of it in Snowdonia and the Brecon Beacons.

Visitors enjoy walking along the miles of rugged coastline – join them and you may be lucky enough to catch a glimpse of new-born seals or dolphins riding the waves. By following one of the hundreds of upland footpaths you'll be guaranteed a breathtaking view of some of the most dramatic and iconic landscapes in Wales.

Superb scenery and ancient history

Pembrokeshire is famed for its superb scenically and geologically varied coastline. Legends of Celtic saints will take you on a mythical journey into the past.

When following the coastal footpath it's hard not to notice that it is studded with Iron Age promontory forts. There are fine examples at Greenala and Fishpond Camp on the Stackpole Estate, and Porth y Rhaw near Solva. St David's Head is a classic prehistoric landscape, complete with chambered graves.

Fine circular walks can be found at Stackpole (lakes and cliffs), Marloes, St David's Head, Dinas Island near Fishguard, Little Milford and Lawrenny Woods on the secluded River Cleddau.

Sweeping beaches and sheltered bays

The Llŷn Peninsula is one of the jewels of Wales. Multicoloured beach huts provide a vibrant backdrop to the long, sweeping beach at Llanbedrog. In the sheltered bay at

Above left: **Marloes Sands and St Anne's Head, Pembrokeshire**
Above right: **Snowdonia**

The headland at Pen Anglas on the Pembrokeshire coast

Previous page: **suitcases in the Luggage Room at Newton House, Dinefwr Park, Carmarthenshire**

Porthor the sand famously whistles underfoot, due to the unique shape of the grains. The fishing village of Porthdinllaen is picture-postcard perfect. An exhibition about its history and traditions is open throughout the season.

For one of the best views in Wales stroll to the Coastguard's Hut on top of Mynydd Mawr – you may even see as far as Ireland on a clear day. Look out for rare choughs flying overhead, dolphins swimming in the bay and seals basking in the sun. A coastal path has recently been opened around the whole peninsula.

Further south, Llandanwg has a beautiful, sandy beach with views across to the Llŷn Peninsula and a medieval church half buried in sand. Egryn, a site of continuous habitation for more than 5,000 years, is only a stone's throw away. The Medieval Hall House and outbuildings are being restored and will be open on certain days later this year.

Legend and majesty

Snowdonia is a land of legend, majesty and breathtaking beauty. The National Trust cares for eleven of its peaks, as well as miles of footpaths. A wheelchair-accessible, riverside path in the village of Beddgelert leads to the grave of the legendary faithful hound, Gelert, mistakenly killed by his master after saving the life of the Prince's young baby.

Historic parkland

The Dinefwr Historic Parkland in Carmarthenshire is a very special place and is now a National Nature Reserve due to its 'Capability' Brown-inspired landscape. Why not enjoy an historic walk with stunning views towards the castle, house and along the Tywi Valley? You may even see some resident fallow deer or some of the stunning white park cattle that have been in Dinefwr for more than 1,000 years.

There are three walks in the upland 1,000-hectare (2,500-acre) Dolaucothi Estate. Glorious views across the Cothi Valley will leave you breathless, and you will almost certainly see red kites.

Paxton's Tower, west of Llandeilo, was built as a folly in the early 1800s,

Newton House sits in Dinefwr Park, Carmarthenshire

and standing on the first floor, you will experience commanding views along the Towy Valley.

An iconic and dramatic landscape

With its spectacular combination of sensational valleys, distinctive flat-topped summits, craggy slopes, tumbling streams and wildlife-rich moorland, the Brecon Beacons is home to some of Wales' most iconic and dramatic landscapes, including some of its most popular gems – Pen y Fan, Sugarloaf, Skirrid and Henrhyd Falls.

The picturesque beauty spot of Henrhyd Falls on the Nant Llech boasts the impressive title of the highest waterfall in South Wales.

A haven for wildlife

The lagoon at Cemlyn on Anglesey is a haven for wildlife and nesting birds. During the winter it is a great place to come and watch the wildfowl,

Paxton's Tower, Dyfed, was built in 1811 as a memorial to Lord Nelson

while the late spring sees the return of a colony of Arctic and common terns for their nesting season.

Unspoilt charm

The coast of Ceredigion has an unspoilt and intimate charm, and is nationally important as a conservation resource. The gently rolling coastline, with occasional striking rocky outcrops and steep wooded river valleys which run inland, is a valuable example of man's long-term relationship with his environment.

Mwnt is a small horseshoe-shaped bay with steep cliffs that run south from the beach. The site is of great historical importance – it was a 13th-century battlefield against the invading Flemish, who left their mark on many place names in the area. This is probably the best place in Ceredigion to spot a bottlenose dolphin.

A few miles north is Penbryn – a golden beach which is a safe and popular magnet for families. The wooded Hoffnant Valley, also known locally as 'Cwm Lladron' (the Robber's Valley), was a well-known destination for illicit Irish cargoes during the 18th century. Cwmtudu,

Llŷn Gwynánt on the Hafod y Llan Estate, Snowdonia

another tiny cove famed for smuggling, is also well worth a visit.

Fabulous walks and dramatic wrecks

One of Gower's most iconic beauty spots is, undoubtedly, the spectacular Rhossili. The three-mile long, sweeping bay is on the very tip of the Gower Peninsula. To add to the drama, wooden ribs of the *Helvetia*, shipwrecked in 1887, protrude from the sand at low tide. There are fabulous walks along the clifftop towards the tidal island of Worm's Head and the old coastguard lookout.

The area has a highly valued and wide range of important habitats and species. Among its gems are the black bog ant, chough, rare marsh fritillary butterfly and brown hare.

My favourite place

My favourite place is where I work. That is Craflwyn, near Beddgelert, Snowdonia. Once a Victorian gentleman's estate, it's now a busy volunteering centre and base for our work in West Snowdonia and Llŷn.

If you follow the footpath up through the mossy woods, you soon find yourself away from all the crowds and among the most beautiful scenery. The best time to visit is in May. The woods are full of the promise of spring, and when you finally come out onto the open hill, the happy call of the cuckoo often echoes among the rocks and scattered rowan trees.

Richard Neale
Property Manager for West Snowdonia and Llŷn

Mae'r wybodaeth sydd yn y llawlyfr hwn am feddiannau'r Ymddiriedolaeth Genedlaethol yng Nghymru ar gael yn Gymraeg o Swyddfa'r Ymddiriedolaeth Genedlaethol, Sgwar y Drindod, Llandudno LL30 2DE, ffôn 01492 860123.

www.nationaltrust.org.uk/coastandcountryside

Aberconwy House

Castle Street, Conwy LL32 8AY

🏠 📷 🎨 🎭 👫 🖼️ 1934   **(4:E2)**

14th-century merchant's house

This is the only medieval merchant's house in Conwy to have survived the turbulent history of the walled town over nearly six centuries. Furnished rooms and an audio-visual presentation show daily life from different periods in its history.

⭐ The house has limited electric lighting and is therefore dark on dull days. No WC, nearest 50yds on quay

ℹ️ **T** 01492 592246
   E aberconwyhouse@nationaltrust.org.uk

🎭 Various musical events

♿ 📷 🎨 **Building** ♿

👫 Family guide. Children's quiz/trail

🖼️ Suitable for school groups

➡️ [115:SH781777] At junction of Castle Street and High Street. **Cycle**: NCN5. **Bus**: from surrounding areas. **Station**: Conwy 300yds

🅿️ No parking on site

NT properties nearby Bodnant Garden, Conwy Suspension Bridge, Penrhyn Castle, Plas Newydd Country House and Gardens

Aberconwy House									
House									
25 Mar–1 Nov	11–5	M	T	W	T	F	S	S	
Shop									
1 Mar–24 Mar	10–5	M	T	W	T	F	S	S	
25 Mar–1 Nov	10–5:30	M	T	W	T	F	S	S	
2 Nov–31 Dec	10–5	M	T	W	T	F	S	S	
2 Jan–31 Jan 10	11–5	M	T	W	T	F	S	S	
Shop closed 25/26 Dec. Shop opens 11 on Suns									

Aberdulais Falls, near Neath, Neath & Port Talbot

Aberdeunant

Taliaris, Llandeilo, Carmarthenshire SA19 6DL

🏠 🛗 ♿ 🎨 🚶 1996   **(4:E8)**

Traditional Carmarthenshire farmhouse in an unspoilt setting

⭐ As the property is extremely small, visitor access is limited to no more than six people at a time. The property is administered and maintained on the Trust's behalf by a resident tenant. The gegin fawr (farm kitchen) and one bedroom are shown to visitors. No WC

ℹ️ **T** 01558 650177 (Dolaucothi Gold Mines)
   E aberdeunant@nationaltrust.org.uk

➡️ Full details are sent on booking

Aberdeunant
Admission by guided tour and appointment only. Tours take place April to Sept: first Sat & Sun of each month 12–5. Tel. Dolaucothi Gold Mines to book. Last booking taken at 5 on Fri prior to opening

Aberdulais Falls

Aberdulais, nr Neath, Neath & Port Talbot SA10 8EU

🛗 ♿ 🏠 🛍️ 🎨 🌳 🎭 👫 🖼️ 🍴 1980   **(4:E9)**

Famous waterfalls and fascinating industrial site with tin workers' exhibition

For more than 400 years the Falls provided the energy to drive the wheels of industry. In 1584 a copper-smelting furnace was established and the remains of the best surviving example of a small water-powered tin works can be seen. It has also been visited by famous artists, such as Turner in 1796. The site today houses a unique hydroelectric scheme which has been developed to harness the waters of the River Dulais. The Turbine House provides access to an interactive computer, fish pass, observation window and display panels. Special lifts enable visitors to access the upper levels, which afford excellent views of the Falls. The waterwheel is the largest currently used in Europe to generate electricity, which makes Aberdulais Falls self-sufficient in environmentally friendly energy. The new visitor building has an air heat recovery unit to heat the building – the first commercial one in the UK.

What's new in 2009 New exhibition

Please remember – your membership card is *always* needed for free admission

⭐ The operation of the fish pass, waterwheel and turbine is subject to water levels and maintenance. Please follow NT brown signs, not Sat Nav

ℹ️ **T** 01639 636674
E aberdulais@nationaltrust.org.uk

🚶 Guided tours by arrangement

📱 Contact property for details

♿ P♿ D♿ 🖼🖼🖼🖼 **Building** 🖼🖼🖼🖼
Grounds 🖼 ➡️

🍴 The Friends of Aberdulais Falls serve light refreshments in the Old Works Library and Victorian schoolroom; other times by arrangement. Bar meals and limited car-parking at Dulais Rock Inn (not NT)

👶 Baby-changing facilities. Pushchairs and baby back-carriers admitted. Children's quiz/trail

🏫 Suitable for school groups. Education room/centre. Adult study days. Artists' days. Private hire

🐕 On leads only

➡️ [170:SS772995] **Foot**: via Neath–Aberdulais Canal footpath. **Cycle**: NCN47 passes property. Access near B&Q Neath to Neath Canal towpath and Aberdulais Canal Basin. **Bus**: First/Veolia X58, 158 Neath–Banwen; First/Veolia X63 Neath–Brecon; First/Hoggans 154 Neath–Cilfrew; all stop outside property. **Station**: Neath 3ml. **Road**: on A4109, 3ml NE of Neath. 4ml from M4 exit 43 at Llandarcy, take A465 signposted Vale of Neath

🅿️ Parking outside and on opposite side of road

NT properties nearby
Dinefwr Park and Castle, Henrhyd Falls, Rhossili Visitor Centre

Aberdulais Falls										
1 Feb–22 Mar	11–4	M	T	W	T	F	**S**	**S**
23 Mar–25 Oct	10–5	**M**	**T**	**W**	**T**	F	**S**	**S**
30 Oct–20 Dec	11–4	M	T	W	T	**F**	**S**	**S**
9 Jan–31 Jan 10	11–4	M	T	W	T	F	**S**	**S**
Christmas shop								
1 Nov–20 Dec	11–4	M	T	W	T	**F**	**S**	**S**
Open BH Mons and Good Fri: 10–5								

Yellow poppies in Bodnant Garden, Conwy

Bodnant Garden

Tal-y-Cafn, Colwyn Bay, Conwy LL28 5RE

🎪 ❄️ 🍴 🚶 📱 👶 🏫 🔔 1949   (4:F2)

World-famous garden noted for its botanical collections

One of the world's most spectacular gardens, Bodnant Garden is situated above the River Conwy, with stunning views across Snowdonia. Begun in 1875, Bodnant Garden is the creation of four generations of Aberconways and features huge Italianate terraces and formal lawns on its upper level, with a wooded valley, stream and wild garden below. There are dramatic colours throughout the season, with fine collections of rhododendrons, magnolias and camellias in early spring, and the spectacular laburnum arch, a 55-yard tunnel of golden blooms from mid May to early June. Herbaceous borders, roses, hydrangeas, water lilies and clematis delight throughout the summer, with superb autumn colours during October.

What's new in 2009 New visitor reception

⭐ The Garden and Pavilion and Magnolia Tea-rooms are managed on behalf of the Trust by the Hon. Michael McLaren QC. Picnics on grass in car park area only

ℹ️ **T** 01492 650460
E bodnantgarden@nationaltrust.org.uk

🚶 Head Gardener tours during season

📱 Varied events throughout the season

[♿] [Pᴅ] [♿ᴡᴄ] [⊡] [♿] [⊡] **Grounds** [♿] [♿] [➡]

[⌂] Shop (not NT). Plant sales, gift shop, art and craft studios. Tel: 01492 650731

[☕] Bodnant Pavilion Tea-room (licensed) in car park, serving a wide range of home-produced food. Morning coffee, lunches and afternoon teas. Magnolia Tea-room adjacent to garden exit, serving light refreshments

[♙] Baby-changing facilities. Pushchairs and baby back-carriers admitted. Front-carrying baby slings for loan. Bottle warmer and microwave in Pavilion Tea-room

[▦] Suitable for school groups. Teachers' resource packs. Activity sheets for school groups

[➔] [115/116:SH801723] **Bus:** Arriva 25, Express Motors X1 from Llandudno (passing [🚆] Llandudno Junction). **Station:** Tal-y-Cafn (U) 2ml. **Road:** 8ml S of Llandudno and Colwyn Bay off A470, entrance ½ml along the Eglwysbach road. Signposted from A55, exit 19

[P] Free parking, 50yds. Tight turning circle for coach access

NT properties nearby
Aberconwy House, Conwy Suspension Bridge, Penrhyn Castle, Tŷ Mawr Wybrnant

Bodnant Garden										
Garden/tea-room										
28 Feb–1 Nov	10–5	M	T	W	T	F	S	S		
2 Nov–15 Nov	10–4	M	T	W	T	F	S	S		
Plant centre										
All year	10–5	M	T	W	T	F	S	S		
RHS members free										

The medieval fortress of Chirk Castle, Wrexham

Chirk Castle

Chirk, Wrexham LL14 5AF

[🍷] [1981]   (4:G3)

Magnificent medieval fortress of the Welsh Marches

Completed in 1310, Chirk is the last Welsh castle from the reign of Edward I still lived in today. Features from its 700 years include the medieval tower and dungeon, 18th-century servants' hall and 20th-century laundry. There is also a 17th-century Long Gallery and grand 18th-century state apartments, with elaborate plasterwork, Adam-style furniture, tapestries and portraits. In the award-winning gardens are clipped yews, herbaceous borders and a stunning shrub garden, with many rare varieties. Other areas are more informal, with a thatched 'Hawk House' and rock garden. A terrace with stunning views looks out over the Cheshire and Salop plains and leads to a classical pavilion and 17th-century lime tree avenue. The 18th-century parkland provides a habitat for rare invertebrates and contains many mature trees and also some splendid wrought-iron gates, made in 1719 by the Davies brothers.

What's new in 2009 Experience conservation in action and discover the new technologies being used to make this 13th-century fortress greener. New tea-room at Home Farm Visitor Centre. Early spring and snowdrop opening of garden and tower

[★] Major re-servicing project of the castle under way. Access to some areas may be restricted at times and some items may be removed from display

[ℹ] **T** 01691 777701
E chirkcastle@nationaltrust.org.uk

[🚶] State Room guided tours 11–12 daily on open days. Special interest tours by arrangement (15), Wed–Fri am only. Connoisseurs tour, veteran trees, Head Gardener tour, historic laundry tour

[🎭] Early spring opening snowdrop weekends. Family events, including living history re-enactments and Family Thursdays in summer school holidays. Lecture programme and escorted walks programme. Christmas at the castle in December. Send sae for details

Unless indicated, last admission is always 30mins before closing time

Chirk Castle

Garden/tower/estate

		M	T	W	T	F	S	S
7 Feb–15 Feb	11–4	M	T	W	T	F	**S**	**S**
18 Feb–22 Feb	11–4	M	T	**W**	**T**	**F**	**S**	**S**
28 Feb–29 Mar	10–5	M	T	**W**	**T**	**F**	**S**	**S**
1 Apr–28 Jun	10–6	M	T	**W**	**T**	**F**	**S**	**S**
1 Jul–30 Aug	10–6	M	**T**	**W**	**T**	**F**	**S**	**S**
2 Sep–30 Sep	10–6	M	T	**W**	**T**	**F**	**S**	**S**
1 Oct–1 Nov	10–5	M	T	**W**	**T**	**F**	**S**	**S**

State Rooms*

		M	T	W	T	F	S	S
18 Feb–22 Feb	11–4	M	T	**W**	**T**	**F**	**S**	**S**
28 Feb–29 Mar	11–4	M	T	**W**	**T**	**F**	**S**	**S**
1 Apr–28 Jun	11–5	M	T	**W**	**T**	**F**	**S**	**S**
1 Jul–30 Aug	11–5	M	**T**	**W**	**T**	**F**	**S**	**S**
2 Sep–28 Sep	11–5	M	T	**W**	**T**	**F**	**S**	**S**
1 Oct–1 Nov	11–4	M	T	**W**	**T**	**F**	**S**	**S**

NT shop/farm tea-room

As garden & tower	10–5**

Farm shop/castle tea-room

As garden & tower	11–5**

Open BH Mons. Last admission to garden & tower 1hr before closing. *Guided tours 11–12, free flow 12–closing. **Closes 4 in Feb, Mar & Oct

🚶 Circular 1¼ml walk through historic parkland, with ancient trees and wild flowers

♿ 🅿 🄳 🛗 🚾 ⬤⬤ 🚣 📖 📷 🔤

Building 🔣 L 🔣 Grounds 🔣

🏪 NT gift shop. Farm shop with local and estate produce. Plant sales, including plants from garden. Second-hand bookshop

🍽 Tea-room and kiosk at Home Farm Visitor Centre. Main tea-room at castle. Children's menu

👶 Baby-changing and feeding facilities. Front-carrying baby slings and hip-carrying infant seats for loan. Family activity rooms. Children's play area. Children's quiz/trail. Children's Tracker Packs for woodland walk. Giant-sized family games in the garden

👥 Suitable for school groups. Education room/centre. Live interpretation. Hands-on activities. Adult study days

🐕 On leads and only in car park and on estate walks

➡ [126:SJ275388] **Foot**: permitted footpaths from Chirk and Offa's Dyke Path, open April–Sept. Entrance and exit drives during season

1½ml to Visitor Centre and castle. 1½ml from Llangollen Canal–moor near Chirk Tunnel. **Bus**: Arriva 2/A Wrexham–Oswestry. **Station**: Chirk (U) ¼ml to gates, 1¼ml to castle. **Road**: entrance 1ml off A5, 2ml W of Chirk village; 7ml S of Wrexham, 6ml S of Llangollen, signposted off A483

🅿 Free parking, 50yds to Visitor Centre, 200yds to castle. Short, steep hill from Visitor Centre to castle and garden

NT properties nearby

Attingham Park, Erddig, Powis Castle

Cilgerran Castle

nr Cardigan, Pembrokeshire SA43 2SF

🔲 🔲 1938 (4:C7)

Striking 13th-century ruined castle

The remains of the castle are perched overlooking the spectacular Teifi Gorge and have inspired many artists, including Turner.

⭐ Cilgerran Castle is in the guardianship of Cadw: Welsh Historic Monuments

ℹ **T** 01443 336104
E cilgerrancastle@nationaltrust.org.uk

➡ [145:SN195431] **Bus**: First/Richards 460/1, Carmarthen–Ceredigan, alight Llechryd, 1½ml by footpath. **Road**: on rock above left bank of the Teifi, 3ml SE of Cardigan, 1½ml E of A478

Cilgerran Castle

		M	T	W	T	F	S	S
1 Feb–31 Mar	10–4	**M**	**T**	**W**	**T**	**F**	**S**	**S**
1 Apr–31 Oct	9:30–6	**M**	**T**	**W**	**T**	**F**	**S**	**S**
1 Nov–31 Jan 10	10–4	**M**	**T**	**W**	**T**	**F**	**S**	**S**

Having fun at Chirk Castle, Wrexham

Colby Woodland Garden

nr Amroth, Pembrokeshire SA67 8PP

| 1980 | (4:C8)

Beautiful woodland garden with year-round interest

Set in a tranquil and secluded valley, this glorious informal woodland garden with a fascinating industrial past, offers a variety of walks along open and wooded pathways. Rhododendrons, magnolias, azaleas and camellias, underplanted with bluebells, provide spring colour. Later highlights are the summer hydrangeas and autumn foliage.

What's new in 2009 Redevelopment and replanting of many garden areas

⭐ The early 19th-century house is not open; Mr & Mrs A. Scourfield Lewis kindly allow access to the walled garden during opening hours

ℹ️ **T** 01834 811885
E colby@nationaltrust.org.uk

💟 Numerous events including guided walks, talks and lunches. Easter trails, family fun days, wildlife events, summer holiday activities

🚶 Beautiful walks through the wooded valleys of the Colby Estate and down to the sea at Amroth

♿ 🅳 🚻 ⏺ 🅰 🅲 **Grounds** 🅱 ➡️ 🅵

🎁 NT gift shop and gallery displaying work of Pembrokeshire artists and craftspeople

🍴 Bothy tea-room (NT-approved concession) (licensed). Serves freshly prepared food using local produce. Children's menu

🚼 Baby-changing facilities. Pushchairs and baby back-carriers admitted. Hip-carrying infant seats for loan. Children's quiz/trail

🏫 Suitable for school groups

🐕 On leads, but not in walled garden

➡️ [158:SN155080] **Foot**: from beach via public footpath in Amroth (beside Amroth Arms). **Bus**: Silcox 350/1 from Tenby (passing ➤ Kilgetty). **Station**: Kilgetty (U) 2¼ml. **Road**: 1½ml inland from Amroth beside Carmarthen Bay. Follow brown signs from

An enticing path through rhododendrons at Colby Woodland Garden, Pembrokeshire

A477 Tenby–Carmarthen road or off coast road at Amroth Castle Caravan Park

🅿️ Free parking, 50yds. Contact property for route map for coaches and cars

NT properties nearby
Stackpole, Tudor Merchant's House

Colby Woodland Garden									
Woodland garden/shop									
14 Feb–1 Nov	10–5	M	T	W	T	F	S	S
Tea-room									
4 Apr–1 Nov	10–5	M	T	W	T	F	S	S
Walled garden/gallery									
4 Apr–1 Nov	11–5	M	T	W	T	F	S	S

For further information, visit www.nationaltrust.org.uk

Coats, hats, boots and shoes arranged in the Brushing Room at Newton House, Dinefwr

Conwy Suspension Bridge

Conwy LL32 8LD

1965 (4:E2)

Elegant suspension bridge and toll-keeper's house

See how trade and travel brought Conwy to life and discover how a husband and wife kept Thomas Telford's bridge open every day of the year, whatever the weather.

What's new in 2009 Guidebook exploring the story of this fascinating bridge and town

No WC

T 01492 573282
E conwybridge@nationaltrust.org.uk

Throughout season

Building **Grounds**

NT shop 600yds from bridge

Family guide

Suitable for school groups

[115:SH785775] 100yds from town centre, adjacent to Conwy Castle. **Cycle**: NCN5. **Bus**: Arriva buses from surrounding areas. **Station**: Conwy ¼ml; Llandudno Junction ½ml

No parking on site

NT properties nearby
Aberconwy House, Bodnant Garden, Penrhyn Castle, Plas Newydd Country House and Gardens

Conwy Suspension Bridge		
25 Mar–1 Nov	11-5	M T W T F S S

Dinefwr Park and Castle

Llandeilo, Carmarthenshire SA19 6RT

1990 (4:E8)

12th-century Welsh castle, historic house and 18th-century landscape park, enclosing a medieval deer park

Land of power and influence for more than 1,000 years, Dinefwr Park and Castle is an iconic place in the history of Wales. Dinefwr Castle, which is where the Lord Rhys, Prince of Deheubarth, held court, overlooks the superb 18th-century designed landscape and Newton House. The ground floor and basement of Newton House are furnished *c*.1912 and there is a new exhibition on the first floor which tells visitors about Dinefwr's past. Visitors will be inspired to explore the park, home to more than 100 fallow deer and a herd of rare White Park cattle.

What's new in 2009 Exhibition on the first floor of Newton House tells the story of the history and landscape of Dinefwr. NT gift shop and small play/picnic area for families

T 01558 824512
E dinefwr@nationaltrust.org.uk

Regular guided tours of Newton House and the deer park. Badger watches can be booked

Food and Country Festival, summer events, Christmas fair and evening events

Five walks leaflets

Building **Grounds**

New NT gift shop

Tea-room (not NT). Children's menu

Baby-changing and feeding facilities. Pushchairs admitted. Children's quiz/trail

Suitable for school groups. Education room/centre

On leads and only in outer park

Dinefwr Park and Castle		
15 Mar–1 Nov	11-5	M T W T F S S
6 Nov–20 Dec	11-5	M T W T F S S

Charges for National Trust members apply on some special event days

→ [159:SN625225] **Bus**: from surrounding areas to Llandeilo, then 1ml. **Station**: Llandeilo ½ml. **Road**: on W outskirts of Llandeilo A40(T); from Swansea take M4 to Pont Abraham, then A48(T) to Cross Hands and A476 to Llandeilo; entrance by police station

P Parking, 50yds. Narrow access

NT properties nearby
Aberdeunant, Aberdulais Falls, Dolaucothi Gold Mines, Llanerchaeron, Paxton's Tower

Dolaucothi Gold Mines: first mined by the Romans

Dolaucothi Gold Mines

Pumsaint, Llanwrda, Carmarthenshire SA19 8US

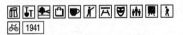
🚴 1941
(4:E7)

Gold mines in use from Roman times to the 20th century

These unique gold mines are set amid wooded hillsides overlooking the beautiful Cothi Valley. The Romans who exploited the site almost 2,000 years ago left behind a complex of pits, channels, adits and tanks. Mining resumed in the 19th century and continued through the 20th century, reaching a peak in 1938. Guided tours take visitors through the Roman and the more recent underground workings. The main mine yard contains a collection of 1930s mining machinery, an exhibition about the history of gold and gold mining, video and interpretation. Gold panning gives visitors the opportunity to experience the frustrations of the search for gold. Other attractions include waymarked walks and picnic areas. There is fishing and accommodation on the estate, including a 35-pitch touring caravan site.

★ Underground tour (charge inc. NT members). Stout footwear essential. Younger children may not be carried on the tours. Pushchairs may be taken on the Long Adit tour, but children must wear a correctly fitting hard hat. Please tel. for advice

i **T** 01558 825146 (Infoline), 01558 650177 **E** dolaucothi@nationaltrust.org.uk

🎭 Roman weekends, vintage machinery day, spooky Hallowe'en tours, Easter trails

🚶 Leaflet showing walks around the 1,000-hectares (2,500-acre) Dolaucothi Estate

♿ 🦽 👓 🦻 Building 🦼 🦽

📷 Welsh gold for sale (including by mail order)

🍽 Tea-room

👶 Baby-changing and feeding facilities. Pushchairs admitted. Children's quiz/trail. Children's parties (booking essential)

🎒 Suitable for school groups. Education room/centre

🐕 On leads only. May go on guided Roman tour

🚴 2½ml of NT permitted cycle route

→ [146:SN662403] **Bus**: Morris 289 from Lampeter. **Station**: Llanwrda (U), 8ml. **Road**: between Lampeter and Llanwrda on A482

P Free parking. Overflow car park available across road from main entrance

NT properties nearby
Aberdeunant, Dinefwr Park and Castle, Llanerchaeron

Dolaucothi Gold Mines									
Mines									
15 Mar–2 Nov	10–5	**M**	**T**	**W**	**T**	**F**	**S**	**S**	
Shop									
15 Mar–2 Nov	10–5	**M**	**T**	**W**	**T**	**F**	**S**	**S**	
Christmas shop									
5 Nov–20 Dec	11–5	M	T	**W**	**T**	**F**	**S**	**S**	
Tea-room									
15 Mar–2 Nov	10–5	**M**	**T**	**W**	**T**	**F**	**S**	**S**	

Groups can be booked at other times. Pumsaint Information Centre and estate walks open all year. Underground tours last about 1hr and involve hillside walking, so stout footwear is essential; helmets with lights are provided. Smaller children will be allowed on the tours only at the discretion of the property staff. Please tel. for advice

Show your card and display sticker for free parking

Erddig

Wrexham LL13 0YT

🏠 🏠 ✚ 🚻 ✨ 🌳 ♨ 🏛 ☕ 🥄 🏠 🎧 🚃 🎭 ♿
🖥 🧑 ♿ ☂ 1973 (4:H3)

Atmospheric house, featuring 485-hectare (1,200-acre) country park and formal walled garden

Winner of UKTV History 'Britain's Best' Historic House, Erddig is a house with a human face. Set within the grounds of a spectacular 485-hectare (1,200-acre) country park bordered by the River Clywedog, and overlooking a restored formal 18th-century walled garden with Victorian parterre, Yew Walk and National Collection of Ivies, Erddig is one of the most fascinating houses in Britain. Celebrating the tale of an unusually close relationship between the family of the house and their servants, the original 'upstairs, downstairs' story comes alive in a series of witty portraits with doggerel verses featuring the servants of the house going about their daily business within and around the striking collection of outbuildings – including the kitchen, laundry, bakehouse, stables, sawmill, smithy and joiner's shop. The house itself presents a stunning example of state rooms with original 18th- and 19th-century furniture and furnishings, including exquisite Chinese wallpaper. There are also horse-drawn carriage rides, cycle hire, circular walks and many events throughout the year to enjoy.

Servants' bells at Erddig, Wrexham

Erddig									
House									
28 Feb–31 Mar	11–4*	M	T	W	T	F	S	S
1 Apr–30 Jun	11–5**	M	T	W	T	F	S	S
1 Jul–31 Aug	11–5**	M	T	W	T	F	S	S
1 Sep–30 Sep	11–5**	M	T	W	T	F	S	S
3 Oct–1 Nov	11–4**	M	T	W	T	F	S	S
7 Nov–20 Dec	11–4*	M	T	W	T	F	S	S
Garden/restaurant/shop									
14 Feb–22 Feb	11–4	M	T	W	T	F	S	S
28 Feb–31 Mar	11–4	M	T	W	T	F	S	S
1 Apr–20 Jun	11–6	M	T	W	T	F	S	S
1 Jul–31 Aug	11–6	M	T	W	T	F	S	S
1 Sep–30 Sep	11–6	M	T	W	T	F	S	S
3 Oct–1 Nov	11–5	M	T	W	T	F	S	S
7 Nov–20 Dec	11–4	M	T	W	T	F	S	S

*Guided conservation tours only. **Guided tours of 'downstairs' 11–12, free flow 12–closing. Restaurant & shop close 1 hour earlier 1 April–1 Nov. Open Good Fri. Last admission 1 hour before closing. Access to house by guided tour only on Thur during July & Aug

What's new in 2009 Accessible horse-drawn carriage rides now available to accommodate less able-bodied visitors and one additional passenger. New virtual tour of the house and collections to complement the existing audio tour. New cycle hire facilities throughout Erddig Country Park. North Wales Mounted Police Unit available to view (subject to operational requirements) on Mondays and Wednesdays. Booking essential

⭐ Most rooms have no electric light; visitors wishing to make a close study of pictures and textiles should avoid dull days. The Small Chinese Room and Tapestry Room are open on Wednesdays and Saturdays only on request

ℹ️ **T** 01978 315151 (Infoline), 01978 355314
E erddig@nationaltrust.org.uk

🧑 Guided tours of the house and garden available, booking essential (charge, inc. NT members). Access to house by guided tour only on Thurs, in July and Aug (booking not required)

🎧 Audio tour of house and collections available from house entrance (charge applies)

🎭 Varied events programme, inc. Victorian and Apple festivals, specialist guest exhibitions, family events and children's activities during school summer holidays

Dogs assisting visitors with disabilities are always welcome

The Naval Monument on The Kymin, Monmouthshire

Three different walks

Building | Exhibition Room | L
Grounds

NT shop. Second-hand bookshop. Garden plant sales. Christmas shopping

Restaurant (licensed) serving traditional home-made food. Available for conferences, banqueting and private functions. Children's menu. Tea-room serving drinks and ice-cream

Baby-changing and feeding facilities. Front-carrying baby slings and hip-carrying infant seats for loan. Children's quiz. Garden Tracker Packs. Garden Art Packs. Family and children's events all year

Suitable for school groups. Education room/centre. Hands-on activities

On leads in country park

Bridleway crosses estate giving cyclists shared access. Cycle hire

[117:SJ326482] **Bus**: from surrounding areas. Alight Felin Puleston, 1ml walk through Erddig Country Park. **Station**: Wrexham Central (U) 2½ml, Wrexham General 3½ml via Erddig Rd & footpath. **Road**: 2ml S of Wrexham. Signposted A525 Whitchurch road. A483 exit 3

Free parking, 200yds from main entrance. Accessible drop-off point. Parking for three coaches

NT properties nearby Chirk Castle

The Kymin

Monmouth, Monmouthshire NP25 3SE

1902   (4:H8)

Landmark hill topped by two interesting Georgian buildings

Set in four hectares (nine acres) of woods and pleasure grounds, this property encompasses a small two-storey circular banqueting house and naval temple, a monument dedicated to the glories of the British Navy. Nelson visited the site in 1802. The grounds afford spectacular views of the surrounding countryside.

★ Croquet set and WC available when Round House is open

ℹ **T** 01600 719241
 E kymin@nationaltrust.org.uk

Offa's Dyke footpath and Wysis Way footpath cross the land

Building | Grounds

Children's quiz/trail

In grounds only

→ [162:SO528125] **Foot**: Offa's Dyke path crosses the property. **Bus**: Stagecoach Wye & Dean 35 Monmouth–Ross-on-Wye, alight May Hill/Kymin access road about 1ml, steep climb. **Road**: 2ml E of Monmouth and signposted off A4136

P Free parking, 300yds. Not suitable for coaches. Steep narrow road with hairpin bends from junction with A4136

NT properties nearby
Skenfrith Castle, Skirrid Fawr, The Weir, Westbury Court Garden

The Kymin									
Round House									
28 Mar–26 Oct	11–4	M	T	W	T	F	S	S	
Temple/grounds									
All year		M	T	W	T	F	S	S	
Open Good Fri. Round House: last entry 3:45									

Fascinated by Erddig? Be sure to visit Chirk Castle too

Llanerchaeron

Ciliau Aeron, nr Aberaeron, Ceredigion SA48 8DG

1989   **(4:D6)**

18th-century Welsh gentry estate – with house, walled gardens and home farm

Mr J. P. Ponsonby Lewes, last of the ten generations of the family to have lived here, bequeathed Llanerchaeron to the National Trust in 1989. This rare example of a self-sufficient 18th-century Welsh minor gentry estate has survived virtually unaltered. The villa, designed in the 1790s, is the most complete example of the early work of John Nash. It has its own service courtyard with dairy, laundry, brewery and salting house, and walled kitchen gardens producing fruit, vegetables, herbs and plants, all now on sale in season. The pleasure grounds with ornamental lake provide wonderful peaceful walks. The Home Farm complex has an impressive range of traditional and atmospheric outbuildings and is now a working organic farm with Welsh Black cattle, Llanwenog sheep and rare Welsh pigs. Visitors can see farming activities in progress, such as lambing, shearing and hay-making. Beyond, the wide expanse of parkland offers breathtaking walks through the beautiful Aeron Valley.

What's new in 2009 Restored saw pit shed and demonstration milking cow in the milking parlour

i **T** 01545 570200, 01545 573024
E llanerchaeron@nationaltrust.org.uk

Guided tours of the garden and Home Farm start 1:30 every Thur, June to end Sept. £1, inc. NT members. Mobile induction loop available on request

Daffodil days, Easter trail, plant fair, shearing day, brewing weekend, children's activity days, learn-about-farming day, apple week

Five walks leaflets (50p each)

Building 🚶 🐕 ♿ **Grounds** 🚶

Shop area in visitor building selling local jams, chutneys and beer, Llanerchaeron farm meat (pork, beef and lamb) and fresh produce and plants from the walled garden. Range of NT gifts and books available

Saying 'hello' to the pigs at Llanerchaeron, Ceredigion

Tea-room (NT-approved concession) in visitor building. Light lunches and teas using local produce

Baby-changing and feeding facilities. Hip-carrying infant seats for loan. Children's guide. Children's quiz/trail. Easter trail, children's activity days, learn-about-farming day

Suitable for school groups. Education room/centre. Adult study days

Cycle track to Aberaeron along old railway line links with NCN82

→ [146:SN480602] **Foot**: 2½ml foot/cycle track from Aberaeron to property along old railway track. **Bus**: Arriva/First X40 ≋ Aberystwyth– ≋ Carmarthen, alight New Inn Forge, ½ml. **Road**: 2½ml E of Aberaeron off A482

P Free parking, 50yds

NT properties nearby
Dinefwr Park and Castle, Dolaucothi Gold Mines, Mwnt, Penbryn

Llanerchaeron									
28 Feb–19 Jul	11–5	M	T	**W**	**T**	**F**	**S**	**S**
21 Jul–30 Aug	11–5	M	**T**	**W**	**T**	**F**	**S**	**S**
31 Aug–1 Nov	11–5	M	T	**W**	**T**	**F**	**S**	**S**

Open BH Mons. Farm/garden 11–5. Guided tours of house on Sat/Sun 21/22 Feb 11:30 & 1:30. House open 11:30–4

For public transport details, see page 377

Penrhyn Castle

Bangor, Gwynedd LL57 4HN

🏰 ➕ ⚡ ❄ 📷 ♦ 🎭 🔊 🗄 🎭 🖼
🍽 1951 (4:E2)

19th-century fantasy castle with spectacular contents and grounds

This enormous neo-Norman castle sits between Snowdonia and the Menai Strait. Built by Thomas Hopper between 1820 and 1845 for the wealthy Pennant family, who made their fortune from Jamaican sugar and Welsh slate, the castle is crammed with fascinating things such as a one-ton slate bed made for Queen Victoria. Hopper also designed the castle's interior with elaborate carvings, plasterwork and mock-Norman furniture. The castle contains an outstanding collection of paintings. The Victorian kitchen and other servants' rooms, including scullery, larders and chef's sitting room, have been restored to reveal the preparations for the banquet for the Prince of Wales's visit in 1894. The stable block houses an industrial railway museum, a model railway museum and a superb dolls' museum displaying a large collection of 19th- and 20th-century dolls. The 24.3 hectares (60 acres) of grounds include parkland, an extensive exotic tree and shrub collection and a Victorian walled garden.

What's new in 2009 'Castle and Quarry' – a fascinating permanent exhibition exploring Penrhyn's industrial past

[i] **T** 01248 371337 (Infoline), 01248 353084
E penrhyncastle@nationaltrust.org.uk

🎭 Specialist guided tours

🎧 In English and Welsh, £1

♿ 📷 🚻 🅿️ 📶 🔴 🎨 🖼 💻 🚪 🔋 🎭
Building 🦽🦽↕🦽 **Grounds** 🦽🦽

💺 Licensed tea-room. Children's menu. Kiosk in grounds

👶 Baby-changing and baby food heating facilities. Front-carrying baby slings and hip-carrying infant seats for loan. Children's play area. Children's guide. Children's quiz/trail. Model railway museum and dolls' museum

🖼 Suitable for school groups. Education room/centre. Hands-on activities. Adult study days

🐕 On leads and only in grounds

➡ [115:SH602720] **Cycle**: NCN5, 1¼ml.
Bus: Arriva 5/5X Caernarfon–Llandudno, KMP 9 Llandudno–Llangefni, 9A/B Llandudno–Llanberis, Padarn 76 from Bangor, all passing close 🚉 Bangor and to castle drive. **Station**: Bangor 3ml. **Road**: 1ml E of Bangor, at Llandygai on A5122. Signposted from junction 11 of A55 and A5

[P] Free parking, 500yds

NT properties nearby

Aberconwy House, Conwy Suspension Bridge, Glan Faenol, Plas Newydd Country House and Gardens, Plas yn Rhiw, Tŷ Mawr Wybrnant

Penrhyn Castle									
Castle									
1 Apr–29 Jun	12–5	M	T	W	T	F	S	S
1 Jul–31 Aug	11–5	M	T	W	T	F	S	S
2 Sep–1 Nov	12–5	M	T	W	T	F	S	S
Shop/museum									
1 Apr–1 Nov	11–5	M	T	W	T	F	S	S

Grounds and tea-room as castle but open 1hr earlier.
Victorian kitchen: as castle but last admission 4:45.
Last audio tour 4

The Lamp Room at Penrhyn Castle, Gwynedd

Plas Newydd Country House and Gardens

Llanfairpwll, Anglesey LL61 6DQ

🏠 ❄ 🌷 🖼 🏛 ☕ 🎭 🗿 🛡 👫 🎒 🚶

🔔 🍸 1976   **(4:D2)**

Home of the Marquess of Anglesey, with spectacular views of Snowdonia

Set amidst breathtakingly beautiful scenery on the banks of the Menai Strait, this elegant house was redesigned by James Wyatt in the 18th century and is an interesting mixture of classical and Gothic. The comfortable interior, restyled in the 1930s, is famous for its association with Rex Whistler, whose largest painting is here. There is also an exhibition about his work. A military museum contains campaign relics of the 1st Marquess of Anglesey, who commanded the cavalry at the Battle of Waterloo. There is a fine spring garden and Australasian arboretum with an understorey of shrubs and wild flowers, as well as a summer terrace and, later, massed hydrangeas and autumn colour. A woodland walk gives access to a marine walk beside the Menai Strait.

What's new in 2009 Two new exhibition rooms

⭐ House is accessible to manual wheelchairs only

ℹ️ **T** 01248 715272 (Infoline), 01248 714795
E plasnewydd@nationaltrust.org.uk

🎭 Connoisseurs' and garden tours

🎭 See website for information

🚶 Woodland & marine walk

Lord Anglesey's bedroom: Plas Newydd, Anglesey

♿ 🅿️ 🚗 🚐 🚻 ⠿ 🔄 📷 👓 🦽 🪜

Building 🦽 🦽 🦽 **Grounds** 🦽

🛍 Second-hand bookshop

☕ Tea-room (licensed). Home-cooked food using local produce whenever possible. Seasonal menu in Nov & Dec. Children's menu. Coffee shop and second-hand bookshop located in the north wing of the house

👫 Baby-changing facilities. Front-carrying baby slings and hip-carrying infant seats for loan. Children's play area. Family guide. High chairs in tea-room

🎒 Suitable for school groups

➡️ [114/115:SH521696] **Cycle**: NCN8, ¼ml.
Bus: Arriva 42 Bangor–Llangefni (passing ≢ Bangor & close ≢ Llanfairpwll).
Station: Llanfairpwll (U), 1¾ml. **Road**: 2ml SW of Llanfairpwll A55 junctions 7 and 8a, or A4080 to Brynsiencyn; turn off A5 at W end of Britannia Bridge

🅿️ Free parking, 400yds

NT properties nearby
Penrhyn Castle

Plas Newydd Country House and Gardens								
Shop/tea-room								
28 Mar–20 May	11–5:30	M	T	W	T	F	S	S
23 May–6 Sep	11–5:30	M	T	W	T	F	S	S
7 Sep–4 Nov	11–5:30	M	T	W	T	F	S	S
7 Nov–13 Dec	11–4	M	T	W	T	F	S	S

House 12–5 (Sat–Wed). Garden 11–5:30 (Sat–Wed). Coffee shop 11–5 (Sat–Wed). Free special interest tour at 11:15 every open day (subject to availability & for a maximum of 12 people). Open Good Fri. *Coffee shop and bookshop as house but open 11:30. Rhododendron garden open early April–early June, 11–5:30. Last admission 4:30

For general and membership enquiries, please telephone 0844 800 1895

Plas yn Rhiw

Rhiw, Pwllheli, Gwynedd LL53 8AB

| | 1952 | (4:C4)

Delightful manor house with ornamental garden and wonderful views

The house was rescued from neglect and lovingly restored by the three Keating sisters, who bought it in 1938. The views from the grounds and gardens across Cardigan Bay are among the most spectacular in Britain. The house is 16th-century with Georgian additions, and the garden contains many beautiful flowering trees and shrubs, with beds framed by box hedges and grass paths. Stunning whatever the season.

[i] **T** 01758 780219
    E plasynrhiw@nationaltrust.org.uk

[X] Specialist guided tours by arrangement

[ ] Plant sales. Easter egg hunt

[ ] ... Building [ ] [ ]

Grounds [ ] [ ]

[ ] Hot and cold drinks available in shop

[ ] Baby-changing facilities. Easter Egg hunt

[ ] Suitable for school groups

[ ] On leads and only on the woodland walk

[→] [123:SH237282] **Bus**: Arriva 17B, Pwllheli–Aberdaron (passing ≋ Pwllheli) to Rhiw village, 1ml. **Station**: Pwllheli 10ml. **Road**: 12ml SW of Pwllheli. Follow signs to Plas yn Rhiw. B4413 to Aberdaron (drive gates at bottom Rhiw Hill)

[P] Free parking, 80yds. Narrow lanes

NT properties nearby
Llanbedrog Beach, Penrhyn Castle, Porthdinllaen, Porthor

Plas yn Rhiw									
26 Mar–3 May	12–5	M	T	W	T	F	S	S
4 May–29 Jun	12–5	M	T	W	T	F	S	S
1 Jul–31 Aug	12–5	M	T	W	T	F	S	S
3 Sep–28 Sep	12–5	M	T	W	T	F	S	S
1 Oct–1 Nov	12–4	M	T	W	T	F	S	S

Open BHols. Garden and snowdrop wood open occasionally at weekends in Jan/Feb

Powis Castle and Garden

Welshpool, Powys SY21 8RF

[icons]
[Y] | 1952 | (4:G5)

Medieval castle rising dramatically above the celebrated garden

The world-famous garden, overhung with enormous clipped yews, shelters tender plants and sumptuous herbaceous borders. Laid out under the influence of Italian and French styles, it retains its original lead statues, an orangery and an aviary on the terraces. In the 18th century an informal woodland wilderness was created on the opposite ridge. High on a rock above the terraces, the castle, originally built *c.*1200, began life as a fortress of the Welsh Princes of Powys and commands magnificent views towards England. Remodelled and embellished over more than 400 years, it reflects the changing needs and ambitions of the Herbert family – with each generation adding to the magnificent collection of paintings, sculpture, furniture and tapestries. A superb collection of treasures from India is displayed in the Clive Museum. Edward, the son of Robert Clive, the conqueror of India, married Lady Henrietta Herbert in 1784, uniting the Powis and Clive estates. The 19th-century State Coach and Livery, the finest in the ownership of the National Trust, is on display in the coach house.

What's new in 2009 Talks and tours led by staff and volunteers throughout the week

[★] All visitors (inc. NT members) need to obtain a ticket from visitor reception in the main car park on arrival. Please note: dogs not allowed at the property or in the deer park

[i] **T** 01938 551944 (Infoline), 01938 551929
    E powiscastle@nationaltrust.org.uk

[X] Guided tours of castle and/or garden by arrangement

[ ] ... Building [ ]

Grounds [ ] [ ] [ ] [ ]

[ ] NT shop. Plant sales

[ ] Licensed tea-room. Serves home-made seasonal menu with fresh local ingredients. Children's menu. Garden tea-room

Unless indicated, last admission is always 30mins before closing time

Powis Castle

Garden/tea-rooms/shop

		M	T	W	T	F	S	S
1 Mar–30 Mar	11–4:30	M	T	W	T	F	S	S
2 Apr–29 Jun	11–5:30	M	T	W	T	F	S	S
1 Jul–31 Aug	11–5:30	M	T	W	T	F	S	S
3 Sep–28 Sep	11–5:30	M	T	W	T	F	S	S
1 Oct–1 Nov	11–5	M	T	W	T	F	S	S
7 Nov–29 Nov	11–3:30	M	T	W	T	F	S	S

Tea-rooms/shop

5 Dec–20 Dec	11–3:30	M	T	W	T	F	S	S

Castle/museum

1 Mar–30 Mar*	1–5	M	T	W	T	F	S	S
2 Apr–29 Jun	1–5	M	T	W	T	F	S	S
1 Jul–31 Aug	1–5	M	T	W	T	F	S	S
3 Sep–28 Sep	1–5	M	T	W	T	F	S	S
1 Oct–1 Nov	1–4	M	T	W	T	F	S	S

Last admission to castle 45mins before closing.
*Admission by guided tour only

Baby-changing and feeding facilities. Front-carrying baby slings and hip-carrying infant seats for loan. Children's quiz/trail

Suitable for school groups

→ [126:SJ216064] **Foot**: 1ml walk from Park Lane, off Broad Street in Welshpool.
Bus: Tanant Valley D71 Oswestry–Welshpool; X75 Shrewsbury–Llanidloes. On both alight High Street, 1ml. **Station**: Welshpool 1¼ml from town on footpath. **Road**: 1ml S of Welshpool; pedestrian access from High Street (A490); vehicle route signed from main road to Newtown (A483); enter by first drive gate on right

P Free parking. Tel. for advice on coach parking

NT properties nearby
Attingham Park, Chirk Castle, Erddig

Exploring the garden at Powis Castle, Powys

Rhossili Visitor Centre and Shop

Coastguard Cottages, Rhossili, Gower SA3 1PR

[icons] 1933 (4:D9)

Large NT shop and Visitor Centre set amongst spectacular countryside and beaches

Rhossili is the ideal location from which to walk along the south Gower coast and discover its rare wildlife, archaeology, unspoilt cliffs and beaches. Rhossili Bay stretches for three miles, behind it the 200-metre climb to Rhossili Down allows you to appreciate the spectacular tidal island of Worms Head and intricate medieval open-field system of The Vile. It is this patchwork of important landscape features which ensured Gower's status as the first Area of Outstanding Natural Beauty in 1956. The Visitor Centre includes a shop, exhibition and information about the area. The Trust cares for 75% of Gower's beautiful coastline and 2,226 hectares (5,500 acres) of its countryside.

What's new in 2009 Refitted shop now enlarged. Updated exhibitions in the Visitor Centre

Rhossili Visitor Centre

Coastline

		M	T	W	T	F	S	S
All year		M	T	W	T	F	S	S

Centre/shop

1 Feb–28 Feb	11–4	M	T	W	T	F	S	S
1 Mar–15 Mar	10:30–5*	M	T	W	T	F	S	S
16 Mar–2 Nov	10:30–5*	M	T	W	T	F	S	S
4 Nov–20 Dec	11–4	M	T	W	T	F	S	S
3 Jan–31 Jan 10	11–4	M	T	W	T	F	S	S

*Closes 6 on Sat/Sun during school hols.
17 Oct–2 Nov closes 4:30

★ No WC, nearest at Rhossili car park

i **T** 01792 390707
E rhossili.shop@nationaltrust.org.uk

Guided walks

Summer events inc. family activities

[icons] **Building** [icon]
Grounds [icon]

Easter egg trails and family events

🖼 Suitable for school groups. Hands-on activities. Booking essential

🐕 Must be under control and only on leads at lambing time; not in Visitor Centre or shop

🚲 Cycling on bridleways

➡ [159:SS418883] **Bus**: Veolia 118 from Swansea–South Gower. **Road**: SW tip of Gower Peninsula, approached from Swansea via A4118 and then B4247

🅿 Parking (not NT), 50yds. Charge inc. NT members

NT properties nearby
Aberdulais Falls, Brecon Beacons, Dinefwr Park and Castle

St David's Visitor Centre and Shop

Captain's House, High Street, St David's, Pembrokeshire SA62 6SD

 1974   (4:A8)

Visitor Centre on the beautiful Pembrokeshire coast

The National Trust owns and protects much of the picturesque St David's Head and surrounding coastline. Situated opposite The Cross in the centre of St David's, Wales's smallest historic city, the Visitor Centre and shop is open all year. Using interactive technology the centre offers a complete guide to the National Trust in Pembrokeshire, its properties, beaches and walks.

⭐ No WC

ℹ **T** 01437 720385
E stdavids@nationaltrust.org.uk

🚶 Local walks leaflets available

♿ **Building** 🔈

➡ [115:SM753253] In the centre of St David's. **Foot**: Pembrokeshire Coast Path within 1ml. **Bus**: Richards 411 from ☒ Haverfordwest. Celtic Coaster & Puffin Shuttle during main holiday season

🅿 No parking on site

NT properties nearby
St David's Head, Porthclais Harbour

St David's Visitor Centre and Shop									
2 Feb–14 Mar	10–4	M	T	W	T	F	S	S
16 Mar–31 Dec	10–5:30	M	T	W	T	F	S	S
15 Mar–27 Dec	10–4	M	T	W	T	F	S	S
2 Jan–30 Jan 10	10–4	M	T	W	T	F	S	S
Closed 25, 26 & 28 Dec & 1 Jan 10									

Segontium

Caernarfon, Gwynedd

🏛 🏞 🚼 🖼 1937   (4:D2)

Remains of a Roman fort

The fort was built to defend the Roman Empire against rebellious tribes and later plundered to provide stone for Edward I's castle at Caernarfon. There is a museum containing relics found on site (not NT).

⭐ Segontium is in the guardianship of Cadw: Welsh Historic Monuments. The museum is not NT and is managed by a local trust on behalf of the National Museums and Galleries of Wales, c/o Institute Building, Pavilion Hill, Caernarfon, Gwynedd LL55 1AS. WC not always available

ℹ **T** 01443 336104
E segontium@nationaltrust.org.uk

♿ **Grounds** 🔈

🚼 Pushchairs and baby back-carriers admitted

🖼 Occasional educational activities

➡ [115:SH485624] **Cycle**: NCN8, ½ml. **Bus**: from surrounding areas to Caernarfon (KMP S4 and Express Motors 93 pass museum, on others ½ml walk to fort). **Station**: Bangor 9ml. **Road**: on Beddgelert road, A4085, on SE outskirts of Caernarfon, 500yds from town centre

🅿 No parking on site

NT properties nearby
Glan Faenol, Penrhyn Castle, Plas Newydd Country House and Gardens, Plas yn Rhiw

Segontium								
All year	10:30–4:30	M	T	W	T	F	S	S
Open BH Mons. Opening times may vary. Closed 24–26 Dec & 1 Jan 10. Museum (not NT) open 12:30–4:30, Tues–Sun. See www.segontium.org.uk								

Skenfrith Castle

Skenfrith, nr Abergavenny, Monmouthshire NP7 8UH

[icons] 1936   (4:H8)

Remains of an early 13th-century fortress

The castle was built beside the River Monnow to command one of the main routes between England and Wales at a time when the two nations were involved in a long drawn-out conflict following the Norman Conquest. A keep and the curtain wall with towers have survived.

★ Skenfrith Castle is in the guardianship of Cadw: Welsh Historic Monuments

[i] **T** 01443 336104
   E skenfrithcastle@nationaltrust.org.uk

[icon] Skenfith is part of the Three Castles Trail

[icon] **Building** [icon]

→ [161:SO456203] **Cycle**: local Three Castles cycle trail starts at nearby Abergavenny castle. **Road**: 6ml NW of Monmouth, 12ml NE of Abergavenny, on N side of the Ross road (B4521)

[P] Free parking (not NT)

NT properties nearby
The Kymin, Skirrid Fawr, Sugar Loaf, Westbury Court Garden

Skenfrith Castle		
All year	Dawn–dusk	**M T W T F S S**

Stackpole Estate

Old Home Farm Yard, Stackpole, nr Pembroke, Pembrokeshire SA71 5DQ

[icons] 1976   (4:B9)

Beautiful and varied stretch of the Pembrokeshire coast

This extensive estate is a coastal property of great contrast, including eight miles of cliff, headlands, beaches and sand dunes, elongated freshwater lakes bordered by trees, sheltered bays and mature woodlands. The Bosherston Lakes and Stackpole Warren are part of Stackpole National Nature Reserve, managed by the National Trust in partnership with the Countryside Council for Wales. Lake wildlife includes otters, herons, wintering wildfowl and more than twenty species of dragonfly. The cliffs are an important site for breeding seabirds and the resident chough. There are eleven species of bat on the Stackpole Estate, some of which live in the outbuildings of the former mansion of Stackpole Court, which was demolished in 1963 – about which there is an exhibition in the old game larder. There is an excellent bathing beach at Broadhaven South. At Barafundle Bay golden sands are backed by dunes and ringed by trees. The beautiful bay is so secluded that it can only be accessed from Stackpole Quay by walking along the cliff path, followed by a steep descent to the beach.

The magnificent limestone cliffs at Stackpole Head, Pembrokeshire

Tudor Merchant's House, Pembrokeshire

What's new in 2009 Improved access and footpaths to west side of the western arm of Bosherston Lakes

[i] **T** 01646 661359
E stackpole@nationaltrust.org.uk

[K] Guided walks

[k] 18½ml of footpaths. Map leaflets available

[&] [P&] [&] [▢] **Building** [&] **Grounds** [&] [➡]

[♨] Boathouse Tea-room (NT-approved concession) (licensed) at Stackpole Quay

[▦] Suitable for school groups. Stackpole for Outdoor Learning runs week-long residential environmental courses for schools and groups. The Stackpole Centre offers accommodation for education groups and others

[➜] [158:SR992958] 6ml S of Pembroke. **Foot**: via Pembrokeshire Coast Path. **Bus**: Silcox 388 ₪ Pembroke–Angle. **Station**: Pembroke 5ml. **Road**: B4319 from Pembroke to Stackpole and Bosherston (various entry points on to estate)

[P] Three car parks, cars £3 at Stackpole Quay, Broadhaven South and Bosherston Lily Ponds (Easter–Sept). Access via narrow lanes with passing places

NT properties nearby
Colby Woodland Garden, Tudor Merchant's House

Stackpole Estate							
All year	M	T	W	T	F	S	S

Tudor Merchant's House

Quay Hill, Tenby, Pembrokeshire SA70 7BX

[▦][K][♥][♣][▦] [1937]   (4:C9)

Late 15th-century town house

Visit this fascinating three-storey house, situated close to the harbour within the historic walled town of Tenby, and discover how the Tudor merchant and his family would have lived. Furnished to recreate the atmosphere of family life in Tudor times, there are costumes for children to try on and replica toys to play with. Features of the house include a fine 'Flemish' round chimney and the original scarfed roof-trusses, as well as remains of 18th-century secco paintings. Access to the small herb garden is available, weather permitting.

What's new in 2009 Staff will be wearing Tudor costume on Bank Holidays. Families can try out the Tenby Discovery Trail and discover more about the town's historic past

[★] No WC

[i] **T** 01834 842279
E tudormerchantshouse@nationaltrust.org.uk

[K] Special out-of-hours tours with staff in costume by arrangement (charged)

[♥] Easter and Hallowe'en family events

[&] [∷] [▨] [▢] **Building** [&]

[♣] Hip-carrying infant seats for loan. Children's quiz/trail. Easter and Hallowe'en family events

[▦] Suitable for school groups. Hands-on activities

[➜] [158:SN135004] In the centre of Tenby off Tudor Square. **Foot**: Pembrokeshire Coast Path within ¼ml. **Bus**: from surrounding areas. **Station**: Tenby ½ml

[P] Parking (not NT). Limited parking on town streets. Town is pedestrianised throughout July & Aug when parking is in pay & display car parks only or via park & ride

NT properties nearby
Colby Woodland Garden, Stackpole

Tudor Merchant's House							
30 Mar–1 Nov		11–5		M T W T F		S	S
Open Sats on BH weekends 11–5							

Show your card and display sticker for free parking

Ty'n-y-Coed Uchaf

Penmachno, Betws-y-Coed, Conwy LL24 0PS
Closed in 2009. Tel. 01492 860123 (NT Wales
office) for further information

Tŷ Mawr Wybrnant

Penmachno, Betws-y-Coed, Conwy LL25 0HJ

🏠🦞🚶🎠🛡️👪📷🚶🚲 1951   (4:E3)

**Traditional stone-built upland 16th-century
farmhouse**

Explore centuries of Welsh living in this
traditional stone-built upland farmhouse. Set in
the heart of the beautiful Conwy Valley, Tŷ Mawr
was the birthplace of Bishop William Morgan,
the first translator of the Bible into Welsh. A
footpath leads from the house through
woodland and the surrounding traditionally
managed fields.

What's new in 2009 Nature walk with wooden
animals to spot along the way. Accompanying
family trail

⭐ No access for coaches. 33-seater minibuses
welcome. Tel. to arrange access

ℹ️ **T** 01690 760213
E tymawrwybrnant@nationaltrust.org.uk

🚶 Introductory talk

🚶 Leaflet available featuring walks around Tŷ
Mawr and the Ysbyty Estate

♿ 🅿️🚾♿ Building 🚶🚶 Grounds 🚶

👪 Pushchairs admitted. Children's guide.
Children's quiz/trail. Children's art pack

🎪 Suitable for school groups

🐕 Under close control

🚲 Newly constructed cycle path around the
Penmachno area

➡️ [115:SH770524] **Bus**: Jones 64 Llanrwst–
Cwm Penmachno (passing ⊠ Betws-y-
Coed), alight Penmachno, then 2ml walk.
Station: Pont-y-pant (U) 1½ml. **Road**: at the
head of the Wybrnant Valley. From A5 3ml S
of Betws-y-Coed, take B4406 to
Penmachno. House is 2½ml NW of
Penmachno by forest road

🅿️ Free parking, 500yds

NT properties nearby
Aberconwy House, Bodnant Garden, Conwy
Suspension Bridge, Penrhyn Castle, Ysbyty Estate

Tŷ Mawr Wybrnant		M	T	W	T	F	S	S
27 Mar–27 Sep	12–5	M	T	W	**T**	**F**	**S**	**S**
1 Oct–1 Nov	12–4	M	T	W	**T**	**F**	**S**	**S**
Open BH Mons								

Tŷ Mawr in the Wybrnant Valley, Conwy: birthplace of Bishop William Morgan, the first translator of the Bible into Welsh

Dogs assisting visitors with disabilities are always welcome

The National Trust in Northern Ireland cares for and provides public access to 40 square miles of scenic countryside and 120 miles of magnificent coastline. World-renowned for its breathtaking natural beauty and sheer diversity of landscape, Northern Ireland has scenery on an epic scale.

There are enticing open spaces, exhilarating challenges and serenely tranquil getaways. From the dramatic granite peaks of the Mourne Mountains and the bucolic wooded glens of Antrim, to the legendary basalt columns of the Giant's Causeway, the pastoral drumlin landscape of Strangford Lough and the idyllic Fermanagh Lakeland – the spectacular scenery speaks for itself. There is something for everyone to explore and enjoy throughout the year at the National Trust gems across Northern Ireland.

Coastal treasures

The Northern Ireland coastline is a wonderful place to explore on foot. It offers a wide range of walks for the serious rambler as well as for those who simply want to take a short stroll.

Bracing coastal walks at that iconic World Heritage Site, the Giant's Causeway, will be rewarded with clear, crisp air and dramatic views. In addition the nearby shoreline is dotted with some of the region's best-loved visitor attractions.

Discover the historic ruins of Dunseverick Castle, or stroll along the majestic sweeping arc of White Park Bay. Brave the elements and cross Carrick-a-Rede rope bridge, or marvel at the bustling seabird colonies at Larrybane, with its views beyond to Rathlin Island and the west coast of Scotland.

There are few better places to experience this diverse coastline than the distinctive headland of Fair Head, which rises 190 metres and gives

Top left: **Fair Head**
Top right: **the Giant's Causeway**
Above: **the rope bridge across the 30m-deep chasm at Carrick-a-Rede. The above are all in County Antrim**

Previous page: **the Laundry at Castle Ward, County Down**

dramatic views of nearby Murlough Bay. On unspoilt Rathlin Island inspirational views across to the Scottish Islands and Mull of Kintyre can be seen from the waymarked path through Ballyconagan.

Other coastal treasures include the tiny village of Glenoe near Larne, with its spectacular waterfall, while the footpath along Skernaghan Point on

High tide at Strangford Lough, County Down

the northern tip of Island Magee leads to open headland, cliffs, coves and beautiful beaches.

Riches for walkers and naturalists

Building sandcastles at White Park Bay, County Antrim

The County Down coastline has much to offer the walker and naturalist, with rocky shore and heathland at Ballymacormick Point and wildfowl, wading birds and gulls at Orlock Point.

Strangford Lough, Britain's largest sea lough and one of Europe's key wildlife habitats, offers bracing coastal walks among delicate wild flowers and butterflies. There are also rock pools bursting with marine life and opportunities for spectacular birdwatching.

Further south, the fragile

6,000-year-old sand dunes of Murlough National Nature Reserve, near Newcastle, is an extraordinarily beautiful dune landscape with a network of paths and boardwalks – perfect for walking.

Wild countryside

Why not escape to some of Northern Ireland's best off-the-beaten-track experiences?

Just a stone's throw from the region's capital, in the heart of the Belfast Hills, the heathland-rich Divis and the Black Mountain provide the stunning backdrop to the city's skyline and a perfect haven for those in search of wild countryside.

Other rural escapes in the Belfast area well worth exploring include the hidden woodland paths of Collin Glen and the fine riverbank and meadows of Minnowburn – a green oasis in the heart of the city – as well as the wonderful waterfalls at Lisnabreeny.

To the west of the region, idyllic County Fermanagh is perfect walking country, boasting a kaleidoscope of tranquil landscapes to discover – including the woodland and wetlands of Crom on the serene shores of Lough Erne.

Or for a real walk on the wild side, the Trust's Mourne Mountain paths allow hikers to enjoy the dramatic scenery of Northern Ireland's highest mountain, the majestic Slieve Donard, as well as neighbouring Slieve Commedagh. Visitors to Ballyquintin Farm, on the Ards Peninsula, can enjoy stunning views of Strangford Lough and learn how this critical site is managed for wildlife and conservation.

Meanwhile, along the geologically rich coastline to the north-east lies the delightful seaside village of Cushendun and the ecologically important raised blanket peat bog at Cushleake Mountain.

Birdlife on the north coast

Traditionally more famous for the Giant's Causeway and spectacular geology, the north coast is also home to some special wildlife, particularly birds. Dotted along the North Atlantic coastline can be found numerous breeding birds – both summer visitors and hardy resident species.

On the western section of this stretch of coastline, marvel at the spectacular birdlife along the mudflats and coastal saltmarsh of the Bann Estuary – a Special Area of Conservation. These rich feeding grounds for waders, wildfowl and nesting birds can be viewed from a well-positioned hide on the west side of the river (key required, telephone 028 7083 6396). Shelduck and Sandwich terns offer good entertainment in summer, with exciting passage birds in the autumn and spring, such as godwits and golden plovers. The site is known by bird enthusiasts as a vagrant hotspot.

Heading east, the soft coastline of the Bann Estuary is quickly replaced by the rugged basalt cliffs of the North Antrim coastline. For twelve miles, from the Giant's Causeway to Carrick-a-Rede Rope Bridge, stretches some of Europe's finest cliff scenery. A waymarked path offers the birdwatcher stunning views of nesting fulmars, as well as black guillemots, oystercatchers and eider ducks patrolling the remote bays.

Inland, skylark song is almost constant, as are the calls of stonechats and linnets. This is also peregrine and raven country, and choughs visit on occasion. The only break in the cliff landscape occurs at White Park Bay – a majestic sweeping arc of white sands.

The sand dunes at White Park Bay are a naturalist's paradise – most noteworthy for the rich variety of orchids. In terms of breeding birds, cast an eye or ear for grasshopper warbler, reed bunting and whitethroat. Breeding ringed plovers and passing sanderlings are also common. Out to sea, you may be able to spot a number of sea ducks, as well as porpoises and even basking sharks.

At Carrick-a-Rede, you will be rewarded with the best and most accessible seabird colony on the mainland. This noisy community has guillemots, razorbills, kittiwakes and fulmars in abundance. Only Rathlin Island offers the birdwatcher more, with the west lighthouse the place to go, where the puffins never fail to impress the visitor and locals alike.

Barry Crawford
Nature Conservation and Access Warden (North Coast)

Top: **fulmar with chick at Carrick-a-Rede** Above: **guillemots on Rathlin Island**

Further information

- Euro notes are accepted by the Trust's Northern Ireland properties.
- Under the National Trust Ulster Gardens Scheme, a number of private gardens are generously opened to the public in order to provide income for Trust gardens in Northern Ireland. For the 2009 programme tel. 028 9751 0721.
- To find out what is happening in Northern Ireland this year, see our 2009 *Events Guide*.

Ardress House

64 Ardress Road, Annaghmore, Portadown,
Co. Armagh BT62 1SQ

🏠 ♨ ❀ 🏠 🍴 🎋 🗷 ♿ 🚼 🏛 🚶 1959   (7:D7)

17th-century house with elegant 18th-century decoration and a traditional farmyard

ℹ️ **T** 028 8778 4753
  E ardress@nationaltrust.org.uk

Ardress House									
21 Feb–22 Feb	12–4	M	T	W	T	F	**S**	**S**
14 Mar–28 Jun	2–6	M	T	W	T	F	**S**	**S**
10 Apr–19 Apr*	2–6	**M**	**T**	**W**	**T**	F	**S**	**S**
2 Jul–30 Aug	2–6	M	T	W	**T**	**F**	**S**	**S**
5 Sep–27 Sep	2–6	M	T	W	T	F	**S**	**S**

Admission by guided tour (last admission 1hr before closing). Open BH Mons & all other public hols in N. Ireland **inc. 17 March**. Grounds ('My Lady's Mile') open daily all year, dawn to dusk. *Easter week

The Argory

144 Derrycaw Road, Moy, Dungannon,
Co. Armagh BT71 6NA

🏠 🚗 ❀ 🍽 🏠 💼 🎋 🎧 🗷 😷 🚼 🏛 🚶 🎭
📺 1979   (7:C7)

Atmospheric Irish gentry house and wooded riverside estate

Built in the 1820s, this handsome Irish gentry house is surrounded by its 130-hectare (320-acre) wooded riverside estate. The former home of the MacGeough Bond family, a tour of this neo-classical masterpiece reveals it is unchanged since 1900 – the eclectic interior still evoking the family's tastes and interests. Outside there are sweeping vistas, superb spring bulbs, scenic walks and fascinating courtyard displays. A second-hand bookshop, adventure playground and Lady Ada's award-winning tea-room provide retreats for children and adults alike.

What's new in 2009 Replica of the original turn of the 19th/20th-century Dining Room carpet. The Red Bedroom will be on view for the first time

ℹ️ **T** 028 8778 4753
  E argory@nationaltrust.org.uk

🎧 Williams Sound Hearing Helper Tour Guide System available

🎭 Craft fairs, walks and family days

♿ 🦽 🚾 😊 🗺 **Grounds** 🦼 ➡️

🍴 Lady Ada's Tea-room. Afternoon teas. All produce baked on the premises

🚼 Baby-changing facilities. Hip-carrying infant seats for loan. Children's play area. Children's quiz/trail

🏛 Suitable for school groups. Education room/centre. Live interpretation. Hands-on activities. Adult study days

🐕 On leads and only in grounds and garden

➡️ [H418640] **Cycle**: NCN95, 7ml.
  Bus: Ulsterbus 67 Portadown–Dungannon (both pass close ₹ Portadown), alight Charlemont, 2½ml walk. **Road**: 4ml from Charlemont, 3ml from M1, exit 13 or 14 (signposted). Coaches must use exit 13; weight restrictions at Bond's Bridge

🅿 Parking, 100yds

NT properties nearby
Ardress House, Derrymore House

The Argory								
Grounds								
1 Feb–30 Apr	10–4	**M**	**T**	**W**	**T**	**F**	**S**	**S**
1 May–30 Sep	10–6	**M**	**T**	**W**	**T**	**F**	**S**	**S**
1 Oct–31 Jan 10	10–4	**M**	**T**	**W**	**T**	**F**	**S**	**S**
House								
14 Mar–28 Jun	1–5:30	M	T	W	T	F	**S**	**S**
10 Apr–19 Apr*	1–5:30	**M**	**T**	**W**	**T**	**F**	**S**	**S**
1 Jul–31 Aug	1–5:30	**M**	**T**	**W**	**T**	**F**	**S**	**S**
5 Sep–27 Sep	1–5:30	M	T	W	T	F	**S**	**S**

Admission by guided tour (last admission 1hr before closing). Open BH Mons and all other public hols in N. Ireland. Grounds open 2–6 on event days. Tea-room/shop open as house. *Easter week

The Argory: magnificent roses in the Sundial Garden

Carrick-a-Rede

119a Whitepark Road, Ballintoy,
Co. Antrim BT54 6LS

 1967   **(7:D3)**

Rocky island connected to the cliffs by a rope bridge

Take the exhilarating rope bridge challenge to Carrick-a-Rede island and enjoy a truly clifftop experience. Near the North Antrim Coast Road, amid unrivalled coastal scenery, the 30-metre deep and 20-metre wide chasm is traversed by a rope bridge that was traditionally erected by salmon fishermen. Visitors bold enough to cross from the cliffs to the rocky island (which is a Site of Special Scientific Interest) are rewarded with fantastic birdwatching and splendid uninterrupted views to Rathlin and the Scottish islands.

⭐ Maximum of eight people on bridge at any one time. Suitable outdoor clothing and footwear is recommended

ℹ️ **T** 028 2076 9839
E carrickarede@nationaltrust.org.uk

🎭 Putting up the bridge, Feb

♿ 🅿️ 🚻 🅰️ �" **Grounds** 🔀 🔀 ➡️ 🔀

☕ Tea-room

👶 Baby-changing facilities. Baby back-carriers admitted. Pushchairs not permitted over rope bridge. Children's Discovery Trail

🏫 Suitable for school groups

🐕 On leads, not permitted to cross rope bridge

➡️ [D062450] **Foot**: on North Antrim Coastal Path and road, 7ml from Giant's Causeway, ¼ml from Ballintoy village and 1½ml from Ballintoy Church on Harbour Rd.
Cycle: NCN93, 5ml. **Bus**: Ulsterbus 172, 177 from Coleraine, Ulsterbus 252 is a circular route from Belfast via the Antrim Glens. Both stop at Carrick-a-Rede.
Road: on B15, 7ml E of Bushmills, 5 ml W of Ballycastle. Giant's Causeway 7ml

🅿️ Free parking. Access all year

NT properties nearby
Cushendun, Giant's Causeway, Hezlett House, Mussenden Temple and Downhill Demesne, Portstewart Strand, White Park Bay

Carrick-a-Rede									
Rope bridge									
28 Feb–24 May	10–6	M	T	W	T	F	S	S
25 May–31 Aug	10–7	M	T	W	T	F	S	S
1 Sep–1 Nov	10–6	M	T	W	T	F	S	S

Final access to Rope Bridge 45mins. before closing time. Car park and North Antrim Coastal Path open all year. Bridge open weather permitting

The splendid 18th-century Castle Coole

Castle Coole

Enniskillen, Co. Fermanagh BT74 6JY

🏠 🏛️ 🌳 🅰️ ☕ 🅰️ 🅰️ 🎭 👶 🏫 🔀 🔔
📶 1951   **(7:A7)**

Magnificent 18th-century mansion and landscape park

Savour the exquisite stately grandeur of this stunning 18th-century mansion set in an historic wooded landscape park – ideal for family walks. Castle Coole is one of Ireland's finest neo-classical houses, and the sumptuous Regency interior, boasting an especially fine State Bedroom prepared for George IV, provides a rare treat for visitors, allowing them to glimpse what

For general and membership enquiries, please telephone 0844 800 1895

life was like in the home of the Earls of Belmore. Discover the story of the people who lived and worked below stairs as you explore the splendid suite of servants' rooms and service quarters of this magnificent property.

What's new in 2009 Guided tours of historic basement

i **T** 028 6632 2690
E castlecoole@nationaltrust.org.uk

Guided tours of historic basement

Classical and popular music events, including opera and jazz

Off the Beaten Track walks series

[icons] **Building** [icons]
Grounds [icons]

Tea-room (NT-approved concession) in Tallow House

Baby-changing facilities. Baby back-carriers admitted. Front-carrying baby slings for loan. Children's play area

Suitable for school groups

On leads and only in grounds

[H378788] **Cycle:** NCN91. Property entrance lies on the Kingfisher Trail, Ireland's first long-distance trail covering approx. 300ml.
Bus: Ulsterbus 95, Enniskillen–Clones (connections from Belfast). **Road:** 1½ml SE of Enniskillen on Belfast–Enniskillen road (A4)

P Walkers' car park. Main car park, 150yds.

NT properties nearby
Crom, Florence Court

Castle Coole									
Grounds									
14 Mar–30 Sep	10–8	**M**	**T**	**W**	**T**	**F**	**S**	**S**	
House									
14 Mar–31 May	1–6	M	T	W	T	**F**	**S**	**S**	
10 Apr–19 Apr*	1–6	**M**	**T**	**W**	**T**	**F**	**S**	**S**	
1 Jun–30 Jun	1–6	**M**	**T**	**W**		**F**	**S**	**S**	
1 Jul–31 Aug	12–6	**M**	**T**	**W**	**T**	**F**	**S**	**S**	
5 Sep–27 Sep	1–6	M	T	W	T	**F**	**S**	**S**	

Admission by guided tour (last tour 1hr before closing). Open BH Mons & all other public hols in N. Ireland **inc. 17 March.** Tea-room/shop open as house, but close at 5. *Easter week

Castle Ward

Strangford, Downpatrick, Co. Down BT30 7LS

[icons] 1953 (7:F7)

Interesting 18th-century mansion, famed for its mixture of architectural styles

Explore this exceptional 332-hectare (820-acre) walled demesne dramatically set overlooking Strangford Lough and marvel at the quirky mid Georgian mansion, home of the Ward family since the 16th century. An architectural curiosity, it is built inside and out in the distinctly different styles of classical and gothic. Children can dress up and play with period toys in the Victorian Past Times Centre or learn about local wildlife at the Strangford Lough Wildlife Centre. Winding woodland, lakeside and parkland walks afford amazing unexpected vistas. Stay at the caravan site or holiday cottage and you'll have longer to explore.

What's new in 2009 New cycle path

i **T** 028 4488 1204
E castleward@nationaltrust.org.uk

Guided and specialist behind-the-scenes house tours, morning and evening by prior arrangement

Jazz in the garden, opera, Pumpkinfest, book fair, dinner and a movie, speciality market, toy trade, murder mystery, 'Dead Men's Tales' boat trips and Santa's house

Free trail maps from leaflet dispensers in car park area, visitor reception and gift shop. All walks are moderate

[icons]
Building [icons] **Grounds** [icons]

Castle Ward, County Down: an architectural curiosity

Unless indicated, last admission is always 30mins before closing time

📷 Gift shop and second-hand bookshop in stableyard

🍽 Tea-room. Children's menu

👪 Baby-changing and feeding facilities. Hip-carrying infant seats for loan. Family guide. Children's quiz/trail. Children's activity packs. Children's play area (adventure playground in woodland). Victorian Past Times Centre; toys & dressing up

🏫 Suitable for school groups. Education room/centre. Live interpretation. Hands-on activities. Adult study days

🐕 On leads and only in grounds

🚲 New cycle path. Free trail maps from leaflet dispensers in car park area, visitor reception and gift shop

➜ [J752494] **Foot**: on Lecale Way. **Ferry**: from Portaferry. **Bus**: Ulsterbus 16E Downpatrick–Strangford, with connections from Belfast (passing close ⬛ Belfast Great Victoria Street); bus stop at gates. Ulsterbus Lecale Rambler (Sat, Sun only) in summer. **Road**: 7ml NE of Downpatrick, 1½ml W of Strangford village on A25, on S shore of Strangford Lough, entrance by Ballyculter Lodge

🅿 Free parking, 250yds

NT properties nearby
Mount Stewart, Murlough National Nature Reserve, Rowallane Garden

Castle Ward									
Grounds									
1 Feb–31 Mar	10–4	**M**	**T**	**W**	**T**	**F**	**S**	**S**	
1 Apr–30 Sep	10–8	**M**	**T**	**W**	**T**	**F**	**S**	**S**	
1 Oct–31 Jan 10	10–4	**M**	**T**	**W**	**T**	**F**	**S**	**S**	
House									
21 Feb–28 Jun	1–5	M	T	W	T	**F**	**S**	**S**	
10 Apr–19 Apr	1–5	**M**	**T**	**W**	**T**	**F**	**S**	**S**	
4 Jul–31 Aug	1–5	**M**	**T**	**W**	**T**	**F**	**S**	**S**	
5 Sep–1 Nov	1–5	M	T	W	T	F	**S**	**S**	

Admission by guided tour. Open BH Mons and all other public hols in N. Ireland **inc. 17 March**. Corn mill operates on Suns during open season. Tea-room open 12–5 daily Jul/Aug, Sat/Sun for the rest of the year. Shop open 12–5 daily May–Aug, Sat/Sun for the rest of the year. Bookshop 2–5 daily May–Aug, Sat/Sun for the rest of the year. For Strangford Lough Wildlife Centre opening times contact 028 4488 1411

Crom

Upper Lough Erne, Newtownbutler,
Co. Fermanagh BT92 8AP

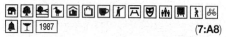

🔔 ⊤ 1987   **(7:A8)**

Romantic and tranquil landscape of islands, woodland and historical ruins

Escape to this breathtaking 810-hectare (2,000-acre) demesne, set amid the romantic and tranquil landscape of Upper Lough Erne. One of Ireland's most important nature conservation areas, Crom's ancient woodland and picturesque islands are home to many rare species, including the elusive pine marten. The award-winning visitor centre offers a huge range of exciting activities and adventures for all the family – from boating and coarse angling to inspirational nature trails. There are also fascinating wildlife exhibitions. Stay for longer in the award-winning holiday cottages or campsite.

What's new in 2009 Licensed for civil weddings in function rooms and ruins of Old Crom Castle

A boat on Lough Erne, part of the Crom demesne in County Fermanagh: romantic and tranquil landscape

⭐ The 19th-century castle is private and not open to the public. WC available only when visitor centre open. Showers available for campsite users

ℹ️ **T** 028 6773 8118 **E** crom@nationaltrust.org.uk

🦇 Family days, bat nights, history and nature walks

🚶 Guided walks to discover wildlife and social history

♿ 🅿️ 🚾 👁️ 🔊 🔤 Building 🏛️ ♿
Grounds 🏛️ ➡️ ♿

📷 In visitor centre

🍽️ Little Orchard Tea-room in visitor centre

👶 Baby-changing facilities. Pushchairs and baby back-carriers admitted. Hip-carrying infant seats for loan. Children's play area. Family activity packs. Family days

🏫 Suitable for school groups

🐕 On leads only

🚲 2ml of NCN91, designated as the Kingfisher Trail, runs through the property

➡️ [H455655] **Cycle**: NCN91. **Ferry**: ferry from Derryvore church must be booked 24hrs in advance. **Bus**: Ulsterbus 95 Enniskillen–Clones (connections from Belfast), alight Newtownbutler, 3ml. **Road**: 3ml W of Newtownbutler, on Newtownbutler–Crom road, or follow signs from Lisnaskea (7ml). Crom is next to the Shannon–Erne waterway. Public jetty at visitor centre

🅿️ Parking, 100yds

NT properties nearby
Castle Coole, Florence Court

Crom										
Grounds										
14 Mar–31 May	10–6	**M**	**T**	**W**	**T**		**F**		**S**	**S**
1 Jun–31 Aug	10–7	**M**	**T**	**W**	**T**		**F**		**S**	**S**
1 Sep–1 Nov	10–6	**M**	**T**	**W**	**T**		**F**		**S**	**S**
Visitor centre										
14 Mar–29 Mar	10–6	M	T	W	T		**F**		**S**	**S**
4 Apr–13 Sep	10–6	**M**	**T**	**W**	**T**		**F**		**S**	**S**
19 Sep–11 Oct	10–5	M	T	W	T		F		**S**	**S**
18 Oct–1 Nov	10–5	M	T	W	T		F		S	**S**

Open BH Mons and all other public hols in N. Ireland inc. **17 March**. Last admission 1hr before closing. Tel. for tea-room opening arrangements

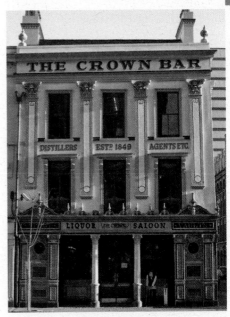
The Crown Bar's façade: showing decorative tiles

The Crown Bar

46 Great Victoria Street, Belfast,
Co. Antrim BT2 7BA

🏠 🍷 🍽️ 1978   **(7:E6)**

The most famous pub in Belfast

With its brightly coloured ornate tile-and-glass interior, period gas lighting and cosy snugs, this atmospheric hostelry is one of the finest examples of a High Victorian saloon still in existence in the UK.

ℹ️ **T** 028 9024 3187 **E** info@crownbar.com

🍽️ Traditional, home-cooked lunch menu

➡️ [J336736] **Cycle**: NCN9, ½ml. **Bus**: opposite Europa Buscentre. **Station**: opposite Great Victoria Street

🅿️ Street parking only

NT properties nearby
Divis and the Black Mountain, Mount Stewart, Patterson's Spade Mill, Rowallane Garden

The Crown Bar										
All year	11:30–11	**M**	**T**	**W**	**T**		**F**		**S**	S
All year	12:30–10	M	T	W	T		F		S	**S**

Derrymore House

Bessbrook, Newry, Co. Armagh BT35 7EF

 `1953` **(7:D8)**

Late 18th-century thatched house in gentrified vernacular style

This elegant 18th-century thatched cottage with its peculiar gentrified vernacular style, rests peacefully in a pleasant landscape demesne. It has a rich history, being built by Isaac Corry, who represented Newry in the Irish House of Commons for 30 years from 1776. The pretty parkland has fine views and boasts impressive spring bulbs.

⭐ No WC

ℹ **T** 028 8778 4753
E derrymore@nationaltrust.org.uk

♿ 🅿 **Grounds** ♿ ➡

👪 Pushchairs admitted

🐕 On leads and only in grounds

🚲 NCN9 passes through estate

➔ [J056280] **Cycle**: NCN9. **Bus**: Ulsterbus 42, 44, 341C from Newry (passing close ⭷ Newry). **Station**: Newry 2ml. **Road**: on A25 off the Newry–Camlough road at Bessbrook, 1½ml from Newry

🅿 Free parking, 30yds

NT properties nearby
Ardress House, The Argory

Derrymore House									
Grounds									
1 Feb–30 Apr	10–4	**M**	**T**	**W**	**T**	**F**	**S**	**S**	
1 May–30 Sep	10–6	**M**	**T**	**W**	**T**	**F**	**S**	**S**	
1 Oct–31 Jan 10	10–4	**M**	**T**	**W**	**T**	**F**	**S**	**S**	

Treaty Room only open 4 May, 25 May, 12/13 July & 13 Aug, 2–5:30. Closed BHols & public hols

Derrymore House, with spring bulbs in the foreground

Florence Court

Enniskillen, Co. Fermanagh BT92 1DB

 `1954` **(7:A7)**

Beautiful 18th-century house and demesne

There is something for all the family at the warm and welcoming 18th-century former home of the Earls of Enniskillen. The house enjoys a peaceful setting in west Fermanagh, with a startlingly beautiful backdrop of mountains and forests. There are many glorious walks to enjoy, as well as fine vistas and play areas in the outstanding grounds. There is even a charming walled garden. Every aspect of life in this imposing classical Irish house, with its fine interiors and exquisite decoration, are brought to life on the fascinating guided tours. Outside there are numerous unusual places to explore, including a sawmill, ice house and the thatched Heather House.

What's new in 2009 Family entertainment on Sundays in July and August

ℹ **T** 028 6634 8249
E florencecourt@nationaltrust.org.uk

🎭 'Living History' tours, Suns in July & Aug

🎭 Events include Easter Egg trails, family fun days, craft fairs, Hallowe'en and Christmas activities. Annual Country Fair on Sun 24 May

♿ 🅿 🇩 ♿ ⋮⋮ 📷 📺 ♿ ♿
Building ♿ ♿ ♿ **Grounds** ♿ ➡ 🚲

Florence Court									
Gardens/park									
21 Feb–9 Apr	10–6	**M**	**T**	**W**	**T**	**F**	**S**	**S**	
10 Apr–1 Nov	10–8	**M**	**T**	**W**	**T**	**F**	**S**	**S**	
2 Nov–31 Jan 10	10–4	**M**	**T**	**W**	**T**	**F**	**S**	**S**	
House									
21 Feb–10 May	1–6	M	T	W	T	F	**S**	**S**	
10 Apr–19 Apr*	1–6	**M**	**T**	**W**	**T**	**F**	**S**	**S**	
16 May–29 Jun	1–6	**M**	T	**W**	**T**	**F**	**S**	**S**	
1 Jul–31 Aug	12–6	**M**	**T**	**W**	**T**	**F**	**S**	**S**	
1 Sep–13 Sep	1–6	**M**	**T**	**W**	**T**	**F**	**S**	**S**	
19 Sep–1 Nov	1–5	M	T	W	T	F	**S**	**S**	

House: admission by guided tour (last admission 1hr before closing). Open BH Mons & all other public hols in N. Ireland **inc. 17 March**. Tea-room/shop: open daily 12–5 (July/Aug 12–6). ***Easter week**

Charges for National Trust members apply on some special event days

All the family will love Florence Court

🖪 The car park and tourist information centre are owned and operated by Moyle District Council

ℹ️ **T** 028 2073 1582
E giantscauseway@nationaltrust.org.uk

🚶 Sensible outdoor footwear recommended

♿ Building 🏛 Grounds ➡️

☕ Tea-room. Children's menu

🚼 Baby-changing facilities. Pushchairs and baby back-carriers admitted

▣ Suitable for school groups

🐕 On leads only

➡️ [C952452] **Foot**: path from Portballintrae alongside steam railway and from Dunservick Castle (4½ml). **Cycle**: NCN93. **Bus**: Ulsterbus 172, 177 from Coleraine. Ulsterbus 252 is a circular route from Belfast via the Antrim Glens. **Station**: Coleraine 10ml or Portrush 8ml. Giant's Causeway & Bushmills Steam Railway, 200yds. Tel. 028 2073 2844. **Road**: on B146 Causeway–Dunseverick road 2ml E of Bushmills

🅿 Parking (not NT), 100yds. Charge includes NT members

NT properties nearby
Carrick-a-Rede, Hezlett House, Mussenden Temple and Downhill Demesne, Portstewart Strand, White Park Bay

---

☕ Stables Restaurant (NT-approved concession)

🚼 Baby-changing facilities. Baby back-carriers admitted. Front-carrying baby slings for loan. Children's play area. Children's quiz/trail

▣ Suitable for school groups. Education room/centre. Live interpretation. Hands-on activities

🐕 On leads and only in garden and grounds

➡️ [H175344] **Cycle**: NCN91. Property entrance lies on Kingfisher Trail. **Bus**: Ulsterbus 192 Enniskillen–Swanlinbar, alight Creamery Cross, 2ml walk. **Road**: 8ml SW of Enniskillen via A4 Sligo road and A32 Swanlinbar road, 4ml from Marble Arch Caves

🅿 Parking, 200yds

NT properties nearby
Castle Coole, Crom

Giant's Causeway

44a Causeway Road, Bushmills,
Co. Antrim BT57 8SU

 1962 (7:D3)

Famous geological World Heritage Site on the North Antrim Coast

Northern Ireland's iconic World Heritage Site is steeped in a wealth of history and legend. All the family will enjoy exploring the renowned amphitheatres of layered basalt stone columns left by volcanic eruptions 60 million years ago, and searching for the distinctive stone formations fancifully named the wishing chair, camel, harp and organ. The centrepiece of an internationally important designated Area of Outstanding Natural Beauty, the Causeway is home to a wealth of local and natural history.

Giant's Causeway							
All year	**M**	**T**	**W**	**T**	**F**	**S**	**S**
Shop/tea-room: tel. for opening arrangements. Open all year, except 25/26 Dec							

The iconic Giant's Causeway, County Antrim

Gray's Printing Press

49 Main Street, Strabane, Co. Tyrone BT82 8AU

🎁 ⬆️ 🚹 📦 🏛️ 1966   (7:B5)

18th-century printing press

Take a step back in time and discover a treasure trove of ink, galleys and presses hidden behind an 18th-century shop front in the heart of Strabane, once the leading printing town in Ulster. See the 18th-century printing press where John Dunlap, printer of the American Declaration of Independence, and James Wilson, grandfather of President Woodrow Wilson, learnt their trade, and hear the story of printing and emigration.

⭐ For opening dates and times tel. Property Manager, 028 8674 8210

ℹ️ **T** 028 7188 0055
   E grays@nationaltrust.org.uk

♿ 🚾 🅿️ Building 🏛️🏛️

🏛️ Suitable for school groups. Live interpretation

➡️ [H345977] **Cycle**: NCN92. **Bus**: Ulsterbus Express 273 Belfast–Derry City, alight Strabane centre; few mins walk.
   Road: situated close to the Omagh road on the main street in the centre of Strabane

🅿️ Parking (not NT), 100yds (pay & display)

NT properties nearby
Mussenden Temple and Downhill Demesne, Springhill, Wellbrook Beetling Mill

---

Gray's Printing Press

Admission by guided tour. Last admission 45mins before closing. For opening dates and times tel. Property Manager, 028 8674 8210

Demonstration of printing at Gray's Printing Press

Hezlett House

107 Sea Road, Castlerock, Coleraine, Co. Londonderry BT51 4TW

🏛️ ❄️ 🅿️ 🚹 🏕️ 🏛️ 1976   (7:C4)

17th-century thatched cottage and garden

Learn about the reality of life in a rural 17th-century Irish thatched cottage told through the experiences of the people who once lived in one of Northern Ireland's oldest surviving buildings. Hezlett's quaint exterior, with its elegant Georgian windows, hides a curious early timber frame dating from 1690, and the cosy interior is simply furnished in mid Victorian style. Guided tours offer an enthralling afternoon treat for all the family. Hezlett House is also home to the Downhill Marbles collection from the Bishop of Derry's Demesne at Downhill.

What's new in 2009 Refreshments available in visitor reception. Roof rethatched and walls limewashed

ℹ️ **T** 028 2073 1582
   E hezletthouse@nationaltrust.org.uk

♿ 🅿️ 🚾 🅿️ Building 🏛️ Grounds 🏛️

🍵 Light refreshments

🚼 Baby-changing facilities

🏛️ Suitable for school groups

🐕 On leads and only in grounds

➡️ [C772349] **Cycle**: NCN93. **Bus**: Ulsterbus 134 Coleraine–Londonderry, alight crossroads, few mins walk.
   Station: Castlerock ¾ml. **Road**: 4ml W of Coleraine on Coleraine–Downhill coast road, A2. Beside Castlerock turn-off at crossroads

🅿️ Free parking

NT properties nearby
Carrick-a-Rede, Giant's Causeway, Mussenden Temple and Downhill Demesne, Portstewart Strand, White Park Bay

Hezlett House									
4 Apr–19 Apr	11–5	**M**	**T**	W	T	**F**	**S**	**S**
25 Apr–28 Jun	11–5	M	T	W	T	F	**S**	**S**
3 Jul–31 Aug	11–5	**M**	**T**	W	T	**F**	**S**	**S**
5 Sep–27 Sep	11–5	M	T	W	T	F	**S**	**S**

Admission by guided tour. Open BH Mons & all other public hols in N. Ireland

---

Dogs assisting visitors with disabilities are always welcome

Mount Stewart House, Garden and Temple of the Winds

Portaferry Road, Newtownards,
Co. Down BT22 2AD

🍸 1976 (7:F6)

Neo-classical house and celebrated gardens

The exotic luxuriance of Mount Stewart's celebrated gardens, created in the 1920s by Edith, Lady Londonderry, has helped make it one of Northern Ireland's most popular Trust properties with all the family. Nominated as a World Heritage Site, the impressive landscape garden makes the most of the unique microclimate of the Ards Peninsula and boasts magnificent views across Strangford Lough from the romantically idyllic Temple of the Winds. Engaging tours of the opulent house reveal its fascinating heritage and historic world-famous artefacts and artwork.

What's new in 2009 Mount Stewart fountains. Sunken Garden parterres restored to 1930s heyday. Heather parterres in the Italian Garden and South American borders in the Lily Wood also restored. Multi-sensory activity trails and hands-on gardening activities with the new gardener

i **T** 028 4278 8387
E mountstewart@nationaltrust.org.uk

🕇 Special behind-the-scenes tours for groups. Available to smaller parties for a higher charge (booking essential)

😃 Drama, music and craft events. Easter Egg trails. Half-term activities for families. Grand Garden and Craft Fair 16/17 May. Food Fayre 10/11 Oct and seasonal themed activities for all

🚶 Programme of specialised garden walks and talks by a member of the garden team throughout the year (some include supper)

♿

Building 🔲🔲🔲 Grounds 🔲🔲🔲

🛍 NT shop selling quality local gifts. Plant sales

🍴 Bay Restaurant (licensed). Serving main and light meals using finest local ingredients. Children's menu

👶 Baby-changing facilities. Pushchairs and baby back-carriers admitted. Hip-carrying infant seats for loan. Children's quiz/trail. Family activity packs. Easter Egg trails. Family half-term activities. Big draw event in October. Children's winter trails and Santa's Grotto

🏫 Suitable for school groups. Education room/centre. Live interpretation. Hands-on activities

🐕 On leads and only in grounds and garden

➔ [J553695] **Bus**: Ulsterbus 10 Belfast–Portaferry, bus stop at gates.
Station: Bangor 10ml. **Road**: 15ml SE of Belfast on Newtownards–Portaferry road, A20, 5ml SE of Newtownards

P Free parking, 100yds

NT properties nearby
Castle Ward, Divis and the Black Mountain, Patterson's Spade Mill, Rowallane Garden

The Italian Garden at Mount Stewart, County Down, now has beautiful heather parterres

Mount Stewart								
Lakeside gardens								
All year	10–sunset	M	T	W	T	F	S	S
Formal gardens								
21 Feb–29 Mar	10–4	M	T	W	T	F	S	S
1 Apr–30 Apr	10–6	M	T	W	T	F	S	S
1 May–30 Sep	10–8	M	T	W	T	F	S	S
1 Oct–31 Oct	10–6	M	T	W	T	F	S	S
House								
7 Mar–29 Mar	12–6	M	T	W	T	F	S	S
2 Apr–30 Apr	12–6	M	T	W	T	F	S	S
10 Apr–19 Apr	12–6	M	T	W	T	F	S	S
1 May–31 May	1–6	M	T	W	T	F	S	S
1 Jun–30 Jun	1–6	M	T	W	T	F	S	S
1 Jul–31 Aug	12–6	M	T	W	T	F	S	S
2 Sep–30 Sep	12–6	M	T	W	T	F	S	S
3 Oct–1 Nov	12–6	M	T	W	T	F	S	S
Temple of the Winds								
5 Apr–1 Nov	2–5	M	T	W	T	F	S	S
10 Apr–14 Apr	2–5	M	T	W	T	F	S	S

Open BH Mons & all other public hols in N Ireland inc. **17 March**. House: admission by guided tour (timed tickets only); opens 12 Sat/Sun. Last admission 1hr before closing. Lakeside gardens closed 25 Dec. Tel. for shop/restaurant opening times

Mussenden Temple and Downhill Demesne

Mussenden Road, Castlerock,
Co. Londonderry BT51 4RP

🔲 🏠 ♿ ❀ 🔺 🚗 🎭 👪 🔲 🚶 🔔
🍽 1949   **(7:C3)**

Landscape demesne and romantic temple in a dramatic coastal setting

Take a stroll around the stunning landscape park of Downhill Demesne, with its beautiful sheltered gardens and magnificent clifftop walks affording rugged headland views across the awe-inspiring north coast. Discover the striking 18th-century mansion of the eccentric Earl Bishop that now lies in ruin, then explore the romantic Mussenden Temple, precariously perched on the cliff edge.

What's new in 2009 Restoration of orchard – old Irish varieties of apple trees planted in the walled garden

⭐ Admission charge at both the Lion's Gate and Bishop's Gate entrances

For public transport details, see page 377

Bishop's Gate at Downhill Demesne

ℹ️ **T** 028 2073 1582
E downhilldemesne@nationaltrust.org.uk

🎭 Midsummer concerts organised by North Coast Members Association

♿ 🅿️ 🔳 Building 🏔 Grounds 🏔

👪 Baby-changing facilities. Pushchairs admitted. Family guide. Children's quiz/trail. Family activity packs

🔲 Suitable for school groups

🐕 On leads only

➡️ [C757357] **Cycle**: NCN93, borders property. **Ferry**: Magilligan–Greencastle Ferry (8ml). **Bus**: Ulsterbus 134 Coleraine–Londonderry. **Station**: Castlerock ½ml. **Road**: 1ml W of Castlerock and 5ml W of Coleraine on Coleraine–Downhill coast road (A2)

🅿️ Parking (pay & display) at Lion's Gate, where information, WCs and picnic tables are provided. Not suitable for 50-seater coaches. Alternative parking for coaches at Bishop's Gate entrance, ½ml from Temple

NT properties nearby
Carrick-a-Rede, Giant's Causeway, Hezlett House, Portstewart Strand

Mussenden Temple and Downhill Demesne								
Grounds								
All year	Dawn–dusk	M	T	W	T	F	S	S
Facilities								
28 Mar–4 Oct	10–5	M	T	W	T	F	S	S

Open BH Mons and all other public hols in N. Ireland **inc. 17 March**

Patterson's Spade Mill

751 Antrim Road, Templepatrick,
Co. Antrim BT39 0AP

1991   **(7:E6)**

The last working water-driven spade mill in daily use in the British Isles

See history literally forged in steel at the last working water-driven spade mill in daily use in the British Isles. Hear the hammers, smell the grit and feel the heat of traditional spade-making. Guided tours vividly capture life during the Industrial Revolution and dig up the history and culture of the humble spade. Then take home one of only 150 hand-made spades produced each year that are on sale.

i **T** 028 9443 3619
E pattersons@nationaltrust.org.uk

Guided tour with the Spade-maker

'Farming in the 40s' and steam working day

P D WC Building

Grounds

No shop but spades for sale

Pushchairs and baby back-carriers admitted. Children's guide

Suitable for school groups. Live interpretation. Hands-on activities

→ [J263856] **Bus**: Ulsterbus 110 & 120, bus stop at gates. **Station**: Antrim 8ml.
Road: 2ml NE of Templepatrick on Antrim–Belfast road, A6; M2 exit 4

P Free parking, 50yds

NT properties nearby
Divis and the Black Mountain, Mount Stewart, Rowallane Garden, Springhill, Wellbrook Beetling Mill

Patterson's Spade Mill								
14 Mar–31 May	2–6	M	T	W	T	F	S	S
10 Apr–19 Apr*	2–6	M	T	W	T	F	S	S
1 Jun–30 Aug	2–6	M	T	W	T	F	S	S
5 Sep–27 Sep	2–6	M	T	W	T	F	S	S

Admission by guided tour. Open BH Mons and all other public hols in N. Ireland **inc. 17 March**. Last admission 1hr before closing. ***Easter week**

Portstewart Strand

Strand Road, Portstewart, Co. Londonderry BT55 7PG

1981   **(7:C3)**

Miles of golden sand

The magnificent two-mile Strand of glistening golden sand is one of Northern Ireland's finest and most popular Blue Flag beaches with all ages. It is the perfect spot to spend lazy summer days, have fun family picnics and take long walks into the sand dunes, which are a haven for wild flowers and butterflies. New environmentally friendly visitor facilities are open at the beach and include WCs, open-air showers, shop and refreshments available.

What's new in 2009 Environmentally friendly visitor facilities, with WCs, open-air showers, shop and refreshments available

i **T** 028 2073 1582
E portstewart@nationaltrust.org.uk

Family Fun Days, 4 July and 15 Aug

Numerous walks

WC

Shop in new visitor facility

Refreshments in new visitor facility

Baby-changing facilities. Family Fun days

Dogs on leads. Dog litter area

→ [C720360] On S side of River Bann, 1½ml E of Castlerock and 5ml NW of Coleraine.
Cycle: NCN 93 runs nearby. **Bus**: Ulsterbus 140 from Coleraine (connections from Belfast route 218). **Station**: Coleraine

P Parking on beach

NT properties nearby
Carrick-a-Rede, Giant's Causeway, Hezlett House, Mussenden Temple and Downhill Demesne

Portstewart Strand								
All year		M	T	W	T	F	S	S
Facilities								
28 Feb–29 Mar	10–4	M	T	W	T	F	S	S
30 Mar–26 Apr	10–7	M	T	W	T	F	S	S
27 Apr–31 May	10–8	M	T	W	T	F	S	S
1 Jun–31 Aug	10–9	M	T	W	T	F	S	S
1 Sep–30 Sep	10–7	M	T	W	T	F	S	S
1 Oct–1 Nov	10–4	M	T	W	T	F	S	S

Please remember – your membership card is *always* needed for free admission

Rowallane Garden

Saintfield, Co. Down BT24 7LH

❖ 🗗 💷 🔏 🎋 🎭 🚻 🕴 1956   **(7:E7)**

A true plantsman's garden in an informal style – with trees, shrubs and plants from around the world

Be inspired by this enchanting garden's dazzling array of exotic species from the four corners of the globe. Created in the mid 1860s by the Reverend John Moore, this informal plantsman's garden reflects the beautiful natural landscape of the surrounding area. There are spectacular displays of shrubs, superb spring bulbs and several areas managed as wildflower meadows. It is also home to a notable natural Rock Garden Wood with shade-loving plants. The outstanding Walled Garden includes the colourful National Collection of Penstemons.

What's new in 2009 Two new walks, the Farmland Walk and Woodland Walk, allow visitors to explore Rowallane Garden and surrounding farmland further. Tree Trail, highlighting 30 magnificent trees

⭐ Tea-room is not open the same hours as the property

ℹ️ **T** 028 9751 0131
   E rowallane@nationaltrust.org.uk

🔏 By arrangement

🎭 Easter trail, plant fairs, craft fairs, workshops and musical events

🕴 Farmland and woodland walks. Tree Trail Walk

♿ 🅿️ 🚻 🍴 **Grounds** ♿ ♿

🗗 Plant sales from spring to autumn

💷 Tea-room (NT-approved concession)

🚻 Pushchairs admitted. Children's quiz/trail

🐕 On leads only. Not permitted on Farmland Walk

Rowallane Garden									
1 Feb–28 Feb	10–4	**M**	**T**	**W**	**T**	**F**	**S**	**S**	
1 Mar–30 Apr	10–6	**M**	**T**	**W**	**T**	**F**	**S**	**S**	
1 May–31 Aug	10–8	**M**	**T**	**W**	**T**	**F**	**S**	**S**	
1 Sep–30 Oct	10–6	**M**	**T**	**W**	**T**	**F**	**S**	**S**	
1 Nov–31 Jan 10	10–4	**M**	**T**	**W**	**T**	**F**	**S**	**S**	

Closed 25/26 Dec & 1 Jan 10. Tel. for tea-room opening times

➡️ [J412581] **Foot**: ¾ml from Saintfield village centre. **Bus**: Ulsterbus 15 Belfast–Downpatrick (passing ➤ Belfast Great Victoria Street). **Road**: 11ml SE of Belfast, 1ml S of Saintfield, on road to Downpatrick (A7)

🅿️ Free parking

NT properties nearby
Castle Ward, Divis and the Black Mountain, Mount Stewart, Patterson's Spade Mill

Rowallane Garden: stone cairn on the entrance avenue

Springhill

20 Springhill Road, Moneymore, Magherafelt, Co. Londonderry BT45 7NQ

🏛️ 🛏️ ❖ 🗗 💷 🔏 🎋 🎭 🚻 🎪 🕴 🔔
🍽️ 1957   **(7:C6)**

Pretty 17th-century 'Plantation' home with a significant costume collection

Experience the beguiling spirit of this inimitable 17th-century 'Plantation' home, with its walled gardens and parkland, full of tempting waymarked paths. Informative 'Living History' tours breathe life into the fascinating past of this welcoming family home. There are ten generations of Lenox-Conyngham family tales to enthrall you, as well as numerous portraits and much furniture to admire – not forgetting Ireland's best-documented ghost, Olivia. The old laundry houses the celebrated Costume Collection, which features some fine 18th- to 20th-century pieces that highlight its great charm and enthralling past.

Unless indicated, last admission is always 30mins before closing time

Springhill

Grounds & Costume Collection

		M	T	W	T	F	S	S
1 Feb–30 Apr	10–4	M	T	W	T	F	S	S
1 May–30 Sep	10–6	M	T	W	T	F	S	S
1 Oct–31 Jan 10	10–4	M	T	W	T	F	S	S

House

		M	T	W	T	F	S	S
14 Mar–28 Jun	1–6	M	T	W	T	F	S	S
10 Apr–14 Apr*	1–6	M	T	W	T	F	S	S
18 Apr–19 Apr*	1–6	M	T	W	T	F	S	S
1 Jul–31 Aug	1–6	M	T	W	T	F	S	S
5 Sep–27 Sep	1–6	M	T	W	T	F	S	S

Admission by guided tour to house. Open BH Mons & all other public hols in N. Ireland **inc. 17 March**. Last admission 1hr before closing. Tel. property for shop and tea-room opening arrangements. *Easter week

What's new in 2009 New Costume Collection exhibition for 2009

i **T** 028 8674 8210
E springhill@nationaltrust.org.uk

Out-of-hours tours by arrangement

GIs on Parade on the last Sat in April

Woodland walk

Building

NT shop. Plant sales

Tea-room in Servants' Hall serving light refreshments

Baby-changing facilities. Pushchairs and baby back-carriers admitted. Hip-carrying infant seats for loan. Children's play area. Children's quiz/trail. Family days at Easter. Teddy Bears' Picnic. 'Clueso for Kids'

Suitable for school groups. Education room/centre. Live interpretation. Hands-on activities. Adult study days

On leads and only in grounds

→ [H866828] **Foot**: from Moneymore village, 1ml. **Cycle**: NCN94/95, 5ml. **Bus**: Ulsterbus 210 & 110 Belfast–Cookstown, alight Moneymore village, 1ml. **Road**: 1ml from Moneymore on Moneymore–Coagh road, B18

P Parking, 50yds

NT properties nearby
Gray's Printing Press, Wellbrook Beetling Mill

Wellbrook Beetling Mill

20 Wellbrook Road, Corkhill, Cookstown, Co. Tyrone BT80 9RY

1968 (7:C6)

Working water-powered mill used in the manufacture of linen

Nestling in an idyllic wooded glen full of lovely walks and picnic spots, the last working water-powered linen beetling mill in Northern Ireland offers a unique experience for all the family. Try some scutching, hackling and weaving with costumed guides at a hands-on demonstration, then, against the thundering cacophony of beetling engines, learn of the importance of the linen industry to 19th-century Ireland.

i **T** 028 8675 1735
E wellbrook@nationaltrust.org.uk

Out-of-hours tours by arrangment

Living History days

Building Grounds

Selection of Irish linen

Pushchairs and baby back-carriers admitted

Suitable for school groups. Live interpretation. Hands-on activities

On leads only in grounds

→ [H750792] **Cycle**: NCN95. **Bus**: Ulsterbus 80 from Cookstown, with connections from Belfast, ½ml. **Road**: 4ml W of Cookstown, ½ml off Cookstown–Omagh road (A505): from Cookstown turn right at Kildress Parish Church or follow Orritor Road (A53) to avoid town centre

P Free parking, 10yds

NT properties nearby
Gray's Printing Press, Springhill

Wellbrook Beetling Mill

		M	T	W	T	F	S	S
14 Mar–28 Jun	2–6	M	T	W	T	F	S	S
10 Apr–14 Apr*	1–6	M	T	W	T	F	S	S
18 Apr–19 Apr*	1–6	M	T	W	T	F	S	S
1 Jul–31 Aug	2–6	M	T	W	T	F	S	S
5 Sep–27 Sep	2–6	M	T	W	T	F	S	S

Admission by guided tour. Open BH Mons and all other public hols in N. Ireland **inc. 17 March**. Last admission 1hr before closing. Tel. property for shop opening arrangements. *Easter week

This section of the *Handbook* provides a range of information that will help you make the most of your visits to our properties. Please also see the questions and answers on page 376, as these contain important information.

Admission fees and opening arrangements

Members of the National Trust are admitted free to virtually all properties (see special information about National Trust membership, page 384). Admission fees include VAT and are liable to change if the VAT rate is altered. The prices for most properties include a voluntary 10% donation under the Gift Aid on Entry scheme – see page 10 for full details. Current admission prices are given in full on our website www.nationaltrust.org.uk or are available from the Membership Department on 0844 800 1895.

Children: under-fives are free. Children aged five to sixteen usually pay half the adult price. Seventeens and over pay the adult price. Children not accompanied by an adult are admitted at the Trust's discretion. Most properties offer discounted family tickets (usually covering one or two adults and up to three children, unless stated otherwise).

Concessions: as a registered charity which has to raise all its own funds, the National Trust cannot afford to offer concessions on admission fees, although we do offer free entry on Heritage Open Days (check website for details).

Education groups: many properties offer educational facilities and programmes. Teachers are urged to make a free preliminary visit by prior arrangement with the property. We highly recommend our Educational Group membership (see page 384).

Group visits: groups are always welcome at our properties. All group visitors are required to book in advance and arrangements should be made direct with the property. Admission discounts are usually available for groups of more than fifteen people, although this can vary and needs to be confirmed with the property when booking. The Travel Trade Office at the Trust's Central Office (see page 386) can also provide general groups information and details on special interest tours

and activities for groups. For further information visit www.nationaltrust.org.uk/groups

National Gardens Scheme open days: each year many of the National Trust's gardens are opened in support of the National Gardens Scheme (NGS). If this is on a day when the garden is not usually open, National Trust members will have to pay for entry. All money raised is donated by the NGS to support nurses' and garden charities, including the National Trust garden careership training scheme. In 2009, National Trust gardens with careership gardeners will open for the NGS on 18 July. The National Trust acknowledges with gratitude the generous and continuing support of the National Gardens Scheme Charitable Trust.

Busy properties: properties can be extremely popular on bank holidays and summer weekends. At some, timed tickets may be issued to smooth the flow of people entering (but not to limit the duration of a visit), and all visitors (including NT members) are required to use these tickets. This system aims to create better viewing conditions for visitors and to minimise wear and tear on historic interiors and gardens. On very rare occasions entry may not be possible on that day. If you are planning a long journey, please telephone the property in advance. At a few places special considerations apply and booking is essential, eg Red House, Mr Straw's House, 2 Willow Road.

WCs

There is always one available, either at the property, when open, or nearby, unless the property entry specifically indicates 'no WC'.

The bathroom at Packwood House, Warwickshire

Please see page 385 for the application for membership form

The *Handbook* can only provide a brief indication of access facilities. Full detailed access information about our built properties is contained in the *Access Guide*, which can be downloaded from **www.nationaltrust.org.uk** and is available free from the Membership Department: tel. 0844 800 1895 or write to FREEPOST NAT9775, Warrington WA5 7WD. This book is also available in large print and on tape.

The National Trust Magazine is available free on tape to members, as are several regional newsletters. If you wish to receive these regularly, please contact the Access for All office at our Central Office address (see page 386), email accessforall@nationaltrust.org.uk or tel. 01793 817634.

Guided tours

Many properties now offer 'taster' tours between 11–1, before opening for free-flow visiting. These tours of particular rooms provide specialist insights into curatorship and conservation issues. Other properties offer guided tours only for groups, so to avoid disappointment please telephone the property in advance or check the website.

Events

An incredible range of events takes place at National Trust properties throughout the year, from springtime estate and wildflower walks, to family fun at Easter and Hallowe'en. There are live summer concerts, living history events, countryside open days and open-air theatre productions. We offer lecture lunches and 'behind-the-scenes' tours, explaining the work of our gardeners and house staff. Also on offer are 'Conservation in Action' events, providing opportunities to see and talk to specialists at work, or experience exhibitions or interpretation. There might also be the chance for visitors to carry out conservation work. See page 380 for details of our Working Holidays. The year ends with Christmas craft fairs and carol concerts. For details tel. 0844 800 1895 or visit **www.nationaltrust.org.uk/events**

For private and corporate events in our properties, visit **www.nationaltrust.org.uk/hiring**

Access information

Property entries are shown using symbols. For a key to the Access symbols please see the inside front cover.

This year we have continued to work with groups from various disability charities – which include MENCAP, Gateway Gardens and RNIB – on various projects around the country to advance our Access for All work. We work closely with Assistance Dogs UK and welcome all assistance dogs at our properties.

Our admission policy enables the necessary companion of a disabled visitor to be admitted free of charge, on request, while the normal charge applies to the disabled visitor. If you are disabled and would like an Admit One Card to save having to request the admission for your companion, please contact the Access for All office on 01793 817634 or email accessforall@nationaltrust.org.uk

Our properties continue with their commitment to develop and promote inclusive access opportunities which are creative and sensitive to the surroundings. Property teams continue to try to make their properties more accessible by installing ramps and purchasing self-drive and wheelchair-accessible volunteer-driven powered vehicles.

Wherever possible, we admit users of powered wheelchairs and similar small vehicles to our buildings. This is subject to the physical limitations of the property and any other temporary constraints which may apply on the day.

Most properties offer Braille and large-print guides, and many have developed sensory information. Properties are continuing to develop virtual tours and more have been commissioned during the past year. Some properties are now offering British Sign Language tours – places are limited on these tours and may need to be booked.

We recommend that if you need further information or wish to reserve a powered mobility vehicle, you contact the property direct.

⬛ 🗨 Shopping and eating

All the Trust's shops and 150 restaurants, tea-rooms and coffee shops are managed by National Trust Enterprises. The profit they generate goes to support the work of the National Trust, and in 2007/2008 contributed £20 million to funds. Every purchase makes a vital contribution to the Trust's work.

Shops: many properties have shops offering a wide range of relevant merchandise, much of which is exclusive to the National Trust. These shops are indicated in relevant property entries by the shop symbol and their times given in the 'Opening arrangements' table. Many are open for Christmas shopping. The Trust also operates a number of shops in towns and cities, which are open during normal trading hours (see below). We also offer many National Trust gifts for sale online at **www.nationaltrust.org.uk/shop**

Restaurants and tea-rooms: the National Trust operates more than 150 tea-rooms and restaurants, which contributed more than £7 million to the Trust in 2007. They are often located in special old buildings – including castles, lighthouses, stables, and even hot-houses! We aim to offer a warm welcome, quality seasonal food and traditional home baking. The properties feature menus which reflect the changing seasons and use locally sourced products from local suppliers. Tea-rooms and restaurants are often open at times of the year when houses and gardens are closed and many offer programmes of events, such as lecture lunches, as well as festive meals in the run-up to Christmas.

Town shops: opening times vary, so please telephone for details if you are making a special journey.

Bath Marshall Wade's House, Abbey Churchyard, BA1 1LY (tel. 01225 460249)

Cambridge 9 King's Parade, CB2 1SJ (tel. 01223 311894)

Canterbury 24 Burgate, CT1 2HA (tel. 01227 457120)

Chichester 92a East Street, PO19 1HA (tel. 01243 773125)

Conwy Aberconwy House, 2 Castle Street, LL32 8AY (tel. 01492 592246)

Dartmouth 8 The Quay, TQ6 9PS (tel. 01803 833694)

Hereford 7 Gomond Street, HR1 2DP (tel. 01432 342297)

Hexham 25/26 Market Place, NE46 3PB (tel. 01434 607654)

Kendal 16–20 Stricklandgate, LA9 4ND (tel. 01539 736190)

London Blewcoat School, 23 Caxton Street, Victoria, SW1H 0PY (tel. 020 7222 2877)

Monmouth 5 Church Street, NP25 3BX (tel. 01600 713270)

St David's Visitor Centre & Shop, Captain's House, 6 High Street, SA62 6SD (tel. 01437 720385)

Salisbury 41 High Street, SP1 2PB (tel. 01722 331884)

Seahouses Information Centre & Shop, 16 Main Street, NE68 7RQ (tel. 01665 721099)

Sidmouth Cosmopolitan House, Old Fore Street, EX10 8LS (tel. 01395 578107)

Skipton 6 Sheep Street, BD23 1JH (tel. 01756 799378)

Stratford-upon-Avon 45 Wood Street, CV37 6JG (tel. 01789 262197)

Street Clark's Village, Farm Road, BA16 0BB (tel. 01458 440578)

Swindon Heelis Café & Shop, Kemble Drive, SN2 2NA (tel. 01793 817600: shop; 01793 817474: café)

Truro 9 River Street, TR1 2SQ (tel. 01872 241464)

Wells 16 Market Place, BA5 2RB (tel. 01749 677735)

York Shop & Tea-room, 32 Goodramgate, YO1 7LG (tel. 01904 659050: shop; 01904 659282: tea-room)

Please remember – your membership card is *always* needed for free admission

A young visitor conducting an experiment at the Science Discovery Centre, Woolsthorpe Manor, Lincolnshire

The National Trust Home Collection: National Trust Enterprises collaborates with leading British designers and manufacturers to create inspiring collections based on the Trust's historical properties, land and archives. Partners include Zoffany furnishings and wallpaper, Duresta furniture, Stevensons of Norwich plaster mouldings, Alitex greenhouses, Marshalls paving, Scotts of Thrapston summerhouses, Vale Garden Houses and Caspari stationery. For further details visit www.nationaltrust.org.uk/homecollection

Family facilities/activities

The National Trust welcomes families. Many properties organise activities specifically for families and family tickets are offered at most properties. Parking is made easy, and many places provide baby-feeding and baby-changing areas, sometimes in purpose-designed parent and baby rooms.

Our restaurants have highchairs, children's menus, colouring sheets and, at some properties, play areas.

In historic buildings, visitors with smaller babies are welcome to use front slings (often available on loan); at some places hip-seat carriers or reins for toddlers can be borrowed. There are usually arrangements for storing prams or pushchairs at the entrance, as it is not possible to take these into fragile interiors.

Some houses are able to admit baby back-carriers at all times; others may admit them on quiet days mid week, at the discretion of staff. We realise that the restriction on back-carriers, prams and pushchairs may be inconvenient for those with older and/or heavier children. As access arrangements vary at each property, we suggest that you telephone in advance to check whether there are any restrictions that will affect you.

Learning and discovery – when places come to life

The National Trust is committed to placing learning at the heart of the organisation. We provide a variety of experiences, which are inspiring, stimulating and fun. We encourage everyone – local communities, young people, families – to engage with us to develop their sense of discovery and their enthusiasm for sharing it.

Our properties welcome visitors from across the educational sector and from special interest groups. Many have an on-site learning officer and a programme of learning activities. For more information email learning@nationaltrust.org.uk or visit www.nationaltrust.org.uk/learning

More than 60 National Trust properties have guides for children and families, some have family activity rooms – and many more have trails, handling activities and other things to do for young visitors and families. Tracker Packs at some houses and gardens provide activities for the whole family as they explore the property. Trusty the Hedgehog, our own children's character, appears at events and has his own website: **www.trusty.org**

At **www.nationaltrust.org.uk/events** you can search by date or location for things to do that are especially suitable for children and families. Many more activities are arranged than may be listed, especially during weekends, bank holidays and school holidays, so do call individual properties for information. The Membership Department can also help, tel. 0844 800 1895 or email enquiries@nationaltrust.org.uk

Dogs allowed

Dogs assisting visitors with disabilities are welcome inside our houses, gardens, restaurants and shops. The dog symbol is used in property entries to indicate places where dogs are allowed in the grounds or other specified areas. If a property does not show the dog symbol, there are no opportunities to take your dog on the visit. Only assistance dogs are allowed beyond the car park.

We endeavour to provide facilities for dogs, such as water for drinking bowls, advice on suitable areas to exercise dogs and shady spaces in car parks (though dogs should not be left alone in cars). These facilities vary from property to property and according to how busy it is on a particular day. The primary responsibility for the welfare of dogs remains, of course, with their owners.

Dogs are welcome at most countryside sites, where they should be kept under close control at all times. Please observe local notices on the need to keep dogs on leads, particularly at sensitive times of year, eg during the breeding season for ground-nesting birds, at lambing time or when deer are calving. Dogs should be kept on a short lead on access land between 1 March and 31 July, and at any other time in the vicinity of livestock.

In some areas we have found it necessary to introduce restrictions, usually seasonal, and particularly on beaches, due to conflicts with other users. Where access for dogs is restricted, we attempt to identify suitable alternative locations nearby.

Clear up dog mess and dispose of it responsibly. Where dog waste bins are not provided, please take the waste away with you.

Weddings and private functions

These symbols at the top of entries in this handbook indicate that the property is licensed for civil weddings (bell symbol) and/or available for private functions (glass symbol) such as wedding receptions, anniversaries, family celebrations and so on. For more information, contact the property, the Membership Department on 0844 800 1895 or visit **www.nationaltrust.org.uk/hiring**

Corporate hospitality and meetings

The National Trust's new portfolio of properties was launched last year and has since welcomed many top companies from Britain and overseas for events including grand dinners, elegant conferences, formal meetings, team-building and family fun days. Each property has been carefully prepared to offer a variety of facilities, striking settings and exclusivity for clients demanding something different. Entertaining is about attention to detail and making each event as individual as the company hosting it. For more information, either email the Functions Team at functions@nationaltrust.org.uk, tel. 01793 817401 or visit **www.nationaltrust.org.uk/hiring**

The Dining Room at Lyme Park, Cheshire

Please remember – your membership card is *always* needed for free admission

Your safety

We aim to provide a safe and healthy environment for visitors to our properties, and we take measures to ensure that the work of our staff, volunteers and contractors does not in any way jeopardise visitors' safety or health. You can help us by:

■ observing all notices and signs during your visit;

■ following any instructions and advice given by Trust staff;

■ ensuring that children are properly supervised at all times;

■ wearing appropriate clothing and footwear at countryside properties and in gardens;

■ wearing appropriate footwear in built properties.

At all our properties the responsibility for the safety of visitors should be seen as one that is shared between the Trust and the individual visitor. The Trust takes reasonable measures to minimise risks in ways that are compatible with our conservation objectives – but not necessarily to eliminate all risks. This is especially the case at our coastal and countryside properties. As the landscape becomes more rugged and remote, the balance of responsibility between the landowner/manager and the visitor shifts. There will be fewer safety measures and warning signs, and visitors will need to rely more on their own skills, knowledge, equipment and preparation. You can help to ensure your own safety by:

■ taking note of weather conditions and forecasts and being properly equipped for changes in the weather. Please note that some properties (or parts of) may close in severe weather conditions. It is always advisable to check opening arrangements before setting out on your journey;

■ making sure you are properly prepared, equipped and clothed for the terrain and the activity in which you are participating;

■ giving notice of your intended route and estimated time of return;

■ making sure you have the necessary skills and fitness for the location and activity, and being aware of your own limitations.

Visitors to Chirk Castle, Wales

The White Lady waterfall, Lydford Gorge, Devon

For general and membership enquiries, please telephone 0844 800 1895

May I use my mobile telephone? The use of mobile telephones can interfere with the correct operation of sensitive electronic environmental monitoring equipment, and so visitors are asked to switch them off when entering houses and other buildings where such equipment is likely to be fitted.

Where can I picnic? Many properties welcome picnics; some have a designated picnic area, a few cannot accommodate them (in which case the 'suitable for picnics' symbol 🚪 is not included in the property entry). Fires and barbecues are generally not allowed. If you are planning a picnic at a Trust property for the first time, please telephone in advance to check.

Is there somewhere to leave large or bulky bags? At historic properties visitors will be asked to leave behind large items of hand luggage while they make their visit. This is to prevent accidental damage and to improve security. The restriction includes rucksacks, large handbags, carrier (including open-topped) bags, bulky shoulder bags and camera/camcorder bags. In most houses where the restriction applies (principally historic houses with vulnerable contents, fragile decorative surfaces or narrow visitor routes) it is possible to leave such items safely at the entrance; this policy reflects standard practice at museums and galleries worldwide. See the Family facilities/activities section on page 373 for additional information on back-carriers and pushchairs.

What types of footwear are restricted? Any heel which covers an area smaller than a postage stamp can cause irreparable damage to floors, carpets and rush matting. We regret, therefore, that sharp-heeled shoes are not permitted. Plastic slippers are provided for visitors with unsuitable or muddy footwear, or alternative footwear is available for purchase.

Please remember that ridged soles trap grit and gravel, which scratch fine floors. Boot-scrapers and brushes are readily available. Overshoes may be provided at properties with vulnerable floors.

Where can I sit down? Seats for visitors' use are provided at various points in all the Trust's historic houses and gardens. Distinctive seat pads will be used to identify chairs available for visitors to use; these will make it easy for you to take a rest, confident that you are not sitting on a fragile historic chair.

Why is it dark inside some historic rooms? To prevent deterioration of light-sensitive contents, especially textiles and watercolours, light levels are regularly monitored and carefully controlled using blinds and sun-curtains. We recommend that visitors allow time for their eyes to adapt to darker conditions in rooms where light levels are reduced to preserve vulnerable material.

Some historic houses offer special tours during the winter months, when house staff demonstrate traditional housekeeping practices. Guided tours explain why National Trust conservation policies require low light levels inside houses and closure to visitors during the winter. Events showing the process of 'Putting the House to Bed' are advertised in the local press and in regional newsletters, or details can be obtained from the Membership Department (see page 386), or www.nationaltrust.org.uk/events

Why is it so cold inside some houses in winter? The heating systems in National Trust houses are not designed for the levels of domestic heating that we have become used to in our own homes. Visitors are advised to dress warmly when they go to Trust houses in the winter.

Where can I take photographs? We welcome amateur photography out of doors at our properties. We regret that photography is not permitted indoors when houses are open to visitors. The use of mobile phones with built-in cameras is also not permitted indoors. At most properties special arrangements can be made for interested amateurs (as well as voluntary National Trust speakers, research students and academics) to take interior photographs by appointment outside normal opening hours. Requests to arrange a mutually convenient appointment must be made in writing to the property concerned. Not all properties are able to offer this facility and those that do may make an admission charge (including NT members). All requests for commercial photography must be channelled through the Broadcast Media Liaison Officer: tel. 020 7799 4547.

What are the rules regarding measurements? Area is shown in hectares (with the acre equivalent in brackets); and distances are shown in yards and miles. Heights where mentioned are shown in metres, except where a structure may have been built to achieve a very specific height in imperial measures (Leith Hill Tower in Surrey being one example).

Please remember – your membership card is *always* needed for free admission

⇥ How to get there

Each property entry includes its OS Landranger (or OSNI) series map number and grid reference, an indicator of its location and public transport/road access.

Car-free days out

Travelling on foot, by bike, bus, train or boat to National Trust properties can be an enjoyable and environmentally friendly way of visiting. In support of car-free travel, a growing number of properties offer incentives for visitors arriving without a car – from a discount on entry to a tea-room voucher. Visit www.nationaltrust.org.uk/carfreedaysout

Public transport

Details of access by public transport were correct as of July 2008. No indication of service frequency is provided. You are strongly advised to check services and timetables before setting out, with www.traveline.info or www.transportdirect.info – both provide multi-modal journey planning services.

The National Trust is grateful to Journey Solutions – a partnership of Britain's bus and train operators – for checking and updating the public transport information. Journey Solutions manages PLUSBUS, Britain's integrated train and bus ticketing system. For details visit www.plusbus.info

Ferry: some properties are best reached – or can only be reached – by boat.

Bus: unless otherwise stated, bus services pass the property entrance (although there may be a walk from the bus-stop). Many bus services connect properties with local train stations – 'passing ⊞' indicates that the bus service passes the station entrance or approach road and 'passing close ⊞' indicates that a walk is necessary.

Train/London Underground: the distance from the property to nearest railway stations is given. Unstaffed stations are indicated by (U).

🚲 Cycling

More than 200 National Trust properties are within $1\frac{1}{4}$ miles or 2km of the UK's 10,000-mile National Cycle Network (NCN). Combined with bridleways, byways and quiet roads, this provides many opportunities for cycling to your favourite places. We work closely with Sustrans, the sustainable transport charity, to promote cycling as a healthy, enjoyable and environmentally-friendly way of reaching our properties.

- *Handbook* property entries give information on the nearest NCN route. For example NCN4, 2ml denotes the property is 2 miles from NCN route number 4.
- Unless otherwise stated, most National Trust properties have cycle parking on site or nearby.
- The bicycle symbol shows cycling opportunities at the property itself.

Further information to help plan your journey

Transport Direct: plan how to get to our properties by public transport or car from any UK location or postcode using www.transportdirect.info

Sustrans: for NCN routes and cycling maps visit www.sustrans.org.uk or tel. 0117 929 0888.

Traveline: for bus routes and times for England, Wales and Scotland visit www.traveline.info or tel. 0871 200 2233.

National Rail Enquiries: for train times visit www.nationalrail.co.uk or tel. 08457 484950.

Taxis from railway stations: www.traintaxi.co.uk

Public transport in Northern Ireland (train and bus): www.translink.co.uk or tel. 028 9066 6630.

For general and membership enquiries, please telephone 0844 800 1895

⎡⚡⎤ Walking

There is no better way to appreciate the variety of places cared for by the National Trust than by exploring on foot. Long-distance walking routes, including thirteen National Trails, link many Trust properties, on top of a scenic web of local paths and access land. We have promoted the freedom to roam over open country, coast and woods for more than a century and continue to work to improve access for all today.

■ Hundreds of guided walks take place at our properties each year. They are a great way to find out more about our conservation work, wildlife, history, farming and so much more, while enjoying a healthy stroll. Many properties also offer waymarked trails, leaflets and maps.

■ Hundreds of walks sheets are available free on the National Trust website to download, print and take on your day out. Before setting out to a property visit **www.nationaltrust.org.uk/walks** for a route map and description of our interesting walks.

Handbook property entries give information on pedestrian access from the nearest town or railway station and details of routes passing through or nearby.

⎡P⎤ Car parks

Visitors use car parks at National Trust properties entirely at their own risk. You are advised to secure your car and not to leave any valuable items in them during your visit.

Parking in National Trust car parks is free for members displaying current stickers, although a valid membership card should always be shown to a member of staff on request. Individual members' stickers cannot be used to gain free parking for coaches. Replacement or additional stickers may be requested from the Membership Department on 0844 800 1895 (terms and conditions apply).

National Trust books, guidebooks and prints

The National Trust publishes a range of titles that promote its work and the great variety of properties and collections in its care. Books and guidebooks are available from most Trust shops or from all good bookshops. Details of new books and guidebooks can be found in the members' magazine and on the website, and are available for purchase via individual property pages or from the online shop.

One of the extensive range of National Trust property guidebooks

www.ntprints.com features carefully selected images available to purchase from the National Trust's very own photographic library. This collection of images vividly illustrates the rich diversity and historical range of properties and collections in the National Trust's care. Whatever the subject – wild moors, craggy cliffs, tranquil gardens, imposing country houses, breathtaking works of art or beautifully conserved interiors – our images have been created to capture the spirit of each location. Prints of the photos featured in the 2009 *Handbook* and in many of our other publications may be ordered direct.

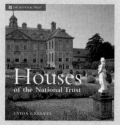

Houses of the National Trust £30
ISBN: 9781905400669

Please remember – your membership card is *always* needed for free admission

The National Trust has selected a group of leading specialist travel operators to offer a range of holidays with special appeal to members and supporters. Every booking made earns important income for the Trust.

The National Trust Holiday Cottages

More than 360 unique properties in outstanding locations make up the National Trust's Holiday Cottages Collection. From the really rural getaway to a city break, a coastal location to apartments in our great houses, this collection contains the widest choice that we have ever offered, either as a main holiday or short break. Our cottages range from cosy hideaways for two, to large rambling farmhouses able to accommodate up to fourteen people for gatherings or to provide the setting to make a birthday or anniversary event special. For a brochure tel. 0844 800 2072, quoting ref. NT HBK. To book or check availability tel. 0844 800 2070 or visit www.nationaltrustcottages.co.uk

The National Trust European Cottages and Villas Collection

This unique collection of self-catering accommodation includes charming cottages, quaint farmhouses and villas with pools in the most beautiful rural and coastal regions of France and Corsica. The hand-picked portfolio of more than 350 properties ranges from a cosy pigeonnier for two, to a chateau in the Loire sleeping sixteen. The cottages and villas in this collection are operated for the Trust by award-winning VFB Holidays, a leading specialist tour operator which first introduced the concept of gîte holidays to the UK market in 1970. For a brochure, please tel. 01452 715326, quoting ref: MNTCT or visit www.nationaltrust.org.uk/frenchcottages

The National Trust Short Break Collection

An award-winning range of European short break holidays which offer something for everyone, from city breaks to country hideaways and from art exhibitions to one-off festivals. This unique collection of short breaks for the independent traveller is operated for the Trust by VFB Holidays, a leading specialist tour operator with 39 years' experience of arranging holidays. With a strong emphasis on cultural themed

Cotehele, Cornwall, where the National Trust has a selection of outstanding holiday cottages

breaks and a wide choice of hotels and travel arrangements, the Short Break Collection is sure to inspire you. For a brochure, please tel. 01452 715324, quoting ref: MNTSB or visit www.nationaltrust.org.uk/shortbreaks

The National Trust Active Holiday Collection

Discover walking and activity holidays that will invigorate, inspire and relax you – holidays where everything is taken care of. Guide yourself or be accompanied by one of our expert guides every step of the way to stunning backdrops, hidden pathways, new friendships and a nice cup of tea. With more than 300 different holiday ideas to choose from, there is something for everyone. You can come with a partner or you can come alone; whatever you choose to do, you can be sure that you'll come away with new friends. For a brochure please tel. 0845 470 7558 quoting NTHF or visit www.nationaltrust.org.uk/activeholidays

For general and membership enquiries, please telephone 0844 800 1895

The National Trust Hotel Reservation Service

A comprehensive range of two- to five-star hotels across Britain, operated for the Trust by leading short break specialist Superbreak. The wide choice of locations makes it easy to get away and find hotels close to faraway Trust properties you've always wanted to visit. For a brochure tel. 0844 800 2076, quoting ref. NTHBK. To book visit www.nationaltrust.org.uk/hotels

The National Trust Escorted Tours and Cruise Collections

The cruises and tours in this programme are operated by Saga, which has more than 50 years' experience of organising holidays, providing the highest standards of service and unbeatable value for money with so much more included in the price. The exclusive cruises and tours have been developed to appeal to members and supporters of the Trust. From a cruise around Britain or exploring the vineyards of France and Iberia, to a tour of Madeira or Italy, there will be a holiday for you! For a brochure tel. 0844 800 2076, quoting reference NTHBK or visit www.saga.co.uk/nationaltrust

The National Trust Working Holidays

The National Trust Working Holidays programme provides great opportunities to make new friends, socialise and work together in a team. You can get away from the day-to-day distractions of modern living to achieve a worthwhile objective and make a significant difference to the preservation of our coast, countryside and historic houses. They are a true learning experience, with activities ranging from hedge laying or drystone walling, to archaeological digs or dragonfly identification. For those of you who like your home comforts, premium holidays offer en-suite accommodation.

Also included are Youth Discovery holidays for 16–18 year olds. Young people wanting to know more about this or other opportunities should email youth@nationaltrust.org.uk

Each holiday is run by Trust staff and trained volunteer leaders, so experience is not necessary – just plenty of energy and enthusiasm! For a brochure tel. 0844 800 3099, email working.holidays@nationaltrust.org.uk or to book online visit www.nationaltrust.org.uk/workingholidays

Bed and Breakfast on National Trust Farms, Camping and Caravan Sites

Enjoy some of the best of our countryside and coastal areas by staying with National Trust tenant farmers or at one of our camping and caravan sites. For details visit www.nationaltrust.org.uk/holidays or tel. for a B&B leaflet (0844 800 1895).

Volunteer on a Youth Discovery Working Holiday in Snowdonia, North Wales

Please remember – your membership card is *always* needed for free admission

As a charity we rely greatly upon additional support, beyond membership fees, to help us to protect and manage the coastline, countryside, historic buildings and gardens in our care. You can help us in several ways, such as making a donation or considering a gift to the National Trust in your Will, or by volunteering.

Volunteering for a brighter future

The National Trust is supported by more than 50,000 incredible volunteers, who last year contributed more than three million hours to support our work in more than 200 different roles.

We would like you to volunteer with us. There are numerous roles available, from welcoming visitors to a built property to tackling countryside conservation tasks. Not to mention taking part in a working holiday (see opposite), joining a supporter group (see right) or taking part in our employee volunteering programme.

By volunteering with us you can: make new friends; gain work experience; use and develop old skills in new environments; see behind the scenes and make a difference.

To find out more, contact your local property, or tel. 01793 817632. Search for opportunities online at
www.nationaltrust.org.uk/volunteering

Don't forget that our volunteers can really enhance your visit with their knowledge and enthusiasm, so do not hesitate to ask them any questions you might have.

Voluntary talks service

The National Trust has a group of enthusiastic and knowledgeable volunteer speakers available to give illustrated talks to groups of all sizes. Talks cover many aspects of the Trust's work, from the Neptune Coastline Campaign to garden history, conservation, individual properties and regional round-ups. Talks can also be tailored to meet your group's particular interests. To find out more, contact the Talks Service Co-ordinator at your local National Trust regional or country office (see page 387).

Donations

You can help us protect the special places in our care by donating to appeals, such as the restoration of Hidcote Manor Garden, or other

Join your local NT supporter group

You can make more of your membership by joining a local supporter group. Tens of thousands of National Trust members and volunteers are also members of one of our 200 independent centres and associations. A small subscription enables you to:

- make new friends and mix with like-minded people with an interest in heritage;
- enjoy a programme of informative talks;
- take part in social and fundraising events;
- go on rambles, day trips, visits and holidays.

You could also join one of our many local Friends groups and advisory bodies, which work in partnership with some Trust houses and countryside properties by providing practical assistance and valuable advice.

All our supporter groups offer great opportunities to get involved as a volunteer in all kinds of ways (see opposite). There are more than 40 National Trust Volunteer Groups which work with properties on conservation and environmental projects. Many of the centres and associations also act as a focus for local volunteering, whether it is organising the group's programmes or directly working on volunteer activities at specific houses and countryside properties.

Want to know more about your local groups? Tel. 01793 817636 or visit
www.nationaltrust.org.uk/supportergroups

projects of special significance to you, or by buying raffle tickets at our properties; raffle funds stay at the property and are used for specific projects.

The Trust organises several programmes to give donors the opportunity to see at first hand the work they support, such as the Benefactor, Patron and Quercus programmes. These include special behind-the-scenes events and the opportunity to talk to Trust experts.

For further information or to make a donation, please contact the Fundraising Department on 01793 817400. The National Trust is grateful to the Art Fund for its continuing support in the acquisition of historic contents, and warmly welcomes Art Fund members to Trust properties.

Legacies

By making provision for the National Trust with a legacy in your Will, you would be providing a lasting gift for future generations, Every sum, whatever the size, will be put to good use and will make a positive difference to our work across England, Wales and Northern Ireland in permanently safeguarding our natural and built heritage. We guarantee never to use a single penny on administration costs or overheads. Choose too where you would like your gift to be directed – the project, property or region which means most to you.

Find out more by requesting the free colour booklet entitled *Guide to Making and Updating your Will*, available from our Membership Department, or visit us today at **www.nationaltrust.org.uk/legacies**

Your gift is as special to us as the unique places it helps to protect.

How you can support the National Trust in the US – join The Royal Oak Foundation

More than 40,000 Americans, including members and donors, belong to The Royal Oak Foundation, the National Trust's membership affiliate in the US. A not-for-profit organisation, The Royal Oak Foundation helps the National Trust, through the generous tax-deductible support of members and friends, by making grants towards its work. Member benefits include *The National Trust Handbook*, three editions of *The National Trust Magazine*, the quarterly *Royal Oak Newsletter*, and free admission to properties of the National Trust and of the National Trust for Scotland. The Royal Oak sponsors lectures, tours and events in the US, designed to inform Americans of the Trust's work, on topics related to English gardens, country house interior design, art, architecture and social history.

The Royal Oak Foundation, 26 Broadway, Suite 950, New York, NY 10004, USA. tel. 001 212 480 2889, fax 001 212 785 7234 email general@royal-oak.org website **www.royal-oak.org**

Heritage Lottery Fund

The Heritage Lottery Fund (HLF) enables communities to celebrate, look after and learn more about our diverse heritage. From museums and historic buildings, parks and nature reserves, to celebrating traditions, customs and history, the HLF has awarded more than £4 billion to projects that open up our nation's heritage for everyone to enjoy.

We have supported the following National Trust projects:

Attingham Park, Shropshire

Beningbrough Hall and Gardens, North Yorkshire

Biddulph Grange Garden, Staffordshire

Birmingham Back to Backs, West Midlands

Croome Park, Worcestershire

Dinefwr Park and Castle, Carmarthenshire

Divis and the Black Mountain, Belfast

Gibside, Newcastle upon Tyne

Glastonbury Tor, Somerset

Greenway, Devon

Hardcastle Crags and Gibson Mill, West Yorkshire

Hardwick Hall, Derbyshire

Holy Jesus Hospital, Newcastle

Llanerchaeron, Ceredigion

Lyme Park, Cheshire

Mr Hardman's Photographic Studio, Liverpool

Nostell Priory and Parkland, West Yorkshire

Prior Park Landscape Garden, Bath

Springhill, Co. Londonderry

Sudbury Hall and the National Trust Museum of Childhood, Derbyshire

Tyntesfield, North Somerset

Wordsworth House and Garden, Cumbria

The Workhouse, Nottinghamshire

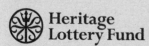

Awarding funds from

If you would like to find out more please visit **www.hlf.org.uk**

Please remember – your membership card is *always* needed for free admission

Governance

A guide to the Trust's governance arrangements is available on our website www.nationaltrust.org.uk A paper copy is also available on request from the Secretary. Copies of our Annual Report and Accounts are also available; contact our Membership Department for more information or to request a copy.

Annual General Meeting

We believe that it is a crucial part of the governance of any large organisation, such as the Trust, that once a year the members have the chance to meet the officers and senior staff of the organisation at the Annual General Meeting (AGM). It is an opportunity for you to comment and make suggestions, to make your views known to the Trustees and the staff both through questions and through putting forward and debating resolutions of real interest to the organisation.

You will receive the formal papers for our AGM in the autumn magazine. The meeting has been held in different towns or cities every year and we hope you will consider attending. However you don't need to come to the meeting to take part. You can listen to the meeting and take part in the debates on our webcast. You can also let us know your views by returning your voting papers – or voting online – ahead of the meeting.

In addition, you have the opportunity to elect members of our Council. The voting papers are distributed with the autumn edition of the magazine. The Council is made up of 52 members, 26 elected by you and 26 elected by organisations whose interests coincide in some way with those of the National Trust. This mix of elected and appointed members ensures that the Trust takes full account of the wider interests of the nation for whose benefit it exists. The breadth of experience and perspective which this brings also enables the Council to act as the Trust's conscience in delivering its statutory purposes.

Privacy Policy

The National Trust's Privacy Policy sets out the ways in which the National Trust processes personal data. This Privacy Policy only relates to personal data collected by the National Trust via our website, membership forms, fundraising responses, emails and telephone calls.

The full Privacy Policy is available on our website www.nationaltrust.org.uk

The Data Protection Act 1998

The National Trust makes every effort to comply with the principles of the Data Protection Act 1998.

Use made of personal information

Personal information provided to the National Trust via our website, membership forms, fundraising responses, emails and telephone calls will be used for the purposes outlined at the time of collection or registration in accordance with the preferences you express.

Consent

By providing personal data to the National Trust you consent to the processing of such data by the National Trust as described in the full Privacy Policy. You can alter your preferences as follows.

Verifying, updating and amending your personal information

If, at any time, you want to verify, update or amend your personal data or preferences please write to:

The National Trust,
Membership Department,
PO Box 39,
Warrington WA5 7WD

Verification, updating or amendment of personal data will take place within 28 days of receipt of your request.

If subsequently you make a data protection instruction to the National Trust which contradicts a previous instruction (or instructions), then the National Trust will follow your most recent instruction.

Subject access requests

You have the right to ask the National Trust, in writing, for a copy of all the personal data held about you (this is known as a 'subject access request') upon payment of a fee of £10. If you would like to access your personal data held by the National Trust, please apply, in writing to:

The Data Controller,
The National Trust,
Heelis, Kemble Drive,
Swindon SN2 2NA

If you have any questions about our Privacy Policy please contact the National Trust on 0844 800 1895.

■ Membership of the National Trust allows you free parking in Trust car parks and free entry to most Trust properties open to the public during normal opening times and under normal opening arrangements, provided you can present a valid membership card.

■ **Remember to display your car parking sticker.**

■ **Please check that you have your card with you before you set out on your journey. We very much regret that you cannot be admitted free of charge without it, nor can admission charges be refunded subsequently.**

■ Membership cards are **not transferable.**

■ If your card is lost or stolen, please contact the Membership Department (address on page 386), tel. 0844 800 1895.

■ A replacement card can be sent quickly to a temporary address if you are on holiday. Donations to cover the administrative costs of a replacement card are always welcome.

■ In some instances an entry fee may apply. Additional charges may be made:

– when a special event is in progress at a property;

– when a property is opened specially for a National Gardens Scheme open day;

– where the management of a property is not under the National Trust's direct control, eg Tatton Park, Cheshire;

– where special attractions are additional and/or separate elements of the property, eg steam yacht *Gondola* in Cumbria, Wimpole Hall Home Farm in Cambridgeshire, Dunster Watermill in Somerset, the model farm and museum at Shugborough in Staffordshire and the Tudor Old Hall and farm at Tatton Park in Cheshire;

– where special access conditions apply, eg 20 Forthlin Road or Mendips in Liverpool, where access is only by minibus from Speke Hall and Liverpool city centre, and **all** visitors (including Trust members) pay a fare for the minibus journey.

■ The National Trust encourages educational use of its properties. Our Educational Group membership is open to all charitable status educational groups whose members are in full-time education. Subscription rates are banded according to the number of pupils on roll. Tel. 0844 800 1895 for further details.

■ Individual life members of the National Trust who enrolled as such before 1968 have cards which admit one person only. Members wishing to exchange these for 'admit two' cards, to include the guest facility, or those wishing to change from one category of life membership to another, should contact the Membership Department for the scale of charges.

■ Entry to properties owned by the Trust but maintained and administered by English Heritage or Cadw (Welsh Historic Monuments) is free to members of the Trust, English Heritage and Cadw.

■ Members of the National Trust are also admitted free of charge to properties of the National Trust for Scotland, a separate charity with similar responsibilities. NTS properties include the famous Inverewe Garden, Bannockburn, Culloden and Robert Adam's masterpiece, Culzean Castle. Full details are contained in *The National Trust for Scotland Guide to Properties* (priced £5, inc. p.&p.), which can be obtained by contacting the NTS Customer Service Centre, tel. 0844 493 2100. Information is also available at **www.nts.org.uk**

■ Reciprocal visiting arrangements also exist with certain overseas National Trusts, including Australia, New Zealand, Barbados, Bermuda, Canada, Jersey, Guernsey and the Manx Museum and National Trust on the Isle of Man **(your membership card is always needed)**

■ Trust members visiting properties owned by the National Trust for Scotland or overseas Trusts are only eligible for free entry **on presentation of a valid membership card.**

Please remember – your membership card is *always* needed for free admission

Application for membership

To: The National Trust, FREEPOST NAT9775, Warrington WA5 7BR

Membership subscription rates for 2009/10 will be available from 1 March 2009. Please visit www.nationaltrust.org.uk or telephone the Membership Department on 0844 800 1895 for details. 2008/9 rates apply until the end of February 2009.

Twelve-month membership

☐ **Individual** One card for each member. Pensioner rate available to those who have held membership for at least five years, aged 60+ and retired. Available on request. Tel. 0844 800 1895 for details.

☐ **Family group** Two adults, living at the same address, and their children or grandchildren under 18. Please give names and dates of birth for all children. Two cards cover the family.

☐ **Family one adult** One adult and his/her children under 18, living at the same address. Please give names and dates of birth for all children. One card covers the family.

☐ **Child** Must be under 13 at time of joining. Please give date of birth.

☐ **Young person** Must be 13 to 25 at time of joining. Please give date of birth.

☐ **Educational Group membership** See opposite. Tel. 0844 800 1895 for details.

Life membership

☐ **Individual** (Reduction if aged 60 or over and retired.) Please note Charities Aid Foundation payments cannot be accepted for individual life membership. One card admits the named member and a guest.

☐ **Joint** For lifetime partners (reduction if either partner is aged 60 or over and retired). Two cards, each admitting the named member.

☐ **Family joint** Two adults, living at the same address, and their children or grandchildren under 18. Please give names and dates of birth for all children. Two cards cover the family.

Full address					
Postcode			Tel.		
Title	First name	Surname		Date of birth	Value £

'I would like the tax to be reclaimed on any eligible donations or membership subscriptions that I have ever made or will make to the National Trust until further notice. I confirm that I pay an amount of UK income or capital gains tax at least equal to the tax that the National Trust will reclaim.' *gift aid it* ☐

Amount attached: £
Cheque/postal order
Delete as appropriate
Please allow up to 21 days for receipt of your membership card and new member's pack

Signature   Date

Credit/debit card/direct debit payments can be made by telephoning 0844 800 1895 (Minicom 0844 800 4410) in office hours, 7 days a week. Immediate membership can be obtained by joining at a National Trust property, shop or countryside information point, or you can join online at **www.nationaltrust.org.uk/join**

I am happy to be contacted by the National Trust by email and email newsletters about conservation, membership, fundraising and other activities. My email address is (please print)

National Trust Enterprises also works with carefully selected organisations and we may contact you by email and email newsletter with special offers from them that will benefit the National Trust. Please tick this box if you do want to receive these offers. ☐

The National Trust collects and processes personal information for the purposes of customer analysis and direct marketing so that we can contact you about our conservation, membership, fundraising and other activities. Please tick this box if you would prefer not to hear from the National Trust in this way. ☐

National Trust Enterprises also works with carefully selected organisations and we may contact you with special offers from them that will benefit the National Trust. Please tick this box if you would prefer not to receive these offers. ☐

The National Trust is an independent registered charity (no. 205846)

Source NT080087M1

The National Trust supports the National Code of Practice for Visitor Attractions.

We are very willing to answer questions and receive comments from members and visitors. Please speak to a member of staff in the first instance. Many properties provide their own comment cards and boxes. All comments will be noted, and action taken where necessary, but it is not possible to answer every comment or suggestion individually.

Enquiries by telephone, email or in writing should be made to the Trust's Membership Department (see below), open seven days a week (9–5:30 weekdays, 9–4 weekends and bank holidays). Detailed property enquiries, eg accessibility for wheelchairs, should be made to the individual property. Business callers should contact the appropriate regional or country office by telephone (0844 numbers are charged at 5p per minute from BT landlines, charges from mobiles and other operators may vary). You can also obtain information from our website, www.nationaltrust.org.uk

Central Office
The National Trust & National Trust (Enterprises) Ltd
Heelis, Kemble Drive, Swindon,
Wiltshire SN2 2NA
Tel: 01793 817400
Fax: 01793 817401

National Trust Membership Department
PO Box 39, Warrington WA5 7WD
Tel: 0844 800 1895
Fax: 0844 800 4642
Minicom: 0844 800 4410
Email: **enquiries@nationaltrust.org.uk** for all general enquiries, including membership and requests for information

National Trust Holiday Cottages
Tel: 0844 800 2072 for brochures
Tel: 0844 800 2070 for reservations

The National Trust Membership Department, where thousands of enquiries are received and dealt with every day, via telephone, email or post

The National Trust online

You can find information about all the properties in this *Handbook* on our website at www.nationaltrust.org.uk Online property information is updated on a daily basis. Most properties show additional information about their history and features, to help you make the most of your visit. The website includes information about volunteering and learning opportunities, hiring a venue for corporate or private functions, events and regional news. We also have a dedicated holiday cottages website at www.nationaltrustcottages.co.uk and an online gift shop at www.nationaltrust.org.uk/shop

For monthly National Trust news, events information, details of things to do and places to visit, updates on our work and suggestions of how you might get involved, sign up for your free email newsletter via www.nationaltrust.org.uk/email

This *Handbook* contains email addresses for those properties which can be contacted direct. General email enquiries should be sent to **enquiries@nationaltrust.org.uk**

Please remember – your membership card is *always* needed for free admission

Regional contacts

Devon & Cornwall
(Devon)
Killerton House, Broadclyst, Exeter EX5 3LE
Tel: 01392 881691. Fax: 01392 881954
Email: dc.customerenquiries@nationaltrust.org.uk

(Cornwall)
Lanhydrock, Bodmin PL30 4DE
Tel: 01208 74281. Fax: 01208 77887
Email: dc.customerenquiries@nationaltrust.org.uk

Wessex
(Bristol/Bath, Dorset, Gloucestershire, Somerset & Wiltshire)
Eastleigh Court, Bishopstrow, Warminster, Wiltshire BA12 9HW
Tel: 01985 843600. Fax: 01985 843624
Email: wx.customerenquiries@nationaltrust.org.uk

Thames & Solent
(Berkshire, Buckinghamshire, Hampshire, part of Hertfordshire, Isle of Wight, Greater London & Oxfordshire)
Hughenden Manor, High Wycombe, Bucks HP14 4LA
Tel: 01494 755500. Fax: 01494 463310
Email: ts.customerenquiries@nationaltrust.org.uk

South East
(Kent, Surrey, East Sussex & West Sussex)
Polesden Lacey, Dorking, Surrey RH5 6BD
Tel: 01372 453401. Fax: 01372 452023
Email: se.customerenquiries@nationaltrust.org.uk

East of England
(Bedfordshire, Cambridgeshire, Essex, part of Hertfordshire, Norfolk & Suffolk)
Westley Bottom, Bury St Edmunds, Suffolk IP33 3WD
Tel: 01284 747500. Fax: 01284 747506
Email: ea.customerenquiries@nationaltrust.org.uk

East Midlands
(Derbyshire, Leicestershire, S. Lincolnshire, Northamptonshire, Nottinghamshire & Rutland)
Clumber Park Stableyard, Worksop, Notts S80 3BE
Tel: 01909 486411. Fax: 01909 486377
Email: em.customerenquiries@nationaltrust.org.uk

West Midlands
(Birmingham, Herefordshire, Shropshire, Staffordshire, Warwickshire & Worcestershire)
Attingham Park, Shrewsbury, Shropshire SY4 4TP
Tel: 01743 708100. Fax: 01743 708150
Email: wm.customerenquiries@nationaltrust.org.uk

North West
(Cumbria & Lancashire)
The Hollens, Grasmere, Ambleside, Cumbria LA22 9QZ
Tel: 015394 35599. Fax: 015394 35353
Email: nw.customerenquiries@nationaltrust.org.uk

(Cheshire, Greater Manchester & Merseyside)
18 High Street, Altrincham, Cheshire WA14 1PH
Tel: 0161 928 0075. Fax: 0161 929 6819
Email: nw.customerenquiries@nationaltrust.org.uk

Yorkshire & North East
(Yorkshire, Teesside, N. Lincolnshire)
Goddards, 27 Tadcaster Road, York YO24 1GG
Tel: 01904 702021. Fax: 01904 771970
Email: yne.customerenquiries@nationaltrust.org.uk

(Co. Durham, Newcastle & Tyneside, Northumberland)
Scots' Gap, Morpeth, Northumberland NE61 4EG
Tel: 01670 774691. Fax: 01670 774317
Email: yne.customerenquiries@nationaltrust.org.uk

Wales
Trinity Square, Llandudno LL30 2DE
Tel: 01492 860123. Fax: 01492 860233
Email: wa.customerenquiries@nationaltrust.org.uk

Northern Ireland
Rowallane House, Saintfield, Ballynahinch, Co. Down BT24 7LH
Tel: 028 9751 0721. Fax: 028 9751 1242
Email: enquiriesni@nationaltrust.org.uk

National Trust for Scotland
Wemyss House, 28 Charlotte Square, Edinburgh EH2 4ET
Tel: 0131 243 9300
Email: information@nts.org.uk

For general and membership enquiries, please telephone 0844 800 1895

THE NATIONAL TRUST
OUTDOOR PROGRAMME

Index of properties by county/administrative area

Properties with no individual entries are shown in italics.
* Denotes properties shown only on maps.

Property and general index

Properties with no individual entries are shown in italics.
* Denotes properties shown only on maps.